VICTOR LAZZARO graduated from New York University in 1941 with a degree in engineering. He subsequently joined the Scovill Manufacturing Company, Waterbury, Connecticut as a junior engineer. In 1943 he was employed by Arma Corporation doing work simplification with Dr. Lillian Gilbreth. After one year, he headed the Time Standards Department which handled the company's time studies and product assembly methods.

Mr. Lazzaro became associated with Merrill Lynch, Pierce, Fenner and Smith in 1946 and is now serving as Manager of the Methods and Procedures Department. The work of this department includes methods and equipment analysis, and the development of various management controls and operating techniques. Over the years, he has participated in many areas, such as factory manufacturing methods, job evaluation, time studies, work simplification, work measurement, office methods and procedures, electronic data processing, and management development and controls.

Victor Lazzaro, the author of several articles on systems and procedures, is also a charter member of the New York Chapter of the Systems and Procedures Association and has served *as the Editor of the Association's Systems and Procedures Journal*. At the present time he is Chairman of the SPA Editorial Advisory Committee.

In connection with his methods and procedures work, Mr. Lazzaro has lectured on systems, management controls and data processing before meetings of various professional organizations and management training groups, the Armed Services and conferences. He has also conducted seminars for the Systems and Procedures Association and the American Management Association.

Mr. Lazzaro was the recipient of the Systems and Procedures Association's 1964 International Systems Award for his contributions to the systems profession.

Systems
and
Procedures

A Handbook for
Business and Industry

CONTRIBUTORS

WILLIAM H. BRUSH

WILLIAM F. BUHL

BENJAMIN CONWAY

CLIFFORD J. CRAFT

ELLES M. DERBY

MARVIN FLAKS

WILLIAM A. GILL

PAUL E. HAMMAN

JOHN W. HASLETT

JAMES G. HENDRICK

GUY L. LANGSFORD

WILLIAM P. LEONARD

ARMOND L. METTLER

WILLIAM R. MULLEE

GIBBS MYERS

RICHARD NEUMAIER

RICHARD W. POMEROY

EUGENE V. REDMOND

MILTON REITZFELD

PAUL R. SAUNDERS

N. LOUIS SENENSIEB

GLENN L. WHITE

PRENTICE-HALL, Inc.

Edited by VICTOR LAZZARO

Systems and Procedures

A Handbook for Business and Industry

SECOND EDITION

Englewood Cliffs, New Jersey

LIBRARY OF CONGRESS
CATALOG CARD NUMBER 68-20370

CURRENT PRINTING (last digit)
10   9   8   7   6   5   4   3

PRENTICE-HALL INTERNATIONAL, INC., *London*
PRENTICE-HALL OF AUSTRALIA PTY. LTD., *Sydney*
PRENTICE-HALL OF CANADA, LTD., *Toronto*
PRENTICE-HALL OF INDIA PRIVATE LTD., *New Delhi*
PRENTICE-HALL OF JAPAN, INC., *Tokyo*

Printed in the United States of America

Preface

Almost two decades ago, Systems and Procedures first achieved recognition as a technique for improving managerial controls and reducing operating costs. During this period its principles and practices have been tested and have proved to be sound. The general acceptance of systems and procedures techniques can be attested by the large number of systems and procedures people serving large and small business organizations and governmental and service groups. Furthermore these principles have played a major role in the application of computers and electronic equipment to today's business needs and total systems concept.

The objective of this Handbook is to bring together information on the various systems and procedures techniques—such as work measurement, EDP, PERT, forms control, and systems analysis—into a single, comprehensive volume that can be used as a ready reference guide by readers interested in acquiring a general knowledge of the subject. The book is particularly useful for students of systems and procedures, and for staff personnel responsible for making management and operating studies and related improvements. Each chapter was written specifically for this book by a recognized authority in the field, thereby making it possible to produce a comprehensive work on systems and procedures. The reader should realize, however, that its contents are not all-inclusive. Many other essential phases could easily have been included, but to have done so would have made the book too voluminous for ready-reference and training purposes.

The editor wishes to extend grateful acknowledgment and appreciation to the authors of the chapters and to the many others who helped to make this volume possible.

VICTOR LAZZARO

Foreword

WHAT DO SYSTEMS AND PROCEDURES OFFER MANAGEMENT?

A system, as I see it, is a series of functions, steps, or plays designed to bring about a desired result. Procedure is the detail of the steps of the system. Through the use of systems and procedures, Management can expect its job—or any job—to operate with greater efficiency, effectiveness, and economy than it could without them.

A business, be it large or small, cannot rely on trial–and–error methods or rule–of–thumb judgments. Management must keep abreast of the everchanging developments of the market and create as efficiently as possible ways and means to compete for a place in the market. The use of Systems and Procedures assists Management in exercising proper judgment and achieving necessary efficiency.

The need for the systematic development of efficiency makes a Systems and Procedures Department more than just a clearing house for the development of office routines, accounting procedures, and new electronic data processing methods. It can be, and frequently is, the key for translating into action the broader policies and needs of Management. In such a situation, a handbook of Systems and Procedures can readily become a handbook of Management.

Mr. Lazzaro's book supplies a sound, firmly-grounded approach to the study of Systems and Procedures, one that can help Management to operate with greater efficiency, effectiveness, and economy.

ROBERT A. MAGOWAN

Chairman of the Board
Safeway Stores, Incorporated

About the Editor

Victor Lazzaro was graduated from New York University in 1941 with a degree in engineering. He subsequently joined the Scovill Manufacturing Company, Waterbury, Connecticut, as a junior engineer. In 1943 he was employed by Arma Corporation doing work simplification with Dr. Lillian Gilbreth. After one year, he headed the Time Standards Department which handled the company's time studies and product assembly methods.

Mr. Lazzaro became associated with Merrill Lynch, Pierce, Fenner and Smith in 1946 and is now serving as manager of the Methods and Procedures Department. The work of this department includes methods and equipment analyses, and the development of various management information systems and operating techniques. Over the years, he has participated in many areas, such as factory manufacturing methods, job evaluation, time studies, work simplification, work measurement, office methods and procedures, electronic data processing, and management development and controls.

In addition to being a charter member of the New York Chapter of the Systems and Procedures Association, Mr. Lazzaro has served as the editor of the Association's *Systems and Procedures Journal*. Among the various activities in S. P. A., he has been a member of the National Board of Directors and served as the chairman of the Board's Publication Committee.

In 1964, Mr. Lazzaro was the recipient of the Systems and Procedures Association's International Systems Award "for his many outstanding contributions to the advancement of the systems profession." Mr. Lazzaro is an adjunct assistant Professor of Management at New York University.

Mr. Lazzaro is a frequent lecturer on systems and management controls before meetings of various professional organizations and groups. He has also conducted seminars for the Systems and Procedures Association and the American Management Association.

Contents

1

SYSTEMS
AND PROCEDURES

William A. Gill

INTRODUCTION, 1; *The Systems and Procedures Role in the Over-all Management Job, 2; Systems and Procedures Responsibilities, 6; Concept and Approach, 10*

2

THE SYSTEMS
AND PROCEDURES
DEPARTMENT

John W. Haslett

CONCEPT OF THE DEPARTMENT, 11; *Systems and Procedures Function Defined, 11; Evolutionary Cycle, 11; Management's Responsibility, 13; Relationship to Other Departments, 13; Staff Assignment, 14; Implementation of New Systems and Procedures, 15;* ORGANIZING THE DEPARTMENT, 15; *Location within the Company, 15; Size of Systems Department, 17; Qualifications of Systems Men, 18; Staffing the Department, 19; Use of Outside Consultants, 21;* PROGRAM AND PROJECT PLANNING, 23; *Phasing the Programs, 23; Office Systems Program, 24; Equipment Standards Program, 24; Records Management Program, 25; Office Appraisal Program, 25; Coordination Program, 25; Research and Training Program, 26; Directing through Projects, 26; Planning the Project, 26;* ADMINISTERING THE DEPARTMENT, 27; *Controls, 27; Manual of Techniques, 28; Progress Revitalization, 29*

3

THE SYSTEMS
STUDY

Armond L. Mettler

INTRODUCTION, 31; *Project Requests, 31; The Project Assignment, 32; Planning the Study, 34; The Preliminary Survey, 34; Redefining the Problem and Adjusting the Study, 35; Fact Gathering, 37; Recording the Facts, 39; Analyzing the Facts, 41; Developing the Solution, 45; Importance of Work Flow, 48; Solution must Fulfill Objectives, 50; Considering Equipment, 51; Effect of Solution on Policies, 53; Evaluating the Solution Against Present Methods, 54; Writing the Proposed Procedure, 54; Preparing the Report, 55; Putting the Recommendations into Effect, 56*

4

SYSTEMS
CHARTING

Richard W. Pomeroy

CHARTING: MAINSTREAM OF SYSTEMS TECHNIQUE, 59; *Charting in Survey, 60; Charts in Design, 61; Charts in Presentation, 61; Charting in Installation, 62;* METHODS OF CHARTING, 62; *Planning and Evaluation, 62; Economics of Chart Costs, 63; Subsidiary Information on Charts, 64;* TECHNIQUES AND MECHANICS, 64; *Methods, 64; Tools of Charting, 65; Materials, 65; Reproduction Media, 66;* TYPES OF CHARTS, 67; FLOW CHARTS, 68; *Operational Flow Charts, 68; Schematic Flow Diagram, 72; Forms Flow Charts, 73; Layout Flow Charts, 73; Punched Card and Computer Procedure Charts, 76; Forms Distribution Charts, 77;* ORGANIZATION CHARTS, 77; SPECIAL PURPOSE CHARTS, 79; *Work Distribution Charts, 79; Right- and Left-Hand Charts and Simo Charts, 81; The Linear Responsibility Chart, 85;* SCHEDULING CHARTS, 85; *Gantt Charts, 87;* PROGRAM EVALUATION AND REVIEW TECHNIQUE (PERT), 87

5

THE MANAGEMENT
AUDIT

William P. Leonard

INTRODUCTION, 90; BASIC ELEMENTS OF MANAGEMENT, 91; *Planning, Organization, and Direction, 91; The Importance of Command, Coordination, and Control, 92;* AP-

PRAISAL OF MANAGEMENT METHODS AND PERFORM-
ANCE, 93; *Management Audit Defined, 93; Specialized Service
to Management, 93; Benefits to Be Derived, 94;* CONCEPTS OF
MANAGEMENT AUDITS, 95; *Measuring and Evaluating Effectiveness of Control, 96; Checking Organization Principles, 96;
Evaluating Policies and Practices, 99; Reviewing and Appraising
Systems and Procedures, 101; Appraisal of Operations, 102; Appraisal of Personnel, 104;* ORGANIZING A PROGRAM, 105;
*Preliminary Planning, 105; Selection of Personnel, 105; Train-
ing Programs, 106; Preparing the Audit Program, 106; Time
and Cost Involved, 107; Audit Findings, 108;* CONDUCTING
THE MANAGEMENT AUDIT, 108; *Review and Appraisal,
108; Interviews, 109; Investigation, Analysis, and Techniques,
109; Techniques Employed, 110; Getting the Facts, 110; Use
of Check Lists, 110; Measuring Performance, 112; Difficulties
Encountered, 112;* PREPARING THE MANAGEMENT AUDIT
REPORT, 113; *Method of Presenting Findings, 114; Facts of
Major Importance, 115; Matters Discussed with Supervisors, 115;
Recommendations, 116; Distribution of Reports, 117;* THE
FOLLOW-UP, 117; *Discussion of Audit Findings with Manage-
ment, 117; Final Action Necessary for Completion, 118*

6

WORK
SIMPLIFICATION

Richard Neumaier and William R. Mullee

WORK SIMPLIFICATION: A PHILOSOPHY, 123; *Introduc-
tion to Work Simplification, 123; Resistance to Affirmative
Change, 124; Development of the Open Mind, 124; Tools and
Techniques, 125; Work Distribution Chart, 126; Flow Process
Chart, 130; Workplace Chart, 131; Multi-column Flow Process
Chart, 131; Records and Report Study, 133; Work Simplifica-
tion Applied to Forms Design, 133; Twenty Principles of Motion
Economy, 137; The Orderly Office, 138; Job Enlargement, 139;
Office Mechanization, 139; Small Office Tools, 140; Work Meas-
urement, 141; Setting Up a Work Simplification Program, 141*

7

WORK
MEASUREMENT

William H. Brush

BASIC CONCEPT OF WORK MEASUREMENT, 143; *Definition, 143; Philosophy, 144; Comparison with Other Management Tools, 144; Objectives, 144; Work Count, 145; Work
Standards, 147; Relationship of Methods Analysis and Work
Measurement, 148; Approaches to Developing Work Standards,*

150; *Engineered Standards, 152; Comparison of Standard and Actual, 169; Application of Work Standards, 169; Administration of Work Measurement Plans, 175; Benefits to Be Derived, 180*

8

FORMS DESIGN AND CONTROL

Gibbs Myers

WHY FORMS CONTROL?, 182; *What is a Form?, 183; Forms Control Responsibilities, 184; Installing a Forms Control Program, 185; Forms Numbering Systems, 187; Forms Classification Systems, 187; Forms Design Techniques, 189; Tools of the Trade, 194; Writing the Specifications, 195; Grades and Weights of Paper, 195; Construction, 197; Printing Techniques and Processes, 200; Relations with the Purchasing Department and the Printer, 204; Checking Proofs, 205; Stockroom Control of Forms, 205; Minimum and Order Quantities, 207; Reordering Procedure, 208; Inventorying, Revising, and Scrapping Forms, 210; Inspecting Forms, 210; How to Handle Forms Problems and Crises, 211; Reporting the Results of the Forms Control Program, 212*

9

RECORDS MANAGEMENT

Milton Reitzfeld

INTRODUCTION, 214; *The Costly Records Problem, 215; Research Impeded, 215; The Clerical Employee, 216; The Records Barrier, 216; Forms Management, 218; Reports Management, 221; Administrative Issuances, 222; Correspondence Management, 225; Paper Work Simplification, 229; Office Equipment, 231; Records Disposal, Storage, and Protection, 233; Protect that Information, 237; Automation and Conclusion, 239*

10

COMPANY MANUALS

James G. Hendrick

NEED FOR MANUALS, 240; *The Manual as a Tool of Communication, 240; Comments, 241; The Use of Manuals in the Management Functions, 242; The Role of Manuals in a Decen-*

tralized Organization, 243;   The Organization Manual, 244;   The Policy Manual, 251;   The Procedure Manual, 253;   Appraising an Existing Manuals Program, 260;   Research in the Field of Manualization, 260

11

BUDGETS
AND COST CONTROL

Paul E. Hamman

INTRODUCTION, 262;   The Need for Budgets and Cost Control, 262;   Budgets, Controls, and People, 263;   Budget Objectives, 263;   Definitions, 264;   PREPARATION OF BUDGET FORECASTS, 266;   Objectives, 266;   Procedure, 268;   COST CONTROL AND CONTROL BUDGETS, 278;   Important Factors for Cost Control, 278;   Budgetary Factors, 280;   Reports, 283

12

PUNCHED CARD MACHINES
AND PERIPHERAL DEVICES
IN DATA PROCESSING

N. Louis Senensieb

INTRODUCTION, 285;   PUNCHED CARD CONCEPTS, 287;   Punched Card Formats, 287;   Basic Card Reading, 289;   Card Fields, 289;   Card Design and Layout, 290;   TYPES OF PUNCHED CARD EQUIPMENT AND FUNCTIONS PERFORMED, 295;   TABULATING PROCEDURE DEVELOPMENT, 302;   Objectives, 302;   Procedure Analysis, 302;   Tentative Plan, 302;   Coding Structure, 304;   Source Information Form, 304;   Card Layout, 304;   Form Layout, 305;   Volume Measurements, 307;   Timing and Scheduling Requirements, 308;   Machine Processing and Specifications, 311;   Controls, 311;   Final Procedures, 313;   TABULATING APPLICATIONS, 313;   Employee Payroll, 315;   Labor Distribution Accounting, 315;   Material Accounting and Control, 315;   MACHINE RECOGNIZABLE MEDIA, 317;   Punched Paper Tape, 317;   Magnetic Ink Character Recognition (MICR), 319;   Optically Recognizable Characters, 319;   Optically Recognizable Printed Codes, 320;   Machine Recognizable Perforated Characters, 320;   Perforated Tags, 321;   Magnetic Tape, 321;   DATA PROCESSING PERIPHERAL EQUIPMENT, 321;   Punched Paper Tape Processing Equipment, 322;   Equipment for Recording and Processing Machine Recognizable Media, 322;   Source Data Recording Equipment, 323;   Data Transmission Equipment, 325;   Data Display Equipment, 326;   BIBLIOGRAPHY, 326

13

ELECTRONICS
IN BUSINESS

Benjamin Conway

THE BACKGROUND, 327; *A Comparison of Processes—the Advantages, 328; The Disadvantages, 329;* GENERAL COMPUTER CATEGORIES, 330; *Analog and Digital Computers, 330; Process Control and Special Purpose Computers, 331; General Purpose Computers, 331; Staffing, 333;* SYSTEM COMPONENTS, 333; *Input-output Equipment, 334; The Central Processor, 335;* PROGRAMMING, 338; *The Hypothetical Data Processor, 339; Flow Chart, 339; The Coded Program, 341; The Software Background, 342; Evolution of Program Languages, 343; Development of Current Operating Concepts, 346; Terminals, 348;* ACCURACY AND CONTROLS, 349; *Built-in Checking Features, 349; Programmed Checks and Controls, 350;* THE FEASIBILITY STUDY, 352; INTEGRATING EDP, 360

14

WORK SAMPLING
IN THE OFFICE

William F. Buhl

CONTROL OF CLERICAL ERROR, 362; *The Need for Control, 362; Costly Additional Operations, 363; Methods of Reducing Cost, 364;* WORK SAMPLING, 365; *Advantages and Uses of Sampling, 365; Sampling Defined, 365;* WORK SAMPLING FOR QUALITY CONTROL, 367; *History of Quality Control, 367; Office Applications, 368; Reducing Error at Source, 370;* WORK SAMPLING IN OTHER APPLICATIONS, 370; *Other Uses of Techniques, 370; Research Reveals Applications, 371; Users of Statistical Methods, 373;* SAMPLING BASED ON STATISTICAL METHODS, 374; *Statistical Methods Applied, 375; The Normal Curve of Error, 375; Probability or Chance, 376; Factors Affecting Sampling, 383;* INSTALLING WORK SAMPLING, 386; *Selling the Program, 386; Installing the Program, 388; Control of the Program, 390*

15

OPERATIONS RESEARCH

Clifford J. Craft and Guy L. Langsford

INTRODUCTION, 393; *History of Operations Research, 394; Definition of Operations Research, 395; Operations Research in the Organization, 396;* TECHNIQUES OF OPERATIONS RE-

SEARCH, 397; *Probability Theory, 397;* *Sampling Theory, 399;* *Linear Programming, 400;* *Queuing Theory, 406;* *Simulation, 407;* *Operations Research and Electronic Data Processing, 410;* APPLICATIONS OF OPERATIONS RESEARCH, 411; *Requirements for Operations Research, 411;* *Administrative Planning and Control, 412;* *Linear Programming Application to Purchasing, 415;* *Matrix Algebra Application to Information Processing, 417;* *Participative Forecasting, 419;* PAYOFFS FROM OPERATIONS RESEARCH, 422; *Conclusion, 423*

16

MANAGEMENT INFORMATION SYSTEMS

Paul R. Saunders

INTRODUCTION, 424; WHAT A MANAGEMENT INFORMATION SYSTEM DOES, 427; NEED FOR MANAGEMENT INFORMATION SYSTEM, 428; *Monitoring Reports, 429; Triggered Reports, 429; Demand Reports, 430; Planning Reports, 430; Report Timing, 431;* DEVELOPMENT OF A MANAGEMENT INFORMATION SYSTEM, 432; *Time and Responsibility, 433;* ANALYSIS OF PRESENT SYSTEM, 434; *Multidimensional Flow, 434; Input-output Data, 434; Short-range Improvements, 436; Subsystem Changes, 437;* DETERMINING MANAGEMENT'S NEED, 438; PRESENTING THE TOTAL PICTURE, 439; DESIGN OF THE NEW SYSTEM, 440; A CORPORATE DATA FILE, 441; *Informational Rather Than Functional Orientation, 441; Single Record or Source of Information, 442; Information Storage Relative to Output, 442; Transaction—The Key to Input, 442; Extraction—The Key to Output, 443; Capabilities and Limitations of Data File, 443; Pros, 443; Cons, 443;* GENERALIZED PROGRAMS, 444; DATA RETRIEVAL, 445; OUTPUT DISPLAY AND AUDIO UNITS, 445; TIME-SHARED COMPUTERS, 446; BETTER INPUT METHODS, 447; IMPROVED REPORTING SYSTEM STRUCTURE, 448; IMPLEMENTING THE SYSTEM, 449; CONCLUSION, 450

17

SELECTING AND TRAINING SYSTEMS MEN

Elles M. Derby

INTRODUCTION, 451; THE REQUIREMENTS, 452; *Salesmanship, 453; The Systems Man as an Analyst, 453; Creativity, 454; Other Qualities, 455;* THE PROBLEM OF SELECTION, 456; *Sources of Systems Men, 456; The Process of Selection, 458; Identifying Analytical Ability, 459; Identifying Creative Ability, 460; Identifying Sales Ability, 461; Evaluating, 463;*

THE BASIS OF SYSTEMS TRAINING, 464; *Training Systems Men, 465; Responsibility for Selection and Training, 468*

18

THE NETWORK SYSTEM
—PERT/CPM

Marvin Flaks and Glenn L. White

INTRODUCTION, 471;   BACKGROUND AND HISTORY, 471;   BASIC CONCEPTS, 473;   *The Planning Phase, 473;   The Scheduling Phase, 474;   The Control-Monitor Phase, 475;*   NETWORK DEVELOPMENT, 477;   *Network Rules and Practices, 478;   Illustration, 482;   Dummy Activities, 483;*   TIME ESTIMATES AND THE CRITICAL PATH, 487;   NETWORK CALCULATIONS, 488;   *Manual Calculations, 488;   Computer Calculations, 491;*   CONTROL-MONITOR PHASE, 492;   CONCLUSION, 492

APPENDIX A

OUTLINE FOR CONDUCTING
AND IMPLEMENTING
A SYSTEMS STUDY

V. Lazzaro

APPENDIX B

CASE STUDY
—THE WALNUT FURNITURE COMPANY

Eugene V. Redmond

Systems and Procedures

WILLIAM A. GILL

Systems Consultant
Alexandria, Va.

WILLIAM A. GILL has been owner and manager of The William Gill Company, Washington, D.C., since 1950. A former federal government official, Mr. Gill has been active in the management engineering field for twenty years, and has specialized in systems and procedures work during the greater part of this period. He has served as instructor or lecturer in several colleges and universities and as leader or lecturer in management seminars and workshops. He has been active in several management societies and associations and served as president of the group that later became the Washington, D.C., chapter of the Systems and Procedures Association.

Mr. Gill's writings on systems and procedures, and other subjects, such as survey principles and techniques, are widely used in this country and abroad. He was commissioned by the International Institute of Administrative Sciences, United Nations, to prepare a booklet on work measurement, entitled "Performance Analysis," which was published in 1953 for the use of all member nations.

INTRODUCTION

In a relatively few years, the phrase "systems and procedures" has acquired considerable meaning in business management and in public administration. Systems men and systems and procedures departments, under a variety of titles or designations, have been increasing in number at an almost phenomenal rate during the past quarter century. Although "systems and procedures," in many instances, hardly embraces all the things that systems men do, it has so implanted itself in the minds of people that it seems to be universally recognized by officials in industry and government as an acceptable title for a field of endeavor that has now become very much a part of business and public life.

Yes, there is a *field* of systems and procedures just as surely as there is a field of accounting or advertising. It may not be one with which the average man on the street has a long-standing familiarity, such as he might have with the fields of law and medicine, because the field of systems and procedures has come into its well-earned prominence on the national scene only in the fairly recent past.

What is this field of systems and procedures? Where does it fit into the total picture of management? How broad or narrow is this field in terms of its functional coverage? Who is responsible for systems and procedures activities? What does a systems man or a systems and procedures department do? These and related questions will be given a general treatment in this opening chapter and a more definitive treatment in succeeding chapters.

The Systems and Procedures Role in the Over-all Management Job

First, let us establish the fact that the field of systems and procedures is an integral part of the job of every manager. By this is meant that every person who supervises, directs, or administers the activities of subordinates (few or many) has a responsibility inherent in his job for the systems and procedures that he and his subordinates employ—the *how* of getting things done, the *ways and means* used to accomplish the tasks assigned, and the *methodology* of the work processes used. Systems and procedures, then, is a field of endeavor that should be classified as one of the several elements of management.

In the simplest form of expression, management involves deciding things, doing things, and then evaluating the things done. Even within the limits of this oversimplification, it should be possible to see that the manager has before him, at any given point in time, any one, several, or all of ten basic considerations. Identifying these ten considerations within the three natural groupings in which they fall will aid in recognizing the placement, the scope, and the content of the systems and procedures job. Briefly, these are the ten basic considerations:

A. *Before-the-fact considerations* (*deciding things*)

1. *What will be done*—planning, policy-making, quantitative work objectives, product specifications, service goals, and the like.

2. *When it is to be done*—priorities, production scheduling, programming.

3. *Who is to do it*—organization, delegation of authority, division and coordination of work, and functional relationships.

4. *How it is to be done*—systems, procedures, methods, qualitative goals, standardization of work practices, and issuance of operating manuals.

5. *The availability of the resources needed to get it done*—supply management, construction, maintenance, personnel management, and financial management.

B. *Immediate consideration* (*doing things*)

Accomplishing what is to be done, in the way it is supposed to be done, at the time it is scheduled to be done, using the resources made available for the purpose.

C. *After-the-fact considerations* (*evaluating things done*)

1. *What has been done*—the evidences of results achieved: reports and statistics on quantitative production and costs, and the comparison of actual results against forecasts.

2. *How well it was done*—qualitative review, consumer reaction, work measurement, surveys, audits, and so forth.

3. *Whether it should continue to be done*—end product review, market analysis, cost analysis, consumer research, and operations analysis.

4. *How what was done could be done better*—product redesign; re-orientation of service; and improvement in the organization structure and the systems and procedures involved in production, personnel management, supply management, financial management, and the processes used to plan and program the future activities of the enterprise.

Within this briefly expressed concept of the considerations involved in the day-to-day job of management, where does the systems and procedures activity fit appropriately? Most certainly in the A–4 and C–4 considerations—this is the customary concept of the breadth and scope of the field of systems and procedures. Actually, however, there are systems and procedures connotations in all the other considerations. This point will be developed later, but before doing so it would be good first to consider two other aspects of the scope that require mention.

Does the field of systems and procedures embrace *all* systems? *All* procedures? To answer this question, some classification of systems and procedures is necessary. For convenience of discussion, and in a more or less arbitrary sense, systems and procedures can be divided into two categories, blue-collar and white-collar.

Blue-collar systems and procedures are those identified with the factory; the shop; the maintenance yard; the construction project; the procedures (manual or mechanical) that are used in fabrication, construction, maintenance, and manufacture of things; and the handling of the parts and materials used.

White-collar systems and procedures are primarily those identified with administrative management, in the broad sense of that term. Included are those procedures generally identified as office operations, such as paper handling, record keeping, accounting, reporting, planning, work scheduling, budgeting, drafting, engineering (office as opposed to shop), job standards, production control, and similar things, whether actually performed in the office proper or in the shop. White-collar systems and procedures may be performed manually or by machines and men.

Using the categorization of blue- and white-collar systems and procedures described above, despite its possible inadequacy for other purposes, the point can now be made that the field of systems and procedures is quite often restricted, both in thinking and in action, to white-collar types of work. The predominant reason for this seems to be that since the latter part of the eighteenth century, and especially during the twentieth century, the field of industrial engineering has been fairly well established, and in popular thinking is usually associated with the shop or factory, or what has been described here as blue-collar systems and procedures. On the other hand, management engineering, which has had a much shorter existence, is in popular thinking associated usually with white-collar systems and procedures. There are known cases in which either industrial engineering or management engineering has been expanded to embrace both blue- and white-collar work, and there are many cases in which the attention of management is concentrated upon either blue-collar or white-collar systems and procedures to the exclusion of the other. These variations in thinking need not be thought of as being detrimental to the growth of either type of engineering; they merely reflect the fact that the growth of interest in the field of systems and procedures, as this field applies to white-collar activities, has occurred in sizable proportions during a much shorter span of years than has been true in the blue-collar area of activities.

Our experience nationally to date in the field of systems and procedures is hardly enough to enable us to draw exact boundaries in terms of blue- or white-collar coverage. There is a wealth of evidence to indicate that concentration upon the review, analysis, and improvement of white-collar procedures is a profitable undertaking in terms of money saved, of improved employee morale, and of customer satisfaction. Whether this is accomplished by using employed or retained industrial engineers or management engineers (i.e., systems and procedures analysts), or by operating supervisors and executives themselves, is a matter to be decided in individual cases. Any universally applicable ground rules offered on this subject must be considered to be primarily theoretical and, in the light of the limited experience data available, suspect. From a purely practical standpoint it appears quite doubtful that useful ground rules on the point in question can ever be devised for general application in industry or in government. As will be demonstrated in a later chapter of this handbook, the organization and operation of a systems and procedures improvement program, regardless of its size and where it is placed in the functional organization, involve giving thought to and making decisions on the blue- or white-collar boundaries of the program.

Still another point to be considered in connection with the scope of systems and procedures activities is the type of effort involved. There are several such types:

1. DESIGNING SYSTEMS AND PROCEDURES FOR NEW WORK PROCESSES THAT ARE LATER TO BE PERFORMED. This might also be termed *procedures planning*. It involves the imaginative creation of a series of procedural steps before the procedure is ever put to use. Although not unusual, this type of systems and procedures effort is met less frequently than the others identified below.

2. PREPARING WRITTEN PROCEDURES FOR THE FIRST TIME FOR WORK PROCESSES ALREADY BEING PERFORMED. When the decision is made to reduce to writing all or most of the systems and procedures used in an enterprise, this type of effort will be employed and, quite often, will be in conjunction with the types of effort identified below.

3. PREPARING, ISSUING, AND MAINTAINING SYSTEMS AND PROCEDURES MANUALS. When a system or procedure is reduced to writing, in either narrative, graphic, or pictorial form (or all three), these procedural documents are issued individually or in series in the form of a manual. Since systems and procedures so issued are frequently in need of change, deletion, or augmentation, continuous maintenance work is necessary to keep these systems and procedures issuances in a current status, a status that always reflects the effect of all procedural decisions made.

4. REVIEWING, ANALYZING, AND IMPROVING SYSTEMS AND PROCEDURES. This type of effort is described in some detail in Chapter 3, "The Systems Study," and in Chapter 14, "Work Sampling in the Office." The systems study, sometimes called a systems and procedures survey, is normally a carefully planned and scheduled project for deliberative and thoroughly detailed study of existing procedures. It should be understood, however, that systems and procedures problems arise which, because of the existing circumstances, must be dealt with so speedily that the normal type of systems study must temporarily be discarded in favor of what is commonly referred to as the "brush fire" treatment. It is usually the aim of any systems and procedures improvement program to keep the brush fire type of effort to a minimum—to emphasize fire prevention rather than fire fighting. This is a sound aim, especially if it takes into consideration the well-established fact that, though brush fires can be kept few in number, they can never be completely eliminated.

Improving systems and procedures is often accomplished in part through mechanization of work steps and processes. The use of tabulating equipment and electronic computer equipment is also dealt with in this handbook.

5. ESTABLISHING AND OPERATING SYSTEMS AND PROCEDURES CONTROLS. This type of effort involves several kinds of controls. First, the centralized control of procedural directives and manuals such as those suggested under Type 3 above. Second, forms design and control as outlined in Chapter 8. Third, records management as outlined in Chapter 9. It is through controls such as these that continuous improvements are being made in forms, reports, and records.

6. CREATING AMONG ALL COMPANY OFFICIALS AN AWARENESS OF THE NEED FOR A CONTINUOUS COMPANY-WIDE ATTACK UPON KNOWN, SUSPECTED, OR ANTICIPATED DEFICIENCIES IN SYSTEMS AND PROCEDURES. This type of effort is important not only in getting a systems program sold and in high gear but as a continuous challenge to those who have a respon-

sibility to keep interest in the program alive. It requires one kind of "selling" to get the program accepted. Once accepted, however, and put into action, the program must sell itself through its accomplishments. In other words, we sell the program initially with words; we keep it sold through deeds— that is, through the things done under the efforts described above as Types 1, 2, 3, 4, and 5.

7. INCREASING THE COMPETENCE OF LINE SUPERVISORS AND MAN-AGERS TO RECOGNIZE AND ADJUST THEIR OWN SYSTEMS AND PROCEDURES PROBLEMS. Any person having the capability to be a supervisor, or to be trained as such, will almost invariably be capable of learning and applying simple tried-and-proven techniques and procedures for reviewing, analyzing, and improving those systems and procedures for which he is responsible. The development of this systems and procedures capability is a most de-sirable objective and will be accomplished through training and through programs designed to put this capability to work.

Up to this point, the scope of the field of systems and procedures has been discussed in two ways: first, in terms of categories of procedures; second, in terms of the types of systems and procedures effort. Now it seems desirable to discuss scope in terms of two questions:

1. Who determines officially the scope of the systems and procedures effort, and what rules, policies, principles, or criteria are used in making this determination?

2. What are the extremes in scope, and when, if ever, can the ex-tremes be utilized advantageously?

Systems and Procedures Responsibilities

The question of *who* makes the final determination and subsequent redeterminations of the scope of the systems and procedures effort intro-duces the corollary question of responsibility for all aspects of the systems and procedures effort.

We often hear the very generalized and theoretical statement that "sys-tems and procedures are in some measure the responsibility of every person in any company or agency." Whether or not an individual accepts or rejects this theory seems to be entirely dependent upon how the general statement is translated into specific terms and the extent to which "every person" gets a clear and plausible explanation of what the phrase "in some measure" means to him wherever he may be, at the top, bottom, or middle rung of the organizational ladder.

The need for spelling out the systems and procedures responsibility seems quite apparent. It is equally apparent that when this clarification of responsibility does not take place, one or both of two things happen: (1) people do little or nothing about systems and procedures, or (2) people who do something establish overlapping, conflicting, or shortsighted objectives. Recognizing these dangers, many companies and agencies have seen to it that their employees have an adequate understanding of the type and extent of effort to be expended in creating, controlling, and improving systems and procedures, and have clarified and assigned responsibilities in this field of endeavor. Numerous measures and devices are used to achieve the degree of understanding sought. Chief among these are: *first,* the document that explains the over-all company program for control and improvement of systems and procedures in other words, the "Company Systems and Procedures Program," expressed in fairly general terms, usually (and preferably) signed by the company's topmost official, and dealing with the matter of responsibility to the extent a company-wide document should; *second,* translations of the company-wide program into more definitive departmental programs, being more specific, especially as to responsibility; *third,* orientation sessions and group discussions of what the program documents have to say, leading to mutual understanding and agreement as to the ways the program will operate; and *fourth,* seeing that all of the job descriptions written contain specific references to the systems and procedures responsibilities attached to every individual or prototype job performed. Where the foregoing measures and devices are used, the resulting responsibilities very often fall substantially into the pattern suggested below.

Responsibilities of the worker (the staff or operating person who supervises no one) as a minimum are: (1) to put to use the procedural instructions he receives, whether orally or in writing, and to deviate from these instructions only to the degree authorized; (2) when the instructions he receives do not embrace fully everything he does, to develop and use his own procedures and systems; (3) to discover and suggest, to his superior, ways in which the procedural instructions he has received can be modified, either for clarity or to effect or ratify beneficial improvements; and (4) to search continuously for and to use ways and means for improving the procedures he himself designed.

Systems and procedures responsibilities of the first-line supervisor (the line official who has direct responsibility for workers and who has no lower-level supervisors under his jurisdiction) as a minimum are: (1) to guide and to direct the people he supervises as they perform their systems and procedures responsibilities; (2) to view all of the systems and procedures needed or used in his unit of the organization as his official responsibility as a manager, to the end that he will see to their preparation, use, expansion, or modification, and will recommend or take action to improve them when improvements are warranted; and (3) to coordinate laterally or vertically with other units of the organization on systems and procedures matters of mutual concern.

Systems and procedures responsibilties for those levels of line supervision between the first-line supervisor and the topmost line official of the company or agency (that is, the supervisors who supervise supervisors) as a minimum are comparable in substance to those of the first-line supervisor.

At these higher levels, of course, the supervisory officials involved have a systems and procedures responsibility that is much broader, since it embraces more people, and thus more functions, and a responsibility that has greater depth in an organizational sense, in that it embraces more levels of supervisory authority. It is these middle-management and next-to-top-level management officials (superintendents, branch chiefs, division directors, department heads) who, as the link between the very top and the very bottom positions in line management, have the very difficult but none-the-less significant responsibility for upholding the company's policies and program for systems and procedures. Indeed, their role is crucial, for unless they discharge their responsibilities fully and well, the first line of supervision— the front line of operations—will not be provided with the leadership motivation that makes for an effective systems and procedures program. Without such a program, management has not taken all the measures it can to reduce costs, increase job satisfaction, and improve upon customer relationships—three of the several essential ingredients in any recipe for greater profits and higher employee morale.

Systems and procedures responsibilities of the topmost line official of the company (the president, the administrator) as a minimum are: (1) to recognize the value of a well-organized and integrated company-wide effort to develop and maintain efficient systems and procedures; (2) to require his staff and line assistants to prepare, coordinate, and submit to him a proposed program (policies and a course of action) for dealing with the systems and procedures aspects of the total management job; (3) to approve the proposed company-wide program, after modification if necessary, and put it into action; (4) to maintain a personal interest in the program continuously; (5) to make his support of the program evident constantly; and (6) to call for periodic briefings by his next-in-line officials on the progress in program implementation. The foregoing responsibilities in the aggregate are in support of three basic principles that of necessity must be a part of the foundation upon which any really worthwhile systems and procedures effort is built: *first,* that though a systems and procedures effort normally produces results in a "bottom-up" direction, the incentives, the motivation, and the leadership for obtaining those results is distinctly a "top-down" matter; *second,* that a company's systems and procedures program is for the line, not the staff, even though staff usually participates in the technical development and execution of the program; and *third,* that the things that are done to bring about improvements in systems and procedures, whether as a suggestion or an action, and whether by the staff or the line, should be seen as being the *responsibility* of the employees who do them and not as a right or a privilege.

Systems and procedures responsibilities of the supervisory head of a staff unit of organization (the chief of a group of *staff* people) are, for the purposes of this discussion, comparable to those of a first-line or higher-level supervisor as described above.

The systems and procedures staff specialist (the full-time systems and procedures technician) who is attached to a line official somewhere in the organization, either as an individual or as one member of a group of staff specialists, may find his responsibilities limited in a functional or organizational sense, but quite varied and probably not limited in terms of the seven types of systems and procedures effort that were described earlier in this chapter. Limitations in the functional or organizational scope of the responsibilities of the systems and procedures specialist, or the group of specialists of which he is a part, will be referred to in Chapter 2, The Systems and Procedures Department. And, as will be seen in other chapters to follow, the systems and procedures specialist may in most instances find that in a functional sense, regardless of the arm of the organization to which he is attached, he will become involved in surveys or developmental work in respect to work simplification, work measurement, forms design and control, reports management, records management, work sampling, office machines, tabulating equipment, electronic computers, organization, budget, cost controls, quality control, production control, space utilization, and many other aspects of the administrative management job.

When the field of systems and procedures is described, and when in this connection the job of the systems and procedures staff specialist is also described, there is always present the remote possibility that the one who provides these descriptions will be an extremist in either of two directions. In one extreme, the responsibilities of the systems and procedures specialist can be so delimited that his potential worth to the company is questionable. This is an unfortunate situation both for the company and the man. In the other extreme, the responsibilities of the systems and procedures specialist can be so broad that he succumbs to the rather human tendency to attach to his job a degree of authority that in his mind gives him the right to command rather than to recommend, to direct improvements rather than to espouse them. This, too, is a most unfortunate situation for both the company and the man.

Naturally, then, a position somewhere between these two extremes is one that has the best chance of being acceptable and workable. It is believed to be entirely accurate to say that this middle position is not apt to be exactly the same in any two companies; and it is just as accurate to say that the presence of these variations in thinking as to the middle position in the scope and responsibilities of the systems and procedures specialist should not be the cause for concern. As in most things, the overriding considerations in the field of systems and procedures are the conceptual foundation upon which the program is built and the methodology of approach used in making the program come alive and produce meaningful and beneficial results. Unless the program is sound in concept, the questions of scope and responsibility become quite academic. Even when a sound concept is established, its benefits can be negated by the line and staff officials and the staff specialists whose job it is to make the concept come alive, if these people attempt to subordinate the over-all objectives of the company program to their desire for personal gain. What, then, constitutes a proper conceptual foundation for a systems and procedures program? What are the major factors to consider in establishing a practical approach to the fulfillment of a well-conceived systems and procedures program? These two basic questions will be touched upon frequently in this handbook.

Concept and Approach

The soundness of the conceptual approach to systems and procedures in any company will be in almost direct proportion to the degree in which it embraces these fundamental principles:

1. Systems and procedures considerations are an essential part of all the processes of management.

2. The application of systems and procedures considerations to the processes of management must be dynamic.

3. The policies, scope, objectives, and responsibilities of the company's systems and procedures program must be clearly set forth in writing.

4. All levels of management and all employees must be told, through the program document or otherwise, what their systems and procedures responsibilities are.

5. Responsibility and accountability for achieving systems and procedures objectives must be placed with *line* executives and supervisors.

6. Responsibility for the technical aspects of the systems and procedures program may properly be placed with systems and procedures staff specialists when it is economically feasible to employ these specialists.

7. The improvement of systems and procedures, through simplification, modernization, or standardization, must not be seen as a start-and-stop drive or campaign; it is a continuous, repetitive function that can pay off in a host of beneficial results, with only a few of these results being of a spectacular nature.

If in the words of the company program document, or a departmental version of the same, the principles expressed above are clearly set forth in the language of that company, and if the deeds of those responsible for the program are suited to the language used in expressing the principles, the foundation will have been laid for a successful program, a program that should convince the officials and employees of the company that, although systems and procedures improvement means work, and sometimes hard work, it is not the mysterious or baffling kind of work that some would have us believe. It would be desirable for the reader to bear these facts in mind as he moves into the more definitive aspects of the field of systems and procedures that appear in the remaining chapters.

2

The Systems and Procedures Department

JOHN W. HASLETT

Management Consultant
Darien, Conn.

JOHN W. HASLETT engages in administrative systems research and development in many capacities: consultant to industry and government, writer on management topics, and educator in the field of business administration. A member of the Management Institute faculty of New York University, he is also executive editor of the Systems and Procedures Journal *and has been associated in advisory and executive capacities with the Shell Oil Company, the New York City LaGuardia administration, and the Management Control Division of the Army Service Forces in Washington, D.C. In 1963 the Systems and Procedures Association designated him "Systems Man of the Year." He is a past national vice-president and national director of that organization. Mr. Haslett is active in the Society for the Advancement of Management and has led numerous seminars of the American Management Association. He is a graduate of Columbia College.*

CONCEPT OF THE DEPARTMENT

Systems and Procedures Function Defined

Although the systems and procedures function may be defined in simplest terms as "organized common sense," a more formal working definition might be "the analysis of corporate policies, procedures, forms, and equipment in order to simplify and standardize office operations." All corporate functions—production, marketing, finance, purchasing, industrial relations, and so on—are performed by means of routines, or systems and procedures, which translate the policies of management into action.

Evolutionary Cycle

Evolutionary influences have been at work for many years, and are still at work upon the systems function itself. In fact, the evolutionary cycle

11

may be observed in the development of the systems function in a typical enterprise that has grown from a small company to one of medium size or large proportions. The cycle may be considered in terms of a number of phases.

The first phase occurs when the growth of an enterprise brings about the need for administrative planning and control. For present purposes, administrative planning and control may be considered to involve non-routine problems of forward thinking, as opposed to the routine and recurring judgments regularly exercised by all levels of management. These may be limited to organization and procedures planning and control, but this is not a hard and fast rule.

The second phase occurs when recognition is given to the need for administrative planning after conditions of growth have brought it about. At this point, usually starting with top management, each managerial level assumes the planning and control function as part of its normal administrative duties. Procedures planning and forward thinking on organizational problems form a basis for anticipating future problems before they occur and devising solutions to these problems which will be ready for use at the appropriate moment.

As the enterprise continues to grow, organization and procedures problems become more numerous and complex, with a consequent increase in their demands on the time of the operating levels of management. As is so often the case, the results that have been obtained from work in this field, combined with the diminishing availability of time on the part of operating supervisors and managers, indicate the desirability of designating full-time specialists to assist all levels of management in the field of administrative planning and control. The need to abandon part-time planning in favor of full-time planning is the third phase of the cycle.

The fourth phase comes into being with the establishment of a special staff within the organization to carry out these functions on a formally organized and systematic basis.

Although there may be others, three fundamental principles underlie the formal methods function. First, the pattern of a systems organization as well as the approach to building such an organization should be tailor-made to the situation existing in the specific company. Otherwise, there will be a dangerous lack of realism from the start. Individual company situations may be judged in terms of numerous factors, such as the number and type of employees, management attitudes, the structure of the company organization, the type of products it makes, its methods of distribution, and many other factors. In the interplay among these factors, each one influences others and is itself influenced. In fact, it takes a good deal of intuition to discern from this complex pattern the best course of approach.

The second fundamental is that the design of the systems department should anticipate revisions in the future as objectives are accomplished and as conditions change. This insures an essential flexibility without which the department might well find itself lagging behind the progress of the company as a whole.

The third fundamental is that building the department should be a continuous process of staff, program, and project planning. Here again, flexibility is of paramount importance, for the analysts, the objectives, and the work assignments must at all times be balanced in terms of the changing needs of the company as a whole. If proper attention is paid to these three principles, the plan for a concrete design for the department will be greatly facilitated.

Management's Responsibility

Before introducing a systems unit into a company, management, together with the person in charge of the new program, should spell out to the satisfaction of each the scope of the function, specific responsibilities, authority, and relationships. While so doing, management will endeavor to put the new group in the proper organizational place to allow it to accomplish its fundamental goals.

The new unit will be effective only if there is *genuine support by top management and key executives.* Management has a fundamental responsibility to the new unit as well as to the whole organization to see that the unit is properly introduced and to make it apparent that it is fully backed by management. To do this, management must be completely convinced of the need for this function and must have confidence in the people it has selected to do the job. This conviction must be conveyed down the line, from key executives who report to top management to the first-line supervisors and the employees themselves. Furthermore, support of the program should be continuous in nature, not subject to spasmodic enthusiasms.

Certainly, however, continuous support must be earned once the program is under way, and the degree of confidence and amount of support forthcoming will be greatly influenced by the effectiveness of the unit. The matter of support is an interacting one. It must be present initially to allow effective action. Effective action must result in order to produce continuous support.

Relationship to Other Departments

The systems and procedures department works closely with and assists all departments on systems problems, as required. Projects may be instituted at the request of the department concerned or at the suggestion of the systems department. Basic objectives, an approach, and a plan of action are usually discussed and agreed upon by the managers of the systems department and the other department or departments concerned. A typical working unit might consist of one or more systems department representatives and several reprsentatives of other departments.

Electronic data processing functions, either developmental in nature or operational, as in the case of computer center operations, are frequently associated with general methods and procedures responsibilities. In some organizations the systems department encompasses the electronic data processing functions. However, where the general systems function and the EDP function are separated, the two groups work together toward the same systems objectives when their projects are related. EDP projects invariably tie in with the systems analyst in the development of an improved method to be processed by the computer and in the preparation of forms, procedures, and instructions needed for the implementation of the computer system. This is particularly the case in preparing the procedures and data required as input for the computer, and in properly processing the EDP output.

There is a complementary relationship between the work of the auditing department and that of the systems and procedures department. The auditing department is concerned primarily with safeguarding the fiscal interests of the company and preventing fraud and deception. This requires a thorough check into the practices of all offices of the company and may reveal deviations from prescribed policy and procedure and areas for systems improvement. Likewise, studies by the systems department may point to questionable activities for investigation by the auditing department.

Staff Assignment

The systems and procedures function is a staff function with the normal responsibility and authority of the usual staff assignment. This includes planning, organizing, coordinating, and evaluating activities within certain designated spheres. The staff unit works as a complement to the operating units. The staff executive consults and advises on problems confronting the line executive who is responsible for results. The staff executive recommends; he has no authority to direct line action, except, of course, within his own department. The staff unit is impartial in attitude; it has no axes to grind. Herein lies one of its greatest values to an organization. As an impartial unit, it can approach a problem with a detached, objective viewpoint, having before it the over-all concept rather than a specialized one. A staff department that establishes a reputation for thorough, complete, and considered recommendations finds that operating management becomes more and more eager to enlist its aid in analyzing problems.

The systems and procedures department follows this general pattern of approach. In addition, it normally makes available concrete assistance to line management in the implementation of a decision by making available trained staff people and by preparing manuals covering policy and procedure.

The accepted principles of effective staff work, staff anticipation, and completed staff action apply as well as to the systems function.

Staff anticipation is the concept that stresses the need for advance thinking and forward planning. It advocates foresight rather than hindsight. The staff department does not wait for operating management to come up with problems of major significance; it plans for them. It tries to foresee problems and anticipate areas for action before they actually become "problems." The principle of staff anticipation thus places upon the staff unit the responsibility of seeing that management is not caught short on any important issue. Examples of areas for such thinking in current systems programs are electronic data processing and integrated data processing.

Completed staff action means doing a job as comprehensively as possible, leaving no loose ends. The project, be it a one-day job for one man, an EDP project or a two-year job for a dozen men, should be so thoroughly planned, developed, and cleared that the executive concerned, if he desires, can merely approve the recommendation and place it in operation. This involves on the part of the staff man a thorough working out of the major elements of the project, consultation and discussion with other staff people concerned, development of possible solutions, and, finally, the preparation of a single, consolidated plan of action. As this concept applies to the total work of the department, so does it apply to the work of any individual members. The systems staff (both general and EDP systems) should be trained in these concepts of staff work.

Implementation of New Systems and Procedures

Although it is the responsibility of the line organization to make the actual installation, the systems department must stand ready to assist in the installation of a plan by supplying manpower and furnishing advice as required.

It is desirable that those concerned with carrying out the new procedures participate in their development. When one takes part in the formulation of a plan, he feels responsible for making it work. On the other hand, resistance to change is a fundamental attitude present in all people in different degrees. The best of plans has been known to fail because those principally engaged in carrying out the procedure were not consulted in its development and, as a result, had made up their minds, before testing, that the change would not work. Consulting with all concerned prior to the installation stage is important to successful installation.

ORGANIZING THE DEPARTMENT

Location Within the Company

Although "ideal" organizational structures look excellent on paper, in practice they may be highly impractical for existing organizational patterns.

Most staff departments would prefer to be lodged in the bailiwick of top management, where they are surrounded by the aura of top management support. However, the peculiar needs of the particular organization must be considered. There are several good reasons why the systems and procedures department might well report to the chief executive or a vice president. One is the fact that the work of this department enters all cor-

PROGRAM

PROJECT

ANALYST

PERCENT OF PROGRESS

| 25 | 50 | 75 | 100 |

BEGINNING DATE

TARGET DATE

PURPOSE AND SCOPE OF PROJECT:

STATISTICAL DATA REQUIRED AND SOURCE OR DATA:

CONDITION NECESSITATING PROJECT:

TYPE OF PRESENTATION:
☐ CHART
Prepared by: _____
☐ TABULATION
☐ WRITTEN REPORT

☐ OTHER (SPECIFY)

REQUESTED BY:

SR-1813-1

PROJECT STATUS CARD

Front

RESULTS OF PROJECT

SAVINGS	ANNUAL RATE		OTHER SAVINGS AND IMPROVEMENTS:
	QUANTITY	COST	
Man Hours			
Floor Space			
Equipment			
Forms (Forms x Copies)			
Reports (Reports x Copies)			
Postings			

Back

Fig. 2-1. A Typical Project Status Card

porate functions and cuts across all departmental lines. Therefore, a logical argument can be offered for having this department report to a top executive who is charged with general administrative duties rather than specialized ones.

In many large organizations, in lieu of reporting to the chief executive, this department is placed in the financial organization, usually reporting to the controller. Since many projects of the systems department are concerned with financial activities, and since the controller is charged with promoting the highest efficiency within the areas of his functional responsibility, placement of the department in this sphere is logical. Often, problems may best be solved in that part of the organization where they are most acute. Here the operational know-how is immediately available to those who have the time and the systems training to take advantage of it. An objective selection of the placement of the department should be based upon the logic of situating it as high in the organization as necessary to gain prompt and universal acceptance.

Wherever the systems responsibility is placed, the scope of activities should be clearly defined by top management and clearly understood by all segments of the entire organization. There should be no mystery about who is going to do what.

Then there is the question of the centralized systems unit versus the decentralized. Should the job be done by a headquarters staff circulating in the field, or should it be done by divisional methods staffs whose programs and techniques would be coordinated by a small systems advisory group in the home office? Here we can revert to a fundamental principle: The unit should be tailor-made to fit the particular company. Size of the company, diversification of its products, and dispersal of its offices should point the way for or against systems staff centralization. Management policies might even suggest that the operating divisions themselves, without their own special staff, be responsible for management improvement programs and projects coordinated by a small advisory group in the head office.

The advantages of systems unit centralization are several. Since systems and procedures problems frequently cut across departmental lines, a centralized group is in a position to recognize these relationships and to coordinate plans and projects with a minimum of effort. Duplication of effort is eliminated and costs lowered.

The chief advantages of decentralization are the familiarity with the particular operation gained by the group and the prompt attention that often can be given to arising problems.

Size of Systems Department

The size of the systems department varies widely from company to company. Several factors account for this. The five fundamental determinants of departmental size are (1) the scope of the department's operation, (2) the depth of study to be made, (3) the volume and complexity of company operations, (4) whether the systems function is to be centralized or decentralized, and (5) whether EDP systems are part of the major systems department or a separate entity.

Attempts have been made to determine the size of the methods staff in relation to the number of over-all company personnel. This is a far from accurate gauge, as can readily be seen. Probably the best way to approach this problem is to set a pattern based upon the systems programs to be undertaken; for example, specialists in the following areas are usually regarded as part of the fundamental staff: forms design and coordination, filing and records management, surveys and procedural analyses, and equipment standards, including punched card and electronic computing equipment. Obviously, the number of forms used within the company and the scope of the forms function—whether it is to be a policing action, whether it aims to review all forms, whether it will cover design through reproduction or merely design and review, and so on—all these factors will determine whether one person can do the forms job or whether ten people will be needed. This same principle applies to the other systems programs.

If the systems function is to be centralized, with the departmental staff "doing" the job, rather than decentralized, with the departmental staff acting mainly in a consulting capacity, the size of the department will be correspondingly larger. The number of EDP systems people and programmers are dependent on the type and size of the computer installation.

Qualifications of Systems Men

The ideal systems man combines several key qualities needed for success in different fields. Certainly the systems man must have a questioning mind; he is the sort of person who seeks answers to the what, when, why, where, who, and how of journalism. He is not content with pat answers, but desires to know what lies behind them and what is to follow.

Complementing this basic and pervading curiosity must be the ability to make use of information by analysis, correlation, and creativity. As a composite of accountant, auditor, and researcher, he must be able to sift the facts, bore to the essentials, fit the pieces into place, and see the whole as well as the parts. The ability to think beyond the immediate, to challenge precedent and come up with a new concept, even though radical, is requisite. In short, the qualities of the thinker are indispensable.

He must, and this is most important, approach his work with somewhat the same objectivity of view as the scientist, banishing prejudice and preconceptions and being honest with himself as well as those he deals with above, below, and on his own level.

Then, and here may be the rub, he must top these definite characteristics with a special polish—the quality of salesmanship. The best idea or system will die a-borning if it is not sold. Although the approach of the systems man is the soft rather than the hard sell, the ability to put his idea across in person and on paper is imperative to success. In fact, the first job of salesmanship for the systems man is to sell himself and faith in the skills and tools of his department and staff. He must have the ability to deal with people on all levels.

To sell himself, he must be worthy of respect and must instill confidence by virtue of his professional and personal qualities. A good dash of humor, enthusiasm, cooperativeness, and energy and tact to counteract the skepticism and control also required is most desirable.

These, then, are some of the personal qualities and aptitudes necessary for the sucessful and happy systems man or woman.

A few words about training. Although today's business programs on the college and university levels frequently offer specialized courses in systems and procedures work, there is no substitute for some experience in the market place. Formal training can also be obtained in adult education centers. Professional management associations, such as the American Management Association, the Society for the Advancement of Management, and the Systems and Procedures Association, broaden knowledge in the field through seminars, workshops, conferences, and publications. Courses in accounting, management, machine accounting, electronic computing, logic, business English, public speaking, and salesmanship offer good background for systems work.

In summary, for this challenging and diversified field, the systems man requires a many-faceted personality and diverse abilities, not the least of which are common sense and a sense of values.

Staffing the Department

He who is to manage and direct the systems and procedures activity should be a seasoned practitioner who has himself been through the course and can guide his people around the multitude of pitfalls that inevitably lie ahead. He should possess all of the qualities—leadership and personality, analytical ability, the facility for fluent speech and writing, patience, the will to horse-trade, and the ability to get along with all types of people— that he will expect of his staff. This man must be willing to give credit to others and able to get the job done using only staff authority.

The systems department is regarded by most management-knowledgeable firms as an excellent training area for future executives, since its activities cut across functional and departmental lines and provide a top management view of company operations. This is a frame of reference to which few other departments have so ready an access.

Therefore, many companies include a tour of duty with the department as part of their management training programs. This results in a periodic turnover of staff with a constant inflow of able, enthusiastic young people, fresh from operating experience. These carefully selected trainees are then thoroughly trained in systems and procedures principles and techniques, both on actual job assignments and by attendance at seminars and conferences of management and professional associations. One disadvantage of constant staff turnover is that the systems department manager cannot train just one set of employees, but must do a continuous job of training.

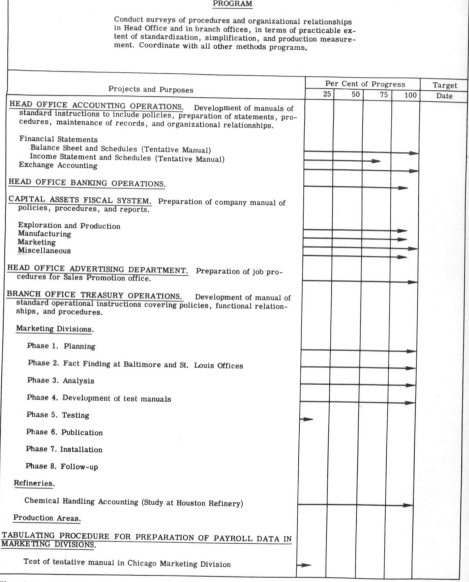

Fig. 2-2. Office Systems Program and Status of Project

There are certain spheres of knowledge that require a longer period of technical training than a company may wish to spend without productivity on the part of the trainee. Most of this knowledge pertains to office equipment, mechanical and electronic. Clerical work measurement and forms design can be taught in less time and with concurrent productivity, although they too are technical in their way. Some organizations make it a practice to hire senior, experienced systems analysts in these specialties as the hard core of the department. Their knowledge is then available as required by the junior personnel.

Use of Outside Consultants

The use of management consultants in business is generally accepted. The consultant may be part of an organization set up solely for the purpose of advising companies on specialized, functional business problems, such as public relations, advertising, sales promotion, organization, finance, data processing, or systems. He may also be part of an organization with other primary functions, such as education or public accounting. Here his services are adjuncts to the main purposes of the organizations. In either event, he is equipped by training, background, associations, and experience to counsel on special problems, to assist in formulating programs, and to train company personnel.

A number of reasons are often given by the systems department for considering the use of such outside services. These include requirements imposed by highly specialized or technical systems programs, the degree of systems staff specialization, time requirements, and organizational or political reasons.

A systems department in a large organization, investigating the application of electronic data processing to company operations, may call in an authority in the field for a preliminary appraisal before making a full-fledged study of its own. Then, after receiving the consultant's comments and recommendations, the department may carry on independently in formulating a program and implementing it.

A small company with a small systems staff may find it most economical and effective to retain a specialist in electronic data processing to perform the entire study, to recommend a suitable program, and to assist in ironing out problems of organization, staffing, and training. Many pitfalls inherent in the trial-and-error method can be avoided by accepting the guidance of specialists possessing substantial related experience.

Other programs that predate electronic data processing in the field of systems work are also frequently treated on a consulting basis. Such specialized programs include records management, forms administration, reporting analysis, work simplification, and the employee suggestion system. Usually, firms will have key staff people work closely with specialists in these fields during their studies. After the study has been completed and implemented, the staff disseminates and perpetuates the basic principles and techniques within the company.

Consultants also are called in to perform a special job when the priority of other systems projects does not permit the assignment of the permanent staff members to a new project. Sometimes, organizations prefer to use an outside consultant for certain types of studies where the resulting recommendations are expected to be unpopular and it is wished to avoid associating any company unit with them. An example of this might be when exten-

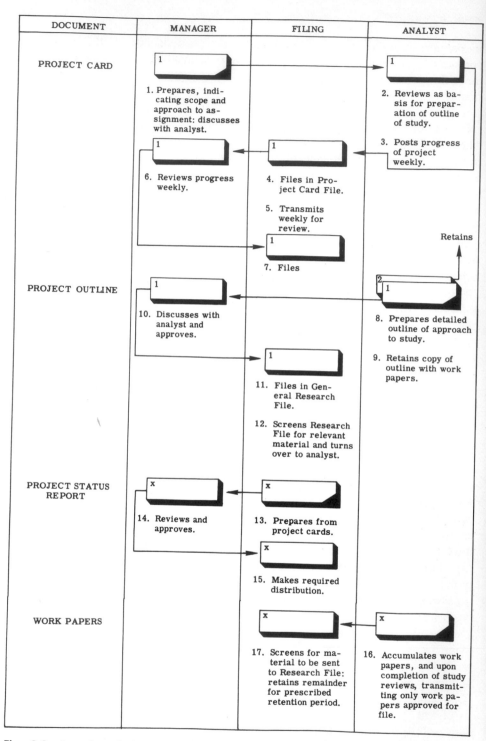

Fig. 2-3. Procedure for Assignment and Control of Methods Projects

sive organizational changes and personnel shifts are anticipated following a complete organization study. Unpalatable recommendations are sometimes more easily and completely accepted by company executives when they are made by an impartial outside group.

Perhaps the most common reason for using a consultant, however, is the desire of management to get the benefit of an impartial, competent outsider's view and advice. This outlook is quite in keeping with that in the professions of law and medicine, where consultations with specialists are a normal and expected occurrence.

These, then, are some of the reasons why consultants are used by systems departments and some of the most common areas of specialization. Some reasons various firms have for not using consultants follow.

There may be a preference for the use of knowledge of company operations by the company's own people. If it is necessary for new technical knowledge to be acquired by its people in order to do a certain job, the company elects to make this training available to them. It feels that a sound and intimate understanding of the company's internal affairs, operations, philosophies, policies, and procedures is of paramount importance, and that no outside consultant can offer this, regardless of his competence within his specialty.

Some companies feel that company employees will resent outsiders, and that the amount of antagonism and ill-feeling that would result from using a consultant would counterbalance the value of his recommendations. Others, for competitive reasons, do not wish certain company information to become known outside the firm. Then, some few have had unfortunate experiences with consultants.

Criteria frequently used for selecting a consultant include the reputation of the firm, results reported by others, and the general caliber of the staff. It is important to know also whether the men who will actually be doing the job are as competent as the men who make the contract. The consultant should be willing and ready to give a fairly accurate estimate of the total cost of the project and the time involved, as well as results to be expected. The best consultants are generally eager to avoid generalities and prefer to have the problem defined as specifically as possible prior to accepting the assignment. Experience within the same industry is also considered a requisite by many firms.

PROGRAM AND PROJECT PLANNING

A program may be considered to be the general plan for carrying out the assigned functions of the department. Projects consist of the detailed work assignments to the staff.

Phasing the Programs

When a systems and procedures department is introduced into an organization, there is generally a wealth of opportunity for accomplishment in profitable areas⌈ The typical department finds that its beginning phase is concentrated at first on the development of manuals covering policy and procedure involved in carrying out the basic programs of the department and, secondly, on the review of basic company procedures and the development of covering manuals.⌋ As these basic jobs are accomplished, the department usually finds itself able to devote more time to refinements and to act more truly as an internal consultant on special projects.

There are commonly six distinct programs: office systems, equipment standards, records management, office appraisal, coordination, and research and training. *Office systems* include both general systems and EDP or computer systems.

Office Systems Program

Conduct surveys of procedures and organizational relationships in terms of the practicable extent of standardization, simplification, and production measurement. The office systems program, although the most comprehensive of all, places its emphasis upon administrative work flows and the organizational relationships established to process the work. In the program, measurable units of work are developed and related to the number of employees required to process a given volume of work. Of necessity, this program is closely coordinated with the other programs. Analysts responsible for the office systems program possess the most general type of methods knowledge, although they must, from time to time, call for assistance from specialists engaged in other programs.

Equipment Standards Program

Conduct detailed studies and test makes and models of office machines and equipment for the purpose of making specific recommendations for practical application, proper utilization, and economical operation of equipment recommended. Establish basic requirements for the justification of purchase and for budgetary control purpose.

The equipment standards program is the most technical of all the programs. It deals with the best applications of office equipment, in accordance with the requirements of the procedures in which they are employed. Since procedural variations frequently govern whether or not a process will be performed manually or by machine, the equipment program is closely allied and coordinated with the office systems program. Likewise, the manner of housing filed records in cabinets becomes a joint consideration of analysts engaged in the records management program and the equipment program.

With the advent of electronic computers, the chief emphasis in recent years has been in this area. The following is a typical statement covering an electronic computer applications subprogram:

Coordinate throughout the company the development of uses for electronic computers to take advantage as rapidly as is practical of the operational and economic activities of the processing of data electronically; conduct research on the equipment and its proper application throughout industry; assist in applying the machines in cooperation with the offices involved.

Records Management Program

Develop filing systems and standards for the effective management of records. Develop recommendations concerning the retention of records in accordance with prescribed company policies.

The records management program comprehends filing systems and the administration of records generally, including their arrangement, accessibility, and preservation. Clearly a specialty, records management as a program must be conducted in terms of the procedures of which the records are a part.

Office Appraisal Program

Follow up new methods installations and periodically review on a comparative basis the effectiveness of office systems, using data derived from the production measurement phase of the office systems program.

The office appraisal program, although it may be considered as a final phase of the office systems program, is developed separately. This is primarily because its emphasis is upon the comparative measurement of work performed, following the standardization that results from the development of revised procedures. The program starts only after sufficient time has elapsed to permit an accurate evaluation of results and final adjustment of procedural and organizational details.

The office appraisal is not to be confused with the financial audit, which is primarily concerned with review of basic policies, procedures, and records for purposes of safeguarding the company's interests.

Coordination Program

Establish a systematic means of correlating forms and reports with related administrative procedures and coordinate the dissemination of information concerning policies and procedures.

Coordination of forms: Within existing company requirements, develop and maintain a system for review and clearance of forms for purposes of analysis and standardization prior to use. Coordinate standardization with the office systems program.

Coordination of recurring reports and statements: Develop and maintain a system for review and clearance of recurring reports and statements initiated or requested, to avoid duplication and overlapping of data. Coordinate operation of the plan with the office systems program.

Coordination of publications: Develop and maintain a system of review and clearance for standardization of format and consistency of content of manuals, instructions, and other publications involving policies, procedures, organization, reports, and statements of forms.

Each of the three segments of the coordination program could of itself become a separate program if the volume of work were sufficient to warrant separate emphasis. The coordination of forms, recurring reports, and publications is basic to administrative management. Without forms coordination, many duplicated forms, ill designed for ease of use, could slow down procedures and retard action. Without reports coordination, independent segments of the organization could impose reporting requirements upon other offices of an unduly burdensome or overlapping nature. Without publications coordination, conflicting instructions could be issued. Coordination provides a clearance that prevents administrative confusion and unnecessary expense.

Research and Training Program

Establish and maintain relationships with professional management societies and other companies for the mutual exchange of information relating to management improvements in policies, organization, procedures, equipment, and methods development techniques.

Develop, by laboratory methods, systems applications to company problems; test the applications; maintain a bibliography and file of data representing the most effective proven solutions to typical methods problems.

Prepare training material on all phases of systems work for the regular use of employees engaged in this field.

Conduct regularly scheduled seminars in systems problems and techniques.

Coordinate activities with all other systems programs.

The research and training program embraces the development and exchange of technical data relating to methods work between internal and outside sources. Data are available for training new analysts and for refresher material for the staff.

Directing through Projects

Projects constitute the nonroutine, nonrecurring studies that are made by methods analysts to further the goals of the programs. The result of a project ordinarily is the development of a new, or the modification of an existing, plan, policy, or procedure. Results normally are accomplished by means of a special report, revision of published instructions, issuance of a manual, or other appropriate media.

It is apparent that the acuteness of the individual problems will play a large part in determining the scheduling of the specific projects. The scope of any given project will be governed necessarily by the size and competence of the methods staff. Another thought that can be overlooked all too easily in the timing of projects is the absorption point of the company. Changes that are too numerous or too frequent cannot be digested by any office, so it is wise for the systems manager to guide himself accordingly.

Planning the Project

Following the assignment of a project to the methods analyst, there are preliminary preparations that must be made prior to the start of the study. Regardless of the type of analytical survey involved, these preparations are basically always the same. Their object is to insure that the course of the project is determined beforehand and that the desired result is kept in sight during all phases of the study.

Step 1: Determine who, what, and how long.

Who—Decide to whom the results of the project will be beneficial. Is the study directed toward management controls or toward assisting operating personnel in performing assigned functions? Decide also whose assistance will be required. Consider asking assistance from specialists in the field under study. Take the opportunity to discuss the problems with those who are most familiar with the project as a prime source of ideas.

What—Determine what the end result of the project will be, such as a report, a manual, or a letter of instruction.

How long—Determine how long it will take to complete the project. It is desirable to set a target date and to try conscientiously to meet that date, although this may be difficult because of unforeseen circumstances and it may later have to be revised.

Step 2: Obtain background data. Review pertinent reference material already available both inside and outside the company. What has already been accomplished? What have the results been? Study reports, manuals, instruction letters, and other reports pertaining to the subject to obtain a broad picture of the problem and to select authoritative reference material for later detailed study. Discuss the problem generally with the persons who have a working knowledge of how the job is performed. Obtain from them their experiences and problems. Ask for constructive suggestions for improvements.

Analyze available statistics. This will assist in evaluating the size of the project, such as the number of employees, number of transactions, monetary values, number of machines, or number of forms.

Step 3: Select location for conducting study. Select the office or area, in which the survey may be made most appropriately.

Step 4: Prepare tentative plans. Develop the course of the project in outline form, setting forth the objectives of the study and the method of attack. The plans should include, in chronological sequence, the steps that are proposed to be followed from the start to the end of the project. Upon completion of the outline, the analyst will be ready to embark upon the actual study.

ADMINISTERING THE DEPARTMENT

Controls

The extent of controls employed in internal departmental operation varies, depending upon a number of factors. These include the stage of over-all systems program, the type of projects undertaken, and the attitude of management toward "loose" or "tight" control.

When rather tight control is required, it may be accomplished through the use of detailed project cards. When a project is assigned to the analyst or analysts concerned, a project card, Figure 2-1, is completed, defining such information as: purpose and scope of the project, department(s) requested by or concerned, condition necessitating project, statistical data required and sources of data, end product planned, and estimated target date. As the project progresses, the assigned analyst records extent of progress and pertinent comments. Sometimes, a percentage type of gauge is used to indicate status. When the project is concluded, final findings and recommendations are noted. Detailed savings in quantity and cost for such items as man-hours, floor space, equipment, forms, reports, and postings may be given. These written reports are usually supplemented by verbal reports, and by periodic summary reports, often quarterly, prepared for advice to top management.

When an over-all systems program has been under way for some time, and management's emphasis is not particularly on dollar savings, a less formal approach to reporting is sometimes taken. As progress occurs, significant developments are presented in verbal reports and discussions. As major phases of a lengthy project are completed, a written report in memorandum form is prepared. Frequently, reports to top management are made on an annual text report basis, supplemented throughout the year, when appropriate, by special reports and discussions.

Manual of Techniques

One of the first projects that a systems department should undertake is the preparation of a manual covering systems principles and techniques. This will serve as a basic source reference for the department and will aid in indoctrinating new staff members. It is also an excellent means of disseminating basic systems information throughout the company.

Although the field of systems is an ever-evolving one, certain fundamental concepts, principles, and techniques have crystallized. A staff manual might well contain sections on the following:

1. Place of the Methods Staff in Management
2. Internal Operations of the Methods Staff
3. Survey Principles and Techniques
4. Production Control
5. Forms Control
6. Work Measurement
7. Work Simplification
8. Records Management
9. Office Appraisals
10. Office Equipment

MANAGER METHODS AND PROCEDURES

<u>Province</u>

Methods analyses.
Office procedures and equipment in all offices of the Company.

<u>General responsibilities and functions</u>

Direct and supervise the activities of the Methods and Procedures Department.

Develop programs involving procedural and methods planning; develop projects for improving effectiveness or co-ordination in assigned fields.

Analyze current policies, procedures, practices, forms and records; review charts and analyses reflecting work flows and performance, distribution of forms, maintenance of records, and specific action taken on such forms and records; ascertain essentiality of existing activities and approve the necessary changes to simplify or reduce clerical and administrative work and processing time.

Direct the preparation of manuals covering new or improved office methods; assist with the installation of such methods and arrange for training of employees in the required techniques.

Co-ordinate studies of office methods and equipment conducted in all offices; keep informed of the progress made on each study and disseminate results to all interested Head Office departments and offices.

Direct the development of job performance standards as a tool for office management and for comparative purposes when evaluating methods.

Maintain continuous research in new methods management practices and disseminate information to improve administrative operations.

Direct detailed studies to test makes and models of office machines and equipment, including electronic computers, for the purpose of making specific recommendations for practical application, proper utilization and economical operation of equipment recommended; establish basic requirements for the justification of purchases and for budgetary control purposes.

Direct surveys in all offices in terms of the practicable extent of standardization, simplification, and production measurement.

Maintain a follow-up on new methods installations and periodically review on a comparative basis the effectiveness of office systems using data derived from the production measurement phase of the office systems program.

Direct the development of filing systems and standards for the effective management of records; develop recommendations concerning the retention of records in accordance with prescribed company policies.

Develop and maintain, within existing Company requirements, a system for review and clearance of forms for purposes of analysis and standardization prior to use.

Develop and maintain a system for review and clearance for standardization of format and consistency of content of manuals, instructions and other publications involving policies, procedures, reports, and statements or forms.

Prepare training material on all phases of methods work for the systematic use of employees engaged in this field.

<u>Relationships</u>

Work closely with all offices of the company and its subsidiaries to develop improved office methods, to establish standards for office furniture and equipment, and to insure full co-ordination in promoting reciprocal use of data and reports.

Maintain external contacts with other companies and with professional management societies for the mutual exchange of information and the development of new ideas and methods.

Authorities

See separate section.

Fig. 2-4. Organization Write-up

Progress Revitalization

From time to time, management must take a careful look at its over-all program to see whether changing conditions have necessitated a change in approach or emphasis. As stated goals are attained, new ones must be set. Complacency is an attitude which above all must be avoided.

3

The Systems Study

ARMOND L. METTLER

E S B Incorporated
Philadelphia, Pa.

ARMOND L. METTLER was born June 1, 1909, at Sleepy Eye, Minn.,
and received his early education in that area. In 1932 he graduated from
Iowa State College with a degree in engineering; two years later he
received a master's degree in economics. He joined the Grinnell Com-
pany, Providence, R.I., in 1935 as a cost accountant, and after six months
was transferred to the firm's Warren, Ohio, plant. In 1937, he was again
transferred, this time to Grinnell's Columbia Malleable Castings Cor-
poration Division at Columbia, Pa., where he subsequently became office
manager and credit manager.

In 1943 he was employed by E S B Incorporated as a staff assistant
in the executive department. He was made administrative assistant to the
vice-president in charge of manufacturing in 1944, and manager of sys-
tems and procedures in 1948. In 1957 he was appointed executive assistant
in the controller's department. He is assistant controller responsible for
systems and procedures, data processing, tax and government reports,
and corporate office accounting.

Authoritative articles under his by-line have been published in
Systems and Procedures Journal, The Office, *and* Office Management and
Equipment *magazines. Mr. Mettler is a member and past president of the*
Systems and Procedures Association.

INTRODUCTION

The nature of systems or methods studies varies substantially between
companies. The organization structure, the place of the systems activity in
that structure, and the management charter under which the systems and
procedures activity operates have an important influence on the types of
studies undertaken. Furthermore, the qualifications of the systems and
procedures personnel may have the effect of limiting or increasing the
degree of complexity of studies entrusted to the systems activity. With well-
qualified personnel and management recognition and support, a systems
and procedures staff might be assigned the responsibility of analyzing the
administrative efficiency of a company being considered for purchase or

merger, whereas a less talented staff, or one without a strong organization position, might be restricted to departmental methods studies of limited objectives.

Ideally, each systems study is part of a carefully planned program covering a long period and carrying the approval of the company management and of the line and functional managers. Operating conditions are then ideal from the perspective of the administrator responsible for the systems and procedures activity. The systems and procedures staff can then be budgeted with a minimum allowance for lost time due to overlapping studies, inopportune timing. of projects, and uncooperative attitudes of functional groups to be studied. The studies programmed are quite likely to lead successfully to planned objectives, and the maximum available savings per dollar of analyst time expended are more nearly realized.

In reality, only a portion of available staff time can be devoted to the long-range program. A certain amount of time must be scheduled for services to management and operating activities in solving short-range operating problems and putting out brush fires. Requests for studies originate with managers and department heads who encounter problems they cannot solve with the aid of personal staff, either for lack of specialized knowledge or because the problems involve organizations outside the scope of responsibility of the requester. Many systems men pride themselves on their ability to promote good relations with lower echelons of supervision as a result of quick studies. There is no doubt that this type of service can pave the way in certain areas for more comprehensive systems studies at a later date as part of the long-range systems program. However, the danger for the systems administrator lies in the fact that success in this area creates a greater demand for this uncoordinated type of service, and he soon finds himself with a backlog of project requests that would require the full-time services of the entire systems staff.

The administrator of a systems and procedures staff must have both an ideal approach to a project and a practical, less formal approach. His experience in the problem areas as well as his professional knowledge of systems work must guide him in the handling of varied studies. The systems man is under a misconception if he contends that he never needs to use charts, work counts, task lists, and other recognized analysis techniques. By the same standard, he is incompetent if he always insists on a formalized study using all the professional techniques regardless of the nature of the problem, the source from which it came, and the study's objectives. (See Appendix A for a detailed "Outline for Conducting and Implementing a Systems Study.")

Project Requests

Recognizing organization channels in accepting requests for studies pays multiple dividends. The most important dividend is the cooperation that accrues to the study when all affected personnel realize that their superiors are parties to the request. Furthermore, the executive takes substantial interest in a report resulting from a study that he personally authorized, or at least approved. Although a systems staff, from the nature of its company's organization, may operate informally as compared with similar groups in other companies, its administrator should make every effort to have all requests for studies come from the top of the organization or division of the function to be studied.

There is an informal as well as formal organization in every company. Clearance of a project request with the informal organization is a matter of simple communications, usually on the part of the systems administrator. The old and influential key man in the sales department, who functions without much formal authority, may be able to supply the real reason for the request for a study of branch record keeping. At any rate, because of his early knowledge of the requested study, it is good to have him, and others like him, on the analyst's side.

Every administrator of a systems staff must be on guard for opinionated and prejudiced requests. Many departmental executives are prone to recommend, with pressure, systems studies in other departments. The administrator must not be trapped into agreeing to study the sales forecasting system without the sympathy of the sales manager just because the manufacturing department claims to be receiving poor forecasts of requirements.

Perhaps the best method of assuring that the requester carefully considers the value of the project is to insist upon written requests that define the problem. Figure 3-1 illustrates a form used as a request for a systems study and as a project assignment sheet. Formalizing in this manner assures some precision in describing the problem. It is also a means of communicating the request through organization channels. The written request serves to set up the project assignment and to define the analyst's authority in pursuing the study.

Getting the request in writing certainly does not eliminate the desirability of discussing the proposed study with the party who initiated it. Discussion, based on the written request for the study, should be extended in most cases to include additional members of the affected organization and members of the informal organization previously cited. The objective is perfection in the definition of the project, its scope and background, in order to make the resulting assignment clear in the mind of the analyst.

The Project Assignment

Many systems staffs work entirely on a project basis. Certainly it is the desirable way of controlling the expenditure of staff time. Even small jobs should be assigned in writing. The larger jobs should be described in greater detail in order to insure a minimum of misdirected effort on the part of the analysts. The project assignment sheet, prepared by the administrator more or less in detail depending upon the complexity of the study, is an aid to clear and precise assignment of projects.

The desired end result of the study should be indicated on the project assignment sheet. It may be a feasibility report, an evaluation report, a computer program, a recommended policy, a procedure, an organization chart, a job instruction manual, or other results, depending upon the objectives and nature of the problem.

The project assignment sheet should spell out the project methods to be followed by the analyst and should indicate the pertinent background of the problem. The systems administrator should have a broad knowledge of the organization and its administrative peculiarities to measurably reduce the research and analysis by spelling out for the analyst the approach to the problem and the underlying factors to be considered. For a more complex assignment, the administrator could readily advise concerning any or all of the points listed on the following page.

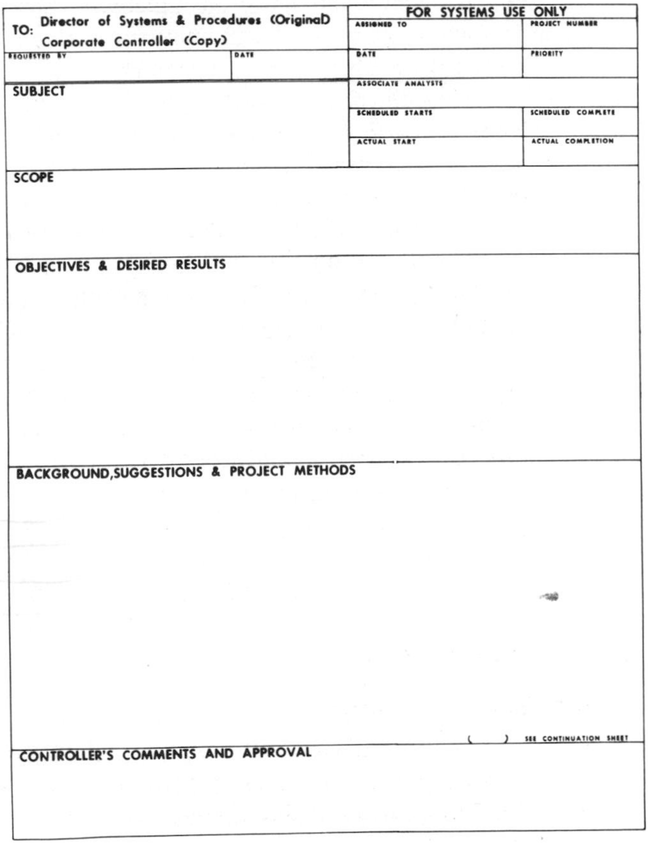

TO: Director of Systems & Procedures (Original) Corporate Controller (Copy)		FOR SYSTEMS USE ONLY	
		ASSIGNED TO	PROJECT NUMBER
REQUESTED BY	DATE	DATE	PRIORITY
SUBJECT		ASSOCIATE ANALYSTS	
		SCHEDULED STARTS	SCHEDULED COMPLETE
		ACTUAL START	ACTUAL COMPLETION
SCOPE			
OBJECTIVES & DESIRED RESULTS			
BACKGROUND, SUGGESTIONS & PROJECT METHODS			
			( ) SEE CONTINUATION SHEET
CONTROLLER'S COMMENTS AND APPROVAL			

Fig. 3-1. Systems and Procedures Project Assignment

1. Other studies completed or in progress that bear on this project
2. Management planning that might alter the project recommendations
3. Organization structure of the problem area
4. Personnel to be interviewed
5. Union agreement considerations
6. Timeliness for reassignment of functions in the company organization
7. Mechanization possibilities to be considered
8. Specific accounting statements and reports to be examined

It is usually good practice to send a copy of the completed project assignment sheet to the executive having the over-all responsibility for the area included in the study. This gives the executive an opportunity to add pertinent information, advise his subordinates of the study, and, generally, add his blessings.

Planning the Study

When the systems analyst receives the project assignment sheet, he uses the "background and project methods" section as a guide for preparing an outline of the study. The administrator should approve the outline before releasing the analyst to start the study.

The outline serves as an aid in coordinating the investigation and development, particularly when a team of analysts handles the assignment. It should be sufficiently complete to prevent overlooking any facts to be gathered or areas to be investigated.

An important part of planning the study is the thorough preparation of the analyst responsible for carrying out the assignment. Whereas the "background and project methods" portion of the project assignment sheet serves as a guide, detailed research will enable the analyst to be at his best when he begins his interviews. To gain the respect of the supervisors he must seem to have an intelligent grasp of the problem and be schooled in the surrounding conditions. For this reason, as well as to aid his fact-gathering efforts, the analyst should consider several points before beginning the study. Examination of manuals, organization charts, and personnel records, review of previous studies in the affected areas, discussion of similar problems with analysts of other companies, perusal of literature on the subject, and discussion of the problem with other members of the systems staff will all prove to be worthy investments of the analyst's time before he starts the actual investigation.

The Preliminary Survey

It is not always possible to assign specific projects without a preliminary survey. There are several situations that indicate the need for this, and a brief review of possible situations will develop the nature of the preliminary survey.

An office may be failing to produce the required results in terms of quality of information, timeliness of information, or economy. A preliminary survey may be conducted to determine the general conditions of the office and establish specific projects with priority for study, projects which should result in recommendations for accomplishing the objectives of the office.

In other cases, the preliminary survey is designed to result in a feasibility report that recommends, or does not recommend, a methods project to develop a specific solution to a problem. In such a case, the preliminary survey *refines* the statement of the problem, breaks it down into workable projects, and recommends a schedule for accomplishment. For instance, if manual methods of timekeeping are costly in the computation of gross earnings based on straight-time rates and a complex incentive system, and it is thought that a computer method could be adopted with resulting economy, a preliminary survey may be required to disclose the real factors that cause the claimed inefficiencies. If the preliminary survey indicates that a methods study would be a good investment of analysts' time, specific projects can be authorized.

The preliminary survey is intended to isolate the problem factors, not to develop solutions. It is, therefore, a quick gathering of data in a broad or general manner for exploratory purposes. Since detail is avoided, the interviews are quite likely to be held with the upper level of supervision. The questions asked and the samples of documents collected vary with the objectives of the survey.

Redefining the Problem and Adjusting the Study

With or without a preliminary survey, the methods study should be opened with an attitude of reconnaissance. The analyst must recognize that the definition of the problem, and the scope, objectives, and desired results of the study, are subject to redefinition until progress indicates that the results of the study will be satisfactory. The problem was probably referred to the systems administrator by an executive who was troubled by a specific failure in his area of responsibility. To a large extent, therefore, the project request represents the diagnosis of the executive, and may be colored by error in facts, or lack of knowledge of systems in other areas that directly affect his operation. Consequently, redefinition is always desirable and sometimes essential, as the following hypothetical case shows.

Assume that the manufacturing executive responsible for an assembly plant of 2,000 workers was troubled by material shortages in spite of a substantial expenditure for the material control function. A conference with the controller and the systems manager resulted in a project to develop a new material control system. The new system was to permit more detailed analyses of parts stocks and to facilitate simplified and prompt reorder of optimum quantities to provide materials at the right time without inflating the inventory investment. Since punched card equipment was being used for other functions, and since more analyses seemed to be required, the systems manager, among other proposals, suggested project methods involving the use of electronic equipment to achieve an integrated system and a management information system.

The senior analyst, through the initial investigation, confirmed the problem, but found several factors that called for a restatement of the project.

First, although it was thought that manufactured parts were an integral part of the shortage problem, a review of past shortages and discussion with the production control manager changed this concept. Shortages of manufactured parts were relatively few and caused little difficulty, because such parts could be produced on a flexible short-term schedule. The real problem was caused by purchased parts.

Second, the purchasing agent had for some time been dissatisfied with the time required to convert a purchase requisition into a purchase order on the proper supplier.

Third, a large percentage of the total number of purchased parts items were small items with relatively little value. These items were being given the same control and purchasing routine as all other items.

Fourth, the production scheduling supervisor wanted a weekly analysis of open purchase orders by part numbers with promised delivery dates. He wanted to relate such promised deliveries to his assembly requirements.

Fifth, the accounts payable supervisor confirmed the purchasing agent's criticism of the slow receiving system.

Before pursuing the study further, the senior analyst conferred with the systems manager to redefine the project. The redefinition was approved by the manufacturing executive and the controller to cover material control, inventory control, and procurement. Since accounts payable routines were so closely associated with procurement, it was decided to include this function in the study. Furthermore, since use of a computer seemed a strong possibility, perhaps it could be used to write the vendors' checks, as well as to charge receipts to stock. With this concept the new "recommended project methods" included the statement: "Explore the possibilities of applying computer processing to parts stock control and attempt to integrate the data processing for requisitioning and ordering stock replenishment, receiving, payables, and inventory accounting functions."

The axiom to be taken from this hypothetical case could be stated as follows:

Within the limitations of available staff time and deadlines for accomplishment, the methods study should be as broad as possible, so that interrelated problems will be solved at one time, and conflict of methods objectives avoided.

If a study becomes overextended in scope, it should be divided into a series of projects.

Fact Gathering

The most important means of gathering facts is the systems interview. The skillful interview is not an easy accomplishment. To some analysts it comes with reasonable naturalness. Others spend years developing the ability to interview workers and supervisors with an objectivity that produces results and a passive, friendly attitude that begets confidence. The obvious characteristic of the natural interviewer is his personality. He is conceded to be not only an intelligent fellow, but a regular guy. He may be earning several times the salary of the operating supervisor, but no one would know it.

The skillful analyst *sells* systems work as he plies his trade. He lets the interviewee "in on" his problem. He explains his approach to the problem. He is always complimentary, never critical. He always finds something about the operation to admire. He casually makes helpful suggestions to the supervisor: "I just happened to see an extra copyholder that your statistical typist might be able to use." He promises to have a minor adjustment included in the next revision of a procedure. He solicits suggestions as to facts needed, how to get them, opinions on probable solutions—and on the outcome of the World Series. Every interview is designed to produce facts and gain a friend to whom the analyst can return on a later assignment.

The second important means of fact gathering is the physical examination of paper—perusing files, counting completed and in-process work, collecting facsimiles of completed documents. Blank forms are of doubtful value; filled-in samples disclose the peculiarities of the work. For this reason, care should be exercised that the samples collected are typical of the work. As a corollary, however, the analyst must take care not to be misled by the supervisor who points out only the extremely complex examples that are not typical of the average.

The analyst carefully notes the workplace and its layout. He obtains the names of key personnel. He notes the organizational arrangement, the type of equipment being used, its condition and age. If the analysis involves all work being done by an organizational unit, the analyst obtains, with the aid of the supervisors and the operators, task lists for each job in the unit. These lists detail all the duties of each job, the frequency of occurrence, time required, and typical volume.

The objectives of the fact-gathering phase of the analysis can be summarized as having to do with all pertinent data concerning the following:

1. Objectives and requirements of the system—what is the system designed to produce? A labor distribution as well as a payroll? Is the outstanding requirement one of speed of information, quality, or cost?

2. The organization and personnel assigned to the system—is the organization proper with respect to accepted principles? How many and what quality of personnel operate the system?

INSTRUCTIONS	Employee Name
	Dept. -Division-Section
1. Number each task. Write or print legibly.	Job Title
2. Start with task you perform most frequently.	
3. Describe each task.	Name of Supervisor
4. Report time in units of 1/4 hour.	
	Date · Approved by

Names of Employees Supervised by you

NO.	LISTING OF DUTIES	FREQUENCY					QUANTITY	TIME
		Day	Wk.	Mo.	Yr.	Other		

Fig. 3-2. Task List

3. Policies involved in the system—pricing policies in a billing system, labor agreements in a payroll system, management's inventory policies in a material control system.

4. Details of the present system—answers to the questions who, what, when, where, how, and why.

5. Cost of the system—number of personnel, salary ranges, depreciation, rental costs of equipment, forms and supplies, space charges.

6. Effectiveness of the system—does it do what it was designed to do in the time allowed, with the proper quality, at the optimum cost?

7. Interrelationships with other systems—does the time study system unnecessarily complicate timekeeping? Does the method of placing purchase orders multiply the work of accounts payable? Are the systems integrated along the principles of automated data processing?

8. Forms, records, and reports—are they useful? Of efficient design? Duplicating other documents? Properly filed? Retained a minimum period?

The fact gathering, on the one hand, must be thorough. No significant facts may be missed without jeopardizing the project. On the other hand, the fact gathering must be strictly within the scope of the project. Generally, fact gathering requires time of supervisors and their clerical personnel. Needless consumption of such time reacts to the discredit of the systems program.

Recording the Facts

The most general requirement, and the only important one, is the exercise of extreme care in the recording. What is clear today may be totally confusing a few weeks later, when the facts are being analyzed. Therefore, charts, graphs, and tables should be used, depending upon the nature of the data. The first rule is always: "Make the record clear enough for someone else to understand."

Obviously, certain kinds of data are best recorded in special forms. When the study applies to all duties of an office, there is need for an understanding of the organization of that office. This can be a position chart, a personnel chart, a functional chart, or, most likely, a combination of such organization charts. In preparing these charts, the analyst is automatically analyzing the possibilities of rearranging the organization for better accomplishment of the objectives.

When the study applies to an entire organizational unit or a specific group of clerks, a basic technique is the task list for each member of the unit. This was referred to earlier in our discussion of fact gathering and is the basis for preparation of the work distribution chart to be used in analyzing the facts (see Figure 3-3).

In contrast to the copious use of scratch-pad notes as prepared by so many analysts, William A. Gill recommends with considerable merit the use of a "Procedure Analysis Work Sheet," as illustrated in Figure 3-4. This is a printed form on which can be filled in all the details of paper flow and processing. It allows for an orderly recording of the who, what, when, where, why, and how of the procedure. It is particularly helpful when there is substantial paper flow to be analyzed in detail. The work sheets make

Work Distribution Chart

ACTIVITY	TOTAL MAN HOURS	Frank Stapelton SECTION CHIEF CAF-6	MAN HRS	Thomas Freeman ANALYST CAF-6	MAN HRS	Wm. Sullivan CASE DIRECTOR CAF-7	MAN HRS	Mary Moody CORRESP. CLK. CAF-5	MAN HRS	Grace Hoffman HEAD-STENO-POOL CAF-5	MAN HRS	Mary O'Rourke STENO IN POOL CAF-2	MAN HRS
ISSUE CERTIFICATES CLASS 127 A	121	Policy review recommendations Final review & sign recommendations	17 6	Preparing recommendations for action	19	Checking drafts for form Checking final statements for form	6 10	Dictating acknowledgments Signing acknowledgments	16 4	Proofreading acknowledgments	6	Checking addresses Type answers, drafts, statements Take dictation	6 20 11
ISSUE CERTIFICATES CLASS 127 B	54	Reviewing and signing	7	Checking for form Re-checking approvals	7 2	Preparing approval notices	13	Tabulating	11	Proofreading Selecting field applications Type "51" forms	2 3 3	Checking applications for address changes Numbering applications	4 2
GENERAL PUBLIC INQUIRY SERVICE	19	Interviewing callers	2	Preparing daily report Interviewing callers Dictating replies to special inquiries	6 2 1	Interviewing callers	1	Interviewing callers Preparing cumulative report	2 1	Assembling printed materials	3	Interviewing callers	1
FURNISHING CASE DATA TO COMPLIANCE DIV.	24	Reviewing	2	Checking for form Gathering data	1 1	Gathering data Dictating Revising	5 2 3	Tabulating and checking figures	3	Check field men's names Laying out reports Code info reports	2 2 2	Tabulating data	1
ADMINISTRATION	34	Confer with pers. off. Conferences Preparing budget request	6 4 3	Staff conferences	2			Posting attendance records Preparing administrative reports	3 2	Hearing grievances Trg. new emp. Proofread stone work	1 3 10		
WAR EFFORT AND EMPLOYEE WELFARE	17	Making speeches	1	Making car pool arrangements Keeping credit unit records	2 3	Arranging blood bank Writing Army newsletter	1 1			Bond selling records Collect hosp. payments Collect health payments	3 2 1	Handling arrangements for girls baseball team	3
MISCELLANEOUS	19			Analyzing operating reports of other sections	2	Making security inspections Controlling routed materials	4 2	Special messenger service Cutting up old forms to use as scratch paper	4 2	Sorting old files Keeping phone directory up to date	3 2		
	288		48		48		48		48		48		48

ACTIVITIES in the order of importance in the first column.

EMPLOYEES by name, grade, and working title in order of their responsibility.

TASKS for each employee for each activity in the proper spaces on form.

TOTAL HOURS for each employee and for each activity.

Fig. 3-3. Work Distribution Chart

easy the preparation of procedures and flow charts, which are recommended for analysis of the facts.

Facsimiles of processed documents are by themselves valuable records of the facts. Careful recording of the facts permits verification of the findings by the supervisor. This is an important step that is often overlooked by inexperienced analysts. Besides the obvious verification, this step accomplishes two important things: it impresses the supervisor with the thoroughness and conscientiousness of the analyst, and it allays his fear that systems men will act with insufficient knowledge of the facts.

Analyzing the Facts

To permit logical analysis, the facts must be organized in a manner that relates them to the objectives of the various major steps of the system, and discloses the reasons for the failure of the system to accomplish its objectives. The purpose of the study and its scope have an important bearing on the organization of the facts. The general rule is to group the facts according to the objective of the system, the external factors that may seriously affect the accomplishment of the objective, and the major steps of the system. As the facts are organized, the analyst can indicate questions to be resolved for each group of facts. For instance, what would be the effect of eliminating the mathematical check of vendors' invoices for charges of less than $10? Could the check of extensions of customer invoices be combined with the quality review of the duplicate copies rather than making the check before the invoice copies are prepared?

Under any method of organizing the facts, the effect should be to break down the study into digestible portions. The portions should permit logical study, treating the most significant features first. The wise systems

PROCEDURE ANALYSIS WORK SHEET			PAGE NUMBER	NO. OF PAGES
PROCEDURE				
FORM TITLE			FORM NUMBER	
TYPE OF FORM Standard ☐ Treasury ☐ CSC ☐ VA ☐ VA Branch ☐ OTHER (Specify)				
VOLUME _____ sets per	NOW PREPARED Manual ☐ Typed ☐ OTHER (Specify)			
REMARKS				

PREPARATION AND PROCESSING			DISPOSITION OF COPIES			
COPY NOS.	ORGANIZATIONAL ELEMENT	DETAILS OF PROCESSING	FOR-WARDS	SUS-PENDS	DES-TROYS	FILES

INSTRUCTIONS TO ANALYSTS
1. Obtain the signature or initials of the person(s) who can verify that this work sheet has been reviewed and is an accurate presentation of fact.
2. Obtain and attach to this work sheet two copies of the form(s) analyzed.

Fig. 3-4. Procedure Analysis Work Sheet

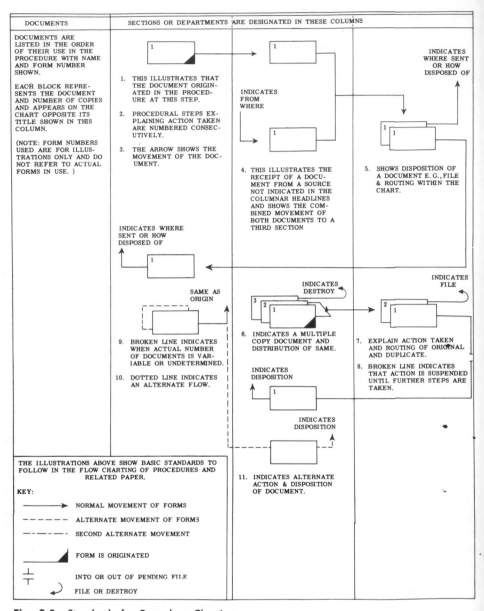

Fig. 3-5. Standards for Procedure Charting

manager will not permit a drawn-out study to accomplish the last ten per cent of an analysis when ninety per cent of the problem contains the essentials and can be resolved with the treatment of only a few significant features.

A great deal of emphasis in systems studies is placed on charting. Many kinds and variations of similar charting techniques are used to advantage. In selecting the type of chart, the purpose to be accomplished is the major consideration. A chart designed to show the over-all paper work flow will not serve as a tool for analysis of motion economy. A chart for the purpose of presenting the data to others must be a great deal simpler than a chart to be used only by the analyst to study the system. Extensive use of symbols in charting may represent a saving in time to the analyst who understands the symbols, but it is completely out of place in charts prepared for presentation to a line manager.

Since charting is a time-consuming job, it should be used only to serve a useful purpose. A chart should be used to clarify the facts, make the facts more understandable, and disclose missing links in the details of the system. The more important types of charts are discussed briefly below.

A procedure chart shows the flow of paper and the operating steps required to process it. It is usually necessary when the study is concerned with a complex paper flow. Each work unit is assigned a column, and the flow of documents is pictured in the proper columns, together with brief descriptions of the processing steps in each work unit. This procedure chart is easy to prepare, particularly if a procedure analysis work sheet has been prepared during the fact-gathering survey. It not only portrays the complete flow and processing of the paper, but assures the analyst that all copies have been brought to a logical procedural conclusion (*see* Figure 3-5).

A forms distribution chart is a simplified version of the procedure chart. It simply shows the flow of forms through columns representing organizational units or clerks, without notation of the processing details. It is a means of accounting for all copies of a form and indicating the units that are concerned with them.

A forms analysis chart is used to determine all the detail that is recorded on a form or group of forms, usually the latter. It is generally called for when there is a possibility of combining two or more forms (*see* Figure 3-6).

A layout flow chart indicates the geographic flow of paper through an office. It is used primarily to analyze the possibility of improving the arrangement of work stations (*see* Figure 3-7).

The organization chart is used to study the possibilities of adjusting the organization structure in an effort to improve the assignment of functions, effectiveness of supervision, and general conformity to organization principles.

The work distribution chart is invaluable for showing compactly the duties of each of a group of clerks and the time required for such duties, as related to the major functions of the group. It can be used as a means of estimating the cost of functions performed.

The process chart, or flow process chart, is used to set forth in fine detail the operational steps required to process information. It also records the temporary and permanent file operations and the transport required in the method. Its purpose is to analyze the efficiency of the processing (*see* Figure 3-8).

FORMS ANALYSIS CHART OF RECURRING DATA		FORM TITLE →								
DATE OF ANALYSIS	PAGE OF PAGES									
ACTIVITY										
ANALYST										TOTAL
ITEMIZED DATA		FORM NO.	FORM NO.	FORM NO.	FORM NO.	FORM NO.	ORM N	FORM NO.		
1.										
2.										
3.										
4.										
5.										
6.										
7.										
8.										
9.										
10.										
11.										
12.										
13.										
14.										
15.										
16.										
17.										
18.										
19.										
20.										
21.										
22.										
23.										
24.										
25.										
TOTAL ☐ CARRIED FORWARD ☐										

Fig. 3-6. Forms Analysis Chart of Recurring Data

Right- and left-hand charts are used in an attempt to analyze in detail the workplace efficiency of processing. Analysis with this technique should result in improved balance of motions and economy of time of processing.

Statistical charts are frequently helpful in analyzing the data. Although statistical analysis is itself a specialty, and a friendly statistician can be of help, the systems analyst should be able to prepare bar and pie charts, and various graphs to determine and demonstrate relationships between data. Because there are so many studies in which frequency of occurrences or values dictates a solution, special consideration should be given to the frequency distribution chart. A simple one illustrating the distribution of sales order values is shown in Figure 3-9. For computer programming, logical charts or block diagrams are used.

Developing the Solution

Probably the first principle in attacking any systems problem is to adopt the broad approach, that is, to examine the problem in relation to the entire organization and to measure it against known standards of good management.

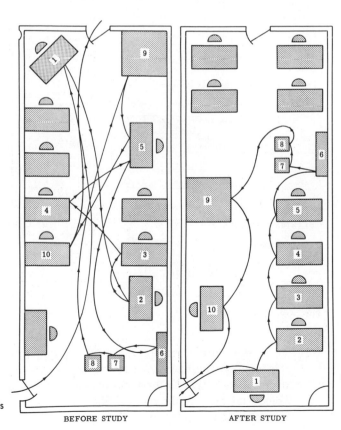

Fig. 3-7. Layout Flow Charts
(before and after study)   BEFORE STUDY   AFTER STUDY

ACTIVITY ANALYSIS CHART

ACTIVITY CHARTED PROCESSING INCOMING MAIL						CHARTED BY JOHN SMITH		DATE 1/16/67
ORGANIZATIONAL UNIT MAIL DEPARTMENT						APPROVED BY L J		DATE 1/25/67

DETAILS OF (PRESENT)(PROPOSED) METHOD	Step No.	Symbols	Distance in Feet	Time in Minutes	NOTES
		○⇨□D▼			
Messenger picks up mail from post office & places it at work table	1	○⇨□D▽	3B	25	Walks to post office (3 blocks away) with special cart
Clerk opens bag and dumps contents on table	2	●⇨□D▽			
Sorts mail into two categories	3	●⇨□D▽			
(1) General mail (company)		◑⇨□D▽			
(2) Individually addressed mail		◑⇨□D▽			
Time stamps envelope of individual mail	4	●⇨□D▽			Uses automatic date time stamp machine
Counts number of individual mail	5	●⇨□D▽			
Posts number in log book by date	6	●⇨□D▽			
Places individual mail in outgoing basket for sorting by department	7	●⇨□D▽			
Sorts general mail by size of envelope	8	●⇨□D▽			
Places in slicer for slicing edge	9	●⇨□D▽			Slicer on work table
Extracts contents, 1 envelope at a time, time stamps contents & staples to envelope	10	●⇨□D▽			If contents contains check, places aside for special handling
Rubber stamps routing stamp	11	●⇨□D▽			Use dept. routing stamp A
Reads contents & checks rating and places in outgoing basket	12	●⇨□D▽			
Delivers all "read" mail to department sorting	13	○◖□D▽	20		
Holds mail until messenger returns from route	14	○⇨□◤▽		30	Average time mail waits
Checks mail for time stamp (continued on next page)		○⇨■D▽			
		○⇨□D▽			
		○⇨□D▽			
		○⇨□D▽			

ELIMINATE! COMBINE! SIMPLIFY! CHANGE SEQUENCE! IMPROVE!	SUMMARY						USE REVERSE SIDE FOR DRAWING IF REQUIRED.
		PRESENT		PROPOSED		DIFFERENCE	
		NO. TIME		NO. TIME		NO. TIME	
	○ OPERATIONS						
	⇨ TRANSPORTATIONS						
	□ INSPECTIONS						
	D DELAYS						PAGE 1 OF 2
	▽ STORAGES						
	DISTANCE TRAVELED	FT.		FT.		FT.	

Fig. 3-8. Process Chart

Many problems can be solved by an analysis of the organization. Can the functions be reassigned to reduce communications, storage delays, and overlapping work? Is the function misplaced and being performed with no "blood interest" in the results? Should a new unit be established to increase specialization? Is the span of control overextended, supervision too thin?

Does the assignment of functions make impossible the operation of internal controls? Can like functions, especially those using the same data, be combined for greater efficiency and better flexibility resulting from a larger, combined work force? Is the delegation of authority so limited that tardy decisions are handicapping the work? Is there a logical function that has been overlooked and for which no one is responsible? Should an organization unit be eliminated because its cost exceeds the value of the function performed? Are line instructions coming from more than one source with confusion resulting? Is there too great a dependence on staff and committee organization? Is the organization handicapped by lack of written procedures and delegation of authorities?

The second guiding principle in systems problem solving is to look for eliminations. Eliminations are more lucrative than simplifications. An entire function is subject to elimination if it does not contribute to the objective more than it costs to perform the function. In other words, each operation within a function must contribute more than it costs.

In analyzing a work unit, a study of the work distribution chart may disclose possibilities for elimination and reassignment. Such a study should provide answers to the following questions:

1. What operations require the most time? Are these operations justified in taking so much time? Are they really important? How could the objectives be accomplished if we were forced to allocate less time to the performance of such operations?

2. Are too many people assigned to the same operation or function? If the jobs are spread too thin, the required coordination is expensive due to excessive handling and comprehension time. There is a high incidence of errors, and it is harder to track down responsibility for errors.

3. Is there too much switching from job to job? Changing jobs involves start-up and clean-up time, which are unproductive.

4. Are highly trained personnel being required to perform unskilled tasks? If so, rearrangement of duties may be required. Similar rearrangement may be required if unskilled personnel are assigned to operations requiring a great degree of skill.

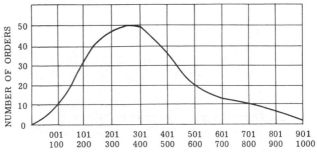

Fig. 3-9. Frequency Distribution Curve

SALES VALUE PER ORDER IN DOLLARS

5. Consultation with supervisors may indicate that the operations as assigned result in unrealistic schedules and peak loads. Reassignment of duties is then in order.

6. Is it possible to mechanize some operations or functions?

In studying the efficiency of a paper flow system, the procedure chart may indicate an excess of many things. Too many different documents, many copies of documents, too many persons or organizational units involved in the procedure, too many temporary files, or too many insignificant operations, such as reviews. The first consideration should be that of elimination. Studies of the organization chart, the work distribution chart, and the procedure chart may readily indicate that a simple reassignment of functions makes further development unnecessary.

Importance of Work Flow

The importance of work flow is not always fully realized. Although a study of the procedure chart and the layout flow chart may indicate possibilities for reducing operating steps and travel of information, there is more to be considered in work flow improvement.

The flow of work may be divided into any one or a combination of three basic patterns. These are the serial plan, the parallel plan, and the unit assembly plan. The nature of the processing of the information, the character of the paper work, and the policy objectives for the system (economy, total cycle time, quality level) largely indicate the plan or combination of plans that will accomplish the objectives most efficiently.

The serial or assembly line plan (*see* Figure 3-10) provides a single channel through which the work flows. Specialists perform the operation steps of the process and should develop a high degree of efficiency with a minimum of skill and training. Since there would be a number of clerks or operators in this channel of work flow, there would be increased "comprehension time," and there could be a rather large amount of material in process with significant delay inherent in temporary storage. Whereas the cost may be at a minimum, reflecting the efficiency of specialists, the total cycle time of the paper work may be excessive.

The parallel or concurrent handling plan (*see* Figure 3-11) divides the

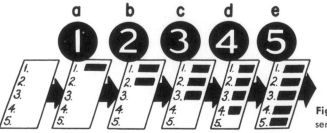

Fig. 3-10. The Serial (or Assembly Line) Plan

work in bulk on an arbitrary basis among two or more clerks or groups, each of them completing all, or nearly all, of the operations of the system. Thus, the clerk is assigned a greater variety of operating steps than would be the case in the serial plan, with resultant potential for increased job interest. This plan tends to reduce the total comprehension time and cycle time and the movement of work in process. It does not provide the advantages of specialization and requires more training than is inherent in the serial plan.

The unit assembly or simultaneous handling plan (*see* Figure 3-12) takes advantage of multiple copies of a form set to divide the work so that two or more clerks simultaneously perform operating steps on a single unit of paper work. The copies are finally reassembled. This plan allows for the advantages of specialization and job simplification and tends to minimize cycle time. On the other hand, it requires the separating, transporting, and reassembling of copies of the paper work.

Generally, any one of the three plans described can be used to distinct advantage in organizing the paper work flow. Many times, a combination of the plans provides the best results. Under any circumstances, the skilled analyst will carefully consider the proper arrangement of the paper work before he commits himself to an investment in costly equipment that must be justified only as an improvement over an efficiently organized manual system.

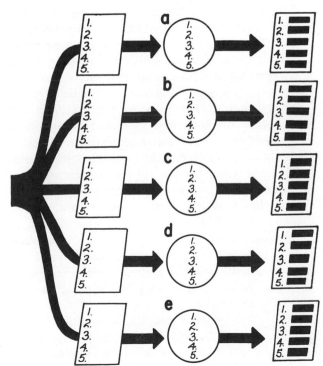

Fig. 3-11. The Parallel (or Concurrent Handling) Plan

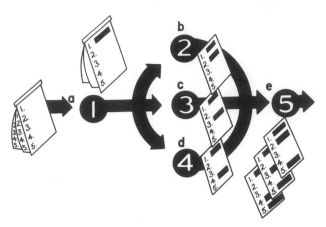

Fig. 3-12. The Unit Assembly (or Simultaneous Handling) Plan

Solution Must Fulfill Objectives

As the facts are analyzed and various analysis charts are prepared, logical methods ideas occur to the analyst, and he attempts to relate all the details to the true objective of the system. The details have been questioned as to necessity, objective, place, time, and personnel to perform the work; the final consideration is, "What is the best way to do it?"

The best way to accomplish the basic objective may be only distantly related to an improved way of doing what is now done. The inexperienced analyst can easily get lost in the maze of existing paper work. He can be trapped into streamlining and speeding up the performance of present paper work when he should be visualizing what should be the fundamental results of a work unit. As a simplified illustration, an analysis of a purchasing function may indicate, on the surface, a need to simplify the method of preparing a large volume of purchase orders. A more enlightened study pointed at the fundamental objective of procurement may determine that a large percentage of the purchase orders are not required to accomplish procurement (blanket orders subject to release, delegation for small cash purchases, and so forth). The person who said, "Be wary of obvious answers and hospitable toward original ones," must have been talking to systems analysts.

Since we are primarily concerned with producing the maximum of *useful* information at a minimum of cost, we must focus our attention on those necessary operations that add the *most* to the cost of accomplishing the *true* objective.

We must have complete information on the volume of work, standards of quality, and time limitations. With these facts in mind, the analyst is ready to consider the various techniques, manual or mechanical, that can be used to accomplish the purpose.

Most information processing consists of one or a combination of the following basic operations:

1. Computing
2. Classifying or distributing
3. Summarizing
4. Recording
5. Storing

To determine the proper technique to best accomplish these basic functions, the analyst must first decide which function represents the principal part of the problem. If computing is major and recording is minor, he may consider a high-speed calculator with pencil recording or a computer-oriented system. If extensive classifying is involved, he may want to use a multiple-register adding or bookkeeping machine or electronic sorting devices.

Considering Equipment

Since any piece of equipment must justify its total cost through savings over alternative methods, first consideration must be given to manual methods and simple devices. Application of work simplification may readily improve manual methods to the point of efficiency that rules out investment in more expensive equipment. Furthermore, the use of so-called manual methods and techniques has certain inherent advantages over highly mechanized methods. Among these are the added flexibility that can be obtained by using more people to accomplish peak loads, and, possibly, a lesser need for extensive and specialized training. (Some mechanized systems claim this, too.)

The aforesaid is not intended to belittle in any way the value of investing in well-chosen equipment. It is intended to stress the need for complete knowledge of the details of the routines under consideration and the wisdom of first considering the simple techniques. A simple illustration may make this clear. Any reasonable volume of computations requiring the multiplying of six digits by six digits would justify, at least, an electric calculator. However, multiplying a large volume of two-digit figures by two-digit figures would be more efficient using a key-driven calculator. Again, however, if these digits are confined to a relatively narrow range, the multiplication probably can be accomplished much more efficiently with the aid of a multiplying chart, even a homemade one. Volume is not the only consideration. All factors must be considered, and the equipment investment must be self-liquidating.

As a generalization, it may be stated that it is usually more profitable to provide equipment that combines two or more of the functions than equipment that only reduces the time required to perform any one of the functions. This is the major reason for the successful applications of bookkeeping machines, which record accounts receivable in ledgers, on customer statements, and on journal sheets while they summarize the debits and credits for control purposes. It is the reason for the development of devices for obtaining punched cards or punched paper tape while a computation or recording or both are being made with an adding or bookkeeping machine

In the end, a decision to use any piece of equipment must be based on the economics of the operation. Spectacular abilities to do things that are not essential to the system have no part in such decisions. Every effort should be made to fit the equipment in such a manner that a minimum investment is needed to accomplish the required results. The cost of the present method must be carefully determined. The total cost of the new method must be sufficiently less than the cost of the present method to justify the investment in the machine equipment unless other objectives justify the investment. The cost of the proposed machine method can be determined by estimating annual factors as follows:

Clerical labor in new method
plus depreciation of installed cost of new equipment
plus interest on investment in new equipment
plus maintenance, power, forms, supplies, and space charges

Professor Barish recommends the following formula [1] for determining the annual interest charge:

$$\text{Average annual interest cost} = CR \left[\frac{N + 1}{2N} \right]$$

where

C represents the original installed cost
R is the required rate of return on investment
N is the number of years the equipment will be used

There is just one caution in estimating the annual cost—don't use the tax accountant's depreciation rate based on the physical life of the equipment. *Use your best systems judgment of obsolescence in this day of rapid developments in the business field.* Also, the period, such as three to five years for recovery of investment, must be considered.

The rate of return on investment to be used in determining the annual interest cost of a machine installation will vary from company to company, and is largely a management determination. The other cost factors are the best estimates the analyst can develop. When the final comparison of the proposed machine method with a current manual method requiring a larger clerical force indicates no appreciable difference in cost, the indirect costs of personnel versus machines become an important consideration. Machines are considerably more reliable than human beings. They require neither controls over attendance nor coffee breaks. The analyst can readily recog-

---

[1] Norman N. Barish, *Systems Analysis for Effective Administration* (New York: Funk & Wagnalls Company, 1951), p. 218.

nize the lower supervisory and administrative cost of a highly mechanized small staff. He can justifiably recommend the machine method over the manual method when the cost comparison shows no difference in costs, provided there are other advantages to be gained.

Then there is the question of fractional personnel savings. Such savings are real savings, in spite of the resistance of many managements to accept them. Supervisors have the responsibility for adjusting work assignments and accumulating fractional savings until a reduction of work force is accomplished or until new work can be absorbed by the same work force. This is not a farfetched proposition in the modern office with its requirement to produce an ever-changing variety and volume of information. Failure to accent it, however, is seriously reducing the productivity of many offices.

Elimination of excess paper work and the improvement of essential paper work is an obvious and important phase of any systems development. The cost of duplication and overlapping of paper work is one of the wasteful practices of business administration. Many systems men earn their keep by their ability to improve the processing of large-volume paper work. With today's high cost of clerical labor, multiple part forms with interleaved carbon paper, flat forms designed for efficient recording of information, and continuous forms designed for efficient use of high-speed writing equipment justify more systems emphasis than ever before.

Effect of Solution on Policies

Company policies enter into every systems development. There is, for instance, great emphasis today on policies for reduction of force, which could result from increased use of electronics in the office. The analyst needs to know if management will or will not use normal attrition as a means of reducing force. He needs to know if management will permit the establishment of service centers for processing information to accomplish functions without reference to departmental prerogatives. When policies are not satisfactory or are not clear, every attempt must be made to adjust them at an early stage of the systems study.

During the entire development of the new method, the analyst should carefully maintain the best of communications with all affected key personnel. In doing so, he develops participation by the key personnel, which not only aids the problem solution, but sets the stage for acceptance of the final recommendation. Exceptions to a routine can be problems in a proposed new method. Often these exceptions can be handled readily by supervisors, without interfering with the new method, if the supervisors have been brought along by the analyst to the point where the new method is sincerely wanted. Lack of participation by supervisors can exaggerate the whole issue to the point that the proposed method may not be accepted, or, if it is, installation may be needlessly difficult. As the final step in developing the solution, conferences with affected personnel must result in no serious faults being found with the proposal.

Evaluating the Solution Against Present Methods

The proposed method must completely satisfy the problem as it was defined for the study. It may, as finally developed, be more comprehensive than the problem as originally defined, but it may not be less.

When the proposed method represents a comprehensive change from the existing method, with significant investment in new equipment and installation cost, the analyst must make detailed comparison of the costs of the present system with the anticipated cost of the proposed system. If the proposal applies to a number of decentralized work units, a pilot run may be necessary to ascertain clerical time and cost factors. When a pilot run cannot be made, the analyst must resort to more ingenious methods of determining anticipated clerical costs. With the help of front-line personnel time standards can be developed by time study techniques or less formal means. This is where the analyst will reap the benefits from the time devoted to obtaining the participation of supervisors.

In evaluating the proposed method against the existing methods, consideration must be given to the quality of results expected, the over-all time cycle, the information needed for decision-making, and any intangible benefits (such as employee morale) that are inherent in the proposed method. It is important that this evaluation be worked out with supervisory personnel, since management will invariably call for the opinions of all key personnel before accepting the proposal. This calls for a high degree of skill in human relations and tact on the part of the analyst.

Writing the Proposed Procedure

Methods changes of any consequence usually require new or revised written procedures or computer programs. Their nature and extent vary generally as follows:

1. None required when the scope of the method is so compact that very little coordination is required and the analyst's report is a sufficient record of the change.
2. Coordination throughout a number of work units is quite significant, and interdepartmental policy and procedure must be recorded and approved to make the new system operative.
3. A series of training manuals is required, in addition to a general procedure, in order that key points will not be overlooked when the new system is installed.
4. Necessary computer programs must be prepared and tested to assure accomplishing the objectives.

The general or interdepartmental procedure is organized to state first the objectives, scope, and policy. It should then set forth the responsibilities of the various organizational units involved in the procedure. Finally, the details of "how to do it" are recorded, generally arranged according to responsibilities clearly indicated. With this arrangement, the reader need

follow through the procedure only as far as it satisfies his need for information.

The language of the procedure must be only that which is pointed
directly at, and understandable by, the reader. It should not reflect the advanced literary development of the writer.

Whenever the paper flow and operating steps of the procedure are
numerous, a procedure chart is recommended. This chart is essentially the
same chart prepared in the development of the new method and compares
with the chart of the present method referred to earlier in discussing the
analysis of the facts. The procedure chart makes a compact presentation
that can be more easily followed and referred to than reams of narrative.
The procedure chart also helps to show the role of the computer or other
mechanical and electronic devices in the over-all system.

In contrast with the general procedure, the training manual is designed
to instruct an operator or group of like personnel how to perform specific
steps of the procedure. When warranted, any number of training manuals
may be prepared—one for the order editors, one for the order typists, one
for key punchers, and so on. These are full of action words and illustrations
designed to guide the operator through the detail in exactly the prescribed
methods.

Preparing the Report

The nature of the assignment and the type of study dictate the type
and extensiveness of the report. Basically, the executive who asked for the
study is entitled to an easily understood report on the results of the study.
When the proposed change affects more than one department, the report
must be directed at the interdepartmental executive who has the approving
authority. Since he will undoubtedly solicit the opinions of his departmental
subordinates, the report must be comprehensive. The comprehensiveness
increases as the size of the investment in new equipment and installation
cost increases.

The report should be packaged in an attractive manner and should
consist of at least the following parts, in the following sequence:

1. TITLE PAGE. The title or subject of the study should be completely
descriptive, but concise and set with plenty of white space. Some authorities
like to add a transmittal message on this or on a separate page. If it is brief,
this is permissible. In fact, this is a good place to include a credit line in
recognition of those people who have been of valuable assistance in making
the study.

2. TABLE OF CONTENTS. The various parts of the report, illustrations,
and special features should be listed, showing page numbers for easy
reference.

3. STATEMENT OF THE PROBLEM. This is preferably a separate page
carrying a concise explanation of the reason for the study, its objectives, and

scope. This must be carefully worded. The executive who reads it has many other problems competing for his time. His reaction at this time can have an important bearing on how he handles the report.

4. SUMMARY OR ABSTRACT. This must be designed for the executive reader who wants to get into the results of the study quickly, the essentials of the story. State major fact findings and conclusions first. Number them. Stick to the essentials. State your major recommendations, why they should be adopted, and what they will cost. Follow up with less important recommendations. If certain of the recommendations are such that the supervisor could adopt them during the course of the study and has done so, mention this fact.

5. MAIN BODY OF THE REPORT. This is supporting detail for the conclusions and recommendations. It sets forth the facts and logic of the study, which can be observed by the careful reader to bring about agreement with the analysis.

6. CREDITS. If a credit line has not been included on the title page as part of a transmittal message, this is the place for it. Be generous, but not flowery.

7. APPENDIX. In this section should be placed a copy of the procedure, if it is prepared prior to submission of the report. In this manner, the analyst can often get the executive's approval of the implementing policy and procedure while the facts of the study are fresh in his mind. This section is also the place for exhibits of technical detail, such as manufacturer's literature describing equipment, and tables and charts of interest to the detailed reader but not requiring the time of the executive reader.

Putting the Recommendations into Effect

Putting recommendations into effect is the joint responsibility of the line and staff organizations, with the planning and coordination being done by the staff analyst. The analyst cooperates closely with supervisors throughout installation.

The analyst prepares a plan of action, including a timetable, that is, the basis for additional planning, scheduling, and follow-through of the steps preparatory to and concurrent with the installation. He prepares procedures and training manuals as required. He prepares purchase requisitions for new equipment required and designs necessary forms.

Without actually taking over the responsibilities of the various supervisors for administering the personnel affected by the systems change, the analyst should constantly audit the performance of supervision in this area of personnel relations. The attitudes of personnel are important to the success of the new methods, and adequate plans must be made for transfers, reductions, and training.

As he works with the supervisor in getting ready for the installation, the analyst should be able to develop numerous work aids and office workplace rearrangements that will aid in the operation of the new system. In this preparatory work there are likely to develop unforeseen problems requiring solution, and there may be some minor modification of the system. All these details should be handled as promptly as possible, and management advised of progress being made toward installation.

The final timing of the actual changeover is important. Whenever possible, it should coincide with slack periods of the year or month or logical conversion period. It must be recognized that a new system requires a certain period of time in which to develop the efficiency expected of it. Additional temporary help may be required during the pilot run or breaking-in period. It is better to use temporary help where possible than to require excessive overtime on the part of the regular personnel. If unforeseen delays make the planned starting date unrealistic, it is wise to delay the start rather than jeopardize the success of the installation.

Care must be taken that replaced functions and duties are actually discontinued at the time of the changeover, or as soon as feasible.

Neuschel provides ten rules for making a major change-over that bear repeating: [2]

1. Be ready before starting.
2. Keep up to schedule.
3. Avoid rash, emergency decisions.
4. Anticipate and eliminate crises.
5. Don't let minor kinks dampen your enthusiasm or your confidence in the plan.
6. Keep all phases of the change-over coordinated by informing executives and supervisors promptly of any changes in the original procedures or the installation plan.
7. Prevent dissension among the personnel.
8. Don't require continuous or excessive overtime work of the installation crew. If the change-over is falling significantly behind schedule because of lack of personnel, get some extra temporary help.
9. Avoid disruption of service.
10. Don't sacrifice thoroughness for speed.

After installation, the methods job is not complete until there has been a follow-up by the systems analyst. This follow-up has several purposes:

1. Determine that objectives of the system are being accomplished. Are anticipated cost savings being realized? Is the quality of the information resulting from the system in accordance with the planned standards? Are time schedules being maintained and is output of the system on schedule?

---

[2] R. F. Neuschel, *Streamlining Business Procedures* (New York: McGraw-Hill Book Company, Inc., 1950), p. 262.

2. Determine that all parts of the new system are actually operating. Sometimes minor phases of the system are left unstarted in favor of concentration of the major parts of the system.

3. Make whatever modifications or refinement in the system and the written procedures as may be justified by actual operating experience.

4. Make sure that *all* replaced routines are actually discontinued.

Subsequent review of the system is desirable at infrequent intervals. However, proper cooperation with and by the internal audit staff should satisfy this requirement.

4

Systems Charting

RICHARD W. POMEROY

National Bellas Hess, Inc.
Kansas City, Mo.

RICHARD W. POMEROY was educated at Columbia College and Columbia and New York Universities. He is now vice-president in charge of administrative services and data processing for National Bellas Hess, Inc., a large retail and mail order firm. His business career has included employment with the General Electric and Otis Elevator companies in systems and production areas, and twelve years in management consulting, mostly with the large CPA firm of Arthur Young & Co.

As feature editor of Systems *and* Procedures Journal *for a number of years, Mr. Pomeroy has contributed frequent articles and reviews to that publication, and since 1962 has written its "Question Box" column. He has taught EDP and advanced systems courses at Bridgeport Engineering Institute and New York University and is a well-known speaker on systems and management subjects.*

CHARTING—MAINSTREAM OF SYSTEMS TECHNIQUE

A number of factors differentiate a qualified systems man from any other person actively interested in bettering a procedural activity. A major difference is that the systems man has the *time* to study an operation and to think about better ways of doing the job or improving business systems. Another factor is the possession by the systems man of a wide knowledge of business procedures and of the facilities that may be used to effect them. However, the most important difference between this man and the supervisor who is continually striving to better his department's performance is that the systems man is familiar with the techniques and tools that enable him to translate the details of a departmental operation into the simplicity of pictures. Graphic presentation is to the systems profession what a numbers system is to the field of mathematics—a language of abbreviation enabling the understanding of complex phenomena in relatively short periods of time.

Charting is by no means the sole province of the systems function. It is an integral part of the activity of almost all professional techniques, a heavily relied-upon device for simplification and presentation in hundreds of different contexts. But outside the field of pure science, few areas rely so much on the use of graphic presentation as does the systems profession.

Charting finds three major areas of usage in systems work: in survey, design, and presentation. In the installation area of systems work, charting again appears, albeit in a lesser role.

Charting in Survey

The survey phase of the systems job is the original investigation into present procedures. At this time, the study is concerned with how the job is now being done. The information the analyst needs must be correct and thorough. The collection of the thousands of detailed facts that will be put together to form so complete a picture is neither difficult nor esoteric. It is done by asking questions of everyone concerned with the job being studied and writing down the answers. But when this is done, the interviewer sets aside his lay techniques and becomes a systems analyst. He now makes use of the flow chart, a simple device that will transform the vast jumble of disconnected details he has assembled into a single, simple roadmap that defines a complete clerical procedure.

The mapmaking process is analogous to the working of a jigsaw puzzle. Each detail is pulled from the pile in turn and made part of the over-all picture. On completion of the picture, the elemental segments have been arranged to form a compact area of complete comprehension. It is important to realize that it is this comprehension the analyst gains—not the chart itself—which is the desired end product. The chart is only the means by which the analyst has *learned* the procedure.

A very important part of this learning is that in seeing *how* the job is done, we come to understand a great deal of the *why*. Training takes over from there. We sense—usually see on the chart, though occasionally we refer admiringly to a man who can "smell" or "feel"—areas of potential improvement. What has been a simple investigation now begins to take on direction; it begins to point out the areas of greatest potential for improvement.

These two phases, comprehension of present procedures and indication of the best paths for future action, constitute the greatest value of the flow-charting method. Flow charts could be destroyed at this point and would still have made their major contribution. Beyond this point, flow charts, although of great usefulness, are of diminishing importance.

A by-product use of flow charts in the survey phase is in sparking employee interest in the systems job and in helping to dispel the fear of changes to come. To dispel the bulk of this fear we need only explain what we are doing and how. In most cases it is necessary that the analyst check the accuracy of his charts by going over them in detail with the persons doing the job. If the analyst will take the few moments needed to explain the chart itself to the employee, he will frequently turn a frightened clerk into an interested ally. It is a well-known fact in the industrial engineering world that there are few standards for production machine jobs for which the operator can not and does not find a short cut. Clerical employees also frequently have sound ideas on how their work could be simplified. If the systems man can find the key to this fund of ideas, his job will be substantially simplified, and the results of his work improved. The clerk (or supervisor) who sees his own suggestions built into a proposal for revision becomes a more co-operative participant in the installation of the revised system that follows.

Charts in Design

The design phase of systems work is perhaps the most important, and certainly the most crucial, stage of a systems assignment. Here will evolve the new methods, new equipment, new forms—in short, the new system itself. At this stage the flow charts the analyst drew in the survey phase come again into active use. The paths to improvement previously pointed out will now be followed. Areas in which effort is duplicated or expended needlessly, where routing is awkward, and where there are other indications that improvement could be made will now be thoroughly investigated. One by one the pieces of a new puzzle are being assembled; the picture will be that of the new procedure; the medium for conveying this picture is again the flow chart.

The charts of the proposed system drawn in this phase of the study will usually become the basis for the finished drawings around which the presentation to management will center.

Charts in Presentation

The presentation phase of the job leans heavily on the use of charts chosen and executed for the sole purpose of explaining to management how the old system works, and why and how it should be improved. Whereas in the previous phases of the systems assignment flow charts were the main type used, the presentation makes use of a wide range of chart types, depending on what material is to be presented and which parts of it are to be stressed. The purpose of charting here is to simplify and shorten. To make a presentation wholly in oral or written form would be a long and tedious task that might lead to general confusion.

The effects of systems analysis are cumulative up to this point. All effort previously expended has built toward this climax—the acceptance or rejection of the proposal.

This decision may rest on seemingly minute details—the routing of a particular copy of a form, for example. If the systems man does not know where it goes, his lack of knowledge may be taken by management as an indication that the study has been poorly conducted. Such a conclusion can shake confidence in the entire presentation.

Charting in Installation

The final step in the systems process is the actual installation of the new system. Here again, charting plays a role similar to that which characterized the survey phase of the job. Charts are used to supply points of reference and to assist the analyst in answering the multitude of questions that will arise about what, who, where, and, particularly, how.

Another type of installation application is the use of charts in procedures manuals to facilitate understanding. Although this usage need not be elaborated upon, a word of caution may be advisable: Do not forget that the persons who are likely to refer to the charts are probably unfamiliar with them and may require instructions on how to read them if the charts are to be of practical value.

METHODS OF CHARTING

Planning and Evaluation

Every well-executed systems analysis stems from careful planning at the start and continuing evaluation as the work progresses. As applied to charting, planning takes the form of deciding which charts will best suit the assignment and accomplish the desired ends, and what information the charts should contain. Not every analysis is concerned with minute details, and the depth to which an investigation should be carried is an important consideration. A decision must be made on the most expedient and least costly approach consistent with doing a comprehensive job. The initial planning indicates to the analyst the type and quantity of information needed.

Evaluation is the process of adjustment, which must be continually and consciously applied as the work progresses and more is learned about the operation being studied. Almost without exception, systems studies depend to some degree on trial and error methods of approach. Very few studies are completed which could not be done better a second time. The analyst must constantly evaluate his present methods and results against the over-all aims of the study, which will be refined as the work progresses.

WHEN TO CHART. During the survey phase of a study the analyst will be primarily concerned with charts of the flow or process type. The question arises here whether interview notes should be written and the charts drawn from them, or whether rough charting can be done directly as the interview progresses, bypassing the intermediate step of written notes. There is no simple answer to this question, because the ability to chart directly depends both on the analyst's knowledge of the operation being studied, or similar operations, and on the complexity of the procedure itself. In approaching a completely unfamiliar procedure, it is often impossible for the analyst to specify the size and number of sheets that will accommodate the charts, let alone chart directly from spoken information.

Where it is feasible, though, this rough charting is a valuable device for three reasons. First, it saves writing time and permits the interview to progress faster, because operations can be described faster in symbols than in words. Second, it permits the analyst to lead the interview along an orderly and logical path; an operator's description of the work he does seldom takes such a path of its own accord. Finally, the roughed-out chart serves to indicate points at which information details have been skipped and flow lines prematurely abandoned. In this connection, the analyst may find it helpful to associate each chart symbol with a check list of questions on the type of information he wants. For example, a file symbol might trigger such questions as: "Filed by whom?" "Retained how long?" "In what order?" "How many per month?" "What type of file housing is used?"

In practice, many analysts use a combination of roughly sketched chart sections and written notes to record interview information. Interviewing improves with practice and knowledge, and, frequently, the experienced analyst slips in and out of the rough-charting technique to suit the conditions of the moment.

WHO DOES THE WORK? The question of who is to do the actual drafting of systems charts is of importance to the economics of a study. Wherever possible in the gathering, processing, and charting of information, tasks not requiring the special skill of a senior analyst should be delegated to a junior or trainee. Experience has shown that operating personnel in the procedures being studied are, when qualified, usually glad to assist in this capacity. Also, it may be feasible to enlist the help of drafting personnel in other departments of the company—for example, engineering—for temporary assignment. Large systems teams usually include charting specialists.

Economics of Chart Costs

Systems charts can be very expensive, occasionally running to hundreds of dollars for a large and complex chart, not including the cost of obtaining and processing information. From a purely monetary point of view, it would seem that there could be little justification for spending even $25 on a chart that may be used for a single presentation to management and then be permanently shelved or destroyed. The same information that appears on a chart of professional and artistic quality could be presented in rough form by pencil or chalk sketches for analysis purposes only.

However, charts used in presentation are the focal point of discussion, and, as such, make an important contribution to the feeling of thoroughness and competence that the systems man is trying to convey to his audience. A proposal is accepted or rejected, depending on whether management feels that the present situation has been studied thoroughly and evaluated soundly, or whether the proposal may be impractical because of incomplete knowledge or improper consideration. Poorly prepared charts imply a haphazard handling of the whole systems assignment. Thus, the expense of charting becomes a secondary consideration to the production of charts that suggest complete and competent fulfillment of the systems assignment.

Subsidiary Information on Charts

A frequently neglected area of charting is the subsidiary information on charts, such as titles, source of references, and legends. The application of improper titles is the reason for unnecessary confusion in many cases. This may result from skimping on words or failing to describe the chart properly, or from generous use of title words. Adjectives such as intradepartmental, geo-operational, and the like may add confusion to the title of a chart and frighten away potential proponents.

Source references should appear unobtrusively on charts if such information (a) aids in understanding the chart, (b) adds validity or emphasis to it, or (c) serves to refresh the analyst's memory at a later date. This last purpose is particularly apparent when information is obtained from more than one source.

Legends, which permit understanding by readers not familiar with conventions used, are necessary where symbols, different line forms, and the like are used.

TECHNIQUES AND MECHANICS

Methods

Although the actual construction of charts can often be assigned to a person specializing in such work, it is important that systems personnel be familiar with the techniques, tools, and materials of systems graphics. The systems man is expected to handle his own work in an efficient and systematic manner. This requires a working knowledge of tools and techniques that make charting easier and more effective.

In this connection, a trip to the table of a professional draftsman may prove rewarding. Because the draftsman has been schooled in the methods of his trade, he is able to supply valuable information, both of a general nature and for a specific assignment. But the methods of professional drafting are not the sole source of systems charting techniques; in many cases the construction of a chart leans heavily toward the trade of a less accessible individual, the commercial artist. A visit to a commercial or industrial art department is both interesting and informative.

The methods of charting have been considerably simplified in recent years by a number of tools and materials designed to facilitate charting, drafting, and commmercial artwork. Periodic browsing sessions in well-stocked artists' supply or stationery stores can keep the systems man up to date on new developments in this category.

A systems department faced with periodic charting assignments should invest in a graphics kit of materials, tools, and related information. The extent and cost of such a kit is proportional to the frequency and scope of its use.

Tools of Charting

Tools of the charting trade may be thought of in two categories: first, drawing and lettering instruments, and second, miscellaneous tools for a variety of other uses. A set of drafting instruments has multiple uses and is therefore a general requisite. The drafting pen itself is being replaced in systems work by recently developed felt pens for drafting. These come in a variety of line widths and use india inks, black or colored. Although the quality of the lines is not quite as good as that of drafting pens, the results are generally good without the need for tedious refilling and careful handling that characterize the use of drafting pens. The fountain pen can be used to trace template figures, although the line width cannot be varied as with a drafting pen.

Lettering devices range from simple letter templates to elaborate, precision-machined lettering tools, such as the Leroy set made by Keuffel & Esser. Although the later are initially expensive, they repay their cost in shortened work time, more versatile application, and excellent results.

A set of pen points for lettering by hand will find frequent use. These should range in width from hairline to poster-lettering widths. A felt-point pen, grease pencils, and drafting pencils with leads of various hardness should serve to round out the kit for most lettering and drawing requirements.

The availability of templates with cutout areas for tracing symbols to assist in a wide variety of drawing assignments is generally known, but the rapid extension of these devices to new areas suggests that the systems man will do well to keep abreast of developments.

Drawing boards are available in a wide variety of sizes, ranging from those designed to accommodate letter-size sheets to elaborate drafting tables with many adjustments and attachments. A board with a sliding horizontal rule attached is best for most systems uses.

The need for scissors is obvious, and the long-bladed type makes it easier to cut long straight lines. A pair of flat-nosed tweezers of the type used by stamp collectors is almost a necessity for handling small pieces of paper, as, for example, when captions are to be cemented onto charts. Electric pencil sharpeners and electric erasers may be advisable where frequency of use justifies the expense.

Materials

The systems charting job has been tremendously simplified through the availability of a large selection of adhesive-backed statistical tapes, pictorial symbols, predrawn charting symbols and shading materials. Tapes come in a variety of line widths, colors, and line types, as well as number increments and months of the year. They are simple and fast to use and may be corrected by the simple expedient of removing or repositioning.

Pictographic symbols of men, coins, telephones, machines, trucks, and a variety of other things may be obtained to cover a wide range of requirements. Charting symbols include multiple form copies, operational symbols, and the like, as well as office and plant layout symbols of furniture and machinery, and organization chart boxes. Shading materials are available for many general and special uses. A number of kits are presented for specialized uses, such as organization charting, plant layout, including conveyor systems and various makes and dimension machines, and so on. Some of these kits utilize their own scaled grids, boards of plastic, or other materials; others can be used on any paper surface, and prices range accordingly. Original illustrations for this chapter were prepared with extensive use of materials available from Chart-Pak, Inc.

Along with the aforementioned materials, lettering aids are available in the form of sheets of printed type in many styles, consisting of a quantity of each letter and number, which may be detached or cut out and laid down to form words. Although the use of such aids is limited by cost and the relatively slow process of application, they are an excellent medium for preparing titles and for other uses requiring a large type face.

The advantage of using water-soluble drawing ink has been learned the hard way by many persons who have overturned a bottle of waterproof ink on papers, clothes, or furniture. Generally, the use of waterproof inks should be avoided unless there is a specific purpose. The appearance of the plastic, eyedropper-type stopper for india ink bottles is a welcome improvement, replacing the old, quill-type filling device.

An insignificant material deserves mention because of its general utility and surprisingly infrequent use—white paint. To prepare charts for photographic reproduction, the use of white paint—for example, moist poster watercolor—is an invaluable device for cleaning up a chart or making corrections. Applied with a fine brush, it can even serve to delete the minute error lines in printing that often detract from the appearance of a final drawing.

The drawing of arrowheads to indicate the direction of flow has plagued many individuals and spoiled the appearance of many otherwise carefully prepared charts. Attractive arrowheads that do not dominate the picture may be drawn freehand if the simple expedient of beginning the arrowhead very close to the flow line is adhered to—as a rule of thumb, no more than a thirty-second of an inch on each side of the line. Failing this, the chartmaker may resort to the use of template arrow symbols or printed tapes.

Reproduction Media

A general familiarity with reproduction methods is a prime requisite, both from a cost standpoint and from consideration of end-use results. In addition to making copies, the ability of some reproduction methods in making enlargements or reductions of source material is frequently helpful in the actual construction of charts. For example, type sizes can be varied by photographic enlargement, or documents can be reduced in size for use as illustrations on a chart. In enlarging type for such use, it frequently saves time and cost to have all items of each desired size typed on a single sheet, which can be blown up or reduced to desired dimensions and then cut apart for cementing onto the chart. Paper negatives of such work can be used for a contrasting white-on-black effect. It should be remembered that enlarging type exposes the minute variations in letters; carbon backing to give an identical reverse image of the original typing will often improve results. Conversely, reducing type will obscure minor defects.

The use of color in charts is often effective, particularly when chart originals are to be used for presentation and copies are not needed. When reproduction is desired, it is best to stick to black components, using different line types or widths to express varying conditions. If copies are to be reduced in size from the original, care must be taken to assure a clearly visible difference in line types, because reduction tends to obscure differences.

A dirty original chart can be cleaned up by treatment of the photographic or xerographic negative. In this connection, it is frequently helpful to explain the use and importance of the finished product to the person handling the reproduction.

It hardly seems necessary to mention that a camera will not differentiate between shades of white. On copies of white forms mounted on white paper, the outline definition is completely lost. This is also true of holes punched in paper; they will not show or will show only indistinctly unless they are backed by a contrasting color. The color blue is usually lost or nearly lost, depending on shade, through photographic processes. This fact can be used to advantage when there are lines on the original that should not appear on the copies, for example, a light blue grid for an office layout. Other colors reproduce with varying degrees of success. Where there is doubt about reproduction results, personnel experienced in photographic work should be consulted.

TYPES OF CHARTS

The literature of the systems profession sets forth a confusingly large number of chart types and combinations of types designed by their authors to fit a wide variety of charting assignments. To catalogue and describe each would add nothing to the literature and lessen the confusion only slightly. We can, however, categorize the basic uses of charting that, alone or in combination, underlie the many chart types in existence:

1. *Operational charting*—to depict the progression of operations
2. *Architectural charting*—to present an outline picture of physical areas
3. *Personnel relationship charting*—to indicate lines of authority, responsibility, and function
4. *Statistical charting*—to summarize numerical and chronological relationships

Although recognition of these underlying types and purposes is of value, presentation of the many kinds of systems charts is facilitated if it is done in terms of the areas described by the various types. The descriptions that follow are in three categories:

1. *Flow charts,* relating basically to the flow of operations and including forms charts that relate to forms handling and logical diagram charts that relate to computer programs
2. *Organization charts,* concerning personnel relationships
3. *Miscellaneous charts,* which lie outside the areas above or which cross area lines in such a way as to make classification difficult

FLOW CHARTS

Flow charts are the most important and most widely used of the charts in systems work. Briefly defined, the flow chart is a symbolic or pictorial representation of a business procedure. Because of its wide use, the flow chart has taken on many variations designed to adapt it to special problems. It appears in many forms and under many titles resulting from the great versatility of the basic method. For that reason, it lends itself to many variations that fit different situations and yield varying results.

The basic kinds of flow charts are presented here to illustrate this versatility and to help in selection and use of those types and conventions best suited to the needs of the particular assignment (some alternate titles are noted in parentheses):

1. Operational flow charts (procedural flow charts), including the many chart types known as process or flow process charts
2. Schematic flow charts or diagrams (pictorial flow charts)
3. Forms flow charts
4. Layout flow charts (forms routing charts), including the records accessibility chart
5. Punched card and computer procedures flow charts (logical or block diagrams)
6. Forms distribution charts, including the forms routing diagram

Operational Flow Charts

It is sometimes difficult to differentiate between flow charts and process charts. Both depict clerical procedures, and the names have been used interchangeably by some authors. For our purposes, and following the most prevalent usage, we can define the process chart as a special case of the flow chart, utilizing a preprinted form with all symbols repeated on each horizontal line, such as is illustrated in Figure 4-1. The process chart has the advantage of being simpler to draw than a regular flow chart, because no layout need be worked out, no templates or other drawing materials used. It has the primary disadvantage of being cumbersome for use with procedures that involve many forms or subsidiary activities branching off the main flow lines. Selected symbols are blacked in with pencil or ink and

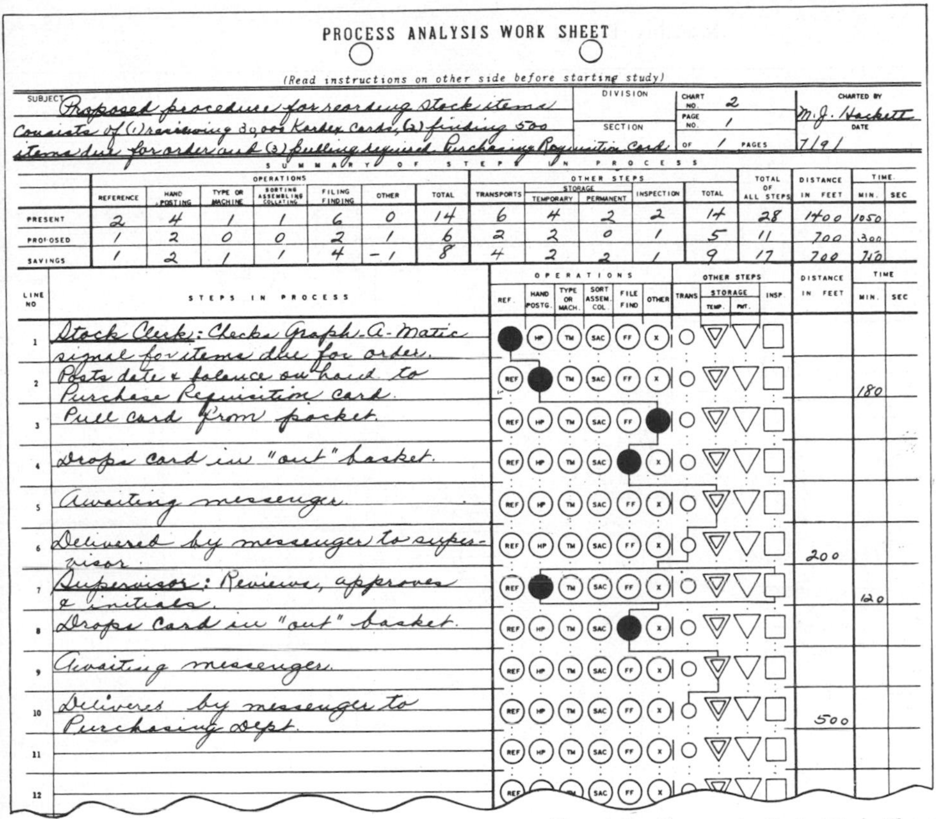

PROCESS ANALYSIS WORK SHEET

(Read instructions on other side before starting study)

SUBJECT: Proposed procedure for reordering stock items. Consists of (1) reviewing 30,000 Kardex cards, (2) finding 500 items due for order and (3) pulling required Purchasing Requisition card.

DIVISION | SECTION | CHART NO. 2 | PAGE NO. 1 OF 1 PAGES | CHARTED BY M. J. Hackett | DATE 7/9/

SUMMARY OF STEPS IN PROCESS

	OPERATIONS							OTHER STEPS					TOTAL OF ALL STEPS	DISTANCE IN FEET	TIME	
	REFERENCE	HAND POSTING	TYPE OR MACHINE	SORTING ASSEMBLING COLLATING	FILING FINDING	OTHER	TOTAL	TRANSPORTS	STORAGE TEMPORARY	STORAGE PERMANENT	INSPECTION	TOTAL			MIN.	SEC
PRESENT	2	4	1	1	6	0	14	6	4	2	2	14	28	1400	1050	
PROPOSED	1	2	0	0	2	1	6	2	2	0	1	5	11	700	300	
SAVINGS	1	2	1	1	4	-1	8	4	2	2	1	9	17	700	750	

LINE NO	STEPS IN PROCESS	DISTANCE IN FEET	TIME MIN.	SEC
1	Stock Clerk: Checks Graph-A-Matic signal for items due for order.			
2	Posts date & balance on hand to Purchase Requisition card.		180	
3	Pull card from pocket.			
4	Drops card in "out" basket.			
5	Awaiting messenger.			
6	Delivered by messenger to supervisor.	200		
7	Supervisor: Reviews, approves & initials.		120	
8	Drops card in "out" basket.			
9	Awaiting messenger.			
10	Delivered by messenger to Purchasing Dept.	500		
11				
12				

Fig. 4-1. Process Analysis Work Sheet

connected by lines. As indicated in the illustration, the process chart may carry time, distance, and personnel information as well as spaces for summarizing. It affords a simple mechanism for illustrating present versus proposed charts of simple operational areas.

The operational or procedural flow chart, or simply flow chart, is the name generally given to charts other than process charts that utilize symbols for depicting the steps of a business procedure. These charts may take on a variety of forms. With some exceptions, flow charts are usually not drawn on preprinted forms. Figure 4-2 is a flow chart of a fictitious procedure, designed to illustrate some of the many conventions in use.

In this and other writings on charting, the reader should not be misled into thinking that complex flow charts are simply dashed off correctly the first time. Most flow charts are and should be hand drawn the first time without the use of charting templates. Usually these first-cut charts are mazes of crossing lines and scribbled notations. Often they are adequate for the purposes they must serve, but to prepare a finished chart for presentation, like the one shown in Figure 4-2, usually requires a tedious rearranging and redrafting process for even the skilled chartist.

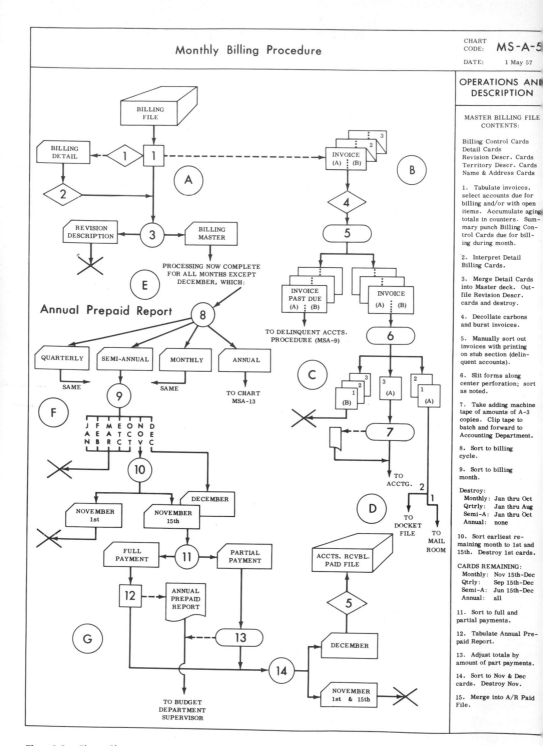

Fig. 4-2. Flow Chart

70

As a result of the widespread uncoordinated use of flow charts, there are many charting conventions in use.

SYMBOL CONVENTIONS. Charting symbols trace their immediate ancestry to the Therbligs, symbols designed by Dr. Frank Gilbreth (the word Therblig is an anagram of his name) for analysis of industrial operations. Charting symbols now in use range from simple outlines of common geometric figures to elaborate pictorial symbols differentiating between many types of clerical operations. Some effort has been made to standardize charting conventions, notably by the American Society of Mechanical Engineers. Selection of a symbol convention depends on the procedure that is to be charted and the use to which the charts are to be put. Obviously, there is a one best way for any given charting assignment, but no one convention has emerged that best suits all needs. The ASME standard, Figure 4-3, is one of the more widely used, and consists simply of a circle for an operation, a square for inspection, an outline letter "D" for delay, an arrow outline for transportation, and a triangle for storage.

With varying degrees of success, a number of equipment and forms manufacturers have sought to get their own symbol conventions into general use.

LAYOUT CONVENTIONS. The question of horizontal or vertical charting, and the question of putting the chart entirely on one sheet or on more than one, are other areas dependent on individual job requirements. When procedures are charted on more than one sheet, it will be found almost obligatory to code the sheets and cross-refer the inter-sheet flow of documents. Frequently, a mnemonic code reference system will facilitate use when letter code designations suggest the names of departments or work units charted. In the chart code A-P-3, for example, the "A" would stand for accounting department, the "P" for payroll section, and the number 3 the third chart in a series.

In cases in which procedures are to be charted on a number of sheets of paper, the analyst might find it helpful to draw the charts horizontally on the paper and arrange the charts in progression on one or more walls

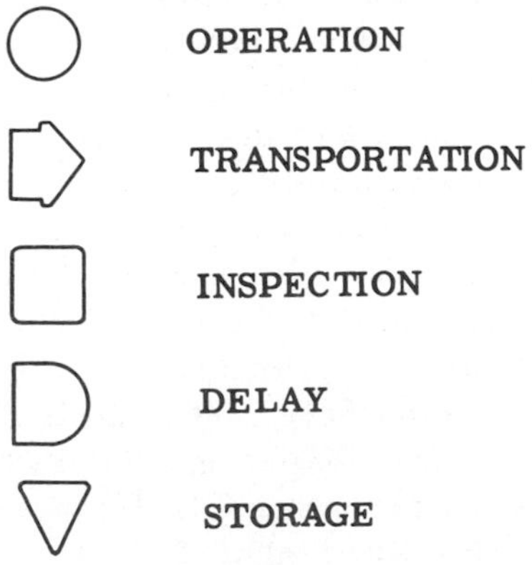

OPERATION

TRANSPORTATION

INSPECTION

DELAY

Fig. 4-3. ASME Standard Flow or Process Charting Convention

STORAGE

of a room. In other cases it will facilitate use if the charts are drawn vertically—for example, to follow the top-to-bottom format of the pages in a procedures manual.

Areas on the chart may be outlined and labeled to represent different organizational units, so that the flow of work between departments or groups is accentuated. Form symbols may be drawn only once at the beginning of a flow line to indicate the creation or initial receipt of a document, or they may be redrawn wherever the form stops for processing. Different line thickness or colors may be used to differentiate types of flow, or this purpose may be served by the use of different line types, such as solid, broken, dotted, and so on. Flow charts may be drawn on preprinted outline forms or on blank paper ruled according to need. A number of these conventions are illustrated in Figure 4-2.

TEXT CONVENTIONS. Textual matter in the form of operation captions, explanatory notes, and the like, also lends itself to various treatment. When a large amount of textual writing is required to describe operations, it may be best to number or letter the operations symbols in sequence and place the descriptions on a separate page or, as in Figure 4-2, in a column to one side of the chart to avoid cluttering and to simplify presentation. An additional advantage of this convention is that frequently repeated operations need appear only once in the text, with the reference number repeated wherever the operations occur on the chart. Conversely, brief textual captions best belong in the body of the chart itself.

Schematic Flow Diagram

The schematic flow chart, or diagram, is similar in nature to the flow chart, but is considerably simplified to present the important highlights of a procedure. Although this type of chart has little place in systems analysis, it is used in the presentation of a proposed system. The presentation of a new systems concept to a group of persons completely unfamiliar with it must be carefully handled. This is necessary to prevent the audience from becoming unduly concerned with details and to focus attention on major principles of the proposal. To permit discussion of details such as form design or minor points of operation at this time may cause the audience to become confused and lose sight of the major system components. The schematic flow diagram serves this purpose very well—it tells only what has to be learned in the first lesson.

It is frequently helpful to use pictures, as shown in Figure 4-4, rather than symbols to accentuate and describe important ideas and facilitate understanding of central ideas. The originals of charts can be constructed using half-size photostats of actual forms and photographs like those available from the sales literature of equipment manufacturers. Captions and title letters may be photographically blown up from Varityped copy before being added to the charts. In this type of chart, the use of colored lines or tapes is frequently of value.

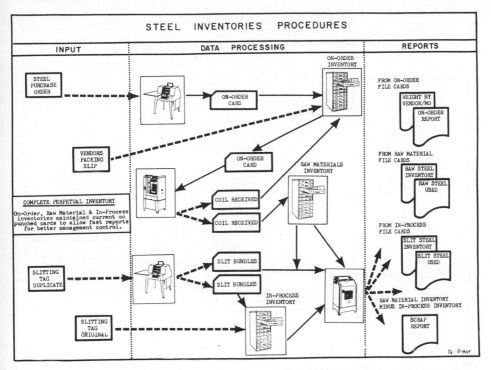

Fig. 4-4. Schematic Flow Diagram

Forms Flow Charts

This type of chart, strictly speaking, belongs in the discussion of forms charts, but is mentioned here because of its close relation to the flow chart type. The forms flow chart (*see* Figure 4-5) consists of actual forms or photostats of forms with characteristic entries made on them. The purpose of the chart is to illustrate the flow of information from one form to the others. The chart is not concerned with extraneous operations or documents not affected. Information filled in on the forms used in the chart relates back to the source document on the chart, and the connecting lines are used to indicate that information is being picked up from one place and posted to another. This type of chart is useful in analyzing and illustrating duplication of posting functions. It is frequently used as a basis for the combination of related forms or elimination of unnecessary forms.

Layout Flow Charts

The layout flow chart, as its name implies, is a simple combination of flow chart and office layout. A diagram of the physical location under study is first drawn, and lines, frequently in color, are superimposed to represent the flow of paper work. The chart is a very useful device for analysis of the physical travel of paper work in a given procedure, and highlights awkward

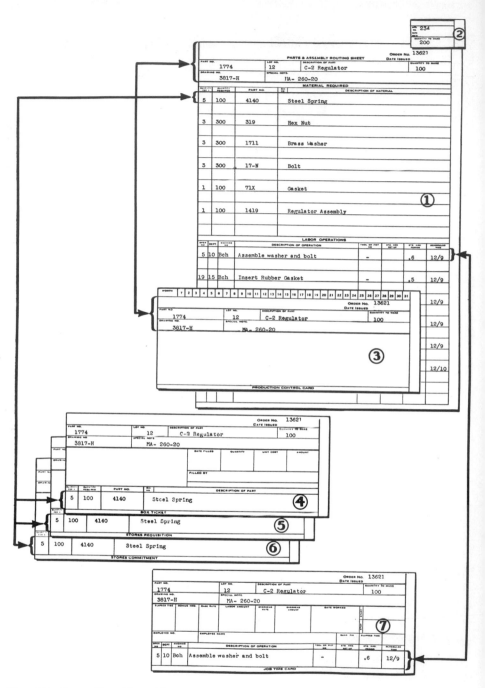

Fig. 4-5. Forms Flow Chart (*Courtesy Ditto, Inc.*)

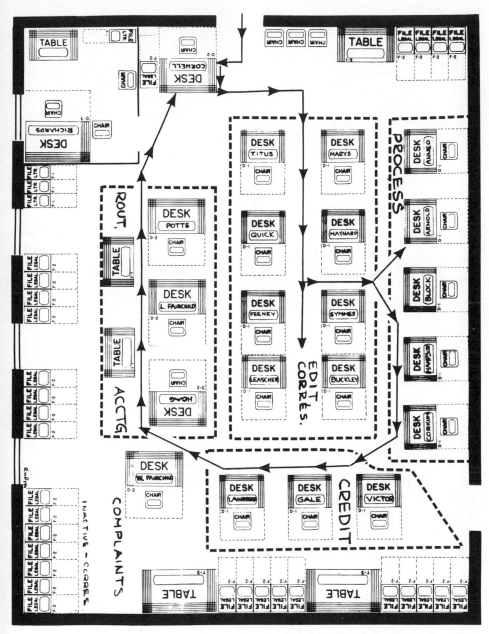

Fig. 4-6. Layout Flow Chart

routings or unnecessary backtracking of papers. It is often used for improving office layout. An example of the layout flow chart is shown in Figure 4-6.

The records accessibility chart is a special case of the layout flow
chart, and is used to determine the best location for filed documents. Instead

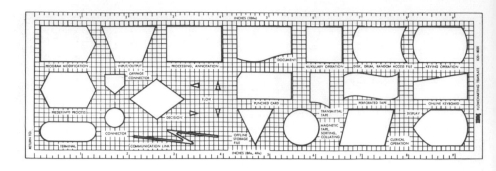

INVENTORY   CONTROL   PROCEDURE

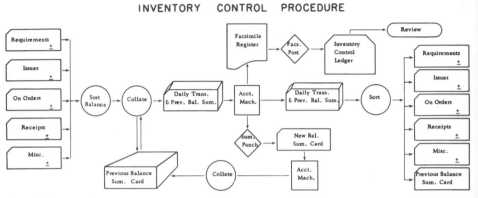

Fig. 4-7. IBM Template and Simple Line-drawing Flow Chart
(*Courtesy IBM*)

of indicating paper work flow, lines on this chart indicate the paths followed
by personnel referring to filed documents. Lines are drawn between desks
and file cabinets and may be labeled with the number of steps involved and
the number of times daily that the trip is made. An analysis sheet may then
be used to arrive at a simple mathematical evaluation of present versus
proposed file and desk locations.

Punched Card and Computer Procedure Charts

FLOW CHARTS OF PUNCHED CARD PROCEDURES. A special charting
symbol convention is in wide use for depicting punched card procedures.
This convention was developed by IBM, and has the advantage of assigning
symbol shapes to categories of punched card machine operations such as
accounting machine operations, auxiliary machines, and so on. A template
is illustrated in Figure 4-7, along with a typical chart drawn with it.

CHARTS OF COMPUTER PROCEDURES, THE LOGICAL OR BLOCK DIA-
GRAM. The logical diagram, or block diagram, is similar to the flow chart in
type and purpose, but with one distinguishing characteristic: whereas the
flow chart depicts procedures performed by personnel working with or with-

out machines, the logical diagram depicts procedures that take place inside an electronic computer. The logical diagram finds much more limited application than the flow chart, because it is primarily an aid in programming for a computer.

The logical diagram consists of three major parts, the entry or start routine, the going case or central procedure, and the exit or stop routine. Inasmuch as the starting and stopping of a computer routine are exceptional procedures, and the vast bulk of the work is done in the going case or body of the procedure, the logical diagram is usually begun in the middle, with the entry and exit routines added on after the central procedure is established. This form of charting permits the analyst to visualize the steps that must be taken by the computer to handle a particular problem.

Figure 4-8 indicates the source of the name "logical diagram," since such charts usually center around a series of logical considerations that the computer performs.

Forms Distribution Charts

The forms distribution chart (*see* Figure 4-9) is another special purpose chart using the basic flow chart procedure, but pertaining only to forms and with little or no description of operations. Although there are a number of variations of the forms distribution chart, all portray the distribution of multiple-copy forms to a number of different individuals or organizational units. Forms may be (a) represented by symbols, (b) reduced photos of the form itself, or (c) simply word descriptions. The form is pictured or designated on the left side of the chart and usually progresses horizontally through the various columns allotted to organizational units or individuals.

The chart serves a useful though limited purpose in presenting the simple story of the disposition of forms so that analysis may be directed toward the elimination of unnecessary copies, unnecessary filing of copies, unauthorized distribution, and so on. In its pictorial variations, the chart is useful for instruction and demonstration as well as analysis, and lends itself well to before-and-after presentations. It has the additional advantage of being quickly and easily prepared. A frequent use of this chart is in conjunction with flow charts, when copy distribution would clutter the flow chart or when particular detail in this area is desirable.

A variation of the layout flow chart is sometimes used in place of, or as a supplement to, the forms distribution chart, wherein the lines representing the distribution of form copies are superimposed on an office layout diagram. This type of chart has been given the name forms routing diagram.

ORGANIZATION CHARTS

The organization chart is a special type of chart used to depict personnel relationships. It is one of the most familiar systems charts and is as simple

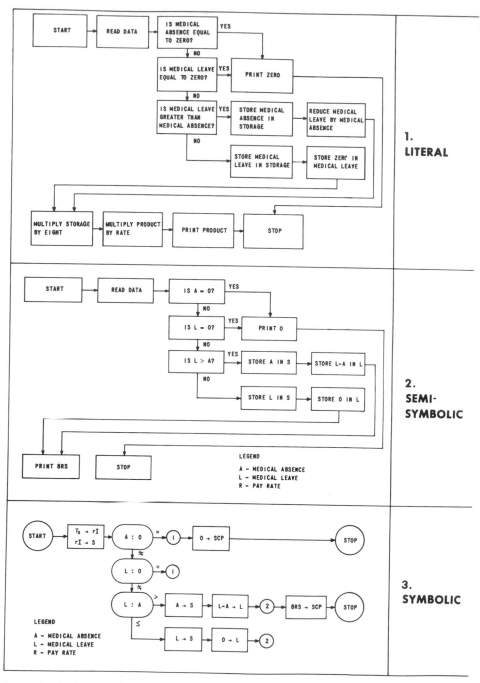

Fig. 4-8. Logical or Block Diagram Indicating Three Types of Charting Conventions (*Courtesy Remington Rand, Sperry Rand Corp.*)

to understand as it is to draw. The chart consists of a number of boxes representing people, jobs, or both, which are connected in such a way as to indicate lines of authority and responsibility. Like flow charts, the organization chart may be drawn horizontally or vertically, the latter being the more commonly used convention. In addition, organization charts have been drawn in the form of lines radiating from a central position in a circular manner. Aside from novelty, however, this format possesses no advantage over the standard horizontal or vertical presentation. Organization charts are sometimes titled with the word "functional," indicating that the major functions of each job are listed on the body of the chart. Generally, solid lines are used to present direct lines of authority, and broken lines to indicate close advisory or open contact between positions.

Names of personnel may or may not appear on the chart, the disadvantage of including names being that such charts must be maintained to reflect personnel changes. Organization charts may also carry other special-purpose information, such as salary or salary range, number of years until retirement, lines of succession to key positions, or staffing requirements, as in Figure 4-10.

SPECIAL PURPOSE CHARTS

Outside the areas of process and organization charting are a number of chart types designed for application to special situations or for general use. Although this list is by no means exhaustive, the following chart types are discussed:

1. Work distribution charts
2. Right- and left-hand charts and simo charts
3. The linear responsibility chart
4. Scheduling charts

Work Distribution Charts

The work distribution chart (also called activity analysis chart) is a useful device for assembling information on group activities into a logical and orderly presentation to facilitate analysis. This chart (*see* Figure 4-11) is a textual rather than symbolic presentation, and deals with all persons in an organizational or functional unit, such as a department or work center. It consists of a left-hand column where activities are listed in order of decreasing importance; on the right side there are individual columns for each employee in the unit. Individual tasks pertaining to each activity are briefly described under each employee's name. The amount of time devoted to each task is noted—usually in hours per week or month, alternately in percentages of total time.

This chart is often drawn on a preprinted form. The information can be gathered from the employees through the use of a simple questionnaire

Flow Chart showing typical A

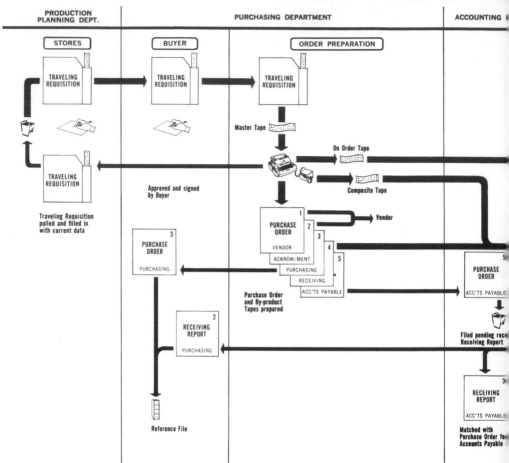

Fig. 4-9. Forms Distribution Chart (*Courtesy Moore Business Forms, Inc.*)

form on which each person concerned lists all his activities and the amount of time devoted to each. Information submitted in such form can usually be cross-checked by comparing questionnaires, through conference with supervisory and other employees, by work count, and by other means. Hours spent on each activity can then be totaled by employee to insure completeness, and by activity to determine total time for each.

When more than one organizational or functional unit is charted, the work distribution charts for all units may be summarized on a separate sheet with organizational unit rather than employee headings.

The work distribution chart serves two useful purposes—in analysis and in costing. In analysis, the chart assists in pointing up poor distribution of work loads, lack of specialization of function, poor utilization of par-

chasing - Receiving System

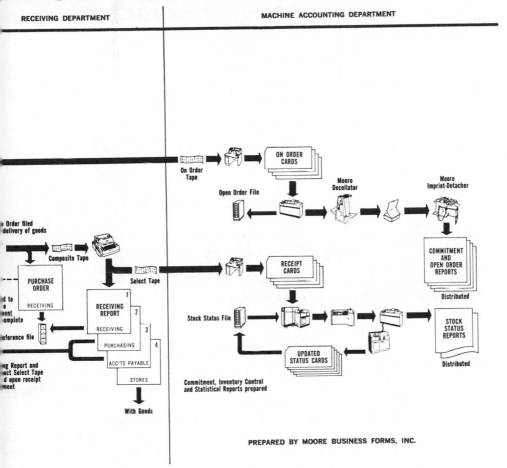

RECEIVING DEPARTMENT   MACHINE ACCOUNTING DEPARTMENT

On Order Tape

ON ORDER CARDS

Open Order File

Moore Decollator

Moore Imprint-Detacher

Order filed delivery of goods

Composite Tape

COMMITMENT AND OPEN ORDER REPORTS

Distributed

Select Tape

RECEIPT CARDS

PURCHASE ORDER

RECEIVING

d to e ent omplete

RECEIVING REPORT

RECEIVING

PURCHASING

ACC'TS PAYABLE

STORES

1
2
3
4

Stock Status File

STOCK STATUS REPORTS

Distributed

eference file

UPDATED STATUS CARDS

ng Report and uct Select Tape d upon receipt ment

Commitment, Inventory Control and Statistical Reports prepared

With Goods

PREPARED BY MOORE BUSINESS FORMS, INC.

ticular skills, and duplication of function. In the costing of operations, it serves as a basis for determining average costs per activity and total costs. This is done by applying salary figures to each employee, and breaking down these amounts by percentage to each activity.

Right- and Left-Hand Charts and Simo Charts

The use of micromotion studies in office systems work is much more limited than the amount of writing on the subject would lead one to believe. In practice, the minute analysis of split-second operations, which has proven so useful to the factory methods and time-study functions, has not, as yet, been widely applied to systems work. The reason for this is not lack of knowledge by systems personnel, for the tools of methods work have been

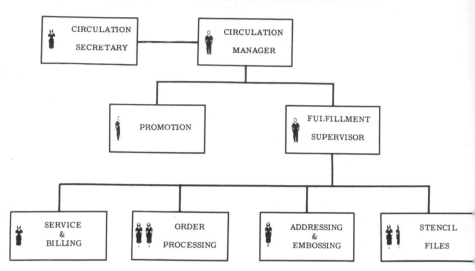

SUBSCRIPTION FULFILLMENT DEPARTMENT

CHART OF PROPOSED ORGANIZATION

Fig. 4-10. Simple Organization Chart Showing Staffing Requirements in Symbols

highly developed and publicized. But the systems function is relatively new, and the application of systems techniques to business operations has not yet standardized procedures to the point where important savings can be effected through microanalysis.

The ideal area for such detailed study would be an office operation in which a very large number of employees were working on identical jobs and using identical machines. This is the very area that is best suited to the application of electronic equipment for data processing. Systems analysis in such an area would probably take the form of a feasibility study for new and different methods of processing data, rather than accepting the present methods and trying to improve them through micromotion techniques. The tremendous volume of new equipment pouring onto the market for the solution of office problems has resulted in a dynamic concern with over-all systems rather than with minute systems details. To conserve his time for more important studies with a greater reward for time spent, the systems man concentrates his attention on the broader aspects of systems instead of on task details.

This situation is closely related to the per-man investment in machinery, which is far higher in the factory than in the office. Whereas the production worker in the plant works with a single machine, costing perhaps $30,000, the vast bulk of office employees has access only to relatively low-cost machines. The entry on the business scene of high-priced computation and special purpose machinery for office work may tend to reverse this

Work Distribution Chart with the following structure:

ACTIVITY	Tot Hrs	SUPERVISOR A 5 (Hrs)	SUPERVISOR A 5	ORDER EDITOR A 3 (Hrs)	ORDER EDITOR A 3	INVOICE EDITOR A 2 (Hrs)	INVOICE EDITOR A 2	ORDER TYPIST B 3 (Hrs)	ORDER TYPIST B 3	FILE CLERK B 2 (Hrs)	FILE CLERK B 2
ORDER PROCESSING	66	2	Answer special inquiries from Sales Office	16	Edit orders for correct cost and selling price	5	Assist with order editing	8	Type purchase orders	23	Maintain open order file
		3	Review orders requiring special processing	6	Direct open order file operations			3	Type letters for supervisor and order editor re: order processing		Maintain follow-up file
											Maintain service file
		(5)		(22)		(5)		(11)		(23)	
INVOICE AUDITING	41	2	Answer special inquiries from vendors			15	Approve and clear routine invoices	4	Type letters for supervisor re: invoice auditing	3	Assist in checking invoices
		2	Correspond with vendors re: major questions of billing, delivery, etc.			2	Review with supervisor invoices requiring special attention	2	Assist in checking invoices		
						6	Process such invoices as directed				
						5	Routine correspondence with vendors				
		(4)				(28)		(6)		(3)	
ADJUSTMENTS CREDITS CLAIMS RETURNS	32	7	Clear adjustment claims with Traffic Dept.	4	Review with supervisor			11	Type letters for supervisor and order editor re: adjustments, credits, claims, and returns		
		4	Review requests for credits, returns, and cancellations	6	Request for credits, returns, and cancellations						
					Process such requests as directed by supervisor						
		(11)		(10)				(11)			
ALLOCATIONS	19	4	Assist Dept. Head in preparation of allocation schedules					4	Type allocation list stencils	5	Run allocation-list stencils
		6	Direct allocation of scarce items								
		(10)						(4)		(5)	
MISCELLANEOUS	42	3	Direct preparation of dept. reports	3	Prepare order, shipment and cancellation reports	7	Typing of telegrams, routine reports, and copy work	4	Type reports for management	1	Distribute mail
		2	Confer with Dept. Head re: dept. operations	5	Assist supervisor			2	Date-stamp incoming mail	1	Collect mail
		5	Assist Dept. Head					2	Sort incoming mail for distribution	4	Sort old files
										3	Messenger
		(10)		(8)		(7)		(8)		(9)	
	200	40		40		40		40		40	

Fig. 4-11. Work Distribution Chart (Courtesy Remington Rand, Sperry Rand Corp.)

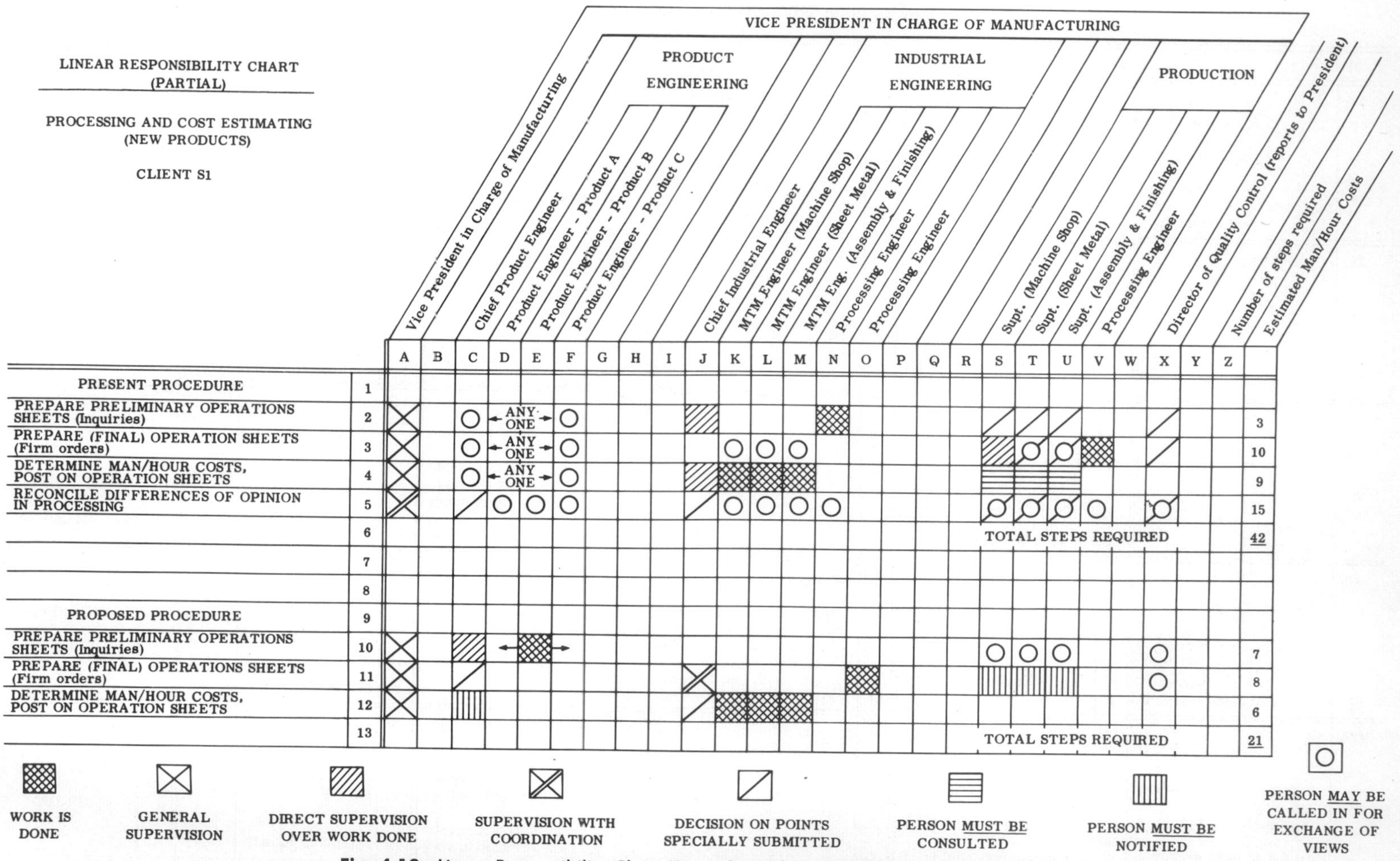

Fig. 4-12. Linear Responsibility Chart (Reproduced from Dun's Review and Modern Industry, Copyright 1953 by The Serge A. Birn Co.)

trend and, perhaps, further the systems use of micromotion techniques in that area.

The right- and left-hand chart is a device used to analyze in detail what each hand does during an operation. The simo (simultaneous motion) chart permits an even more minute analysis of the same thing. Both these charts result from the use of a stop watch, even film clock, or wink counter, devices that are anathema to many systems people. The latter chart utilizes Therblig symbols and codes. The interested reader will find excellent and detailed explanations of these charts in time-study literature.

The Linear Responsibility Chart

The linear responsibility chart is a device designed to portray graphically information relating to the degree of responsibility of key individuals for the performance of various functions. The chart was devised by Ernst Hijmans and Serge A. Birn and copyrighted by the latter in 1953. The chart itself is best described by the illustration of Figure 4-12, and is used to supplement or replace completely the organization manual.

As in the layout of the work distribution chart, operational areas or activities are listed vertically on the left side of the linear responsibility chart. A column to the right is assigned to each individual with any degree of responsibility for the performance of the work. The main contribution made by this chart is the derivation of a symbol or code convention for the designation of degrees of responsibility. This enables the chart to portray concisely a great deal of information formerly confined to the text of organization manuals. In one variation of the chart illustrated, the symbol convention is replaced by a simple letter code.

The linear responsibility chart is of primary usefulness to management as an operating device for control and instruction. It is also useful to systems personnel in much the same manner as the work distribution chart— in pointing out areas of duplication or weakness (in this case, of responsibility), in facilitating management audit, and in the comparison and analysis of organizational units that are similar in organization and function.

SCHEDULING CHARTS

To a large extent, the success of a systems project is dependent on the planning and scheduling which is done at its outset and the control exercised during its conduct. In simplest terms, planning may be defined as listing the steps in the project; scheduling means applying a time requirement to the performance of the steps; and control is the administration of the project after it is begun. Project scheduling and control are carried out through the use of either or both of two types of charts, the Gantt chart and the more recently developed network charting of PERT or CPM. These are discussed in turn.

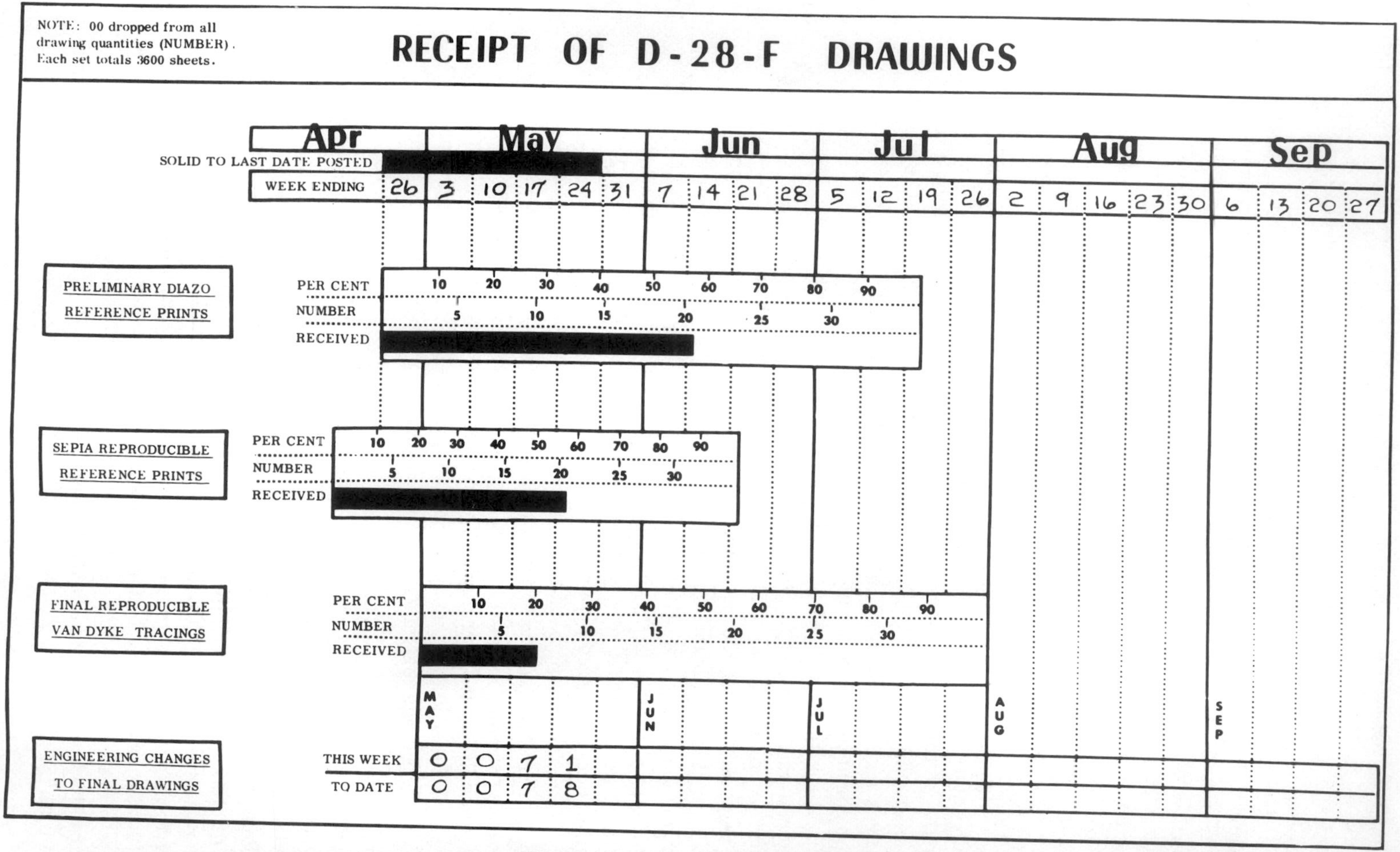

RECEIPT OF D-28-F DRAWINGS

NOTE: 00 dropped from all drawing quantities (NUMBER). Each set totals 3600 sheets.

	Apr	May					Jun				Jul				Aug					Sep			
WEEK ENDING	26	3	10	17	24	31	7	14	21	28	5	12	19	26	2	9	16	23	30	6	13	20	27

SOLID TO LAST DATE POSTED

PRELIMINARY DIAZO REFERENCE PRINTS
PER CENT — NUMBER — RECEIVED

SEPIA REPRODUCIBLE REFERENCE PRINTS
PER CENT — NUMBER — RECEIVED

FINAL REPRODUCIBLE VAN DYKE TRACINGS
PER CENT — NUMBER — RECEIVED

ENGINEERING CHANGES TO FINAL DRAWINGS
THIS WEEK — TO DATE

Fig. 4-13. Gantt (or Scheduling) Chart

The Gantt chart was formulated in 1917 by Henry L. Gantt, noted pioneer in the field of industrial management, as a device for controlling the production of war materiel. It is now in wide use for a variety of purposes where it is desired to portray performance or output against a time requirement. As applied to systems work, the chart finds its greatest usefulness as a tool for planning and scheduling analyst performance during a systems project and for machine and supplies delivery during the installation phase of a project. Where it is used for scheduling an employee training program, it is frequently known as a training timetable. Figure 4-13 shows such a chart—a schedule for the receipt of drawings.

The horizontal axis of the chart is used to depict time, with activities, items, or personnel listed vertically in the left-hand column. The chart is often used to compare actual with planned performance by periodically adding line increments representing the accomplishments of the latest period. Different colors may also be used to contrast planned with actual performance. The current date, or the date of the last entries to the chart, is characteristically noted on the chart in the form of an inverted "V" along the top horizontal axis or, as in the illustration, as a solid bar to the date of the last posting.

PROGRAM EVALUATION AND REVIEW TECHNIQUE (PERT)

PERT is a relatively recent development for project scheduling and control which has achieved widespread use since its declassification by the Navy Department in 1960. Essentially, it is a combination of the network charting techniques, used in specialized industrial applications for many years, and a simple arithmetic formula discussed below. PERT is an outgrowth of CPM (for Critical Path Method) and differs from it mainly in the use of three time estimates rather than a single estimate of how long a task will take.

The PERT network centers on "events," *points in time* at which tasks are completed, and "activities," the *spans of time* during which the work is done which leads to events. Alternately, events may be defined as starts rather than as completions of tasks, in which case the activity line would emanate from the event symbol in the left-to-right progression. Time is stated in man-days, man-weeks or man-months, depending on the project.

Although a detailed explanation is beyond the scope of this chapter, a review of the network presented in Figure 4-14 should convince the reader of the simplicity and major advantages of the technique. First, it should be noted that the purpose of the activity lines on the diagram is to connect the event symbols and indicate precedence, so that the length of the lines is meaningless. Solid lines may be used to represent the time an activity takes, and broken lines, called "zero time" lines, may be used to indicate that an

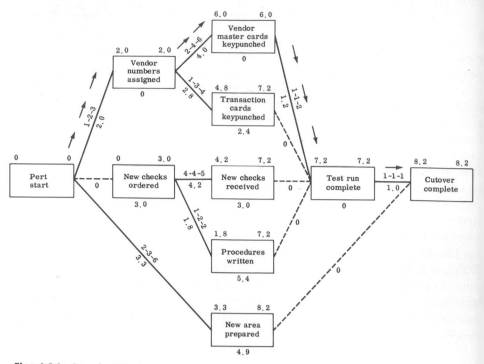

Fig. 4-14. Sample PERT Network for Accounts Payable Mechanization Project (*Reprinted, by permission, from* The Arthur Young Journal, *April 1963*)

activity does not take a significant amount of time but is prerequisite to another. Two or more activity lines converging into one event symbol indicate that both or all the previous events *must be* completed before the latter event can be completed. Conversely, two or more activity lines coming out of one event symbol indicate that the completion of that event is prerequisite to the events which follow. By specifying which events *must* precede others, PERT provides one of its major advantages over the Gantt chart, that of clarifying the interdependent relationship of tasks in the project. The Gantt chart tells us only that one event is scheduled for completion before others, not that it must be.

The duration of each project step is estimated in terms of optimistic, most likely, and pessimistic conditions (noted as T_o, T_{ml}, and T_p) and these estimates are posted above each activity line. The probable of expected time (T_e) is then derived from the formula

$$T_e = \frac{T_o + 4T_{ml} + T_p}{6}$$

and this is posted below each activity line.

Once this is done it is a simple matter to accumulate the estimated times from the start of the project to the finish, using the larger accumulated time where more than one line converges into an event symbol, and post accumulated times to the upper left space above each event symbol. The total expected duration of the project will be posted over the final event. At this point the so-called Critical Path, the particular sequence of events which will take longest to complete and which therefore determines the total duration of the project, can be easily identified (it is indicated in Figure 4-14 with arrows). Reversing the procedure from finish to start, the decreased times are posted to the right above each event symbol, and the difference between the accumulated and decreased times is posted below the event symbol. This difference is called slack time and it represents the amount of time each event can be delayed without delaying the completion of the project.

Detailed explanations of basic PERT methods are available from many publications but much of the literature also concerns advanced refinements and applications which may intimidate the student. For the systems man and for most others the great bulk of the value of PERT lies in the simple, basic method. No computer is required to handle networks of up to about 250 events effectively—a limitation which would apply to very few systems projects. The very simple procedure of drawing the network will alone teach the planner a great deal about his project that he would not learn from Gantt charting. Also, routine use of PERT will provide a degree of control over a systems project not previously attainable.

5

The Management Audit

WILLIAM P. LEONARD

Bendix Aviation Corporation
Teterboro, N.J.

*WILLIAM P. LEONARD began his business career as a public ac-
countant and systems analyst with Lybrand, Ross Brothers and Mont-
gomery, CPAs. Later, he joined the General Motors Corporation, where
he held executive positions in accounting, sales, and management control
sections. In the spring of 1942 he was on special assignment with the
War Production Board handling liaison work between the Army, Navy,
and other war agencies. Since that period he has been associated with
Bendix Aviation Corporation in Philadelphia, Pa., and Teterboro, N.J.,
handling systems and procedures, electronic data processing, and various
administrative functions.*

 *Born in Springfield, Mass., Mr. Leonard received his early educa-
tion at Boston University, Suffolk Law School, and Northeastern University. Later he took post-graduate work in management engineering at
Stevens Institute of Technology.*

 *He is a member of the Systems and Procedures Association of
America, having joined the Northern New Jersey Chapter in 1951; and,
after assisting in the organization of the Palisades Interstate Chapter,
he became its first president in 1955. Along with his other SPA assignments, he has been active in such professional groups as the Institute
of Internal Auditors, the National Association of Accountants, and the
Society for the Advancement of Management.*

 *From time to time he has conducted seminars and lectured on
various management control subjects before both professional associations
and college groups.*

INTRODUCTION

  Time changes many things. Customs considered adequate in former
years for an examination of a business or other organization were limited
mostly to the financial position and the financial operations. For many
years, auditing was associated with and considered a part of accounting.
The purpose of the audit, in the main, consisted of an examination by a
firm of outside auditors to ascertain the financial condition and to detect
fraud or errors. As a business expanded in size, the managerial burden

became greater, and with a wider delegation of authority and responsibility to functional heads, the significance of internal check and control became of greater importance. Thus, management became aware of the need for a change in its methods of management.

Today, modern management in business, with its many problems and complexities, demands a much closer check on controls and performance. In addition to ascertaining the accuracy and reliability of its controls over accounting data, management seeks better means of control over all areas of the business. The objective is to achieve the most efficient administration of the business operations with continuous improvement in policies and procedures.

This new approach in management has brought about the need for review and appraisal of management methods by individuals who are not only basically capable, but who have also the required specialized education, training, and experience to perform such tasks.

BASIC ELEMENTS OF MANAGEMENT

To operate a successful business today, management must specify its objectives, establish plans and a system of procedure to accomplish them, delegate responsibilities and authorities, set up adequate methods and standards of performance, apply a scientific attitude, and evaluate results.

Management's task of governing, coordinating, and controlling the various functions of a business is not an easy one. Its aim is to get things done in the most efficient manner. It must control the enterprise into a going, profitable operation. The main job would appear to consist of three major elements, namely, planning, organization, and direction.

Planning, Organization, and Direction

Planning is accomplished by formulating a system of procedure and policies that reflects the basic objectives and goals of management. The system, properly planned and utilized, will aid in obtaining the desired results in the best manner, with the least expenditure of both time and effort. Policies, once established, designate the aims of the enterprise. They establish the pattern to be followed and the process whereby a top executive reduces the necessity for making routine decisions.

Organization consists of the act or process of defining the lines of authority and responsibility of individuals, and coordinating their individual efforts for harmonious attainment of the predetermined objectives.

Direction means to command, coordinate, and control. To *command* is to issue definite orders, release instructions, or establish rules and regulations under which the operations are to be carried out. To *coordinate* is to design the structure by which the various units can best operate together for the best interests of the enterprise. It is the process of getting all of the different work routines to move along together, and smoothly, toward a common goal. To *control* is to evaluate, appraise, examine, and investigate. It is the necessary action for ascertaining whether or not the plans and objectives are being achieved.

The Importance of Command, Coordination, and Control

Difficulties will arise unless definite orders, instructions, rules, and regulations are carefully predetermined and set up to guide the conduct of each function. For example, without established methods for carrying out repetitive activities, employees become confused and often have an inclination to use variable judgment without following any degree of consistency. The result is a lack of teamwork and coordination.

Coordinated management is necessary in order that all functions of a business may work in harmony to give better over-all management control. Without coordination, each job is likely to get out of hand.

Control by management is necessary in order to accomplish the desired goals. This concerns preplanning of work, policy formulation, predetermining objectives, the delegation of authority and responsibility for the accomplishment of results, and the comparison and evaluation of results with the predetermined objectives.

Control is actually checking to make certain that everything is in order as intended. Some of the checking can be performed by the supervisor and others who are responsible. If so instructed, they can make the necessary reports and take action to correct unsatisfactory conditions.

The following are only a few conditions that contribute to poor management or a poorly run business:

Organizational defects
Unbalanced financial structure
Ineffective marketing of product or service
Inaccurate reports
Inadequate physical equipment and/or layout
Lack of enforcement of policies and regulations
Bad production planning
Non-compliance with governmental regulations
Poor methods, systems, and procedures
Lack of adequate operating standards
Incompetent supervision
Poor or inadequate records
Little or no internal control

In regard to poor internal controls, it is interesting to note that dishonesty of employees does not necessarily occur as the result of employees' having access to cash receipts. Some losses, for example, come about by reason of an employee's receiving a "kickback"—the return of a part or all of a sum of money, or the acceptance of the equivalent in merchandise, following a transaction of a confidential nature with another party through coercion or otherwise.

The establishment of controls always involves some degree of uncertainty about the final results. Unexpected conditions may develop. There is always an element of experimentation, of test or trial, in any new method of control. Because of uncertainty, management has begun to realize more and more the importance of making provision for periodic reviews and appraisals. A greater number of business firms and other organizations are beginning to appreciate the advantages of the management audit.

APPRAISAL OF MANAGEMENT METHODS AND PERFORMANCE

Management Audit Defined

The management audit may be defined as a comprehensive and constructive examination of an organizational structure of a company or its components, such as a division or department, its plans and policies, its financial controls, its methods of operation, and its use of human and physical facilities.

The primary objective of the management audit is to reveal defects or irregularities in any of the elements examined in that portion of the organization that is under study and to indicate possible improvements. A management audit may cover a company as a whole or an organizational component—down to the lowest level of supervision. Generally, the audit is tailored to fit the area being studied. For example, adherence to government regulations may not apply to a specific department, but may apply to the company as a whole.

The examination of management's methods and performance involves a review of the objectives, the procedures, the delegation of responsibility, the standards, and the accomplishments. The operating effectiveness of the area under study can be ascertained by a comparison of the present conditions with those that were intended by policies, procedures, and so forth.

Scientific appraisal involves the process of measurement, and the checking of principles, to ascertain whether or not the plan, the policy, the system, or the procedure is best under the particular circumstances. After securing the facts, the process is to evaluate the data in order to make sound recommendations for improvement. An important point here is not to accept or reject hastily any plausible approach to a solution. A high degree of imagination is important and necessary. It might be possible to test out various solutions that offer the greatest promise.

Specialized Service to Management

Audits serve as a check on the abilities of management at all levels. It is a service designed to determine potential danger spots and to highlight opportunities to eliminate waste or unnecessary loss. It is a means of deter-

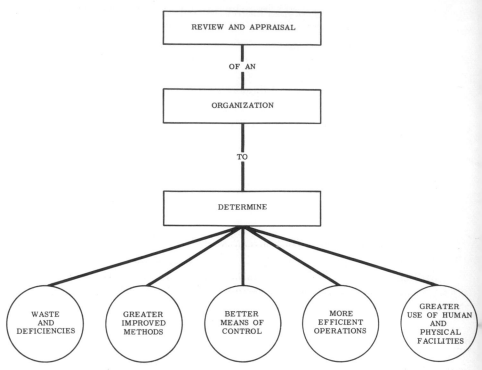

Fig. 5-1. Purpose of Management Auditing

mining whether or not federal, state, and local governmental regulations are being adhered to, of assuring management that company policies and procedures are complied with, and that observations are made for the purpose of improving the company's economic position. The nature of the work, performed by individuals with specialized training, expert knowledge, and ability, is such that it renders a specialized service to management that is distinct and apart from any other type of service. This specialization, over a period of time, becomes more and more beneficial to a company in that the auditor is capable of performing management audits more and more effectively by reason of his greater experience.

Benefits to be Derived

Defects in the organizational structure of a business can be the cause for the difference between successful and unsuccessful business results. The defects may be due to poor or no leadership, internal friction, little or no cooperation, inadequate or poor coordination of activities, and a general lack of knowledge or disregard for the principles of good organization.

Nothing so restrains the enthusiasm and the energy of an organization as the lack of definite instructions and the disregard for control. As the business expands and operations become more and more complex, the problem of control becomes greater and greater.

By constantly aiming for greater efficiency, management can find ways for reducing costs and increasing profits. Poor methods of marketing the product, inadequate physical equipment, lack of training and development of personnel, loose standards of performance, and poor records of operations are only a few of the factors that can contribute toward high costs and poor profits.

Some of the results that might be expected from a management audit are:

1. Spotlighting deficiencies in production controls
2. Improvements in systems and procedures
3. Clarification and better understanding of basic objectives and responsibilities as they pertain to the area under study
4. Better control over physical inventory
5. Improving supervision through sound training programs
6. Reduction in waste through realistic performance standards
7. More effective organization methods through clarification and improved arrangement of individual duties and responsibilities

As a result of the success already attained by some firms, the trend toward adopting management audit programs is increasing more and more in organizations. Some have established a management audit function as a key control and evaluation device, and others have allotted the various specialties to senior staff personnel. Each man is trained to be particularly conversant with matters in his field.

CONCEPTS OF MANAGEMENT AUDITS

The management audit may be made of a specific function, of a department or a group of departments, of a division or group of divisions, or of the entire business. Some audits may include a combination of any two or more of such areas, such as a specific function as well as an examination of the organizational group or groups performing the work. For example, in the study of a sales order routine, the investigation might include the various routines maintained in processing the paper work in the sales department as well as the procedure and qualifications of the personnel approving the customer credit in the accounting department.

The area of study could involve the economics of production, including such elements as specialization, simplification, standardization, diversification, expansion, contraction, and integration, or such factors of production as the supply of raw material, procurement of parts, labor supply, plant layout, job standards, and so forth.

A matter of importance that cannot be overestimated is that a complete understanding with management must be secured beforehand concerning both the size of the audit staff and the limitation of the audit work. This is necessary before starting any audit assignment.

It should be borne in mind that the functions of the auditor differ in some companies. In most cases the work consists of making an examination, reporting defects or irregularities, and presenting recommendations for improvements. The responsibility for actually making changes to bring about improvements is generally assigned to a methods analyst. On the other hand, it is not unusual to find, on occasion, that management in some companies has charged the management audit group with the full responsibility for making changes and revisions in systems and procedures.

Measuring and Evaluating Effectiveness of Control

For efficient control in any undertaking, there must be continuous and detailed measures of accomplishment. This is particularly true of operations, costs, methods, products, wages, and salaries. The function of the management audit is to check the performance and evaluate the effectiveness of control. To appraise is to find out how well it was done. In this connection, the observation may imply a lack of control, or at least not a very tight control.

Poor control may be the result of a breakdown in the records and procedures, lack of adequate supervisory enforcement, or inefficient standards of measurement. The auditor is forced to make a study of both the records and the procedures, and, where necessary, to make recommendations for revisions in the procedures. He may find that supervision requires additional instruction in order to enforce compliance. After evaluating the standards, he may find it necessary to recommend the re-establishment of standards according to current conditions.

If an audit review of management methods reveals no major deficiencies and no opportunities to increase effectiveness, there is, at least, a feeling of satisfaction and security.

In his review, it would be good for the auditor to have a knowledge of and apply, wherever possible, the methods of quantitative and qualitative measurement. Hence, he should develop, through questionnaires or otherwise, measures, tests, scales, and the like, and apply them in his work in order to satisfy himself whether or not something is good, bad, high, low, average, and so on.

Certain information and material will be required for quantitative data, such as the number of measurable units of each type of work performed and the man-hours required to process a given number of units of each type. An example of a requirement for qualitative data is the relative frequency of errors occurring in each type of operation.

Checking Organization Principles

Experience shows that a major weakness in many companies is the failure by management to give full application to the principles of good organization. In general, the cause is due to indifference, or lack of understanding or appreciation of the value of organization principles.

In checking organization principles, due regard must be given to the over-all plans and objectives of a business, to the basic fundamentals necessary for getting work done and results accomplished, to the organizational structure, to the essential requirements for functionalization and departmentalization, to the manner of selection and development of personnel, and to the orderly arrangement of teamwork, in order to provide unity of action in meeting the desired goals.

The auditor should include in his study a check on the advantages of centralization or decentralization of certain functions. For example, in a business with a number of manufacturing plants, it might appear on the surface to be far more economical to centralize all purchasing activities at a main point rather than maintain purchasing departments at each plant. On the other hand, the types of products manufactured at each plant may differ greatly, with absolutely no similarity in basic materials or requirements. As a result, it may be more advantageous to maintain a decentralization of the purchasing function. In studies involving centralization versus decentralization, it may be necessary for the auditor to recommend additional studies, such as one calling for operations research techniques.

Another point to consider is that no organization remains static. Changes in product, methods of operation, channels of distribution, increase or decrease in volume, and even changes in key personnel, all demand a review and evaluation, to some degree, in order to point out any defects, and to suggest possible improvements.

Communicating the requirements necessary for getting work done is not easy. Organizational communication involves the complete program of communication policy, planning, and procedure. Communication involves the transmission of information upward, downward, and across. Decisions depend upon facts that are derived from communications. Action is achieved through instructions that are conveyed through communications.

Of vital importance to successful business operation is the communication of basic information by means of the organizational structure—the organization chart showing graphically the relationship of functions and the flow of authority and responsibility.

The auditor, in examining the organization chart of a business, must first ascertain whether or not it reflects correctly the true, current status of the organizational functions. He must analyze each and every element and complete his evaluation to determine whether or not the organizational structure is sound and effective. In some cases, he may find it necessary to prepare and present a new chart showing recommended changes.

The important step in the process of analyzing organizations according to functions is the recognition of the activities of which the business is comprised. There is the question of determining what functions are necessary or desirable. The importance of each function must be ascertained so

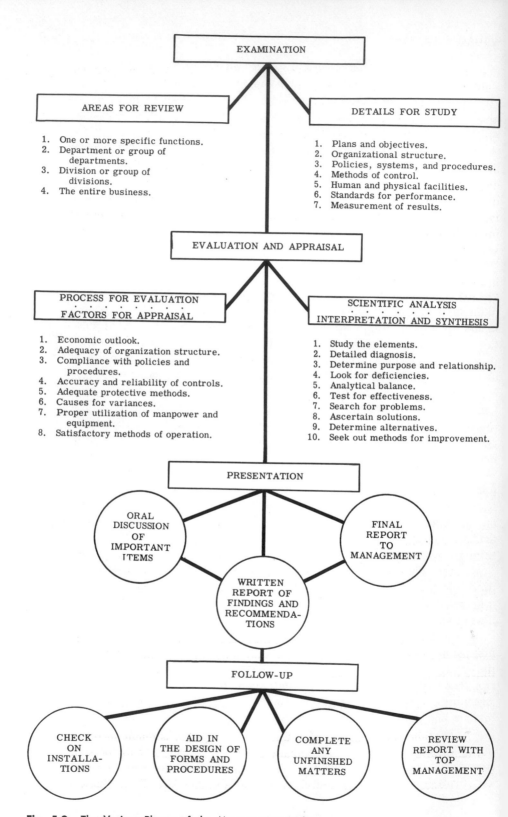

Fig. 5-2. The Various Phases of the Management Audit

that major functions may be properly separated. The need for assigning similar or related minor functions under a single functional head is likewise important. The auditor should look for possible overlapping and duplication of effort, and concentration on one or more functions. The existence of this situation could result in an unbalanced organizational structure.

Instances will be found where important functions are being neglected and others of far less importance are receiving major recognition. Other defects, found occasionally, generally reflect that certain executives are overburdened, positions of importance are assigned to individuals who lack the ability to perform the work, persons of unusual ability are handling minor functions, and a staff assistant to a corporate officer may be responsible for several unrelated functions.

The auditor is often confronted with such problems as dissension among management, lack of or poor leadership, rivalry between department heads, favoritism by corporate officers toward one executive or department, unofficial "top brass," little or no cooperation, the idea that "production comes first," and others.

Evaluating Policies and Practices

Sound policies with strong leadership are, of course, basic and essential for effective management. They outline intent and represent the guiding principles that help the business to follow a planned course in reaching its objectives. Policies, put in writing and properly communicated throughout an organization, create a means for uniformity and coordination, of getting things done through people in an economical and consistent manner.

Many times, so-called "policies" come about by custom or precedent, not necessarily by planned action of top management reduced to writing. Actually, they represent practices created at one time or another, possibly at a lower level in the organization and not necessarily known or having official sanction of top management.

Definite, clear-cut policies, in writing and distributed to all concerned, will avoid misunderstanding, waste, friction, and lost motion. Of course, they must be understood and have the respect of everyone in the organization. Respect at lower levels of the organization, with disrespect or lack of consideration at the higher levels, will not bring about effective management.

Policies are like standards in that they represent the best thinking that can be devised at the particular time and must be complied with at all times until good reasons suggest a change. Hence, under no circumstances should policies be so inflexible as to resist a change. They must be modified, when necessary, to fit into any new condition beneficial to the business.

Policies, unless enforced, can break down and become uncontrollable and cause difficulties. For example, unless a strict policy is maintained over the removal by employees of company product and property for personal use, the business will suffer losses in both its product inventory and fixed assets. Hence, enforcement is needed in order to make any policy effective.

The stronger the enforcement by management, the greater the possibility of the business achieving successful results.

There is, of course, no positive assurance that policies, although issued in writing, will be complied with. Although the intent may be good, management, due to the pressure of other matters, often fails in its responsibility to follow up and enforce major policies in operating a business. Some persons with authority who could easily delegate responsibility for follow-up and enforcement fail to do so, feeling that their successors have less experience and may lack good judgment.

Clear statements of policy are indispensable. Each and every decision and step of action should be based upon sound thinking with a positive approach toward the company's objectives. Statements of policy are needed as a basis for decision in the areas of product lines, finance, personnel, research, procurement, wages, selling price, channels of distribution, and so forth. The selection of a course of action must be made so as to accomplish a definite purpose.

Actual periodic examination by the auditor is necessary in order to assure compliance with company policies. For example, in the evaluation of a purchasing department, basic policies for the auditor to examine and appraise would include, among other things, the following:

> Responsibility for purchasing
> Authorization for each purchase
> Adherence to required specifications
> Orders placed as the result of competitive bidding
> Availability of sources of supply
> Reliability of the supplier

The auditor should look for the lack of effective policy in any area. In his review, he must check the soundness of the policy. Is it directed toward a definite objective? Is it positive, clear, and understandable? Does it recognize economic principles?

In checking policies and practices, the auditor should consider all elements. For example, an evaluation of the sales policies of a business would involve getting into the quality, design, and style, as well as the number and variety of products. In addition, it would involve an examination of the channels of distribution, type and location of customers, determination of selling prices, training and selection of salesmen, and sales promotion activities. Each element must be examined comprehensively and constructively. The auditor looks for defects and irregularities in every element. His aim is to indicate possible improvements.

Actually, to insure compliance with policies one must first have a clear understanding of the objectives. Are they completely sound and practicable? What are the limiting and determining factors? The next step is to ascertain whether or not the policies are being followed by all concerned. Are they guiding the organization in the achievement of its objectives? Is there a conflict as to the method of attaining the objective? The auditor reviews the policies through the various levels of management. He checks performance for proof of policy. He seeks areas for possible misinterpretation. And, finally, he must appraise each policy. Is each policy sound and effective? Is it being implemented in accordance with the program? Is it presenting the most effective results?

Reviewing and Appraising Systems and Procedures

In reviewing any business system or procedure, the management auditor must concern himself with its purpose as well as whether it is designed in the best interests for efficient administration. A poor system or procedure can be costly and may prevent carrying out the policy for which it was intended. A system may have outgrown its usefulness. A procedure may be confusing, misunderstood, and inadequate to fit the particular need. The flow of the paper work may reveal backtracking, congestion, poor working conditions, and the need for mechanical aids.

Evaluation of a system or a procedure actually includes three separate considerations. First, is the system or procedure meeting all of the current requirements? Second, is it operating effectively? And, third, what is the degree of effectiveness?

To determine whether a system or procedure is meeting current requirements, the following, among other things, should be considered.

1. Is the procedure designed to promote the achievement of the company's objectives, and is it accomplished effectively?
2. Does the procedure operate within the framework of the organizational structure?
3. Does the procedure provide methods of control so as to obtain maximum performance with minimum expenditure of time and effort?
4. Do the routines designated in the procedure indicate performance in logical sequence?
5. Does the procedure provide the means for effective coordination between one department and another?
6. Have all required functions been established?
7. Has authority been designated to carry out responsibilities?
8. Can any changes be made to improve effectiveness?

The important thing is to make sure that the system or procedure is designed to meet desired end results. One must determine what is actually done as well as where, how, when, and by whom. Each individual step in the process must be studied and consideration given to its effectiveness. At the same time, one must be constantly alert for possible improvements.

Although a precise measurement of how effective a system or procedure operates may be difficult to determine, the degree of effectiveness can be ascertained somewhat by checking on the activities from the standpoint of speed, accuracy, and orderly flow of the paper work. Do bottlenecks and delays occur from time to time? Does the paper work reflect a few or a large number of errors? Is the work neat and the writing readable? Are the schedules, reports, or end results promptly completed and furnished on time? Are operations proceeding well or better than expected? What is the relationship between the volume of work and the number of employees performing the work, and how does it compare from month to month?

The auditor must always be on the alert for possible defects and irregularities. He must check the activities with the instructions to see if the instructions are properly complied with. All deviations must be called to the attention of the supervisor responsible for the proper adherence to the instructions, and the necessary action must be taken for correction. On occasion, due to some unusual circumstances, the auditor may find that good judgment often dictates a deviation from an instruction, possibly to achieve a desired objective better.

Management must be constantly alerted to the importance of the systems and procedures function as an element of good organization and management. No business can continuously achieve success without giving consideration to maintaining proper systems of control and current, written procedures to guide all concerned in performing their work assignments.

Appraisal of Operations

Business success is gained chiefly by performing all operations effectively and by consistently striving for improvements. Such accomplishment can result only if there is a keen awareness on the part of management of the necessity for promptly translating good judgment into decisive action. If management is alert to the advantages that modern control techniques afford, and applies them intelligently, it has little fear of results. Maintaining good control over operations is one of management's principal problems.

The problem of the auditor is to determine whether or not the business is operating as profitably as it should. He must study and analyze all the factors that pertain to the operation of the business, including its profits and volume relationship, the products or services, the market, the organization, the facilities, and the finances. There must be adequate controls established to bind the elements of the business into a going, profitable operation. Methods are necessary in order to compare actual performance with predetermined standards. Causes for variances must be ascertained and the necessary steps set up for applying corrective action.

Often, an audit examination, proceeding from one deficiency clue to another, leads to finding a defective objective or policy and the need for a revision of the system or procedure. Deficiences may be attributable to the fact that the employees are not qualified to perform the work, and require training. Other points requiring examination for possible deficiencies are working conditions (ventilation, light, floor space, and temperature control). The auditor must keep in mind that operating objectives are not reached unless plans are made and are kept up to date constantly. Forward planning should be carried on in every phase of business operations—engineering, manufacturing, selling, and the rest. Planning includes the forecasting program representing the thinking of management. Planning establishes advanced goals and indicates what is needed to reach these goals. It reflects the cost levels to be maintained. It represents the guide for good, efficient operation and proper utilization of manpower and equipment.

The management auditor should concern himself with an appraisal of the forecast, and with its comparison with operating results. If a current day-to-day comparison of the budget figures with actual performance is not in use, he should stress the establishment and use of this management tool. Its principal advantage is that it shows the daily amount and the trend for actual performance as compared with that projected, making known any detrimental conditions so that corrective steps may be taken almost immediately.

Cost controls play an important part in many types of businesses; here, the auditor should look for defects and irregularities in operating performance. Present practices should be carefully reviewed for possible weaknesses in the procedures, and the facts should be presented, in report form, to those concerned. The following is a typical example of a brief report of this nature:

> On making a preliminary survey in connection with the new scrap procedure to be established November 9, I found that the physical setup in Department #401 is not conducive to obtaining the best results. It is doubtful whether the procedure could even be partially inaugurated in the department involved.
>
> I found that we are not securing proper control on counts. The present practice is for the employee, at various times during the day, to bring work up, have it counted, and noted on the back of his time ticket. At the end of the day, the counts are totaled and the employee is given credit for the full amount thus handled. The catch to this procedure is that the employee takes the work back with him, and there is nothing to prevent him from bringing the same pieces up and having them counted over and over again. The reason for this procedure's being followed is that the dispatch and inspection facilities have not been properly set up as elsewhere in the plant.
>
> In discussing this situation with both the factory manager and his assistant, it was the consensus of opinion that proper control cannot be established until an "inspection and dispatch" crib is set up for each department. It is highly recommended by all concerned that immediate steps be taken to see that this is accomplished. The savings, even for the next month or two, will more than offset the small amount of expense involved.

It is most important that a careful evaluation be made of all control techniques of a business to determine their effectiveness. Control is the final step in the cycle of administration. It checks actual results against plans or policies to ascertain whether or not the plans or policies have been carried out as intended. Control is built upon previous planning and provides the basis for subsequent planning. Good examples are physical controls, such as watchmen and plant protection, and such statistical records that may be kept by sales, production, engineering development, maintenance, or other departments.

Appraisal of Personnel

In almost every type of business, there is need for frequent scrutiny and evaluation of personnel policies and practices in order to maintain effective personnel administration. The appraisal of personnel includes an evaluation of the personnel practices, and a review to determine the abilities, strengths, and weaknesses of the people on the payroll. A close check should be made of working conditions, employee morale, training programs, employees' service activities, methods of record keeping, job evaluation, merit rating, and employee development.

The auditor will find many instances in which the average personnel director needs help in finding a solution to the problems pertaining to the personnel function. One will find problems due to faulty company policies, poor or inefficient supervision, inadequate parking space, poor ventilation, insufficient cafeteria facilities, ineffective employee-relations service, and so on. An effective way to get a good, broad picture of the things that concern the feelings of the average employee is through an employee opinion poll.

Personnel policies and procedures should be in writing. They should be reviewed carefully by the auditor for completeness and to see if they currently reflect the industrial relations philosophy of the management. The auditor should also check for possible deviations from established federal, state, and local regulations. Following an appraisal of the policies and procedures, every effort should be made to point out possible methods for improvement.

It is important that employees have knowledge of the various employee service activities in force, for these are the things that help to attain maximum results in improving employee morale. The auditor must check these services for purposes of ascertaining their effectiveness.

In the audit of personnel administration, due regard should be given to the method of maintaining records and to the preparation and release of personnel reports. The report on turnover should be given special attention.

Other matters requiring evaluation include job specifications, interviewing methods, placement methods, and methods for reclassifying employees. The auditor should seek out causes for job dissatisfaction, lack of compliance with company policies and procedures, poor coordination, and the like. His objective is to reveal shortcomings, weaknesses, errors, deficiencies, failings, and irregularities. The complete facts must be obtained and the details, with recommendations, presented in the auditor's report.

ORGANIZING A PROGRAM

In organizing a program for management audits, consideration must be given first to a statement of policy, indicating therein the objectives, and secondly to the careful preparation of a plan to achieve the objectives. The latter includes the matter of selecting the right type of personnel to perform the work, establishing a good staff training program to improve the effectiveness of the work, determining methods of procedure for work accomplishment, setting forth a basis of control over time and costs, and preparing the audit outline.

The essential step, of course, is to obtain management's approval of the plan and its full support in carrying out the program. Without complete understanding and support, difficulties are bound to arise later, causing discouragement and confusion.

Preliminary Planning

Although the management audit might be described as a comprehensive and constructive examination of a business activity to determine defects or irregularities and to indicate possible improvements, the important element is to determine what factors are necessary for carrying out the objective. What are the best methods for the business and the individuals responsible for performing the function? What are the limiting and controlling factors? What means can be established to appraise performance? The answers to these questions will give at least a starting point preliminary to the selection of a final plan. To build a successful program, whether for a large or small organization, the scope or intent is basic. The problem most common is that of extent of coverage. A management audit group can handle many assignments provided they have enough qualified personnel. They can perform appraisals in almost any area of the business if permitted to do so. There must be a definite understanding with management as to the nature of audits to be performed, the scope and detail of the auditing work, the methods employed, and the manpower requirements.

Another matter is the location of the audit function. It may be a part of the activities of the methods department, the internal auditing section, or the management planning group. It could be a staff function.

Selection of Personnel

Whatever the size of the company, it is important that each person selected to perform management audits have a thorough knowledge of the fundamentals of organization and management, the principles for effective methods of control, and the requirements for conducting scientific appraisals. He must have experience in systems and procedures work and the ability to conduct surveys and make examinations in the various areas of a business for the purpose of disclosing inefficiencies or weaknesses, if called upon to do so. He should be able to make constructive recommendations, pointing out better or more effective methods to eliminate waste and unnecessary loss.

In addition to the foregoing, the individual should have certain personal characteristics, namely, good judgment, an inclination toward analysis, a high degree of imagination, and ability to write and express himself clearly and logically. A college education and a broad business background are advisable.

If possible, the individual who is to appraise the activities of a business should be selected from within the organization. He could be one who has advanced through the ranks in the organization.

Training Programs

For quality in performing audit assignments, a continuous training program is necessary, since the management auditor must keep abreast with the many new business techniques being currently released.

The type of training required for the more experienced staff member will differ somewhat from that required for the new, inexperienced man. For example, the latter will require sufficient time to get familiar with the over-all activities of the company. He must have some knowledge of the organizational structure, the various functions, the outlook for the business in matters of product demand or services, competitive conditions, and the like. He should be instructed thoroughly in the method of handling audit assignments, in making an appraisal, and in recommending improvements. Some of his training may be obtained on the job, but a large part of the training must be secured by individual study or from group meetings and discussions held by his supervisor.

An experienced management auditor generally improves his knowledge and efficiency by handling more complex assignments and by keeping up with new techniques. He finds it necessary to do a great amount of reading on new ideas, and to attend and participate in conferences and discussions held by the various professional business organizations. For example, to keep abreast of electronic computer systems, time must be devoted by the auditor to reading much material and attending various training courses on equipment and business applications.

Preparing the Audit Program

Before beginning a management audit in connection with any assignment, it is good to sit back and outline briefly an audit program as it relates to the area being studied. This is merely a matter of listing the points to be covered and the procedures to be followed in performing the assignment. It is most important that the points be directed toward the principal objectives, but it is not necessary that the auditor follow the program rigidly, for in some instances there may be occasion and opportunity for him to exercise his own imagination and judgment.

The audit program may be reduced to a number of important steps. A knowledge of these steps represents the real crux of an efficient management audit program.

A. *Organization*

    1. Study the organization structure in the area under appraisal.

    2. Compare the existing structure with that shown on the company's organization chart (if one exists).

    3. Ascertain whether or not full appreciation has been given to the principles of good organization and functionalization.

B. *Policies and practices*

Make a study to find out what action, if required, must be taken to improve the effectiveness of the policies and practices.

C. *Regulations*

Determine whether or not due regard has been given by the company for full compliance with all local, state, and federal regulations.

D. *Systems and procedures*

Study the systems and procedures for possible defects or irregularities in the elements examined and seek out methods to bring about possible improvements.

E. *Operations*

Evaluate operations to ascertain what is necessary for more effective controls and efficient results.

F. *Personnel*

Study the general personnel requirements and their application to the work in the area under appraisal.

G. *Layout and physical equipment*

Determine whether or not improvements could be made in the layout and in better or greater use of physical equipment.

H. *Report*

Prepare a report of findings with suggested recommendations.

Time and Cost Involved

The time required to carry out a management audit will vary depending upon the extent and nature of the assignment. For example, the time required to perform an audit of the entire activities in the purchasing department of a business might take a few weeks, whereas an audit of the entire business could take several months. The cost will vary for each assignment depending somewhat upon the number of auditors assigned to perform the work and whether or not one or more specialists in a particular field is required. An audit of a production planning and control department, for example, because of its size and other factors, could require an audit staff of several men, and, in addition, a specialist in production planning and one in production control.

Audit Findings

A very important part of the management audit is the method of handling the audit findings. These may involve deviations in procedures, bad practices, inadequate controls, poor policies, and so on, some of which are of major importance and require immediate action to bring about corrections. The correction may or may not be one that can be made by the local personnel involved. In any event, it must be discussed with the personnel directly in charge or those responsible at a higher level, and the necessary action taken to bring about a correction. It is always good to indicate in the management audit report the results of the discussion on audit findings, as well as a statement of the action taken by those concerned to correct the situation immediately. Should further steps be required, it is necessary for the auditor to establish a system of follow-up until the matter has been properly disposed of by all parties concerned.

CONDUCTING THE MANAGEMENT AUDIT

Management audits can be performed efficiently if care is taken in the planning stage. This means the establishment of systematic methods of procedure in bringing together certain information of importance and interpreting its meaning. It means making interviews to obtain information, conducting investigations, performing various analyses, applying modern techniques, determining the real facts, using check lists, measuring performance, and finding solutions to various types of problems.

Review and Appraisal

To review is to make a survey of the past—to take a closer look at the business activities for the purpose of ascertaining whether or not they are being carried out with maximum effectiveness and economy, to check on compliance with company policies and procedures, and to appraise the method of control.

Although the management auditor may not be an expert in all fields of management, he should be an expert in the appraisal of control, and, in this position, be able to examine and offer constructive suggestions regarding the control of any phase of company operations. He knows, for example, that the organization chart is not an end in itself. The organization chart is of little importance without an efficient organization.

Interviews

Before making an interview, adequate preparation is necessary in order to avoid wasted effort and loss in time. The auditor should have a good idea of the type of information desired and should be prepared to ask a number of direct questions. To obtain factual information, care must be taken in selecting the proper person or persons. The time and place should be pre-arranged. The person or persons to be interviewed should be notified before-hand of the subject matter to be discussed and properly informed as to what, if anything, should be made available at the time of the interview in the way of records, reports, and the like.

The interview should be conducted in an informal manner, and the approach should be through a proper channel of authority, clearing with the supervisor before dealing with his subordinates. It is important that the auditor be tactful and diplomatic at all times.

In starting the interview, the auditor should state its purpose and point out that he is only seeking specific information that may aid in his review and appraisal. He might indicate that opinions may be expressed but that they will be disregarded unless substantiated by evidence.

During the interview, the auditor should not commit himself, nor should he make any recommendations, even though he may tentatively favor, one way or another, the matter under discussion. He will find it necessary to verify doubtful points by asking questions, the answers to which may require study later on in his examination. His notes on all matters discussed must be supported, whenever possible, by sample forms, reports, and so on, and these should be made a part of his work papers. Whenever time and circumstances permit, it is advisable for the auditor to check and digest the information received from one interview before starting another. In some cases, it is advisable to verify the accuracy of data obtained at an interview, by requesting the person interviewed to read the notes taken and place his initials thereon.

Investigation, Analysis, and Techniques

Investigation is a careful inquiry, search, or examination for the purpose of collecting pertinent facts. The purpose of analysis is to prepare for synthesis. *Analysis* is the separation of anything into elements. *Synthesis* is the process of combining the separate elements—the opposite of analysis.

Following an investigation, the facts are analyzed into elements in order to ascertain their relationship and their bearing upon the matter at hand. In other words, an analysis is made to determine whether or not all of the facts have a bearing upon the plan or the objective. If they do, they should be arranged in order of importance for interpretation. Discrepancies in facts require further investigation and analysis.

The value of any analysis may be determined by the care and thoroughness with which the analysis is made. Each step must be performed carefully and all matters verified to make certain that subsequent steps are not predicated upon incorrect bases. For a good analysis, the best technique is actually to chart the various activities, in detail form, step by step.

Interpretations made from an analysis are not necessarily conclusions. They must be related to other inferences and, possibly, reformulated for one reason or another. It is not good practice to attempt to formulate a conclusion without giving consideration to every element.

Techniques Employed

There are a number of techniques employed in recording facts in order to facilitate analysis and interpretation. Some of them are as follows:

1. Organization charts (structural, functional, position)
2. Process charts (product, operation, procedure)
3. Man-machine time charts
4. Motion picture films (motion studies)
5. Layout charts (machine, equipment, building, floor, workplace)
6. Forms distribution charts
7. Questionnaires (operation, requirements, etc.)
8. Comparison charts (Gantt, relationship, line and staff)
9. Graphic charts (progress, line, surface, bar, map, pie)
10. Statements, exhibits, etc.

Getting the Facts

Good audits can be obtained by a complete gathering of facts—facts concerning objectives and requirements to be met, the organization structure, the company policies and practices, systems and procedures, actual operations, and personnel.

The various techniques indicated previously are the means of gathering facts. It is better to gather too many rather than too few facts, for the excess facts may be helpful later when making interpretations.

It is important that the auditor be on the alert constantly for new sources of factual data, for any new information may influence his viewpoint in the evaluation.

Use of Check Lists

A check list is an essential tool in making an appraisal. It serves as a guide in seeking answers to various questions. It is one good method for a plan of action, something to follow or modify if necessary. It is of consider-

PROCEDURE INTERVIEW

By: *John Brown*

DATE: *August 20, 1967*

SUBJECT: MANUFACTURING PROCESS SHEET—FORM #387

PURPOSE:	To detail the complete information regarding the method of manufacturing each part.
ORIGINATION:	Tools and Methods Department.
SOURCE OF INFORMATION:	Procedures and tool data.
INFORMATION ENTERED:	Operation number, operation, department, machine, feed, speeds, cut, and tools by Processing Section. Tool numbers and material requirement data by Tooling Section. Machine and man-hours by Time Standards Section.
NUMBER OF COPIES:	Five or more as required.
FREQUENCY:	With each part released by Engineering and revised as required.
DISTRIBUTION:	Copy #1 – Retained by Processing Section in part folder as historical record.
	Copy #2 – Retained by Processing Section in part folder as aid in preparing revisions. After revised process in effect, copy #2 to be destroyed.
	Copy #3 and #4 – To Production Control for planning purposes. To be destroyed when superseded.
	Copy #5 and as required – To Production Control only as its request for distribution to departments concerned, including Cost Accounting, in accordance with effective date, to be filed for reference and destroyed when superseded.

CHANGE IN PROCEDURE: *None*

VERIFICATION: *Information correct as*
(PLEASE INITIAL) *written. A.C.D. 8/29/67*

Fig. 5-3. Typical Example—Information Received as a Result of an Interview

able help in checking back later when one arrives at a point to define precisely a problem that requires solution.

Each management audit program is unique, and should be adapted to the particular conditions and problems encountered. For this reason, the check list must be designed to include only those specific questions pertinent to the particular type of audit examination being made at the time. Each case has its individual aspects; therefore, it is not possible to establish a check list that can be used for all situations.

A number of major factors in every management audit that the auditor should concern himself with when preparing a check list are as follows:

1. Are the plans or objectives sound in principle?
2. Are the policies and practices properly established, and are they in harmony with the objectives?
3. Is the organization set up to carry out the objectives effectively?
4. Are the controls adequate and working effectively?
5. Is there full compliance with the system or procedure?
6. Are there any problems pertaining to personnel requirements and work load?
7. What is the quality of the work performed?
8. What can be done in the matter of improvement?

Measuring Performance

Measuring performance involves a study of work volume in a particular work area or unit. The study is made to ascertain the work effort, to get facts on how effective the work is performed, to determine requirements for eliminating backlog, and to seek improved methods.

Measuring performance is the result of establishing an equitable relationship between the volume of work performed and the manpower utilized in completing that volume. It is another technique that the auditor can use, if so directed, in connection with his studies of any operation.

Difficulties Encountered

During the audit, and sometimes as the result of the audit, difficulties will arise owing to various reasons. For example, one may find management to be slow in accepting recommendations for improvement, mainly because of resistance to change.

Improvements sometimes cause intense resistance. One audit revealed a problem of resistance to a recommendation in which the head of a purchasing department objected to the task of preparing a form authorizing the transfer of material on consignment from the plant to a vendor. Actually, the material was needed by the vendor in order to process certain work requested by the head of the purchasing department. Formerly, the routine of preparing and issuing the material transfer form was a responsibility of the storekeeper, but the practice was found to be unsound from the standpoint of internal control.

The immediate reaction of the head of the purchasing department was violent objection, mostly due to the idea of making out the paper work and checking for accountability of the material. The problem was finally resolved by pointing out to the department head the important need for strict accountability and internal control.

A problem found frequently in business is the one in which management fails to correct the department head who makes changes in systems and procedures without prior notification. Many times the changes are made irrespective of the needs of other departments. As a consequence, the management auditor is constantly confronted with the job of reporting the fact so that the necessary action may be taken as soon as possible to bring about any corrections.

There is the problem in which a plan is accepted and installed but later, for one reason or another, fails to work. Sometimes an apparently good plan may not be good under certain circumstances or with certain personnel. An auditor may spend a number of days, sometimes weeks, in training a supervisor or a section chief for the proper handling and control of a certain function, only to find out in making a contact at a later date that the supervisor or section chief has resigned and left for parts unknown.

All verified facts and other pertinent data must be recorded on working papers during an examination, as the working papers represent a record of the audit work performed and are very valuable when it is necessary to refer to them at a later date. Should the occasion arise where exceptions are taken (by a department head or a supervisor) to statements made in a report, the auditor must be in a position to substantiate such statements by reference to his working papers. In addition, carefully prepared working papers facilitate the preparation of clear and concise management audit reports.

PREPARING THE MANAGEMENT AUDIT REPORT

The careful preparation of the audit report, containing details of the auditor's findings and recommendations, plays an important part in the completion of an audit assignment. There are basic elements to be considered in the writing of the report, and the method of presenting findings requires special attention. Facts reflecting detrimental conditions, defects, irregularities, and so forth, should be arranged and indicated in the sequence of their relative importance. Recommendations should be clearly formulated.

During the course of an examination, the auditor may, depending upon the circumstances, meet occasionally with supervisors and others concerned, and whenever possible with management, for the purpose of discussing freely any aspects or findings pertaining to the examination. This practice may aid in obtaining a better understanding as well as determining the best methods for the prompt correction of any disclosures. It is most important sometimes that the audit findings be acted upon as quickly as possible in order to overcome any deficiencies effectively. When corrective action is not taken, or is not complete, the matter might be discussed with top management for its decision.

Words are the means by which information is conveyed, and unless the auditor uses care he cannot effectively communicate his thoughts to those receiving and reading his report. Clear thinking must precede clear writing

The report should be written in good English and written so clearly that it cannot possibly be misunderstood. The auditor must do his very best to convey his thoughts with correctness, conciseness, and courtesy.

Correctness means accurate statements based upon definite information.

Conciseness means clear presentation of the information.

Courtesy means the use of words and phrases that avoid unnecessary sharpness or implication.

Method of Presenting Findings

Various methods are in use for reporting findings resulting from management audits. The usual practice is to issue a complete report following the completion of each examination. In some instances, a preliminary report is issued during the assignment or just as soon as there are sufficient findings to report. In such cases, the final report, when issued, includes details of the action taken to correct detrimental conditions. In other instances, the method of presenting the findings of a management audit is covered by a series of reports—one report covering the examination of the enterprise as a whole, a separate report for the examination of each functional activity and a report dealing with future requirements of the enterprise.

The form of report should be somewhat uniform in design, that is, in outline but not in content. The important point is that the adoption of a report that is uniform in design should not under any circumstances contemplate uniformity in the manner of stating certain conditions encountered on an assignment, nor should it stifle individuality in report writing. A typical example of an outline of a management audit report follows:

Outline—Contents of Management Audit Report

    I. Purpose and scope
   II. Facts of major importance
  III. Matters discussed with supervision
  IV. Current practices (detail)
   V. Discussion or comments
  VI. Recommendations
 VII. Exhibits

The written report must include the purpose and the scope of the auditor's examination, any limitations made or encountered, and the auditor's findings, opinions, conclusions, and recommendations.

Comments presented in the report should be arranged in a manner that provides proper balance and presents to the reader the various subjects in the order of their importance.

The use of informative headings and subheadings is most beneficial in presenting subjects of particular interest. Detrimental conditions, defects, and irregularities, summarized briefly, should, of course, take a prominent position in the report. By presenting the more important subjects in the early part of the report, the auditor will get at least a part of his message over to the reader and arouse interest to read further.

Facts of Major Importance

This section of the report is designated to summarize for management's review the most important detrimental conditions and improper practices. Simple terminology should be used, technical terms and expressions avoided. Brevity is essential. Caution should be exercised in order to maintain a proper balance between clarity and brevity.

Detrimental conditions should be reported in the sequence of their relative importance. Too much emphasis cannot be placed on this point. If the first item impresses the person reading the report, the rest of the report will receive more attention than if the first item is of minor importance.

Management wants to know when a detrimental condition exists or when it becomes aggravated—in other words, unfavorable trends or indications.

The statements reflected under the heading of "Facts of Major Importance" are, of course, dwelt upon in detail later in the report, in the same order of their appearance. Any conditions of a favorable nature should not be included under "Facts of Major Importance."

The auditor should review his report and satisfy himself that the report is acceptable. He should ask himself:

1. Have I brought out all important facts available?
2. Have I included all important facts disclosed by the report?
3. Are the statements presented as briefly as possible, and does the report show originality?
4. Are the statements included under "Facts of Major Importance" described in more detail later in the report and in the order listed?
5. Is the report written so clearly that my statements cannot possibly be misunderstood?

If the auditor can answer these questions in the affirmative, he may be assured that the report, as written, will be acceptable.

Matters Discussed with Supervisors

The auditor's discussion with the supervisor and/or department head at the conclusion of the audit is perhaps the most important part of an audit assignment and affords an opportunity to prove the value of the management audit service. Therefore, the auditor should confine his discussion to important items and detrimental conditions, and be tactful and diplomatic in presenting the subjects.

In preparing his audit report, the auditor should present the details of the discussion and indicate fully what action, if any, has been taken or

---

From the Office of the   Date: July 20, 1967
Manager of Management Audits

                                                Subject: Audit of the Factory
                                                                   Operating Centers
To: Mr. J. R. Smith, General Manager

   As requested by you, we have made an examination of the activities of the Factory Operating
Centers for the purpose of making recommendations with regard to the general planning and
control, the organization, and both the procedures and clerical routines in the handling of the
various activities.

Facts of major importance

   1. Poor records were maintained in Incoming Inspection for incoming raw materials and parts
      and, as a result, numerous charges to suppliers were not made for defective items.
   2. Operations were not planned by means of load charts, thus causing waste in both machine
      and man-hours.
   3. No policy was in existence in respect to the authorization for rework and, as a result, many
      loose practices occurred in rework activities.
   4. The functions of the Industrial Engineering Department and the Tools and Methods Depart-
      ment were not defined clearly, causing much confusion and friction in the proper conduct
      of these activities

Fig. 5-4. Typical Example of a Part of a Report Reflecting "Facts of Major Importance"

will be taken by the supervisor or head of the department to correct unfavorable situations.

A few examples of reporting the action taken are as follows:

1. During the course of the audit, it was found that no dispatch racks or boards were in use in the shop as an aid in the preparation and assignment of work to the various machines. This was discussed with the general foreman and the factory manager, and steps have been taken for the purchase and installation of new dispatch racks throughout the plant.

2. The problem of planning operations by means of load charts was reviewed with the production manager, and we were informed that immediate action will be taken to correct the condition.

3. We stressed the importance of the tool inspection section being responsible for checking the tools aaginst the tool drawing. Positive assurance was received from the head of the department that the condition will be promptly corrected.

Recommendations

Instances will be found where audit tests and observations reveal suggestions for improvements in procedures and work performance, policies and standards, organizational structure, personnel development, operating reports, and other areas. Some suggestions may be put in effect during the course of the audit through the efforts of the auditor (provided he is authorized to do so). Other suggestions may require special handling or a real selling job.

Recommendations, in general, should be presented in the order of their possible acceptability. In other words, present to the organization those new ideas that appear to have greater acceptance possibilities.

The auditor should strive for acceptance of recommendations regardless of the fact that delays may occur because of personalities, organizational problems, or for other reasons.

Whenever possible, it is wise to have an alternative to a basic recommendation, so that if the original idea is not accepted, a close alternative may be presented. Upon acceptance of ideas, the auditor should obtain a definite date for putting them into operation.

Distribution of Reports

Following the competion of an examination, an audit report should be made out immediately, in final form, and distributed to those concerned as soon as possible. From the viewpoint of top management, no report is ever received too soon. Reports that are not issued promptly can delay management in making important decisions that could reduce and possibly eliminate waste and unnecessary costs.

Audit reports should be delivered to the supervisor and/or department head directly concerned and responsible for the matters reported. A copy should be presented to top management and to any other person or persons of authority in the organization who may have a particular interest. Because of the possible confidential nature of the material contained in it, no management audit report should be exposed, under any circumstances, to anyone who has not been authorized to receive a copy.

THE FOLLOW-UP

The principal objective of the follow-up is to complete unfinished matters pertaining to the recommendations made in the audit report. The auditor may find it necessary to follow up and check on the installation of some recommendations, aid in the design of new forms and procedures, and modify or formulate policies. In the follow-up, the auditor may find it necessary to discuss with management certain aspects of the report in respect to operations or activity, with the idea of furthering improvements. This discussion also presents an opportunity to offer any explanations or to clear away possible misunderstandings.

Discussion of Audit Findings with Management

Matters of importance that have not been corrected should be discussed with top management. Having made all of the facts available, the auditor should seek a decision, but not be disturbed if it is not forthcoming immediately. Top management is frequently confronted with many complex problems requiring decisions; therefore, it may not be possible to receive an immediate decision. What may seem to be a very simple request may require much study. A change in policy could mean first obtaining the necessary approval of the board of directors. A proposed outlay of money might require a capital appropriation. Do not press for immediate decisions on points not accepted; they may be accepted readily a little later.

Final Action Necessary for Completion

The important point in management auditing is to strive continuously for perfection. A well-conducted audit, the presentation of a good report, and a discussion of facts of major importance are essential, but not enough to bring about the necessary results to achieve final completion. Any recommendations not readily accepted must be followed up regularly for final action.

Top management is generally in accord with putting recommendations into effect that will reduce costs and improve profits. A change or modification to improve the means for more effective control may often be worked out over a considerable period of time. For example, improved methods for control over a company's line of products may mean organizing a competent staff agency to devote full time in analyzing market needs and simplifying the product line to meet those needs.

The successful business executive of today has recognized that management auditing is a tool of management, instrumental in examining and determining the quality of performance. It is also an instrument for measuring the effectiveness of a company's organization structure, its policies and practices, its systems and procedures, and its personnel. The proper use of this instrument can be the means of equipping the business for better achievement of predetermined objectives. It can also do much, through review and appraisal, in finding improved methods of reducing costs and increasing profits.

Following is an example of a management audit check list:

Department: Purchasing   *Name of Department Head:* John Fisher
Assignment No.: 136   *Date:* January 29, 1967   *Auditor:* I. B. Wright

A. *Plans and objectives*

1. Have definite plans and objectives been established for the department?

2. Are the plans and objectives of the purchasing department in harmony with those of other departments as well as with the company as a whole?

3. Has adequate time been allotted by those concerned in respect to forward planning and better ways of meeting objectives?

4. Is there a clear understanding of objectives as to soundness and practicability?

5. Is top management entirely in accord with the purchasing department's plans and objectives?

6. What points should be considered to bring about an improvement in the plans and objectives of the purchasing department?

B. *Organizational structure*

1. Is an organizational chart available and maintained currently? (If not available, the auditor must prepare an organization chart.)

2. Is the organization structure sound and effective?

3. Does the organization reflect the program and objectives?

4. Are the various duties and responsibilities delegated properly and defined clearly?

5. Are the lines of authority effective from the standpoint of control?

6. Is there any overlapping or duplication of functions?

7. Can any organizational elements or functions be eliminated? Transferred to other departments?

8. Can changes be made in the organizational setup to bring about increased coordination of activities?

9. Is there proper balance between the functions assigned to key personnel?

10. Is there a lack of coordination or cooperation between the various functions?

11. Do the personnel concerned have sufficient understanding of responsibilities and authorities assigned?

12. What steps should be taken to increase the effectiveness of the organizational structure?

13. Does the average employee in the purchasing department have knowledge and understanding of the organizational structure?

14. Is there provision within the department for regular reviews of the organizational structure?

C. *Policies, systems, and procedures*

1. How are the purchasing policies determined?

2. Have all purchasing policies been reduced to writing?

3. Do the purchasing policies reflect the basic objectives and goals of management?

4. Are the purchasing policies positive, clear, and understandable?

5. Are the policies made known to the purchasing department personnel?

6. What provisions are set up to insure compliance with established policies?

7. What is the policy pertaining to the selection of vendors?

8. Is the function of procurement entirely centralized?

9. Do purchasing requisitions properly reflect the necessary approvals by authorized personnel? Within dollar limits?

10. What is the policy in respect to vendor overshipments?
11. How are defective items handled with a vendor?
12. Are all purchasing policies complied with?
13. Is the purchasing system meeting all current requirements and operating effectively?
14. Can the general routine in processing the paper work be improved?
15. Can improvements be made in the system to bring about a cost reduction?
16. Are the purchasing procedures reduced to writing?
17. Have adequate controls been established over material rejections?
18. Has sufficient consideration been given to internal control?
19. What is the general condition of the records?
20. Have definite procedures been established to guide the conduct of each and every function?
21. Are the procedures fully complied with?
22. Check for non-compliance with governmental regulations.
23. Have the purchase order terms and conditions been checked adequately by legal counsel?
24. Can any records be eliminated?
25. What specific procedures require immediate study and revision?

D. *Personnel*

1. What policies are established for selection, training, and assignment of personnel?
2. Review the working conditions. What improvements are recommended?
3. Is the maximum use made of personnel? If not, what greater use can be made of the personnel?
4. Review the practices for the handling of personnel, including job specifications, interviewing, placement, etc.
5. What activities are in force for the development of personnel for promotion? For executive positions?
6. Are new employees given sufficient orientation and training?
7. Are purchasing specialists used?
8. What is the morale of the personnel in the purchasing department and their attitude toward the company?
9. What is the rate of turnover?
10. Are there understudies for supervisory and key jobs?
11. What is the status of absenteeism, sick leave, and requests for transfer?
12. What percentage of routine clerical work is performed by supervisory personnel?

E. *Layout and physical equipment*

1. Prepare general layout of office space and equipment.
2. Is the office laid out in a manner to get maximum utilization of space and efficient work areas?

3. Has provision been made for reception and interviews with salesmen?
4. What is the general condition of the office equipment?
5. Describe all mechanical equipment in use.
6. Is the maximum use made of the present mechanical and general office equipment? (List types of excessive equipment.)
7. Is the equipment located for most extensive use?
8. Has provision been made for adequate storage space?
9. Are the files reviewed regularly for transfer to storage? Records retention?

F. *Operations and methods of control*

1. What consideration has been given to the adequacy, clarity, and promptness of management reports?
2. Is the normal lead time for procurement generally adhered to?
3. Review the methods established for expediting.
4. What safeguards are established against possible irregularities?
5. What, if anything, has been done toward greater standardization?
6. What are the causes for overtime and what can be done to eliminate them?
7. What are the principal means of control?
8. How can the various operations be improved?
9. Are the purchase orders placed as the result of competitive bidding?
10. To what degree is there adherence to required specifications?
11. Can any operations be eliminated, simplified, combined, or improved by changing sequence?
12. Are there any bottlenecks? What is being done to eliminate them?
13. Can or should any operations be mechanized?
14. What methods are established to measure productivity?
15. Are work units identified and standards developed? Are the standards obtainable?
16. Is there need for work simplification training?
17. Are forecasts established to reflect future trends?
18. Is there budgetary control over all expenditures?
19. Do reports give comparisons with past periods? With predetermined objectives?
20. Is there a means of ascertaining the cost variance on material purchases?
21. Has a clerical work measurement program been established? Is it working effectively?
22. What clerical cost controls should be established? Expanded?
23. What is needed to increase the purchasing efficiency?
24. What can be done to increase the quality of the work performed?

6
Work Simplification

RICHARD NEUMAIER

Systems Consultant
Philadelphia, Pa.

WILLIAM R. MULLEE

Professor of Industrial Engineering
New York University

RICHARD NEUMAIER has been a consultant on office systems and procedures since 1945. He counts among his accomplishments the calling of the first systems and procedures meeting, held in 1944. This led directly to the foundation of the Systems and Procedures Association of America, an organization that devotes its entire effort to the improvement and training of systems and procedures men employed in industry and commerce. Mr. Neumaier has been active as a national director of the association at various times because of his special interest in education.

As a staff member of the Round Table for Work Simplification at New York University, he has been lecturing on paper work simplification since 1947. He also has participated in the refresher courses at the Wharton School of the University of Pennsylvania. A round table meeting, once a week for sixteen weeks, on systems and procedures, is his annual assignment at the Management Institute of Temple University.

He is a charter member of the Systems and Procedures Association, Philadelphia Chapter and Keystone Chapter. He is a member of NOMA and also of the Association of Professional Consultants. His clients are in the industrial and commercial fields, but include also a great number of charitable institutions to which he is greatly devoted.

WILLIAM R. MULLEE, prior to appointment to his post at NYU in 1946, practiced industrial engineering for more than twenty years, heading engineering departments, installing wage payment plans, conducting work simplification programs, plant management, marketing, and so on. One of the pioneers in the field of work simplification, he started programs for factory supervisors in 1931. Later these programs were extended to other plants, and by 1941 he had conducted or supervised programs for engineers, supervisors, and other management personnel in more than seventy-five different companies, with product lines from aircraft to zippers.

In the field of wage incentives, Professor Mullee was among the early users of the standard data method of establishing time standards, starting in 1929. Budgetary control, product design, cost control, tool design, quality control, and other management techniques were developed from this data. In 1941 he was a member of the eight-man panel under Glenn Gardiner, who originated the Job Instructor Training (J.I.T.) program.

Working with Professor D. B. Porter, he helped to start the NYU Work Simplification Round Tables in 1947. Hundreds of companies have participated in these programs, in banking, insurance, services, and other office areas. In recognition of his contributions to the management field, he received the 1952 Gilbreth Medal. A licensed professional engineer in the State of New Jersey, Professor Mullee is the author of numerous articles on work simplification, incentives, cost reduction, training, and other topics.

WORK SIMPLIFICATION: A PHILOSOPHY

Basically, the difference between systems and procedures analysis and office work simplification is the difference between the expert advice of specially trained personnel or consultants and "do it yourself" improvement by supervisory and lower echelon personnel. The do it yourself approach requires a short training period and simple tools in the hands of the supervisor and his people. A procedure studied for a work simplification approach requires the full participation of all involved. It is this spirit of a combined effort and understanding of current procedures and possible improvements, understood by all, with the definite knowledge of job security and a spirit of cooperation, that makes work simplification such a successful tool of management in reducing cost.

In many cases, it is not possible for the systems and procedures personnel to analyze, improve, and polish all intradepartmental procedures and follow through on proposed improvements. It therefore becomes desirable to have outposts throughout the entire organization to improve a workstation job load. The systems man in most instances can concern himself only with the analysis and improvement of over-all procedures affecting major jobs and interdepartmental functions.

Historically, work simplification became a necessity because of enlarged clerical operations and the multiplicity of functions, together with the red tape, which is a cancerous growth of bureaucracy. We have to be thankful to the industrial engineers who developed this philosophy that we are now adapting to the office. Frederick W. Taylor, Frank B. and Lillian M. Gilbreth, David B. Porter, and Allan H. Mogensen are the names of pioneers in this philosophy. The tools that they have invented and adapted are described in later sections.

Introduction to Work Simplification

There is nothing mysterious about work simplification, and there are no secret tools or abracadabra connected with its applications. It is just the application of common sense, a rather rare commodity, to the daily operations of any business, with the object of arriving at a better way to render a business service. To accomplish this, we must carefully choose our projects for analysis, analyze them through charting, and, finally, measure our productivity for effectiveness. A knowledge of techniques is necessary, and this knowledge should be in the hands of all supervisors and employees affected by work simplification improvements. The basic factors with which we have to deal are the analysis questions—why, what, where, when, who, and how; and the actions that must follow our questioning are: eliminate, combine, change sequence, change place, change person, and improve. We also want to know the number of units, the time element, distribution, and method of transportation, wherever they are involved.

Resistance to Affirmative Change

All proposed improvements are not worth the paper they are written on if we do not have the good will of the employees affected to carry out recommended changes. It is in this area that work simplification differs most from any other approach in improvements and cutting costs. The employee who criticizes management, or its representative assigned to bring about improvements, and who does not understand the purpose of recommended changes, will not help to ease his own work load or accept more responsibilities to improve the operation in an over-all picture. Human beings think first of themselves, and, therefore, job security becomes a very vital factor in their own thinking toward anything pertaining to changes in their own daily work. To overcome this resistance to affirmative change, we have to establish job security as a positive policy of job improvement, and we have to respect the dignity of our personnel and their loyalty toward the company and their jobs to assure ourselves of their continued loyalty in changed or improved operations. Therefore, success can be achieved only with the positive assurance by management that job security is the number one concern of management, that dignity and loyalty are the second consideration, and that job improvement will be carried out only if it is possible within the first and second considerations. This does not mean that we cannot change employees from one job to another, and it does not mean that attrition and turnover of personnel cannot take care of improved functions and reduction of work load, but it means that without employee cooperation, no work simplification program can ever be successful.

Development of the Open Mind

Overcoming resistance to change does not mean that we have also developed an open mind. The open mind is best explained in some classical examples of negative thinking. The farmers of New Jersey said, back in 1787 when the cast-iron plough was invented, "We can't use cast-iron ploughs. They might poison the soil and promote growth of weeds." When Westinghouse approached Commodore Vanderbilt about an air brake, he said, "I have no time to listen to fools who want to blow air on wheels to stop trains." The trials and tribulations of Charles Kettering in convincing people about the self-starter, quick-drying paint, and many other projects are well known. Although our everyday thinking may not be confronted with such dramatic changes, it is still necessary to have an open mind. It is just as important to have an open mind about the elimination of an extra carbon copy as about a change of responsibility in a billing operation. In both cases it is fundamental that we see what we are doing now and that we be willing to see what could be done under changed or different circumstances. Again, it is we, or the individual, who must transpose ourselves into different, and perhaps currently nonexisting conditions, to appraise, approve, and cooperate with new thinking. To gain this open mind, and the basic thinking behind it, is just as necessary as the willing participation of the employee. It is possible to be willing to participate but still have a closed mind, so that we are confronted with a dual need of understanding. We cannot be afraid of job security, and we must at the same time also be willing and able to understand new approaches. This open-mindedness can very often be accomplished only through an educational process starting with top management and filtrating down to the lowest echelon. In many organizations, a senior officer is often identified with the closed mind; and if it exists at the top of the organization, it will also exist in multiplicity in lower echelons. Unless work simplification and the open mind necessary for its success are given more than lip service by top management, they cannot succeed in the lower echelons where their actual application and performance take place.

Tools and Techniques

After understanding the importance of creating an open-minded environment and reassuring those who may resist change because of insecurity, we are ready to examine the tools and techniques to be used in a work simplification program.

The application of work simplification usually proceeds along a five-step pattern:

1. *Select an important job.* Selecting a job requires sound thinking, as only a job with large enough volume or difficult techniques will offer the opportunity for considerable work simplification. We are confronted, actually, with two problems: the job with possible large benefits from improvements, and the improvements that can be made on practically each work station but very often cannot be measured with tangible results. Both improvements are necessary for the benefit of management and personnel, but the job with measurable improvements is of major importance, owing to management's need to measure the results of work simplification.

2. *Break it down.* This is the process of charting details or parts of a job, system, or procedure so that it can be minutely examined. The listing of these individual steps very often causes an immediate visualization of things that can be improved. There are various charting tools that must

be used to break down the job so that both the over-all picture and the detailed operation can be seen.

3. *Question every detail with an open mind.* This is an absolute requirement for preparing the aforesaid charts, since only complete knowledge can produce a complete job for the subsequent analysis toward improvements.

4. *Develop an improvement proposal.* This is the end result of our breakdown, charting, and questioning, and requires a good deal of ingenuity, imagination, and logical thinking. It is here especially that the open mind is important. The selection of the best method and the proposal for elimination of unnecessary steps and combining of others are all part of the development of the improved method.

5. *Install the improvement.* This is the final step after it has been accepted. However, here we deal with the important factor of the work simplification philosophy, and that is wholehearted participation of the employees concerned. Only cooperation and complete understanding by the employees will insure success of an improved operation. Lip service and a negative attitude by the employees involved are a deterrent and can seldom be overcome to produce positive results.

Work Distribution Chart

Many times we cannot solve problems because we "can't see the forest for the trees." However, this inability to see the over-all picture can readily be overcome through the preparation of a work distribution chart of all the functions of a specific segment of an office. The work distribution chart, with its subsidiary forms, activities list and task list, produce all the necessary factors for recording the activities of one organization unit. The preparation of the work distribution chart will give us the mountaintop view that we need for an analysis of the many elements that are so important in the entire picture, without confusing us with all the details.

The preparation of a work distribution chart actually requires detailed information about the functions and responsibilities of all supervisors and clerical employees involved in the analysis. This recording is prepared on the task list, which is sometimes called a "duty list." This detailed form is used to record each separate item of work performed by an individual and the average number of hours spent on each task per week. Each employee and supervisor prepares his own list. The list must be complete, the wording brief and to the point.

The departmental functions are summarized on the activity list. This shows the activities or functions performed by all people who have filled out task lists. It defines the range of activities that take place in the segment of the organization being analyzed.

The individual functions recorded on the activity list are now transferred to the work distribution chart in descending order of importance. The

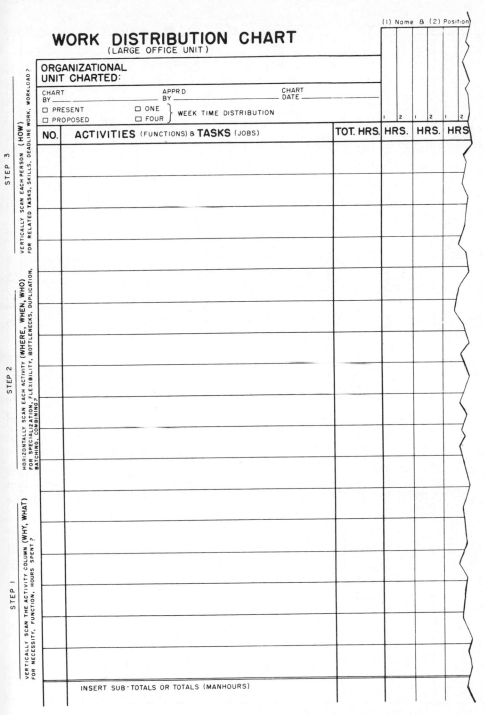

Fig. 6-1. Work Distribution Chart

The chart contains the following text:

WORK DISTRIBUTION CHART
(LARGE OFFICE UNIT)

(1) Name & (2) Position

ORGANIZATIONAL
UNIT CHARTED:

CHART BY _____ APPR'D BY _____ CHART DATE _____

☐ PRESENT ☐ ONE
☐ PROPOSED ☐ FOUR } WEEK TIME DISTRIBUTION

NO.	ACTIVITIES (FUNCTIONS) & TASKS (JOBS)	TOT. HRS.	HRS.	HRS.	HRS
			1 2	1 2	1 2

INSERT SUB-TOTALS OR TOTALS (MANHOURS)

STEP 3 (left margin): VERTICALLY SCAN EACH PERSON (HOW) FOR RELATED TASKS, SKILLS, DEADLINE WORK, WORKLOAD?

STEP 2 (left margin): HORIZONTALLY SCAN EACH ACTIVITY (WHERE, WHEN, WHO) FOR SPECIALIZATION, FLEXIBILITY, BOTTLENECKS, DUPLICATION, BATCHING, COMBINING?

STEP 1 (left margin): VERTICALLY SCAN THE ACTIVITY COLUMN (WHY, WHAT) FOR NECESSITY, FUNCTION, HOURS SPENT?

ORGANIZATIONAL UNIT CHARTED

EXISTING ORGANIZATION

RECOMMENDED ORGANIZATION

DATE

APPROVED BY

CHARTED BY

ACTIVITY

ACTIVITY NUMBER

HOURS PER WEEK

NAME

POSITION

GRADE

TASKS

HOURS PER WEEK

NAME

POSITION

GRADE

TASKS

HOURS PER WEEK

NAME

POSITION

GRADE

TASKS

HOURS PER WEEK

NAME

POSITION

GRADE

TASKS

HOURS PER WEEK

INSERT SUB–TOTALS OR TOTALS (MANHOURS)

STEP 1

VERTICALLY SCAN ACTIVITY COLUMN (WHY, WHAT)
(NECESSITY, FUNCTION, HOURS SPENT?)

STEP 2

HORIZONTALLY SCAN EACH ACTIVITY (WHERE, WHEN, WHO)
(SPECIALIZATION, FLEXIBILITY, BOTTLENECKS,
DUPLICATION, BATCHING, COMBINING?)

STEP 3

VERTICALLY SCAN EACH PERSON (HOW)
(RELATED TASKS, SKILLS, DEADLINE WORK, WORKLOAD?)

DEPARTMENT:	SECTION:	SUPERVISOR:	DATE:

ACTIVITY NO.	ACTIVITY (FUNCTIONS)

DEPARTMENT: Cost Dept.	SECTION: Cost Control	SUPERVISOR: Al Thorndike	DATE: 7-1-67

ACTIVITY NO.	ACTIVITY (FUNCTIONS)
1	Labor Budgets and Control
2	Labor Distribution
3	Administration & Training
4	Suggestion System
5	Maintain Stock Records
6	Miscellaneous

Figs. 6-3 and 6-4. Activity List for Work Distribution Chart

NEW YORK UNIVERSITY — DEPARTMENT OF INDUSTRIAL AND MANAGEMENT ENGINEERING

NAME:		OCCUPATION or TITLE:		CLASSIFICATION:
DEPARTMENT:	SECTION:	SUPERVISOR:	DATE:	

TASK NUMBER	DESCRIPTION	QUANTITY	POSTED TO ACTIVITY NO.	HOURS PER WEEK

NAME: Henry Jones		OCCUPATION or TITLE: Labor Clerk Eagle Division #6		CLASSIFICATION: Labor Clerk
DEPARTMENT: Cost Dept.	SECTION: Cost Control	SUPERVISOR: Al Thorndike	DATE: 7-1-67	

TASK NUMBER	DESCRIPTION	QUANTITY	POSTED TO ACTIVITY NO.	HOURS PER WEEK
1	Post #6 Labor Distribution	2		11
2	Code #6 Labor Cards	2		6
3	Weekly Labor Cards	1		5
4	Chart efficiencies	1		5
5	Prepare Control Charts	1		5
6	Assist Cost Accounting	3		5
7	Deliver #6 Labor Cards	2		1/2
			TOTAL —	37 1/2

Figs. 6-5 and 6-6. Task List for Work Distribution

information from the task lists of the individual employees is then also transferred, in the activity list sequence, to the work distribution chart. The tasks of as many as six employees can be recorded on one work distribution chart. For larger departments, several charts can be pasted together. The great advantage offered by the work distribution chart is its ability to point out obsolete and duplicate operations, total hours involved, and the general work distribution among all employees recorded. The questioning attitude of why, where, when, who, and how, is the analytical approach to get better procedures with less effort.

Flow Process Chart

There is no better or simpler tool available for the analysis of a procedure than the flow process chart. It is a form on which the details of present and proposed procedures (method) can be recorded, where the activities are symbolized and can be charted and counted, where there are places for travel distribution, quantity performed, time consumed, notes, and for checking off of analysis questions and resulting action. Naturally, more than one form may be required to record a procedure, but not more than one procedure can be recorded at one time on a form. The symbols used are sign language for operation, transportation, inspection, delay, and storage.

The first symbol, a large circle, denotes an *operation*. An operation occurs when information is arranged and prepared and when an actual action takes place, such as opening mail, time stamping, manual adding machine posting, and so on.

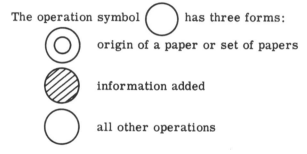

The operation symbol ( ) has three forms:

(⊙)   origin of a paper or set of papers

(▨)   information added

( )   all other operations

The second symbol, the arrow, denotes *transportation*. Transportation may cover as short a distance as from one desk to the adjoining desk or as large as the entire mailing service. It is indicative of the fact that the paper work has left one employee for additional work on it by another employee.

The third symbol, a square, denotes *inspection*. It is used for all work having to do with examination and checking of work performed by somebody else.

The fourth symbol, the letter "D," stands for *delay*. Delay may occur in batching work as compared with continuous flow. Delay also occurs when searching files, waiting for an answer, or simply awaiting necessary production in its predetermined cycle. It is the symbol of a waiting period, and does not denote a failure to accomplish.

The fifth symbol, an inverted triangle, denotes *storage*. A storage occurs when a flow is terminated for temporary or permanent safekeeping of the paper work in files or other designated places of storage.

Although there are exceptions to every rule, it is possible to make these symbols do for almost all operations that occur in an office procedure. As a matter of fact, flow process charts are used with machine and EDP systems.

In the actual preparation of the flow process chart it is necessary to fill in the identifying information at the top of the form. It is essential that the description be brief and accurate. The analysis of a well-prepared flow process chart will point out any duplication of effort, all backtracking, all delays, and any excessive checking and inspection that might take place. Although there may be more than one chart required to record a procedure, it provides with one set of forms a complete method for analysis of all factors involved in the fulfillment of its performance from beginning to end. It can be established how many operations are involved, how often these operations occur, how many transportations are required, how many different people are needed, the distances covered, the delays occurring, the existing multiplicity of checking, and the temporary and final storage of the papers involved. Through its symbols and check marks, a great number of factors pertaining to analysis and action can be noted for quick review. The flow process chart is the most important single tool of work simplification.

Workplace Chart

The workplace chart is also known as a right- and left-hand chart, and should be used to analyze the motions of an employee at a workplace. It is only of advantage where jobs are repetitive enough to warrant a detailed study. However, a workplace chart will readily point out inaccessibility of tools, records, and forms. It will very often point out that the modern flat-top desk is least suitable for some work that has to be performed, since it does not offer enough ready access and storage areas for quick handling. The industrial engineer has proven to everybody's satisfaction that an employee will develop a one-hand method, using the other hand as a vise or fixture, whenever not instructed to coordinate his motions into simultaneous actions by both hands. This fact can often be applied to great advantage in office operations.

Multi-column Flow Process Chart

The regular flow process chart is designed to follow one man or one procedure. However, in office operations we are frequently confronted with simultaneous action in one procedure in more than one segment of the organization. To show the physical location and participation of other segments of the organization in their simultaneous or consequent action on the same procedure, it becomes necessary to use the multi-column flow process chart, which records the actions not only in a vertical listing, but also in a horizontal distribution. The final result is a two-dimensional visualization of the activities, personnel, and locations involved. The same symbols are used as on the flow process chart, except that, in the case of the multi-column chart, the symbols have to be reproduced as needed and are not preprinted.

Dramatic effects can be created by using varicolored pencils to chart

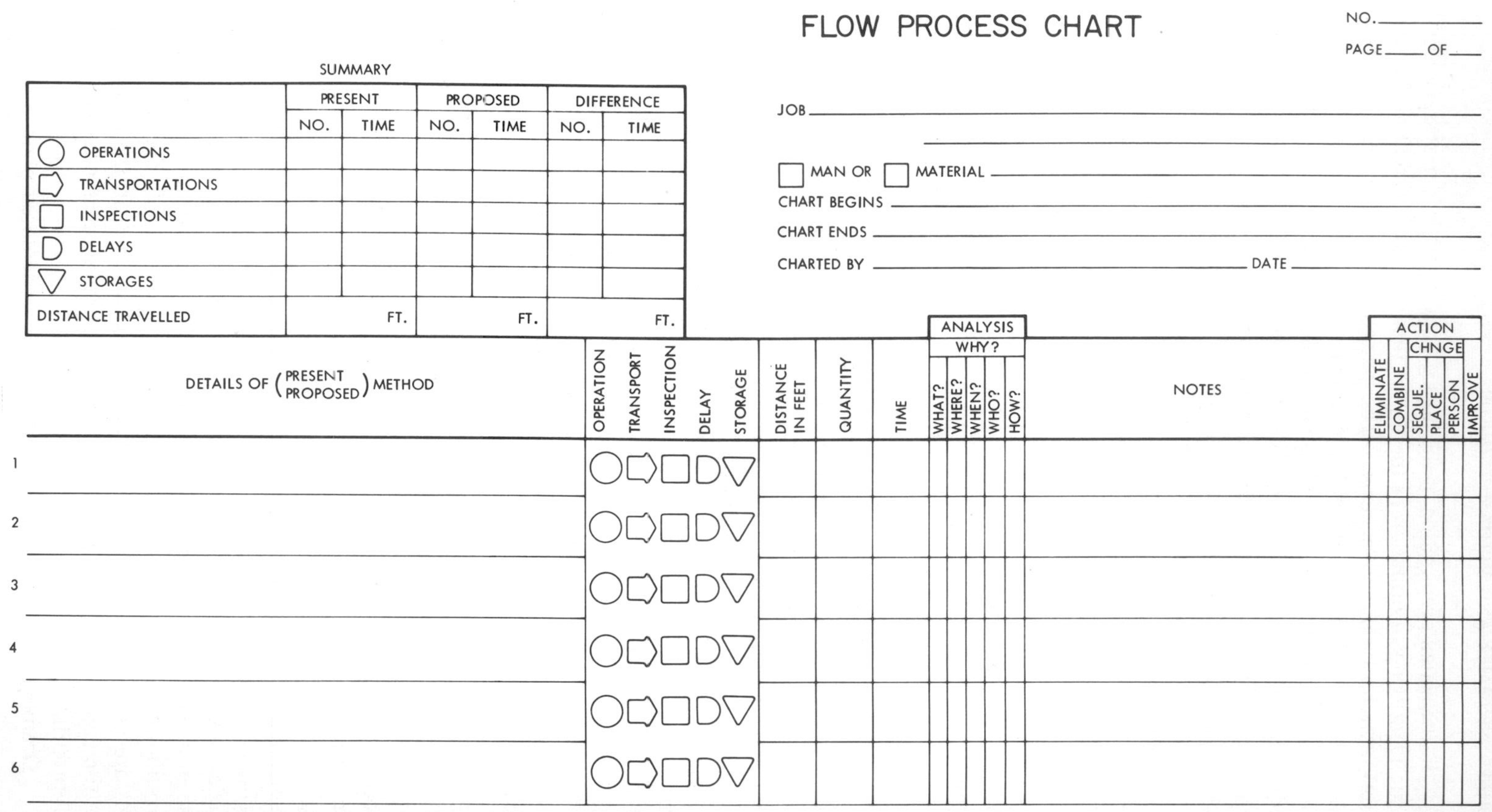

FLOW PROCESS CHART

JOB _____

NO. _____
PAGE ____ OF ____

☐ MAN OR ☐ MATERIAL _____

CHART BEGINS _____

CHART ENDS _____

CHARTED BY _____ DATE _____

SUMMARY

	PRESENT		PROPOSED		DIFFERENCE	
	NO.	TIME	NO.	TIME	NO.	TIME
◯ OPERATIONS						
⇧ TRANSPORTATIONS						
☐ INSPECTIONS						
◗ DELAYS						
▽ STORAGES						
DISTANCE TRAVELLED	FT.		FT.		FT.	

DETAILS OF (PRESENT / PROPOSED) METHOD

	OPERATION	TRANSPORT	INSPECTION	DELAY	STORAGE	DISTANCE IN FEET	QUANTITY	TIME	ANALYSIS						ACTION						
									WHY?					CHNGE						
									WHAT?	WHERE?	WHEN?	WHO?	HOW?	ELIMINATE	COMBINE	SEQUE.	PLACE	PERSON	IMPROVE	NOTES
1	◯	⇧	☐	◗	▽															
2	◯	⇧	☐	◗	▽															
3	◯	⇧	☐	◗	▽															
4	◯	⇧	☐	◗	▽															
5	◯	⇧	☐	◗	▽															
6	◯	⇧	☐	◗	▽															

Fig. 6-7. Flow Process Chart

the multiple copies of forms. After charting, the analysis is again founded on the questioning attitudes and the resulting changes.

Records and Report Study

A study beginning with a list of all records and reports prepared in any given segment of an organization will readily point out duplication of effort and superfluous reporting. There is nothing complicated in the preparation of such a list; however, it often requires considerable determination to bring about the discontinuance of records and reports. This is primarily due to an alibi attitude that some information may be needed "in case somebody asks for it." Unfortunately, a great many of these alibi records are being maintained today for no other reason, and, therefore, offer a real challenge for actual reduction of work loads.

Work Simplification Applied to Forms Design

There is no management function that is not recorded on paper. Therefore, an analysis of the paper work performed offers a wonderful opportunity to make a critical analysis of all business activities. Less than 10 per cent of the forms used in business are actually bought in large enough quantities to make their initial cost important. The other 90 per cent, in variable quantities of hundreds of thousands, represent probably 60 to 70 per cent of all clerical records operations.

A form is a printed or duplicated piece of paper with "open spaces" to be filled in. It is this filling-in action with which we are concerned as a time-consuming operation. The cost of forms has been estimated at about 7 per cent of the clerical expense of using them. In other words, the authorization of a purchase requisition for $70 worth of printing is also the authorization for $930 worth of clerical labor. The following forms-design check list breaks down the analysis into six sections:

1. General description
2. Purpose
3. Necessity
4. Text
5. Design
6. Specifications

An additional factor in reducing the clerical cost connected with the printed form is the application of time- and labor-saving methods, such as:

1. Carbonized forms
2. No-carbon-required forms
3. Snap-out forms
4. Continuous carbon interleafed forms
5. Form-feed devices
6. Registers
7. Sales books
8. Window envelopes
9. Translucent paper for diazo copies
10. Spirit carbon forms for duplicating
11. Papermasters for offset reproductions
12. Peg-forms for processing various-sized papers in one writing and also for the accumulation and distribution of figures in horizontal and vertical alignment without recopying.

RIGHT- AND LEFT-HAND CHART

NO. _____

PAGE _____ OF _____

OPERATION _____

☐ PRESENT METHOD ⎱ OPERATOR _____
☐ PROPOSED ⎰

CHARTED BY _____ DATE _____

PARTS SKETCH

LEGEND

ROW or LEVEL		
	1ST	2ND(A)
R7		
R6		
R5		
R4		
R3		
R2		
R1		
C		
L1		
L2		
L3		
L4		
L5		
L6		
L7		

SUMMARY

PER _____ PIECES	PRESENT		PROPOSED		DIFFERENCE	
	LH	RH	LH	RH	LH	RH
◯ OPERATIONS						
⇧ TRANSPORTS						
▽ HOLDS						
D DELAYS						
TOTAL						
DISTANCE						

LAYOUT

NORMAL WORK AREA

28 24 20 16 12 8 4 0
30 26 22 18 14 10 6 2 0 2 6 10 14 18 22 26 30

LEFT HAND

RIGHT HAND

DISTANCE	OPERATIONS	TRANSPORTS	HOLDS	DELAYS		DISTANCE	OPERATIONS	TRANSPORTS	HOLDS	DELAYS
	◯ ⇧▽				1		◯ ⇧▽			
	◯ ⇧▽				2		◯ ⇧▽			
	◯ ⇧▽				3		◯ ⇧▽			
	◯ ⇧▽				4		◯ ⇧▽			

TWENTY PRINCIPLES

1) START THE MOTION SIMUL.

2) STOP THE MOTION SIMUL.

3) OPPOSITE SYM. DIRECT

134

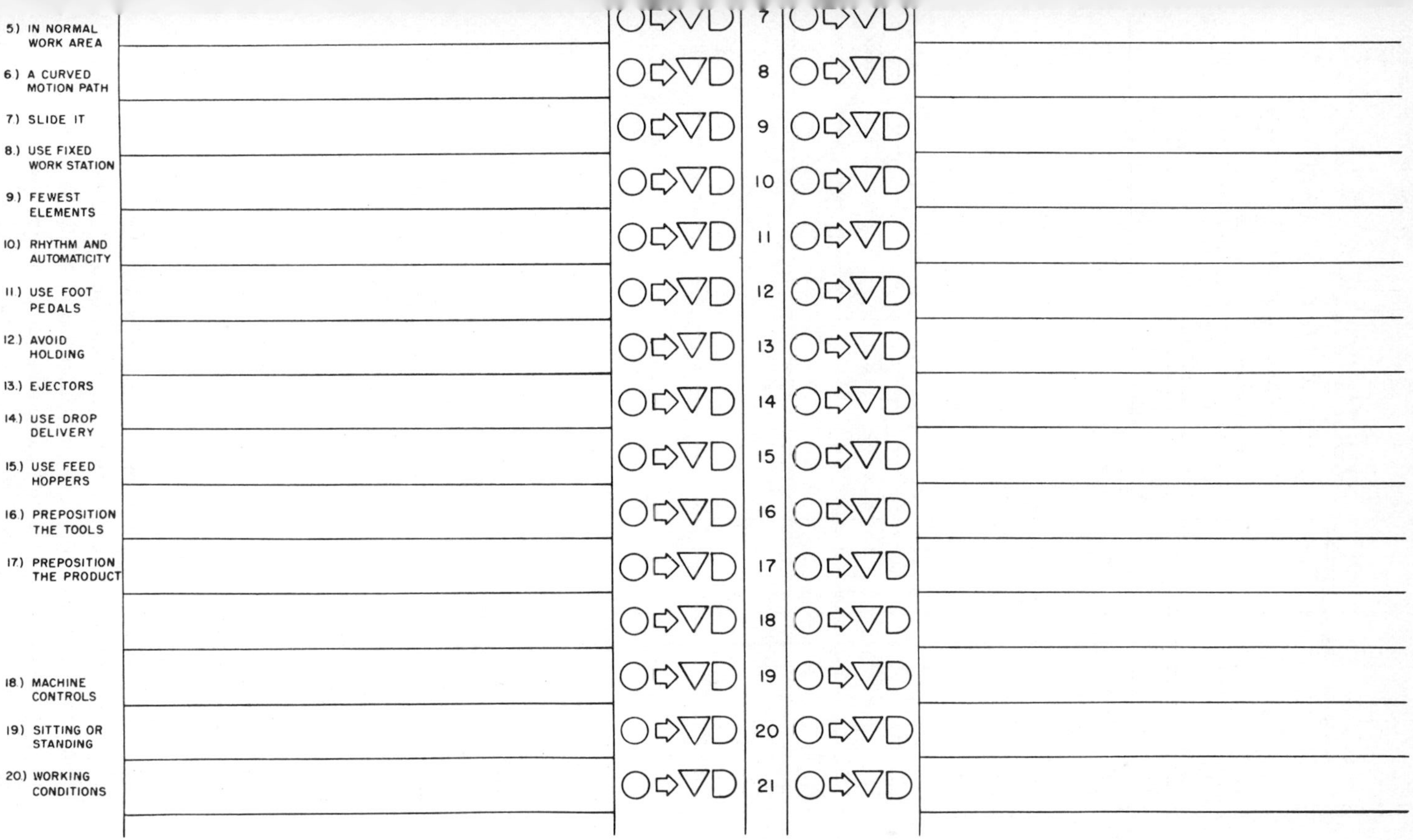
5) IN NORMAL WORK AREA
6) A CURVED MOTION PATH
7) SLIDE IT
8.) USE FIXED WORK STATION
9.) FEWEST ELEMENTS
10) RHYTHM AND AUTOMATICITY
11) USE FOOT PEDALS
12.) AVOID HOLDING
13.) EJECTORS
14.) USE DROP DELIVERY
15.) USE FEED HOPPERS
16.) PREPOSITION THE TOOLS
17.) PREPOSITION THE PRODUCT
18.) MACHINE CONTROLS
19) SITTING OR STANDING
20) WORKING CONDITIONS
7
8
9
10
11
12
13
14
15
16
17
18
19
20
21

Fig. 6-8. Right- and Left-hand Chart

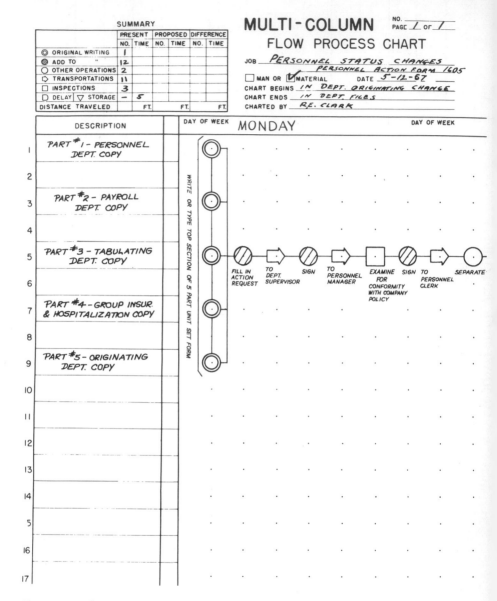

Fig. 6-9. Multi-column Flow Process Chart

All these methods offer a great number of variations and combinations whereby information can be deleted, added at a later time, or reused when required. The use of the handwritten form with its original data entry is very often a good source for additional processing without recopying and offers great opportunities for saving. The elimination of recopying saves writing and proofreading time, and averts copying errors.

Designed, 1950, by William Robert Mullee
Published by Work Simplification Round Tables — New York University, N.Y.C.

A-PURPOSE: For a bird's-eye view of a number of events and their chronological relationships. To develop a better product or procedure at a lower cost.

B-CONSTRUCTION: Use A.S.M.E. symbols ◯▷□D▽ **(MODIFICATIONS :◉ ORIGIN OF RECORD, ⊘ ADD TO RECORD)**

  1-Material Type Chart (use passive voice, i.e., Typed, Data entered, Checked, etc.)

    a-Multicopy or Multiproduct: Chart each on a separate line. Use the major item as line no. 8.

    b-Single Copy or product: Use a separate line for each station and indicate movement from station to station.

  2-Man Type (use active voice, i.e., Types, Enters data, Checks, etc.)

    a-Multi-Person: Use a separate line for each person, and chart like a chronological series of snap shots.

    b-Single Person: Chart from station to station to show travel.

C-IDENTIFICATION: To dramatize different items, fill out symbols with colors shown.

D-ANALYSIS: Steam shovel approach. Use 6 questions (why, what, where, when, who, how) to get the actions (eliminate, combine change sequence, simplify). If detailed analysis is required, prepare a regular Flow Process Chart for each paper, material, or man.

This is one of the greatest areas for work simplification connected with paper work.

Twenty Principles of Motion Economy

Most people work productively with one hand by holding the object with the other hand. Generally, this is not desirable. The hands should work together, each beginning the motion and completing the motion at the same time. The motion of the hands should be simultaneous and symmetrical. In many activities more work can be accomplished by using both hands than by using one hand. The symmetrical movements of both arms help balance each other, thus reducing the strain and physical effort. Although motion economy does not play as large a part in the office operation as in the shop, we still do a great deal of work, such as filing, turning pages while adding, and typing, in which both hands are needed and should be used in the best possible manner. Following is a list of the twenty basic principles, as adjusted for the use of clerical employees:

1. *Move hands simultaneously*—start and stop both hands at the same time.
2. *Balance motion pattern*—use symmetrical motions, in opposite direction.
3. *Rotary wrist motions*—avoid fatiguing upper-arm motions.
4. *Relax work tensions*—vary motion patterns; relax muscle tensions.
5. *Convenient work area*—keep all work within arc of forearm motions.
6. *Curved motion path*—avoid sharp changes of direction.
7. *Slide—don't carry*—save half the time and effort.
8. *Fixed work stations*—build habit patterns; save eye travel.
9. *Batch to save "make-ready"*—combine several lots, or several days, into one lot.
10. *Rhythm and automaticity*—reduce fatigue and increase productivity.
11. *Foot pedal action*—relieve hands on simple repetitive jobs like stapling.
12. *Use holding devices*—free both hands for useful motions.
13. *Orderly disposal*—release into a drop delivery chute to reduce travel.
14. *Use sampling techniques*—calculate the risk; improve quality control.
15. *Shorten transport distance*—bring work close to point of use.
16. *Pre-position tools, supplies*—reduce, select, and grasp; save eye travel.
17. *Pre-position work papers*—use collators, racks, feeding devices.
18. *Use touch system*—save eye travel; build good work habits.
19. *Improve workplace height*—try alternating sitting-standing arrangements; check seating posture.
20. *Improve working conditions*—check illumination, temperature, dust, noise, orderliness, and working environment.

The Orderly Office

Orderliness can save considerable time in almost any office. A simple example of orderliness is prompt filing of records in an accurate manner in a properly subdivided file. A time-consuming and possibly fruitless search for desired information is thus avoided.

The flat-top desk lends itself extremely well to the orderly *appearance* of an office, but does not offer sufficient storage space for ready access to records and supplies as needed. A solution to this problem is the L-shaped office unit, which has been in general use for some time under the name of the secretarial desk, with the typewriter extending out of either the left or the right pedestal. Just as it is practical for a typist to have the full surface of the desk available and still have a space for the typewriter, it is also important for clerks to have space for telephones, adding machines, calculators, price books, reference charts, and storage places. A neatly hand-written record can be used throughout an operation without recopying. Accuracy and orderliness go hand in hand, and greater accuracy reduces errors, eliminates checking, and speeds up production of all work. Too often do we have 100 per cent checking where greater accuracy of the original work and spot checking would improve the quality of our work and reduce the time element. Statistical quality control as practiced in industry can very often be applied in the office in a work simplification program.

Job Enlargement

Job enlargement requires greater job knowledge than the split-up of the assembly line operation. However, although the assembly-line operation might be suitable for industrial work, it does not always lend itself well to the office. A piece of paper traveling through a group of several persons requires recognition by each one. Technically, this recognition might be called "make-ready," and this make-ready time can add up to a considerable loss of time when too many individual work stations are involved. The assembly-line operator is confronted with only one specific function and no variance. The clerical employee always has a variance to consider, and a time-loss of recognition before the actual operation can start. Training employees to do the work of several work stations can often speed up the work flow and actually reduce the total number of employees required. However, we must consider that a longer training period and perhaps higher caliber personnel may be required to do the job better. In general, fewer errors and faster processing are the result of job enlargement.

Office Mechanization

The lack of mechanization in an office is due partially to a management attitude requiring quick amortization entirely out of proportion to the amortization requirement for manufacturing equipment. The daily saving of twenty minutes is equivalent to the ten-year amortization charge on a $1,000 office machine. It does not show a profit, but it can readily be seen that if the time saving is more than twenty minutes a day or the capitalization is less than $1,000, many applications of office machinery and timesaving equipment can be justified. After all, we do not use our automobiles and washing machines constantly, simply because we own them, but put them to use only when necessary. The same thinking should apply to office machines that may not be in constant use eight hours a day.

Small Office Tools

Aside from the major office equipment which requires expert advice, there are many devices available for work simplification, such as:

Copyholder—a very useful office device but not in general use because it is not very well known. It advances one line at a time on the copy, enabling the person typing, posting, or billing to align a single line at a time successfully. It is one of the many tools available that are economical in price, are real time savers, and add greatly to the accuracy of office work.

Collator—gathering of many sheets may be accomplished with this kind of rack or machine. It is particularly adaptable to the preparation of a catalogue or brochure when as many as ten papers may be gathered in proper sequence as a set. Mechanical collators are still greater in their productivity, yet not expensive.

Uniticket recorder—a manifest sheet combining journal sheet and a single line record. Particularly adaptable to accounts receivable, material requisitions, scrap material control, sales analysis, time and job tickets, long distance call records, and the like.

Spirit-carbon correction—a self-adhesive tape for corrections of spirit-carbon masters, eliminating the messy erasures.

Shelf file—another space saver; shelf filing does not permit an elaborate system of indexing, but readily lends itself to alphabetical breakdown by date on terminal digit filing. This method of filing is acceptable in most instances, because accumulation of data referring to one special subject is rare.

Numbering machines—a little-used office device that is a great aid in cross reference indexing or identification. One numbering machine on the market will imprint a set of forms with carbon between the sheets.

Address stencil—may be attached to a ledger card permitting a variety of uses, such as eliminating additional typing or duplication of address or description (such as inventory specification).

Spiritwriter—a duplicating device for addresses or short text messages; a time and money saver particularly applicable to direct mail advertising, duplicating, and recording.

Stapler—a long arm stapler that permits stapling in the center of a sheet, which cannot be done with the average stapler found in most offices.

Electric stapler—permits fast stapling of a quantity of papers without any physical effort.

Hanging folders—a file folder that hangs from guide bars extending along both sides of the file drawer. Makes for neater filing by allowing the papers in the folder to remain in proper vertical order. Eliminates bulging and out-of-shape files.

Tally counter—provides the simplest and most modern method for counting and recording vital facts in single units. When the cover is depressed, the dials register your recording. It may be grouped in banks up to a total of seventy-two units, and it is especially useful in restaurants and cafeterias to record the quantity of each dish or food item sold.

Folding machine—for quantity circular letters, invoices, statements, catalogue sheets, and announcements. It is small, portable, and electrically driven; may be adjusted to any size parallel fold.

Parallel rule—a device for ruling forms. By means of a setting knob, the proper distance between lines is accurately measured; operated by slight pressure of thumb and forefinger.

Noise eliminator—a cushion for business machines prevents creeping and eliminates noise.

Calculating charts—supply pre-calculated, verified answers. Useful for percentages, discounts, and commission calculations. Rates are graduated ½ per cent to 200 per cent in ½ per cent steps, 420 rates, and one-tenth hours to 99.9 hours.

Automatic line finder—permits spacing of continuous forms in typewriter from last line on one form to first typing position on next form.

Dual feed—permits two records at one typing, one typing for two separate records of different height and spacing with common information. Entries on one set of forms may be registered automatically on another set of different size with independent spacing as required for each form. Each record may progress at different speeds, such as checks and payroll records.

Work Measurement

Work measurement as part of work simplification concerns itself primarily with a work count. It is a simple method of establishing the present productivity of one or many people performing the same work and analyzing the result of this count. Such an analysis will uncover the fact that the work load is distributed unevenly, and that some of the employees are producing the major work load while others are merely coasting. Not only will the work count increase the quantity produced, but it will also point out the employees who show superior productivity for future recognition of their greater value.

Setting up a Work Simplification Program

Work simplification as a philosophy is not the task of the expert or trained systems and procedures man. It is the means of reducing the work load in the areas where the systems man cannot spend enough time and effort to bring about the necessary reduction of work load.

The most successful approach to work simplification is a training program for the supervisory personnel. This training program should be conducted by personnel who are qualified to inspire their co-workers, and in small groups not exceeding fifteen, to insure active participation and lively discussion. The training program should cover about eight or ten two-hour sessions, and part of each session should be devoted to discussion of actual problems existing among the employees of the supervisory personnel. Flow process charts and all other analysis material should be used by the trainees and reviewed as a group project. The training sessions should culminate in a final meeting attended by a representative of top management. Here the unhesitating and wholehearted assurance of job security and management's cooperation is required. Work simplification is not theory, but proven fact. It can work for anyone who really tries.

7
Work
Measurement

WILLIAM H. BRUSH

The Atlantic Refining Company
Philadelphia, Pa.

WILLIAM H. BRUSH began his career in industrial engineering in 1933, when he went to work for Radio Condenser Corporation as a time study engineer. Later he held industrial engineering positions with the Carrier and Philco corporations. In 1938 he joined The Atlantic Refining Company, where he has held several positions at the management level in the Methods and Standards Department. Currently he is manager of the Marketing and Product Pipe Line Division, directing the work of engineers conducting studies of distribution, sales, accounting, and related functions. The work of his division includes systems and procedures studies as well as the development and application of a wide variety of management control data.

Mr. Brush, a member of the American Management Association for many years, has been a member of the Planning Council of A.M.A.'s Office Management Division. A member of the Society for the Advancement of Management, he has been active at the national level in its managment research program. He is also a member of the production committee of the Philadelphia Chamber of Commerce.

Mr. Brush is a recognized pioneer in the field of clerical work measurement. During the past twenty years he has contributed several articles describing his development work in this area. He has been called upon many times to lecture on this subject at universities and to technical societies.

BASIC CONCEPT OF WORK MEASUREMENT

Definition

In its broadest definition, clerical work measurement is the comparison of a standard with the result of the expenditure of physical or mental effort. The greatest importance lies in the words "comparison with a standard." The essential value of work measurement is that it provides a basis for determining the extent of progress and improvement in productive effort by comparing what has been done with what is being done. Measurement of clerical activities may range from a simple count of pieces of paper handled by a clerk to a more complex measurement based on time study. The rough or precise form of measurement for each has its place and importance depending upon economic justification and needs of the enterprise at the time.

Philosophy

In everyday affairs, the importance of yardsticks to gauge results or establish dimensions is well recognized. The woodsman pacing off distance along a tract and the atomic physicist employing delicate and complex calculations to identify rare elements are both exhibiting the practical need to know "how much." Whether the yardsticks are crude, like the woodsman's, or refined, like the physicist's, their ultimate purpose is a quantitative expression of "how much" that is meaningful, objective, consistent, and verifiable. In the context of clerical effort, work measurement provides the gauge that meets these criteria and the need to know "how much." Work measurement minimizes the varying influence of subjective judgment and provides practical, trustworthy, objective gauges of clerical performance.

Comparison with Other Management Tools

Work measurement can be likened to many other tools of management. Job evaluation, for example, is a means for measuring the dollar worth in terms of wages for a given set of responsibilities assigned to an individual. Quality control, as another example, provides a basis for measuring and controlling the quality of product. Each of these can be found among a wide range of management tools that, as their basic purpose, provide guides for measuring the results of various activities of business. Work measurement takes its place among these as a device for gauging results of productive effort of human beings. Without such measurement, there would be a serious gap in management's "tool kit" used for appraising the effectiveness of activities in the enterprise.

Objectives

The primary objective of work measurement is the establishment of yardsticks for determining extent of progress and improvement of productive effort in clerical activities. Work measurement also provides an improved basis for accomplishing the following subordinate objectives:

1. Planning and scheduling work more effectively
2. Improved forecasting of manpower requirements
3. Determination of most economic work methods
4. Determination of proper work assignments
5. Determination of time and cost of work to be performed
6. Selection of employees and determination of an employee's worth to the company
7. Locating areas of operation that require investigation for improvement
8. Determination of the point of economic justification of clerical activities as they are currently performed

Accomplishment of such objectives provides management with factual information for making improved decisions concerning use of clerical effort. Such improved decisions result in lower cost of operation, thus enhancing the competitive position of the enterprise.

Work Count

FOUNDATION FOR WORK MEASUREMENT. The work count is the foundation for measurement application. In fact, it is a form of measurement in itself. Knowledge of the number of units produced in a given time period provides the basis for comparing the production of one period with another.

SELECTING THE WORK COUNT UNIT. Since an hour of clerical effort is usually composed of types of work that differ one from another, a unit to measure work must be selected to take care of these differences. Selection of these units is most important. They must, within practical limits, truly indicate the effort (time) expended by the worker as volume of work varies. The proper selection of these units is probably the most difficult part of clerical work measurement. In many cases, they are not so apparent as those found in manufacturing operations. For example, determination of the proper unit for measuring the production of an operation involving computations on a company financial statement is much more difficult to discern than the production unit for a punch press operation. This can be attributed to the greater variety and number of constant and variable work elements to be considered in clerical measurement. The combinations in which these elements are found have a significant effect upon the amount of effort and time required to produce a unit of work. If the work count itself is used as a basis for making comparisons of worker output, it is axiomatic that work content should be reasonably consistent from unit to unit.

Examples of typical clerical work count units are as follows:

Orders	Reports	Punch cards
Typing keystrokes	Postings	Computations
Invoices	Time cards	Reports
Checks		Requisitions

In addition to properly considering work content in selecting the work count unit, it is also important for such units to be easily understood and recognized by the worker as the proper measurement unit.

USE OF EXISTING COUNTS. Before work counts are established, study should be made to determine if there are satisfactory counts already existing. In many instances, counts are made in clerical functions for purposes other than work measurement. For example, a count of orders billed may have already been made to determine dollars billed per order for accounting control purposes. If this count proves to be satisfactory for work measurement purposes, it is a gift to the measurement program, since no additional time or money need be spent to obtain it. Although the use of these counts depends upon the preciseness of the measurements needed, counts should be tested for applicability. Some examples of these are:

Invoices	Production reports
Orders	Units of product produced
Punch cards	Time cards
Accounts	Sales dollars
Sales tickets	Freight tickets

The value of such work counts is no secret to clerical supervisors. Many supervisors have used similar counts for reporting production and have tested them over a period of time. Such counts may have already gained employee acceptance, and their continued use in the measuremnt application will promote acceptance of the program.

SUPPLEMENTARY COUNTS. Where additional counts are needed to supplement existing counts, they can be obtained in several ways. The most obvious method is to have someone make the count manually. A less obvious, but yet a very important, method is to obtain the count by mechanical or electrical counting devices. When office machines are involved in the measurement application, study should be made to determine the possibility of using such devices. Mechanical or electrical counters are more accurate and, in the long run, less costly than the manual method of counting production. Some that have been used sucessfully are:

A. *Mechanical impulse counters for obtaining:*
   1. Typing keystrokes
   2. Number of cards inserted in a mechanical bookkeeping machine
   3. Addressograph plate impressions
   4. Graphotype keystrokes
   5. Checks processed through a check writer

B. *Electrical impulse counters for obtaining:*
   1. Punch cards keypunched or verified
   2. Holes keypunched or verified
   3. Punch cards sorted
   4. Punch cards printed on tabulator

Opportunities also exist for facilitating a manual count. Study will reveal a variety of aids to this method of counting. Use of the simple tape measure to ascertain inches of cards, which are then converted to number of cards in a file drawer, will reduce manual counting time by at least one half. A weighing device for determining pounds of mail handled instead of counting each piece of mail will cut counting time by at least two thirds. The strictly manual method, that is, physically counting the units produced, is less desirable than other means because of the time it takes to make the count plus the possibility of lower accuracy. However, it is considered a satisfactory method for making the count. Experience and study have shown that the time consumed counting by this method is not prohibitive. Results of studies made for the purpose indicate that the time required for counting in this manner will range from 1 to 3 per cent of an operator's eight-hour workday depending upon the detail of the count made. Also, the accuracy of such counts can usually be verified with other counts made in the function.

USES OF WORK COUNT. The primary use of the work count is for comparing production of one period with another to watch trends in output. In addition to this use, the work count also provides information needed in a number of other important phases of production, such as establishment of unit costs, determination of proper distribution of work, planning and scheduling work, and evaluation of alternative methods of performing work.

Although it is an important factor in work measurement, the use of the work count by itself to determine extent of progress and improvement of clerical effort has its limitations. The major limitation is lack of information concerning the time it takes to perform the work. Trends in work counts could be misleading, because the time consumed in producing the work count unit may vary from period to period as a result of changes in the amount of work performed on the unit.

ASSIGNING A VALUE TO THE WORK COUNT. The next step in approaching true measurement is the assignment of a value to the work count unit. A number of different values could be used, including a dollar value or even an arbitrary numerical value. However, in assigning a value to a work count, a common factor is needed. Time is the factor that is common to all work. Therefore, the time per unit of work is generally accepted as the proper expression for evaluating the unit. It is less affected by outside influences, such as changing wage rates or price considerations than, for example, the use of dollars.

ACTUAL TIME PER UNIT, A BASIS OF MEASUREMENT. The time per work count unit can be determined by using records of time and production. If time and production records do not already exist for doing this, they can be set up to give the desired data. Improvement in measurement is obtained through establishing unit times that provide a basis for review and analysis of variable work content. They also provide additional information for comparison of what has been done with what is being done. Although the actual time per unit is an improved basis for measurement, it also has its limitation, since the time established in this manner expresses what is being done or what has been done and not what should be done.

Work Standards

PRIMARY PURPOSE. The primary purpose of a work standard is to provide a basis for evaluating performance against a benchmark. Establishment of the benchmark in terms of goals or pars for the work count unit expresses the level of production that should be attained by the worker.

DEFINITION. A work standard is a measure of accomplishment that *should* be attained in a specified activity under specified methods and conditions affecting the activity.

FAIR DAY'S WORK CONCEPT. In setting work standards, determination of an equitable relationship between the volume of work produced and the manpower utilized is most important. It is in arriving at this equitable relationship that the proper production requirement for a "fair day's work" is determined. A fair day's work is the degree of production attainment that is fair to both the company and the employee for a full day's operation. Such an expectancy should represent the amount of work that can be produced during a working period under specified conditions by a qualified employe working steadily and consistently at a normal pace. A fair day's work represents the level of performance that should be expected for base wage or salary paid to a worker. In establishing this level, the company sets forth the attainment goal expected of individual workers; thus the company and the worker know where they stand at all times with regard to production requirements.

Implicit in establishing the production level for a fair day's work is the provision for uniformity and consistency of this level between operations, functions, and areas of the company. Such uniformity and consistency provide the basis for equitable treatment of all workers. Since performance based on comparison with this goal may be used in making decisions regarding payment of extra awards, merit increases, or promotion recommendations, the importance of uniformity and consistency of goals is accentuated. In making such decisions, harmonious relationships between employees and employers are enhanced if they are based on uniform and consistent performance goals.

Relationship of Methods Analysis and Work Measurement

THE ONE BEST WAY. Probably the question most frequently raised with respect to work measurement and methods analysis is whether study and determination of proper methods, the "one best way," is an absolute requirement prior to measurement. When the measurement is applied to the individual worker and is used to evaluate him, use of this principle is mandatory. Measurements involving broader applications to groups of workers or operations do not require such methods analysis, except where these measurements are used as a basis for financial incentive payments. When broader applications of nonfinancial measurements are made, it is necessary at least to establish a method of operation that is reasonably fixed and specific concerning the way the work is to be performed. To wait until improvements in methods are made before measurement is applied may be a waste of time and loss of cost reductions when needed.

In all of the foregoing, it should be remembered that seriously fluctuating methods will eventually destroy reliability of any work measurement. Therefore, adjustments must be made in measurements for changing methods. Although some minor fluctuations can be tolerated for practical reasons, measurements, within reasonable limits, must reflect actual work requirements.

WORK MEASUREMENT IN METHODS ANALYSES. Frequently, in the evaluation of alternative methods of performing work, it becomes necessary to

```
Weekly & Monthly Billing Section              1-2
Sort Service Station Sales                    Procedure 2
Tickets by Ledger # and
Classification Stamps Other
Than Cycle Billing Accounts


Effective:  9/1/68

        1       EACH TICKET

        1.1     Go to storage bin and remove tickets and place
                in the measuring device.

        1.2     Carry ticket stack to work area, and place in
                position for sorting.

        1.3     Pick up handful of tickets from stack.

        1.4     Read numerical code, first two digits, and
                thumb-off ticket and lay aside in number order
                on table.

        1.5     Unstamped tickets are Monthly Bill.

        1.6     Sort from pack, into related piles on table, tickets
                showing the appropriate stamp.

        1.7     Disregard all other stamps and sort tickets by
                code.

        1.8     Place unidentified tickets in separate pile.

        2       WHEN ALL SORTING IS COMPLETED

        2.1     Arrange ticket piles by criss-crossing each,
                starting with the highest ledger number on the
                bottom.

        2.2     Pick up a convenient stack and carry to Sorting
                Table.  Make two trips if necessary due to
                volume.

        2.3     Pick up each criss-cross pack and place in
                related code compartment, or stamp compartment.

        2.4     Give unidentified tickets to Supervisor.
```

Fig. 7-1. Job Breakdown in Steps

obtain information dealing with time for the methods being evaluated. Work measurement is a valuable tool in making these time evaluations. Time to perform an operation or an element of work provides a factual basis to evaluate the entire operation or the portion of it being considered for improvement.

STANDARD PRACTICE INSTRUCTIONS AND PROCEDURES. Written instructions outlining the method of performing work provide a valuable guide to the establishment of work standards (Figure 7-1). They provide necessary information concerning work operations that are to be included in the standard for the job. Such documentation also facilitates making changes to standards when work methods change. Job instructions written in sufficient detail make it a relatively easy matter to determine those elements affected by the change. Evaluation of the effect of the change can then be made and standards altered accordingly. Standard practices or procedures take on added importance when standards are questioned. By comparing work done against written job instructions, it is possible to know in detail if the standards properly cover actual work requirements.

"POLICING" THE METHOD BY WORK MEASUREMENT. Since the standard includes time to do all work specified to be done on the unit, deviations from the prescribed method can be detected. For example, if a worker performs additional operations not specified to be done on a unit, his performance record will indicate lower production output. Investigation of this lower performance will reveal the deviations from procedures so that steps can be taken to determine whether they are justified.

With continuing changes made to improve work methods, the need increases to obtain a means to effect potential cost reductions to be derived from these new methods as well as to determine magnitude of cost improvement resulting from their installation. Revised work standards reflecting the changes in method provide the basis for meeting such needs. Generally, method improvement changes result in lowering the time required to perform the work. In such cases, standards are adjusted accordingly and a new standard is established. The time difference between the old and new standard provides the basis for computing potential benefit to be derived from the new method. In addition, comparison of the operations performance against the lower standard will give an indication of the extent to which reduction in time has been effected under the new method.

Approaches to Developing Work Standards

KINDS OF APPROACHES. Approaches to developing work standards can be classified under three general headings:

1. Subjective
2. Statistical
3. Engineering

Each of these has its place, depending upon the preciseness of measurement method and the stage of development of the work measurement program in the company.

SUBJECTIVE APPROACH. Simply stated, this approach is the determination of rule-of-thumb standards based upon the experience and opinion of individual supervisors. Sometimes such "standards" are better than none at all, but supervisors are ready to admit that production goals established in this manner cannot be factually supported or justified. Probably the most serious complaint with this method is that judgment of supervisors can be markedly different with respect to performance goals.

Generally, work counts are made to take some of the guesswork out of the subjective approach. When this is done, the supervisor has in mind a production figure that he expects from individuals or groups of workers. Records of production are kept and used by him to match output with his opinion of good production. Although this approach can be questioned with respect to accuracy and equitability of standards set in this manner, it should not be overlooked as a possible rough means for determining extent of production progress and improvement.

STATISTICAL APPROACH. Generally speaking, in this approach past records of time and production are used to ascertain the average time per unit of work. These records can provide unit times that, although based on past performance, are an improvement over subjective judgment. These unit times at least establish what has been done and give guidance for improving this performance. Some companies consider such unit times as their production "standards," realizing that they are an expression of what has been done. Although this approach does not establish what the production goal should be, it lays the groundwork for such determination. In some companies, the smaller ones in particular, this step might profitably be taken before more precise methods are used. In so doing, the company can then appraise the need and desirability for greater precision in measurement. The data and experience derived from use of the rougher approach can be used to justify a more searching analysis.

The average time per unit, described above, is a starting point for development of further refinement of statistical "standards." Analysis of these averages from period to period may disclose opportunities for investigation to reduce controllable variations in procedures and working conditions. For example, investigation of an unusual (high or low) unit average may reveal that work being performed is not in accordance with the specified method or is being done under abnormal working conditions. Knowledge of causes for unit time variations resulting from work differences is important in further analyses of these times. Adjustments in unit times can be made for these variations and the unit times observed over a number of periods with assurance that work differences are not causing wide fluctuations in average times.

Having reduced the effect of a major cause for variation in unit times, the remaining reason for variation is primarily differences in performance of workers. It is in the treatment of these differences in performance that the performance goal (standard) is established. Assume, for example, that an array of average times per unit for checking invoices by different workers or groups of workers is as follows:

minutes per invoice

1.0	1.7
1.2	1.8
1.2	1.8
1.4	1.8
1.5	2.0
1.5	2.2

Some means of selection must be used to arrive at the "standard" unit time. Based on experienced judgment, the "standard" unit time may be derived by a statistical approach, such as one of the following:

1. Select from the entire array of unit times the one that, in the opinion of the person making the selection, is most reasonable to attain.
2. Select the median time.
3. Select, from the upper quartile of times, the one considered most reasonable to attain.

Each of these methods is an attempt to find the time that represents the proper goal for the qualified employee working continuously and consistently at a normal pace. Generally, careful use of such methods results in more nearly approaching the level of performance that should represent standard. However, additional study and analysis is required to obtain assurance that the level selected is the correct one.

ENGINEERING APPROACH. Standards established by this method involve scrutiny of detail in analysis and greater precision in development of measurements. When the engineering approach is considered appropriate for developing standards, it can be looked upon as an extension of the statistical approach. In many cases, the two approaches complement each other. Generally, in the development of engineered standards, an individual job or operation is analyzed in detail to reduce the work involved to only its necessary parts. In doing this, individual work elements are identified and studied for possible elimination or combination with others. In addition, equipment, machines, workplace layout, and work flow are standardized. After standardization, additional analyses are made to establish the normal (standard) time for the work elements of the job or operation. These elemental times can be determined in four ways:

1. By employing conventional time study procedures.
2. By using predetermined motion times.
3. By using standard elemental times.
4. By application of statistical sampling techniques (usually referred to as "work sampling.")

Upon establishment of the base time for the work elements, they are arranged in appropriate measurement units and necessary allowances are included for personal needs of the operator and justifiable work contingencies to establish the final unit standard.

Engineered Standards

WHEN TO USE ENGINEERED STANDARDS. Since the engineering approach gives more refined and precise standards, development and use of engineered standards should be dependent primarily upon their economic justification. Generally, the intended use of standards will reveal whether or not the expense of refined standards is warranted. Greater refinement and preciseness of measurement provide closer control of operations for obtaining optimum production output per man-hour. Resultant cost reductions from this increased production will provide a substantial return for development and use of engineered standards. In addition to providing closer control of operations, engineered standards make available a greater amount of information and data for explaining and justifying standards to employees and supervisors.

SKILLS AND EXPERIENCE NEEDED. Use of the engineering approach to measure work requires employment of people who have skill and experience in time and motion study. Because of the precise analytical nature of the work involved, it is highly desirable that such skill and experience be made available at the beginning of the program. They can be made available in several ways, for example:

1. By hiring people skilled in engineering clerical standards.
2. By using company personnel skilled in standards development for plant operations. This requires proper indoctrination of such individuals in office procedures and practices.
3. By using management consultants skilled in this work to start the program. Usually, consulting firms will train their client's personnel to carry out the program after their work has been completed.

There is no cut and dried way for getting started with the engineering approach to establishing measurements. The exact approach will be dictated by study and analysis of the measurement needs in the company. Setting forth the program objectives based on these needs will provide an orderly and systematic approach to achieving the best results. No two companies are alike in their needs; therefore, the program must be tailored to fit the individual company.

PRIMARY OBJECTIVE OF STANDARDS. Prior to the development of standards, a decision should be reached as to the main purpose for which standards will be used. The intended use of standards dictates the extent of refinement needed in the measurements. For example, use of standards for calculation of incentive pay for individual workers will require more refinement than standards designed for measuring group performance on a non-incentive basis.

In deciding upon the primary objective of standards, consideration should be given to the experience the company has had with controls and other forms of measurements. In an atmosphere of close control over costs and operations, clerical measurements can be established in greater detail almost at once, even to the extent of measuring individual performance. However, in an atmosphere of looser control, it may be necessary to go more slowly by first installing broader measurements for determination of the required number of people in a group or function. Reaching a decision on the primary purpose of standards requires consideration of two general uses of standards. Proper consideration of these will give direction and meaning to the program for development of standards. These are:

1. Continuing application—for determination of performance on a continuing basis. This method for applying standards requires the neces-

sary system and procedures for making performance comparisons from period to period. In addition, it requires continuing maintenance of standards.

2. One-time application—for determination of manpower requirements, methods evaluation, cost analyses, and so forth. Applications of this type are usually made to solve an immediate problem and do not require continuing attention to standards.

A one-time application of standards serves an important and worthwhile purpose in quickly making improvements in performance. However, as in the case of many approaches of a one-time nature, there is the tendency to backslide after the application is made. The continuing method provides the same benefits of the one-time application, with the added advantage that the basis for making improvement is available from period to period.

THE START OF STANDARDS WORK. Standards development for office work must, of course, start with those things that can be definitely measured. Work that is more difficult to measure, but which is still measurable, should follow, stopping with those operations clearly not measurable. Establishing these general guides will avoid many pitfalls and will eventually provide full extent of measurement by standards.

A good starting point for development of standards is in an office area or function that has a substantial volume of repetitive work. Standards can be established more quickly for such work and put into use at an earlier date. Experience gained with this application will be useful in future applications. Following this course of action, before measurement of less repetitive operations, will pay dividends and will make available knowledge and experience that will be invaluable in the development of standards for more complex work.

STEPS IN SETTING STANDARDS. The following steps should be taken in the establishment of standards:

1. Study existing method to acquire sufficient familiarity and knowledge of the operation, equipment, working conditions, and method.
2. If needed, develop a new method, discarding the useless or inefficient work elements, combining others, and making suggestions for improvements in equipment and working conditions.
3. Observe and study the operation to obtain necessary data for standards development.
4. Set the standard.

These steps, taken in the sequence above, will provide necessary information and data for establishment of the initial standard, and will also make available documentation that will be needed in the event the standard is questioned. Such documentation is an absolute necessity for proper maintenance of standards as work changes take place.

COLLECTION OF DATA FOR STANDARDS DEVELOPMENT. Since time is the basic quantitative measurement of clerical effort, a method or combination of methods for collecting these data must be selected. Several recognized methods may be used for obtaining these data. These are as follows:

1. Time study
2. Predetermined motion times
3. Standard data (predetermined elemental times)
4. Work sampling

In the collection of time data for standards development, it is necessary that times be developed for the smallest practical increments of the job or operation studied. These time increments are known as work elements. A work element is an increment of work that is practicable of separation and for which beginning and ending points can be clearly identified for observation, timing, and analysis.

These elemental times provide the necessary flexibility for their proper arrangement and combination in development of base standard times for appropriate measurement units. They also provide the needed flexibility for addition, deletion, or rearrangement of work elements when changes in work occur. Selection of the method or combination of methods to be used to obtain these elemental times is largely dependent upon the facility and relative cost of the method. Use of predetermined elemental times, for example, may be the quickest and least costly method for obtaining data for a simple keypunch operation, whereas, in a more complex operation, such as compiling a financial statement, the use of time study may be the best method.

TIME STUDY. This method for obtaining time data involves the use of the stop watch for timing work elements as the work is being performed by the operator. There are a number of differently calibrated stop watches that can be used. The two most generally used are:

1. The minute decimal watch, calibrated in increments of 1/100 of a minute—the large sweep hand of this watch makes one revolution in a minute, which is recorded on a small dial for accumulating number of minutes.
2. The hour decimal watch, calibrated in increments of 1/100 of an hour—the large sweep hand of this watch makes one revolution in thirty-six seconds, or 1/100 of an hour. A smaller dial revolves once for each thirty revolutions of the large hand.

Each of these watches has its advantages; for example, the hour decimal watch is favored when a faster watch is needed for timing smaller elements, whereas the minute decimal watch is favored because a direct reading can be made in the same unit of time in which the standard is to be expressed. There are two methods of stop-watch timing:

1. *Snap-back timing*—a method of timing the duration of each element directly without requiring arithmetic calculation. The large sweep hand is started at zero as each work element is begun, and is allowed to run while

the work element is being performed. When the work element is completed, the time consumed is recorded and the sweep hand is immediately snapped back to zero, ready to begin timing the next work element. This method requires swift finger movements in order to get the sweep hand instantaneously back to zero ready to start timing the next element. Some time-study observers prefer this method, because no computations are necessary to obtain elemental times; the direct watch reading itself gives the elemental time. However, some inaccuracies may result in using this method. Mental lag and slowness of finger movement in snapping the watch hand back to zero can introduce errors in timing that will result in inaccurate standards.

2. *Continuous timing*—a method of timing the duration of an entire study, the elemental readings being made wherever the watch hand happens to be as each work element is completed. The sweep hand is started at zero at the start of the study and is allowed to run without interruption throughout the entire operation. Elemental times and descriptions are recorded in sequence as they occur while the watch is running. This method gives a series of readings, each of which must be subtracted from the preceding reading in order to show elapsed elemental time. The continuing method requires concentration and mental agility in order to observe the exact time when elements are completed, but this effort is not affected by preoccupation with getting the sweep hand back to zero to start the next element. Concentration is also required to describe the elements that can occur with great rapidity, a factor that makes advance familiarity with both work operation and the probable sequence of elements extremely helpful. Among most time-study observers, the continuing method of timing is believed to give the more satisfactory results. It facilitates obtaining the exact time for each element and provides for recording them in the order of their performance. Further advantages are: It accounts for every minute of time for the duration of the study; being physically simpler, it helps prevent mentally anticipating the completion point of elements, thereby introducing error into the watch readings; it minimizes the danger of omitting elements; and it eliminates inaccuracies caused by finger manipulations in the snap-back method, and the attendant mental concentration on handling the watch in addition to observing and recording.

In recording times on the observation sheet (time-study form), two methods are usually employed, depending upon the nature of work being studied. Each of these recording methods requires use of a different form appropriate to its manner of arranging elemental description and recording time observations.

1. *Repetitive recording*—a repetitive recording of time observations is an arrangement that lists individual work elements in sequence vertically and cycles of these elements horizontally. When work elements are in a reasonably fixed order and these elements recur in the same general sequence, this method of recording is suitable. When elements are known to take place in this order, they can be listed on the form prior to taking the study. A

10-5602	REPETITIVE FIELD DATA SHEET												Sheet No.	1-1
Operation _Posting Debits-Monthly Bills_				Location _Mechanical Bookkeeping_								File No.	101-7
Operator's Name_____ Clock No._____			Observer_____				Date_____						
Time Start _3:01_ Time Stop_____			Remarks _Burroughs #110 Bookkeeping Machine_							Study No.	79

No.	OPERATION	1	2	3	4	5	6	7	8	9	10	11	12	13	14	15
	Dispose Previous Work	.70 / .70	9.41 / .05													
	Position New Work	.95 / .25	9.63 / .22													
	Pick up Card from Box & Insert in Mach.	1.06 / .11	.41 / .06	.65 / .07	.85 / .04	2.04 / .05	.23 / .04	.48 / .06	.72 / .06	.94 / .05	.12 / .05	.30 / .07	.52 / .04			
	Post Debits	1.21 / .15	.58 / .12	.75 / .10	.92 / .07	.13 / .07	.35 / .12	.61 / .13	.82 / .10	3.03 / .09	.20 / .08	.45 / .15	.61 / .09			
	Remove Card from Mach. & return to Box	.35 / .14	.58 / .05	.81 / .06	.99 / .07	.19 / .06	.42 / .07	.66 / .05	.89 / .07	.07 / .04	.23 / .03	.48 / .03	.85 / .04			

Remarks: _Operator skill & effort - 105%_
12 cards posted

Fig. 7-2. Repetitive Field Data Sheet

single listing of the elements is all that is necessary, since the time recordings for successive cycles are made on appropriate lines in each of the columns to the right, one column for each cycle. This method avoids the necessity of writing down the elemental description during the study and permits full concentration on recording the times (Figure 7-2). In clerical work, this method is particularly useful for highly repetitive operations. However, its application to clerical operations is more limited than its use in the study of manufacturing operations. Clerical work usually entails a greater number and variety of work elements. Although these elements may occur over and over again, they generally do not recur in the same fixed order.

2. *Continuous recording*—a continuous recording of time observations is an arrangement of elements in unbroken sequence as they occur during a study. In this method, work elements are described and the times recorded on the observation sheet in the order of their occurrence (Figure 7-3). In using the continuing method of recording time observations, satisfactory identification of elements may involve considerable writing. Therefore, symbols may be advantageously used to reduce the amount of writing and permit full concentration on timing.

In both methods described above, it is important to understand exactly what constitutes a work element. Beginning and ending points of elements must be clearly identified. This is particularly important when more than one observer is used to time the same job. Indefinite elemental identification in time studies is misleading and will usually result in the establishment of incorrect standards.

OPERATION Prepare Monthly Listing of Errors made by Price & Station Clerks	CONTINUOUS OBSERVATION SHEET STOP 3²⁷ DATE 5-2-66
LOCATION Billing & Journals Group JOB NO. 8.0	START 3¹⁸ STUDY 6s
OPERATOR W. Green OBSERVER M. E. Dolan	ELAPSED 9 SHEET 1 OF 1

OPERATION	TIME	E	R	S		OPERATION	TIME	E	R	S
Sort 26 journals						Joggle & attach orig. set				
into 5 piles - ⊗	.60	.60	80	.48		Get punch & fasteners	.83	.13	70	.09
re-type error						Punch journals & put				
Pick up each pile -	1.02	.42	50	.21		in fasteners	.99	.16		.11
joggle, lay aside						Look thru journals & count	5.19	.20		.14
operator error	.25	.23	X	23		interruption	6.60	1.41	X	1.41
						Obtain 2 sheets paper -				
Obtain 2 sheets paper *	.50	.25	70	.18		insert carbon - joggle	6.88	.28	70	.20
insert carbon, joggle						Insert - line-up	6.99	.11	80	.09
insert in typewriter						Read journals - pile 5				
line-up	.60	.10	80	.08		Type listing ‖‖ 1				
						6 journals	7.59	.60		.48
Open drawer - search	.75	.15	70	.11		Aside journals				
Remove sample	.90	.15	80	.12		Remove set - separate	7.79	.20		.16
						Get ruler - tear set	8.02	.23	70	.16
Read journal - pile 1-4						Pick up journals -				
for error	3.80	1.90		1.52		joggle & attach orig. set	8.23	.21		.15
Type listing						Pick up punch - punch				
(20 journals)						pack & fasten	8.40	.17		.12
Aside journal										
‖‖ ‖‖ ‖‖ ‖‖						Look thru journals - count	8.48	.08		.06
(Not all journals						Aside packs	8.52	.04		.03
in piles listed)										
Remove from typewriter						Put file copies &				
Separate sets	4.00	.20		.16		sample in drawer	8.55	.03		.02
Get ruler - tear set	.25	.25	70	.18		Observer - interruption	9.00	.45		.45
Pick up journals										
(1 pile now)	.70	.45	50	.23						

REMARKS:

⊗ Piles - 4 different clerks / 1 Station clerk / 5

* clerk errors, 1st set / station " 2nd set   always 2 listings/mo. / only variable is no. of journals listed / 26 journals corrected

10-5601C 1/55

Fig. 7-3. Continuous Operation Sheet

To complete the documentation of the time study, it is important to include other pertinent facts concerning the operation under study. The following items should be clearly indicated on the observation sheet for each study:

Operation title (include job number, if one exists)
Department or location
Operator's name (include employee number, if any)
Observer's rating of operator's performance
Machine (include model number)
Other equipment
Materials
Start and stop time
Elapsed study time
Notation of working conditions

In addition to the above, it is advisable to prepare rough sketches of the workplace layout. This is important when the workplace differs from the ordinary desk arrangement. Since many clerical operations involve the use of forms, a copy of such forms should be attached to the observation sheet. Complete documentation lays the groundwork for a thorough analysis of the work method and the time to perform the operation as well as providing adequate reference material in the event of work changes.

The proper length of the study is also an important consideration in good time-study practice. In order to obtain a representative sampling of the work during the time study, careful consideration should be given to the number of work cycles to be studied. The observer can usually judge satisfactorily the proper number of cycles to be studied based on his experience and knowledge of the operation. However, as a rule of thumb, a work cycle of less than one minute will usually require a time study of approximately fifteen minutes duration. In the case of short work cycles, a representative sample may be obtained in a shorter time.

PREDETERMINED MOTION TIMES. This method for obtaining time data involves the use of pre-established motion times. Several motion time systems have been developed that include time values expressed in minute detail. These systems generally include basic movement (finger, arm, leg, and so on) times as well as times for appropriate combinations of motions. Time expressed in terms of the motion or inches of movement in these systems makes it possible to analyze the method in considerable detail in addition to providing time values for establishing the standard.

Consulting firms have taken the leadership in the development of these motion time systems and make them available to business organizations at an installation fee. Two of the more popular systems are MTM (Methods Time Measurement), available through The Methods Engineering Council, and Work Factor, available through Work Factor, Inc. The use of these systems requires many of the same steps taken in time study, without the use of the stop watch, but analysis must usually be made in greater detail. Precise operation analysis is required, as well as complete documentation of the method, equipment, and working conditions.

Analysis of the work using this method involves listing the basic movements or combination of moves for a representative work cycle of the job or operation. Time values for these motions are then obtained from the appropriate motion time tables.

Because of the precise nature of this method for obtaining time data, care should be exercised in the selection of the job or operation to be analyzed in this manner. Generally, repetitive large-volume jobs are more susceptible to the application of motion time data.

STANDARD DATA. Standard data are similar to pre-established motion times, except that they cover and are applied to larger increments of time. Usually, these time values are expressed in terms of the work element, which is composed of a group of motions. Some companies have developed their own clerical standard data, which have proved very successful in method analysis and in the determination of work standards. These companies usually develop these data through the use of time-study procedure. In the development of standard data, time studies are made of operations, using watches and sometimes several observers to break the job down into the smallest possible elements. The elements must be described and expressed in terms common to the kinds of operations in which they may be found. Only in this way can they be accurately used to analyze and measure different jobs at different workplaces. The development of standard data on the basis of small elements or grouping of elements common to many kinds of operations gives them a flexibility that permits quick and low-cost development and maintenance of standards. Probably the most difficult aspect of standard data development is the selection of the proper size time increment appropriate for use. How well these time increments are selected will determine how practical the standard data will be for measuring work. Elemental times that are too small require operation analysis in more than necessary detail. Elemental times that are too long give insufficient detail for widespread methods analyses and standards determination. Experience has shown that a proper balance between the too long and the too short time elements can be achieved that will give the desired accuracy and economy of use.

In building standard data, particular emphasis should be placed on the interchangeability of data. Before starting to develop time data, it is essential to prepare a list of different kinds of work elements that recur frequently enough to warrant the expense of developing standard time values. For example, the list might include the following types of work, which could be found in a variety of clerical functions in different locations of the company:

> Fastening operations (e.g., stapling, paper-clipping, pinning)
> Paper-handling at desk
> Writing numerals, letters, and so forth
> Machine calculations (e.g., key-operated calculators by type)
> Carbon insertion
> Insert paper in machine (e.g., typewriter, bookkeeping machine)

With such a listing prepared, the first step has been taken in planning the development of standard data. By themselves, the types of work listed lack the flexibility needed for interchange of data. Each of the types of work has different combinations of work elements, depending upon materials, equipment, or workplace layout used. Therefore, a subdivision of work elements is needed to isolate the element or elements of work that have application in a number of different clerical functions. For example, in a simple operation such as stapling papers it would be desirable to determine time values for at least the following elements:

> Procure papers from desk top
> Joggle papers
> Insert in stapler and staple
> Remove and place aside

In the foregoing illustration, each element should be reviewed to determine if it is reasonably constant as to its work composition, so that the time value, when established, can be used again when the element occurs in different functions or areas of the company.

These two steps will lay the proper groundwork for establishing the time value for the work element. With such planning, necessary observation and study steps for developing standard elemental time values can be taken in a more logical sequence.

Several methods can be used to develop time values for work elements consistent with the planning steps outlined above. Four methods that have been successfully used are as follows:

1. Special time studies taken of "mock up" or "dummy" operations under "laboratory" conditions. In this method, the study is so arranged that elements can be easily segregated and recorded. When using this approach, work elements must be simulated under conditions as near to actuality as possible.
2. Time studies made of actual operations. This method requires careful advance planning of the study so that the desired standard data elements are clearly defined and can be timed. In addition, the observer must take extra care in making his watch readings.
3. Use of predetermined motion times. This method requires study and analysis of the motions that make up the work element. Predetermined motion time values can then be inserted for each of the motions and a time value for the work element determined.
4. Use of statistical methods (work sampling). Use of this method for obtaining standard data will be described later in this chapter.

The foregoing methods can be used separately or in combination with others. In many cases the use of one of these methods to supplement another will give desired results in minimum elapsed time and at lowest cost. Each method has its place in development of standard data, based on the relative ease and cost of using the method to obtain the desired accuracy of results. As in the case of predetermined motion times, use of standard data requires detailed operation analysis to develop work standards. In the process of doing this, standard data time values are assigned to each work element in the frequency of their occurrence during the work cycle being measured. The primary advantage of using standard data as well as predetermined motion times is that they give consistency in development of standards because like elements are always given the same time value. In addition, use of such methods will prove, in many cases, to be less time consuming and less expensive than other methods of developing and maintaining work standards (Figures 7-4 and 7-5).

WORK SAMPLING. This method for obtaining time data is an extension of statistical sampling techniques to the measurement of work. The basic principles of work sampling have been used for many years in such activities as inspection, production control, and quality control. As in the case of

ARM MOVEMENT

Select Time Expressed in Decimal Minutes

Inches Moved (Measured at Knuckles)	Select Time	Inches Moved (Measured at Knuckles)	Select Time
1	.00310	15	.00830
2	.00330	16	.00840
3	.00370	17	.00860
4	.00430	18	.00880
5	.00490	19	.00900
6	.00540	20	.00920
7	.00580	22	.00950
8	.00620	24	.00980
9	.00660	26	.01010
10	.00700	28	.01040
11	.00730	30	.01070
12	.00760	35	.01150
13	.00790	40	.01210
14	.00810	45	.01270

INSTRUCTIONS:

1. The above table of Select Times covers those normal arm movements generally found in clerical operations. Each individual time includes a start and stop and the times are based on exercising the normal amount of precision, care and control of direction. These times cannot be used if arm movements do not fall within these qualifications.

2. To obtain the distance moved, measure the chord of the arc made by the knuckle of the forefinger.

3. These times cannot be used when the arm is transporting weights of over five pounds.

Fig. 7-4. Arm Movement

other methods for obtaining data, observations are required in work sampling to obtain data for analysis. In work sampling, data are created for analysis by statistical sampling techniques by having an observer record flash observations of work being performed at a preselected moment of time. Simply stated, data obtained from flash observations are a record of the number of times work components occur during the period of time that the work sampling study is made.

Careful programming of the observations is the key to a successful work sampling application. Most important among the steps taken in this programming are:

1. Selection of the practical time increments of work to be observed.
2. Determination of sample size of observations. Statistical formulae are available to calculate sample size based on the predetermined percentage of reliability required to obtain desired accuracy for the smallest time increment to be observed.

GRASP & RELEASE (COMBINED)

Select Time Expressed in Decimal Minutes

	Select Time	Object Handled
Single Isolated Object	.00110	Pencil, Pen, Rubber Band, Ash Tray, Eraser, Scissors, Roll Tape, Staple Remover.
	.00360	Ruler, Paper Clip.
	.00460	IBM Card.
	.00480	Phone Receiver, Cradle or Upright.
	.00700	Bond or Tissue, Single Sheet.
	.00810	Loaded or Empty Folder.
One Object From Group	.00920	Rubber Band or Paper Clip, in Pile.
	.01130	Tissue Paper, Pile on Desk.
	.01330	Bond Paper or Loaded Folder, in Pile.
	.01580	Tissue Paper, Pile in Basket.

DOCUMENTATION:

1. The above table is to be used for Grasp & Release of objects generally found in clerical operations.

2. The Select Time is the Combined Time for Grasp & Release only.

3. The Select Times may be applied to either right or left hand operations.

INSTRUCTIONS:

1. Do not attempt to break the above times down into separate Grasp & Release times. Always use the full value, as the release portion of the time is negligible.

2. These times do not include any fumble allowance. Normal fumble time for the individual operation should be included in the standard as either an operational or error allowance.

3. The above table should be used as a guide for establishing times for unlisted objects.

4. When determining time values:
   (a) If the object is in a group, pile, etc., use the lower portion of the table as designated.
   (b) If the item is a single object, use the upper portion of the table as designated.

Fig. 7-5. Grasp and Release (combined)

3. Selection of random moments of observation. The value of work sampling results hinge on elimination of bias. By using random numbers (established by statistical methods) for selecting the proper moments for observation, bias can be minimized.

The essential steps to be taken for obtaining the data are as follows:

1. Of all the work elements that are to be measured, estimate the percentage of the total time consumed by the smallest element for which reliable measurement is desired.

2. Establish the percentage of reliability desired for the final measure of the smallest element.

3. Calculate the number of random observations required to obtain the desired reliability for the smallest element.

4. Select moments of observations at random from a table of random numbers.

5. Observe the elements at the selected moments.

The number of times each element occurs during the observation period establishes the basis for calculation of time for each work element. The total number of times the element occurs during the observation period divided by total observations of all work components establishes the percentage of its occurrence during the period. This percentage is an index of the total actual time consumed by the element during the period. By applying this percentage to the total hours in the observation period, the total actual time consumed by the element is obtained. Dividing the total time the element consumed by a count of the number of times it actually occurred during the period gives the time for the work element. For example, if the total time population were forty hours, the percentage of occurrence of the element 10 per cent, and the number of times the element actually occurred one hundred, the average actual time for the element would be calculated as follows:

$$40 \times 10\% = 4.0 \text{ hours}$$
$$4.0 \div 100 = .04 \text{ hours (2.4 min.) per work element}$$

It becomes obvious from the discussion and example given, that the underlying principle involved in work sampling is that work components occurring more frequently consume more total time during the period of observation. The opposite is true for those occurring less frequently.

Experience has shown that there are two distinct advantages in using this method to obtain time data.

A. Generally, this method is a more economical study approach for obtaining:
   1. Greater sample of work under study
   2. Better coverage of workers performing the work
B. Data from which standards are developed can be tested mathematically for reliability.

There are limitations on the use of work sampling that should be properly weighed before applying the techniques:

1. It is sometimes difficult to distinguish between productive and non-productive work in flash observations.
2. It is sometimes difficult to explain the technique to employees unfamiliar with statistical methods.
3. Its use is limited when observation points are widespread. In such cases, it may be impossible to make observations at random moments.

Experience with this technique has indicated that certain conclusions can be reached with respect to its usefulness as a tool for obtaining time measurement data.

1. When physical layout and other working conditions surrounding the job are such that flash observations can be made properly, this technique gives final results substantially the same as obtained by other study methods.

2. Reliable time values for specific elements of work within a job can be obtained when the element represents 5 per cent or more of the whole time population sampled.

3. Time values for elements constituting a small unit of time, but a sufficiently large percentage of the total time population, are sufficiently reliable for development of clerical standard data exclusively by this technique.

Besides its use in developing standards, work sampling can be employed:

1. To determine the number of people required to operate tabulating machines in relation to cards keypunched for a given, normal "mix" of work

2. To determine unavoidable delay and machine down-time factors in such functions as duplicating, mailing, and tabulating

3. To determine current effectiveness of a group of workers prior to application of standards

4. To plan and schedule operations in a variety of clerical functions

RATING OBSERVED PERFORMANCE AND LEVELING TIME DATA. In the data-gathering methods described so far, the resulting time values have been or will have to be adjusted to normal (standard), representing the time that is expected for a fair day's work.

It is obvious that the time taken per work cycle by one worker will vary from the time taken by another worker because of differences in pace of working. Therefore, an adjustment is made of the data to level it to the time the normal qualified worker should take. While taking a time study, the observer judges the pace of movement of the operator. This judgment is made in terms of percentage of normal—normal representing 100 per cent. If, for example, a keypunch operator were to average .25 minutes per card keypunched in a given type of work and the observer were to rate this performance at 90 per cent of normal, the average base time per card would be leveled to normal as follows:

$$.25 \times 90\% = .225 \text{ minutes/card}$$

During the course of the study, whenever the operator varies his pace of working, the observer changes his rating accordingly. By doing so, each work element in the study can be leveled to normal.

Some benchmarks for judging the normal rate of working have been established as guides for the observer. For example, dealing cards at the rate of fifty-two cards in twenty-seven seconds and walking three miles in an hour represent the normal pace of movement. In addition, a number of motion pictures taken of operations at different paces of movement are available for training time-study personnel in the proper pace concept of normal.

Rating performance has been a subject of research in the industrial engineering field for a number of years. This research has made available to industry valuable data in support of the normal pace concept and for guiding the judgment of observers in rating performance.

In addition to the guides established for judging performance, judgment involved is conditioned by the repetitive experience of the observer, to the point that a rating by skilled observers can be relied upon for accurate determination of standards.

Predetermined motion times and standard data are adjusted to normal prior to their use, whereas time studies must be leveled as they are made. Therefore, pre-established time data can be used directly in the development of standards without the intermediate step of adjusting time values to normal. Work sampling studies also require rating of performance as they are made. In this case, the observer rates the performance of the operator at the moment the flash observations are made. Calculation of the composite rating for a work element is made by averaging the different ratings by their frequency of occurrence during the observation period. Time derived for the work element is then adjusted to normal by multiplying it by the composite rating.

ALLOWANCES FOR WORK DELAYS AND PERSONAL NEEDS OF THE OPERATOR. Up to this point in the discussion of engineered standards, explanation has been given of the various means for deriving base times for the work cycle. Base times by themselves are not sufficient for development of the final standard, since they do not include allowances for legitimate delays that will occur during the work, nor do they include allowance for personal needs of the operator. In clerical function, unavoidable delays occur in a number of ways. For example, the normal work cycle may be interrupted by:

1. General instructions by supervision
2. Interruption in the normal flow of work
3. Special requests for information on data concerning the work
4. Justifiable errors in the work
5. Machine breakdown
6. Supervisory questions on the work

Allowance must be made for these delays to establish an equitable standard for the work. Two approaches can be taken to establish the extent to which these factors affect the normal work cycle: special time studies or work sampling studies. In both approaches, studies are so arranged as to obtain time data for these delays over a fairly long period of study. Because these conditional times occur infrequently, it is also necessary to cover a reasonably long calendar time. Normally, in the office, several all-day time studies spaced out over a month's period of time will give the desired results. Covering a whole month assures a representative sample of the delays that occur during the work. The work sampling method involves making observations in a similar manner to those made for deriving base time data. However, with this approach it is difficult to predetermine the sample size.

Therefore, observations are made on a continuing basis until it is determined that the extent of effect of these delays starts to level off in a consistent pattern. The period of time over which this will occur is largely dependent upon the nature of the work. Less time will be needed in the more repetitive clerical functions than in the less repetitive. Usually, the leveling-off process will occur within a given month's operating cycle.

The extent to which these delays affect the work cycle is expressed in terms of percentage of time they represent in relation to the total time of the cycle. Under normal conditions, this percentage will range from 5 per cent to 8 per cent in clerical operations.

Determination of allowance for personal needs can also be made through the study methods described above. However, in a good many companies, the allowance that should be made for personal needs is determined by judgment guided by thorough knowledge of conditions surrounding the work operations being performed. For instance, management of a company may feel that 5 per cent of an eight-hour workday or twenty-four minutes is a reasonable allowance for personal needs, and will set their personal allowance policy accordingly. Irrespective of the method used to determine personal allowance, general experience indicates that a range of 5 per cent to 10 per cent is reasonable.

DEVELOPING THE FINAL STANDARD. After leveled time values are obtained for the various elements of the job, several important steps must be taken in order to arrive at a final standard. In brief, these steps are as follows:

1. Arrangement and grouping of leveled elemental time values in appropriate units of measurement (previously referred to in this chapter as work count units)
2. Application of necessary allowances
3. Documentation of data to support the standard

How well a standard conforms to the work that it will be used to measure depends largely upon how well the elemental time values are grouped to form the various units of measure. There must be a reasonably fixed relationship between the element of work and the unit selected. For example, in the handling of time cards in a payroll department, selecting the time card as the measurement unit would depend upon whether the number and kind of work elements performed on each time card occur with a reasonable amount of regularity from card to card. For practical reasons, some averaging of number and kind of elements can be tolerated without seriously affecting measurability of the unit. The amount of averaging permissible depends upon the degree of variation in time needed to complete the work on one card as compared with another. Generally, a plus or minus 10 per cent variation should be questioned. It is doubtful that a variation of this size would average out over a given volume of work. Within the tolerance given, time for irregularly occurring elements must be averaged in the unit time in accordance with their frequency of occurrence. For instance, if an element occurred once in ten time cards, each card would be given one-tenth of time of the element.

As mentioned previously, allowances for contingencies and personal needs are usually developed in terms of percentage of the work cycle. For this reason, the correct arithmetic for applying allowances in the following example would be:

$$
\begin{array}{rl}
.25 & \text{Minutes per time card} \\
\times\ 1.05 & \text{Allowances for contingencies} \\
\hline
.263 & \\
\times\ 1.07 & \text{Allowances for personal needs} \\
\hline
.281 & \text{Final standard per card (expressed in three} \\
& \qquad\qquad\qquad\qquad\text{significant figures)}
\end{array}
$$

In the development of the final standard, certain statistics and data that are used must be recorded on work-up sheets. Documentation of such items as the following are necessary for explanation and justification of the standard, as well as for future reference purposes when standards need revision because of work changes:

1. Number of units observed
2. Average total volume of units for given period of time—day, week, month
3. Frequency of irregularly occurring elements
4. Necessary explanation of method used, if one, to check reliability of unit times

CRITERIA FOR ESTABLISHING STANDARDS. Before engaging in a program of standards development, the following questions should be considered:

1. Is it possible to provide a fairly even and constant flow of work? If not, can provisions be made for shifting employees to other kinds of work when idle?
2. Can the amount of judgment required in doing a task be reduced by standardizing the method or by presenting the employee with a pattern of choices?
3. Can the operation be described by a unit of work that will be recognizable and usable to the operator as a "measured unit"?
4. Will it be possible for the unit of work to be assigned to employees by the supervisor and can output be recorded easily?
5. How will the quality of this work be controlled, and can it be evaluated by spot check?
6. Can production be checked and audited?
7. Can provision be made for proper documentation of method and standard?
8. Does size, repetitiveness, and volume of job justify the expense of measurement?
9. Are facilities available for proper job instruction?
10. Can control over the use of accepted method be established?

Careful consideration of these questions relating to criteria will help avoid many pitfalls in any type of standards application, whether the standards are in the roughest or most detailed form. As the standard and its application are made more precise, finding satisfactory answers to these questions becomes more important. Where standards are used to determine an individual worker's performance, an affirmative answer to all of these questions is a prerequisite to their development and use.

Comparison of Standard and Actual

A standard has many uses in the effective planning of work. Its most important use is computing the performance effectiveness of individuals or groups of individuals to determine the extent to which productive output can be improved. The index of performance is obtained by multiplying the standard for each unit of work by the number of units produced in a given period of time. This calculation gives the total standard time allowed, which is compared to the total actual time consumed in producing that volume of work. Indexes of performance are usually expressed in one of two ways (sometimes both are used):

1. Percentage of effectiveness, by dividing the standard time by the actual time
2. Variance between standard and actual, expressed in time (hours, minutes, and so on) by subtracting whichever is smaller

When the actual time is greater than the standard time, the amount of difference between the two indicates the degree to which improvement in productive output can be obtained when the standard has been met.

Application of Work Standards

TYPES OF APPLICATION. Standards applications fall under two general headings:

1. "One-time" applications. Generally speaking, one-time applications are made to solve an immediate problem involving productive output or costs of production. Standards can be of considerable help, for example, in determining manpower required to perform a new job, in estimating the cost of one way of performing a job as opposed to another way, and in ascertaining the proper distribution of work among operators to smooth out the flow of work.
2. Continuing applications. Application of this kind involves installation of methods and procedures for making comparisons of actual and standard performance from period to period on a continuing basis. In addition to the advantage of being able to plan work from period to period, this type of application affords an opportunity to observe worker performances regularly. To obtain optimum improvement in production on a long-term basis, this type of application should be made.

A place can be found for both types of application in the office. Selecting the right application for the right situation is largely dependent upon the desired degree of control over worker performance at the time.

DESIGN OF PLAN OF APPLICATION. In designing a continuing standards application there are several basic procedural requirements that must be included to obtain a well-organized plan. Methods and procedures are required for:

1. Obtaining the production and actual time consumed producing the work

2. Arranging and compiling production count in a manner suitable for applying the standards

3. Applying standards and determining the effectiveness index

Format and style used in the foregoing requirements should be tailored to fit prevailing company customs and practices.

Design of the continuing plan for applying standards is also affected, to a large extent, by the period over which the measurement will be made and by the precision or sensitivity required for measuring the individual worker or group of workers. Selection of the proper measurement period is based primarily on one factor; that is, the normal cycle or period of elapsed time during which all elements and conditions of the work occur. Since the standard is a representation of the time that should be taken to perform all elements and conditions involved in producing the unit of work and will be used to predict what should occur in the future, it is axiomatic that the standard cover whatever is expected to be done within the period of measurement.

Methods for making one-time applications range from a simple calculation of the time required to perform a given job to making elaborate plans for laying out the work in a newly formed clerical unit of the company. In each of these applications, production count and related standards are needed in sufficient detail to solve the immediate problem at hand. Full understanding of the nature of the problem will help in deciding what approach to follow to evaluate the time factors involved.

It is self-evident that preciseness of measurements materially affects the design of the measurement plan. Plans for measuring individual workers require considerably more detail in production counts, compilation, and computation of data than group measurement plans. Therefore, cost of administering such plans becomes a factor of importance to be considered in comparison with the potential benefits that can be derived from each type of application. Potentially, individual measurement plans offer the greatest benefit possibilities. From the technical point of view, selection of individual measurement application should be made when productive output is clearly the result of the effort of the individual worker. Group measurement should be used when output depends upon teamwork of a number of individuals.

ILLUSTRATIVE METHODS FOR MAKING APPLICATION OF STANDARDS. Although the style and format of the following application methods may vary in different companies, the principles involved are essentially the same in each application.

1. Manpower utilization (manloading). Manpower utilization studies serve the purpose of a quick appraisal of the number of people required to perform the work in a given clerical unit of the company. Requirements are based on existing methods of operation. The determination of the standard number of men is based on time-study data, and this figure is usually given by major types of work or by groups of people. No attempt is made to measure an individual's effectiveness in this program. These measurements tell the supervisor whether he is overmanned or undermanned, based on the total actual number of people on the payroll, and in which areas, if any, he can reduce his personnel as opportunities arise. Where possible, the manager is provided with tables or charts that show him, based on rough overall yardsticks, such as the number of invoices, what his manpower requirements will be if his work volume should increase or decrease without significant changes in method of operation (Figure 7-6).

2. Cost standards. Cost standards are more detailed. They are used to obtain, where practical, the best economic balance of the entire function, covering both labor and other expenses, such as material and equipment. The same techniques are used to develop the basic time standards. As a second step, not found in the manpower utilization studies, the appropriate practical labor-dollar value is assigned to the various types of work performed and the time standards converted to dollars accordingly. In addition, the proper amount of equipment and material and any other significant costs are determined and standards developed for use with the expected labor costs. Finally, a system for reporting and accounting for results is developed so that standard and actual costs can be compared and variations justified. Here the attempt is to measure the cost of a piece of work—for example, the clerical cost of an order shipped involving work at many different locations and by different people at different times. Here again, no attempt is made to measure individual effectiveness. Cost standards plans are of a continuing nature, which require more attention to the maintenance of standards so that actual and standard can be compared properly each cost period (Figure 7-7).

3. Wage incentives. Wage incentives are used to obtain increased labor productivity per man-hour and to share the value of this increased productivity with the workers. Wage incentive plans may be designed to measure an individual's performance, or the performance of a group of individuals. Again, time studies, production studies, standard data, and other techniques are used. Since money may be paid to an individual on the basis of the standards, a greater degree of preciseness in the standards is required. This is achieved by a greater sampling of the work or people to be studied and by giving more consideration to the details of the work measured. Standards are expressed in terms of time per unit, and measure only labor efficiency, including some control over quality. Because of the degree of

I.B.M. MOTOR DRIVE DUPLICATING KEYPUNCH — TYPE 16
I.B.M. ELECTRIC PUNCHED HOLE VERIFIER — TYPE 52

Select Times Expressed in Decimal Minutes

HANDLING OPERATIONS

Applies To	Description of Operation	Unit of Measurement	Select Time	Elements Included in Operation
KP&V	Insert Cards in Magazine	Each Occurrence of Filling Magazine	.12370	Move hands 2" to cards, grasp, move 2" to jogger, jog 3 times, simultaneously lift weight and transport cards 6" to magazine and insert. Replace weight, simultaneously return right hand to key-board and left hand to work source.
KP&V	Change Skip Bar	Each Skip Bar Changed	.09520	Move hands 2" to bar, grasp, remove 2" clear of machine and re-lease - grasp other bar, transport 2" to machine, insert and release.
KP	Cut and sight verify each Hole in Master Card	Each Hole Cut and Verified	.01344	With hands positioned for keypunching, keypunch hold in Master Card and sight verify with work source. (Verify while in machine.)
KP	Remove Master Card from card bed and insert in Master Card Rack	Each Master Card	.05790	Move hands 2" to release key; press key and lock turnover latch simultaneously; grasp Master Card as it flips over, transport and insert in Master Card Rack, latch Duplicating Bar, simultaneously move right hand to keyboard and left to turnover latch, unlock turn-over latch and await completion of feed cycle.
KP	Remove Master Card from Master Card Rack	Each Master Card	.01240	Move hand 2" to Master Card Rack, unlatch, grasp Master Card, raise 3" above rack and release.
KP&V	Remove Finished Cards from Stacker	Each Occurrence	.01530	Move 2" to Stacker, grasp cards, raise 2" above stacker and re-lease. (Cards must be removed for each job and for each 230 cards in the same job.)
KP	Remove Cards from Magazine	Each Occurrence	.04060	Move hands 2" to magazine, simultaneously lift weight and grasp blank cards remaining in magazine, move cards 8" clear of magazine, and simultaneously replace weight in magazine. Release cards and weight. (Remove cards each time a change in card type occurs.)
V	Sight Verify 1 Column through 75 cards	Each Column	.00492	With cards positioned in front of eyes, sight through each common hole.

Fig. 7-6. IBM Motor Drive Duplicating Keypunch Handling Operations

ADDITION AND SUBTRACTION - FELT AND TARRANT ELECTRIC COMPTOMETER
Select Times Expressed in Decimal Minutes

NO. OF DIGITS	EACH NUMBER IN ADDITION DOWN / EACH MINUEND IN SUBTRACTION DOWN	EACH NUMBER IN ADDITION ACROSS / EACH MINUEND IN SUBTRACTION ACROSS	EACH SUBTRAHEND IN SUBTRACTION DOWN	EACH SUBTRAHEND IN SUBTRACTION ACROSS	FROM MACHINE WINDOW TO WORK SOURCE	
					WRITE DOWN – PENCIL OR INK	COMPARE
1	.0036	.0038	.0164	.0166	.0428	.0147
2	.0076	.0080	.0231	.0235	.0522	.0162
3	.0120	.0125	.0329	.0334	.0615	.0182
4	.0167	.0174	.0452	.0459	.0709	.0215
5	.0218	.0227	.0592	.0601	.0802	.0259
6	.0273	.0283	.0762	.0772	.0895	.0310
7	.0332	.0343	.0920	.0931	.0989	.0365
8	.0394	.0406	.1097	.1109	.1082	.0423
9	.0460	.0473	.1283	.1296	.1176	.0480
10	.0530	.0543	.1471	.1484	.1269	.0548
11	.0604	.0617	.1660	.1673	.1362	.0615
12	.0682	.0695	.1851	.1864	.1456	.0681

INSTRUCTIONS:
1. Select the time required to insert each addend or minuend, according to the number of digits, in the comptometer for addition or subtraction down or across.
2. Select the time required to insert each subtrahend, according to the number of digits, in the comptometer for subtraction down or across.
3. Add the constant (.0071) for positioning hand. This time includes time to move hand from "Clear Machine" position to position for inserting first number in machine.
4. Add the constant (.0056) for clearing machine.

Write down time includes: Focus on number, read, move hand to work source, position hand, write down, return hand to machine.

Compare time includes: Focus on number, read, focus on duplicate number, compare.

When ink is used for write down, refer to "General Write Down" table for additional allowances.

Fig. 7-7. Addition and Subtraction—Felt and Tarrant Electric Comptometer

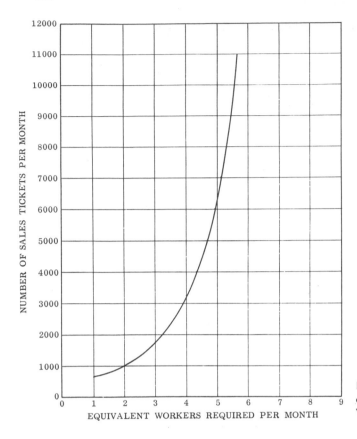

Fig. 7-8. Sales District Standard Manning at Various Work Volumes

accuracy required, and because the best practical operating methods have to be installed and documented prior to the establishment of standards, it takes longer to complete the development of a wage incentive plan than either a manpower or cost standards study. Like cost standards studies, the wage incentive plan is continuing and requires constant and diligent maintenance of standards so that the company and the employee may obtain equitable benefits from it (Figure 7-8).

The applications described above are not necessarily in the order of their importance. Each differs in measurement precision and sensitivity of application. Wage incentives, for example, are considered by many to be the best application of standards for obtaining maximum benefit. However, wage incentives require more detailed standards and application methods for proper operation. Each of the three illustrations of applications can be made separately or in sequence starting with the rougher manpower utilization approach running through wage incentives.

CRITERIA FOR INSTALLING WORK MEASUREMENT. Before embarking upon a program of work measurement, careful consideration should be given to the following criteria. A successful program depends to a considerable extent upon close adherence to these rules:

1. First and foremost, make sure that management is sold on such plans.
2. Educate management and workers in the objectives and workings of the program. Remove the mystery.
3. Find competent people to develop and maintain the measurements.
4. Base the measurement on sound principles and practices.
5. Do not attempt to apply measurements where a practical unit of measurement cannot be found for the operation. The work count should be clearly defined and easily made.
6. Make the measurements fair to both the worker and the company.
7. Where wage incentives are applied, make the reward for extra production sufficiently attractive to interest the worker. Keep it separate from the company's base wage program.
8. Find a way to make the program simple and easily understood. A simple program is the most effective.
9. Install a good program for maintaining standards. More than one program has failed because standards were not properly adjusted when the method changed.
10. Establish a policy of not changing standards unless there is an error in the original calculation of the standard or there is a change in method. Nothing will break down a measurement plan faster than changing standards for other reasons; employees will resist arbitrary changes in standards.
11. Establish an acceptable basis for determining results of the program. A sound basis for comparing costs before and after measurement goes a long way toward establishing confidence in the plan.
12. Establish a good personnel policy for handling displaced persons. Indiscriminate layoffs or transfers will eventually wreck such a program. In many instances, normal turnover will take care of this problem.
13. Help the worker find his full potential under the program. Encourage and assist him to attain standards.
14. Finally, after a decision has been made to apply measurement in one unit of the company, have the courage to go forward with similar plans in other areas where measurements can be applied. It will pay dividends and will reassure the workers that all are being treated alike.

Administration of Work Measurement Plans

CLERICAL REQUIREMENTS. Clerical requirements for administration of work measurement plans fall under three major headings:

1. Time and production reporting
2. Compilation of time and production
3. Application of standards and computation of performance effectiveness index (and calculation of incentive earnings where wage incentives are applied)

TIME AND PRODUCTION REPORTING. At the outset, it is necessary to design a means for obtaining the production count and time consumed in performing the work. Records of work counts and time spent on the work

DUPLICATING GROUP - STANDARD COST REPORT

PERIOD July

1	2	3	4	5 LABOR COST		6 MATERIAL COST		7 TOTAL LABOR & MATERIAL COST		8 TOTAL UNIT COST		9 CURRENT MONTH'S VARIATION		10 PREVIOUS MONTH'S VARIATION	
JOB	JOB NAME	UNIT	ACTIVITY	ALLOWED	SPENT	ALLOWED	SPENT	ALLOWED	SPENT	ALLOWED	SPENT	FAVORABLE	UNFAVORABLE	FAVORABLE	UNFAVORABLE
5	Blueprint	Print	13,285	703	762	1,003	886	1,706	1,648	.12842	.12405	.00437			.02695
10	Photostat	Print	27,801	923	819	2,203	2,146	3,126	2,965	.11244	.1065	.00579		.00679	
14	Xerox	Plate	1,531	589	657	119	119	708	776	.46244	.50686		.04442	.06628	
14-1	Multilith	Impression	83,975	583	645	314	324	897	969	.0168	.01154		.00086	.00011	
15	Davidson	Impression	287,374	1,014	951	555	561	1,569	1,512	.00546	.00526	.00020		.00014	
22	Mimeo #80	Impression	2,955	54	72	12	14	71	86	.02403	.02910		.00507		.00361
23	Mimeo #87	Impression	3,385	36	33	32	25	68	58	.02009	.01713	.00296			.00241
25	Marr	Impression	145,942	535	600	263	287	798	887	.00547	.00608		.00061		.00037
27	Fluid Dup.	Impression	77,304	483	546	172	156	655	702	.00847	.00908		.00061	.00026	
30	Flat Bed Dup.	Impression	2,696	119	158	-	-	119	158	.04414	.05861		.01447		.00517
35	Collating	Sheet	98,319	232	257	-	-	232	257	.00236	.00261		.00025		.00102
40	Micro 35 MM	Exposure	24,433	195	135	123	123	318	258	.01302	.01056	.00246		.00288	
45	Micro 16 MM	Exposure	65,189	212	259	147	147	359	406	.00551	.00623		.00072		.00035
690	Ret. of Rec.	Container	1,097	774	820	37	37	811	857	.73929	.78122		.04193		.70629
TOTAL			736,967	6,457	6,714	4,980	4,825	11,437	11,539						

Fig. 7-9. Duplicating Group—Cost Standards Report

may already be part of existing operating procedures and should be used to the fullest extent practicable. In many instances, however, it will be necessary to establish procedures for obtaining such data. Usually it is found that having the operator keep the records is the most practical means for procuring time data and production count (Figure 7-9). Although this method is subject to attack from the standpoint of its ability to be audited, it nevertheless has been proved to be a satisfactory method. In almost every case in which individual productivity is being measured, this method is an economical necessity. Group measurement on the other hand does not normally require such detail in timekeeping and production counting. Sometimes, when time and production records are compiled by the supervisor, these data may be all that are needed for group measurement purposes. Studies of time and production reporting by the operator indicate that the time consumed in keeping the records does not exceed 3 per cent of an eight-hour workday. Record keeping for measurement of group performance will run substantially less in time taken to keep the records.

COMPILATION OF TIME AND PRODUCTION. Records of time and production kept on a daily, weekly, monthly, or like basis are summarized for the measurement period in the same arrangement in which standards are established. Assembling these data should be adapted to company practices and facilities that are used for making similar summaries. In the establishment of procedures for producing these records, consideration should be given to the use of office machines that can be adapted to the purpose. Tabulating equipment, for example, has proved to be an accurate and economical means for compiling the data. In addition, cards keypunched in this method provide the basis for obtaining data, when needed, for a number of different analyses of production and performance.

APPLICATION OF STANDARDS AND COMPUTATION OF PERFORMANCE EFFECTIVENESS INDEX. Computations involved with application of standards and determination of effectiveness index can usually be integrated with methods used for compilation of time and production data. This is particularly true where tabulating equipment is used. Cards keypunched for time and production can be assembled with related, pre-cut standards cards so that computations can be made during tabulation of the summaries.

MAINTENANCE OF STANDARDS. Once the standard is developed and is used to measure performance, the company takes on an obligation to keep the standard up to date. More than one program has failed because standards were not properly adjusted when methods changed. Also, a policy must be established of not changing standards unless there is an error in the original calculation of the standard or there is a change in method affecting the time to perform the work. Arbitrary changes in standards will break down confidence in the plan and will be resisted by supervisors and employees alike.

Organizing for adequate maintenance of standards starts with developing a system for bringing changes in methods to the attention of those re-

OFFICE INCENTIVE REPORT
COMPTOMETER SECTION

OPERATOR NAME _Jane Doe_   OPER. NO. _87_   PERIOD ENDING _June 3, 1967_

JOB NO.		UNITS OF MEASURE			ACTUAL MINUTES		STANDARD MINUTES	Percent Effectiveness
		1	2	3	Non-Incentive	Incentive		
21	S	.46	.26			543	692	127
	P	1142	642					
22	S	.12				703	771	110
	P	6429						
23	S	.16				351	435	124
	P	2716						
40	S	.11				1022	1314	129
	P	11944						
80	S	.06				415	504	121
	P	8398						
94	S	2.42				161	150	93
	P	62						
100	S				1605			
	P	840	160					
	S							
	P							
	S							
	P							
	S	= STANDARD MINUTES PER UNIT					(S x P)	(Std. Mins. / Act. Inc. Mins.)
	P	= PRODUCTION COUNT PER UNIT						
				TOTALS	1605	3195	3866	121

Incentive Pay Calculation:

A. $\frac{3195}{4800}$ = **67** % of time on incentive

B. **67**% x $140 (2 weeks base wage) = **$93.80** (base wage on incentive)

C. **121**% Effectiveness pays **21**% incentive
$93.80 (B above)   x **21**% = **$19.70** Incentive earnings

D. **140.00** (2 weeks base wage)
19.70 (Incentive earnings)
$ 159.70   TOTAL EARNINGS

Fig. 7-10. Office Incentive Report

sponsible for keeping the standards up to date. The office supervisor is usually in the best position to observe changes in work and should be expected to notify the responsible persons of the changes. Notification can be given by way of a memorandum or by submittal of a revised procedure. The latter method is preferred, since it provides the basis for complete analysis of the change. In any case, notification of the change should be made a matter for the record.

DAILY PRODUCTION RECORD

COMPTOMETER SECTION

OPERATOR NO. _87_

DATE _6-1_   NAME _Jane Doe_

TIME START 8:30	ACTUAL MINUTES		JOB NUMBER	UNITS OF PRODUCTION		
	IN-CENT	NON INCENT		1	2	3
9:30	60		21	120	70	
10:45	75		22	712		
11:10	25		23	281		
12:00	50		40	508		
12:30			Lunch			
1:35	65		40	612		
2:17	42		80	830		
2:32	15		94	6		
5:00		148	100	79	15	
480	**332**	**148**				
TOTAL MINUTES	COLUMN TOTALS					

ig. 7-11. Daily Production
Record

Standards should be revised, where necessary, as soon as possible after notification of change in work. Significant delays in revising standards may result in using performance computations that are misleading. Where individual measurements are used, additional importance should be given to making changes promptly.

Cost of maintaining standards depends primarily upon two factors: the preciseness of measurements used and the frequency of work changes. Since these factors vary widely between measurement applications, no rule-of-thumb costs can be given.

SUPERVISORY FOLLOW-UP. Supervisory follow-up of a measurement plan does not rest with making sure that proper notification is given of changes in work. At the end of each measurement period the supervisor holds the responsibility for checking over the reports to see that, in general, time and production recording is correct. He should investigate questionable items and take steps to make necessary corrections. He should also give credit to the better performers and encourage poorer performers to make improvement. In no case should he use the measurement plan as a whip over the workers. The best results will be obtained if the supervisor helps the worker to find his full potential under the program. Although the immediate supervisor is the key person in the successful follow-up of any standards program, upper levels of management must also give evidence of interest in and backing of the program. Usually, they can make their support of the program evident to all through the immediate supervisor.

Benefits to Be Derived

TANGIBLE BENEFITS. The primary reason for application of work measurement is to improve the effectiveness of the working force and thereby reduce the cost of performing the function. Better planning and implementation of the work through work measurement will reduce costs of operation in either of two ways, or a combination of both:

1. By reduction in payroll hours
2. By absorption of increased volume of work without increasing payroll hours proportionately

Although cost reductions obtained through the absorption of increased volume are less obvious, since they do not show up as actual payroll dollars saved, they are nonetheless tangible savings to the company. In either of the above cases, cost reduction is reflected in lowering unit cost of operation.

BASIS FOR DETERMINATION OF COST REDUCTION. In order to determine the economic justification of measurement plans, a sound basis must be established for computing reduction in unit costs after measurement has been applied. This means that unit costs prior to application must be obtained for comparison with post-application unit costs. Obviously, the difference between the two unit costs extended by current volume of units will give dollars cost-reduction for that volume of work. To obtain pre-measurement unit costs, production and time reporting are installed prior to the application of standards. A three to four months' reporting period is usually sufficient to establish good pre-measurement unit costs in a clerical function.

Some companies prefer using percentage of improvement in performance as the basis for calculating cost reductions. In this method, standards are applied to pre-measurement production and time data to obtain percentage of effectiveness, which is used as the basis for comparison with post-application effectiveness figures. The percentage of improvement is then converted to dollars cost-reduction at current wage levels and column of work. This method has two primary advantages over the unit cost method in that it is not affected by either changing wages or production in the post-application period.

Experience with clerical applications of work measurement indicates that pre-measurement performance will range from about 50 per cent to 60 per cent of standard performance expected under wage incentive conditions. Using this as a rough guide, the large potential improvement possibilities of work measurement can be readily visualized. Since base wage performance (nonincentive) measurement plans do not include the stimulus of extra pay for extra production found in wage incentive applications, expected (standard) output should be somewhat less. Some companies have set their output expectancy in this type of plan at 80 per cent of the wage incentive standard. This being the case, pre-measurement effectiveness would fall in the range of approximately 60 per cent to 75 per cent of standard. A substantial percentage of improvement possibility is also evident under these circumstances.

INTANGIBLE BENEFITS. Reduction of man-hours and/or the absorption of increased volume of work with the same number of man-hours produces additional savings, which are less obvious and much more difficult to calculate. Because the work is performed with fewer people than would be required under non-measurement conditions, some of these intangible savings take the form of:

1. Lower requirement for working space
2. Fewer pieces of clerical equipment and office supplies required
3. Lower dollar outlay for fringe benefit expenses related to payroll
4. Less handling of records and matters pertaining to personnel administration

USES FOR OBTAINING FURTHER BENEFITS. In addition to its use as a means to obtain cost reductions through improved worker performance, other almost equally important uses can be made of work measurement to more effectively plan work. Some of the most important of these uses are as follows:

1. To locate and point out areas of operation resulting in variances from standard that require investigation and correction of the causes
2. To determine expected time and costs for jobs to be done
3. To determine most economic work methods and equipment
4. To determine relative economy of using company clerical labor versus outside clerical labor
5. To serve as a guide for selecting clerical employees and for determination of an employee's worth to the company
6. To determine proper work assignments
7. To plan and schedule work effectively
8. To forecast manpower requirements
9. To determine break-even points that would indicate at what specific volumes of business it becomes economical or not economical to maintain clerical functions or units as they are operated at present

8

Forms Design and Control

DR. GIBBS MYERS

General Precision, Inc.
Little Falls, N.J.

GIBBS MYERS has been connected with the Aerospace Group of General Precision, Inc., Little Falls, N.J., since 1956 as manager of systems and procedures. Prior to this association he served a long tour of duty with the ITT Federal Division, where he held the positions of manager of general services and director of methods and procedures. Elsewhere in his career he has carried out assignments as an industrial engineer, records management consultant, forms control specialist, data processing supervisor, archivist, editor and accountant.

A native of Washington, D.C., Dr. Myers was educated at the University of Maryland, where he received his A.B. and A.M. degrees; he later took advanced graduate work at Yale University, which awarded him a Ph.D. degree in 1943.

In addition to his business duties, Dr. Myers has also served as coadjutant lecturer on accounting systems at the Rutgers University School of Business in Newark, N.J., and has spoken and written on systems and accounting subjects for various professional and academic groups, with frequent attention to problems of forms design and control.

Dr. Myers is a past International Director and Publication Chairman of the Systems and Procedures Association, and is a founder and past president of the association's Northern New Jersey chapter. In 1960 the Systems and Procedures Association named him "Systems Man of the Year."

WHY FORMS CONTROL?

The printed form has become, within the last hundred years, so common a means of transmitting data that it is hard for us to conceive how men were able to carry on their business transactions in the pre-forms era.

Printed forms, like interchangeable parts, helped to spark the industrial revolution. In the pre-forms era, two documents for recording the same type of transaction were about as much alike as two hand-forged horseshoes. They were similar but seldom identical.

Two factors that led to the development of business forms were the expansion of printing and the specialization of work. Printing made forms possible. Specialization of work made them necessary.

Wherever repetitive clerical operations occur, you will find transactions being recorded in a uniform manner. The pattern that guides this uniformity, while contributing to the efficiency of the operation, is the printed form.

Today, with the extensive use of punched cards, paper tapes, magnetic tapes, discs and drums, character reading devices, automatic plotters, and other marvels of the electronic age, one might expect some change in the role of forms in the systems drama. Once a computer program is perfected, work can now be processed from entry of data to finished output without the intervention of human beings. What, then, is the effect on the forms that once were such important cogs in this process?

Two trends may be detected. On the output end, there is much more paper being used, but a higher percentage of it is plain stock paper rather than printed continuous forms. This trend is due to the versatility of the computer programs in the area of printout. Within the stored program can be included instructions that will imprint column headings and other forms indicia on each sheet as it rolls through the high-speed printer. Even vertical and horizontal rules can be simulated. There are still plenty of printed output forms required for computer-based systems, but a growing percentage of the total computer print-out will utilize only plain continuous stock paper.

The second trend relates to the input end. Here there is a proliferation of forms. Data can be introduced from a growing variety of media, and invariably there are printed forms required in the process. These, for example, may be tab cards, documents with magnetic ink encoding, edge-punched cards, merchandise tickets, and numerous formats for data transcription or entry. The strong need for precision and controls which is inherent in computer-based systems will extend the forms requirements in this area.

Forms control is really a specialized kind of systems work. In some offices it is looked on as an apprenticeship to a regular systems berth, but preferably it should be considered a career in itself. Just as a good dentist must also be a physician, a good forms control man must also be a systems analyst. To do an adequate job in designing and maintaining a company's forms, he not only must be a clever and accomplished craftsman in his special field, but must also have a wide knowledge of the organizational relationship and the systems impact of each form he handles.

It is principally through the printed form that positive and visible guidance and control of clerical work are exercised by management. The printed form on a clerk's desk or in a typewriter is often a more eloquent device for directing the flow of work than the written procedure that is filed away in the supervisor's bookcase.

What Is a Form?

Before outlining the responsibilities of forms control, it would be a good idea to define the thing to be controlled. A form—it might be further distinguished as a "printed form" or a "business form"—is nothing more than an object having constant information printed on it and having spaces for the entry of variable information. It is generally printed on paper or some similar substance; it may be printed by any of many reproduction processes (it may be reproducible itself); and it may be constructed of several similar or different parts or attachments.

Some of the more common types of forms, with which almost every person is familiar, are letterheads, employment applications, payroll checks, and income tax reports. On the other hand, such complex forms as manufacturing orders, bills of material, operation sheets, and engineering change requests are seldom seen by persons not directly involved in their preparation or processing.

In general, certain items should be excluded from the forms definition to keep the picture clear. Instances have occurred of such items as advertising circulars, product labels, price lists, and customer's instruction sheets being considered as printed forms and put under the jurisdiction of forms control. It should be quite evident that each of the items mentioned above consists of completely printed advice and would not ordinarily carry any spaces for entry of additional data. To items such as these the forms control man can contribute very little, and their development and usage seem to fall outside the scope of the systems and procedures operation. Conditions differ in various types of business, but a good general rule is to exclude such extraneous material from the forms control activity.

On the other hand, there may be forms that, strictly speaking, are not written on, yet they very definitely fall within the scope of forms control. The most common of these is the tab card, but there are others, such as inspection tags, which are stamped only, or items such as ticket forms, which are hand punched rather than written on, to introduce data.

Probably the best criterion for judging whether a piece of paper is a form is its function in relation to a business procedure or system. Any printed document that is not an essential link in an operating procedure or a medium for business communication should be excluded from the forms control group's responsibility.

Forms Control Responsibilities

The purpose of forms control, on the positive side, is to provide and improve all forms essential for the conduct of the company's business; on the negative side, it is to eliminate unnecessary and duplicatory forms. More fully stated, the forms control activity is responsible (a) for ascertaining that each form fulfills a basic requirement of an approved operating procedure, (b) for designing it so that it will perform its purpose effectively, (c) for specifying the most economical method of manufacture, and (d) for establishing a system of stock control and replenishment that will make forms available when needed, in economic quantities, at advantageous prices.

In short, this means that the forms control group is normally responsible for controlling the design, revision, specifications, nomenclature, numbering, classification, provisioning, and obsolescence of all company forms.

The forms control specialist does not necessarily approve the application of a form; this is the systems analyst's function. The latter determines whether a proposed new form is essential to carrying out an approved procedure before turning it over to the forms man for action. Likewise, the forms man refers any procedural problem relating to a form that has come to his attention to the systems man.

When systems and forms work are carried out by the same group, the dividing line between these two functions does not have to be drawn. But when forms control is split off from the systems group, it is important that the responsibilities of each group be defined so as to prevent any overlapping or neglect of duties. There is much to be said for placing the forms control activity as a subunit or sister unit of the systems and procedures group.

Preferably, each systems man should know the basics of forms design. Too marked a cleavage between systems and forms control can weaken the effectiveness of the former. Such a setup develops an incomplete kind of systems man—one who is incapable of recognizing forms deficiencies when he sees them and thus may admit poorly designed forms into his procedures.

To establish control over the design and revision of forms, the forms control program must necessarily have the backing of management and must also win the cooperation of the various departments of the company. The group can win this cooperation by proving that it knows its business and is out to render technical assistance in this specialized field of systems work. The group must develop a reputation for helping rather than hindering the forms author in developing his ideas into a capable and efficient form.

In carrying out its responsibility for specifications and construction, the forms group exercises the technical know-how of forms design and of reproduction methods, which it must possess to do an adequate job.

The nomenclature, numbering, classification, and cataloguing of forms are factors that contribute to an orderly system of control. Titles and numbers provide needed handles for forms. Classification and cataloguing are tools used by the forms control unit to carry out its program of bringing like forms together and weeding out duplicates.

The provisioning of forms involves the establishment of quantity requirements; methods of stocking, distribution and replenishment; and reviews of usage for the purpose of detecting changes in requirements and also for dealing properly with slow-moving or nonmoving items. This significant area of forms control is one of the most neglected by writers in this field. The most perfectly designed form is of little use unless it is there when it is needed—in the right place, at the right time, in the right quantity, and of the right quality.

Installing a Forms Control Program

Practically all writers and workers in the forms control field agree that the best way to start up a program from scratch is, with proper management backing, to announce the program and its purpose and to request each department to send in samples of every form that it originates. Usually, two samples are needed—one for a numerical file and one for a functional file. Emphasis must be placed on the fact that *all* forms are requested, whether they have been purchased from an outside printer or run off on the department's (or internal) duplicating machine.

One set of forms from each department should be kept in a separate jacket, identified by the department name. This will be used later to set up the functional file. Meanwhile, the other set of forms should be arranged by form number and put in the numerical file, which will be useful for cross-reference purposes. Any form that lacks a number can be identified by a temporary number until such time as a regular one is assigned.

The next step is to classify the forms in each departmental jacket according to the organizational functions to which they are related. To accomplish this, reference should be made to the forms classification system, which is outlined later in this chapter. As soon as this has been done, the analysis of each department's form can be started to see what improvements are in order. Initial efforts should be directed toward those departments that (a) have the most clerical employees, (b) have the most forms and systems trouble, (c) have the biggest bottlenecks and most frequent crises in their activities, (d) have the most apparent need for forms improvement, and (e) are most receptive to your efforts to help them.

It will be necessary to consult each department to establish quantities of forms used, how prepared, how used, to whom distributed, how filed, and other information not readily apparent from a review of the forms themselves. Once this information has been gathered, the forms samples can be arranged and classified in the manner provided in the following sections, a program of forms and systems integration can be planned, scientific redesign can be undertaken, and procedures established for requesting new and revised forms and for controlling forms provisioning and issuance.

An airtight plan for assuring that all requests for new or revised forms are reviewed by the forms control group is to get management to issue an order that all requests for forms, whether printed inside or outside, whether stock replenishments or new designs, are to be routed via forms control for clearance prior to the placement of a print shop or purchase order.

The forms unit must act promptly in reviewing these requests if it is to maintain the confidence of the various operating departments. Once it acquires a reputation for needlessly delaying orders, ways will be found to bypass it. Reorders without change should be scanned and cleared promptly, provided no apparent improvements are called for or no organizational or procedural changes are pending that might affect the use of the form. Even when improvements appear to be in order, it is unwise to hold up a print request if the delay could result in a forms shortage. The best course is to clear the present request and earmark the form for action before it comes up the next time.

Forms Numbering Systems

A simple forms numbering system, under which numbers are assigned from number one up, in sequence as required, has many advantages, and is preferable to trying to make the form number do double duty as a functional classification number. One should keep in mind that the primary purpose of the form number is to identify the form and provide a ready index for use on stores requisitions, stock records, purchase requisitions, purchase orders, and receiving tickets, as well as in written procedures and instructions.

The easiest way to store most forms is on stockroom shelves in form number sequence. Hence, when form numbers are assigned in regular order, the stock room has to reserve space for expansion in only one place—after the highest number previously assigned. By contrast, if each department uses a separate series of form numbers, the central stock room has to allow shelf space at various points for expansion and, frequently, has to shift the stock around to make room where needed. An alternative is to store new stock on the next open shelf, regardless of form number, and to post the storage location on the stock record.

In addition to the form number, a prefix is useful to identify the company and to indicate that the number represents a form. This can be a one or two-letter prefix that is distinctive from other prefixes used within the company for other purposes. Following the form number, the revision date can be indicated by a number or letter in sequence, or merely by giving the month and year of the revision. However it is shown, the revision indicator is essential to control forms in the stockroom and to provide assurance that samples of the latest revision are submitted to the printer when replenishing stock.

Forms Classification Systems

The purpose of classifying forms is to relate them to the organizational functions with which they are used. By arranging forms in this manner it becomes possible to see forms relationship better, and also to detect duplications of activity more readily.

The functional form file also serves as a reference tool for the forms control or systems man who is looking for information on a certain function. He may find the data he needs here for integration with other forms, or he may find a form already in existence that will meet the need for which a new form has been requested.

A method of classifying forms, which has been used effectively in several companies, is to set up a four-digit base code, with the first three digits identifying the departmental functions of the company, and the final digit indicating the purpose of the form. For example, the 0200 series might cover the accounting department, the 0600 series the industrial relations department, and so on. Within each department a further breakdown is made to identify subfunctions. Under accounting, 0210 is general ledger, 0220 accounts payable, 0230 accounts receivable, 0240 payroll, and so forth. Figure 8-1 illustrates a forms classification coding system.

As for the fourth digit, which is shown only as zero in the examples just cited, it can be made to signify the purpose of the form by setting up a list of ten categories applicable to the type of business involved. For example, a manufacturing organization might use those listed in the accompanying table (Figure 8-1). Actually, there are eighteen generally recognized forms purposes, namely: (1) to acknowledge, (2) to agree, (3) to apply, (4) to authorize, (5) to cancel, (6) to certify, (7) to claim, (8) to estimate, (9) to follow-up, (10) to identify, (11) to instruct, (12) to notify, (13) to order, (14) to record, (15) to report, (16) to request (17) to route, and (18) to schedule. However, these can usually be condensed into ten or fewer categories, as shown below, so that a one-digit code will suffice.

Once the code has been established, the forms within each departmental classification can be grouped according to these functions so that those having similar purposes are thrown together for study to eliminate duplication and overlapping.

Another useful refinement of the forms classification system is to include a code to designate the construction of the form. This is a significant addition to the classification code, since there are many times when it is helpful to refer to all forms of a certain type of construction, such as tab cards, hecto masters, snapouts, continuous, and the like. An example of how the stockroom could make use of this construction classification for adjusting minimum quantities would be when the lead time on all tab card forms has to be increased from thirty to forty-five days. Through the use of this code, all stock records covering tab cards could be reviewed to adjust minimum and order quantities to meet the changed delivery conditions. The use of the digits 0 to 9 for this purpose is shown in the accompanying table (Figure 8-1).

One should keep in mind that the forms classification code does not have to be printed on the form. It is of interest only to forms and systems people and to the stockroom; they can write it on the form samples in their forms classification file or they can list it in the forms catalogues and on the stock record cards.

A complete forms catalogue, incidentally, is needed only by the group mentioned above. The various departments should be provided, at most, with listings of their own forms. A good way to prepare a forms catalogue, if punched-card equipment is available, is to run it from tab cards into which the form number, form name, and classification code have been punched. Two runs will be needed—one in form number sequence and one in classification sequence. For the use of the stockroom, an additional run by type of construction will be helpful. The tab cards can be brought up to date and new runs made once a year.

FORMS CLASSIFICATION SYSTEM

type of construction (1-digit prefix)	*purpose* (final digit of 4-digit base code)
0 Outside purchased (not classified otherwise)	0 General and other
1 Company printed (up to 8½ x 13)	1 Requests
2 Company printed (over 8½ x 13)	2 Orders
3 Duplimats	3 Records
4 Hecto masters	4 Movement of material
5 Envelopes	5 Notifications
6 Tags	6 Identifications
7 Tab cards	7 Reports and analyses
8 Multipart units	8 Schedules and tables
9 Continuous strip	9 (open)

ORGANIZATIONAL FUNCTION

(first 3 digits of the 4 digit base code)

0100	Executive and General	1000	Sales Department
		1100	Sales—product A
0200	Accounting Dept.—basic functions	1200	Sales—product B
	0210 General ledger	1300	Contract and order service
	0220 Accounts payable	1400	Market research
	0230 Accounts receivable		
	0240 Payroll	2000	Engineering Department
	0250 Timekeeping		2100 Laboratory A
	0260 Cost accounting		2200 Laboratory B
			2300 Drafting
0300	Accounting Dept.—related functions		2400 Blueprint and drawing control
	0310 Auditing		
	0320 Budget control	3000	Production Department
	0330 Systems and procedures		3100 Industrial engineering
	0340 Forms control		3200 Production control
	0350 Cashier		3300 Purchasing
			3400 Material control
0600	Industrial Relations		3500 Machine shop
	0610 Personnel		3600 Assembly shop
	0620 Medical		
	0630 Labor relations	4000	Inspection Department

Fig. 8-1. Coding System for Classifying Forms

Additional use can be made of these cards by punching into them the unit cost and estimated annual requirements. By extending these figures you can obtain a forecast of departmental forms expense for use in preparing expense budgets and in projecting overhead costs.

Forms Design Techniques

The fundamental purpose of forms design is to provide standardized media for the efficient processing of business information. This includes the layout of the form and the specifications for its construction and manufacture.

The forms designer's craft calls for a combination of practical and aesthetic qualities, plus an understanding of the underlying system. Above all, the forms designer must be meticulously thorough. Realism is another necessary trait, for this person will face numerous problems that require significant answers with really short times. The quality of his performance will have a distinct and durable effect on the image of the company that emerges from its paper work.

Of prime importance to the forms designer is the purpose of the form, which is to record and convey information. As such, it is an instrument of human activity. It acts upon and is acted upon by people. This factor may be called the facility of use. Forms should be so designed that it is easy for the human users to do the right thing with them. Forms, therefore, should be easy to write, easy to read, easy to process, and easy to dispose of.

To make the form easy to write, sufficient space is needed for each entry. Entries should be in sequence of data being transcribed. Captions should readily indicate what is to be entered. As much information as possible should be pre-printed on the form to reduce the time required to prepare it. All variables should be questioned to see if some of them are not really constants. Entries frequently but not always applicable should be pre-printed with a "ballot box" preceding them, thus making it necessary for the clerk to make only a check mark or type in an "X," rather than fill in the complete data called for.

The boxed design, with upper left captions for data entries, is usually an improvement over the caption followed by a dotted line, particularly if entries are made on a typewriter (*see* Figure 8-2). This method conserves both space and clerical effort, and is also easier to read. When using the boxed design, it is also a simpler matter to line up many of the boxes vertically so as to reduce the number of tab stops to be set on the typewriter.

Lines should be spaced at ¼″ intervals for most handwritten entries. If a form is sometimes prepared by hand and sometimes by typewriter, ⅓″ spacing should be used. If prepared entirely on the typewriter, horizontal lines should be omitted unless needed to aid the eye in following successive entries across the sheet. If space is limited, ⅙″ can be allowed for typewritten entries and ⅕″ for handwritten entries.

Another way to make forms both easier to write and easier to read is to use variations in the weight of columnar rules to set information apart. Use hairlines for several breakdowns under one category column, then put a heavy or double rule before the next categorical grouping. The same technique can be used for horizontal rulings.

Use colored inks and colored papers advisedly. Stick to one color of ink throughout unless there is a good reason for changing colors. Although black ink is the accepted standard for most forms, some companies have

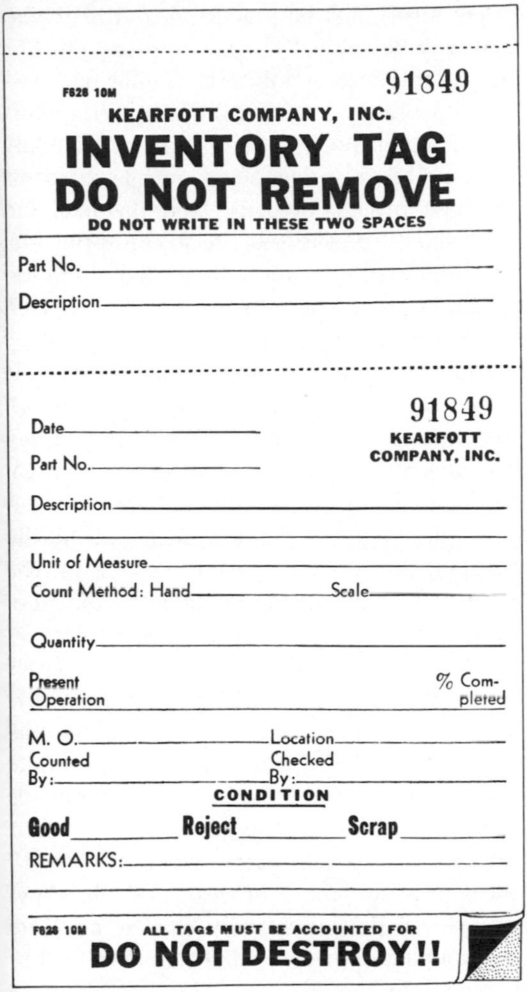

F628 10M 91849

KEARFOTT COMPANY, INC.

INVENTORY TAG
DO NOT REMOVE

DO NOT WRITE IN THESE TWO SPACES

Part No.

Description

91849
KEARFOTT COMPANY, INC.

Date

Part No.

Description

Unit of Measure

Count Method: Hand Scale

Quantity

Present Operation % Completed

M. O. Location

Counted By: Checked By:

CONDITION

Good Reject Scrap

REMARKS:

F628 10M ALL TAGS MUST BE ACCOUNTED FOR

DO NOT DESTROY!!

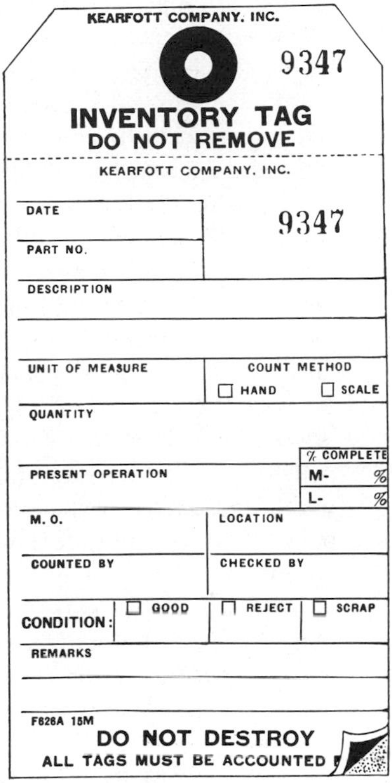

KEARFOTT COMPANY, INC.

9347

INVENTORY TAG
DO NOT REMOVE

KEARFOTT COMPANY, INC.

DATE 9347

PART NO.

DESCRIPTION

UNIT OF MEASURE | COUNT METHOD ☐ HAND ☐ SCALE

QUANTITY

PRESENT OPERATION | % COMPLETE M- % L- %

M. O. | LOCATION

COUNTED BY | CHECKED BY

CONDITION: ☐ GOOD ☐ REJECT ☐ SCRAP

REMARKS

F626A 15M

DO NOT DESTROY

ALL TAGS MUST BE ACCOUNTED F

Fig. 8-2. Form Design, Illustrating Boxed Arrangement for Data Entries Before and After Form was Redesigned

switched to brown because it affords a better contrast to the handwritten or typewritten entries. Red ink is used frequently on credit memos, rejection tickets, rework orders, and so on, where it affords a marked contrast to similar forms or serves as a flag to indicate trouble. Gray ink is sometimes used for printing contract conditions on the backs of such forms as purchase orders or sales order, but the print must be dark enough to be legible.

Colored papers are used principally in multi-part forms to identify the various departmental copies and to facilitate distribution. Sometimes, especially on fanfold forms, colored inks are substituted for colored papers, usually with a solid triangular block of color at one corner of each part of the form.

All wording that is put on the form must be precise. Avoid abbreviations or incomplete phrasings that may be subject to misinterpretation. For example, "Oper. No." on an operation sheet or job ticket could be interpreted as "operator number" or "operation number." Form titles must likewise be concise, yet indicative of the purpose of the form. The company name should appear prominently on all forms distributed outside the company, such as sales orders, purchase orders, invoices, and the like. On internal forms, the company name should be subordinate to the form title, or omitted altogether. While form titles are conventionally placed at the top of the form, the bottom location can be used when the top position is given over to filing indicia or other identifying information.

Margins are important for both usage and appearance. Binder margins vary from ½″ for ring binders to 1½″ for post binders. Top and bottom margins are essential to good appearance as well as for facility in printing and use; they should normally be at least ½″ each, but if space is critical they can be reduced to $\frac{5}{16}$″. Side margins, where no binders are involved, should be at least ¼″. However, if the form is a snapout with stub on the left, a ½″ gripper edge for snapping the copies apart is needed on the right, and only a negligible margin is needed on the left next to the stub.

Most forms printers make use of gothic type faces, and the choice can generally be left to the printer. For internally printed forms, gothic types can be had on the VariTyper or on manual and electric typewriters. Other type faces can be used if gothic is not available, but if a machine is purchased specifically for forms preparation, the selection of an appropriate type face is an important matter to be decided before the machine is ordered.

With all kinds of forms, it is good advice to limit the size to 8½″ x 11″ if possible. This size is economical to print, stock, process, and file. Anything larger results in higher costs, slower deliveries, more shelf wear, more costly handling, and bulkier filing equipment. Sizes smaller than 8½″ x 11″ should by all means be used wherever they are adequate. Good results have been obtained by reducing the size of 8½″ x 5½″ forms to 7″ x 4¼″. In a surprisingly high percentage of cases, the smaller size gives enough space for the information previously printed on the larger size, and the cost is about 20 per cent less (*see* Figure 8-3). Whenever sizes larger than 8½″ x 11″ are required, go as far as 11″ x 17″, but fight tenaciously against anything larger. It is especially important to avoid odd sizes that are difficult or expensive for the printer to handle.

To lay out the form with proper spacing, both vertical and horizontal, it is necessary first to have a rough sketch or previous design of the form with all normal entries written in for guidance. After deciding on the best sequence for entry of the data, resketch the form roughly, then enter the minimum width of each box or column, preferably in tenths of an inch. Add these up, remembering the margins, and see if they come within the allotted space. If additional space is available, increase the width of those

SALARY ADJUSTMENT
AND/OR RECLASSIFICATION OR RATE ADJUSTMENT

☐ UPGRADE   DATE
☐ DOWNGRADE

EMPLOYEE NAME		BADGE NO.	SEX	DATE OF HIRE
DEPT. NO.	DEPT. NAME	LOCATION	SHIFT	RECORDS OF SALARY ADJUSTMENTS DURING PRECEDING 12-MONTH PERIOD.

JOB TITLE	CODE	LABOR GRADE	RATE	PER	DATE	RATE	JOB TITLE AND REASON FOR ADJUSTMENT
FROM			$	☐ HOUR		$	
TO			$	☐ WEEK		$	
DATE EFFECTIVE	AMOUNT OF INCREASE $			☐ YEAR		$	

IS REPLACEMENT NECESSARY?   IF SO, ENTER PERSONNEL REQUISITION NO.

REASON FOR ADJUSTMENT OR RECLASSIFICATION

IF REJECTED, STATE REASON

ORIGINATED BY	DATE	APPROVED	DATE	APPROVED	DATE
SALARY AND PROMOTION SECTION		WAGE AND SALARY ADMINISTRATION		DIRECTOR INDUSTRIAL RELATIONS	

FP 79 (REV. 6-53)   FEDERAL TELEPHONE AND RADIO

1. PAYROLL

FEDERAL TELEPHONE & RADIO
FP79

EMPLOYEE RECLASSIFICATION
AND/OR RATE ADJUSTMENT

☐ UPGRADE   DATE
☐ DOWNGRADE

EMPLOYEE NAME		BADGE NO.	SEX	DATE OF HIRE
DEPT. NO.	DEPT. NAME		LOCATION	SHIFT

JOB TITLE	CODE	LABOR GRADE	RATE	PER
FROM			$	☐ HOUR
TO			$	☐ WEEK
DATE EFFECTIVE	AMOUNT OF ☐ INCREASE ☐ DECREASE $			☐ YEAR

REASON FOR CHANGE (IF REJECTED, STATE WHY).

ORIGINATED BY	DATE	APPROVED	DATE	APPROVED	DATE
SALARY AND PROMOTION SECTION		WAGE AND SALARY ADMINISTRATION		DIRECTOR INDUSTRIAL RELATIONS	

1. PAYROLL

Fig. 8-3. Form Reduced from 8½" x 5½" (above) to 7" x 4¼" (below)

boxes or columns that could use the extra space, such as name, description, remarks, and so on. If not enough space is available, check carefully to determine which areas can be reduced slightly without seriously affecting the usefulness of the form. Repeat this operation for each horizontal line, then make whatever adjustments are possible to line up the various boxes or columns vertically for the purpose of reducing tab stops to a minimum and improving the form's appearance.

Horizontal spacing is best computed in sixths of an inch, allowing ⅙″ for columnar headings and from ⅖″ to ⅗″ for most lines. Of course, if entries are to be handwritten, the body of the form can be spaced off in quarter inches.

By working out all of these dimensions on the rough sketch, it will be possible to make up the final design with a minimum of time lost by trial and error. Although there are many tricks used by the skilled forms designer in crowding extensive entries into a limited area, one device that should be shunned is the vertical or diagonal caption. All printing should follow the conventional horizontal arrangement, because this is the way the forms writer and the forms reader will look at it. Exceptions are filing indicia, which may be printed at right angles to the rest of the printing if the form is to be filed on its side.

When forms are to be prepared on special types of machines or filed in special equipment, the designer must make a study of the equipment and the process so that he understands fully all critical dimensions and tolerances involved. Any details that are left to chance will probably come back to haunt him later.

Forms for high-speed data processing equipment need special attention to both their design and construction. Probably no two machines have exactly the same specifications for writing area, printing and ejection speeds, carriage length, line spacing, print pressure, etc. Therefore, it is essential to make a carefully simulated test of a new form on the actual equipment in order to ascertain that both the design and the proposed construction of the form will be adequate for the purpose intended.

Last but not least, forms should be made attractive. One should not be satisfied with a purely functional design that is totally lacking in aesthetic qualities. Forms should create a favorable mental attitude. The persons handling them will be more likely to have a pleasant reaction to their tasks. Their work will be more accurate and more thorough, and they will probably complete it in less time. How can one design attractiveness into a form? This is the combined effect of layout, type fonts and sizes, headings, the weight of horizontal and vertical rules, the use of color and shadings, and the employment of white space in margins and elsewhere. All of these should add up to an uncluttered design that subtly but surely accomplishes its business purpose.

Tools of the Trade

Only a few basic tools are needed by the forms designer in plying his trade. These are a drawing board with a straightedge attached, a 30/60 degree triangle, a scale with graduations in sixths, eighths and tenths inches, a ruling pen, and a supply of drawing pencils. Useful adjuncts are an X-Acto knife, duck-bill tweezers, scissors, and plastic templates for drawing ballot boxes, arrows, etc.

Layout sheets for machine-printed forms may be obtained from the forms manufacturers and printers. Some forms designers prefer to print their own design guide sheets for use in laying out their forms. Others like to sketch their forms designs on plain paper. Any good surfaced paper that will withstand erasing may be used.

Transfer types can give the designer an assist in putting headings on his forms. These come in a variety of type styles and sizes, and also provide a large selection of symbols, borders, patterns, and tones. They are available from several manufacturers and are sold under such trade names as Instantype, Craf-type, Prestype, and others.

If forms are being designed for in-house printing, a cold-type setting machine will help to do a professional job. A VariTyper machine, for example, provides a large selection of type fonts with sizes ranging from 3 to 13 points. A companion machine, the Headliner, will provide larger sizes (up to 80 points) in photo reproductions suitable for stripping in as headings.

Writing the Specifications

A convenient way to convey printing specifications, particularly to an outside printer, is to prepare them on a specification sheet printed on vellum or all-purpose bond. From this, reproductions can be made and given to the buyer for attachment to requests for quotations and to purchase orders. This method not only saves the purchasing department the trouble of retyping these specifications on the two forms mentioned, but it assures the correct transmission of the complete forms specifications to the printer.

An example of a forms specification is shown in Figure 8-4. This sheet attempts to answer almost every question the printer may ask on how to set up the form so that it will come out the desired way. Both the spec sheet and the accompanying form sample or design must be clear in every detail so that nothing is left to chance or misunderstanding.

The specification sheet illustrated has spaces for entering construction, carbons, punching, numbering, and packing. There is also a space for other, less common, information, which may be required on certain specialized forms. On the left is a form revision column in which should be shown, for each revision, what you changed *from*. The current specification sheet will show what you changed *to*. This historical information is especially important if it affects cost, such as a change in size or in the number of parts, and it will be useful in making cost comparisons later.

Grades and Weights of Paper

The grades of paper most commonly used for forms are bond, manifold, duplicator, ledger, index bristol (commonly called index), and tag stock. Bonds are of rag or sulphite and vary in quality according to the percentage of rag content or finish. Rag papers, with 25, 50, or 100 per cent rag content, are specified where appearance, durability, and permanence are required. Sulphite bonds are the work horses of the business forms

PRINTING SPECIFICATIONS

NOTICE TO BIDDER OR VENDOR: No deviations are to be made from these specifications unless they are noted in your quotation. Such deviations should be made only to lower the price, shorten the delivery period, or facilitate production on your equipment. If these specifications are changed as the result of a bidder's request, a revised specification sheet will be sent to the successful bidder attached to our Purchase Order.

PART NO.	SIZE (INCHES) WITHOUT STUB	WGT.	PAPER COLOR	GRADE	INK BLK	OTHER	BACK PRINTING NONE	SAME	DIFF	HEAD TO	MARGINAL CAPTIONS
1	8½ X 11	12	WHITE	SULPHITE BOND		BLUE			✓	HEAD	1. ORIGINAL
2	8½ X 11	9	CANARY	SULPHITE BOND		BLUE			✓	HEAD	2. ACKNOWLEDGMENT
3	8½ X 11	20	WHITE	HECTO MASTER	✓		✓				3 RECEIVING MASTER
4	8½ X 11	9	PINK	MULTICLEAR or EQUIV.		BLUE	✓				4. COST ACCOUNTING
5	8½ X 11	9	SALMON	MULTICLEAR or EQUIV.		BLUE		✓		HEAD	5. PURCHASING DEPT.
6	8½ X 11	9	WHITE	MULTICLEAR or EQUIV.		BLUE		✓		HEAD	6. ACCOUNTS PAYABLE
7	8½ X 11	9	BUFF	MULTICLEAR or EQUIV.		BLUE	✓				7. INSPECTION
8	8½ X 11	9	BLUE	MULTICLEAR or EQUIV.		BLUE	✓				8. DATA PROCESSING
9	8½ X 11	9	GREEN	MULTICLEAR or EQUIV.		BLUE	✓				9. REQUISITIONER
10	8½ X 11	12	WHITE	SULPHITE BOND		BLUE			✓	HEAD	10. COORDINATOR

FORM REVISIONS

A 2/65
PART 1 BACKER
REVISED

B 4/67
RECEIVING
MASTER
ADDED

CONSTRUCTION: ✓ SNAPOUT SET, STUB AT ___TOP___ WIDTH ✓ OPTIONAL STUB ✓ INSIDE GLUED / OPTIONAL METHOD

☐ TAG ☐ ENVELOPE ☐ HECTO MASTER ☐ TAB CARD ☐ CUT SHEETS ☐ NOT PADDED ☐ SHEETS

☐ CONTINUOUS ☐ CRIMPED ☐ STAPLED AT ☐ OTHER EXPLAIN ☐ PADDED AT ___ QUANTITY PER PAD ___ ☐ SETS

CARBONS: ✓ ONE-TIME   ✓ TYPEWRITER   ✓ BLACK

☐ NONE TYPE: ☐ REGULAR ☐ PENCIL ☐ BLUE

SIZE (INCHES) ** ✓ HECTO

8½ X 9 Interleaved, Facing Parts __2__   X Interleaved, Facing Parts ___
8½ X 10½ Interleaved, Facing Parts __3 TO 10__   X Interleaved, Facing Parts ___
  X Interleaved, Facing Parts ___   X Interleaved, Facing Parts ___

*(EXCLUSIVE OF STUB) ** 8½ X 10½ HECTO BLUE NON-SMEAR FACING BACK OF PART 3

PUNCHING: ☐ ROUND HOLE (NUMBER OF HOLES ___ ; CENTER-TO-CENTER ___
✓ NONE (DIAMETER ___ ; CENTER-TO ___ EDGE ___

NUMBERING: COLOR OF INK ☐ OPTIONAL ✓ RED ; SERIAL NOS. (Range) LOWEST NO. _1001_ HIGHEST NO. _99999_
☐ NONE NUMBER OF PLACES ON EACH FORM ___ Never go outside this range of numbers. See Purchase Order for specific numbers assigned to the forms covered by this order.
CUT SHEETS OR PADDED FORMS TO BE NUMBERED IN ☐ SING. ☐ DUP. ☐

OTHER INSTRUCTIONS: ① PARTS 1, 2 + 10 HAVE CONDITIONS OF PURCHASE AS BACKER; PARTS 5+6 HAVE RECEIVING + PAYMENT RECORD AS BACKER — ALL PRINTED IN GRAY INK.
② COPY CHANGE ON PART 2 PER SAMPLE. ③ PART 3 IS HECTO MASTER, KISS-PRINTED. ④ CHINESE BLOCKOUT OF ITEMS 26, 27 + 28 ON PARTS 3 + 7.
⑤ BLUE INK MUST BE REPRODUCIBLE ON THERMOFAX.

TYPES OF EQUIPMENT ON WHICH THIS FORM WILL BE PROCESSED ✓ TYPEWRITER ☐ FLEXOWRITER ☐ STD. REGIS BURSTER IMPRINTER ☐ PIT. BOWES FOLDER INSERTER ☐ SPIRIT DUPLICATOR ☐ OTHER NCR ACCTS. MACH.

DESIGN: ☐ PER ATTACHED DRAWING ✓ PER ATTACHED SAMPLE FORM ☐ AS PREVIOUSLY PRINTED / ✓ AS MARKED UP

PACKAGING: WRAP _100_ ☐ SHEETS ✓ SETS ☐ PADS, PER PACKAGE
MARK FORM NO., QUANTITY AND SERIAL NOS. (IF ANY) ON EACH ONE SHORT END OF EACH INDIVIDUAL PACKAGE, PACK IN CARTONS NOT LARGER THAN 13" X 16" X 19½".

PROOF: ✓ REQUIRED ☐ NOT REQUIRED | FORM TITLE | FORM NUMBER |
PAPER & CARBON DUMMY ✓ REQUIRED ☐ NOT REQUIRED THREE COMPLETED SAMPLE FORMS REQUIRED | PURCHASE ORDER | F 206 |
SEND TO: J. M. CHERICC

F 1382 B

Fig. 8-4. Form Specification Sheet

world, being used widely for numerous types of internal forms where appearance, body, and durability are not critical factors. Sulphite grades 1, 2, and 4 are generally available, the last mentioned being an economical paper suitable for most types of office forms. Bonds range in weight from 10 to 24 lbs., the higher weights usually being rag content papers. Lighter than the bonds is manifold, or onionskin, of which the 9 lb. weight is most widely used. Duplicator papers are specially calendered for hectographic reproduction, and usually come in 16 and 20 lb. weights. Ledgers usually run in weight from 28 to 36 lbs. and are used for posting ledgers, checks, visible record forms, and so on. Index stocks, ranging from 72 lbs. upward, are used for printing all types of card forms. Tag stocks come in various finishes and run from ten to twenty points in thickness.

The knack of knowing which grade and weight of paper to specify comes only from extensive study and practice in the forms control field. Fundamentals to be remembered are that light papers are difficult to print and to handle; therefore, they should be specified only when essential to obtain legible carbon copies or to conserve filing space. Heavy papers are expensive and space-consuming; therefore, they should be used only when appearance or durability is of particular importance. For most one-, two-, or three-part forms, a 16 lb. sulphite bond is satisfactory. Legibility of the four-part form will be improved by using 12 or 13 lb. paper for the last three parts. If the form has five parts or more, all except the first and last parts should be either 9 lb. manifold or 10 lb. bond.

To improve the legibility of multi-part forms, special papers and carbons have been developed that make it possible to obtain six to eight readable copies of a handwritten form, and up to twenty copies of a form prepared on an electric typewriter. These special papers are thin, with high tensile strength, and they are treated with a finish that has an affinity for the carbon. The carbons in turn are brilliant, with strong transfer characteristics.

Another type of paper that is useful in certain multi-part applications is the carbonless type that transfers the image by chemical action or through the release of minute particles of encapsulated dye. A familiar example is the NCR or "no carbon required" paper that produces a copy through the interaction of the coated back of the first part with the coated front of the second part, under the pressure of a pencil or keystroke. This process is useful in applications in which the insertion or removal of carbon paper would cause procedural problems or costly delays in processing.

Needless to say, most of these specially processed papers are premium items. The forms specialist must weigh the increased cost against the expected advantages to determine whether they should be specified.

Construction

Paper specifications become especially important with respect to multi-part forms, and it is here that the ingenuity of the forms man must come into play. He has to consider such factors as method of preparation, subsequent processing, and quantities required to determine whether the form should be padded or stubbed, whether one-time carbon (or carbonless paper) should be used, what order the parts should be arranged in, and where the stub should be located. The quantity of a form to be prepared by one clerk during a day's work is an important index, as is the total daily or weekly requirement of the form. If a clerk prepares only half a dozen sets of a two- or three-part form daily, a simple padded form is sufficient, with carbons to be inserted as required by the clerk. But if several clerks prepare similar quantities daily, or if one clerk devotes several hours a day to preparation of these forms, a snapout form interleaved with one-time carbons, or possibly a continuous form (for machine preparation), will generally be more economical. Quantity becomes an important factor because of the high production costs in manufacturing snapout and continuous forms. In quantities less than 5,000, the cost may be so high as to be prohibitive for certain uses, but in quantities of 50,000 and over they may become almost as economical as padded forms without carbon. However, if 10,000 or more of a carbon-interleaved snapout form are ordered at one time, rotary press manufacture will, almost without exception, afford the best job and the lowest price.

Location of snapout stubs should be given careful consideration. Most forms authors will put the stub at the top. It is up to the forms designer to consider whether a bottom stub would not be preferable in order to make typing corrections without removal of the entire form from the machine. Forms measuring 8½″ x 5½″ or less are more economical if the stub is placed at the side, usually on the left. However, a form of six or more parts that has to be inserted in a typewriter may not feed in properly unless the stub is in the top position. Incidentally, the same considerations for location of the stub apply to hectograph master units.

Other details of construction, such as punchings, perforations, scoring, folding, and die-cutting, must be given special attention by the forms designer and spelled out clearly on the specification sheet.

Certain of the more complex types of forms construction call for special care in preparing the specifications. For example, multi-part continuous data processing forms are fed through the data processing machines so as to print at speeds ranging from 100 to more than 1,000 lines a minute, and these machines pass and eject paper at even higher rates. Obviously, the specifications for paper quality, pin-feed perforations and paper fastening are very exacting for this type of form. Paper and carbon specifications must be related to the equipment, since machines differ in paper-handling devices and in printing mechanisms. Various models print from bars, wheels, cylinders, chains and matrices. Paper fastening is critical; this may be accomplished by stapling, gumming, crimping, flexible fastening, or other process. Unfastened forms may prove best in certain limited applications—

e.g., on low-speed printers when only one or two carbon copies are required. Consideration should also be given to the use of carbon backing, or carbonless paper with chemical coatings that simulate carbon backing. These reduce form thickness, eliminate carbon removal, and may even be lower in price.

When designing hectographic master forms, it is necessary to specify the color and grade of carbon, location of stub or fold-over, use of slip sheets, and whether the master is to be fully printed or "kiss-printed" (face printed only). Purple is the preferred color of carbon because of its durability and economy. Other colors, such as black, green, and red, are available, but they usually cost more and will reproduce only a limited number of copies. Purple carbon comes in a number of grades that will give short, medium, or long runs. It also comes coated with wax or plastic to reduce staining of the typist's hands and to retard the drying out of the carbon. Slip sheets are usually provided in all unit hectographic forms to prevent the carbon from bleeding onto the back of the master, and also to protect it from accidental transfers of carbon deposits during the handling process. Continuous-strip hectographic masters, however, come without slip sheets, because of the impracticability of removing them. A hard or coated carbon should be used in this case to retard bleeding prior to use.

Tabulating cards are available in natural (manila) and colored stocks, as well as white, post card, and plastic. The last is used for machine posting or in other applications where heavy usage is expected. Plastic cards are much higher priced than conventional cards. In preference to colored stocks, you can use natural with a colored horizontal stripe printed on the card. This is cheaper and the card will have a higher salvage value. Round-cornering may now be obtained at or near the price of square-cornered tab cards. Many additional features are available on tab cards, such as pre-numbering, pre-punching, back printing, and detachable stubs; but all of these cost more and require considerably longer lead times. One important point to remember is that the normal minimum order quantity is 30,000 cards. You can get lower quantities (in multiples of 2,000), but your order will be subject to additional special charges.

Money can be saved on tag forms by reducing the size to the minimum standard and by using a cheaper tag stock. Unless you specify the grade of tag stock to be used, the printer will usually furnish a heavy, durable paper suitable for outdoor use. However, you will probably find that most tags are used indoors, and generally for short periods of time, for which an inexpensive ten-point tag stock is adequate. Wire and string ties cost extra, and should be specified only when they will be used to advantage. Standard tag sizes are illustrated in Figure 8-5.

Tracing forms are on the expensive side, particularly the larger sizes, for which quantity requirements are usually the smallest and printers' setup charges are the highest. With proper cooperation by the using departments,

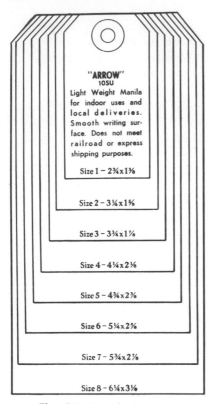

Fig. 8-5. Standard Tag Sizes

the forms specialist can work out some extraordinary savings in forms costs. One step is to standardize as many as possible of the forms used by the various engineering sections with respect to design, size, and type of paper (or cloth) used. A second step is to eliminate as many as possible of the printed sizes that are larger than 11″ x 17″. These larger sizes, which frequently are as large as 34″ x 44″, are slow and costly to print, clumsy to handle in the stockroom, and subject to excessive shelf wear. As a substitute, the draftsmen can be furnished with blank sheets of tracing paper cut into the standard drawing sizes, to which adhesive, transparent, title and tolerance blocks can be affixed. All that the draftsman then has to do is rule in the border.

Printing Techniques and Processes

An essential part of a forms designer's education is a firsthand knowledge of printing techniques and processes. There is no doubt about his need to know all about the various types of office duplicating equipment—hectograph or Ditto, mimeograph or stencil, Multilith or offset, contact or diazo, Xerox, and so on.

A knowledge of industrial printing presses and methods is equally important—letterpress, pen-ruling, offset, flat-bed, rotary, and others. If possible, the designer should visit various kinds of printing establishments to see how they operate—the corner print shop using flat-bed presses, the larger printer using rotary web presses and automatic collators, the tag and envelope printer, the hectographic master producer, the continuous forms printer, and the tab card manufacturer. From such visits he can learn how his own printing specifications affect printing processes, costs, and deliveries; what copy changes can be effected at little cost as well as those that will cost a great deal; how numbering, back printing, and colored ink printing are done on both flat-bed and rotary presses; the significance of sizes, inside-glued stubs, double stubs, strip carbon; use of special types of paper; and related pertinent information.

The forms specialist should know how a small print shop can simulate the inside-glued stubs of the rotary press equipment by using a Mendes machine or other similar devices for collating and gluing flat sheets and carbons into snapout sets.

Regarding rotary presses, especially for continuous forms, the forms man should learn what cylinder sizes are available and how these affect form costs—how the length of finished forms must go evenly into the total cylinder size or they cannot be printed. In Figure 8-6 are listed the most commonly available cylinder sizes and the form lengths that can be produced on them.

press cylinder size	length of form	widths available
17"	4¼", 8½", 17"	8½", 9⅞", 10⅝", 11¾", 13⅝", 14⅞", 16¾", 17²⁵⁄₃₂"
20"	5", 10", 20"	
22"	3⅔", 5½", 7⅓", 11", 22"	
24"	3", 4", 6", 8", 12", 24"	
28"	3½", 7", 14", 28"	

Fig. 8-6. Commonly Available Sizes of Continuous Strip Forms

Remember that if you choose a length that must be produced on a rare cylinder size that only one or two printers have, you limit the availability of sources for this particular form. However, a few companies have "pull" or "stop-and-go" presses that can print any length. This is accomplished by pulling a web of paper intermittently through a series of percussion-type printing heads, rather than pulling the paper continuously around cylinders on which the printing plates are mounted.

Gang runs are worth knowing about because they enable you to combine several forms in one order, to get a package price. If you are ordering two or more forms having the same number of parts and the same color sequence, your printer can possibly produce them on a combined plate requiring only a single press run. You do not necessarily have to order identical quantities of forms combined in this manner. For instance, you may be able to order 7,500 of one and 2,500 of another, provided the printer can run them four-up through his press. He will do this by making a plate with three images of one form and one image of the other. Consult your large printing houses for more information on gang runs.

Another way to get good quality snapouts in small quantities is to buy blank sets all made up and have a flat-bed printer run the unit sets through his job press. Part one will look just like a regularly printed form, but the succeeding parts will be printed as carbon copies, which are suitable for internal use.

On continuous forms an advantage can sometimes be gained by using so-called "imprints" as opposed to "tailor-made" forms. The imprint is accomplished by overprinting stock tab forms with titles, rules, and columnar headings. The advantages are three-fold: faster delivery, lower price, and smaller minimum quantity. As a matter of fact, some printers will take an order for as few as 1,000 imprints, while the minimum quantity on an order for tailor-made forms is usually 5,000.

There are other printing processes and techniques, too numerous to mention here, with which the forms specialist should be familiar. He should know how numbering is done on both flat-bed and rotary presses. He should know that on the former enough space is required on the form for insertion of the numbering head; otherwise two press runs will be required. On the latter, the numbering is done from a separate device over which the web of paper passes. He should know whether his hectographic master form is to run from type, from a photoengraving, or from a wax plate. He should understand how special die-cutting of forms is done (as required to make the forms fit certain proprietary types of processing or filing equipment) and how it raises costs and limits sources and availability. He should realize the price advantages that can be obtained by using such stylized methods of construction or production as are represented by the salesbook type of form and the fan-fold method of production, particularly when large quantities are involved.

The forms designer should also keep his knowledge up to date on the uses and specifications for the printing of machine-recognizable characters. The most familiar of these is the MICR (magnetic ink character recognition) type which appears at the bottom of most bank checks. This type face is called E-13B by the American Bankers Association. The requirements for printing it are very exacting. It is best to get a spec sheet from the bank and deliver it, properly filled out, to a printer who is qualified to handle this kind of printing. More widely used in the future will be OCR (optical character recognition) types. These may vary for different makes of OCR readers. However, the U.S.A. Standards Institute has developed a standard type font for OCR forms, which is set forth in their Standard X3.17-1966. Character recognition type fonts are shown in Figures 8-7 and 8-8.

LAYOUT CHART FOR PAPER FORMS PRINTED WITH MAGNETIC INK

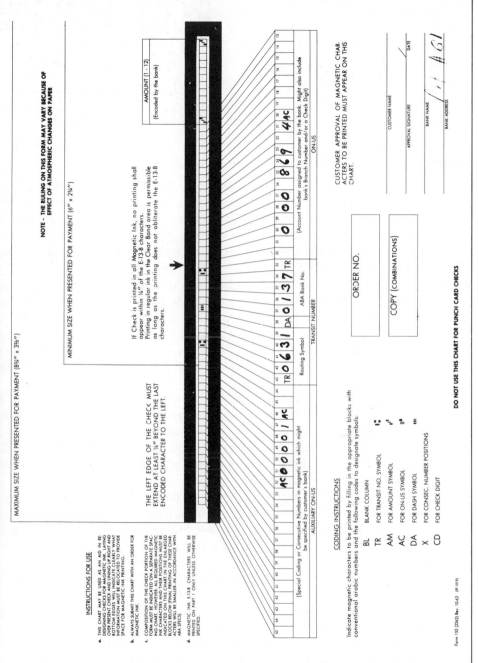

Fig. 8-7. MICR Specifications

ABCDEFGHIJKLM
NOPQRSTUVWXYZ
0123456789
· ⌐ : ⌐ = + / ⑀ * " & |
' - { } % ? ∫ ५ �ᚽ
ÜÑÄØÖÆ£¥

Fig. 8-8. Standard OCR Character Set

Relations With the Purchasing Department and the Printer

In a company that has no systems or forms control section, the purchasing department frequently exercises a certain amount of forms control through the efforts of the printing buyer. The quality and thoroughness of his work will, of course, vary according to his knowledge of forms design and construction, the extent of his authority, and the amount of time he can give to this activity.

Once a forms control group has been established, it should utilize the printing buyer's knowledge and experience as a valuable adjunct to its work. All contacts with forms salesmen and printers should be made through the buyer and should be handled entirely by him on all routine purchases. Direct contacts by the forms specialist with the printer or forms salesman are occasionally necessary to keep the forms man abreast of new developments and processes.

Direct contacts are also justified when the forms or systems man is working out a complicated procedure involving unusual forms constructions or provisioning. In such cases, the forms specialist and the salesman have to work together over details of design, specifications, and installation schedules, but all such contacts should be made with the knowledge and consent of the purchasing department.

It should never become the routine thing for forms control men to contact salesmen and place orders for every new item or rush requirement that comes up. That is what the buyer is being paid to do. If the buyer is a competent person, the necessity for direct contact between the forms specialist and the salesman should occur infrequently. Otherwise the forms man will merely succeed in downgrading himself into becoming a buyer's assistant, and the more important phases of his work will go neglected.

Many forms salesmen are ready and able to help their customers in designing forms and to assist them in working out systems problems, particularly where specialized forms are involved. Such efforts, if accepted, should be recognized by the purchasing department when it places the order for the form on which the salesman has put in a great deal of work. In some companies the systems group recommends the printer to the purchasing department, and he usually gets the order unless his price is abnormal. In other companies the forms control group is allowed to select the printer for the first order of a new form; thereafter, the purchasing department takes over.

Forms salesmen are often experts in forms design and construction, and they have the advantage of a wide knowledge of various companies' forms problems and applications. They can frequently be of immense help, but basically their interests are not identical with the customer's; therefore, they should not be given carte blanche to design all of a company's forms.

Checking Proofs

One of the forms man's jobs is checking the printer's proofs. This responsibility should be his alone, and should never be surrendered to the buyer, the stationery store clerk, or the department that requested the forms. Although the last-named will frequently ask to see proofs of new forms, a firm rule should be established that the using departments must submit definitive designs or approve copy prepared by the forms section before it goes to the printer. They must be convinced that they have to make a final decision on how they want the form before it is ordered; otherwise they will plague both the forms designer and the printer with "author's alterations."

After a final design has been approved by the requesting department, the responsibility rests with forms control to see that the printer produces a form that meets all the requirements. Sometimes it is a big responsibility, especially when the cost of an order runs into several thousand dollars, but this responsibility should not be weakened by sharing it with other departments.

Carbon and paper dummies should always be tested under actual operating conditions in the department where they will be used, and the legibility of carbon should be carefully checked before an approval is given to the printer. Corrected proofs should be returned to the printer promptly, together with the printer's original copy. If numerous corrections have been made, it might be a good idea to summarize them in a letter and request revised proofs.

Stockroom Control of Forms

The stationery stockroom is a microcosm of the production parts stockroom, with most of the same functions and the same problems. Activities include maintenance of stock records, processing and filling withdrawal requisitions, watching stock balances when they fall to or below minimum quantities, originating purchase requisitions or print shop orders for replenishment of stock, following up to obtain deliveries on time, receiving and storing material, and making inventory counts as required to verify stock record balances.

Here are some important principles to remember in running a stationery stockroom effectively and efficiently:

1. Fill requisitions promptly. This will save call-backs, follow-ups, personal pickups, and lost time caused by forms shortages in operating departments.

2. Establish regular schedules for the various requisitioning departments to follow. Almost without exception, various forms are used in fairly consistent quantities by every department of the company. They know their monthly or weekly requirements and can order in advance on specified days of the week or month.

3. Make deliveries of forms and stationery. When the requesting department sends a clerk with a requisition to pick up forms, a great deal of time is lost because the clerk has to wait for the order to be filled, the stationery store's personnel have to interrupt other activities so as not to keep the clerk waiting, and, finally, the clerk may have to make several trips to carry the forms and stationery back to his or her department. On the other hand, if requisitions are sent in by intracompany mail, the stockroom can organize its work efficiently so that no one is kept waiting while stock is assembled for each requisition, and stockroom personnel can accumulate orders for a particular area of the building or plant and deliver them on a single trip. This last point should be remembered in assigning schedules for departmental ordering, especially if the stockroom serves a large plant. Have all departments on the first floor, or the east wing, order on Monday (or the first Monday of the month), have the second-floor order on Tuesday, and so on. The schedule should be arranged so that all working days are not delivery days. Save two or three days of each week for the stockroom to devote to the work of storing incoming material and processing replenishment orders. More can be accomplished if the personnel do not have to jump from one job to another every half hour.

4. Watch fluctuations in usage. The stockroom can be a big help to forms control by noting any unusual changes in the usage of a form, such as increased or decreased quantities withdrawn, withdrawals by new departments, or returns of excess quantities to storage, as well as noting lack of movement of a form. An alert stockkeeper can thus prevent shortages from developing on items whose usage increases, can notify forms control or systems and procedures of an unannounced change in clerical procedures, and can start action to rid the stockroom of obsolete items.

5. Maintain special controls on critical items. The critical items in a stationery stockroom are the forms that take a long time to procure. Needless to say, these forms will be critical to the clerical operations that require them. Watch out for things such as multi-part carbon-interleaved forms, continuous tab forms, tab cards, check forms, and specially designed or die-cut record forms that must be obtained from a particular manufacturer

because of their propietary design to fit proprietary housing equipment (such as Kardex, Postindex, Acme, Visi Record, McBee, and Victor).

6. Do not overcontrol. The aforementioned control of critical items should normally be confined to less than 10 per cent of all forms. The preponderant forms are single sheets or cards that can be quickly procured, from your own print shop or from a local printer, with rather short lead times. If you have a print shop, do not even bother to keep a stock record of these items; just tie up a minimum quantity with a flash card telling you to reorder when the package is broken, or merely depend on the using department to give you a week's notice. At most, post withdrawals to the stock record only in bulk quantities, not for each individual withdrawal. If forms are received in cartons, upon opening one of the cartons, charge the whole quantity off on the stock record. However, on critical items, where usage fluctuations can upset things, a detailed record of withdrawals should be kept.

Minimum and Order Quantities

Too many companies pay high prices for forms because the using departments never take a realistic viewpoint about the lead time required for the economical purchase of printed matter. This is particularly true in companies lacking a forms control staff. One of the most important functions of the forms control group is to see that realistic lead times and economic order quantities are established for all company forms. Here, very tangible savings can be made. Granted they are not so great as the savings to be made in clerical processing time, but this is the kind of savings that is easiest to count and prove.

If management sees this kind of savings in dollars and cents, it is more likely to believe in the less tangible and more difficult-to-measure savings of systems work in forms processing improvements.

Lead times vary in different regions, at different times of the year, and according to the business climate, but an average pattern is represented in Table 8-1. An additional week or two of lead time should generally be provided for on new or revised forms to allow time for the printer's composition and your approval of the proofs.

What quantity of a form to order can be worked out by the same mathematical formula used for any type of stock item, based on factors of cost, storage space required, rate of consumption, cost of placing an order, cost of receiving and storing, shelf wear, and possibility of obsolescence. If you do not have time to go through all this, get quotes on a three-month, six-month, and twelve-month supply; then compare unit costs in these three quantities and check available storage space and the chance of obsolescence. If the price advantage is significant and you have sufficient funds in your budget, buy the six- or twelve-month quantity. Most printers will permit you to take partial deliveries of the forms as you need them, provided you pay them a small warehousing charge.

TABLE 8-1. SUGGESTED LEAD TIMES FOR REORDERING
PRINTED FORMS

Working Days Required

type of form	stationery stores	forms control	purchasing department	printer	delivery	total working days	suggested lead time (weeks)
Single-part (up to 11" x 17")	2	1	5	5	1	14	3
Single-part (over 11" x 17")	2	1	5	10	1	19	4
Hecto Masters	2	1	5	10	1	19	4
Tags	2	1	10	20	2	35	8
Envelopes (printed)	2	1	5	10	2	20	5
Multi-part Snapouts (less than 5,000)	2	2	10	20	2	36	8
Multi-part Snapouts (5,000 or over)	2	3	10	30	5	50	12
Continuous Strip	2	3	10	40	5	60	15
Tab Cards	2	1	5	20	5	33	8
Die-cut Cards	2	1	5	20	5	33	8

In computing minimums to be posted to stock record cards, make
them equal to the lead time requirements plus a thirty-day cushion for long
leads, and half that time for the short leads. This is needed to cover unforeseen delays in purchasing, printers' deliveries, and unexpected shortages, and should reduce the annual number of forms crises by about 90
per cent.

One simple way to figure order quantities is to relate them to minimums—say double or triple, depending on your stock policy. Thus, if the
minimum covers a sixty-day requirement, by ordering double the minimum
quantity you get a four-month supply.

Reordering Procedure

A tested procedure for reordering forms is as follows:

1. Storeroom clerk posts form numbers that have reached minimum to
   a "low stock notice," at the same time marking "LSN" on the stock
   record and entering the balance, minimum, and three-month's usage
   on the low stock notice (*see* Figure 8-9).
2. Stock handler makes counts and enters actual quantity in the column
   next to the stock record quantity.
3. Clerk pulls the purchase requisition traveler or prepares a purchase
   requisition form, entering all information except quantity and date
   required.

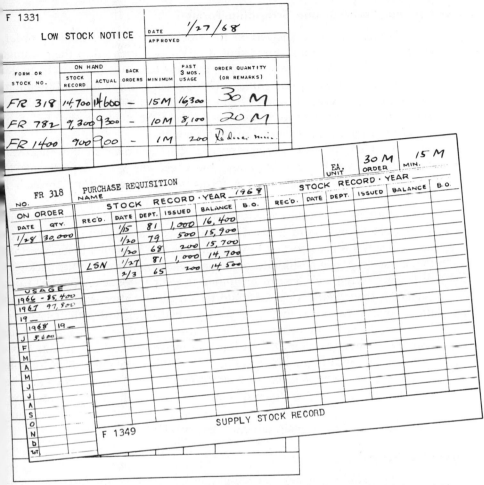

| F 1331 | LOW STOCK NOTICE | DATE APPROVED | 1/27/68 | | | | |

FORM OR STOCK NO.	ON HAND STOCK RECORD	ACTUAL	BACK ORDERS	MINIMUM	PAST 3 MOS. USAGE	ORDER QUANTITY (OR REMARKS)
FR 318	14,700	14,600	–	15M	16,300	30 M
FR 782	9,300	9,300	–	10M	8,100	20 M
FR 1400	900	900	–	1M	200	Reduce min.

PURCHASE REQUISITION

FR 318   NAME

STOCK RECORD · YEAR 1968

NO. ON ORDER		REC'D.	DATE	DEPT.	ISSUED	BALANCE	B.O.
DATE	QTY.						
1/28	30,000		1/15	81	1,000	16,400	
			1/20	79	500	15,900	
			1/20	68	200	15,700	
		LSN	1/27	81	1,000	14,700	
			2/3	65	200	14,500	

USAGE
1966 - 85,400
1967 97,800
19 –
1968 19 –
J 5,600
F
M
A
M
J
J
A
S
O
N
D
Tot

F 1349

| EA. UNIT | 30 M ORDER | 15 M MIN. | | | | |

STOCK RECORD · YEAR

REC'D.	DATE	DEPT.	ISSUED	BALANCE	B.O.

SUPPLY STOCK RECORD

Fig. 8-9. Low Stock Notice and Stock Record Forms

4. Supervisor or the forms control department reviews low stock notice, checks any questionable items, and enters order quantity and date required on the purchase requisition.

5. Low stock notice is returned to the storeroom clerk as notice that items have been ordered.

6. After action by the purchasing department, the storeroom clerk receives a copy of the purchase order and checks off the item on his low stock notice. He follows up the purchasing department on any items not ordered within ten days.

7. The forms control department, if it is necessary to hold up any requisition for further review or revision of the form, must check the balance in stores and in the using department at frequent intervals to make certain that the supply does not fall below the minimum lead time requirement.

Inventorying, Revising, and Scrapping Forms

Forms should be shelved in the stockroom in form number order, except that items in bulk stores should be cross-referenced to their storage location(s). When inventory is taken, all locations must be checked to get the correct count. Many companies have paid out much in toil and premium prices to rush in critical forms of which they had a plentiful supply all the time, but of which they were unaware because the stock handler failed to cover all storage areas when he made his count.

If an unexplained shortage occurs, the supervisor should check all transactions, search the storerooms, and check the using departments to try to find out where the missing forms went, before putting through a costly rush order.

When taking inventory, efforts should also be made to straighten out stock, remove shelf-worn items if unusable, see that serial-numbered items are correctly stacked (so that lowest numbers can be issued first), see that the oldest stock is in position to be moved out first, and watch for packages of forms covered with dust in testimony to their infrequency of use. Concurrently, the storeroom clerk should review all stock records and refer to the supervisor any items that have not been called for during the past year.

If a form is not being used, get rid of it. Ask the original user to approve an order to scrap it. If it has no salvage value, throw it out. Most carbon-interleaved forms are no good for anything else—not even for sale as waste paper. Obsolete continuous forms, however, can sometimes be used for proof runs and other listings that are usually run on stock tab paper. Old tab card forms can always be used by the data processing department in place of plain tab cards or "5081's."

Inspecting Forms

The stockroom supervisor should inspect all incoming forms for general appearance and, in particular, compliance with critical specifications. Complex jobs should always be checked with the forms control group to make certain there will not be trouble later when the forms are put into use. A good practice is to take samples from several cartons to the head of the using department and get him to test them under actual conditions. This is of particular importance on a new, specially designed form, and will help to resolve a problem before it becomes serious.

Here are some things to look for when inspecting forms:

1. Identical serial numbers on all parts of a multi-part form
2. Registration of the various parts of a multi-part form
3. Proper locations, sizes, and types of punchings and perforations
4. Legibility of carbon copies (tested under actual conditions of usage)
5. Correct sequence of parts in a multi-part form
6. Proper weights and grades of paper

7. Proper location of carbon strips and blockouts
8. Copy changes, when specified, on various parts of a multi-part form
9. Proper location of back printing, when called for
10. Proper gluing of snapout stubs
11. Correct packaging and labeling
12. Any special features listed on the form specification sheet

Continuous data processing forms should be checked to make sure the marginal pin-feed perforations are free of confetti, which may foul up the high-speed printer and may also be the cause of spotty impressions on carbon copies. The forms should also be examined to see that the pin-feed perforations in the carbons are in register with the perforations in the paper —otherwise the forms will not feed properly.

Although the list of points to be checked may appear imposing, the experienced forms man can usually spot the significant ones relative to a particular type of form, and can make an adequate inspection in a matter of a few minutes.

How to Handle Forms Problems and Crises

A career in forms control will bring the specialist face to face with many problems and crises, such as those caused by printer's mistakes, unexpected shortages, rush revisions, and crash programs, as well as those resulting from his own errors of omission or commission. The resourceful forms man will always have an ace up his sleeve to help him solve whatever problem arises. Through his knowledge of techniques and processes, his contacts with printers and form salesmen, and his familiarity with business systems requirements, he can usually work out whatever temporary solutions are necessary to keep clerical operations going while he gets things back on the track.

When a shortage of a critical form occurs, he will immediately find out whether the stockroom count is correct, whether any other departments have surplus quantities, whether some other form can be substituted, whether internally duplicated forms can be temporarily used, or whether work schedules can be rearranged; and, at the same time, he will put as much pressure as is required on the buyer and the printer to rush through a delivery in time to prevent a breakdown of operations. His responsibility is not merely to see that the necessary forms are provided "as soon as possible," but to see that they are provided in time to prevent a work stoppage.

To keep himself forewarned of the kind of thing that might affect the forms picture, it is necessary for the forms control man to obtain prompt notification of organizational or product changes, fluctuations in work loads, and changes in company names, locations, addresses, telephone numbers, and so forth.

A real poser for every forms man is a sudden shortage of multi-part snapout or continuous tabulating forms. In most cases, the latter can be improvised by using plain stock tab paper with stripped-in headings. An other method is to divide the continuous-strip tab paper, after it has gone through the tabulator, into individual forms, and to overprint each of these with the form design, using the company's offset machine. To improvise multi-part, carbon-interleaved snapout forms in a hurry is usually more costly. To prevent a work stoppage, it may be necessary to rush through a printing of the individual parts, obtain a supply of one-time carbon, and assemble these by hand into enough sets to keep the office operating until a partial delivery of the regular forms can be obtained. Concurrently with these emergency methods, all possible strings must be pulled to rush the delivery of the needed items. If the forms specialist and the forms buyer do not cry wolf too often, they will find that most of the forms manufacturers will make every effort to get them off the hook when a real emergency arises. Not to be overlooked are such aids to speedier delivery as pickups, air express shipments, rescheduling of other jobs with the printer, and authorizing the printer to deviate from the original specifications in order to shorten production time.

Shortages of printed tab cards are troublesome only on those forms that are originated outside the tab department, such as clock cards or job tickets. Usually, blank tab card forms can be picked up in a hurry and overprinted by the company print shop or local printer.

Hectographic master forms can be improvised by printing the form on duplicator paper and, using one sheet of duplicator paper as the master (backed up with a sheet of hectographic carbon), running off copies on the same forms. This method requires careful registration of the runoffs with the master and will produce shorter runs than can be obtained from a regular master unit.

Many other problems will arise that the experienced forms man will take in stride under his own *modus operandi*. Each problem that he handles not only equips him better to meet the next one, but broadens his knowledge of the various factors to be considered in forms designing and provisioning to reduce the number of crises to a minimum.

Reporting the Results of the Forms Control Program

The tremendous impact of the forms control program on clerical operations and costs may not be fully realized by management without an occasional report. At least quarterly, the forms group should prepare a summary of its operations, reporting the number of forms designed, revised, reviewed, rejected, and rendered obsolete. Sometimes it is helpful to keep a running balance of the total number of active company forms, especially when a campaign is under way to reduce the variety of forms in use.

Significant savings achieved in the cost of forms through redesign should also be reported. These are over and above the clerical savings that result from the installation of improved systems using improved forms.

which should more properly be reported by the systems group as systems savings.

In the report, the savings in forms costs should be projected on an annual basis, and the fact that these savings will recur in each subsequent year should not be understated. In the course of normal operations, the forms group may not be able to make annual savings in forms cost equivalent to the group's annual payroll, but the cumulative effect of these savings year after year will soon start to run well in excess of the annual cost of operations. Savings on forms purchased outside the company can be verified by checking the company's monthly reports of stationery expense. On forms printed by the company, the savings in costs are not usually as significant as the clerical savings, but if the cost of print shop supplies is set out as a separate item on the expense reports, it can serve as an index to savings in this area.

Improved forms-provisioning operations, as evidenced by safe minimum stock quantities, realistic lead times, and economical order quantities, will help to make definite inroads on costs. These can be reported by citing the decrease in rush orders (for which you often have to pay premium prices), and by showing the savings in unit prices achieved.

Once the forms control supervisor has everything going smoothly, he should look about for new areas in which to improve his performance. Some things that may add to the stature of his program are listed here:

- Survey of latest available tools for forms designing
- Cultivation of close relations with purchasing and stationery stores
- Studies of printing papers and their special qualities for various forms purposes
- Studies of latest developments in commercial printing equipment and processes
- Analysis of forms-provisioning and reorder trends to detect incipient changes in requirements
- Closer knowledge of such related fields as records management and reports control
- Studies of MICR- and OCR-type characteristics and printing specifications
- Up-to-date information on specifications and characteristics of all types of paper and forms handling equipment, such as typewriters, teletypewriters, special filing devices, inserters, signers, bursters, folders, collators, sorters, tab and high-speed printers, etc.

But the chances are that the sheer dynamics of the forms control program, as constantly buffeted by advanced systems techniques and equipment changes, will keep the forms manager stepping at a lively pace in order to stay abreast of the times.

9
Records Management

MILTON REITZFELD

Third Naval District,
United States Navy,
New York, N.Y.

MILTON REITZFELD, a native New Yorker, has spent the last twenty years as a management consultant to industry and government in improving business organization and procedures and conducting training programs. A pioneer in the field of paper work improvement and records management, he is the author of various articles and brochures, a member of the faculty of New York University's Management Institute, and a frequent lecturer at national conferences sponsored by professional societies. He is the director of the Management Assistance Office of the Third Naval District. He received the bachelor of science and master of business administration from New York University.

Some of Mr. Reitzfeld's professional affiliations include: the Systems and Procedures Association of America, the Records Management Association of New York, the Society of American Archivists, the Armed Forces Management Association, the American Management Association, the American Institute of Management, and the Interagency Records Administration Conference of New York.

INTRODUCTION

A major task confronting top management is the simplification of paper work burdens in order to release sorely needed time for creative thinking. Business, government, and social activity depend on accurate records. In this "paper dynasty," man is regulated by documents from the day he is born until the time he dies. Records are akin to man's memory and can be considered an extension of his brain. In them are stored knowledge from which decisions are made and plans are formulated. Small enterprises operate with a minimum of records. However, as ventures grow, the need for records multiplies. Executives removed from the scene of operations are in desperate need of information on business administration. Each increase in the control gap between executives and workers aggravates the need for communicating information. Without paper work most communication dies. Employees can receive no direction, performances cannot be reviewed, and managements cannot control.

The Costly Records Problem

The volume of records created and held by all business and government, and the enormous amount of time, money, and material that go into its preparation are staggering. The actual number of full-time clerical workers and the true cost of paper work are elusive figures. Nevertheless, there are considerably more persons in the United States engaged full time in the creation of records than there are farmers. Our annual paper work cost is a multi-billion dollar figure that exceeds the annual federal budget. A mountain of paper casts a shadow of inefficiency and waste over the land. Documents, the majority of which become worthless in less than five years, are stored in expensive containers in costly space long after they have fulfilled their purposes. Another less publicized problem is the lack of adequate documentation procedures. Unimportant items and policy matters dealing with the same subject are usually filed together. The large volume of records created makes it impossible for administrators to know the value of all records at any given time. Thus, unless unimportant records are systematically removed from files, basic decisions may be based on incorrect information.

Research Impeded

The affinity of research to recorded information is often ignored. The wisest talent can do little with a jungle of unclassified papers. There is a genuine need for civilization to locate, inventory, classify, and publish the vast amount of important records existent. Because of the lack of coordination in this area, not only is government and private research impeded, but there is also no real assurance that any research in process is not being duplicated elsewhere. The continuous efforts of archivists and librarians to gather and catalogue important information is a step in the right direction, but the support of industry and the public is necessary to achieve profitable results.

Results of a questionnaire directed to top-level research managements of one hundred metal companies indicated a high positive correlation between earnings and the degree of knowledge in the use of recorded information. The American Management Association took cognizance of the research paper work problem in an article by Paul W. Kearney:

> A defense plant maintained a costly staff of 800 engineers for original research on a multitude of projects. A management expert, wondering about the necessity for this outlay, investigated fifty sample research projects. To the amazement of the top officers, he demonstrated that in half the cases he could have obtained the same, or better, information by going to the library.[1]

[1] "Try Your Company Library First!" *The Management Review*, November, 1955, p. 764.

The Clerical Employee

The cost of paper work is appalling, and the quality of many records is notoriously poor. Inept administration and recording are responsible for a sizable percentage of business errors. Responsibility for the situation rests squarely on the shoulders of management. Conditions that would not be tolerated in production and service areas are often accepted in administrative departments. A cause of costly, inept paper work is the failure to secure and properly supervise skilled clerical employees.

The Records Barrier

The mushrooming expansion of federal, state, and local government and industry binds this age to paper work, L. F. Urwick gave vent to his thoughts on this matter by stating:

> There must, of course, be official records, but the recording procedure is a secondary one. It is the tendency to regard it as all-important which makes so many of our large businesses excessively bureaucratic, and it is because some chiefs elevate paper work to a position of significance which it should not occupy that they are overworked. Many managers spend too large a proportion of their time mulling over documents and too small a proportion cultivating good individual relations with their subordinates. The resulting lack of confidence between people forces them into an elaborate machinery of committees which further restricts their time for personal contacts.[2]

THE SCIENCE OF RECORDS MANAGEMENT. The underlying purpose of all records is the communication of or reference to necessary information. The absence of one of these reasons is not infrequent in paper work. The absence of both precludes the need for any documnt. By predicating the management of records on this simple doctrine and the use of the symbols R for records, C for communication, and Re for reference, the following formulae can be drawn for analysis:

$$R \text{ equals } C \text{ and/or } Re \qquad R \text{ equals } C \qquad R \text{ equals } Re$$

Documents that do not communicate necessary information, and that are not referred to, do not meet the definition of a record and should not be prepared. Papers that communicate required information should be destroyed as soon as the matter they contain is no longer referred to for business operations. An exception is material that must be held because of statutory requirements.

ORGANIZING A RECORDS MANAGEMENT PROGRAM. Although the typical executive despairs of the maze of paper he is required to handle, he

---

[2] L. F. Urwick, "The Manager's Span of Control," *Harvard Business Review,* May-June, 1956, p. 44.

usually has no knowledge of its cost. In order to win the top-level support necessary to establish a records management program, executives must be apprised of the amount of money and man-hours involved in creating records. Quick and dramatic presentation of paper work costs can be made by employing the statement of paperwork costs set forth in Table 9-1. The items under equipment, space, and supplies pose no difficulty if proper accounting records have been kept. However, arriving at personnel costs may require judgment and skill.

TABLE 9-1. ANNUAL STATEMENT OF PAPER WORK COSTS

I. *Personnel*

    A. Clerical Salaries $0,000,000
    B. Portion of Salaries of personnel engaged part
        time in paper work 000,000
    C. Portion of Salaries of executives engaged part
        time in paper work 000,000

        Total $2,000,000

II. *Equipment*

    A. Depreciation .... $ 000,000
    B. Rentals 00,000

        Total .... $ 240,000

III. *Space*

    A. Rent .... $ 000,000
    B. Maintenance 00,000
    C. Taxes 00,000

        Total .... $ 235,000

IV. *Supplies and Miscellaneous Expense*

    A. Stationery and Supplies .... $ 00,000
    B. Postage 00,000
    C. Telegraph and Cable Service 00,000
    D. Printing 000,000

        Total .... $ 525,000

        TOTAL PAPER WORK COSTS $3,000,000

Once the actual cost of paper work is known, it acts as the "open sesame" for business to engage in sound records management. A position of information engineer, records manager, or the like should be established at the highest possible level. The expense of creating records and their direct connection with the products and services sold make it imperative that records managers report directly to chief executives. Placing the position on a middle management level is one way of assuring that the program will never really get off the ground—or take it twice as long to achieve results. Still worse is tying a paper work management program to the apron strings of a disinterested official.

A description of the position of an information engineer would include the following duties:

1. Development of over-all information-gathering and information-processing organization, policies, and procedures
2. Administration of a continuous program for control, improvement, and simplification of recording
3. Establishment and current maintenance of paper work plans for activity expansion due to peacetime or wartime conditions, including the protection of records against disaster
4. Compilation of current business history
5. Direction of records depository operations
6. Promotion of records management via training and publicity campaigns
7. Authorization for the selection and purchase of office equipment
8. Presentation of staff assistance to operating personnel on all matters dealing with paper work

Managing records requires coverage on many fronts. It is absolutely vital that policy and procedure be developed for the following areas:

1. Creation and use of forms
2. Creation and use of reports
3. Creation and use of administrative issuances
4. Creation and distribution of correspondence
5. Paper work simplification in general
6. Filing and retrieval of documents
7. Procurement, utilization, and maintenance of office equipment
8. Storage and disposition of inactive record holdings
9. Protection against destruction and unauthorized disclosure of vital information

Forms Management

The most common and most widely used type of record is the form. It enjoys wide popularity because it requires less time and effort to prepare. This apparent ease of preparation allows countless numbers of unnecessary forms to be placed into circulation without any questioning upon the part of management. The relatively small amount of time involved to complete one form tends to screen the huge total required to complete them all. A program to control, improve, and simplify the use of forms, as well as of administrative issuances and reports, may be established by carrying out the following steps:

1. Inventory all forms (issuances and reports).
2. Classify each by function.
3. Evaluate each by need.
4. Analyze and improve the format and writing system.
5. Install functional and numerical files.

6. Centralize control over all reproduction equipment.
7. Audit all writing systems annually.
8. Hold periodic "crash" (review) projects as often as necessary.

A forms inventory is taken by requesting each department to submit two copies of each form in use. Forms should be submitted with the name of the using section, the number of copies prepared in one writing, and the annual usage written across the face of each document. As each set is received, it is arranged by department or section of origin. During this phase, sharp observation may disclose forms of common function with different formats. These are placed aside for further scrutiny during the evaluation step. Organization charts, procedure and policy manuals, and job descriptions are important tools for ascertaining the value of any form to an organization.

EVALUATING AND IMPROVING THE FORMS. The utility of a form can be determined by measuring it against the following criteria:

1. Does the record pertain to an authorized responsibility of the originator?
2. Is the information available in total or in part in some other accessible document?
3. Does the record serve a useful purpose to the originator, some other department, our customers, or the general public?

Forms that do not meet these standards are highly questionable and are set aside for discussion with department supervisors. Records not justified to the complete satisfaction of the survey committee are then removed from operation. Analysis for improvement in design and procedure is not undertaken until a form is deemed necessary.

Examination of the preparation, distribution, reading, and filing of forms is essential to create efficient design. Filling in data requires sufficient space for rapid, uninterrupted hand or machine writing. The use of manual, semiautomatic, or automatic writing methods depends on the nature, quantity, and value of the information to be recorded. The number of copies prepared at one writing and the total number used annually affect the type of paper, need for carbons, and the type and quality of printing. The level of management served and circulation outside the company confines are additional factors that require consideration.

Filing systems, housing equipment, retention periods, and rate of reference determine size and quality of paper. They also affect margins, headings, serial numbers, and types of punching. A well-designed form must be more than a utilitarian record: it must be attractive and command attention. There is a definite psychological aversion on the part of people to complete or read officious, ugly-looking records.

CONTROL NUMBERS AND FUNCTIONAL FILES. In addition to a definite descriptive title, each form is assigned a control number to indicate that it has been approved. Control numbers can be as simple or as detailed as necessary. Alphabetical prefixes and decimal endings can be employed to indicate functional areas. A functional file, which supplies important assistance to any forms improvement program, is established by placing all forms dealing with a common subject or function in folders or jackets under a common heading. Headings in a functional file reflect the nature of business in which any organization engages. A typical file might include the following broad titles, in addition to certain specialized subjects:

Accounting	Furniture and Fixtures	Real Estate
Administration	Inspection	Sales
Advertising	Legal	Security and Plant
Buildings	Management	Protection
Collections	Paper Work	Services
Communication	Personnel	Shipping
Equipment and	Production	Travel
Supplies	Purchasing	Utilities

Under each broad category additional subdivisions may be created as needed. A handy numerical file that acts as a cross index to the functional file may be set up simply by filing a copy of each form according to its control number.

CONTROLLING REPRODUCTION EQUIPMENT. A forms control procedure will remain effective only as long as the administrative, service, and production departments refrain from unauthorized operation of duplicating equipment. Uncontrolled reproduction devices allow a procedure to be circumvented via unauthorized printing. Whenever possible, remove and centralize all duplicating equipment, and establish a system to insure that only requests that bear the approval of the forms analyst will be honored. Because of a need for reproduction equipment in certain standard operating procedures, it is not always possible to centralize all printing machinery. In such instances, technical control may be centralized under one official.

STORING AND ISSUING FORMS. Storing and issuing forms should not be the cause of any elaborate warehousing and accounting system. Completing and processing forms represents a large investment in personnel, but the printing cost is a mere fraction of that expense. Intricate inventory and accounting procedures to control blank forms are wasteful. The simpler the system, the better. Charging off the entire cost of printing forms to a specific expense account should eliminate bookkeeping details. Usage figures to establish reorder levels can be obtained from operating departments.

PLACING THE PROGRAM IN MOTION. When all forms have been inventoried, reviewed, and simplified, a procedural instruction (see Administrative Issuances) is prepared and distributed to all departments, establishing the following routine:

1. All requests for new forms to be submitted to a forms control desk with a rough draft of the proposed form and its operating procedure
2. All requests to be checked against a functional file for duplicate items

3. All operating procedures to be analyzed to determine the "one best way"
4. All approved forms to be assigned an identification or control number
5. All approved forms to be designed for expeditious preparation and maximum utilization

Forms have a tendency to outgrow their usefulness. Failure to follow up approved forms results in an accumulation of unnecessary, obsolete paper work. The validity of previously approved forms and writing systems can be detected by analyzing specific forms on a scheduled basis.

Reports Management

Reports are the most vital tools of administration, and represent key information fed back from all working levels. This information feedback is necessary to determine and compare the status of every operating business and government. Management policies and decisions are usually based on the information carried back via reports. Information feedback systems depend upon many daily records, some prepared exclusively for summarization into periodic reports. Reports are therefore the most expensive type of records created. When reports are canceled, much more is saved than the obvious time and effort spent in summarizing and analyzing data. It is the elimination of countless daily feeder records that pays big dividends when reports are properly controlled. Since reports cover the entire scope of business and are the backbone of many decisions, it is imperative that they be current, simple, and clear.

REPORTS CONTROL SYSTEM. The procedure to control reports is organized along the same lines as the system to control forms. An inventory of reports is made. Each report is then evaluated as to need, makeup, scope, and clarity. It is important to assure that reports are requested from recognized authorities and that the documents are not the result of empire building on the part of requesting offices or absent-mindedness on the part of receiving offices. This is entirely possible when management does not have sufficient time to review all reports, or has failed to notify departments of a report that is no longer necessary.

The contents of reports materially suffer when preparing offices do not have written guides to aid them. Reports submitted by more than one department show wide variance in scope and detail when standards that cover purpose, source for obtaining information, and method of abstracting data are not available. Preparation instructions are also necessary to indicate receiving offices and submission dates. Basic instructions for sound, economical reporting systems are:

1. Be brief and to the point.
2. Submit timely, accurate information.
3. Employ a format to insure the minimum amount of reading and writing time.
4. Include summaries with all voluminous reports.

REPORT INDEX AND TICKLER FILE. After eliminating, combining, and simplifying them to the maximum extent, approved reports are assigned control numbers. Numerical, functional, and follow-up files are established, and the index or inventory is published. A reports index lists all documents alphabetically by subject matter, and includes such items as due date and the authorizing, preparing, and receiving offices. It is an invaluable reference and research aid and is most useful in the indoctrination of new executives. In addition to samples of each report and instructions for its preparation, the functional file contains cost analyses for each report. These show the approximate number of feeder records required, the cost of each feeder record, the cost to summarize, and the total cost of each report.

REPORTING BY EXCEPTION. Even though reports convey information necessary to the conduct of business, they may actually be unnecessary. Strange as this may seem, it is very easy to prove. Many reports convey operating conditions of some sort or other. These usually fall into three broad categories: normal, above normal, and below normal. Why normal conditions are ever reported is one of the unsolved mysteries of business administration. Management should be concerned only with improving unsatisfactory conditions and taking lessons in application from those that are better than satisfactory. Thus, if written standards are developed to describe normal or satisfactory conditions, and departments are instructed to report only when these situations deviate from the norm, the absence of a report would indicate the absence of any problems. Preparing criteria to depict satisfactory circumstances poses no problems for many measurable business functions. Others will require much thought and analysis. The ever-changing interests of business and government and their constant growth necessitate that standards be constantly amended. When reporting is conducted on the exception basis, it is estimated that 30 to 50 per cent of costly report documents can be eliminated.

ACTIVATING THE REPORTS MANAGEMENT PROGRAM. A plan to manage and improve reports requires promulgating instructions calling for:

1. All requests for new reports to be submitted to a reviewing authority together with written justification and preparation instructions in draft form
2. All new requests to be checked with the functional file for duplication
3. All new reporting procedures to be reviewed for simplification
4. All newly approved reports to be assigned control numbers

Administrative Issuances

A large section of business is guided by directives and memoranda generally referred to as administrative issuances. This is still another portion of the over-all paper work mass and represents large current and future clerical costs. The immediate cost of administrative issuances stems from the fact that they are products of the efforts of middle and top management.

These records cause future paper work and technical operations, and as such represent far more dollars and cents than are normally considered. They take on many names. Some common terms are: instructions, memoranda, circulating letters, operating sheets, and standard operating procedures. Issuances fall into three basic communication channels:

1. Those that distribute policy
2. Those that disseminate "how to do it" information
3. Those that release general news items

Since administrative issuances are the bases for action at all levels of employment, they should be built on a structure of terse, simple language. Whenever they convey policy or procedural information they must clearly state and "sell" the purpose for which they have been issued. Policies and procedures that do not have the understanding and support of employees will receive only lip service.

Pyramiding departments causes overlapping of authority and is not uncommon in large organizations. When this condition is present, conflicting directives dealing with the same subject are likely to be issued to operating employees—with disastrous results. Administrative issuances should be distributed on one basis only—*the need to know.* "Shotgun" circulation instead of selective distribution only serves to increase clerical costs and deter personnel from normal routines. Distributing issuances without control is welcomed by empire builders. In addition to establishing files and employing personnel to service unnecessary information, many are bold enough to participate in and carry out duties entirely out of their sphere of responsibility. Whenever administrative issuances are a sizable portion of a company's paper work, it is a good business practice to install methods to control and coordinate these records.

A CONTROLLING SYSTEM. Except for some minor changes, the steps for establishing an administrative issuance control system are the same as those employed to install the forms and reports control procedures. All policy and procedural guides are inventoried, classified by subject matter, and sorted by function. Each communication is reviewed to determine justification, conflict, duplication, obsolescence, and ambiguity. Issuances that cannot be justified are eliminated, those that overlap are combined, and those that are ambiguous are clarified.

A STANDARD FORMAT AND CLASSIFICATION SCHEME. Issuing directive material in standardized format facilitates rapid preparation and speeds the reading of data. It makes possible quick scanning of records and enables busy executives to skip over information deemed unimportant. An excellent issuance format is the type used in the armed forces. It includes space to indicate type of issuance, originating office, an abbreviated list of addressees, subject of the issuance, and the reason for issuance, as well as the body of text. An important aspect of the issuance format is a cancellation clause. The issuance conveying ephemeral information requires a cancellation date to prevent the accumulation of worthless memoranda. The voluminous amount of policy and procedural information required by larger organizations demands a classification system that will promote rapid retrieval and act as an identification scheme to prevent "bootleg" issuances. The Dewey Decimal System is excellent for this purpose. It is suggested that policy issuances be titled "directives," procedural issuances "instructions," and general news issuances "memoranda." Since more than one directive or instruction may be issued on any given subject, it is necessary to separate the basic classification number by a hyphen, and then follow it by a number indicating the numerical order of issuances published. Thus, directives or instructions may be classified as 5000-1, 5000-2, 5000-3, and so on. Because of the one-time nature of memoranda, and the fact that they are canceled when no longer necessary, subordinate numerical series are not recommended for these records. Different memoranda dealing with the same subject matter that may be in effect at any one given time are identified by the addition of the date of publication and issuing office.

DISTRIBUTION LISTS. The responsibilities and functions of business personnel vary with positions. Top policy and confidential information are not widely circulated, nor are the routines of business a matter for key officials. Among other objectives, an issuance system aims for minimizing the amount of paper work handled by all employees. Distribution lists that foster selective circulation are developed by coding departments, sections, and job titles. For example, the letter "A" might indicate all personnel in the administration department, and "A1" the department chief. Material to be released throughout the company might be addressed "to all personnel." An example in which job titles alone are used for distribution lists might be the address "to heads of all departments." The use of codes is recommended for varied and complex organizations. They also aid in routing mail.

FILING ADMINISTRATIVE ISSUANCES. Directives and instructions should not be filed with other types of business records. Memoranda should never be stored in closed file cabinets. Short-term records of this nature are best kept on clip boards and pinned to bulletin boards so that they may be removed and destroyed when cancellation dates reach maturity. When directives and instructions are distributed on a "need to know basis" and filed functionally in loose-leaf binders, a series of policy and procedural manuals are created in the exact detail necessary for each position title. The addition of new and revised issuances assures the administration that these key publications are always up to date. Two copies of all instructions and directives should be maintained in a company information center or library, from which they may be withdrawn temporarily by local offices that do not use them often enough to require separate maintenance.

Lists of instructions and directives published, including the distribution of each document, are issued periodically. This enables holders of policy and procedure manuals to keep their publications current. At least once a year, general indexes to all current instructions and directives are published. These are placed in binders for use as rapid reference media.

PLACING THE PROGRAM IN ACTION. After all preparatory steps have been completed, the continuing system is introduced in the form of an instruction setting forth the following requirements:

1. Submission of new issuances in draft form to a designated staff authority
2. Review of the issuing offices' functions to determine authority for promulgation
3. Check of new issuances against a current index to prevent conflict of interest, duplication and so on
4. Review of the accompanying distribution list to prevent excess circulation
5. Modification of language in the text to enable understanding and compliance
6. Simplification of procedures outlined in the document to reduce the cost of paper work

Correspondence Management

In terms of volume, the letter is second only to the form. Except for the report, the letter is the most expensive document produced. Our economy's great need for communication is revealed in the billions of letters, radiograms, and telegrams that are transmitted each day. Most letters are personally dictated by key or senior executives. Theirs are the most valuable man-hours available to any organization. The correspondence function is broad, and encompasses other duties in addition to the dictating, transcribing, and transmitting of information. It includes the necessary chores of reading and storing information.

LETTER CONTENTS. Letters are nothing more than conversation reduced to writing. They must, therefore, convey facts and thoughts in simple, readable, and understandable language. Ambiguous correspondence only serves to confuse readers, and creates the need for further explanatory and costly paper work. The archaic third person form still used in the correspondence of some government agencies and commercial firms should be discarded along with obsolete material and equipment. Many persons hesitate to use the first person style on the grounds that their statements represent organizational policy and that the addressees will interpret such usage as representative only of the writer's ideas. However, it is a recognized fact that most executives are delegated emissaries, and their statements are actually implementations of some predetermined organizational policy. Correspondence should be written in a positive vein; use of the first person helps to attain this condition. Nothing is more distressing than to receive letters written in a negative fashion, skirting around issues and leaving the addressee wondering what his correspondent has in mind.

The negative approach is employed as a face-saving device when a correspondent does not wish his lack of knowledge on a specific matter to be clearly stated in his reply. It is also used to deny requests indirectly, and requires the reader to wade through a series of stilted paragraphs only to find that his request has been denied. Handling every piece of correspondence as if it were the only document between survival and failure is foolish. There are, of course, vital policy letters that must take into consideration all the facets of diplomacy, politics, and protocol. However, these constitute a minute fraction of administration and should pose no real paper work problem. Persons seeking information that is not available should be told the facts immediately in short, courteous letters. When company policy forbids the release of certain information, the resolution should be directly stated in polite fashion.

SEMANTICS. The world has yet to master the art of written language. A modern Tower of Babel exists in the realm of written communication. There is little difficulty in conveying thoughts orally. No matter what levels of intelligence are concerned, one usually adjusts his language to the other's. However, circumstances are reversed when it comes to reducing thoughts to writing. The prose of chemists, doctors, engineers, scientists, and other technical professionals are often difficult for laymen to comprehend. Technicians fail to take into consideration the lack of familiarity addressees have with certain technical terms. Composing records in such fashion has the effect of restricting rather than communicating information. Unless this is specifically desired, the restriction of information defeats the very idea of communication and paper work.

Short sentences composed of simple, positive, monosyllabic words are far more effective than highly technical or ornate language. Mr. Average Executive spends much of his time reading, usually at a rate of less than three hundred words a minute. There is no better way of getting written ideas across to him than brief, positive correspondence. The best method for reducing the amount of time executives spend in reading correspondence and other records is to prevent paper work from reaching their offices. Another solution is to require administrators to improve their reading rate to at least five hundred words per minute. By concentration and practice, this speed can easily be attained by the average person.

CORRESPONDENCE PRODUCTION. The average stenographer is not engaged full time in correspondence production. A good deal of her time is spent in answering the telephone, acting as receptionist, filing records, and in other miscellaneous duties. The compensation to stenographers is based primarily on the ability to take and transcribe dictation accurately and rapidly. A corporation employing a large number of stenographers would do well to investigate the amount of time they spend in non-stenographic work and the possibility of assigning that work to lower salaried personnel. One method is to emphasize the very speciality for which stenographers are employed and establish stenographic and typing pools. The average letter production rate and the total number of letters required each year may be obtained via work measurement studies and business forecasts. The number of stenographic positions required to staff the stenographic pool is calculated from these figures. Except for secretaries assigned to top-ranking officials, stenographers and typists may then be centralized for full-time acceptance of dictation and typing of finished copy.

A centralized secretarial department or stenographic pool improves the production of correspondence by providing:

1. Full-time supervision of stenographers
2. Maximum utilization of stenographic personnel
3. Measured correspondence production
4. Standard operating procedures for dictation and transcription
5. Formal training of new employees
6. Personnel reserve for peak loads and vacation periods
7. Improved utilization of correspondence production equipment

FORM LETTERS. Devoting valuable time and effort to personally dictate and transcribe routine, stereotyped correspondence is uneconomical. The use of form letters is strongly recommended for such information. Form letters may be designed to cover one or a variety of situations. They can be printed to match any type of writing equipment so that salutations, addresses, and other changing data may be inserted in a manner which will make the entire document appear to be personally typed. The United States General Services Administration has developed common standards for using form letters in government agencies. These standards appear equally applicable to many business correspondence operations.

A form letter is appropriate if:

It is about a routine business or informational matter.
It is not, in fact, a personal letter.
It is not a message that will bring grief or keen disappointment to the reader.

On the basis of a three-month supply, a form letter is economical if:

Line count is:	Monthly usage is:
5	30 or more
10	20 or more
15	15 or more
20 or more	20 or more

CORRESPONDEX. Pattern or guide letters are a further refinement of form letters without any of their inherent disadvantages. Pattern letters can be advantageously employed when individual letter production is low and outgoing correspondence reaches a volume of at least 250 letters per week. Each pattern letter prepared is assigned a code relating to the subject matter and is typed on card stock and filed visibly by code number. An index by subject is prepared and distributed with each set of guide letters. Visible sets of pattern letters or paragraphs, more commonly known as "Correspondex" in many government agencies, are placed on the desks of typists and stenographers. A properly executed Correspondex procedure can reduce as much as 50 per cent of executive dictating and reading time. With a Correspondex system, routine mail requiring replies bypasses top and middle management. It is reviewed, instead, by clerk-correspondents who note the number of the pattern reply, together with any changing data that must be added, on the face of each incoming letter. Letters are sent to the secretarial pool, where the proper reply cards are flipped and the answers are typed. The total time involved in personally dictating a letter may be from a few minutes to several hours or more. A pattern letter reply of 175 words can be completely processed in less than ten minutes. When Correspondex copy is reduced to punched cards, punched tape, or magnetic tape for use with robot typewriters, letter writing becomes automatic. Correspondex eliminates the need for dictation and stenographers.

LANGUAGE STYLE. Executives who sign correspondence prepared by staff assistants must exercise particular care and judgment. It is wrong to demand an exact style of language. Perfectionists often return letters to subordinates for improvement in language style, but correspondence that is readily understandable and couched in good grammar should be approved. Certain personalities express themselves in writing better than others. This should not be cause for average letter writers to be criticized. The administrator who continues to be a slave to one style of language may find his staff beginning to "lose" letters that are continually returned for improvement. People improve their writing with experience and practice. As they mature, they develop individual styles of their own. To restrain this affects personality, production, and morale.

MAIL AND FILE SYSTEMS. Two common paper work functions that never seem to keep pace with modern simplification techniques are the distribution of mail and the filing of records. Mail should be routed in straight-line fashion direct to action or information desks without regard for any organizational hierarchy based on the principle of management by exception. Only those letters containing matters of extraordinary importance are fit subjects for routing to top management and key individuals. Adherence to this philosophy keeps the desks of senior administrators free of routine papers. Direct routing is accomplished by the use of a guide arranged by subject matter and position title.[3]

Files have the unusual faculty of duplicating themselves throughout an organization. This would not be half so bad if it merely increased record-keeping costs. However, when duplicate storage exists, files tend to overlap one another and fail to document accurately entire transactions in one

---

[3] M. Reitzfeld, "The Mail Routing Guide," *The Office*, November, 1951, pp. 58-153.

place. Thus, when one refers to a folder concerning a completed action, he cannot obtain a complete picture without first referring to other records, other files. In the large company, this is difficult and time consuming. Complete transactions must be documented in one dossier even if it is necessary to merge other folders at a specific time following the event. An effective way to eliminate duplication in files is to decentralize all files belonging to one unit and to centralize those used by more than one unit. Then an inventory by title and location is made, published, and distributed.

Paper Work Simplification

Even under rigidly controlled systems, paper work often begets more paper work. Ambiguous, inaccurate, or tardy records foster explanatory or corrective documents. When paper work is uncontrolled, clerical empires quickly form. The burdensome cost of record making and the large percentage of errors prevalent in the finished product are caused by paper work's own complicated processes. Ornate, overlapping, complicated routines are customary in the average administrative division.

Information is the lifeblood of every organized enterprise and government. Paper work is created to maintain, control, process, and transmit that information. Therefore, before any effective program can be established to improve and simplify paper work, it is essential to determine what information is required. Business planning is another important factor, since it is just as easy to create an organization that operates on a minimum of paper work as one that requires the maximum. For example, in one instance, centralization of an operation might eliminate the recording, storage, and transmission of data. In another situation, decentralization of a section might exclude one set of files by utilizing the existing records of a branch, contractor, customer or the like.

COMPOSITION OF INFORMATION (PAPER WORK) SYSTEMS. There are two basic methods for simplifying paper work. The first is to ignore all existing organization and systems and determine the exact information necessary to engage in business, and, from this information model, devise organization, policies, and procedures to circulate the right information to the right person at the right time. The second is to analyze existing procedures, weed out unnecessary steps, improve pertinent operations, and improve work flow. This approach also requires review of organization and policies for the elimination of duplicated, unauthorized, or useless information. The former, or *work revolution,* approach makes a clean break with custom and tradition to produce outstanding, economical record systems. It requires absolute support from all levels of management and employees. The latter, or *work simplification,* approach improves paper work in a piecemeal, evolutionary fashion. Constant chipping away at ingrained, obsolete routines is required.

FLOW AND PROCESS CHARTS. Analyzing procedures step by step can become an arduous and complicated task. To simplify the portrayal of

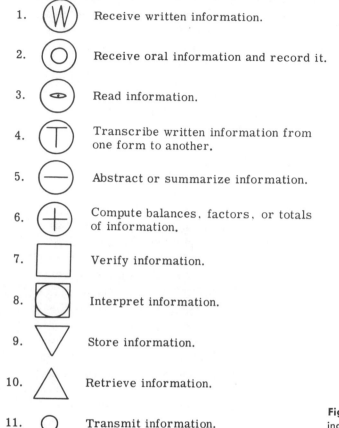

1. Receive written information.

2. Receive oral information and record it.

3. Read information.

4. Transcribe written information from one form to another.

5. Abstract or summarize information.

6. Compute balances, factors, or totals of information.

7. Verify information.

8. Interpret information.

9. Store information.

10. Retrieve information.

11. Transmit information.

Fig. 9-1. Symbols for Charting Paper Work Steps

procedures and work flow, various symbols have been created as a short-hand and a visual aid. When procedures are presented in charts made up of these symbols, duplicate and unnecessary operations are more easily observed. Using these symbols as a base, the symbols depicted in Figure 9-2 for charting the eleven paper work steps were designed.

QUALITY AND PRODUCTIVITY. Two reasons for engaging in work improvement are low productivity and quality. To determine the true status of these conditions, it is necessary to measure and inspect the number of transactions or documents completed. There are several methods to measure and inspect work. Continued examination and measurement should lead to fair production and quality standards. When work load forecasts are compared with production standards, equitable personnel and supporting budgets are prepared. When production and quality standards are available, individual employee performance can be properly rated.

INSPECTING QUALITY. Incorrect paper work leads to errors in administration, production, and sales, and, finally, to monetary losses. Records are often inspected at each step in a procedure and are then given a final, over-all check when they are completed. Such inspection is costly and is no guarantee of good quality. No matter how many inspection stations are established, perfect accuracy at all times is impossible. Boredom and fatigue take their toll in any inspection process. As management strives to increase paper work quality by inspection alone, costs may climb out of proportion to the value of the record itself. For example, time and effort spent in revealing strike-overs in typed interoffice memoranda should be the basis for criticism by a cost-conscious management. On the other hand, errors in production and shipping orders are intolerable. It follows that a degree of accuracy for all types of paper work must be determined. Policies and methods may then be developed to maintain these pre-established quality standards. The best and most economical way to sound quality control is by sampling methods rather than 100 per cent inspection.

Office Equipment

The proper use of office equipment increases productivity and quality, and reduces paper work costs. Improper application of office equipment complicates record making and increases costs. Procurement of paper work equipment and supplies represents large outlays of money, and should be carefully screened by competent personnel. The annual sales of the office equipment and supply industries is a multi-billion dollar figure, which again points up the extreme cost of paper work. The sole objective of these two industries is to serve the paper work function. Controlling the selection and use of office equipment and supplies is another essential of a sound records management program.

OFFICE EQUIPMENT PROGRAM. By installing a formal office equipment program, another link is forged in a chain to control rising paper work costs. The first requirement is an inventory of all furniture and equipment. A form should be designed that lists the name, description, manufacturer, supplier, serial number, date of purchase, and location in the company. Provision can be made for inspection and maintenance data, depreciation, and residual and scrap value. Forms may be designed for individual items or for many like items, as for example a master form for all typewriters of a certain make and model. The procedure is installed by means of an instruction that requires requisitions to be reviewed by the paper work methods staff against proposed usage and an inventory of material on hand. Approved requisitions are turned over to the purchasing unit for procurement.

There is a vacuum in the field of operating standards for office equipment. Some governmental agencies and a few of the larger corporations have made attempts in this direction, but the application of operation criteria in purchasing equipment is far from universal. Although this type of research is sorely needed and should be encouraged, a simpler method of insuring that equipment meets company needs is to buy on approval. Many equipment manufacturers and distributors will place their products in organizations for a trial period without any obligations on the part of that organization. Inspection of equipment on a regularly scheduled basis will reveal deficiencies that, when repaired, will prevent breakdowns and work stoppages and protect investments. By posting all repair costs to inventory cards and by periodically reviewing these records, replacement or continuation of office equipment is judiciously decided.

MICROFILM. The technique for reducing records by $\frac{1}{15}$ to $\frac{1}{60}$ their normal size on the almost perfect medium known as microfilm plays an important role in many phases of paper work management. The obvious application is the reduction of a mountainous mass of records to film in order to effect sizable reductions in storage costs. The microfilm process is much more versatile than mere physical reduction of documents. Recording information on film supplies more or less permanent records that resist deterioration. High-speed, automatic film processors rapidly produce inexpensive copies of negatives, positives, and photo prints to make microfilming an economical reproduction technique.

Automatic microfilm cameras can, in certain procedure applications, eliminate the need for manually reading and recording information. Using specially coded microfilm with specially designed automatic reading and printing equipment results in an automatic information filing and retrieval system. Microfilm and other forms of photo records are usually admissible in courts as secondary evidence when the destruction or the loss of original records can be legally accounted for, or it can be shown that such records have been destroyed as a regular course of business. However, federal law prohibits photographic reproduction of many records, such as:

1. Obligations or securities of the United States government
2. Stamps, paper money, coins, and other representations of value, of whatever denomination, which have been or may be issued under any Act of Congress
3. Licenses—drivers', marine, amateur radio operators'
4. Certificates of citizenship and naturalization, immigration papers, passports, draft cards

Like any other management tool, microfilm is no panacea for all paper work problems. Misuse of the technique leads to poorer methods and higher costs rather than to improved methods. Some shortcomings that sometimes preclude the microfilming of records are:

1. Cost of preparing (removing from files and reports and assembling in the desired order) records for filming may be higher than the cost to store them.
2. Detailed indexes may be required to expedite reference to specific portions of the film.
3. Microfilm cannot be adequately viewed with the naked eye in its basic form; readers or magnifiers are required.
4. Reference to microfilm may be slower and more complicated than reference to the original records.

Interfiling of records requires film splicing when roll film is employed. Standard-size records that are filed loosely, in simple numerical or alphabetical systems, are relatively inexpensive to film with automatic cameras that photograph thousands of documents in a few hours. Bound registers and complicated files require unfastening and sorting before they can be recorded. When the size of documents vary, they usually must be hand fed into the camera. Standard-size documents can be automatically fed to speed the process. Oversized documents are filmed on non-automatic equipment, and require special handling. Records that are to be kept a relatively short period of time are not proper subjects for microfilming when space saving is the sole objective.

Rapid microfilm filing and retrieval systems can be developed with the use of cut, rather than roll, film. Individual cut frames of film are fitted in die-cut apertures, or strips are attached to card stock or in specially designed glassine envelopes, and so on. Each of these microfilm frame-holding records provides a space for the description of the film. Records are available in standard sizes; reference indexes are not required. Special readers for reading mounted microfilm are available from most microfilm camera distributors. In addition to using 16, 35, or 70 mm film as the storage media, reduced copy may be reproduced through offset printing on standard size sheets of paper, or as photographic prints on index card stock. Individual 16 mm photographic paper prints with gummed backing can also be obtained for pasting to standard paper forms, cards, and the like. For example, an entire fifty-page report can be stored on one 3″ x 5″ index card. Certain publications are available in one or more forms of microfilm from organizations that specialize in this service.

Records Disposal, Storage, and Protection

Business executives frequently procrastinate in the disposition of old records. There is no doubt about the difficulty of ascertaining the value of a given record when documents are produced on a mass basis. The possibility of requiring in the future some record, already destroyed, is another cause for reluctance on the part of business to destroy old records. However, as records increase and take up expensive cabinet and floor space, decisions must be made before saturation points are reached. Frequently, the decision is made to retain all the records and move the older files to some less desirable areas, such as the attic or cellar. Paper kept in dark, damp areas deteriorates because of climate, insects, and rodents. Overexposure to the sun will bleach out certain inks. Another solution is to rent space from one of the commercial record centers available in most large metropolitan areas. The opposite solution is to destroy all records of a certain vintage. Destroying records in one fell swoop may purge vital as well as unimportant documents.

Eliminating obsolete files is no easy task. Criteria must be established for the removal of superannuated information. Periodic review of inactive records by a records committee is one course of action taken by many organizations. Although better than allowing obsolete documents to continue to accumulate, a disposal program dependent on the decisions of a periodic board often lags behind the company's actual disposal needs. There are also difficulties that are encountered owing to the lack of written disposal standards. Although the values of records change with the passage of time, their importance does not fluctuate often enough to necessitate calling a meeting each time old records are removed from the files.

RECORD RETENTION SCHEDULE. A schedule of established retention periods for each type of record is the best way to clean house continually in the filing section. Each record series must be evaluated in terms of its importance to the functions and objectives of the organization. Records that transmit information that is of no concern to business operations now or in the future ought to be destroyed after their contents have been noted. Records that contain information actively referred to for the conduct of business are kept in operating areas until it is no longer necessary to refer to this information. Records that contain information occasionally referred to for the conduct of business are kept in inexpensive storage areas or record centers. Exceptions are documents that must be kept, regardless of usage, by public law. A summary of a detailed description for preparing a records retention schedule states: [4]

1. Hold an opening conference with all department heads
2. Inventory all records by type, quantity, location, method of file, and type of storage container
3. Determine the value of each record series
4. Prepare a rough draft of the schedule
5. Submit the draft for approval by top management and all department heads at a final conference
6. Publish, issue, and add to the schedule

Points to earmark in the flow are:

1. When records are prepared, why records are prepared, who prepares them
2. When subordinate records are prepared (subordinate records that hinge upon this primary record), why they are prepared, who prepares them
3. When records are posted to other documents, why they are posted, who posts them
4. When records are summarized

---

[4] M. Reitzfeld and D. Merriman, "Records Management," in *Workshop for Management: Proceedings of 1954 Systems and Procedures Association of America—Annual Systems Meeting* (New York: Management Magazines Inc., Book Division), pp. 185-213.

Seven values to help determine retention periods:

1. Values for administrative use
2. Values for legal use
3. Values for fiscal use
4. Values for policy use
5. Values for operating use
6. Values for historical use
7. Values for research

GOVERNMENT REGULATIONS. From time to time the *Federal Register* publishes a summary of the various record retention requirements of all federal agencies. A commercial index on federal record keeping requirements is available from the National Records Management Council, New York City. Regulations of local and state organizations are obtainable by corresponding with the proper records management officials.

A CENTRAL DISPOSAL PROGRAM. Once the schedule is prepared, it is promulgated in the form of a company instruction and is applied to all records. The attitude that records belong to the department in which they are created or maintained must be dispelled. All records are the property of the mother organization and should therefore come under the technical control of the paper work manager. In the larger organization, a records disposal officer is added to his staff, along with a forms management officer, reports management officer, and others. He is responsible for coordinating the company-wide disposal of records. He may also be assigned the function of operating a records depository, or that duty may be the responsibility of still another position. There are three methods for removing outdated records from busy administrative, productive, and service areas:

1. Via destruction
2. Via mutilation and sale as waste paper
3. Via storage in low-cost record depositories

From a tickler file based on the items and dates in the record schedule, the disposal officer issues memoranda to holders of documents to carry out the provisions of the schedule. It is unnecessary to keep account of the destruction of routine administrative and operational documents. It is a good idea to account for important files destroyed. This may prove useful in future investigation or litigation. Accounting of this nature is limited to a brief, summarized entry, including inclusive dates of the records. This register is kept permanently. Future searches for destroyed records will be eliminated by referring to the schdule, which will indicate that the records are no longer available, or whatever the case may be.

RECORDS DEPOSITORY. Noncurrent or semicurrent records that must be kept permanently, or for long periods of time, must not occupy active floor areas and expensive filing equipment. They may be placed in inexpensive warehouse space on a rental basis, or in commercial record depositories. When the volume of this material is sufficiently large, it is more economical for the organization to establish its own record center. The storage center may be installed in a specially built building, in unused space, or in leased space. Whatever the cause of action, a depository must allow for normal protection of records from the hazards of fire, flood, storm, and theft, and against deterioration from dust, insects, light, and mildew. Economically operated depositories are located in inexpensive areas, and have facilities for storing the maximum volume of records in highly accessible fashion. The maximum utilization of a building's cubic content is obtained by storing records packed in cardboard boxes on open metal shelving from about one foot off the floor to about three or four feet from the ceiling. Keeping records off the floor is a partial protection against the danger of floods. Storing records in cubic-foot cardboard boxes minimizes the hazards of dust, insects, light, and mildew at a nominal cost.

A horizontal layout is preferred over a vertical layout; a one-story building with a twenty-foot ceiling is preferable to a multi-storied building. The structure should contain inside railroad sidings and a sufficient number of inside truck ramps to allow railroad cars and vehicles to transport records a minimum distance away from processing, cataloguing, and shelving areas. Conveyors, fork-lifts, mechanized ladders, dumb-waiters, chutes, and other material-handling equipment and fixtures expedite and simplify operations in a large record depository. Storing records fifteen feet high in inexpensive containers takes advantage of the cubic content and reduces storage costs to less than one tenth of the charges for maintaining records in expensive administrative space.

DEPOSITORY PROCEDURES. The transfer of records from operating to storage areas is accomplished by:

1. Removing records from files and placing them in cubic-foot cardboard containers.
2. Placing a general description on the face of the carton by grease pencil, waterproof crayon, or the like, and numbering each carton one through infinity. (Avoid the use of labels; they dry up and fall off.)
3. Preparing a descriptive list of the shipment by box numbers in triplicate. Descriptive lists need not be in any great detail if the contents of each box can be summarily described.
4. Forwarding the original list to the disposal officer for permanent file.
5. Sending the second copy with the shipment as the packing list.
6. Retaining the third copy in the department transferring the records.

Upon arrival at the storage center, the shipment is examined for records that may be destroyed immediately, in accordance with the disposal schedule. Shipment of these types of records, however, should be avoided since they may be destroyed locally. Archivists may remove and merge files, for example, to more accurately document completed transactions. Records processed for shelving are given a library number that is posted to a locator card maintained for each organization unit. This same number is placed on the copy of the descriptive list that is filed numerically. Locator cards contain information pertaining to the number of boxes, shelf location, and shelving date for each shipment. Available shelf locations are obtained from a space inventory chart before the records are stored. Assigned library numbers are mailed on pre-printed post card forms to the record disposal officer as receipts for shipments. Library numbers are posted to the original and duplicate copies of the descriptive lists. From then on, any referral to stored documents is made by library and box number. Under this system, retrieval of a specific document in the depository takes place in a few minutes.

Providing for microfilm and photographic laboratories is an important aspect in planning the establishment of a records depository. Better than 90 per cent of all records stored should eventually be destroyed, and at least half this amount within five years of receipt at the depository. Therefore, the establishment of a records center should never be cause for the accumulation of a large body of useless information.

Protect that Information

Fixed and liquid assets are zealously guarded day and night. A variety of protective devices and systems are used by government and business to check on all persons who handle money and important and valuable material. Additional safeguards in the form of bonding and insurance coverage are employed. A good deal of the know-how that produces business success and good government is found in that small percentage of our paper work known as *vital records*. Despite all this, much less attention is given to the protection of valuable papers than is afforded expensive raw materials and supplies. The explosive nature of World War II, and the invention of nuclear weapons, prodded government and big business to take steps to correct this glaring fault in managerial control, but continual effort is required to preserve the sciences of business and government for posterity. Each year, vital documents are lost because of the destructive ravages of fire, flood, wind, theft, and vandalism. Significant information can be protected from disasters by training personnel to salvage and secure documents when disaster strikes, by duplicating and dispersing vital records to well-protected rural or nontarget areas, and by storing documents in underground vaults.

Commercial record depositories offer the services of storing vital records in underground vaults and caves. Microfilm service agencies and consultants will enter into contracts to duplicate, disperse, and store important documents. The mechanics for dispersal and storage are not difficult to establish. The problem lies in delineating the small portion of basic records present in any large paper mass. The Civil Defense Administration issues technical bulletins dealing with the protection of records. One has the following to say:

> In general, the following types of records should be considered in a protection program. The list is not all-inclusive. Some businesses might find it necessary to add more types.
>
> Accounts payable, accounts receivable, audits, bank deposit data, capital assets list, charters and franchises, constitutions and by-laws, contracts, customer data, engineering data, general ledgers, incorporation certificates, insurance policies, inventory lists, leases, legal documents, licenses, manufacturing processes data, minutes of directors' meetings, minutes of stockholders' meetings, notes receivable, patents and copyright authorizations, payroll and personnel data, policy manuals, purchase orders, sales data, shipping documents, social security receipts, special correspondence, statistical and operating data, stockholder lists, stock transfer books, tax records.[5]

The National Archives, the National Fire Protection Association, the Atomic Energy Commission, manufacturers of microfilm equipment, and paper work management consultants have published a variety of brochures dealing with the protection of vital records.

That old adage of locking the barn after the horse has been stolen is pertinent to the protection of records. Care must be taken to assure that outstanding information is recorded in the best ink and on the best paper stock. No amount of safeguarding will retain information placed on cheap sulphite stock in ink that is subject to fading. The best source for the proper paper stock and ink to record vital information is the manufacturer of this material. Valuable information placed on low-grade paper or written with inferior ink can be protected by microfilming. Information available from vital records is invaluable to business competitors in the same way that information in secret government documents would materially benefit an unfriendly foreign power. The federal government spends a great deal of time and effort guarding against unauthorized disclosures of vital information. Too many commercial organizations ignore the possibility of business espionage. Many would be astonished to learn the amount of traffic in this nefarious business. Organizations that discover leaks of vital information are reluctant to make the matter public, and little information has been released.

It is good business practice to develop classification systems to distinguish secret and vital papers from routine records. It is equally important to make sure that only persons worthy of trust handle confidential documents and that controls are established to prevent unauthorized disclosures.

---

[5] Civil Defense Technical Bulletin TB-16-2 (Washington, D.C.: Government Printing Office, May, 1955).

Automation and Conclusion

New and revolutionary concepts for the processing and utilization of information were released with the application of electronics to computers, readers, and ordinary office machinery. All the paper work steps pictured in Figure 9-1 can be accomplished automatically through electronic equipment. However, electronic equipment cannot improve paper work conditions when the proper organization, policies, and procedures are not present. The adoption of the various management techniques and controls described in this chapter is a prerequisite for installing machinery for automation of paper work operations. The director of automation of information must strive to keep the creation of hard copies to a minimum. This is not always the result of automation.

Paper work management continues to grow in stature with the increase of paper work costs. However, recognition on a piecemeal basis is a deterrent to attacking the entire problem on an organized, full-scale basis. The only and most obvious answer is the establishment of paper work managers with broad authority who report directly to executive officers of business and government.

10

Company Manuals

JAMES G. HENDRICK

Columbia Broadcasting System, Inc.
New York, N.Y.

JAMES G. HENDRICK is director of the Systems and Procedures
Services Department at Columbia Broadcasting System, Inc. He is
responsible for all phases of systems and procedures work, including the
appraisal of electronic data processing applications. He was formerly a
member of the faculty of New York and Rutgers universities, where he
taught "Advanced Principles of Systems and Procedures," and is a past
president of the New York Chapter, Systems and Procedures Association
of America.

Mr. Hendrick has done systems and procedures work within the
food, heavy machinery, and aircraft industries. His contributions to the
profession of systems and procedures include numerous articles, and
lectures to the American Management Association.

NEED FOR MANUALS

The Manual as a Tool of Communication

Essentially, manuals represent one means of communicating management decisions concerning organization, policies, and procedures. In modern management the volume and frequency of such decisions is increasing. Progressive enterprises have come to regard their organizational structures, policy statements, and procedural practices simply as elements of administration that can and should change as often as required to capitalize on new business opportunities and to meet competition. This concept of management has increased the need for and changed the role of manuals. Emphasis is now placed on using the manual to communicate information concerning "change." Manuals are now designed with a view toward readability, simplicity, and flexibility. The job of manual development is looked upon as one of keeping key personnel informed of changing management attitudes rather than that of doing a one-time job of drafting the organizational chart and putting policies and procedures into permanent book form.

POTENTIALS AND LIMITATIONS OF MANUALS. At an American Management Association seminar, representatives of eighty companies agreed that there are ten basic benefits to be derived from the use of company manuals. Discussion of these benefits leads to an appraisal of each, as shown below:

Benefit of Manuals	Results Normally Attainable (Manual Limitations)		
	excellent	good	fair
1. Flow of management information			X
2. On-the-job reference guide	X		
3. Indoctrination			X
4. Supervisory and executive training			X
5. Clarification of organizational structure and responsibilities	X		
6. Uniformity in interpretation and administration of policies	X		
7. Coordination of activities		X	
8. Elimination of unnecessary duplications		X	
9. Constant review and improvement of policies and procedures	X		
10. Internal auditing of policies, procedures, and controls	X		

Comments

1. Flow of management information. A complete flow of such information requires that data be communicated up and down the line of organization. Manuals may be used to communicate down the line. Other means, however, must be sought out for communicating upward.

2. On-the-job reference guide. Experience has demonstrated that management personnel have need for almost daily reference to written policies and procedures in the normal course of administrative operations.

3. Indocrination. Indoctrination cannot be accomplished merely by giving the new employee a manual, no matter how well designed it may be. The manual will help, but it must be supplemented by a reference to selected subjects of primary interest to the new employee and by personalized indoctrination techniques.

4. Supervisory and executive training. Effective training requires repetition and reference to case histories, both of which must be avoided in manuals if they are to be effective reference tools.

5. Clarification of organizational structure and responsibilities.

6. Uniformity in interpretation and administration of policies. There is no substitute for putting organizational and policy subjects down on paper.

7. Coordination of activities.

8. Elimination of unnecessary duplications. In the process of preparing a manual, substantial progress will probably be made in coordinating activities and eliminating duplications of functions.

9. Constant review and improvement of policies and procedures. Assuming that manual data is referred to and adhered to, thinking will be

stimulated toward improving operations, particularly when supervisory personnel are requested to recommend a change in policy or procedure if their experience indicates that current instructions contained in the manual are impracticable.

10. Internal auditing of policies, procedures, and controls. Systems and auditing work is invariably more effective and is accomplished more expeditiously when manuals are available to guide those doing this work.

The Use of Manuals in the Management Functions

SALES MANUALS. Sales executives recognize and accept the need for policy and training manuals. They are, however, opposed to the development of detailed procedure manuals. This attitude is by no means arbitrary or impractical. It stems from long experience with attempts to manualize sales operations. Appreciation of the attitude that accepts sales policy and training manuals and rejects sales procedure manuals may be found in the following suggestions contributed by seasoned sales executives in several industries:

> Sales people are of necessity given substantial latitude in making day-to-day decisions. Only when they have the benefit of policy guidelines will the sum total of local decisions be profitable and consistent. Hence, the policy manual is a valuable tool of sales administration.
>
> New salesmen appreciate receiving a training manual that earmarks the essentials of their job and gives official recognition to the importance of their contribution. For maximum appeal to sales personnel such a manual must, of course, be written in the best traditions of good advertising copy. (*Note:* These manuals are usually developed by advertising personnel, printed in color, and contain a variety of illustrations.)
>
> To *detail* the elements of a sales job in book form is to admit that the sales force has not been trained on the job or is simply lacking in initiative and ingenuity.
>
> If it becomes necessary to manualize the paper work and reporting routines involved in a sales job, a procedural study is needed to streamline the paper work. The solution to burdensome or complex sales paper work cannot be found by writing a manual of instructions for the salesmen.

PRODUCTION AND ENGINEERING MANUALS. The necessity for coordination between production control, manufacturing, inspection, and engineering personnel is so widely recognized that manuals are accepted and used extensively in plant operations. It is not unusual for a plant manager to issue several bulletins a week on subjects pertaining to this coordination. The production and engineering manual usually evolves from a file of such bulletins and is thereafter supplemented by bulletins that interpret instructions in the light of day-to-day operating problems.

FINANCE MANUALS. The responsibilities of the controller and treasurer require them to give numerous and specific instructions to those in the organization associated with the protection of company assets. Subjects of this nature are so vital to the financial success of the enterprise that manuals must be used to insure understanding of financial responsibilities at all levels of management.

INDUSTRIAL RELATIONS MANUALS. The primary responsibility of an industrial relations director is to assist in the formulation of the attitudes of the higher executives concerning the manner in which supervisory personnel will direct the effort of their subordinates. Having accomplished this, he then has the responsibility of communicating these management attitudes or policies. Industrial relations manuals are used:

1. To announce fixed company policies on such items as vacations, pay periods, and benefits
2. To indicate the circumstances in which local supervision may exercise judgment in handling individual personnel problems
3. To specify the steps to be taken to refer extraordinary personnel matters through the line of organization for decision

The dissemination of industrial relations policy in manual form represents a major step toward assuring consistency among supervisory personnel in protecting the most important company asset—people.

The Role of Manuals in a Decentralized Organization

Decentralization calls for wide delegation of responsibility and authority from the headquarters organization to operating divisions or subsidiaries. Almost without exception, the success of decentralization depends upon the chief executive and his staff people maintaining sufficient control to prevent delegation from becoming abdication.

The balancing of control activities in a decentralized organization is delicate indeed, and it calls for a very special understanding on the part of headquarters systems and procedures personnel, particularly in their role of developing and issuing manuals. The basic rules for manualization under a decentralized mode of organization are as follows:

A. With the advent of decentralization, headquarters staff executives have an immediate responsibility to formulate policy statements relating to their fields of activities. Through these statements the chief executive and his immediate staff members clarify the extent to which decentralization of responsibility and authority actually has been affected.

B. Financial and related control procedures should be published so that authority for specific actions is delegated in accordance with the decentralization plan.

C. Headquarters procedural instructions should be confined almost exclusively to stating, "What is to be accomplished?" Procedural details on the "how" of instructions should be avoided in a decentralized organization, except where company-wide standardization or uniformity is required:

1. To obtain consistent accounting treatment and accurate consolidation of financial and statistical data
2. To assure uniform compliance with laws and governmental regulations
3. To effect important operating economies resulting from method or equipment standardization

D. Provision should be made for operating divisions to develop and maintain their own manuals in which they interpret data from headquarters manuals and tailor instructions to their local objectives and conditions.

The Organization Manual

IMPORTANCE OF THE ORGANIZATION MANUAL. The job of a manager is to organize, deputize, supervise, and energize. This oversimplified but nevertheless effective statement emphasizes an accepted sequencing of managerial actions. The statement fundamentally indicates:

1. That the human and material assets of an enterprise must be organized for work before work assignments can be delegated
2. That delegation which includes the establishment of work standards must precede the act of supervision
3. That people are motivated when work standards are delegated and energized and when performance is appraised and rewarded by supervisors

The act of organizing is by no means limited to or directed solely toward the development of an organizational manual. Organization planning, on the contrary, involves the crystallization of company objectives; the analysis of specialized product, engineering, marketing and other functional considerations; the appraisal of affordable manpower budgets; and a consideration of the skills and potentials of available personnel. From an appraisal of these and related factors, a plan of organization evolves and is usually expressed in organizational chart form.

The manuals of many companies contain only organization charts. Others supplement these charts by material designed to clarify:

1. Corporate objectives
2. The difference between lines of organization and lines of communication
3. The corporate concept of "control"
4. The basis upon which organizational structure has been designed (by products, geography, industries, and so on)
5. The relationship between line and staff organization
6. The specific duties and responsibilities of managerial personnel

An organization manual is not the end product of organizational planning. The extent to which the manual contains up-to-date charts and supplementary material, such as that previously outlined, however, indicates in many cases the amount of consideration that top management has given to its basic responsibility of organizing the human assets of the business and announcing its decisions on this subject to all persons concerned. The organization manual is, therefore, one tangible end product of organizational planning. When the manual does not exist, when it is not current, or is limited to charts alone, it is reasonable to assume that organizational planning has not been given adequate attention.

MANUAL PREFACE. The most common and justified criticism of organization manuals is that they commence with a lengthy preface that details the elements of administration and pleads for cooperation and teamwork among managerial personnel.

An examination of some fifty organization manuals showed introductions containing four to nine pages of "pep talk" material. Many went so far as to compare the management organization with a football team. Detailed examination of these manuals indicated that the theme of teamwork and cooperation was overemphasized in the introduction or preface because the material that followed failed to specify the duties and responsibilities of individuals and then to clarify the means by which individuals would work together.

When the manual is well designed and tailored to the needs of the organization, the preface, signed by the chief executive, can be as brief as the following example.

> If there was ever a subject on which I want to be specific, crystal clear and positive, it is "Organization at the ABC Company."
>
> From experience it is obvious that little, if anything, need be said about teamwork, cooperation, constructive attitudes, unification of objectives, and the like. The maturity of our managerial personnel is such that we need not write about such matters.
>
> The corporate organization structure is charted on the following page. Opposite this, I have interpreted those matters that are not obvious by lines and boxes. If this leaves any questions unanswered, bring the subject up for immediate clarification. Nothing will exceed it in importance.

MANUAL DESIGN. The following check list outlines major items that may be considered in designing the organization manual:

A. Preface or introduction
B. Top management organization chart
C. An interpretation of the basic organization structure in which the chief executive explains such things as:
   1. The mode of organization (geographic, product, and so on)
   2. The extent of centralization or decentralization
   3. The relationship between line and staff personnel
D. Divisional or departmental charts
E. Summarized job descriptions for every member of management

F. Organizational policies relating to fundamental management subjects, such as:
1. Planning
2. Communications
3. Control
4. Development of management personnel
G. Index (alphabetical list of managerial personnel cross-referenced to organization chart numbers)

Figure 10-1 illustrates a design in which organizational charts and summary job descriptions are integrated to facilitate understanding and reference.

Figure 10-2 exemplifies a method of portraying relationships between the corporate staff organization and line of operating divisions where such relationships differ widely by operating divisions.

Table 10-1 demonstrates the manner in which duties and responsibilities can be set forth in the manual by functions or major activities. The

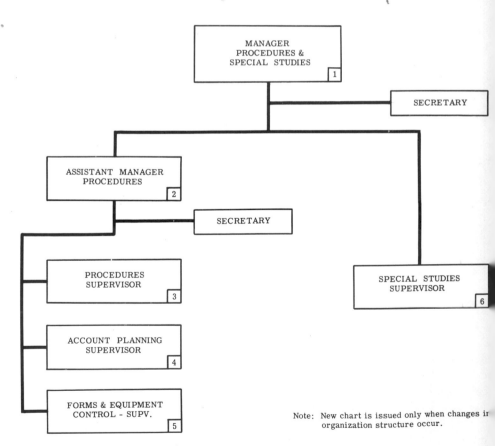

Note: New chart is issued only when changes in organization structure occur.

Fig. 10-1(a). Organization Chart

1.	*Manager Procedures and Special Studies*	Plan, organize, and direct activities relating to special management studies; the analysis and improvement of office systems, procedures, and methods; manualization; account planning; punched card and electronics research; forms control; equipment standardization and the purchasing of office equipment and supplies.
		The services above are provided on a continuing and initiating basis to all members of the comptroller's staff and, on a request basis, to the heads of other divisions.
2.	*Assistant Manager Procedures*	Supervise the activities of procedural analysis, manualization, and account planning. Direct the functions of forms and equipment control and purchasing.
3.	*Procedures Supervisor*	Appraise office procedures and methods within the comptroller's division to ascertain that they are in conformance with company policies and that they employ the most economical and effective techniques of comptrollership. Provide procedural and methods services to other divisions on a request basis. Also provide the comptroller's division, and other divisions upon request, with required instruction manuals on organization, policies, and procedures.
4.	*Account Planning Supervisor*	Provide a chart of accounts covering all routine accounting activities and related policies and controls. Also provide interpretations and instructions for special accounting transactions. Keep abreast of the latest techniques of account planning and apply improved procedures and methods where practicable.
5.	*Forms and Equipment Control Supervisor*	In accordance with corporate purchasing policies, supervise all activities relating to the establishment of standards and the procurement and delivery of: office supplies, printed forms, mechanical office equipment, office furniture.
6.	*Special Studies Supervisor*	Conduct special studies on selected business problems and major business systems. Initiate suggestions for such studies on the basis of observations and experience stemming from regular analyses made of current administrative and clerical activities.

NOTE: Changes in personnel are announced by bulletin and are noted above by the manual holder.

Fig. 10-1(b). Responsibilities

activity used in this example is that of sales promotion. This method of defining responsibilities is recommended when the activity involved concerns many people and requires substantial coordination among specialists (such as salesmen, product managers, and advertising personnel).

KEEPING THE MANUAL UP TO DATE. When organizational planning is given consideration by top management, organization changes are made as frequently as may be required to solve current business problems and capitalize on opportunities for improving operating results. Routine changes in personnel should be announced by bulletin and reflected promptly in new organizational charts.

Figure 10-1 illustrates one means by which personnel changes can be made by organization chart holders directly from announcements received. This minimizes the work of preparing and distributing new organizational charts, by limiting such revisions to the instances in which organizational structure has been changed.

Major organizational changes should likewise be reflected promptly in the organization manual, even if it means rewriting or supplementing the document on interpretation of the organization structure. So long as change is not so spasmodic as to become confused with progress, organization manual revisions should not be resisted. Organizational planning is a dynamic management activity, and all revisions should therefore manifest this vital phase of management planning.

MANUAL DISTRIBUTION. It is recommended that a copy of the entire organization manual be provided for every member of management from first level of supervision to members of the board of directors. Selective

TABLE 10-1. RESPONSIBILITIES RELATING TO PRODUCT PROMOTIONS

	Oper. Div.	Sales Division	
		product mgr.	region mgr.
DETERMINATION OF NEED AND OBJECTIVES			
1. Report trend information for use in determining need, purpose, and length of promotions.			X
2. Consult with operation divisions in determining need for and objectives of promotions, bringing to bear organized field facts.		X	
3. Determine the need for and objectives of assigned product campaigns.	X		
PROMOTIONAL MEDIA			
1. Determine need for deals, samples, premiums, display materials, etc.; objectives to be accomplished by them; and expenditure affordable.	X		
2. Provide information pertinent to trade attitudes, local franchise strengths, and competitive situations that will be helpful in deciding need for and types of sales inducements and tools.			X
3. Consult with operating divisions on the practicability of contemplated promotions.		X	
4. Decide precisely what tools will be used.	X		
5. Within established limits of affordability, estimate quantities the field force will use.		X	
6. Procure purchased promotional materials and services.	X		

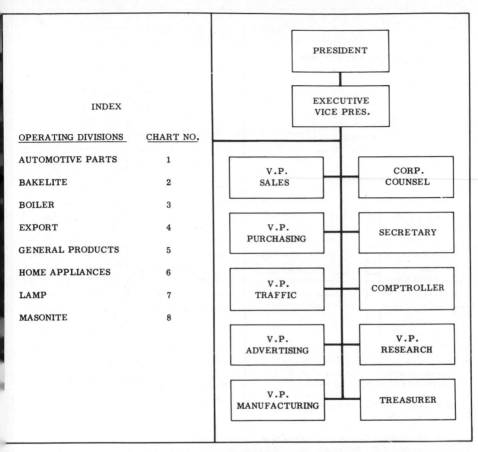

Fig. 10-2(a). Organization Manual Format Designed to Show Variations That Exist in Relationships Between the Corporate Staff Organization (See Fig. 10-2(b) and 10-2(c) as well)

distribution of organization charts and related material implies that some management people need know only their own responsibilities. A complete distribution recognizes that management people at all levels would be interested in knowing how the entire organization functions.

A BY-PRODUCT OF THE ORGANIZATION MANUAL. Organization planning establishes "what is to be done" and "who will do what." Systems and procedures work then follows through to determine "how" authorized and assigned activities will be performed.

Organizational planning work concluded by issuing an organizational manual minimizes the following management problems:

1. Line personnel resent systems people developing a procedure that automatically delegates responsibility that has not yet been defined and delegated by top management.

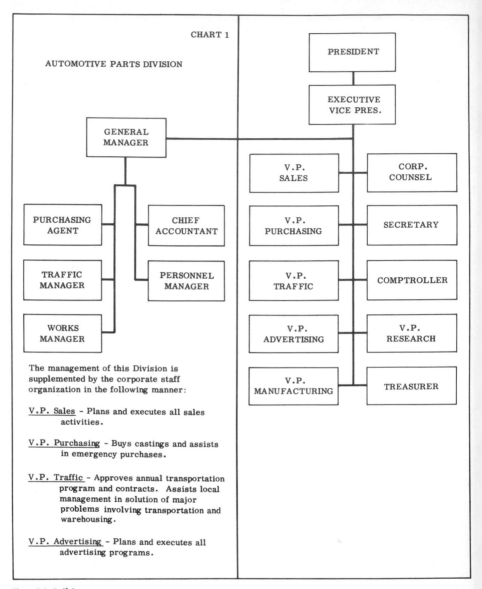

Fig. 10-2 (b)

2. Systems projects are deferred or terminated pending clarification of jurisdictional questions.

3. Systems and procedures program gives top priority to pure paperwork problems rather than to the all-important relationship problems that are earmarked in the process of doing organizational planning.

Effective systems and procedures work stems from, and is so dependent upon, organizational planning work that it may be classified as a byproduct of organizational planning activities.

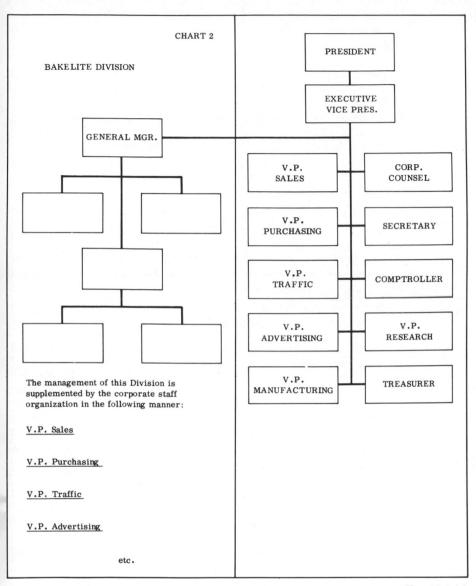

CHART 2

BAKELITE DIVISION

PRESIDENT

EXECUTIVE
VICE PRES.

GENERAL MGR.

V.P. SALES	CORP. COUNSEL
V.P. PURCHASING	SECRETARY
V.P. TRAFFIC	COMPTROLLER
V.P. ADVERTISING	V.P. RESEARCH
V.P. MANUFACTURING	TREASURER

The management of this Division is
supplemented by the corporate staff
organization in the following manner:

V.P. Sales

V.P. Purchasing

V.P. Traffic

V.P. Advertising

etc.

Fig. 10-2 (c)

The Policy Manual

THE VALUE OF WRITTEN POLICIES. Policy is simply management's
attitude. It is reasonable to assume that the chief executive officer of a company has, from experience, arrived at attitudes concerning how the operations under his jurisdiction will be conducted. It is likewise reasonable to
assume that his attitudes must be communicated continually down the line
of organization if operations are to proceed according to his plan. Written
policies are one means of transmitting management's attitudes.

In large companies the chief executive often delegates the job of formulating and revising policy statements to his major staff executives or vice-presidents, and thereafter asks them:

1. How many important subjects have you reduced to writing as of today? In other words, how well are you doing in providing field people with the means of exercising consistently good judgment?

2. In the process of developing policies, how have you improved operations? Have you simply been recording present practices, or are you constantly finding a better set of management attitudes?

3. Has experience proven your policies to be practicable in every sense? Do the field people respect and follow them, or are they looking for ways and means of circumventing them?

4. To what extent are policies molding effective working relationships between headquarters and field personnel?

Written policies establish guidelines, a framework within which managerial personnel may operate to balance top management attitudes and objectives in the best interests of local conditions.

PLANNING POLICY MANUAL CONTENTS. The approach to the development of a comprehensive company-wide policy manual may be:

A. Develop a list of policy subjects, by functions, applicable to the company concerned. Use specialized texts and handbooks on finance, sales, manufacturing, purchasing, personnel, and so on. Examination of "purchasing handbooks," for example, would highlight such policy subjects as relationships with vendors, purchase vs. manufacture, concentration vs. spreading of purchases, quality, forward buying, and centralized vs. branch purchasing.

B. Discuss the above lists with the appropriate company executives to:

1. Establish a list of policies required.

2. Ascertain the extent to which policies are now in existence.

3. Determine a priority of policies to be developed. (A desirable priority listing is based on the immediate needs of the company as expressed by the appropriate executives.)

4. Arrange for staff specialists to develop policy drafts in consultation with the appropriate line personnel.

5. Have final policy drafts approved by executive management.

6. Issue policies in manual form as they are developed. (Since the task of formulating policies is long and difficult, it is inadvisable to withhold needed written policies until the total job has been completed.)

DIVORCING POLICY FROM PROCEDURE. On many subjects and in many areas of a business, substantial policy work must be accomplished before procedures may be effectively designed. Expediency, however, may require that many procedures be written before policies are established. The paper work routines for some procedures, for example, often must be set up before policies may be fully crystallized. In view of the necessity of this overlapping, many companies have found it advantageous to divorce policies from procedures in manuals. Whenever this is done, cross-referencing is beneficial.

POLICY INTERPRETATION. No policy statement can be so all-inclusive or crystal clear as to obviate the necessity of interpretation. If policy is limited to providing a framework within which line executives can operate, questions of applying policy to exceptional situations undoubtedly will occur from day to day. In many organizations these questions are referred to the staff executive who assists the chief executive responsible for:

1. Deciding on the application of policy to current conditions
2. Recommending policy revisions to the chief executive when circumstances indicate the need for a change in management attitude

The Procedure Manual

PLANNING THE MANUAL CONTENT. Development of the average written procedure involves five days of work for an experienced procedures analyst. This includes time for determining the present flow of paper work, making minor paper work improvements, preparing a draft, obtaining approvals, and editing for publication. Thus, if there are five hundred procedures to be written, which appears to be minimum for many companies, the job of preparing a complete procedure manual involves more than ten man-years of tedious work.

Considering the investment required to prepare a procedure manual, it is appropriate to devote at least several months to planning the manual contents item by item.

Planning the table of contents *pro forma* is usually accomplished by conferring with departmental chiefs and listing procedural subjects that, in their judgment, need to be put in writing. Discussion with the payroll manager, for example, may result in a decision to write procedures on the following subjects:

PAYROLL SYSTEM PROCEDURES

1. Calculation of earnings, deductions and net pay
2. Payroll writing
3. Weekly salary
4. Monthly salary
5. Straight hourly rate
6. Combination time-and-incentive hourly rate
7. Piecework rate
8. Computation of gross pay
9. Compute deductions
10. Withhold deductions
11. Remit deductions to proper agency
12. Rendering to employee a statement of deductions made
13. Records of deductions
14. Reporting deductions to government agencies involved
15. Assessments for group insurance

16. Assessments for hospitalization
17. Company purchases
18. Repayment of company (personal) loans
19. Savings plans
20. Bond purchase plans
21. Stock purchase plans
22. Union dues
23. Creditor's legal assignment or garnishment of wages for past due debts
24. Paycheck
25. Earnings statement
26. Earnings record
27. Payroll journal and check register
28. Calculating the payroll
29. Gathering attendance time obtained by timekeepers
30. Social security tax deduction
31. Gathering incentive pay production data
32. Allowances for sick pay
33. Allowances for portal-to-portal pay
34. Allowances for clothes, tools, etc.
35. Allowances for pieceworker's makeup
36. Errors of undercollection or overcollection
37. Payroll journal (and check register)
38. Paycheck or envelope
39. Pay stub or employee's earnings statements
40. Employee's quarterly earnings records
41. Income tax withheld for governmental agencies
42. Employer's tax and employees' tax—F.I.C.A.
43. Profit sharing
44. Anticipated layoff
45. Temporary and permanent passes to enter plant
46. Preparation of clock cards
47. Tardiness
48. Overtime payment
49. Payroll accrual
50. "Confidential" payroll
51. Payment in advance
52. Wage change
53. Salary change
54. Annual earnings statistics
55. Absence pay procedure—wage
56. Absence pay procedure—salary
57. Meal allowances
58. Separation pay allowance
59. Savings bond ledger
60. Uncalled-for checks or pay envelopes
61. Payroll check enclosures
62. Employee called for military service
63. Overtime pay—holiday and unworked time
64. Payments of amounts owed to deceased employees

After planning the manual department by department and subject by subject, the next steps are to:

1. Program procedures in the order of importance and estimate the time required to complete the manual.

2. Determine the staffing requirements.

3. Provide management with a manual development timetable against which progress can be measured.

4. Schedule procedural work so as to capitalize on natural work-sequencing opportunities; for example, an analyst may expedite his work on one procedure because of the background that he has acquired on the subject from working on related procedures.

5. Decide on the physical details of the manual (type binder, format, etc.) with a full recognition of how these details may affect the end product and later revisions.

6. Request a specific appropriation for the total job to be done.

EXECUTING THE LONG-RANGE PROCEDURE MANUAL PROGRAM. As a result of planning the manual contents, many managements hesitate to embark on an all-out program that aims primarily at putting procedures in manual form. Such action may come about after considering:

1. The need for doing substantial organizational planning and policy development work prior to procedural writing work
2. The limited value of a manual that details procedures that are already in the process of change due to mechanization or the introduction of electronics
3. The benefits of manualization in relation to the cost involved in staffing for the activity

Therefore, it is necessary to appraise objectively the long-range effects, costs, and benefits of a manual program for management. Often this requires that the conventional approach of preparing written procedures subject by subject be tailored to fit the specific needs of a company. If manualization activities need to be geared directly to the company's program of organization planning and work simplification, for example, a long-range program as outlined in Figure 10-3 may be more practicable.

INTERDEPARTMENTAL PROCEDURES. The flow chart format illustrated in Figure 10-4 is recommended for the interdepartmental procedures manual. The advantages of this format are:

1. Procedure analysts must develop and present facts, not memoranda.
2. The procedures department, engaged to assist operating departments, works out details rather than general statements.
3. Management and department heads are given details in comprehensive and quick reference form.
4. Flow chart procedures serve as operation sheets for workers, informing them about their specific duties, as well as the flow of paper work, before and after they process it.
5. The full benefits of illustration are gained. Repetitious reading of stock procedure phrases is eliminated. The flow chart section headings fix the work responsibility, the lines show the work sequence, and words must be well chosen to conserve space.

Figure 10-5 provides another example of flow chart format adaptable to manual purposes. This technique is used to record written procedures when complicated clerical routines are involved or numerous exception routines exist.

DEPARTMENTAL PROCEDURES. The forms manual format is used extensively in the preparation of departmental procedure instructions. Ordinarily, this is accomplished by illustrating a sample of the form, record, or report, and noting instructions thereon concerning:

1. Method of forms preparation
2. Time of form preparation

Objective NO. I	Objective NO. II	Objective NO. III
To reduce excessive overhead cost by determining:	To control and administer operations by determining:	To improve operating efficiency and further reduce costs by determining:
WHAT THINGS ARE BEING DONE THAT NEED NOT BE DONE	WHAT THINGS ARE NOT BEING DONE THAT SHOULD BE DONE	WHAT NECESSARY AND AUTHORIZED THINGS CAN BE PERFORMED MORE EFFECTIVELY, IN LESS TIME, AND AT A REDUCED COST

CONCURRENT ACTION PROGRAM

USING THE CHECK LIST OF DEPARTMENTAL FUNCTIONS PREPARED FROM ORGANIZATION MANUAL, SAMPLE FORMS, RECORDS, AND REPORTS
+
INFORMATION OBTAINED IN THE PROCESS OF ACCOMPLISHING OBJECTIVES I AND II

1. Using job descriptions established in organizational manual, prepare a check list of functions by departments or cost centers.

2. Obtain from each department a copy of every form, record, and report that it initiates or processes.

3. On each form, record, and report submitted, note the following: purpose, frequency of use, distribution, whether initiated or processed.

4. By departments, examine each form, record, and report used and see if you can tie each of them into one or more of the authorized functions appearing on the check list for that department.

    a. When you discover a working instrument (form, record, or report) that does not tie into a function, question its existence and use. Chances are you have uncovered *something being done which need not be done.*

    b. When you discover a *function* that is not associated with any form, record, or report, or with instruments that appear to be inadequate, question the extent to which the *function* is being performed. Chances are you have uncovered *something not being done that should be done.*

5. Conduct thorough investigation of questionable functions and instruments. Prepare, then coordinate, recommendations with executives and department heads concerned.

This phase of the program may be classified as a management audit designed to ascertain that all established administrative and operating functions are being performed with the pattern and limits established and delegated by management.

In addition to effecting a substantial reduction in overhead costs, this audit provides the procedures department with the information and background required to accomplish Objective III as outlined above.

1. List all duplicating and split functions existing among departments (e.g., 3 departments maintaining stock records; 13 departments preparing and issuing statistical reports). Investigate practicability of combining like functions for better control and lower costs.

2. Analyze the number and type of forms, records, and reports per function within each department. Such analysis may show, for example: receiving function engaging 8 forms with 28 copies; 6 records; and 4 reports; receiving inspection function engaging 6 forms; 4 records; and 5 reports with 26 copies.

Fig. 10-3. Long-range Program for the Procedures Department

3. From the above analysis determine which functions are obviously overburdened with paper work and schedule these for detailed study and improvement. Give careful consideration to the sequence in which these problem functions will be studied. For example, if both the receiving and receiving inspection functions are to be examined, schedule receiving first because each improvement in this area may automatically effect two improvements in the receiving inspection area. *To expedite work simplification, schedule studies in their order of natural operation or interrelationship rather than purely in terms of their relative importance or cost reduction possibilities.*

4. As each function is improved, prepare and publish a Standard Practice Instruction, outlining the policies, systems, and methods involved in its execution. These instructions authorize and clarify the revised system and give life to the controls established.

ORGANIZATION CHARTS AT WORK

Organization charts and descriptions of the duties and responsibilities of executive and supervisory personnel have long been accepted by progressive organizations as a fundamental management tool. In the process of developing, publishing, and revising organizational material, management performs its prime function of ORGANIZING, DEPUTIZING, SUPERVISING, and ENERGIZING. Since the program above stems from the development of this material, many of the resulting work simplifications, operating improvements, and cost reductions can be attributed to the very tangible and profitable function of *organization planning.*

Fig. 10-3. (Cont.)

ABC CORPORATION
No. E - 7

STANDARD PROCEDURE
Section 1 of 1

TITLE: Preparation of Production & Spare Parts Requirements
Page 1 of 1

SERVICE ENGINEERING	PRODUCTION PLANNING	PURCHASING
(1) Break down blueprint into assemblies, subassemblies, and spare parts.	(5) Compare part requirements with stock balances. (Balances reflect actual less committed.)	(7) Receive purchase requests; obtain management approvals and place purchase orders.
(2) Investigate all parts to determine interchangeability, substitutions, and spare parts requirements.	(6) Post total requirements to stock records and prepare purchase requests for all stock that is at minimum balance. Forward requests to purchasing.	
(3) Prepare a summary of total requirements showing production, spares, interchangeability, and substitution facts thereon.		
(4) Forward copy of summary to Production Planning.		

Fig. 10-4. ABC Corporation Standard Procedure Chart

FORM 02/46.28
PRINTED IN U.S.A.
1.37

FLOW CHART

OFFICE	SYSTEM	AREA NO.	DIV. NO.
Sales Accounting	Grocery Billing	08	1

LOCATION	PROCEDURE	SYSTEM NO.	PROCEDURE NO.
Chicago	Invoicing	03	01

DATE	FREQUENCY	PAGE
5/7/67	Daily	1 OF 1

FORMS

NAME	FORM NO.	ORIGINATED THIS PROCEDURE	TRANSFERRED COPIES	(List System and Procedure Nos.) FROM	TO	MONTHLY VOLUME PROCESSED
Order-Invoice	23/39-38	1/	"	05-1	08-3	3000
	39-33			01-06	03-03	2700
	39-42			"	"	450
	39-45			"	"	30
Manifest Disposal Report	23/69-01		/2	06-5	"	200
Bills of Lading	23/39-38		/2	"	"	1300
Manifest (Indianapolis Plant)	NF#		/2	13-5	"	90
Product Invoice	56/28-13		/2	02-1	"	200

PERSONNEL

JOB CLASSIFICATIONS	NO. OF PERSONS	% OF TIME	ANNUAL PAYROLL COST
Settlement Clerk	3	50%	
"	1	75	

PROBLEMS IDENTIFIED

PROCEDURAL STEP NO.	TIME	QUALITY	COST	CONTROL
3	X			X
5	X			X
11		X		
17	X		X	
19	X			

SETTLEMENT CLERK WILL

FOR WAREHOUSE SHIPMENTS

1. Receive order-invoice from Order Processing Clerk and file in unshipped order file by:
   a) Territory
   b) Shipping Date

2. Receive Manifest Disposals Report together with Bills of Lading representing previous day's shipments from the shipping warehouse.

3. Match and compare quantities on each Bill of Lading (received with the manifest) to the applicable order copy in the unshipped order file. (Exception 3, 4, 5, 6)

4. Sort invoices representing Plant Direct Shipments by District and all invoices by territories and products when a sales promotion campaign (hereinafter referred to as a deal) is in effect.

FOR PLANT SHIPMENTS

1. Receive order from Order Processing Clerk and file in unshipped order file by:
   a) District
   b) Product type
   c) Shipping date

2. Receive Product Invoice representing previous day's shipments from the shipping plant (Exception 1, 2)

   Note: A Product Invoice may represent a shipment to one customer or a pool of orders to various customers. In the latter case it would indicate all the order numbers in the pool and a summarized total of products shipped.

3. Pull invoice(s) from the unshipped file listed on the Product Invoice. (Exception 3, 4) Summarize pulled invoices by product and compare total with amount on Product Invoice. (Exception 6)

EXCEPTION ROUTINES
(00% = Rate of Exception Incidence)

1. Receive a shipping manifest from the Indianapolis Plant. (30% or 90 orders monthly)

2. Write applicable sales district on Product Invoices representing shipments from Indianapolis Plant. (30% or 90 orders monthly)

3. If order is not in file expedite it from Order Processing Clerk or Credit Department. (6% or 400 orders monthly)

4. If order is not with Order Processing Clerk or Credit Department follow it up each day for three days. (1% or 60 orders monthly)

5. If missing order invoice does not show up within 3 days, prepare an order form and issue it to the Order Processing Clerk for pricing, extending, and booking in accordance with booking procedure and return to the Settlement Clerk for invoicing. Request Duplicating Machine Operator to prepare an extra office copy of the invoice and forward it upon receipt to the Order Processing Clerk where ultimately it will be matched against the incoming order-invoice to assure that the order-invoice will not be booked a second time. (.5% or 32 orders monthly)

6. If there is a difference in amount originally ordered and amount shipped determine reason to be either:
   a) Back Orders (6% or 390 orders monthly) Delete back ordered products from the original order.

6. allowance is to be given to customer. (*Exception 7*)

7. Date invoice.

   Check invoices to special instructions list to determine which customers require extra invoices. Write number of invoice copies required on bottom of invoice as notification to Bruning Machine Operator.

   Pull back order from the unshipped file. If back order is not in file, request that Duplicating Machine Operator prepare an extra office copy of the original order and file the extra copy until formal back order is received.

   If Back Order Is A Plant Shipment
   Write up back order (or "B" order) from available information, since plants do not write back orders.

   Using the same bracket price as on the original order, extend the back order and file in the unshipped file.

   b) Cancellation (4% or 230 orders monthly)

   c) **Package Size Changed By Plant** (.2% or 13 orders monthly) Make applicable quantity and dollar adjustments to the invoice. Request Duplicating Machine Operator to prepare an extra office copy of invoice and forward upon receipt to Order Processing Clerk in order to adjust bookings.

   Note: If shipment was made from a warehouse or Indianapolis Plant check manifest and contact warehouse or plant only if difference cannot be determined from manifest. Contact all other plants to determine differences.

9. of copies required.

   Mark each completed invoice master in red to assure that it will not be processed through the machine again.

10. Count the original order invoice masters to determine that all the invoices received from the settlement clerks have been processed.

11. Distribute invoice copies as follows:

Order Invoice Master	Extra C/s	White Copy	Blue Copy	Yellow Copy
(14)			(12) Mail to District (Procedure)	(13) Mail to Salesman (Procedure)

15. Verify that all invoices originally forwarded for Bruning Machine processing have been prepared as requested.

16. Forward invoice masters to the billing control clerk (Procedure 08-1-03-03). (*Exception 8*)

17. Stamp all customer invoice copies with "Locked Box" address. *Note:* "Locked Box" address is a post office box which is controlled by the commercial bank handling SBI's account. Thus, the customer when paying the invoice will remit directly to the bank.

18. Combine all invoices to the same customer, if any.

19. Issue invoices to customers via mail room. (*Exception 9, 10*)

7. If deal allowance is to be paid by check (560 checks monthly) request extra office copy. File all extra copies until the end of the deal, at which time summarize all credits and charges of deal product(s) for each customer and extend the summarized totals at the deal (allowance) rate. (This amount will later be typed on a check which in turn will be forwarded to the customer (32% or 1950 orders monthly)

   Note: Customer may also receive deal credit off the "face" of the invoice. If this is the case then the deal amount should have been previously calculated, by the Order Processing Clerk, and is already reflected on the invoice. Return any deal invoices not calculated to the Order Processing Clerk.

8. Extract all government orders and have accountant certify correctness according to government regulations. (1% or 63 orders monthly)

9. If "shipped to" address is different from "invoiced" address, envelope invoice(s) in right hand window envelope. (18% or 1100 orders monthly)

10. If "shipped to" and "invoiced" address are identical forward invoice(s) to mail room unenveloped. (Mail room will issue these in left hand window envelope.) (82% or 5100 orders monthly)

Fig. 10-5. Flow Chart

3. Distribution of form copies
4. Responsibility for form preparation
5. Special instructions

MANUAL DISTRIBUTION. The contents of procedure manuals are invariably distributed on a selective basis because of the volume of written procedures involved. Departments and individuals receive a copy only of those procedures that relate to their particular responsibilities. It is advisable, however, to issue a complete index of procedures to all manual holders and permit anyone to request a copy of procedures in which he may have an interest.

KEEPING THE MANUAL UP TO DATE. Considering the need for written procedures and the investment made to develop them, specific provisions should be made to keep manuals up to date. Many companies employ one or a combination of the following manual revision control techniques:

1. Direct that written procedures be followed without exception, but make it the responsibility of manual holders to point out the need for revisions when operating experience indicates that current instructions are impracticable.
2. Establish regular audit schedules to determine if current practices coincide with written procedures (the auditing and/or procedures department may perform these reviews).
3. In staffing the procedures department, provide for personnel needed to prepare, clear, and issue manual revisions.
4. Issue revised content and index pages frequently, with a request that manual holders check their manuals for completeness.
5. Have the forms control unit point up changes in procedure that result from new or revised forms. Follow through with necessary manual revisions.

Appraising an Existing Manuals Program

Today, most companies that employ a thousand or more people have already had substantial experience in the use of policy and procedure manuals. Few systems and procedures managers, therefore, are called upon to develop an initial manuals program. They usually inherit a set of manuals and are required to consider the following questions:

1. Are existing manuals too numerous or voluminous? Should manuals be consolidated?
2. Are existing manuals worth revising and improving, or should they be made obsolete in favor of an entirely new manual?

Research in the Field of Manualization

SOME UNSOLVED PROBLEMS. Many problems are inherent in planning and executing a comprehensive manuals program. As evidence of this, efforts are continually being made to:

1. Reduce the cost of publishing and maintaining manuals.

2. Speed the preparation of initial policy and procedure drafts.
3. Facilitate policy and procedure interpretations.
4. Provide complete manual data, but minimize reading time required of executives and supervisory personnel.

EXPERIMENTS BY TAPE RECORDING. Research aimed at the solution of the above problems need not be limited solely to the development of improved techniques involving manual format, indexing, writing styles, and so forth. Considerable thought should be given to communicating policies and procedures by means of tape or disc recordings. This technique has been employed so far in the recording of manufacturing inspection routines and in disseminating technical information to medical personnel.

It is conceivable that manuals of the future will be limited to basic outlines and that the details will be on tape rather than written. Reference to policy and procedure details will be made by telephoning a centralized tape center and asking for a playback of that portion of the policy or procedure outline to which reference is desired.

11

Budgets and Cost Control

PAUL E. HAMMAN

Touche, Niven, Bailey & Smart
Detroit, Mich.

PAUL E. HAMMAN, a partner in the firm of Touche, Niven, Bailey & Smart, has had a career entirely within the practice of public account- ing. Following his graduation from the University of Illinois in 1933 with a bachelor of science degree in accounting, he joined the staff of Scovell, Wellington & Company in Chicago. In 1940 he joined the staff of Ernst & Ernst in Detroit, where he remained until 1947. He was one of the original partners of George Bailey & Company, which was formed early in that year. This firm was merged with Touche, Niven & Co. and Allen R. Smart & Co. later in that year to form Touche, Niven, Bailey & Smart.

Mr. Hamman holds CPA certificates in the states of Illinois, Michigan, and New York, and was awarded the Silver Medal by the Illinois Society of Certified Public Accountants in connection with the examination for his Illinois certificate. He is a member of the board of directors, Executive Committee, and Finance Committee of Junior Achievement of Southeastern Michigan, Incorporated.

Much of his work has been concerned with the use of accounting and industrial engineering by management. His publications include numerous papers in the areas of systems, management reporting, cost control, cost accounting, budgets, and electronic data processing. A mem- ber of many business, accounting, and engineering societies, he has served in an official capacity in several of them. He has served as chairman of the Committee on Electronic Accounting of the American Institute of Certified Public Accountants.

INTRODUCTION

The Need for Budgets and Cost Control

Costs in a manufacturing enterprise are not static; they are subject to continuous change, and, depending upon the nature of the operations, the controls that are used, and a host of conditions that can affect operations, they are likely to vary from what was planned or what should be attainable under ideal conditions. Accordingly, budgets and cost control measures are used to determine what costs should be, the nature of differences from what the costs actually are, their cause and responsibility, and to provide the necessary information for corrective action.

Budgets, Controls, and People

Human factors are important in relation to costs and their control. It is certainly possible to control costs without formal budgets and cost control programs. An individual worker in a manufacturing plant knows when he is working effectively. His foreman and other production supervisors can observe conditions that cause excessive costs. True, the abilities of individuals to observe conditions and mentally measure their effect in terms of dollars of cost are limited. It must be recognized, however, that control of costs commences with physical events and that the first line of defense in controlling costs inevitably involves the worker and his supervisor. Physical factors, such as plant layout, working conditions, machines, and tools, are obviously important. It is only after adequate attention has been directed to all of these factors that it becomes logical to consider more sophisticated engineering and accounting techniques described as budgets and cost control programs.

Budget Objectives

CONTROL VERSUS PREDICTION. It is important to distinguish control measures from purely prediction techniques. This distinction is particularly applicable to the term "budget," but in varying aspects it also applies to the terms "costs" and "cost control." Control measures inherently involve planning and the determination of goals and objectives. Prediction, on the other hand, implies an objective attempt to measure what is most likely to happen and, hence, should recognize all of the contingencies, in proper perspective, that can with reasonable probability be expected to affect operations and costs. Since controls involve goals and objectives, it can be observed that they must, of necessity, involve an element of optimism. Prediction requires striking a balance between optimism and pessimism with respect to future events.

WHY ARE BUDGETS PREPARED? Since the word budget is a general term that acquires specific meaning only when it is further described, it is essential to consider the reasons for preparation of a budget as a background for the determination of what a particular budget is to mean and what it is to accomplish. For example, a budget of the income and expenses of an enterprise as a whole may be prepared for a period of perhaps five years in advance as part of the planning of working capital requirements and financing. Here, perhaps, the emphasis is on a conservative determination of working capital or cash that should be made available as a result of anticipated profitable operations. It may be important not to overstate such amounts, since the financing plans based thereon may be inadequate. In such a situation, the term "forecast" or "budget forecast" has greater clarity than the term budget alone.

Consider another example: In planning a new product and operations for a short period ahead, emphasis may be placed on what the new product may reasonably be expected to accomplish under a set of conditions that anticipate attainment of cost and other objectives. These objectives may represent a substantial achievement or accomplishment from previously existing levels of performance. The conditions may represent rather optimistic goals, which may or may not be reached in full. Under such conditions, this form of budget (commonly described as a profit-planning budget) can be thought of as a statement in dollars of what can be expected to happen if the stated conditions and objectives are achieved. It is often helpful and desirable in a case such as this to prepare such budgets on alternative bases to permit evaluation of the consequences of variations in the accomplishments. Some forms of budgets may be thought of as allowances or authorizations for spending, in the sense of an appropriation.

These limited examples point out the need for considering *why* a budget is to be prepared as a basis for determining *how* it is to be prepared.

WHY ARE COST CONTROLS NECESSARY? Reference has previously been made to the human elements and physical factors in controlling costs. Budgets and cost control programs can be said to be necessary because of limitations in these human and physical factors.

The performance of individual workers may be below normal. Supervisors may not adequately carry out their functions. Materials may be substandard or not available at the instant they are needed. Machines and tooling may be substandard or defective.

Budgets and cost control programs provide a means for planning what the costs should be and for comparing these planned costs with the actual costs experienced. Most important of all, they provide the information needed for corrective action.

Definitions

Because of the variety of practices, policies, and techniques involved in the concept of budgets and cost control programs, it is desirable to define some of the terms that are frequently used. It should be observed that, in common usage, some looseness exists as to the exact meaning of each of these terms.

BUDGETS AND BUDGETARY CONTROL. The terms budget and budgetary control are frequently used in a rather broad sense to include the organization, personnel, and practices that, working together, may perform control and prediction functions.

BUDGET FORECASTS. Prediction is emphasized in budget forecasts, whether of sales, production costs, or expenses. Budget forecasts may also emphasize or be directed to cash requirements or facility programs. They are frequently described as a financial budget or forecast. Although forecasts may assist in developing control measures (perhaps because of predicting undesirable results), they inherently imply prediction rather than control.

COST CONTROL BUDGETS. Cost control budgets emphasize planning and a disciplined predetermination of costs and expenses. They analyze what should be accomplished and how it can be accomplished. They usually imply a striving for the ideal budget and goal that may require coordinated effort and considerable improvement of past performance for accomplishment. They may be "tight" in the sense that accomplishment may be difficult.

PROFIT-PLANNING BUDGETS. Careful and critical planning of proposed operations, including thorough analysis and consideration of alternative courses of action, are some of the more essential elements of profit-planning budgets.

SALES BUDGETS. Sales budgets may represent sales quotas, goals, or objectives. Alternately, they may embody prediction. They may analyze anticipated sales by products, by territories, or by salesmen, may be stated in units of product as well as in dollars, and may reflect varying degrees of optimism as to probability of accomplishment.

PRODUCTION BUDGETS. Production budgets may take at least two forms, one involving units or quantities of products to be produced and the other dealing with costs and expenses required for production of product.

ADVERTISING BUDGETS. Advertising budgets represent a planned or authorized program for advertising expenditures that may detail various elements of the program and, perhaps, relate the dollar amounts to products and product volumes.

INVENTORY BUDGETS. Inventory budgets represent planned inventory programs that are generally associated with formulae and policies for inventory control. The budget may be stated in dollars or in units and other quantitative factors, with detailed segregation by product groupings or by plant location.

CASH BUDGETS. Banks and other lending institutions frequently require projections of cash requirements (sometimes described as cash flow sheets) that summarize anticipated cash receipts and disbursements for a future period. Their objectives generally include (1) determination of amount of financing required, and (2) analysis of planned repayment of obligations.

FLEXIBLE BUDGETS. Flexible budgets describe budgetary data that are prepared in such a manner that budgeted amounts (usually cost and expenses) can be determined for varying levels of volume and other conditions subject to change. This facilitates comparison of incurred costs and expenses with budgeted amounts, since the budgeted amounts can be stated to correspond to the levels of volume and other conditions actually experienced. This permits comparisons of actual accomplishment against the budget data in a variety of conditions that may be experienced.

PREPARATION OF BUDGET FORECASTS

Objectives

This section describes how a budget forecast can be prepared. Attention is directed to problems and questions that are likely to arise, and a step-by-step procedure is outlined.

In considering how to proceed with each of the steps, it is first necessary to ask these questions:

1. Why is the budget forecast needed, and who is to use it?
2. What answers or points are expected to be disclosed?
3. What future period should be covered?
4. How much detail is required in the presentation?
5. What degree of accuracy is required?

Since the answers to each of these questions have an important bearing on how to proceed, each question will be analyzed to indicate its implications.

WHY IS BUDGET FORECAST NEEDED? Why is the budget forecast needed and who is to use it? The answer to this question will affect the course of action in preparing the budget forecast. The answer may fall into one of the following groupings:

1. *Management Planning:* A budget forecast may be needed as part of over-all management planning. The request to prepare such a budget forecast or establish a budgetary control program may originate with the board of directors, the president, or the chief financial officer, usually the treasurer or the comptroller. A budget forecast may be needed to determine cash or capital requirements in connection with plant expansion, new major contracts, mergers, curtailment programs, or other prospective major changes in operations. Corporate policy with respect to payment of cash dividends may be involved. The request or need may be internal or external in origin.

2. *New financing:* A budget forecast may be needed to secure new financing or in connection with existing financing. Here, the request may originate with a bank, an insurance company, an underwriter of securities, or perhaps some other outside financial institution. The particular requirements of any such outside interests should be ascertained.

3. *Overhead rates:* A budget forecast may be needed as a basis for the establishment of standard burden rates or rates for general and administrative overhead. These rates may be needed for cost accounting purposes or for use in estimating costs for the quotation of selling prices to customers.

4. *Control:* A budget may be needed to control revenues—sales quotas are a form of budget—or to control expenditures, either of a capital

or an expense nature. Advertising budgets fall within this category. Bu
may need to be broken down by territories, by departments, by cl;
item, and so on.

It is obvious that the purpose for which a budget forecast is pre
should influence the manner of preparation. There may be a special re
ment for some conservatism in approach, with the objective that income be
stated on a moderate or conservative basis, although allowances for costs
and expenses may be liberal. On the other hand, a budget forecast that is
primarily intended to emphasize control may be established on what could
be described as a tight or restrictive basis.

A complete budgetary control program should include both the forecast and control types of budgets. This does not necessarily mean that the
forecast type of budget, intended to forecast cash requirements for perhaps
a year in advance, need necessarily be predicated upon and rigidly tied in
to control budgets set up for departmental expenses. The objectives are
likely to be different in each instance, and, accordingly, it may be desirable
to establish one on a basis that is easy to attain and the other on a basis
difficult to attain.

WHAT IS THE BUDGET FORECAST TO DISCLOSE? What answers or
points is the budget forecast expected to disclose? This is closely related to
the first question, "Why is the budget forecast needed and who is to use it?"
The major emphasis may be upon one or more of the following:

1. *Cash requirements:* Future cash requirements may be disclosed and,
   hence, the amount of required financing, or perhaps the effect of a
   specified dividend policy.

2. *Earnings:* The objective may be to disclose future net earnings, perhaps by monthly or quarterly periods.

3. *Financial condition:* The future financial condition as disclosed by
   budgeted balance sheets may be desired. The future balances of receivables and inventories may be of particular interest.

4. *Selling prices:* The relationship of prospective income and expenses
   may be an important objective for use as a guide to setting selling
   prices.

5. *Break-even data:* Data may be desired relating to break-even points
   and the effect of volume on net income.

6. *Sales quotas:* The amount of prospective gross income may be important. Sales quotas are an example.

7. *Expense control:* Totals of expense related to specified levels of activity
   may be desired—stated in terms of dollars, manpower, or other convenient units of measurement. This is the "expense control" concept.
   Data on manpower may be desired in planning personnel requirements.

8. *Appropriations:* "Amounts appropriated" may be the objective when
   particular emphasis is placed upon authorizing and limiting expenditures. Governmental budgets have this characteristic.

LENGTH OF BUDGET PERIOD. What future period should be covered? A budget forecast should ordinarily extend as far in the future as management's planning and the available data will permit. Usually, forecasting a year in advance is practicable. Sometimes this is too far ahead, but there may occasionally be good reasons for forecasting several years ahead. Forecasting one year in advance in some detail is probably the most common practice.

Special considerations may suggest an appropriate period. For example, a model year, such as is typical in the automobile industry, may indicate an annual budget. A style season, in the case of clothing or shoes, may favor a six-month budget.

AMOUNT OF DETAIL. How much detail is to be included in the budget forecast? A simple answer may be: as much as is informative to those who will use the budget. Brevity has merit; much of the detailed data can be analyzed in supporting work sheets and need not be included in the budget presentation. Certainly, rounding out of dollar amounts is desirable. Pennies should be omitted, and often the hundreds or thousands of dollars have no significance. It is often desirable to group certain accounts for budget purposes.

ACCURACY. What degree of accuracy is required in the budget forecast figures? In considering this question, it is easy to conclude that a useful budget forecast cannot be prepared because the facts on which it is based cannot be completely accurate. Although reasonable accuracy is desirable, neither the forecast type of budget nor the control type of budget requires a high degree of accuracy to be useful. If the budget is carefully prepared from the best data available to management, it should be useful, even though numerous differences may be observed when comparing actual experience with the budget forecast.

It might be noted, for example, that in preparing a budget forecast to secure a bank loan of $1,000,000, a difference or error of as much as $25,000 or $50,000 in estimated cash requirements is not likely to be significant.

Procedure

An outline of a procedure for preparing a budget forecast is presented in the following paragraphs. Many points and techniques must be worked out for a particular industry or type of business and for a specific company, but there is a pattern of rather general application that can be followed.

Assume, for example, that a budget forecast is to be prepared for a manufacturing company in connection with new financing. What will it look like, what data will be needed to prepare it, and how should each step be undertaken? Assume that the company has been in business for at least several years, that it has reasonably good accounting and cost records, and that monthly financial statements are available. It can be a large company or a small company. The approach need vary only as to details.

BUDGET FORECAST SCHEDULES. When budget forecasts are prepared in connection with new financing, a determination of the amount of future cash requirements is usually the prime objective. Other projected financial data, such as balance sheets, statements of net earnings, and statements of cash receipts and disbursements, are also helpful in portraying the probable result of plans for the future. Assume, therefore, that a budget in report form is to be prepared which contains budgeted statements of net earnings, a statement of earnings retained for use in the business (earned surplus), budgeted balance sheets, and a budgeted statement of cash receipts and disbursements for a period of a year in the future. Although statements of cash receipts and disbursements are not ordinarily included in the monthly or annual reports of most companies maintaining their records on an accrual basis, this particular statement should be included in any budget forecast in which emphasis is placed upon cash requirements. It is not a difficult statement to prepare after the budgeted balance sheets and budgeted statements of net earnings are completed.

PERIODS. Assume that it has been decided to prepare budgeted figures on a monthly basis for the first three months of the year in the future and on a quarterly basis for the remaining three quarterly periods of the year. This is an optional matter. If sharp seasonal peaks and valleys in activity are anticipated during certain months, it may be desirable to prepare budgeted figures for each month of the year, rather than condensing the last nine months into three quarterly periods. This will permit a determination as to the month in which the peak cash requirement would fall. Sample statements that illustrate a simple form that can be used as work sheets and also as budget report forms are presented in Figures 11-1, 11-2, and 11-3. Figure 11-4 illustrates a method of presenting the same data in a form that emphasizes trends for report purposes.

ORGANIZATION OF REPORT SCHEDULES. It is generally desirable, in deciding upon the form of the finished budget forecast, to provide columns in each statement for historical data related to previous periods. This will allow anyone to compare the historical figures in the balance sheets, statements of net earnings, and statements of cash receipts and disbursements with the budgeted figures. This can be readily accomplished by preparing all of the statements on a columnar basis, as shown in Figures 11-1, 11-2, and 11-3. The first three or four columns can be used for the historical period, three columns can be used for the three budgeted months, and three columns can be used for the budgeted quarterly periods. Another column could be used for the totals of the budgeted year, if this is desired.

DATA REQUIREMENTS. Having made the basic decisions outlined above, what data are needed to prepare the budget? There will be special problems in each particular company, but usually, the following essential

$000 OMITTED

	ACTUAL			BUDGETED					
	YEARS ENDED JUNE 30			MONTH OF			QUARTER ENDING		
	1964	1965	1966	July 1966	Aug. 1966	Sept. 1966	Dec. 31, 1966	Mar. 31, 1966	June 30, 1967
Net sales	$761	$877	$910	$ 80	$ 82	$ 85	$275	$325	$350
Miscellaneous income	1	2	1						
TOTAL	$762	$879	$911	$ 80	$ 82	$ 85	$275	$325	$350
Cost of sales	$444	$530	$547	$ 48	$ 50	$ 53	$166	$196	$211
selling expenses	77	80	82	8	8	8	27	32	35
Administrative expenses	114	132	135	13	13	13	41	49	52
Other deductions	46	51	55	3	3	3	12	14	15
TOTAL COSTS AND EXPENSES	$681	$793	$819	$ 72	$ 74	$ 77	$246	$291	$313
NET EARNINGS BEFORE TAXES ON INCOME	$ 81	$ 86	$ 92	$ 8	$ 8	$ 8	$ 29	$ 34	$ 37
Percent to net sales	10.6%	9.8%	10.1%	10.0%	9.8%	9.4%	10.5%	10.5%	10.6%
Provision for taxes on income	31	32	35	3	3	3	11	14	14
NET EARNINGS FOR PERIOD	$ 50	$ 54	$ 55	$ 5	$ 5	$ 5	$ 18	$ 20	$ 23
Percent to net sales	6.6%	6.1%	6.3%	6.3%	6.1%	5.9%	6.5%	6.2%	6.6%

STATEMENT OF EARNINGS RETAINED
FOR USE IN THE BUSINESS
(EARNED SURPLUS)

	1964	1965	1966	July 1966	Aug. 1966	Sept. 1966	Dec. 31, 1966	Mar. 31, 1966	June 30, 1967
Balance at beginning of period	$ 11	$ 11	$ 15	$ 22	$ 27	$ 20	$ 25	$ 31	$ 39
Add net earnings for period	50	54	57	5	5	5	18	20	23
TOTAL	$ 61	$ 65	$ 72	$ 27	$ 32	$ 25	$ 43	$ 51	$ 62
Payment of dividends:									
Preferred Stock	$ 10	$ 10	$ 10	$-0-	$ 2	$-0-	$ 2	$ 2	$ 2
Common Stock	40	40	40	-0-	10	-0-	10	10	10
TOTAL DIVIDENDS	$ 50	$ 50	$ 50	$-0-	$ 12	$-0-	$ 12	$ 12	$ 12
Balance at end of period	$ 11	$ 15	$ 22	$ 27	$ 20	$ 25	$ 31	$ 39	$ 50

Fig. 11-1. XYZ Manufacturing Company Statement of Net Earnings

ASSETS	ACTUAL As Of June 30,				BUDGETED AS OF					
	1963	1964	1965	1966	July 31, 1966	Aug. 31, 1966	Sep. 30, 1966	Dec. 31, 1966	Mar. 31, 1967	June 30, 1967
Cash	$104	$102	$132	$127	$130	$145	$145	$150	$155	$155
Marketable securities	10	10	10	10	10	10	10	10	10	10
Trade accounts and notes receivable	33	40	33	36	35	35	32	32	32	32
Other accounts receivable	5	7	7	8	7	7	7	7	7	7
Inventories	160	176	80	202	210	220	230	211	228	228
Prepaid taxes, insurance, etc.	5	11	12	11	10	10	10	10	13	13
TOTAL CURRENT ASSETS	$317	$346	$374	$394	$402	$427	$434	$420	$445	$445
Cash surrender value of life ins.	$ 3	$ 3	$ 3	$ 4	$ 4	$ 4	$ 4	$ 4	$ 5	$ 5
Investments	5	5	5	5	5	5	5	5	5	5
Miscellaneous other assets	6	7	6	7	7	7	7	6	5	6
TOTAL OTHER ASSETS	$ 14	$ 15	$ 14	$ 16	$ 16	$ 16	$ 16	$ 15	$ 15	$ 16
Property, plant, and equipment	$562	$579	$607	$652	$655	$655	$660	$700	$700	$730
Less accumulated depreciation	156	180	204	241	244	247	250	262	270	282
PROPERTY, PLANT, AND EQUIPMENT	$406	$399	$403	$411	$411	$408	$410	$438	$430	$448
Patents and licenses	152	130	111	90	89	87	86	81	76	70
	$889	$890	$902	$911	$918	$938	$946	$954	$966	$979

LIABILITIES	1963	1964	1965	1966	July 31, 1966	Aug. 31, 1966	Sep. 30, 1966	Dec. 31, 1966	Mar. 31, 1967	June 30, 1967
Notes payable within one year	$-0-	$-0-	$-0-	$-0-	$-0-	$ 10	$ 10	$ 10	$ 10	$ 10
Trade accounts payable	32	30	39	40	40	45	43	40	34	25
Accrued expenses	16	15	15	14	13	17	18	15	14	14
Federal taxes on income	30	34	33	35	38	6	10	20	33	47
TOTAL CURRENT LIABILITIES	$ 78	$ 79	$ 87	$ 89	$ 91	$ 78	$ 81	$ 85	$ 91	$ 96
Long-term indebtedness	-0-	-0-	-0-	-0-	-0-	40	40	38	36	33
Preferred Stock	$150	$150	$150	$150	$150	$150	$150	$150	$150	$150
Common Stock	650	650	650	650	650	650	650	650	650	650
Earned surplus	11	11	15	22	27	20	25	31	39	50
TOTAL STOCKHOLDERS' INVESTMENT	$811	$811	$815	$822	$827	$820	$825	$831	$839	$850
	$889	$890	$902	$911	$918	$938	$946	$954	$966	$979
Net working capital	$239	$267	$287	$305	$311	$349	$354	$335	$354	$349
Current ratio	4.1 to 1	4.4 to 1	4.3 to 1	4.4 to 1	4.4 to 1	5.5 to 1	5.4 to 1	4.9 to 1	4.9 to 1	4.6 to 1

Fig. 11-2. Balance Sheets

$000 OMITTED

	ACTUAL Years Ended June 30			BUDGETED MONTH OF			BUDGETED QUARTER ENDING		
	1964	1965	1966	July 1966	Aug. 1966	Sept. 1966	Dec. 31, 1966	Mar. 31, 1967	June 30, 1967
CASH RECEIPTS:									
Collections from sales and accounts receivable	$754	$884	$907	$80	$82	$88	$275	$325	$350
Proceeds of notes payable	-0-	-0-	-0-	-0-	50	-0-	-0-	-0-	-0-
Miscellaneous income	1	2	1	-0-	-0-	-0-	-0-	-0-	-0-
TOTAL CASH RECEIPTS	$755	$886	$908	$80	$132	$88	$275	$325	$350
CASH DISBURSEMENTS:									
Materials, pay rolls, and other operating payments	$633	$744	$787	$74	$70	$84	$216	$306	$306
Federal taxes on income	27	34	32	-0-	35	-0-	-0-	-0-	-0-
Dividends on:									
Preferred Stock	10	10	10	-0-	2	-0-	2	2	2
Common Stock	40	40	40	-0-	10	-0-	10	10	10
Additions to property, plant, and equipment	17	28	44	3	-0-	4	40	-0-	30
Reduction of notes payable	-0-	-0-	-0-	-0-	-0-	-0-	2	2	2
TOTAL CASH DISBURSEMENTS	$757	$856	$913	$77	$117	$88	$270	$320	$350
INCREASE OR (DECREASE) IN CASH	($2)	$30	($5)	$3	$15	$-0-	$5	$5	$-0-
Cash balance at end of period	$102	$132	$127	$130	$145	$145	$150	$155	$155

JUNE 30-63 ..... $104

Fig. 11-3. Statement of Cash Receipts and Disbursements

Period	Net Earnings	Net Sales	Cost of Sales	Gross Profit	Selling Expense	Administrative Expense	Other Deductions	Net Earnings Before Taxes	Provision For Taxes on Income	Per Cent to Net Sales			Period
										Net Earnings	Gross Profit	Net Earnings before taxes	
Actual Fisc. Yr.													Actual Fisc. Yr.
1964	50	762	444	318	77	114	46	81	31	6.6%	41.7%	10.7%	1964
1965	54	879	530	349	80	132	51	86	32	6.1	39.7	9.8	1965
1966	57	911	547	364	82	135	55	92	35	6.3	40.0	10.1	1966
Monthly Average													Monthly Average
1964	4.2	63	37	26	6.5	9.5	3.8	6.8	2.6	6.6	41.7	10.7	1964
1965	4.5	73	44	29	6.6	11.0	4.2	7.2	2.7	6.1	39.7	9.8	1965
1966	4.7	76	46	30	6.6	11.2	4.6	7.7	3.0	6.3	40.7	10.1	1966
Budget Month													Budget Month
Jul	5.2	80	48	32	8.0	12	3.7	8.4	3.2	6.5	40.0	10.5	Jul
Aug	5.3	82	49	32	8.2	12	3.8	8.6	3.3	6.5	39.0	10.5	Aug
Sep	5.5	85	52	32	8.5	13	3.9	8.9	3.4	6.5	37.6	10.5	Sep
Quarter													Quarter
Sep	16	247	149	98	25	37	11	26	10	6.5	39.7	10.5	Sep
Dec	18	275	166	109	27	41	12	29	11	6.5	39.6	10.5	Dec
Mar	20	325	196	129	32	49	14	34	14	6.2	39.7	10.5	Mar
Jun	23	350	211	139	35	52	15	37	14	6.6	39.7	10.6	Jun

Fig. 11-4. Budgeted Trends of Net Earnings

pieces of information will supply the basis for the preparation of a budget forecast:

1. *Sales forecast:* Many companies have sales forecasts available as part of their sales or production planning programs. If not, the chief sales executive can be requested to prepare a forecast, which should be reviewed and approved by top management. Generally, the more detailed the sales forecast, the better. It should certainly detail sales dollars by months, and it will be helpful if data as to unit quantities and estimated unit selling prices can be secured. Totals by product lines may be helpful. Attention should be directed to seasonal fluctuations that may influence monthly sales totals. Data as to unfilled orders are also useful in appraising the reliability of sales forecasts.

2. *Capital expenditures:* Information will be needed as to contemplated capital expenditures for property, plant, and equipment and tooling. Use should be made of any appropriation system in effect. It may be possible to have an estimate of such expenditures prepared for the budget year by the plant engineer, master mechanic, or other individuals responsible for this activity. Their estimates should be reviewed by top management, and reasonable provision should be made for contingencies.

3. *Inventory data:* Data will be required as to future inventory balances. Such data are seldom easy to obtain. Sometimes a planning or scheduling department is able to forecast future inventory totals in dollars. In other instances only data on quantities are obtainable. A check within the organization will disclose what information is available or can reasonably be compiled. As a last resort, it may be sufficient to develop a relationship between inventories in previous periods and either sales or cost of sales. This relationship can then be used to project the amount of future inventories. The effect of seasonal fluctuations should be considered in relation to inventory planning.

4. *Financial program:* Policies should be determined concerning payment of dividends, contemplated financing, possible sale of facilities or liquidation of investments, and so on. This information should be secured by consultation with the top management group.

5. *Historical data:* Copies should be secured of the company's monthly financial statements for a reasonable historical period. A period of three years was selected in Figure 11-3, for the purpose of developing data as to trends. It may be desirable to shorten or lengthen the period selected.

6. *Costs and expenses:* Cost reports, standard costs, labor performance reports, factory burden analyses, and other similar data may be needed.

The items enumerated are generally sufficient as a starting point for the preparation of a budget forecast. To the extent that they are unavailable or incomplete, or where special problems exist, improvisation will be necessary. A little imagination and considerable ingenuity can be very helpful, particularly if some of these basic data are not readily available in the company.

SCHEDULE CAPTIONS. The next step is to lay out the form of the budgeted statements. These should follow the general pattern of the balance sheets and statements of net earnings normally prepared for the company. It is usually desirable, however, to condense or combine certain of the items. For example, items under the current assets caption in the budgeted balance sheet may well be limited to:

Cash on hand and in banks
Marketable securities
Accounts receivable and notes receivable
Inventories
Prepaid expenses

The classification for property, plant, and equipment may be limited to one figure for the total cost and one figure for accumulated depreciation and amortization.

These are typical examples. It is usually easier to budget items such as these in total, and, although some detail may be desirable in underlying work sheets or in supporting schedules, the totals are probably all that are needed in the final presentation.

HISTORICAL DATA. Mention has been made of the desirability of reflecting a comparison of historical data in the budgeted statements. This technique, in addition to being useful to anyone reviewing the budget, tends to insure that the budgeted figures are assembled on a basis consistent and comparable with previous monthly and annual reports.

SEQUENCE OF SCHEDULE PREPARATION. Under the method outlined, the sequence in which the basic statements are prepared is of fundamental importance for reasons that will become apparent. This sequence is as follows:

First—Statement of net earnings (profit and loss)
Second—Statement of earnings retained for use in the business (earned surplus)
Third—Balance sheets
Fourth—Statement of cash receipts and disbursements

BUDGETED STATEMENT OF NET EARNINGS. Turning first to the statement of net earnings, each of the items should be budgeted or computed in sequence. Budgeted net sales can be determined and entered from the sales budget. If miscellaneous income is significant, a special study may be necessary. Usually, miscellaneous income can be estimated from past experience or from a review of the sources that produce it.

Estimating the amounts for cost of sales may present problems, since this is a complex figure influenced by changes in prices paid for materials and services, labor rates of pay and labor efficiency, volume of production, and so on. Specific provision can be included in the estimated amounts to cover contemplated changes in material costs, labor rates of pay, and other significant cost factors.

As a matter of mechanics, there is usually a choice of one or two methods in estimating cost of sales:

1. Use of a percentage relationship of cost of sales to sales dollars, based upon past experience and adjusted for anticipated changes—this can be described as a "gross profit" method.

2. Pricing individual items included in the sales budget from cost records, cost estimates, or other data. It may be practicable to estimate cost of sales at standard cost and then add (or deduct) an estimated provision for cost variances. This second method may be more accurate than the gross profit method.

Details will vary for each company. Other methods may prove more appropriate.

Attention should next be directed to commercial expenses—selling expenses, perhaps engineering, and general and administrative expenses. If departmental expense control budgets, advertising programs, or other data are available, they should be considered for use. Any special items and known changes should be provided for. The budgeted amounts for commercial expenses can be established, based upon all the available data, using past experience as a guide and applying judgment. It is often helpful to schedule and study each account making up the commercial expense totals and to estimate the future expenses account by account. Consultation with the company's top executives will usually be helpful in establishing budgeted amounts for commercial expenses.

"Other deductions" will usually include interest on borrowed money, which can be computed from the estimated borrowings. Any other items includable under this caption can usually be estimated from past experience.

All items in the statement of net earnings have now been budgeted or computed except income taxes. It is a relatively simple matter to compute the taxes on income at current or anticipated rates and arrive at the net profit for each budget period.

This completes the statement of net earnings. At this point, it is wise to review the figures, particularly the relationship between costs, expenses, and net sales in the historical period, and the same items in the budgeted period. To the extent that new factors, such as changes in prices, changes in volume, and so on, have occurred, it is reasonable to expect to find a different pattern in the budgeted period when it is compared with the historical period.

BUDGETED STATEMENT OF EARNINGS RETAINED. After determining that the statement of net earnings is in final form, prepare the statement of net earnings retained for use in the business (earned surplus). This is simply a procedure of starting with the last actual balance, adding the budgeted earnings or deducting the budgeted losses for each period, and then deducting the estimated amount of dividends to be paid. The end result is a balance for net earnings retained for use in the business (earned surplus) at the close of each budgeted period.

BUDGETED BALANCE SHEET. Turning now to the balance sheet, the problem is to determine how best to budget each item in it, leaving cash on hand and in banks until the last. Balances for net earnings retained for use in the business (earned surplus) have already been determined. Capital stock balances can be estimated for the budget period to reflect any new issues or anticipated changes. Each item in the balance sheet should be analyzed to apply all of the available knowledge and data of future plans.

In the case of accounts receivable, the budgeted sales for each period as recorded on the statement of net earnings are available at this point. These figures represent, in effect, the "debit" to the accounts receivable during each period. The next problem is to estimate the collections on accounts receivable. This can be done in most instances by comparing the net sales and accounts receivable balances in previous periods, perhaps going back as far as two or three years, and determining the percentage relationship. Stated another way, the factor needed can be expressed as the average number of days' sales remaining in accounts receivable at the end of each period. Consideration should be given to seasonal influences and to changes in payment terms that may have occurred or can be anticipated during the budget period.

Some of the methods of estimating inventory balances have already been mentioned. Fixed asset balances at the end of each period can be determined by adding the estimated expenditures for new items and providing for any contemplated dispositions. Depreciation on the new fixed asset balances can then be computed.

Accounts payable can sometimes be estimated by establishing a percentage relationship between cost of sales in previous periods and accounts payable balances. This percentage factor can then be used for the budget period.

Having established a reasonable basis for estimating or budgeting each item in the balance sheet except cash, it is then possible to enter figures for "cash on hand and in banks" in amounts necessary to bring the balance sheets into balance. Although this is a "plugged figure," if the other balance sheet figures are realistically determined, the cash figures determined by this method will be equally realistic. If the cash requirements are such as to require additional financing in the form of loans, minimum and maximum cash balances can be assumed and the difference reflected on the liability side of the balance sheet as the amount of loans that will be required. Such loans will ordinarily be made in round amounts.

Here, again, it should be noted that the showing of historical balance sheet figures in addition to the budgeted figures tends to provide a means for checking the over-all reasonableness of the budgeted figures. The comparison tends to help prevent overlooking of some important item.

BUDGETED STATEMENT OF CASH RECEIPTS AND DISBURSEMENTS. At this stage, three sets of statements have been prepared that are in agreement with each other—statements of net earnings, a reconciliation of earnings retained for use in the business (earned surplus), and balance sheets. Having completed these statements, it is relatively easy to prepare a simplified statement of cash receipts and disbursements by analyzing the cash transactions that would result from the changes reflected in the balance sheets.

In doing this, use can be made of the work sheets previously prepared for such items as accounts receivable, fixed assets, federal taxes on income, and so on. The work sheet for accounts receivable can be designed to disclose the amount of cash collections for each period. The item of miscellaneous income in the statement of net earnings can be adjusted to a cash basis if necessary.

The statement of cash receipts and disbursements serves to highlight the principal factors contributing to the change in cash position, particularly the sources of cash receipts and the major expenditures, including additions to property, plant and equipment, payment of income taxes, payment of dividends, and so on.

BUDGET COMMENTS. Having prepared the three budget schedules, presumably for presentation to management or outside parties, it is helpful and informative to prepare brief and concise comments outlining the source of budget figures, the assumptions that have been made, and any other points deserving comment. This completes the budget forecast.

COST CONTROL AND COST CONTROL BUDGETS

Important Factors for Cost Control

Although cost control is commonly thought of in terms of time studies, cost standards, and control budgets, effective cost control requires attention to a great many factors, including:

1. Facilities—buildings and machine tools suitable for low-cost production

2. Special tools, dies, jigs, and fixtures—economically designed with regard to planned production volume to manufacture a quality product with minimum effort and cost

3. Environmental and working conditions—factors such as temperature, ventilation, lighting, dust, and humidity

4. Industrial relations—employee morale and *esprit de corps,* an intangible but important relationship to product costs

5. Engineering design—design of product to facilitate low-cost production

6. Organization—assignment of clearly defined functional responsibility for all factors affecting production and costs

7. Planning and scheduling—over-all management planning and forecasting as well as the day-to-day balancing of work schedules with machines and manpower—having machines, materials, and workers available when and where they are needed.

8. Capable supervision at all levels—the first line of defense in controlling costs

9. Training programs—both for workers and for supervisors

10. Production methods—determining the best method for performing each operation

11. Work measurement and cost standards—determining how much time should be required for each operation and how much the product should cost—engineered standards desirable for all material, direct labor, and overhead factors that comprise product costs

12. Quality control—measuring the quality of product produced, altering process controls before defective product is produced, and minimizing scrap and spoilage

13. Cost control budgets—as part of the planning for low-cost production, as part of the determination of what the product should cost, and as part of the follow-up to make certain that planned operations and costs are achieved

14. Reports—summary of what has been accomplished, comparison of results with plans, disclosure of excess costs, and assignment of responsibility

15. Wage incentives—listed last to emphasize that, in controlling costs, wage incentives are not a substitute for adequate attention to all other factors

ENGINEERED STANDARDS. Effective cost control can be summarized as being dependent upon:

1. Provision of the right kind of facilities, machines, tools, organization, and supervision

2. Planning and determination of what costs should be incurred

3. Follow-up to ascertain that planned objectives are met. (If they are not met, it becomes important to isolate the causes and responsibility for differences.)

It is in the planning and determination of what costs should be incurred that engineered standards become important. The term "engineered standards" is used to describe basic data and cost determinations for material, direct labor, and the various elements of overhead that are based upon careful engineering analysis and study (rather than, for example, past performance and historical accounting data).

The character of adequate engineered standards makes it possible to use them to determine, with reasonable certainty, what levels of costs and expenses should be attainable.

INCENTIVES. Incentive wage compensation (for direct and indirect labor, supervisors, and executives) can be an important factor in controlling costs. Numerous practical problems often limit its effectiveness. For incentives to be effective, adequate measurements must exist of a "fair day's work" (time study or methods time measurement), the effort must be properly applied (facilities, tools, and methods), and there must be an employee relations atmosphere that will permit a fair and equitable administration of the incentive program. When all of these factors are not present, it is possible, and not uncommon, for incentive compensation to be paid for effort or output that, at best, is no better than could reasonably be expected without incentive compensation.

Incentive wage compensation should not be overlooked as a means of controlling costs, but it should not be expected to be a substitute for good management of plant operations and other basic control measures.

Budgetary Factors

FLEXIBLE BUDGETS. Most cost control budgets must, of necessity, be prepared on a basis that will permit their application to changed conditions, particularly with respect to changes in product mix and in volume of production. Almost every manufacturing program is subject to changes in volume. Since volume can have an important effect on the requirements for indirect labor, supplies, and other expenses of a variable or partly variable nature, it is essential to establish the requirements for each cost element and the relationship of each volume. A budget that accomplishes this is known as a flexible budget.

FIXED AND VARIABLE EXPENSES. Although preparation of a flexible budget can be described as involving the identification of fixed, partly variable, and variable expenses, this can seldom be accomplished effectively solely on the basis of data abstracted from historical accounting records.

It is seldom practical, for example, to classify arbitrarily each account for manufacturing expenses as between fixed, partly variable, and variable classifications. The items recorded in each account are seldom homogeneous with respect to this characteristic of costs. Moreover, historical data are seldom more than one of several criteria that should be considered in establishing desirable levels of expense for the future. Too often, historical data embody undesirable practices, excessive costs, and the effect of conditions that should be altered in the future.

PARTICIPATION OF SUPERVISION. An essential factor in establishing and operating cost control budgets is to provide for participation of each departmental supervisor. This participation by the supervisor should start with the planning of his future departmental activities. He should participate in the analysis of data and the setting of standards, and he should concur in the budget allowances that are finally established. It is important that each supervisor know how the budget for his department was established. Moreover, he should be convinced of the attainability of the budget performance levels.

BUDGETING ON BASIS OF RESPONSIBILITY. In analyzing and selecting organizational segments and cost elements for budgetary control, consideration should be given to the direct individual responsibility in each instance. As a general rule, for example, departmental cost control budgets should be limited to those elements of expense that are directly controllable by the departmental supervisor concerned.

Any strict application of this principle is rather difficult in most companies. The difficulty arises, in part, because responsibilities are often not clearly defined. At best, some degree of joint responsibility may exist for many elements of cost or expense.

In the case of direct labor, for example, it may seem that control of direct labor costs in any department is the direct and primary responsibility of the foreman. However, many factors, such as materials and parts shortages, defective tools and equipment, schedule changes, or industrial relations disputes, may prevent full attainment of optimum levels of direct labor costs. The foreman may have only partial control over, or responsibility for, such factors.

A somewhat similar problem may arise with respect to expense elements, such as inspection, material handling, and maintenance, which may be charged as departmental expense although originating in a separate service department with its own supervisor.

Decisions involving most fixed expenses, such as depreciation, property taxes, and insurance, are not made by departmental supervisors, although these items are charged to their department for cost accounting purposes.

UNIT DATA. In setting standards for costs and expenses, developing basic data as to product mix and volumes, and in reporting operating results in comparison with budget allowances, attention should be directed to unit data as well as dollars whenever practicable. For example, number of people, hours, unit quantities of supplies, and other basic information can be particularly helpful. Unit data are usually more understandable to supervisors and others who are concerned with budget comparisons. It can be particularly helpful in analyzing differences between actual results and budget and in future revisions of budget allowances.

ALTERNATIVE LEVELS OF VOLUME. Cost control budgets are ordinarily established on a flexible basis. The basic data are stated in a manner to disclose what the costs and expenses should be at various selected levels of volume. For example, in budgeting manufacturing expenses (factory burden), these selected volume levels may be stated in terms of units of product per hour, day, week, or month. Alternatively, the selected levels of volume can be stated in terms of dollar totals of direct labor (or hours), dollar totals of product costs, or perhaps even dollar totals of sales, although this is seldom desirable. The selected levels of volume can also be stated in terms of a percentage of capacity, selected at increments of 5 or 10 per cent.

MANPOWER REQUIREMENTS AND MANNING TABLES. Having established as a prerequisite the respective levels of volume for budget purposes, the next step is ordinarily to analyze, plan, and set standards for the number of people in each occupational classification for each department. A convenient way of doing this is to state the manpower requirements in the form of manning tables, which provide a summary of the manpower requirements at each production level, with respect to both direct and indirect labor. In the case of direct labor (and desirably in the case of most, if not all, indirect labor classifications), the manpower requirements should be determined by work measurement techniques such as time studies. Industrial engineering studies can also be made of the requirements for indirect labor classifications, such as timekeeping, checking, inspection, setup, and material handling.

DIRECT LABOR. Direct labor is ordinarily thought of as being controlled by direct labor standards stated in terms of units per product. Accordingly, a direct labor budget per se is not the primary basis for control. It is generally necessary, however, to analyze, plan, and budget direct labor in order to establish cost control budgets for the related manufacturing overhead. The budgeting of direct labor is necessary, for example, to provide a basis for estimating burden rates that may be desired as part of the budget procedures. Moreover, certain of the elements of manufacturing expense may be more or less directly dependent upon the amount of direct labor. Examples would include overtime, shift premiums, and other fringe wage benefits.

DETERMINING EXPENSES AT SELECTED LEVELS OF VOLUME. Practices of companies vary rather widely as to how they budget individual expense accounts or groups of accounts. Assuming that manpower requirements have been established for both direct and indirect labor in terms of number of people and that appropriate volume levels have been selected, for some categories it may only be necessary to convert the number of people and scheduled working hours to dollars by application of appropriate hourly or salary rates.

In actual practice, some companies tend to rely too heavily on the analysis of historical data in budgeting levels of expense in relation to volume, perhaps with some percentage reduction for anticipated improvement. This practice tends to be arbitrary and is generally undesirable as a logical or "engineered" approach.

A better alternative is to analyze each element of expense, determine its components, plan what should be required under the conditions in each instance, and develop an objective standard. Expense levels for both indirect labor and supplies are most appropriately set based upon such analyses and engineered studies. Some elements of expense, such as overtime premiums and other fringe wage costs, taxes, insurance, and depreciation, are based largely on accounting or arithmetical computations.

In the case of service functions, such as maintenance, inspection, and material handling, which are often allocated as a charge to productive departments, it is generally desirable to budget these expenses in detail and in total under their separate departmental divisions. This permits a reporting of these expenses to each responsible service supervisor. A separate reporting or analysis can be given to supervisors of departments receiving the benefits of such allocated service charges.

Reports

Although the form of cost control budget reports depends to some extent upon the facts and circumstances in each particular company, there are some points that deserve particular attention:

1. Reporting to departmental supervisors should be limited to those elements of costs and expenses for which they are responsible.
2. Unit data should be provided in addition to dollars wherever possible.
3. Principles of good report design should be observed, including such points as limiting the reports to reasonable amounts of detail, showing trends, and making use of charts and graphs to improve communication.

Figures 11-5 and 11-6 illustrate report forms that can be used in reporting to departmental supervisors.

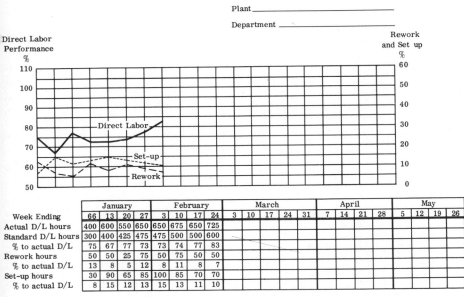

Fig. 11-5. Direct Labor Efficiency Report

DOLLARS

Wk. Edg.	Total Var.	Total Bud.	Total Act.	Spec. Tools Var.	Spec. Tools Bud.	Spec. Tools Act.	Std. Tools Var.	Std. Tools Bud.	Std. Tools Act.	Abrasives Var.	Abrasives Bud.	Abrasives Act.	Paint Var.	Paint Bud.	Paint Act.	Lubricants Var.	Lubricants Bud.	Lubricants Act.	Maint. Mat. Var.	Maint. Mat. Bud.	Maint. Mat. Act.	Other Var.	Other Bud.	Other Act.
Jan 6	100	400	500	34	100	134	34	100	134	6	40	46	9	40	49	6	40	46	7	50	57	4	30	34
Jan 13	75	500	575	16	120	136	32	170	202	7	40	47	4	40	44	6	50	56	6	60	56	4	30	34
Jan 20	75	550	625	13	160	173	35	180	215	8	40	48	0	40	40	10	50	60	5	50	55	4	30	34
Jan 27	100	600	700	25	170	195	35	180	215	7	50	57	4	50	54	17	60	77	9	60	69	3	30	33
Feb 3	70	600	670	10	160	170	30	190	220	10	50	60	2	50	52	7	60	67	7	60	67	4	30	34
Feb 10	40	650	690	5	210	215	12	190	202	3	60	63	3	50	53	6	50	56	6	60	66	5	30	35
Feb 17	50	650	700	7	200	207	20	200	220	5	60	65	4	50	54	6	50	56	5	60	65	3	30	33
Feb 24	10	750	760	0	265	265	5	200	205	0	60	60	0	50	50	2	70	72	2	75	77	1	30	31
Mar 3																								
Mar 10																								
Mar 17																								
Mar 24																								
Mar 31																								

ACTUAL DOLLARS PER ACTUAL DIRECT LABOR HOUR

Wk. Edg.	Total	Spec. Tools	Std. Tools	Abrasives	Paint	Lubricants	Maint. Mat.	Other
Jun 6	1.25	.33	.33	.12	.12	.12	.14	.09
Jan 13	.96	.23	.34	.08	.07	.09	.09	.06
Jan 20	1.14	.32	.39	.09	.07	.11	.10	.06
Jan 27	1.07	.30	.33	.08	.08	.12	.11	.05
Feb 3	1.03	.26	.34	.09	.08	.10	.10	.06
Feb 10	1.02	.32	.30	.09	.08	.08	.10	.05
Feb 17	1.07	.32	.34	.10	.08	.08	.10	.05
Feb 24	1.05	.37	.28	.08	.07	.10	.11	.04
Mar 3								
Mar 10								
Mar 17								
Mar 24								
Mar 31								

Fig. 11-6. Usage of Nonproductive Materials and Supplies

12

Punched Card Machines and Peripheral Devices in Data Processing

N. LOUIS SENENSIEB

Universal Data Systems, Inc.
Los Angeles, Calif.

N. LOUIS SENENSIEB is the director, Information Systems Division, Universal Data Systems, Inc., in Los Angeles, Calif. His responsibilities encompass the direction of consulting efforts for the design and implementation of computer-based management information systems and of computer software development. Prior experience includes some fifteen years in management systems and business data processing. He has held positions as vice-president of Automation Services Corp. and manager of systems for TRW Systems, RCA, Hughes Aircraft Co., and Burroughs Corp.

Mr. Senensieb is a member and past international president of the Systems and Procedures Association, and is currently a member of the editorial advisory board of the Systems and Procedures Journal. *He also holds membership in the Data Processing Management Association, and is active in the field of management systems education. Mr. Senensieb has taught systems courses at U.C.L.A. and Pierce College, Los Angeles, served as guest lecturer at various universities, and has presented papers at professional conferences. Currently, he is a member of the Council of Education and Business Advisors of the International Business Academy in Des Moines, Iowa. He holds B.S. and M.B.A. degrees from U.C.L.A. and the Certificate in Data Processing.*

Mr. Senensieb is the author of a monograph on "The Role of Operations Research in Business," and is a contributing author to Business Systems, *published by the Systems and Procedures Association, the* Encyclopedia of Management, *and the* Total Systems *anthology. He is also the author of several articles in professional journals.*

INTRODUCTION

Punched card machines, also referred to as electronic accounting machines (EAM) or tabulating equipment, have been utilized for a wide variety of record-keeping tasks in government, industry, and business since the late 1880's. These machines consist of a series of electromechanical office machines, each of which performs a specific function of processing data recorded on individual punched cards for the purpose of organizing and tabulating such data into required business information reports.

The basic principle of punched card data processing is to record source data once in the medium of a punched card. That data can then be used time and time again by classifying and summarizing it to produce a variety of desired business information reports.

While this chapter discusses primarily the use of punched card machines for processing business data converted into the form of punched cards, it should be noted that the punched card remains also the prime medium for the initial recording of source data for use by electronic computer systems. It likewise remains a major medium for the communication of data between various types of punched card and electronic computer systems. In turn, some punched card machines perform many functions as peripheral or auxiliary equipment to larger electronic computer systems.

The initial use of punched cards to represent information and control machine operations is credited to Joseph Marie Jacquard, a French weaver. In 1801 he developed a method of using various patterns of holes punched into cards to control his looms to produce automatically different patterns of cloth. However, the application of the punched card for the machine processing of statistical data has its origin in the work of Dr. Herman Hollerith at the U.S. Census Bureau in 1887.

Following the 1880 census, the U.S. Census Bureau had to manually process statistical data handwritten on millions of cards and to sort these cards by various classifications. This final compilation of the 1880 census into useful information was not completed until 1887. To speed up this process and to assure greater accuracy in the final compiled data, Dr. Hollerith developed machines and methods for first representing data in the form of holes in cards, and subsequently mechanically sorting and tabulating this data from the punched cards. The use of punched cards and punched card processing equipment permitted processing of the data from the 1890 census to be completed in less than half the time of the previous census, even though the volume of data had grown to reflect an increase in the U.S. population from 50 million to 62 million.

Dr. Hollerith recognized the potential of the punched card method of data processing for business and industry, and subsequently formed the Tabulating Machine Company for the leasing of such equipment. A later merger led in 1911 to the formation of the Computing-Tabulating-Recording Company, forerunner of the International Business Machines Corporation (IBM), the leading firm in the punched card and computer system field. The code system developed by Hollerith for representing numbers, letters, and other symbols in punched cards remains the basis of the eighty-column card system still in use by IBM and the majority of data processing users.

In 1911 James Powers developed another card code system, the ninety-column card, for punched card data processing and formed the Powers Accounting Machine Company. In 1927 this company was merged to create Remington Rand, Inc., precursor of the present-day Sperry Rand Corporation and its Remington Rand Univac Division, the other major manufacturer of punched card equipment and a prominent computer manufacturer.

There is a variety of other media for recording data for subsequent machine processing besides punched cards. The peripheral devices for processing them normally serve as specialized pieces of auxiliary equipment either to punched card or to electronic computer systems for the purpose of recording data in a machine-processable language medium for communication between different data processing equipment systems.

PUNCHED CARD CONCEPTS

Punched Card Formats

The punched card forms the common medium for representing data in a format that different machines can read and process mechanically. The relative position of the holes in the cards, or their absence, is recognized by various processing machines, and the punching of the data in the form of these holes must be made before any machine processing of the data can take place.

Punched cards have two relative directions in which holes may be located for machine identification—lateral and vertical. Lateral positions, individually referred to as columns, and in combinations of columns as fields, identify the type of information recorded for predetermined system designs, i.e., invoice number, customer number, quantities, dates, etc. Vertical positions or rows, or combinations of them, form the machine codes for actual characters for the type of information to be represented by the punched card medium.

There are two basic punched card formats: the IBM eighty-column and the Remington Rand Univac ninety-column cards. The only similiarities between the cards are the same physical dimensions of 7⅜″ by 3¼″ and .007″ in thickness, and that both represent data by means of codes in the forms of holes. However, the IBM eighty-column card uses the Hollerith code in rectangular holes across the width of the card and the Remington Rand ninety-column card uses the Powers code of round holes in two sets of forty-five columns each across two sections of the card. Figures 12-1 and 12-2 illustrate the IBM and Remington Rand card formats and codes, respectively.

The IBM card provides spaces for eighty columns from left to right and for twelve rows of possible vertical positions from the nines at the

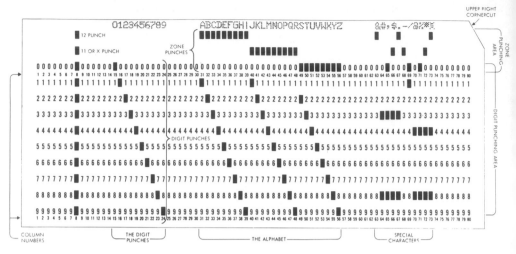

Fig. 12-1. IBM 80-Column Card *(Courtesy IBM)*

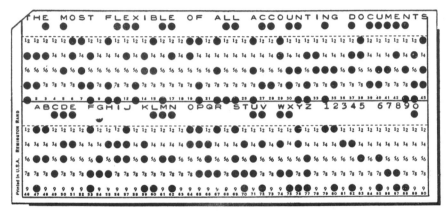

Fig. 12-2. Remington Rand 90-Column Card *(Courtesy Remington Rand, Sperry Rand Corp.)*

bottom to the three rows of "zone" punches at the top. The representation of numbers zero through nine is accomplished by punching the same labeled rows. These "number" rows of the card are known as the "digit" area. The "zone" portion of the card, consisting of the top three rows, is used in combination with the digit area punches to represent letters and special characters. It consists of the zero, eleven, and twelve punches, with the zero punch being considered as both a digit and a zone punch. The eleven punch is sometimes called the "X" punch. Figure 12-1 illustrates the combination of digit and zone punches to represent letters. For example, an "A" is represented by a twelve zone punch and a one digit punch; "B" is represented by a twelve and a two; "J" is represented by an eleven and a one; and "Z" is represented by a zero and a nine. Certain other punch combinations represent special characters.

The Remington Rand card is arranged in two sets of forty-five columns, left to right across the upper and lower halves of the card, each with only six vertical rows. Because the card has only half the number of rows as the eighty-column IBM card, a more condensed code is required to represent numbers. Zero and the odd numbers of one through nine are represented by a single punch in the 0, ½, ¾, ⅚, ⅞, and 9 rows respectively, while the even numbers of two through eight are represented by a nine punch in combination with the ½, ¾, ⅚, and ⅞ rows respectively. In the Remington Rand code there are no zone punches but, as in the IBM card code, multiple punches in the same column are used to represent letters. There is no apparent logic to the arrangement of vertical row combinations. However, the row combinations in the Remington Rand code were selected on the basis of internal operation requirements of the processing machines. Figure 12-2 illustrates the row combinations to represent numbers and letters.

Basic Card Reading

In IBM punched card machines, fine brass brushes drop through the holes in the punched card to make electrical contacts. These electrical contacts then link the card-reading mechanism to the printing and adding devices with the equipment.

It should be noted that a data processing system is set up either to utilize the IBM eighty-column card with IBM punched card equipment to process it or the Remington Rand ninety-column card with Remington Rand Univac punched card equipment to process it. In any one punched card system, only one of the two formats can be used. It should be noted, though, that certain Univac computer systems can have separate sets of card-reading equipment to read both types of punched card formats and codes. However, while all computer manufacturers produce card-reading equipment to read the eighty-column card and codes, only Remington Rand Univac manufactures equipment to read the ninety-column card and codes.

Card Fields

Card fields represent a predetermined combination of card columns to represent specific items of information. Thus, for example, in an accounts receivable application the following data may be required:

Customer number
Customer name
Invoice date
Invoice number
Invoice amount

Before card fields can be assigned for each of the above items, standard digit lengths will have to be established for each as part of the over-all system design for the application. The card field locations and lengths then become fixed for that application. If the following digit lengths are established, specified card column combinations for card fields can be set up as illustrated in Figure 12-3.

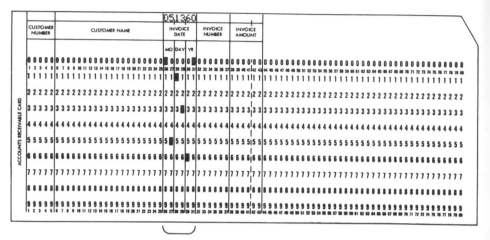

Fig. 12-3. Illustrates Punching Date "5-13-60" in the Data Field in Columns 26-31

card field name	field length	card columns
Customer Number	5 digits	1 through 5
Customer Name	20 digits	6 through 25
Invoice Date	6 digits	26 through 31
Month	2 digits	26 and 27
Day	2 digits	28 and 29
Year	2 digits	30 and 31
Invoice Number	6 digits	32 through 37
Invoice Amount	6 digits	38 through 43
Dollars	4 digits	38 through 41
Cents	2 digits	42 and 43

Card Design and Layout

A punched card can contain a variety of combinations of numerical, alphabetical or alpha-numerical fields that may utilize part or all of the available eighty or ninety columns, depending on the use of the IBM or Remington Rand card formats. However, the column availability on a single card is frequently insufficient to record all data unless some types of data that would require multiple-column card fields can be represented by briefer numerical codes. Because punched card machines process only one digit at a time in sorting, it is preferable to use as few digits as possible in any code to permit faster sorting. Also, numerical codes require fewer punched digits in comparison to alphabetical codes, thereby permitting faster processing.

Three basic types of coding arrangements may be described as follows:

1. *Straight numerical assignment by item.* Items are assigned numbers in ascending order as they occur. No classification provision is made, and additional items merely receive the next highest number. The codes can be used to group and select alphabetical description for the items. For example:

number code	name of employee
1	John P. Alden
2	James K. Brown
3	George L. Camay

2. *Straight numerical assignment by groups.* Items are assigned numbers according to classes, with consecutive numbers within each class. A numerical listing of the data automatically groups the data by classes. Reservation of some numbers in each group provides room for additions to each class as follows:

number code	description	class
01	24/2½ sliced peaches	
02	24/303 sliced peaches	
03	12/10 sliced peaches	
04	48/Buf sliced peaches	sliced peaches
05	reserved	
06	reserved	
07	24/2½ halves peaches	halves peaches

3. *Digital position assignment.* Most appropriate for machine application, this arrangement provides for the succeeding digits of a code to identify classes of the data according to the digit position in the code. For example:

number code	description
6000	Department A
6100	Direct Labor
6110	Machine 1
6111	Job A
6112	Job B
6120	Machine 2
6121	Job A
6122	Job B

Another very important consideration in the organization of the card fields is the coordination of the sequencing of the fields on the card with the source documents from which the data are to be recorded via keypunching. If the sequence of data on the original source document and the sequence of the card fields are the same, keypunching becomes much easier

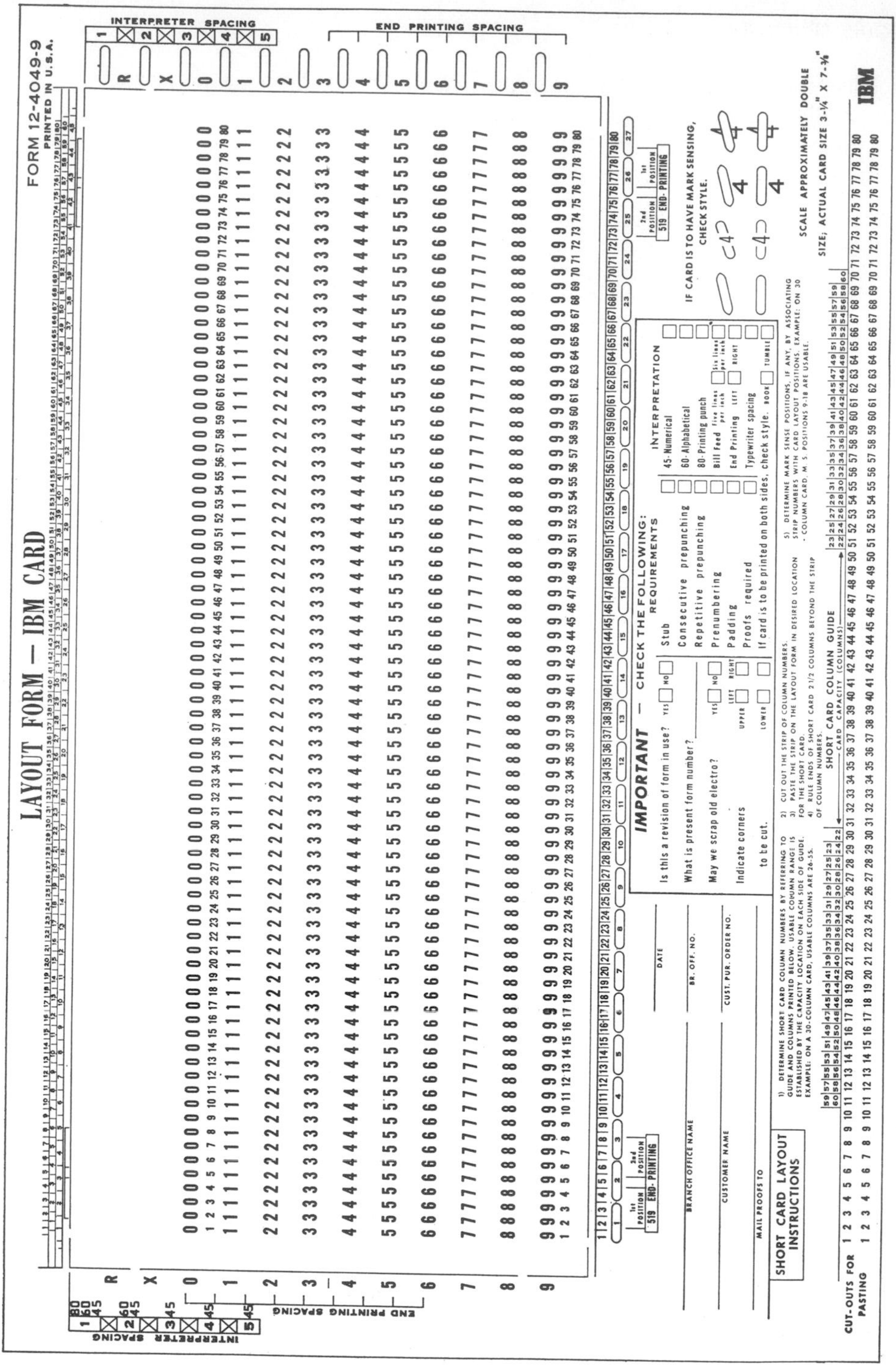

Fig. 12-4. Card Layout Form (Courtesy IBM)

and faster, and less subject to punching of erroneous data. When the source document has also been designed with subsequent keypunching of data in mind, such punching can be handled in the natural left to right sequence by the operator as she reads the source document. Such optimum design and field layout could enable keypunch operators to punch at a rate of 10,000 keystrokes per hour. Keypunching production in turn depends on the number of card columns to be punched in a particular application. Assuming the punching of fifty columns, good document and card design can facilitate the production of two hundred cards per hour.

A major tool in card layout design is the card layout form. A typical example of one for the IBM eighty-column card format is illustrated in Figure 12-4.

Punched cards may be designed according to the manner in which information is entered manually on the card and punched in the card. There are three basic types of information entry methods:

1. *Straight punching*—cards used for the entry of punched data only (*see* Figure 12-5).

2. *Source of entry*—cards that provide an area for a written entry of source information as well as for the entry of punched information in the same card (*see* Figure 12-6). A version of this type is the mark-sensed card that provides an area for a graphite pencil mark. The marks may then be machine read and punched at high speeds.

3. *Business transaction*—cards that are punched, machine printed, and used to effect business transactions. Checks, bills, receipts, and the like may be prepared in card form by machine, used to transact the business, and processed by machine to record transaction completion (*see* Figure 12-7).

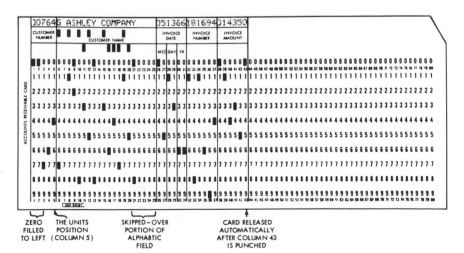

Fig. 12-5. Example of Straight Punching Practices

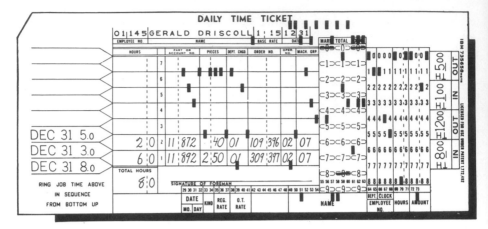

Fig. 12-6. Daily Time Card Used as a Source Entry Card and Mark Sensing Card

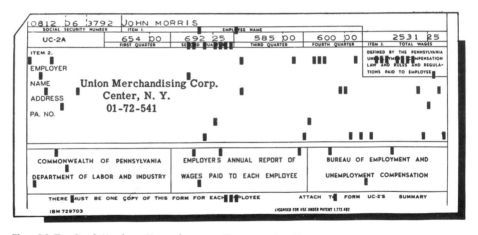

Fig. 12-7. Card Used as Unemployment Compensation Report

Punched cards may also be classified according to their use in machine processing. Six basic types of card by function performed are:

1. *Detail transaction cards*—punched individually to record detail transactions, the data being specific.

2. *Master cards*—punched and checked individually, but, unlike transaction cards, containing basic information, such as descriptions and name and address, and used repeatedly.

3. *Prepunched cards*—punched mechanically with basic information and in groups from master cards at high speeds.

4. *Heading cards*—consisting of all types, but used to print descriptive titles for a series of entries.

5. *Body cards*—used to write the body portion of documents. Transaction cards for invoice items showing quantities, descriptions, prices, and extensions are examples.

6. *Summary cards*—developed automatically by machine containing the net results of many like transactions. Subsequent processing is simplified, since each summary card replaces many detail cards.

TYPES OF PUNCHED CARD EQUIPMENT
AND FUNCTIONS PERFORMED

Nine types of machines constitute the basis of conventional complements of punched card equipment. They are:

1. *Keypunches*—manually operated machines used to punch holes in cards from a keyboard, very much as a typewriter is used to print numbers and letters on paper. Punching location follows the card layout. Keypunches may provide features to expedite punching. For example, IBM provides a fast means of skipping areas not punched and punching information from other cards (duplicating) as well as printing the information directly above the punched position. Remington Rand provides a means of punching repetitive data, which is stored in the machine. Remington Rand's alphabetical numbering punch can also be used to print serial numbers or a group code number in bold figures on the end of the punched card, and these numbers may also be punched into the card or omitted from punching at the option of the keypunch operator. In the case of IBM, such end printing and sequential numbering functions must be performed separately by means of a reproducer. Portable card punches are also available for limited amounts of special purpose punching.

2. *Key verifiers*—manually operated machines much like keypunches, used to check the accuracy of keypunched cards. Key verification is the principal method of checking punches. In the case of IBM equipment, verifiers are separate pieces of equipment on which, normally, an operator re-keys the same information on a deck of punched cards punched initially by another operator. As each card is verified, a "verification notch" is punched in the right edge of the card to indicate that all punching in it is correct.

If there is any discrepancy between the information keypunched initially and that keyed in by the verifier operator, an "error notch" is punched over the column (*see* Figure 12-8).

In the case of Remington Rand Univac equipment, verification punching is normally performed on the same equipment as initial keypunching by means of a verification attachment. The verification punching elongates all previously punched round holes to identify any columns with a discrepancy. Cards with errors can then be identified manually or processed mechanically by an automatic verifier machine. The latter compares the original and verification punched entries in the same card and interfiles a colored signal

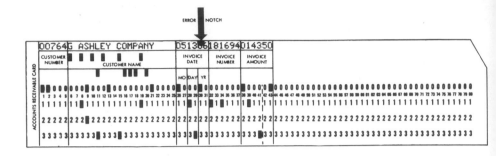

Fig. 12-8. Verification and Error Notches on IBM Punched Cards

card following any card with a discrepant entry. Subsequent stacking of the verified deck of cards permits identification of all discrepant cards by means of the colored signal cards. The automatic verifier also perforates a small "proof hole" in the right edge of each card that has passed through the mechanical verifying process.

3. *Reproducers*—machines that punch one or more cards from a previously punched card, usually a master card. Reproducers are quite flexible in operation. They also provide for interspersed gang punching, the copying of punched information from master cards to detail cards, single or groups of which each follow the master [*see* Figure 12-9(a) and 9(b)].

Reproducers are also used to read and punch the mark-sensed source entry type of card. The latter is a punched card that provides an area for manual recording of a limited amount of numeric data by means of graphite pencil marks in predetermined card rows representing zeroes to nines. The electrically conductive graphite pencil marks can then be read by the reproducer and translated at high speed directly into standard punched holes in another predetermined area of the same punched card that is being read. Mark-sensed cards thus facilitate the manual recording of simple numeric data (such as inventory counts) at any location, and the machine conversion of data into punched cards for subsequent machine processing without manual keypunching.

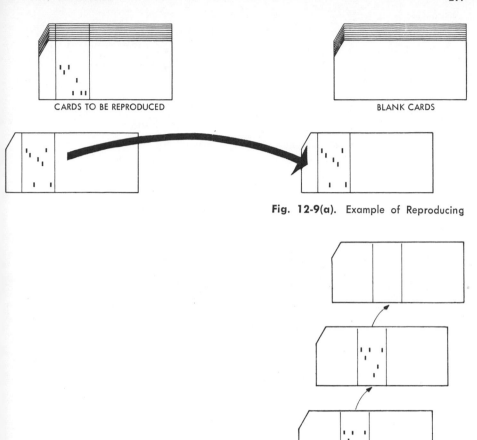

CARDS TO BE REPRODUCED

BLANK CARDS

Fig. 12-9(a). Example of Reproducing

Fig. 12-9(b). Example of Gang Punching

4. *Sorters*—machines used to group cards in numerical or alphabetical sequence, or to select cards of certain classes. In preparing account number cards bearing four-digit account numbers (for an accounting report, for example), cards would be sorted four times—once in each column from minor to major digit, usually right to left in card column position. The cards, properly removed each time from pockets, would then be grouped, like numbers together, from 0000 to 9999. Alphabetical sorting may require two sorts in the same column. Sorters have card counters that provide data on the number of cards sorted as well as the number of cards entering each pocket [*see* Figure 12-10(a), (b), and (c)].

5. *Collators or interpolators*—machines that compare two different stacks of cards, both in given sequence, in order to file all cards in sequence as well as to combine or identify cards that have the same punches. Segregation of cards is thereby possible also [*see* Figure 12-11(a)].

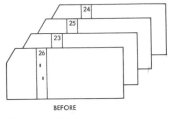

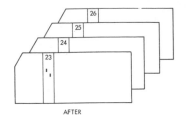

BEFORE

AFTER

Fig. 12-10(a). Example of Sequencing

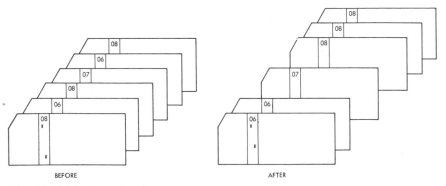

BEFORE

AFTER

Fig. 12-10(b). Example of Grouping

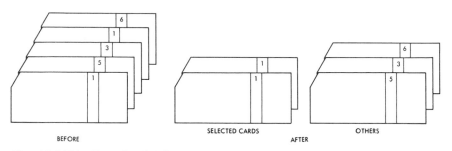

BEFORE

SELECTED CARDS

AFTER

OTHERS

Fig. 12-10(c). Example of Selecting

6. *Calculators*—machines that perform arithmetical operations on basic data punched in cards. Available equipment ranges from electromechanical through small-scale electronic punched cards to large-scale data processing machines. The average small machine can perform arithmetical operations, single and in combinations, as well as accuracy checks. Speed range up to 120 cards per minute and may vary according to the number of digits and type of arithmetical operation the machine is performing [*see* Figure 12-11(b)].

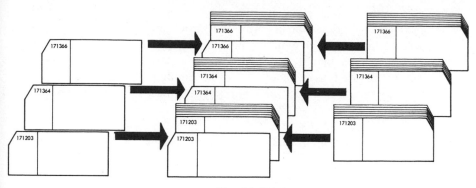

Fig. 12-11(a). Example of Collating or Merging

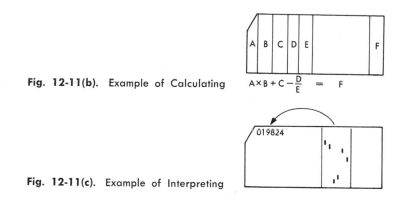

Fig. 12-11(b). Example of Calculating $A \times B + C - \dfrac{D}{E} \; = \; F$

Fig. 12-11(c). Example of Interpreting

7. *Interpreters*—machines that print the meanings of the punched holes in prescribed positions on the cards or other cards fed through the machine after the punched cards. IBM and Remington Rand both provide for the posting of entries from punched cards to a ledger collated with the punched cards, automatically posting on the next open line. IBM has an alphabetical interpreter that will print up to sixty characters on one of the twenty-five lines on the face of each card in one pass through the machine [*see* Figure 12-11(c)].

8. *Tabulators or accounting machines*—machines that read cards and print information a line at a time on forms usually fed continuously through the machine. The machines can print one or more lines from each card or one line from several cards. They contain counter positions and can be controlled to add, subtract, and crossfoot totals. The work horses of the tabulating system, accounting machines are available with a variety of features and speeds covering a wide range of requirements.

9. *Summary punches*—machines that punch cards from total information developed in tabulators. The summary punch is connected by

cable to the tabulator circuits. Thus, when totals developed in a tabulator operation are printed on a form, the information may be transmitted by cable to the summary punch, where the information is punched with the identifying data into the summary card. A large number of detail cards may be reduced to a relatively small number of summary cards. The summary punch may be used separately as a punch for gang punching and as a reproducer.

The nine basic machines may be supplemented by an assortment of accessories:

1. *Combination and special purpose machines not considered as conventional*—machines used to perform particular functions peculiar to a system or an industry. Examples are bank proof machines, test scoring machines, typewriter card punches, card to tape punches, and tape to card punches.

2. *Control panels*—plug boards wired by operators for individual jobs or groups of jobs and placed in position on the accounting, calculator, reproducing, and similar machines to control the movements and processing of the machine for the particular jobs. Panels may be wired permanently (covered and with inset plugs) for jobs of a recurring or complicated nature. Temporary wiring (exposed and with easily removable plugs) for jobs of a one-time or simple nature is used to permit economical reuse of the boards for other jobs. Figure 12-12 shows a wiring diagram from which a control panel may be wired.

3. *Carriage attachments*—devices used for accounting machines to provide faster and more flexible means of feeding and printing forms. Automatic tape controlled and dual feed tape attachments are examples.

4. *Bill feed*—devices used for accounting machines to print information in specific positions on ledgers, cards, and other items not in continuous form. The first line and the totals can be set to print in predetermined positions on the form.

5. *Form processing*—varieties of equipment available from form manufacturers for use in processing prepared documents and reports. Such functions as carbon separation, copy splitting or bursting, data imprinting and pin-feed hole stripping may be completed with this equipment.

6. *Storage*—equipment used to store quantities of cards, forms, and other supplies for efficient tabulating operation. Companies such as Tab Products Company, the Wright Line Division of Barry Wright Corporation and Diebold Inc. provide an assortment of storage facilities designed to cover a wide range of requirements. Equipment varies from loose-leaf binders through card tub files and trucks to large storage cabinets.

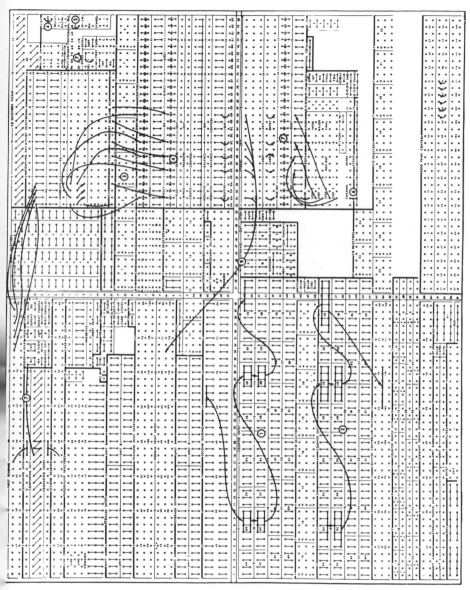

Fig. 12-12. Sample Wiring Diagram for IBM Type 407 Accounting Machine Control Panel (*Courtesy IBM*)

TABULATING PROCEDURE DEVELOPMENT

Objectives

Tabulating procedure development has two major objectives:

1. To provide facts indicating that the tabulating method is the best way of establishing the task
2. To establish the most efficient tabulating operation in fulfilling the mission of the system

The extent and sequence of the steps taken to develop the tabulating procedure vary according to the needs and scope of the system.

Procedure Analysis

The same basic approach used in procedure analysis should be followed, with special consideration given to:

A. Process charting workflow so that the process can be paralleled with a punched card flow chart. Timing requirements should be shown.
B. Identifying and evaluating characteristics of the system particularly appropriate for tabulating application. The greater the degree of the following characteristics of the procedure, the more appropriate the application is for tabulating equipment:
   1. Cost—Are there a large number of clerks, or is overtime involved?
   2. Mechanical—Is the system of an automatic nature?
   3. Stable and constant—Is the system fixed and uniform?
   4. Voluminous—Are large amounts of data and documents involved?
   5. Repetitious and of high frequency—Do the data repeat often?
   6. Vital—Is the information essential?
   7. Continuous—Is the data flow unbroken?
   8. Derived—Is considerable data subject to being developed from an original source?

Tentative Plan

Experience, vendor contact, and reviews of outside company applications point the way towards the best tabulating procedure:

A. The general tabulating procedure should be "blocked" or flow charted showing the major steps by which source documents are converted into documents and reports (see Figure 12-13). Volumes and timing should be entered on the procedure.
B. Tentative personnel, forms (including cards), and equipment needs should be estimated and compared with current requirements.
C. Tentative present and proposed costs should be estimated sufficiently to cover all phases.
D. The proposed plan should be developed to the point where project approval can be secured. Although approval may be subject to further analysis, it is necessary at an early stage so that:

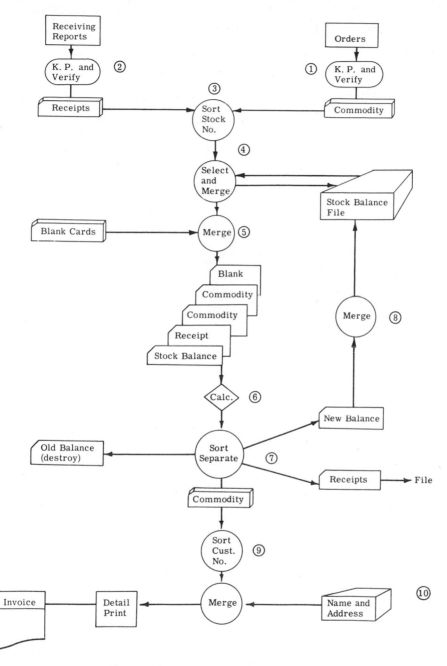

Fig. 12-13. General Flow Chart for Typical Batch-billing (and Inventory Control) Procedure

1. Costly details of the study can be developed under management approval with full knowledge of the stake involved.
2. Equipment subject to long delivery schedule can be placed on order while details of the procedure are being developed.

Coding Structure

Three main coding considerations exist:

1. To provide for the most efficient internal tabulating operations—Sorting, merging, calculating, summarizing, controlling, and like operations can be appreciably reduced with the use of proper codes. Use of master cards bearing efficient processing codes may prove economical.
2. To secure company acceptance by simplifying the coding and decoding of data—Use of pre-printed coded source documents and reports bearing descriptive information are examples.
3. To extend the use of codes into other company activities—Acceptance of codes, otherwise considered necessary solely for tabulating usage, will become a company-wide requirement. One manufacturer based its entire warehouse storage, carloading, and inventory control system on the tabulating codes for its products with considerable savings in handling and increased control.

Source Information Form

Source documents constitute key factors in successful tabulating operation. Keypunching and verifying are relatively time-consuming processes and every effort should be made to simplify and expedite the punching of cards from source documents.

The information must be accurate, legible, and in sequence for punching entry. Under ideal conditions, each line on the source document would contain all of the data to be entered in each card.

The documents should require a minimum of hand processing in the recording process. Entry of correct codes on pre-printed forms or the use of duplicating features of keypunch would reduce keypunch time.

Some verification may be eliminated by establishing "batch" controls or totals of prices, quantities, sizes, and the like for a group of documents to which the batch of cards can be quickly listed on accounting machine and balanced as a means of checking punched data.

Card Layout

The forms of source documents and final product, together with the machine processes to be used, are factors essential to card layout. The factors involved are varied, and considerable experience is required to design the most efficient layouts.

A. Planning is expedited by the use of a card design work sheet like that shown in Figure 12-14. Information required is listed.
B. Evaluation factors for card design are entered in the various column

CARD DESIGN AID

Form 22-6214-1
Printed in U.S.A.

TYPE OF CARD: CARD NAME: SOURCE DOCUMENT:

Information Available and Required for Reports	Columns in other Cards	Sequence on Source Documents	Method of Punching	R-Reference C-Classification Q-Quantitative	Card Field Size		Final Design		Interpretation		
					Trial	Final	Field	Sequence	Field	Size	Sequence
Order No.		6	KP	C	6	6	54-59	8	✓	6	1
Employee No.	64-68	1	KP	C	5	5	64-68	11	✓	5	11
Dept No.	64-65		KP	C	(2)	(2)	64-65				
Clock No.	66-68		KP	C	(3)	(3)	66-68				
Regular Rate	35-37		GP	C	3	3	35-37	3			
Overtime Rate	38-41		GP	C	4	4	38-41	4			
Part or Account No.		4	KP	C	5	5	47-51	6	✓	5	2
Pieces		3	KP	Q	5	5	42-46	5	✓	5	6
Operation No.		5	KP	C	2	2	52-53	7	✓	2	3
Machine Group		7	KP	C	2	2	60-61	9	✓	2	4
Department Charged		8	KP	C	2	2	62-63	10	✓	2	5
Kind of Labor	33-34		GP	C	2	2	33-34	2	✓	2	10
Amount	72-75		Calc P	Q	4	4	72-75	13	✓	4	9
Hours	69-71	2	KP	Q	3	3	69-71	12	✓	3	8
Date	29-32		GP	R	4	4	59-32	1	✓	4	7
Month	29-30		GP	R	(2)	(2)	29-30				
Day	31-32		GP	R	(2)	(2)	31-32				
				TOTALS →	47	47				40	

Fig. 12-14. Card Design Work Sheet

C. If the trial card field size exceeds the number of columns available, a revision of the data or the use of two cards may be necessary.

D. Card column assignment requires the evaluation of many factors. Some considerations include assigning:

1. Data to be duplicated in consecutive columns of the cards
2. Calculated results in consecutive columns of the cards
3. Keypunched fields separately
4. Columns skipped during punching operations on a uniform basis
5. Identical data appearing on various cards, the same fields on each of the cards
6. Fixed control fields in different cards to same columns

E. Individual card layouts can be drawn on vendor specification sheets (*see* Figure 12-4).

F. Use of solid colors should not be overlooked as a means of easy identification for multi-purpose cards.

G. Manufacturers' stock card forms should be considered to avoid designing special cards.

Form Layout

The tabulating system payoff comes in the form of documents and reports issued. The design must accomplish the objective of the program with compliance to machine and user requirements. Regular form layout principles should be followed, with emphasis on the following:

A. The form must be readily readable.

1. The sequence of items should follow user requirements in reading data. The flexibility of accounting machine printing permits in-

formation entry in almost any sequence, although alphabetica
areas may be limited.

2. Items to be read together should be placed together.

3. Only necessary data should be shown. With the considerable data
   available in cards, the tendency is to print additional information
   "just in case." Such action detracts from the value of important
   information on the form and clutters the data.

4. Guidelines should be used to aid eye travel.

B. A minimum of machine spacing and printing should be planned.

1. Use of pre-printed information may save cards; card savings
   extend into machine processing economy.

2. Use of pre-printed information and such devices as lines for
   decimals saves card columns and removes the need for special
   type bars if unusual characters, fractions, etc., are desired.

C. Machine requirements must be fulfilled.

1. Vertical spaces should match machine line spacing.

2. Horizontal spaces should match the position of machine digits.

3. Length and width of the forms should conform to standards for
   economy and efficient operation.

4. Feeding and form ejection requirements should be considered for
   maximum efficiency.

5. Vendor form specification layout sheets should be used to aid
   form design.

D. Physical handling of the forms should be simplified.

1. Alignment symbols, guide marks, or lines for horizontal and
   vertical positioning of the machine carriage and form should be
   printed on the form.

2. Distribution of the copies may be improved by identifying each
   copy with distinguishing figures or colors.

3. If subsequent entries require carbon impressions on two or more
   copies, the copies should be fastened together.

4. Filing procedures should be simplified by adopting standard filing
   sizes and placing information for filing purposes in areas of immediate recognition.

5. Approval should be obtained to leave feed holes on the final form
   to avoid trimming the side strips.

E. Copies should be furnished in readable form.

1. Accounting machines are limited in the number of clear readable
   copies that can be furnished.

2. Special lightweight, high clay content papers and high quality
   carbon paper will improve copy readability.

3. Use of duplicating masters, gelatin, spirit, multilith, and so on
   can be made where more than ten or twelve copies are required.

4. Accounting machine printing permits copy increase by printing
   forms "two up," each part containing two copies separated by
   perforations.

Volume Measurements

The critical balance between a minimum number of machines and full conformance to output time schedules requires accurate measurement of work volume (*see* Figure 12-15).

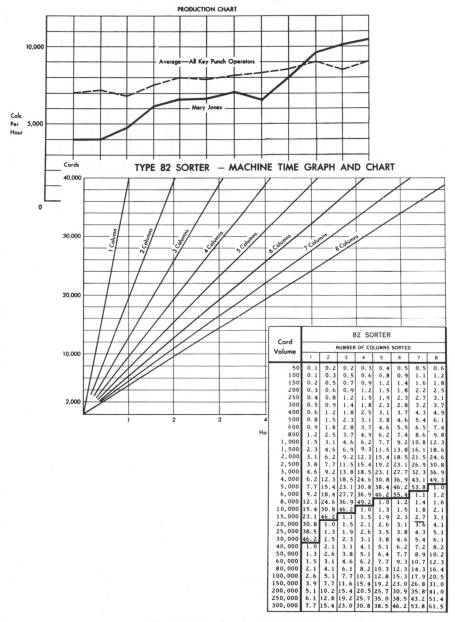

Card Volume	82 SORTER							
	NUMBER OF COLUMNS SORTED							
	1	2	3	4	5	6	7	8
50	0.1	0.2	0.2	0.3	0.4	0.5	0.5	0.6
100	0.1	0.3	0.5	0.6	0.8	0.9	1.1	1.2
150	0.2	0.5	0.7	0.9	1.2	1.4	1.6	1.8
200	0.3	0.6	0.9	1.2	1.5	1.8	2.2	2.5
250	0.4	0.8	1.2	1.5	1.9	2.3	2.7	3.1
300	0.5	0.9	1.4	1.8	2.3	2.8	3.2	3.7
400	0.6	1.2	1.8	2.5	3.1	3.7	4.3	4.9
500	0.8	1.5	2.3	3.1	3.8	4.6	5.4	6.1
600	0.9	1.8	2.8	3.7	4.6	5.5	6.5	7.4
800	1.2	2.5	3.7	4.9	6.2	7.4	8.6	9.8
1,000	1.5	3.1	4.6	6.2	7.7	9.2	10.8	12.3
1,500	2.3	4.6	6.9	9.3	11.5	13.8	16.1	18.6
2,000	3.1	6.2	9.2	12.3	15.4	18.5	21.5	24.6
2,500	3.8	7.7	11.5	15.4	19.2	23.1	26.9	30.8
3,000	4.6	9.2	13.8	18.5	23.1	27.7	32.3	36.9
4,000	6.2	12.3	18.5	24.6	30.8	36.9	43.1	49.3
5,000	7.7	15.4	23.1	30.8	38.4	46.2	53.8	1.0
6,000	9.2	18.4	27.7	36.9	46.2	55.4	1.1	1.2
8,000	12.3	24.6	36.9	49.2	1.0	1.2	1.4	1.6
10,000	15.4	30.8	46.2	1.0	1.3	1.5	1.8	2.1
15,000	23.1	46.2	1.1	1.5	1.9	2.3	2.7	3.1
20,000	30.8	1.0	1.5	2.1	2.6	3.1	3.6	4.1
25,000	38.5	1.3	1.9	2.6	3.5	3.8	4.3	5.1
30,000	46.2	1.5	2.3	3.1	3.8	4.6	5.4	6.1
40,000	1.0	2.1	3.1	4.1	5.1	6.2	7.2	8.2
50,000	1.3	2.6	3.8	5.1	6.4	7.7	8.9	10.2
60,000	1.5	3.1	4.6	6.2	7.7	9.3	10.7	12.3
80,000	2.1	4.1	6.1	8.2	10.3	12.3	14.3	16.4
100,000	2.6	5.1	7.7	10.3	12.8	15.3	17.9	20.5
150,000	3.9	7.7	11.6	15.4	19.2	23.0	26.8	31.0
200,000	5.1	10.2	15.4	20.5	25.7	30.9	35.8	41.0
250,000	6.1	12.8	19.2	25.7	35.0	38.5	43.2	51.4
300,000	7.7	15.4	23.0	30.8	38.5	46.2	53.8	61.5

Fig. 12-15. Charting Volume Measurements (*Courtesy IBM*)

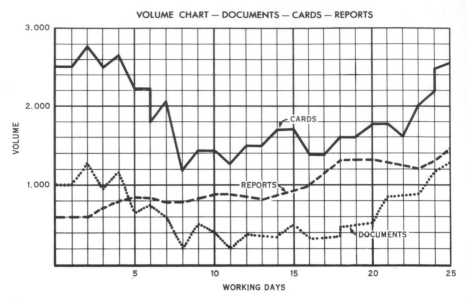

Fig. 12-16. Developing Operation Times (*Courtesy IBM*)

1. The number of source documents should be counted together with the maximum and minimum volumes and the periods of incidence, by hour and day.
2. The volume of cards punched from the source documents may be computed by multiplying the average number of cards punched per document by the number of documents.
3. Card volume before and after each machine step should be determined. The volume is usually greater than that punched from source documents because of the many uses of the cards during machine processing.
4. Reports and documents issued by the tabulating section should be coordinated with the hours and days of issuance.

Timing and Scheduling Requirements

Based upon volume measurements and operator or machine speeds and capacities, each of the tabulating steps may be converted to a time basis. Provision for handling in selecting and restacking the cards in various machines, securing forms, setting up machines, wiring temporary boards and so on, must be included.

Some of the factors influencing timing include:

1. The ability and training of the operators. More experienced operators reduce timing requirements through their ability to work faster and eliminate superfluous processing steps.
2. The volume of work involved. The greater the volume, the better the machine application.

3. The layout of the documents. Particularly in keypunch operations, the sequence and method of entry has a direct effect upon timing.

4. The movement and supply of work. Uninterrupted movement of the data, with a reasonable amount of unprocessed data on hand, lowers timing requirements.

5. Properties of the machines used. Machine features influence timing considerably. The combination of certain operations on machines will reduce times. Setup requirements are also involved.

6. Installation layout and physical features. Timing is directly affected by physical movement. Bordering upon the intangible, the effects of noise, ventilation, safety hazards, and the like on timing develop in the form of operator efficiency.

7. The amount and types of controls. Timing is influenced by the number of records kept by operators, the number of machine steps added to verify transactions, and so on.

Measurement of operating times on machines is determined by the volume of cards processed and the rate of processing of the cards by a given machine for a given operation. The number of machine hours is equal to the number of cards divided by the number of cards that the machine can process per hour for the operation. Machine setup time remains fairly constant and becomes significant when small volumes of cards are involved. Handling time for the stacking of cards in the machine, balancing of data, and so forth is directly related to operating time and is usually measured as a percentage of the total of operating and handling time. For example, in sorting 40,000 cards at 650 cards per minute on ten columns, ten hours' operating time would be required. If 30 per cent of handling time is considered to cover the removal and restacking of cards and minor machine adjustment, operating and handling time is computed to be 14.3 hours:

$$(1.00 - 0.30) \times (O + H) \text{ Time} = 10 \text{ hours}$$
$$O + H \quad \text{Time} = 14.3 \text{ hours}$$

Setup time would be added to operating and handling time to arrive at the total time consumed for the operation. With a setup time of 0.3 hours, total sorting time would be 14.6 hours.

Efficient operation requires the control of documents, machines, and operators in the form of a schedule. Scheduling is necessary:

1. To meet report deadlines and processing schedules such as conversion of cards to magnetic tape for computer processing

2. To minimize machine and man requirements by leveling the work load and preventing avoidable backlogs

3. To eliminate machine conflicts, jobs competing for the same process step at the same time.

4. To provide records of performance as a basis for timing adjustments and changing types of equipment or devices

5. To eliminate overtime by reducing peak periods .

6. To permit the scheduling of important special machine and maintenance jobs

SCHEDULE OF REPORTS   DATE

	EXHIBIT	DUE IN	FROM	DUE OUT	TO
BILLING					
*Customer Orders	A	DAILY 10 AM	Order Dept	DAILY 4:30 PM	Order Dept
Shipping Orders	B			DAILY 4:30 PM	Shipping Dept
Invoice	C			DAILY 1:00 PM	Customers
Register	D			DAILY 5:00 PM	Supervisor
ACCOUNTS RECEIVABLE					
*Remittance Advice	E	DAILY 2 PM	Cashier	DAILY 10 AM	Cashier
Cash Receipts	F			DAILY 2 PM	Chief Acct.
Aged Trial Balance	G			MONTHLY 1st	
Statements	H			MONTHLY 5th	Mail Room
SALES ANALYSIS					
Cost of Sales	I			MONTHLY 10th	Sales Mgr.
Sales by Customer	J			MONTHLY 15th	Sales Mgr.
Commission Statement	K			MONTHLY 15th	Sales Mgr.
Sales by State	L			MONTHLY 20th	Sales Mgr.
Sales by Salesman	M			MONTHLY 25th	Sales Mgr.

*Sou...

MACHINE LOAD WORK SHEET

NO.	MACH.	OPERATING DATA FOR MACHINE LOADS	NO. CARDS	TIME
		Daily Balancing Procedure		
1	Rep.		1200	.3
2	Print.		1200	.5
3	Cler.	Timekeepers	1300	—
1	Sort.	1 col.	1300	.1
2	K.P.	5 col.	100	2
3	Sort.	5 col.	1300	.3
4	K.P.	30 col.	3600	11.0
1	A.P.		4800	1.0
2	Sort.	1 col.	4800	.3
3	Mult.	3 digit multiplier	4560	2.3
4	Mult.	3 digit multiplier	240	.1
5	Col.	1 field open	4800	.4
6	List.	1280 Mi., 50 Det.	4800	1.7
7	Cler.	Check 400 totals per hr.	1200	3.0

SCHEDULE WORK SHEET AND PERFORMANCE RECORD

Fig. 12-17. Examples of Scheduling Aids (*Courtesy IBM*)

Schedules may be developed by machine, job, or both. In any case, it is important to show exactly when the machines are used and the steps of procedures being taken at a particular time. To know how much time is available on machines is not nearly so important as knowing when time is available. From the times established and the flow charts developed, written schedules, graphs, and so on may be constructed to simplify schedule control.

Part of the scheduling requirement includes a written record of all documents in order to establish timing responsibility and provide for corrective action when necessary. The record should show the due time and the actual time source documents are received and completed reports are issued. In many cases more elaborate control is necessary, and times of the completion of the various processing steps are recorded.

Machine Processing and Specifications

It is necessary to prepare machine processing steps completely:

1. Determine the detailed operations to be conducted, the volumes to be processed, and the timing to be met.
2. Chart the individual machine steps (*see* Figure 12-18). The symbols used need not be standard as long as they are understood.
3. Consider all machine steps on the complete process—simplifying, combining, and changing process sequence for maximum efficiency.
4. Determine the types of machines and the features necessary to provide the most efficient operation.

Controls

A most important aspect of tabulating procedure development is that of controls. Control requirements increase in direct proportion to the degree of automatic operation. The highly automatic nature of tabulating systems demands complete and continuing controls. Controls must be established to insure that all documents are received, all information is recorded properly, all information is processed correctly, and all results are reported correctly and in proper form. Factors to bear in mind when establishing controls are:

A. Making certain that all documents are received and that they are recorded accurately
B. Identifying the data and maintaining arithmetical control of cards, forms, tickets, and so on, during processing
C. Reporting the results correctly and in the proper form
   1. The documents issued must balance to controls and be checked for proper entries. The cash receipts book, for example, can be balanced with total receipts. Omissions and errors can be quickly detected.
   2. The controls can be balanced directly at any time. A listing of the open receivable cards, for example, should equal the net balance of the accounts receivable control sheet.

ACTION UPON RELEASE OF SCHEDULE

When a schedule is released, a schedule card is punched for each type of model scheduled. This card is punched with model number and the quantity scheduled for each month. Step by step, the following procedure is used:

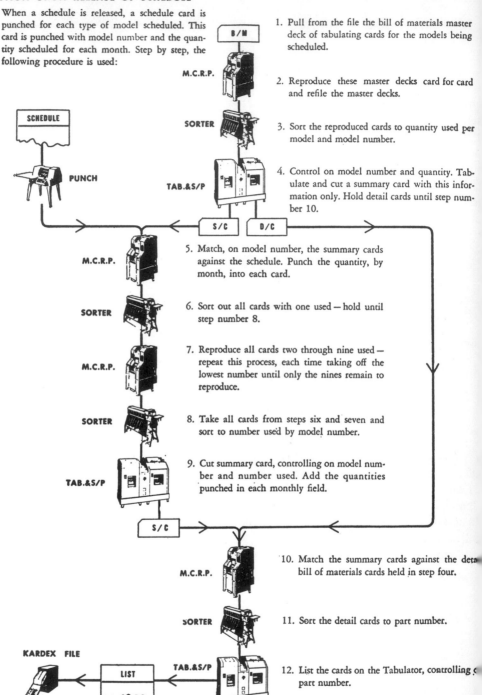

1. Pull from the file the bill of materials master deck of tabulating cards for the models being scheduled.

2. Reproduce these master decks card for card and refile the master decks.

3. Sort the reproduced cards to quantity used per model and model number.

4. Control on model number and quantity. Tabulate and cut a summary card with this information only. Hold detail cards until step number 10.

5. Match, on model number, the summary cards against the schedule. Punch the quantity, by month, into each card.

6. Sort out all cards with one used — hold until step number 8.

7. Reproduce all cards two through nine used — repeat this process, each time taking off the lowest number until only the nines remain to reproduce.

8. Take all cards from steps six and seven and sort to number used by model number.

9. Cut summary card, controlling on model number and number used. Add the quantities punched in each monthly field.

10. Match the summary cards against the detail bill of materials cards held in step four.

11. Sort the detail cards to part number.

12. List the cards on the Tabulator, controlling on part number.

Fig. 12-18. Machine Processing Steps for Materials Control
(*Courtesy Remington Rand, Univac Division, Sperry Rand Corp.*)

Regardless of procedure simplicity, effective operation requires a written procedure:

A. To provide instruction that can be understood and followed

B. To place responsibilities in specific form

C. To describe in relatively simple terms the use of the complex equipment for each operation

D. To instruct substitutes and new personnel in the procedures

E. To disclose interrelationships, standards of operation, and uinformity

F. To establish the basis for the refinement of current procedures, the extension of applications, and the development of new procedures

G. To provide a basis for active supervision in:
   1. Seeing that the work is being done properly
   2. Scheduling or revising schedules
   3. Exercising proper controls
   4. Evaluating machine and employee performance
   5. Answering questions from other sections

Figure 12-19 illustrates a recommended outline of manual development.

TABULATING APPLICATIONS

The use of tabulating equipment in business covers a wide assortment of systems and segments of systems. Some of the applications include:

1. Employee payroll
2. Labor distribution of accounts
3. Employee records
4. Material accounting and control
5. Accounts payable
6. Billing
7. Sales accounting
8. Inventory control
9. General acounting
10. Capital asset accounting
11. Dividend accounting

Punched card machines and peripheral devices are particularly adaptable as input to computer processing. However, where volume is not large enough for electronic data processing, tabulating equipment is usually the most practical process.

Two samples of results from an employee payroll procedure appear in Figure 12-20. General descriptions of several other applications follow.

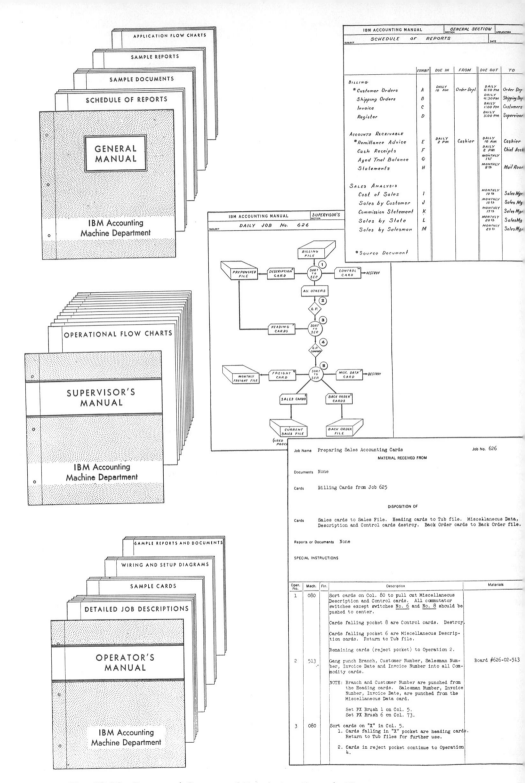

Fig. 12-19. Types and Contents of Tabulating Manuals (Courtesy IBM)

Employee Payroll

The mechanical nature of payroll procedures makes tabulating particularly appropriate for payrolls not practical for computer processing. Weekly attendance and job cards punched with hours, employee codes, job codes, and the like may be balanced for each employee in the preparation of a payroll earnings summary. Job cards are placed in a working file for later use in labor distribution accounting.

The summary current earnings cards for each employee are matched with master cards prepunched with deduction data, and used to calculate net pay, deductions, and so forth, for the current period. Name cards and year-to-date earnings cards developed at the close of the previous pay period are merged, and the cards are used to prepare the payroll register and the employee paychecks (see Figure 12-20).

New year-to-date earnings cards are prepared at the same time and filed for use in the subsequent pay period. Additional records that may be developed from the cards include:

1. Employee earnings records
2. Social security and tax reports to government agencies
3. Registers of deductions
4. Bank account reconciliation reports
5. Various reports on employees
6. W-2 forms

Labor Distribution Accounting

Usually developed with employee payroll procedures, the accounting of labor distribution is appropriate for tabulating application when considerable compilation for account codes in various breakdowns is required. Labor distribution or job cards are filed for the end of the accounting period after they have been balanced to payroll attendance cards. At the end of the period, the cards are balanced to controls, sorted into desired report categories, such as direct vs. indirect charges, and used to prepare accounting and performance reports. Examples of reports are:

1. Direct labor charges by job number (see Figure 12-21)
2. Indirect labor charges by account and department
3. Performance records by employee
4. Various types of efficiency reports by departments or types of labor

Material Accounting and Control

The use of tabulating equipment to provide reports for the control of material inventories and costs becomes desirable when the number of items and amount of activity are high.

1. Purchase orders prepared for materials shown at reorder point from the stock status report are used as source documents in punching

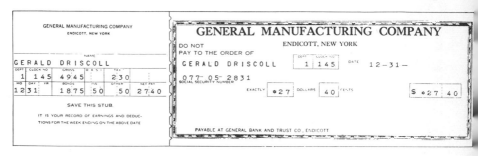

Fig. 12-20. Deduction Register and Payroll Check

"on order" cards. Controls are established in the preparation of a transaction register.

2. Receipt cards are punched from receiving reports, and controls are established.

3. Requisition and return cards are punched from material orders, and the cards are duplicated.

4. The "on order," receipt, and requisition or return cards are placed in a perpetual inventory card file and used with previous balance cards to prepare a new stock status summary report at specified intervals. New balance cards are produced in the summary process and held for the subsequent report period.

5. The original sets of return and requisition cards are punched with prices, calculated for cost amounts, and used to prepare a transaction register that establishes material charges control. The cards are used to credit inventory and to prepare material charge reports. The cards are then filed for later use in the preparation of cost reports.

DETAIL COST STATEMENT

5012 CYLINDER LINER   61538   DATE _____

ORDER NO.	MATERIAL CODE CLASS OPER.	MATERIAL CODE ASSEMBLY NO.	DEPT	QUANTITY	HOURS	MATERIAL	LABOR	BURDEN	TOTAL
5012	1	1 1	3	7	3 4		2 21	4 42	6 63
						*	2 21 *	4 42 *	6 63 *
5012 8 21		1 2		7		8 29 22			8 29 22
5012	1	1 2	6		1 9 3		1 5 44	3 0 88	4 6 32
5012	1	1 2	6		1 4		1 1 90	2 3 80	3 5 70
5012	1	1 2	6	7	1 9 6		1 6 66	3 3 32	4 9 98
5012	1	1 2	6		2 6		2 0 80	4 1 60	6 2 40
5012	2	1 2	6	2	5 4		5 13	1 0 26	1 5 39
5012	2	1 2	6	5	1 3		1 2 35	2 4 70	3 7 05
5012	4	1 2	7		2 7		1 35	2 70	4 05
5012	4	1 2	7		3 1 5		1 5 75	3 1 50	4 7 25
5012	4	1 2	7	7	1 6		80	1 60	2 40
5012	5	1 2	6	2	8 5		8 08	1 6 16	2 4 24
5012	5	1 2	6		7 1		6 74	1 3 48	2 0 22
5012	5	1 2	6	5	1 7 6		1 6 72	3 3 44	5 0 16
5012	6	1 2	1	7	2 2 6		1 1 30	2 2 60	3 3 90
5012	7	1 2	1		1 6		1 3 60	2 7 20	4 0 80
5012	7	1 2	1	1	1 9 7		1 5 76	3 1 52	4 7 28
5012	7	1 2	1	6	1 9 7		1 6 74	3 3 48	5 0 22
5012	7	1 2	1		1 3 6		1 0 88	2 1 76	3 2 64
5012	8	1 2	4		2 4		96	1 92	2 88
5012	8	1 2	4	7	1 6 1		6 44	1 2 88	1 9 32
5012	9	1 2	1	7	1 6 2		1 5 39	3 0 78	4 6 17
						8 29 22 *	22 79 *	4 4 58 *	1 49 7 59 *
5012 4 23		1 3		3 1 5		5 95			5 95
						5 95 *	*	*	5 95 *
5012 7 20		2 5		2 1		23			23
						23 *	*	*	23 *

Fig. 12-21. Report of Direct Charges

MACHINE RECOGNIZABLE MEDIA

While the punched card is the most common medium for processing data in a machine recognizable language adaptable for subsequent use in either punched card electronic accounting machines (EAM) or electronic data processing (EDP) computer systems, other machine recognizable media may be used in a wide variety of information system applications.

Some of the principal machine recognizable media besides punched cards are:

Punched paper tape
Magnetic ink character recognition (MICR)
Optically recognizable printed characters
Optically recognizable printed codes
Machine recognizable perforated characters
Perforated tags
Magnetic tape

Punched Paper Tape

Various types of punched paper tape coding are classified by the number of channels or number of rows of holes punched. Data in paper tape can be punched in five-, six-, seven-, or eight-channel coding systems.

Five-channel paper tape [*see* Figure 12-22(b)] uses the five-channel Baudot teletypewriter code employed by the telegraph industry for about one hundred years. This code does not contain a check or parity bit to assist in verification of accurate transmission of valid characters.

Most other paper tape coding systems use a binary-coded decimal character representation similar to that used in many magnetic tape character representations in computer systems. For input to computer systems, the eight-channel coding system illustrated in Figure 12-22(a) is typical.

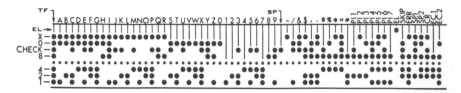

Fig. 12-22(a). Paper Tape—Eight-Channel Code

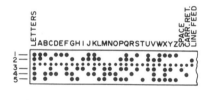

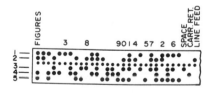

Fig. 12-22(b). Paper Tape—Five-Channel Code

In the eight-channel coding system, a hole in the bottom row forms the binary digit or bit with a value of one. A bit in the second row or channel has a value of two; in the third channel, four; and in the fourth channel, eight. The decimal numbers 3, 5, 6, 7, and 9 are made up of a combination of bits in appropriate channels. Zeroes are punched in the sixth channel and combinations of punches from the sixth and seventh channels, together with numeric character punching in the first four channels, are used to form alphabetic letters. The fifth channel is normally reserved for a check or parity bit on either an even or odd basis. Thus, if parity is odd, a hole is punched in the fifth channel whenever the number of bits or holes in channels one through seven is even. Paper tape reading and transmitting machines then check that there is always an odd number of bits punched, and if this is not so, the machine stops, indicating an incorrect transmission of a character, i.e., a parity error.

The eighth channel is used for machine operating codes. Edge-punched cards are a variation of punched paper tape. They are produced and read by the same equipment as punched paper tape and use identical channel coding systems. They are normally used to store repetitive data in a format for insertion into a system reading punched paper tape input.

In addition to data transmission, information in paper tape form is most frequently produced as a by-product of other office equipment (which has been modified for this purpose), such as typewriters, adding machines, cash registers, bookkeeping equipment, etc. Normally, the intent is to capture data at the source as a by-product of another operation for direct input into a computer system without interim data conversion process into a machine recognizable medium such as keypunching of punched cards.

Magnetic Ink Character Recognition (MICR)

Magnetic ink characters are a form of stylized characters in which portions are exaggerated to provide a greater intensity of magnetism, permitting differentiation on reading by special MICR readers. The quality of imprinting must be very rigid to permit such reading, and this limits the use of MICR largely to banks and financial institutions. The banks, through the American Bankers Association, have adopted a standard MICR type face and enforce rigid magnetic ink imprinting requirements.

MICR coding is widely used on checks and bank deposit tickets to permit machine processing. Figure 12-23 illustrates the use of MICR coding as commonly used on the bottom edge of checks for pre-coded bank and account identification information and for encoding of the amount of the check at the time of processing it.

USE OF MAGNETIC INK CHARACTERS ON CHECKS. If an MICR character in the depositor's account number or amount fields of a check is unrecognizable by the MICR processing equipment, the check is rejected and an MICR encoded slip is manually typed and attached to the bottom of the check in the area underneath the unrecognizable MICR characters.

Optically Recognizable Characters

Various type faces of stylized characters permit optical scanning equipment to recognize specific characters by determining the presence or absence of ink in certain positions. A typical set of optically recognizable characters is shown in Figure 12-24(a). In optical scanning applications, data in optically recognizable characters are read directly from source documents, saving an interim manual data conversion step of manually keypunching such data into punched cards. Optically recognizable characters are frequently used on embossed cards for imprinting on transaction documents, such as those used with many credit card point-of-sale recorder applications.

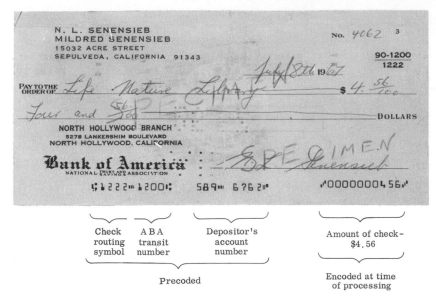

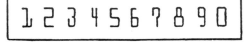

Check   ABA   Depositor's   Amount of check–
routing   transit   account $4.56
symbol   number   number

Precoded   Encoded at time
                            of processing

Fig. 12-23. Specimen Check With MICR Coding

Optically Recognizable Printed Codes

Other applications of optical scanning involve the reading of various pre-printed codes to represent specific characters. An example of an optically recognizable printed bar code is shown in Figure 12-24(b). Such optically recognizable coding is used for similar applications as in optically recognizable character systems.

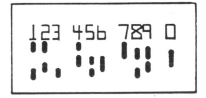

Fig. 12-24(a). Optically Recognizable Characters

Fig. 12-24(b). Optically Recognizable Printed Code

Machine Recognizable Perforated Characters

Perforated characters, such as shown in Figure 12-25(a), are an example of another machine recognizable medium. Recognition is accomplished by reading from five to nineteen possible perforation positions.

Perforated Tags

The perforated tag is a special form of machine recognizable perforated medium, designed primarily for the retail industry. One of the common perforated tag machine recognizable codes used in this industry is the five-channel code, with each character represented by perforations in two channels, as shown in Figure 12-25(b).

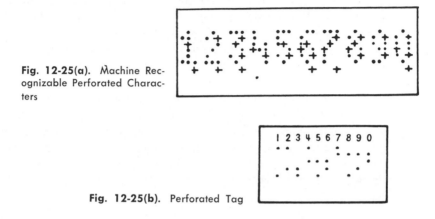

Fig. 12-25(a). Machine Recognizable Perforated Characters

Fig. 12-25(b). Perforated Tag

Magnetic Tape

Magnetic tape is usually considered as a data storage medium to handle input of data for computer processing after conversion from another medium, and for handling output of data from the computer to other peripheral devices. However, magnetic tape can also be used as a medium for some data transmission systems where no computer is involved. Likewise, magnetic tape can be used as the recording medium directly from source documents by means of manually operated keyboard machines. The latter may also produce a typed copy for verification of the recorded data.

Magnetic tape coding has channels similar to punched paper tape, recording data in binary-coded decimal and other coding systems, depending on the computer system used.

DATA PROCESSING PERIPHERAL EQUIPMENT

While keypunch and other punched card processing equipment remain the most common types of equipment for preparation and processing of input data to punched card and computer systems, a variety of peripheral devices complement such equipment for preparing and processing other machine recognizable media, converting data between such media, and for special purposes of source data recording, data transmission, and data display. The major functional types of such peripheral equipment include:

1. Equipment for recording and processing punched paper tape
2. Equipment for recording and processing machine recognizable media
3. Source data recording equipment
4. Data transmission equipment
5. Data display equipment

Punched Paper Tape Processing Equipment

Other than the punching of five-channel teletype code on a teletype machine, most punched paper tape, in five-, six-, seven-, and eight-channel codes, is normally produced as a by-product from the operation of specialized equipment of the office machines type, such as typewriters, adding machines, calculating machines, bookkeeping machines and cash registers. In the case of these machines, typed-copy text, adding machine tapes, and postings on bookkeeping forms can be used for other purposes as well as for verification of the input data captured in the punched paper tape. However, equipment such as the Friden Flexowriter, the Remington Rand Synchro-Tape typewriter, the Monroe Add-Punch, and other similar machines are also used for straight punching of punched paper tape input data directly from source documents in the same manner as punched card keypunching.

The intent of recording data in a by-product punched paper tape medium is again to capture data as early as possible at the source of its production. Thereafter, it is read by either a paper tape reader, for direct input into a computer system, or converted into punched card format by tape to card equipment for subsequent processing by either punched card or computer systems.

Some of the same machines that are used to punch paper tape can be used to reproduce paper tape copies. Also, the typewriter type of tape punches can be used to read strips of punched paper tape and to produce typed copies of the recorded data.

Sorting of data in punched paper tape format cannot be performed. However, a limited amount of selection can be accomplished by splicing the punched paper tape into an endless loop of tape and reading it for one classification at a time for each complete revolution of the tape.

Equipment for Recording and Processing
Machine Recognizable Media

Specific pieces of equipment are required for processing the other machine recognizable media mentioned in addition to punched cards and punched paper tape. Included in this category are optical scanning and MICR equipment, magnetic tape writers, and equipment for punching and reading machine recognizable perforated characters and perforated tags.

Other than magnetic tape and MICR, the data in these other media usually require conversion to punched card or magnetic tape format for any further processing, such as sorting and collating.

Optical scanning equipment of different types is used for reading optically recognizable printed characters or optically recognizable printed codes directly from source documents, and converting the data into punched cards or magnetic tape formats for subsequent processing. Frequently, optical scanners are linked for direct input to computer systems.

Optical scanning facilitates the direct processing of key information on return documents, such as invoices, without interim keypunching or tape punching, in the same manner as pre-punched data or mark-sensed data on punched card return documents. Most of the output from imprinters, such as used for gasoline service station credit card sales tickets, is read and converted by optical scanning equipment. It is a major tool in facilitating source data recording of transaction data. While most optical scanning is performed on printed characters or codes, efforts are being made to optically scan handwritten data in prescribed formats.

Magnetic ink character recognition (MICR) equipment represents a special family of equipment for the banking industry. Included are MICR imprinters as well as MICR reader-sorters. MICR is also the only medium other than punched card and magnetic tape that permits the machine sorting of the encoded data without conversion to another medium.

Magnetic tape writing is normally considered a function of the computer in converting from other input media to magnetic tape or, in output, from computer memory into magnetic tape storage. However, manually operated keyboard equipment does exist for recording data directly on magnetic tape from source documents in the same manner as keypunching of punched cards. Such equipment also produces as a by-product typed copy of the data for verification and other record-keeping purposes. Additionally, verification is possible by comparing two magnetic tape recordings of the same data on the magnetic tape writing equipment. Mistakes can be erased and corrections substituted on tape on a character basis.

Source Data Recording Equipment

This category of source data collection equipment, consisting of such devices as transaction recorders, point-of-sale recorders, imprinters and perforators, is based on the concept of automatically capturing key transaction data directly into machine sensible media as early as possible in the processing cycle, and with minimal manual transcription of data. Basic groups of such equipment include:

A. *Transaction recorders* are input devices which collect data directly from multiple remote locations for continued processing in a computer system. They have two common characteristics:

1. The input of fixed data is by means of a medium that can be read directly by the recorder.

2. The recorder compiles the input data into a standard machine recognizable medium for continued processing.

Most transaction recorders provide for a limited amount of manual input of variable data by means of keyboards, levers, or dials, and for recording automatically constant or repetitive information such as dates and department numbers. The media used for fixed input data include punched cards, edge-punched cards, and embossed plates for printing a machine recognizable printed code.

Individual transaction recorders are normally cable-connected with a central compiler which compiles the input data, generally in the form of punched cards or punched paper tape. Some individual transaction recorders can be used to compile its input data on a tape within the machine, while others are linked directly on-line with a computer system.

Transaction recorders are normally limited to large operations, such as factory operations involving job control and time-card recording. A typical application would provide for recording the receipt of a job in a department by inserting the identification information accompanying the job, probably in a punched card of edge-punched card form into the transaction recorder. When a machine operator starts working on the job itself, he will insert a plastic identification card which contains his employee number, and either key or dial in an operation number and a start-of-job code, or insert another prepunched card for entering all this data into the transaction recorder. On completion of the job, the operator will again insert his identification card and the job number card, and key or dial in or use other prepunched cards for entering such variable data as operation number, quantity produced, and a job completion code. Such fixed and repetitive information as department number and date will be added automatically, and start and finish time will be provided by a wired-in clock.

B. *Point-of-sale recorders* are a specialized type of transaction recorder for use in retail operations. They range from simple intercoupling of a cash register with a paper tape punch or with a perforated tag reader to devices that also read credit cards (which are linked to a central computer and report back when credit limits are exceeded for a potential sale). In typical applications the perforated tags attached to the merchandise are placed in a reader and the amount of the sale is recorded on the cash register, simultaneously producing a punched paper tape as a final by-product for sales analysis and inventory accounting.

C. *Imprinters* are among the most common source data and point-of-sale recording devices. The most common type (such as used in gasoline service stations) imprints recognizable characters or codes from customer credit cards, station data from fixed embossed plates, and additional data such as date to multiple-part sales tickets. The characters and code are then usually read by optical scanning equipment. Another type of this equipment duplicates perforations from an imprinting plate into a punched card. Some imprinters can also enter variable data such as amounts by means of levers.

Data Transmission Equipment

Data in machine recognizable media can be transmitted over teletype or telephone lines, as well as by microwave transmission at various speeds. The transmitting and receiving media may consist of punched paper tape, punched cards, magnetic tape, or computer memory to computer memory.

The most common and oldest type of data transmission is via five-channel punched paper tape transmitted via regular telegraph services. This is the lowest capacity of transmission service, with a maximum rate of transmission of ten characters per second. Regular teletype equipment can be used to create and receive the punched paper tape data. Other punched paper tape devices, as well as punched card devices, can be connected to teletype circuits.

Standard voice or telephone grade channels permit data transmission rates of up to several hundred characters per second, depending on the type of input, receiving, and transmitting devices. Systems vary from simple devices that transmit a manually fed punched card over a regular telephone line to punched paper tape input and receiving devices. Such systems may use six-, seven-, and eight-channel tape that permits transmission speeds up to 150 characters per second to magnetic tape inputs that are received on magnetic tape for immediate computer input. The data may be transmitted via TELPAK on a high-grade leased circuit at speeds of up to 60,000 characters per second.

Two of the more frequently used transmitting services over voice or telephone grade channels are the Dataphone and TELPAK services provided by the American Telephone and Telegraph Bell Telephone System. The Dataphone data set consists basically of a telephone that can be used either for voice or data transmission. It is used to dial the number of the station to which data is to be sent. When answered by the receiving station, the transmitting party can indicate that it is ready to start data transmission. Both parties then depress buttons marked "Data" on their respective Dataphone sets. This suppresses the voice transmission capability and data can then be transmitted. Dataphone sets can be either transmitters or receivers, or a combined transmitting and receiving unit.

TELPAK is another Bell Telephone System service which provides a group of high-grade channels between pairs of points in the United States on a leased circuit basis. These high-grade channels can permit transmission at speeds up to 60,000 characters per second from input on magnetic tape.

Beyond high-speed transmission systems using telephone lines, some companies have set up private *microwave* systems with speeds well over those achieved by the fastest telephone line transmission. However, the costs of such systems are high as they require relay stations at intervals of ten to twenty miles.

Data Display Equipment

With more and more data capable of storage in computers, a variety of equipment has come into use to facilitate real-time inquiry into such computer-stored data and its report back to the inquirer via some form of written output or visual display. Inquiry devices vary from simple computer console typewriters to specially designed inquiry consoles, such as those used by the airlines for reservations and by savings banks. Coming into wider use are also various types of cathode-ray tube visual display devices that can display requested numeric and alphabetic information, as well as information in graphic format. Some of these units provide for a means of "input" by the use of an "electric pen." The operator can place the latter directly on the display unit screen to alter or insert data in the computer stored data.

BIBLIOGRAPHY

Awad, Elias M. and Data Processing Management Association, *Automatic Data Processing, Principles, and Procedures.* Englewood Cliffs, N.J.: Prentice-Hall, Inc., 1966.

Casey, R. S., Perry, J. W., and Berry, Madeline, *Punched Cards, Their Application to Science and Industry.* New York: Reinhold Publishing Corporation, 1958.

Davis, Gordon B., *An Introduction to Electronic Computers.* New York: McGraw-Hill Book Co., 1965.

Gregory, Robert H., and Van Horn, Richard L., *Business Data Processing & Programming.* Belmont, Calif.: Wadsworth Publishing Co., Inc., 1963.

Sippl, Charles J., *Computer Dictionary and Handbook.* Indianapolis, Ind.: Howard W. Sams & Co., Inc., 1966.

Systems and Procedures Association, *Business Systems.* Cleveland, Ohio: Systems and Procedures Association, 1966.

Van Ness, Robert G., *Principles of Data Processing with Computers.* Elmhurst, Ill.: The Business Press, 1966.

————, *Principles of Punched Card Data Processing.* Elmhurst, Ill.: The Business Press, 1962.

Electronics in Business

BENJAMIN CONWAY

International Business Machines Corp.
Harrison, N.Y.

BENJAMIN CONWAY is a graduate of the University of London, where he majored in mathematics and physics. For three years after his graduation he was an industrial engineer with Lever Brothers in England. In 1953 he joined the Electronic Computer Division of Underwood Corporation, where he was employed as a mathematician and programmer. He then joined the electronics group of the Management Advisory Services of Price Waterhouse & Co., for whom he has carried out feasibility studies in many types of industries and businesses.

Mr. Conway has also acted in an advisory capacity to two computer manufacturers concerning various aspects of machine design and marketing.

He has addressed the Systems and Procedures Association, the American Management Association, and the National Association of Accountants, and has had several articles on electronics published.

Mr. Conway is currently a senior systems consultant at IBM's Data Processing Group Headquarters at Harrison, N.Y.

THE BACKGROUND

Business data processing with the electronic computer is now well into the second decade. When the first electronic data processors were introduced in the early 1950's, a well-known business publication estimated that perhaps fifty companies in the country "could eventually use electronic brains." By 1958, however, there were more than 2,000 electronic data processing systems either installed or on order. As of 1968, there were some 30,000 EDP systems installed or on order.

To some, the words "electronic data processing," still conjure up a picture of the completely automatic office, with push-button production, almost instantaneously, of complex reports for management's consideration. To these people, electronic data processing is the panacea for all their clerical ills.

To others, electronic data processing is just another improvement in mechanization, with the same basic concepts as other forms of clerical mechanization. They use the processor only for those applications that have been previously mechanized, or that have been considered generally suitable for mechanization by more conventional methods.

This second concept, that of transition from one type of equipment to another, represents a common use of electronic equipment. There has now been, however, a broadening of functions and record keeping. The actual situation lies somewhere between the two concepts, although modern systems are beginning to approximate the automatic office.

Despite these differing ideas of how to use EDP, there is a unifying factor underlying each of view through the management information system (MIS) approach. In many instances a major by-product of the development of EDP applications such as payroll, billing, inventory control, etc., was the so-called "data base" by means of which management could be supplied with up-to-date information on many facets of the company's business for decision-making and planning purposes. Nowadays the establishment of a data base to serve the needs of all areas of the organization, including marketing, manufacturing, finance, procurement, personnel, etc., is a major goal of most EDP systems with provision for the dissemination of information through MIS.

A Comparison of Processes—the Advantages

What are the major differences between processing data on electronic equipment and processing by other mechanized methods? What are the major advantages and disadvantages of the newer type of equipment? They include:

1. *The speed of processing.* Many thousands of calculations can be performed each second, and masses of data can be processed or rearranged for various requirements or reports in a fraction of the time required by clerical or conventional mechanized methods.

2. *The accuracy of the equipment.* These machines offer an accuracy for each unit of work produced that cannot be matched by any other means. One error in 300 hours of operation, which has been cited in actual practice, may not sound extremely good, but this fact is brought into better perspective when it is realized that the 300 hours represent many hundreds of man-years of operation by nonelectronic means.

3. *Greater processing control.* Data needs to be introduced into the processor only once and is then handled completely automatically. This eliminates the loss of control from transcription and retranscription as well as the loss of control that arises from cards being transferred from machine to machine, or from files getting out of sequence.

4. *Small external storage requirements.* Information can be recorded with accuracy and permanence on magnetic tapes or discs, which generally form the major medium for mass data storage in an electronic system. Tape reels take up little space, one 2,400' reel of magnetic tape, 10″ or 11″ in diameter by ½″ in width being able to hold more information than 25,000

fully punched cards. Removable disc packs and cartridges can store from 20,000,000 to over 400,000,000 characters.

5. *Decision-making ability.* Most clerical operations offer processing variations. If one number is greater than another, then one course of action must be taken; if smaller, another. These minor decisions must be made, often without realization, whenever clerical work is performed. The electronic data processor has the ability through programming to make this type of decisions to select one course of action or another depending on given criteria, and thus becomes a tool of great flexibility. This ability can be clearly seen in the programming example given later. It enables the processor, if correctly programmed, to handle any and all variations of input data, and to perform all the processing automatically on heterogeneous data from the raw state to the finished product.

6. *Internally stored program.* A program is a series of instructions to the processor enabling it to receive or select data, process it, and then produce a desired output. As the program is stored in the processor in the same manner as the data that is to be processed, the program itself is also capable of being processed or modified. This ability to modify an existing program to produce what might be effectively considered as a new program enables the total number of steps to be greatly reduced. The processor can go through the same series of instructions many times, but each time that the instructions are modified, different results are produced.

The Disadvantages

Disadvantages of electronic data processing also exist, but they have often been underestimated by potential users. Among them are:

1. *The relatively high cost of equipment.* While there have been spectacular increases in speeds and capacities of EDP equipment and a broadening of the number of available combinations of systems, ranging from very small to very large, the annual cost of typical systems in many medium-size companies may be reckoned in hundreds of thousands of dollars. This often represents a very large investment for management, and its recoupment in a reasonable period requires additional expenditures for manpower in systems analysis, programming, and conversion tasks.

2. *The cost and difficulty of programming.* Programming, which includes the original analysis of the problem, the planning for a solution, the encoding of these solutions, and assurance of their accuracy and correctness, may take many man-years of effort. As an example, the payroll application of a public utility took twelve man-years of programming before it became fully operational, and a customer billing operation has taken in excess of twenty man-years. A broad, sophisticated system involves several hundred man-years. The major difficulties of programming are to state the task in terms from which coding can be done, to foresee every possible exception in an application, and to provide all necessary means for dealing with the application. This forces an incredibly thorough scrutiny of the

operations to be processed, and sends the time and cost of programming soaring.

3. *The channeling of work.* In normal mechanization, the work load is spread out over a number of machines and, generally, if one machine breaks down the work can be transferred to another. With the high cost of electronic equipment, few companies are able to afford the luxury of stand-by equipment, and thus a breakdown can assume the proportions of a major catastrophe. Furthermore, all the company's varied operations have to be channeled through one piece of equipment, and this causes many machine-scheduling problems not hitherto encountered. It is necessary to carefully plan ahead, to allow specific times for each of the operations that have to be performed, and to establish priorities for each operation in case a break-down should occur.

4. *Conversion to an electronic system.* Conversion poses a twofold problem. The first problem is a purely physical one. It includes such details as site preparation, air conditioning, adequate power supply, sufficient space, and, finally, the actual equipment installation. These costs have climbed as high as $200,000 in some large installations.

Space is an important consideration at the commencement of an electronics program. At this time it is usual to run parallel operations to insure the accuracy of the new processing methods. This creates a need for extra space as both old and new equipment must operate simultaneously. Thus, even though space saving is considered one of the benefits to be derived from electronics, the immediate result is to increase space requirements.

The second problem relates to the conversion of source documents, file records, and the like, to media that are suitable for electronic processing. This conversion generally involves a great amount of keypunch work. A public utility with 1,000,000 accounts, and with partial records for these accounts already maintained in punched card form, spent close to $100,000 to expand these records into the desired integrated master file and to prepare the expanded records for conversion to a magnetic file. If there had been no previous punched card record, this cost would have been many times greater.

GENERAL COMPUTER CATEGORIES

Analog and Digital Computers

The main division to be found in the computer field is that between the analog and digital computers. The analog computer reaches its solutions by replacing arithmetic operations by some other operation bearing a physical analogy to them, the digital by counting. For example, an analog method of multiplication is suggested by Ohm's Law, $E = IR$. With a simple electric circuit containing a variable voltage source, a voltmeter, an ammeter, and a rheostat, a multiplication can be effected. If the resistance is adjusted to equal the value of the multiplier in ohms and the voltage supply adjusted until the ammeter indicates the multiplicand value in amperes, then the product will be shown, in volts, by the voltmeter. Such a circuit will not allow a completely accurate result to be obtained, and this is generally the main disadvantage of the analog computer. Accuracy is limited by the measuring instruments and physical analogies that are employed. For most business applications, a more accurate system of computing is required. This accuracy can be found in the digital computer, which is completely accurate within the limits imposed by the lengths of its arithmetic registers. In some processors this can mean the entire capacity of its memory. Inaccuracy is introduced only when a number exceeds the workable length and has to be truncated or rounded off.

Scientific and business computers. The digital computer has evolved in two ways, as a scientific computer and as a business processor. The major differences between the two lie in the approach to the problems of getting data into and out of the system, the transferring of data within the system, generally for editing or rearrangement, and the scope and flexibility of decision-making. Most scientific problems involve much processing on very little input material, and the desired results can normally be stated succinctly. So, for a scientific computer, multiple high-speed magnetic tape units, high-speed printers, and other high-speed input-output equipment are generally unnecessary. In business problems, on the other hand, although the volume of processing may again be great, this volume is derived from large amounts of input data. The required end result is also a large amount of printed or punched data. Thus, for a business processor, high-speed input-output equipment is necessary both in order to get through the desired volume of work and also to minimize idle processor time, since the amount of processing for each individual item of input and output is generally small.

Process Control and Special Purpose Computers

A special class of EDP equipment has been developed for the purpose of controlling physical processes or providing rapid response in complex man-machine environments. For example, process control systems today are formed in steel mills where they are used to control steel-making, or to operate rolling mills. In chemical plants and oil refineries they are used for process control for a variety of products. A special type of process control is the numerical control computer for machine tools.

General Purpose Computers

The general purpose computer is a completely flexible device. The amount of processing that it can perform is bound by only four physical limitations:

1. The speed of the input devices that control the amount of data that can be fed into the system

2. The internal processing speed that controls the total work potential of the system

3. The storage capacity of the system controls the amount of information that can be processed at any one time without having to call on the input devices for further data or program steps

4. The speed of the output devices controls the amount of processed data that can be removed from the system in order to release storage capacity to start the processing cycle again

The type of processing that can be performed is generally limited only by the skill and imagination of the systems and programming group. Almost every type of business problem can be programmed for processing by electronic equipment. A good systems and programming group is essential for this work, because a qualified analyst not only can handle most business problems, but, by good systems design and coding that takes every advantage of the machine's logical design, he can offset somewhat the four physical limitations on the volume of work that can be performed.

Large-, medium-, and small-scale equipment. To return to the classifications of the computer, the business processor has commonly been categorized as large-, medium-, or small-scale equipment. This is obviously a more artificial type of classification than those previously described and is not so clear-cut. Machines in one category may show some of the characteristics ascribed to the other two categories. However, with this proviso, the characteristics quoted for each category are those most commonly accepted:

1. The large-scale equipment has an outright sales price of above $500,000, or a monthly rental above $15,000. The internal speeds of operation are extremely rapid, the time for most operations being measured in microseconds. The program repertoire, or total number of different operations that can be performed, is large; most processors in this large-scale category are able to perform more than forty different operations. High-speed and extremely flexible input-output equipment is generally associated with these systems. Today's large-scale equipment is characterized primarily by the size of internal storage and by the number of channels or links available for attachment of auxiliary storage, input-output units and communications terminals. Typical large-scale systems have internal storage well in excess of 100,000 characters.

2. Medium-scale equipment has an outright sales price between $50,000 and $500,000, or a monthly rental between $3,000 and $15,000. While internal operating speeds may be almost as fast as large-scale equipment, the internal storage for medium-scale equipment is in the range of 20,000 to 100,000 characters. Hence, medium-scale equipment does not have the capacity to utilize large, complex programs to the same extent as large-scale equipment.

3. Small-scale equipment is generally priced below the $50,000 bracket and has a rental range below $3,000 monthly. In fact, at the lower

end of the price range it is difficult to distinguish between small-scale EDP systems, and the most modern electronic bookkeeping and accounting machines, and desk calculators. The basic characteristic of small-scale equipment is the size of internal storage, usually under 10,000 characters. Among other limitations, this precludes using a large number of peripheral units. Most small-scale systems support a slow speed input such as a card reader, some form of auxiliary store, either disc or tape, and a line printer and card punch. Relatively simple programs are run on small-scale systems. To the extent practical larger programs can be processed on a segmented basis, utilizing auxiliary storage for program residence.

The divisions and subdivisions of the equipment discussed are diagrammed below.

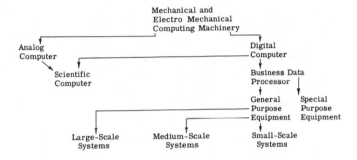

Staffing

Staffing for each of these systems varies greatly. The previous systems and analysis work of a company, the number of different operations to be programmed, and the amount of peripheral equipment required have a considerable bearing on the number of people who will be required. Most companies with electronic data processing have widely different staffing requirements, and the following figures show the range of personnel used:

	operating staff	analysis and programming staff
Large system	6 – 20	10 – 35
Medium system	2 – 10	8 – 30
Small system	1 – 4	1 – 4

SYSTEM COMPONENTS

The major components of an electronic system are:

1. The input and output equipment
2. The central processor
3. The storage systems employed

Input-output Equipment

It was stated earlier that for most business operations there is a great volume of raw and processed data. Thus, the development of the central processor had to be matched by the development of input-output equipment in order that the work volume might be processed.

CONTROL CONSOLE. Probably the simplest form of input equipment is the toggle switch, or its equivalent, which is available to the operator through the computer control board or console. Information can be inserted into the system by the setting of these switches. Obviously, this is a very slow procedure and is used only for very special purposes, generally connected with machine maintenance. The equivalent output device also on the control board usually consists of a set of visual displays that light up to show the coded data held in various portions of the system.

KEYBOARD DEVICES. Next in speed of operation and duality of function (input and output) is the keyboard device. This is normally a modified typewriter keyboard. When used for input, information is typed, using the keyboard, and entered automatically into the system, with visible copy prepared at the same time. When used for output, the keyboard device is operated directly by the computer. This method is slow, input speed being governed by normal typing speeds, and ten characters per second is an average output rate. It is normally used for machine testing and the answering of random interrogations, as well as for remote entry via a terminal.

PAPER TAPE. A punched paper tape can be produced as a by-product of the typing operation, and can also be originated by other equipment not directly connected to the computer. This latter mode of preparation is called "off line." To get information from the tape into the system, a tape reader is required. The reader normally operates by photoelectric sensing of the holes punched into the tape, and reads them at an average rate of 200 to 2,000 characters per second. A second off-line operation, transcribing from paper tape to magnetic tape, can also be performed. The equivalent output device is a paper tape punch which can operate at speeds from ten to over 300 characters per second. The system of coding in paper tape varies from five to eight channels, and will probably be decided by other components of the system. If the tape is to be used only internally, an eight-channel code designed to be completely compatible with the magnetic characters code might be used in order to minimize conversion difficulties.

PUNCHED CARDS. Card-reading and card-punching equipment also form part of the input-output equipment. Data from the cards is either taken directly into the computer through the card reader as an on-line operation, or transcribed to magnetic tape through auxiliary off-line equipment. Reading speeds vary, but 200 to 2,000 cards per minute is a reasonable range. The card punch is the output device, and can be operated directly from the computer, or can be used off-line in conjunction with magnetic tape. Punching speeds vary, but 100 to 400 cards per minute is a realistic range.

PRINTERS. The high-speed printers can print documents at the rate of 500 to 1,100 lines per minute, with up to 160 character positions per line. They can be directly controlled on-line by the computer but are often activated off-line by magnetic tape.

DOCUMENT READERS. A variety of input devices is available to read information contained on documents and either process it on-line or transfer it off-line to magnetic storage. The most widely used document reader for character reading is the MICR (Magnetic Ink Character Recognition) reader used for reading encoded information in a special font printed at the lower edge of a bank check. The characters are sensed magnetically in this case. Optical character readers (OCR) read information printed by mechanical means, typewriter, line printer, etc., usually in a stylized type font. Recently introduced readers can read handwritten numeric characters and a limited number of alphabetic characters and symbols. Mark readers of various kinds are also in use. Document speeds for MICR documents such as checks are well in excess of 1,000 per minute.

MAGNETIC TAPE. One major input and output medium for an electronic data processing system is magnetic tape. Information is recorded on the tape in the form of magnetic spots arranged in a coded pattern, each alphabetic, numeric, or special symbol having its own unique code pattern. Information can be read into and out of the computer at speeds ranging from 15,000 to in excess of 200,000 characters per second. The magnetic tapes, in addition to forming a primary input-output system, can be used to operate high-speed printers or other devices on an off-line basis.

BUFFER UNITS. Although the rate of reading characters from magnetic storage devices to the central processing unit is very high, it is still well below the speeds at which the data can be manipulated internally by the computer. To overcome this speed limitation, an intermediate storage unit, the buffer, was developed.

The buffer is loaded with data at normal reading speeds. The data are transferred to the computer at electronic speeds, and the processing of this data is started. The input buffer can then be reloaded from magnetic storage while the processing is performed, thus permitting overlap of operations, and circumventing the comparatively slow reading speed.

This process can also be applied to output, and thus overlap between tape reading, processing, and tape writing is possible.

The Central Processor

The major differences in central processing units are:

A. The internal speed of operation.

B. The program repertoire, that is, the number of different operations that can be performed. As an example, in some machines a "divide" routine is incorporated into the program repertoire, and the circuitry is designed so that such an operation can be performed automatically. In other computers such circuitry does not exist, and the operation of division has to be performed by a program (subroutine).

C. The mode of programming can also vary. Most systems use either a one, two, or three address system for instructions. The one and two address modes, at least for the arithmetic instructions, refer to the number of operands that can take part in an instruction. The three address mode generally uses two operands, with the third address indicating the position in which the result of the instruction is to be stored. Relative or indirect addressing is also a common feature of most modern processors. Usually an internal register contains a constant which is used to compute an address, or refers to another location for the specific address.

D. Many processors can deal with variable length records and instructions, while others use fixed records and instructions. The "byte" or eight-bit record has come into general use as the unit of information accessed. The value of a byte can be either an eight-bit binary word, an eight-bit alphanumeric character, or two four-bit numeric characters, depending on its use in a program.

E. One of the more significant features of a modern processor, which distinguishes it from earlier models, is its ability to perform concurrent operations in a variety of modes. This ability depends to a large extent on "operating system" programs discussed later. The hardware features required, in addition to adequate internal storage, often include "scratch pad" memory, a variety of registers, interrupt capability, and high- and low-speed channels or buffers, as well as a sufficient number of peripheral devices for the requirements of each of the concurrent tasks.

RANDOM ACCESS SYSTEMS. Before the transformation of the scientific electronic computer to the business electric data processor, the capacity for storing information and the speed at which this stored information could be made available to the computer were not too important. The amount of information was generally small, and could be read into the computer at one time.

Business problems, however, involved large quantities of information set up in ordered files. This information had to be made readily accessible to the processor if business processing was to be handled at all.

The internal storage capacity of most processors is limited in size, even though larger, high-speed memories have become available. To accommodate all the mass of required information, auxiliary methods of storage had to be designed. The past few years, with their emphasis on adapting computers to business needs, have seen the development of many new methods of storing information.

Magnetic tape is considered one of the best auxiliary memory systems associated with electronic processing systems because of the speed with which information can be transferred between the tape and an electronic computer. From the point of view of space conservation also, magnetic tape

s a desirable storage system, since one reel of tape can hold as much in-
ormation as several thousand punched cards. Other advantages of magnetic
ape systems include: permanence, ability to check the information as it is
ead or recorded, accuracy, and low cost—and as a result of this low cost,
ts unlimited capacity, since new tape reels can be added when required.

There are, however, disadvantages also, and in some types of opera-
ions one of the major difficulties when maintaining information on mag-
tetic tape files is the problem of interrogating any particular item of
nformation, and getting the answer to that interrogation in a short enough
nterval of time. The difficulty stems mainly from the fact that individual
tems in a magnetic tape file cannot be immediately identified and inter-
ogated. Instead, the computer must scan the section of the tape file that
contains the particular item, and through programming look at each item
n the file until it determines that it has reached the desired item. Having
lone this for one item, the same procedure must be repeated for others.
If the next item for interrogation is recorded at the start of the same reel
ıs the previous item, the motion of the tape must be reversed in order to
ırrive at the second desired position. This process must be continued for
:ach interrogation. In some systems, scanning is possible only in the forward direction of the tape movement.

It is the scanning of the file that creates the time lag associated with
nagnetic tape file interrogation. For a 2,400-foot reel of tape, assuming
:hat scanning can take place equally well in both the forward and reverse
directions, the average time for access to any part of the file may be several
ninutes. This time does not, at first sight, appear to be very long. However,
'or most magnetic tape systems the act of interrogation is one in which only
)ne interrogation can be performed at a time, a second interrogation being
held up until the first is completed, and thus the time delay becomes
:umulative.

To overcome this type of difficulty in electronic data processing ma-
:hines, random access systems were developed. The name "random access"
is not very accurate—"rapid access" would be better. However, in this
:ontext, what exactly does random or rapid access mean? It means that
regardless of its position within a file, any item of information can be found
rapidly without lengthy searches, the time taken being approximately the
;ame in all cases. There have been several methods of achieving this random
accessibility of information. In one method the information has been stored
on large magnetic drums, in another on discs that look like phonograph
records, and in yet another method the information is stored on small,
addressable sections of magnetic tape. For the random access drum the
term "rapid" represents a time delay of between 10 and 30 milliseconds.
This type of delay can easily be tolerated in meeting many requirements,
and this and other types of random access systems find favor in many
business applications.

In addition to overcoming the time delay difficulty, large, random-

access storage systems enable information to be sorted with comparativ
ease by the processor. The operation of sorting by using a magnetic tap
system is not considered very efficient. The method generally adopted i
that, in each pass of the tape file through the system, the processor create
longer and longer sequences of sorted items, until the entire file is finall
sorted. However, since the physical moving of the tape file must occur fo
each sorting pass, the operation is mainly a mechanical one, rather tha
electronic. Thus, the over-all efficiency of the operation is greatly reduced

By a random access device, however, if the capacity for storing in
formation is great enough, each item as it is read is directed to and recorde
in its correct position in the file, regardless of the fact that other items o
the file may be absent. Then the entire system is read off and recorded o
magnetic tape or some other storage device, with all the empty space
suppressed. By this means, sorting can be accomplished.

None of the methods mentioned so far is truly random access, since
in all cases some file scanning is performed. In the case of the magnetic
drum system, for example, once the correct reading head has been activated
it is still necessary to scan the selected drum channel until the required item
appears beneath the reading head. For the disc system, it is necessary to
select both the correct disc and the required item of information on the disc
These auxiliary search operations require some time to perform.

PROGRAMMING

The repertoire of instructions for any processor indicates the number
of different operations that it can perform. A series of these instructions
listed together in a logical sequence to perform a specific operation is called
a program. In order to illustrate how a computer is programmed, let us
assume a hypothetical computer with the program repertoire in Table
13-1.

The problem that is to be programmed is a simple account posting
program. In this problem it is required to:

1. Prepare a new account tape with balances reflecting the transaction
   debits and credits
2. Detect transactions whose posting would result in debit balances; omit
   posting in these cases and print out the account and transaction records
   for special handling
3. Detect transactions for which there is no corresponding account record, halt and signal the operator

The following assumptions are made:

A. The machine used will have magnetic tape input and output.
B. An account tape will contain for each account an accounting record
   consisting of:
   1. Account number
   2. Balance

C. A transaction tape will contain for each transaction a transaction record consisting of:

1. Account number
2. Credit amount
3. Debit amount

D. Both account records and transaction records will be in account number sequence on the account and transaction tapes.

E. Not all accounts will have transactions.

The Hypothetical Data Processor

The portions of a simple hypothetical machine that are relevant to this illustration are shown in Figure 13-1, and its instruction repertoire is shown in Table 13-1. The organization and operation of the assumed machine will be largely apparent from an examination of this table.

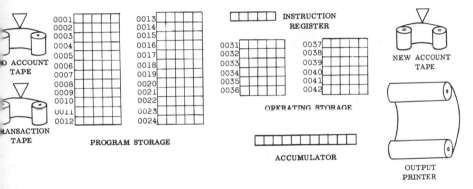

Fig. 13-1. Diagram of Simple, Hypothetical Data Processor

All operations performed by the machine are governed by the program of instructions stored in the program storage. Instructions are read from program storage to the instruction register and executed one by one. Normally the instructions are executed in the sequence in which they are stored, but this sequence may be departed from by means of the conditional and unconditional branch instructions as indicated in the instruction repertoire shown in Table 13-1.

Flow Chart

Having determined the requirements of the problem and the characteristics of the machine to be used, the next step is to prepare a flow chart of the operations to be performed by the machine. A flow chart for the assumed posting problem is shown in Figure 13-2.

The flow chart serves to specify in a graphic way the exact sequence of operations that must be performed during the processing run to achieve the desired results.

TABLE 13-1. REPERTOIRE OF A HYPOTHETICAL PROCESS

Instruction		Operation Performed
opera- tion code	storage address	
T	xxxx	Read a transaction record from the transaction tape unit into storage beginning at address xxxx and continuing until a record mark is sensed on the tape.
A	xxxx	Read an account record from the account record tape unit into storage beginning at address xxxx and continuing until a record mark is sensed on the tape.
W	xxxx	Write on the new account tape from a storage starting at address xxxx and continuing until a record mark is sensed in storage.
Y	xxxx	Type out from storage starting at address xxxx and continuing until a record mark is sensed in storage.
X	- - - -	Clear the accumulator.
P	xxxx	Add the contents of storage address xxxx to the present contents of the accumulator.
S	xxxx	Subtract the contents of storage address xxxx from the present contents of the accumulator.
R	xxxx	Store the contents of the accumulator in storage address xxxx.
U	xxxx	Branch unconditionally—take the next instruction from address xxxx.
B	xxxx	Branch unconditionally—take the next instruction from address xxxx only if the number in the accumulator is zero.
C	xxxx	Branch unconditionally—take the next instruction from address xxxx only if the number in the accumulator is negative.
H	- - - -	Halt and signal the operator.

TABLE 13-2. PROGRAM OF INSTRUCTIONS FOR SIMPLE ACCOUNT POSTING PROBLEM

Instruction			Operation Performed
program storage location	operation code	storage address	
0001	T	0031	Read transaction record to storage.
0002	A	0034	Read account record to storage.
0003	X	0000	Clear accumulator.
0004	P	0031	Add transaction account number to accumulator.
0005	S	0034	Subtract account record number from accumulator.
0006	C	0010	Branch to 0010 if accumulator is negative.
0007	B	0011	Branch to 0011 if accumulator is zero.
0008	W	0034	Write unaltered account record to new account tape.
0009	U	0002	Branch unconditionally to 0002.
0010	H	0000	Halt and signal operator.
0011	P	0035	Add present balance to accumulator.
0012	P	0032	Add transaction credit to accumulator.
0013	S	0033	Subtract transaction debit from accumulator.
0014	C	0018	Branch to 0018 if accumulator is negative (over-draft).
0015	R	0035	Store new balance in place of old balance.
0016	W	0034	Write undated account record to new account tape.
0017	U	0001	Branch unconditionally to 0001.
0018	Y	0031	Type out overdraft details.
0019	U	0016	Branch unconditionally to 0016.

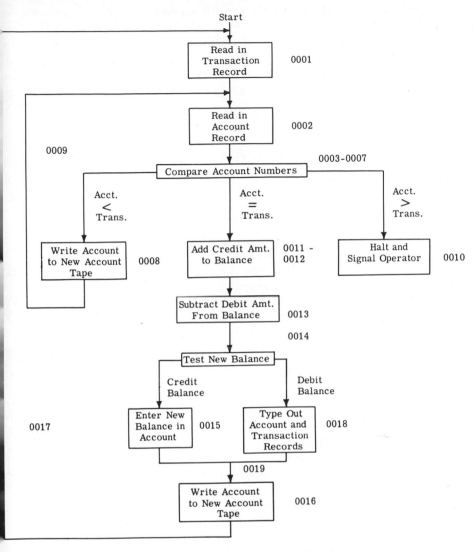

Start

Read in Transaction Record	0001

Read in Account Record	0002

0009

Compare Account Numbers — 0003-0007

Acct.
<
Trans.

Acct.
=
Trans.

Acct.
>
Trans.

Write Account to New Account Tape	0008	

Add Credit Amt. to Balance	0011 - 0012

Halt and Signal Operator	0010

Subtract Debit Amt. From Balance	0013

0014

Test New Balance

Credit Balance

Debit Balance

0017

Enter New Balance in Account	0015

Type Out Account and Transaction Records	0018

0019

Write Account to New Account Tape	0016

Note: Numbers are instruction numbers from
detailed program, Table 13. 2

Fig. 13-2. Flow Chart for Simple Account Posting Program

The Coded Program

After the flow chart has been thoroughly checked and is known to
accomplish what is desired, the detailed program of coded instructions is
prepared. The completed program for the assumed account posting problem is shown in Table 13-2.

In preparing the program, the programmer translates each functional box in the flow chart into the exact instruction to carry out the function noted. Some boxes will require only one instruction to carry out the func tion noted, whereas others may require a number of instructions. During this phase of the programming, the programmer must assign specific storage locations to the various factors involved and take these assignments into account in determining the address portion of each instruction. The storage location assignments used in the account posting program are shown in Table 13-3.

TABLE 13-3. CONTENTS OF STORAGE ADDRESSES

storage address	contents	
0031	Account number	
0032	Credit amount	Transaction record
0033	Debit amount	
0034	Account number	
0035	Balance	Account record
0036	Record mark	

It can be seen that the first box in the flow chart, which is "Read in Transaction Record," is translated from the program repertoire to T 0031 where 0031 is the beginning of the transaction storage area.

The Software Background

EARLY DEVELOPMENTS. As is shown in this example, the steps to be followed in the solution of a problem are the same whether the problem be scientific or commercial:

1. Define the problem.
2. Analyze the problem.
3. Outline a solution (block diagrams).
4. Detail the solution (detailed flow charts).
5. Encode the solution to permit processing by the computer.
6. Eliminate errors from the coded routines—commonly known as "de bugging."

The performance of these six steps, from the statement of the problem to its solution by the computer, is called the programming of the problem. Steps 1 through 4 take about 85 per cent, and steps 5 and 6 take about 15 per cent of the preparation time.

Since steps 1 through 4 are largely creative in nature, very little has been attempted up to the present to utilize the assistance of the computer in performing them. Steps 5 and 6, coding and debugging, however, are mechanical techniques. The coding of a problem, for example, is essentially one of translation, in which the detailed solution of the problem is put into a series of sequential instructions. The instructions must be in a orm in which they can be accepted, understood, and operated upon by the computer. To enable as much of the work as possible in these steps to be aken away from programmers and to be performed instead by the computer, certain techniques have been evolved.

It may seem that in view of the fact that only 15 per cent of the preparation time is taken up by steps 5 and 6, these techniques cannot be very valuable. However, if, as in some cases, the total preparation time for a commercial application is approximately 30 man-years, 15 per cent of this still represents four and a half man-years.

Evolution of Program Languages

The term "software" generally refers to a variety of programming facilities which aid the user in (1) producing object code or machine language, (2) which perform a number of common tasks such as sorting, merging, editing, controlling input-output functions, or (3) which enable the user to maximize the utilization of the system components.

The first programs employed the direct machine language, and generally appeared when written by the programmer as a series of numbers and letters. Such a program could look like this although within the computer it might be a binary string:

instruction address	op code	A address	B address
7030	15	6050	4020
7040	17	3020	1050
7050	22	7030	7040

It is obviously difficult to use, and equally obviously open to all sorts of errors in writing numbers, transposing them, etc. One of the early changes was to introduce the concept of *relative coding* in program writing. In the above program example, the numbers at the left, 7030, 7040, 7050, represent the addresses in memory at which the program was to be stored. If extra instructions were to be added, it was difficult to insert them since then all subsequent instruction addresses needed to be changed. Another difficulty was that such a program had to be placed into the computer at the instruction addresses given by the programmer.

If another program segment was located in these positions, it was necessary for that segment to be cleared out before the new program could be used. Both of these difficulties, and also some errors due to transposition, etc., were avoided by relative coding. Instead of writing 7030, 7040, 7050, symbols would be used. The first instruction in this series (7030) might be given a symbol such as A1, 7040 would be A2, 7050 would be A3, etc. Where the instruction itself, in its A or B address position, referred to an instruction address, these would also be replaced by the new symbol.

Each logical segment of the program is given a different reference letter. For example, in a payroll program there might be sections dealing with:

Calculation of gross pay
Calculation of federal taxes
Calculation of FICA, etc.

All the program steps associated with the calculation of gross pay might be referred to as A1, A2, etc., those dealing with calculation of federal taxes, B1, B2, etc. Thus, the original three program steps shown:

7030	15	6050	4020
7040	17	3020	1050
7050	22	7030	7040

might now appear as:

A1	15	d4	b2
A2	17	e7	f4
A3	22	a1	a2

To insert a new instruction between A2 and A3, we would use a number like A2.5. Further insertions might require numbers like A2.55. When the program is completed, it will be entered into the system where through a translating program the system will assign real machine addresses. This same translating program will, as its first job, sort the instructions in the correct sequence, thus taking care of the inserted instructions, which will now fall in their correct place.

A further refinement to programming was the adoption of mnemonic codes for the operation codes, and tags (data names) for certain data fields or program sections.

The mnemonic codes may replace an operation code like 15 with ADD, an operation code 25 with MPY, etc. A data field that contained an employee number could be referenced by the tag EMPNO or MANNO. A section of the program dealing with FICA could be tagged FICA-RT, etc. Thus a program sheet might now appear as follows:

GROSS-R	MPY	REG—HR	HR. RATE
	MPY	OVER HRS	OV. RATE
	ADD	REG PAY	OV.—PAY
	TRF	NET—R	

When it was realized that many lines of coding appeared unchanged except for their location in memory in many different programs, it became obvious that these "subroutines," as they are called, could be referred to in a program by a tag. Each time the tag was recognized by the translation program it would call in, from a program library that it controlled, the set of instructions that the tag represented. It would then position these instructions in the correct place in the program as called for by the programmer, and in the correct place in memory, depending upon where the program was to be located. The translator program had changed from translating one line of coding to one instruction in machine language, to an *assembler* which could create from its program library a set of instructions far longer than the terms written by the programmer. The instruction which calls in the subroutine instructions from the library of subroutines is called a *Macro*. The type of coding in which macros, tags, etc., are used is called an *assembly language,* of which AUTOCODER is an example.

Most assembly languages include the input and output instructions in their library of Macro instructions.

The evolution of program languages also spread to scientific work, and languages of the type of FORTRAN (Formula Translator) were developed. This consists of a *compiler* which can take coding in the form of highly stylized mathematical equations and translate it to the necessary machine instructions.

From the assembly languages referred to earlier it was a simple conceptual step, although an extremely difficult programming job, to develop compilers which could translate statements which approximated the English language. Such a language is COBOL (*C*ommon *B*usiness *O*riented *L*anguage). In this language, statements like:

Multiply hours worked by hourly rate, giving normal pay
Multiply overtime hours by "1½", giving OT factor
Multiply OT factor by hourly rate giving OT pay
Add OT pay and normal pay giving gross pay

can be recognized by the COBOL compiler and translated to machine language. The compiler is able to recognize operation codes, multiply, add, etc., and to ignore nonessential words such as by, the, etc. It is, of course, necessary for the programmer to define terms, such as hourly rate, normal pay, overtime hours, etc. One such definition, e.g., for hourly rate, might say:

Hourly rate, numeric field, positive sign, four digits, two decimal places.

The compiler, when compiling the program from the COBOL statements would set aside a 4- or 5-digit field (depending on how the particular computer for which this program was being compiled handled signs) for hourly rate, and would "remember" that it was a field with two decimal places. This is important if it were necessary to add this field to another with three decimal places. The compiler would align the numbers correctly to allow the addition to take place properly. If 2842 containing two decimal places is added to 14183 containing three decimal places, then the answer is 42603 containing three decimal places, not 17025, which is the answer that would be derived if the decimal points were not aligned.

A feature of COBOL is that it is a language that is capable of being used on machines of different manufacturers. Theoretically, the data division (the field description section) and the *procedural* sections (the programming section) are unchanged from machine to machine, and it is necessary for the programmer to describe only the particular machine that he would be using in an *environment* section. In practice, the manufacturers found it necessary to develop some COBOL instructions and formats that made good use of their computers, but could not be transferred to another. Thus, COBOL is divided into standard and elective COBOL. The first is translatable from machine to machine; the second is oriented to a particular processor or family of processors. However, the moving of a program to completion is greatly facilitated by the use of COBOL.

The final evolutionary step, bringing us more or less up to date, was to combine COBOL and FORTRAN features into a single language. An example of this is PL/I, which will accept either type of statement. Almost all the high-level languages such as COBOL, PL/I, etc., allow the user to slip out of the high-level language to an assembly language or direct machine language to handle special programming activities that the high-level language cannot deal with.

Development of Current Operating Concepts

The modern EDP system has speeded up the processing of data by a factor of several thousands over previous methods. However, its full processing capabilities could not be exploited in many cases because internal processing speeds permit the processing of data at a far greater rate than it could be received and disseminated through the peripheral devices. Early attempts to improve utilization led to the use of the batch processing mode with off-line data preparation and sequential organization. Data were assembled in some machine sensible format (usually punched cards or punched paper tape) through off-line equipment, i.e., devices not directly connected with the processor. Then the data were transferred from the slow input media such as punched cards to high-speed media such as magnetic tape. Input speed increases up to several hundred thousand characters per second could result. Thus, off-line batch processing was an early means of attempting to match internal processing speeds with input-output.

In time, magnetic tape as a storage media for input-output was augmented by mass storage devices such as disc files, disc packs, and removable cartridge storage devices. These could receive and transfer data at higher rates than most magnetic tape units, and also permitted random operation as well as sequential operations. The RAMAC is a good early example. For the most part, however, batch processing methods continued to be used because, even though input-output speeds were increasing, internal speeds were increasing at an even greater rate. Thus, the imbalance between internal speeds and input-output still continued.

One early method of increasing throughput was to provide for overlapping input-output functions with each other and with internal processing. As an outgrowth of this early overlapping technique, we now find EDP systems with a considerable degree of flexibility in permitting simultaneous operations and sharing of various processor and storage components. Those features and techniques involving simultaneous operations and sharing of capabilities, such as multi-programming and multi-processing, involve the ability of the processor to start an input or an output operation which would then proceed independently while the central processor could perform a full work load without waiting until the input or output device was ready for another operation.

These abilities were further developed to allow the processor to control a large number of more or less independently operating input-output devices on-line, and at the same time, because of the larger size and high speed of available internal storage, several programs could be stored in memory at the same time and executed concurrently in an interleaved manner so that several jobs could be accomplished in the same time interval.

By means of internal logic and through program control, the processor can supervise or monitor the status of input-output units and schedule their performance for the particular program(s) being executed. In some systems, when more than one demand is made on a device, the processor has the capability through its supervisory or monitor program to queue up the various jobs and perform them as they arrive or in some priority sequence.

As can be visualized, the processor in this type of operation, whether using a plain queue, or some type of priority, or a combination of these methods to activate input and output devices, is in the position of a juggler with many balls in the air, keeping absolute control over them, and disposing of them under a predetermined plan. To accomplish this the processor needs a fairly complex control program to transfer control between the pulling or selection program, the input-output commands, and the processing, or application to insure continuous operation. This control program, often known as the *operating system,* resides permanently in processor storage, and is usually provided by the manufacturer, although users can adapt it by program modifications to their own situation if they so require.

The operating system may also provide a *time-sharing* mode of operation. In this mode, the on-line input-output devices can be used in such a way so that each user may appear to be the sole occupant of the processor. The work of several users can be completely unrelated, and the users will not normally be aware of each other. In special situations in which each of the terminal users is using the same programs, as in the case of an airlines reservation system, for example, where a common data base stored internally is also involved, and where more than one processor is in use, the system is in a *multi-processing* mode. Several processors may be employed to support the multi-processing mode. Where users with different programs are sharing the same system, the term *multi-programming* is applied.

The more terminals that are attached directly to the processor (i.e., on-line terminals), the less rapid is its response time to each. If the response time is such that in a given situation the response is received in sufficient time for it to control subsequent user actions, the operation is known as a *real-time* operation. Real-time response requirements vary greatly by application, and what might be real-time for one operation could not be considered real-time for another. For example, in a banking operation, a real-time response of several seconds would be more than adequate to insure that a customer did not cash a check for more than his balance, and to flag that account so that an accomplice could not cash a second check against the original balance. In a missile control operation, on the other hand, a response time of several seconds would be far too long to enable guidance control decisions to be made to correct error conditions. Here real-time response is probably required to be of the order of microseconds.

Terminals do not need to be in the same room or even in the same building as the processor. Telephone circuits, microwave, etc., can all put distant terminals into direct contact with a processor. This is known as *remote processing* or *teleprocessing*.

Terminals

The terminals vary widely in type and capability. They can vary in the type of data they receive and accept, in the display of data, in method of operation, etc. The simplest type of terminal might be some sort of analog device; for example, temperature falling outside certain limits could cause a thermostat signal device to send data to a processing system for corrective action. More complex types of terminals would allow the transmission of much more sophisticated data; for example, a complete text can be transmitted from a keyboard terminal, with all the editing characteristics necessary, and stored within a processor.

Similarly, output terminals vary widely. Again, the terminals might be a simple switch device that opens and closes on a processor command given as the result of data received by the system. It could also be a remotely located high-speed printer on which long reports can be printed remotely after being generated by the processing system. Keypunches, typewriters, high-speed printers, even the telephone with computer audio response, can be used as terminals.

The terminal with the most potential for future expansion seems to be the video display terminal. This type of terminal allows the processing system to project reports, charts, diagrams, etc., on the display screen. In some types of video terminals the user can make changes on the screen which will interact with the system to change data stored therein; in others, new or changed data are entered through a keyboard and verified by being shown on the screen before being transmitted to and stored in the system. The full potential of the video display terminal as a remote device is just beginning to be realized, but it is certain that it will be making its appearance in many types of systems before long.

A system can be programmed to help the user at a terminal to avoid errors in on-line data entry by providing him with a set of guidelines. For example, in an accounts receivable operation the processor might generate or show on a screen a message such as "enter customer number." After the customer number is entered and has been verified by the system, it may then transmit the message "show type of transaction," or "enter amount," etc. This type of interactive operation between the processor and user is called the *conversational mode* because it puts the user and processor into a dialogue with each other.

ACCURACY AND CONTROLS

The correctness of all information that is being processed by the electronic system is insured in two ways:

1. By the inherent accuracy and circuitry controls built into the system and its peripheral equipment by the manufacturer
2. By the use of programmed controls

A brief indication of some of these control features is given. It is not all-inclusive, but should give a general picture of the accuracy and control that is possible.

Built-in Checking Features

The most widely used check is the parity bit. This is a redundant bit (binary digit) that is added, if necessary, to the character code to make the number of bits for all characters either all odd or all even. Whether the odd or even number of bits is used in any given system is not important so long as it remains consistent throughout the system. As an example, in a system employing an odd parity check, if a character has four bits, an extra bit is added by the processor in the parity bit channel. If the character has five bits, the parity bit channel is left blank.

Information is recorded on magnetic tape with this parity check channel also present. Any time that information is passed from processor to tape, the number of bits is counted, and should always be odd, if that is the convention used. If dust or a tape flaw results in the loss of a bit, the parity check will operate to transfer the processor to an error routine. If the error is purely transient, rereading the information may correct the situation. However, if the error persists, the operator can be signaled for the necessary action to be taken. Most systems use the parity check for reading from magnetic tape, recording on magnetic tape, and also at all internal points where transfer of information takes place.

Accuracy checks in peripheral equipment are necessary to insure that the input units have correctly accepted the information from cards, paper tape, magnetic tape, or discs, and that the output units have correctly printed, recorded, or punched the information.

Punched paper tape in some systems is verified in the same manner as punched cards. A tape prepared by one punching unit is read by a verifying unit at the same time that the data is being retyped. A comparison is made with the original, and the correct data is punched into a second tape; any differences lock up the typing unit so that a correction can be made. The second tape, which has now been verified, is used as an input to the machine.

Card input is checked by using two reading stations so that comparison can be made between the data read at one station and then at the other. If both readings agree, the information is transferred into machine storage.

Output to cards is checked in a similar manner, but in the reverse order to input checking. Outputs to a printer use a system in which an electrical signal caused by the mechanical operation of printing is compared to the input signal from the computer or tape. This is the so-called "echo check." The error routine can be programmed to cause rereading to eliminate most transient errors, and to stop after a specified number of reread cycles if the error persists.

These systems of comparison checks on transfer operations are a most important inclusion in any EDP system. Often, data from the computer are stored on tape to be used as the input to other devices to provide off-line output facilities, which allow more efficient scheduling of the computer operation. Thus, the system of checking must be continuous and consistent from the verification of input media to the final check of the mechanical or electrical positioning of the printing units.

Programmed Checks and Controls

These can be as varied and complex as any methods group desires. However, only some of those most frequently used are described.

RECORD COUNT. A record consists of all the information relating to a particular transaction or a particular account balance. For example, all the information relating to one employee's weekly pay in a pay register tape would be considered a record. It is possible to insert on the tape a count of the number of records held on this tape. The machine automatically checks this total each time the tape is read. Thus, should data be transferred from one tape to another and a record or group of records be lost, the machine would automatically indicate to the operator that the record count did not agree. The count is made when the file is written, and each time thereafter that the tape is read, the count is checked.

HASH TOTALS. Hash totals consist of arithmetic totals of data that would not ordinarily be added together; for example, stock numbers and amounts may be added for all records. The hash totals are therefore similar to the record count, but have the added advantage that a check is made to see that descriptive or insignificant information has been read into the machine correctly. Hash totals may be computed for an entire file as an additional record at the end of the file, or they may be incorporated in a single record for a selected portion of the file.

THE LABEL. It is possible to incorporate on a magnetic tape a record that will serve to check on the librarian and other computer employees. In addition to entering on the tape the identity of the tape, it is possible to record the number of a tape machine that tape must be mounted on to process it correctly. Technically this is described as the "address" of the tape unit. The label can be used to include a range of dates within which the tape must be used. If a tape is part of a file that is to be updated regularly, the machine cycle on which the tape was made can be recorded. If the file is to be updated on the next cycle, the machine will automatically check the sequence of cycle numbers to check whether the latest tape is being used as input in the updating process. The label can include a notation as to the "purge" date. This would be the earliest date on which the tape could be used as a new output tape. In other words, for a safety factor, the information on a tape may be retained for a selected period even though the tape itself is superseded. Using the tape as a new output tape automatically erases the information appearing on it. The purge date feature would prevent the erasing of information it was desired to retain for a certain period. The label may also record the number of times the information on the tape has been read. It is desirable not to reuse master tape indefinitely without transcribing the information to a new tape. By the use of the label the machine can indicate on the console each time a designated multiple number of uses is reached.

PROOF FIGURES. A proof figure is used to check an important multiplication in a program. The proof figure is arrived at by inserting in the record of information an artificial figure that has no meaning. An example of the meaning of proof figures is as follows: "An example of this is multiplication of quantity of cost required in grocery billings. The check is based on a relationship between cost and a so-called proof cost. An arbitrary figure larger than any normal cost is set up. Then the proof cost is expressed by the formula cost plus proof cost equals Z."

"When quantity is multiplied by cost it is also multiplied by proof cost. Normally, two of the totals needed for the check, quantity and quantity times cost, are accumulated during the program."

The description goes on to say that the proof is arrived at by adding the total of quantities extended by cost to the total of quantities extended by proof cost, and comparing the aggregate total with the total of quantities extended by figure Z. The purpose of making these artificial calculations is to obtain assurance that the individual multiplications have been performed correctly.

LIMIT CHECKS. This is a check of a field in a record or a total in a calculation to see whether certain predetermined limits have been exceeded.

A limit check can be built into a payroll calculation program so that no amount of gross pay may be allowed to exceed a predetermined limit.

CROSSFOOTING BALANCE CHECKS. These checks are similar to those ordinarily employed by accountants in the preparation of work sheets. They are equivalent to crossfooting individual amounts, vertically adding detail amounts, and crosscasting totals to prove.

USE OF CHECK POINTS. Check points may be used in combination with certain of the other checks, such as crossfooting balance checks to make interim proofs during the course of an operation. In order that a lengthy calculation may not have to be recomputed because it does not crossfoot, a program of check points may be built into the program so that the accumulated totals can be crossfooted at intervals during the processing. One company, for example, makes this proof at intervals of 1/20th of the payroll.

SEQUENCE CHECK. As any item from a master file is read into the processor, its identifying tag is compared with the identifying tag of the preceding item (if any) that was read into the processor. This comparison will tell whether the file is in correct sequence. As the identifying tag can be either numeric (e.g., an account number), alphabetic (e.g., a customer name), or alphanumeric (e.g., a part number containing both alphabetic and numeric information), the comparison has to be programmed to recognize an ascending sequence for all these possibilities. If the master file is found to be out of sequence, the processor jumps to an error routine. Here it may attempt to correct the error itself or it may signal the operator in order that appropriate external action be taken. The same control can also be exercised over items in a transaction file if the transaction file is supposed to be in sequence.

THE FEASIBILITY STUDY

In view of the high cost of electronic data processing equipment, the long preparation period necessary to insure the complete operational planning, and the difficulty of obtaining high-caliber personnel to run, maintain, and improve the installation, it would appear that the advantages of the electronic system over any other would have to be very clearly defined.

To determine these advantages, most prospective users of electronic equipment undertake a feasibility study. The term "feasibility study" is probably an unfortunate one, since almost all business applications are operationally feasible. It is necessary to speak of "a feasibility study to determine a given objective" before much meaning can be attached to the phrase.

The given objective is, of course, management's objective in the proposed use of the equipment, and it is essential that this be very clearly defined before the study is undertaken. Too many studies have been started and then come to a halt because the objectives were not known. The most common objectives that various managements have put forward include:

1. Economic advantages over present methods by the use of the equipment.
2. Greater speed in preparation of reports and processed data to allow more timely management decisions to be made.
3. Greater accuracy in the processing of work, especially where this work has a direct consumer relationship, such as in public utility customer billing where mistakes in billing can create bad public relations.
4. Improved equipment reliability. Most electronic installations operate with a very low percentage of machine downtime. Thus management's investment is not made in idle equipment.
5. Improved systems control, because in an electronic system human intervention, with consequent errors, is at a minimum.
6. Greater ease in expected expansions. Electronic equipment allows volume expansion to be handled more easily than any other systems of mechanization.
7. The desire to perform work, possibly of an operations research nature, which because of its magnitude had not previously been susceptible to attack.
8. The computer is part of an over-all management information system.

It can be seen that some of these objectives may well clash with others. For example, to obtain an advantage in speed of reporting may be possible only at increased cost. Greater control through programming may be possible only at the expense of speed or other factors; therefore, it is necessary for management not only to state the objectives, but also to give appropriate weight to each so that a study group can decide which aim is paramount, and which aims can be subordinated, if necessary.

There are many ways of conducting a feasibility study. One of the most practical methods is in two stages, the first merging into the second as the study proceeds. The first stage is conducted primarily by a small, highly specialized group, probably composed of three or four people. The skills of this group should include systems analysis, systems development and integration, and a broad appreciation of the limitations and abilities of electronic data processing equipment.

Considering the fact that some of these skills may be foreign to company personnel, it may be necessary to look for outside help in order to obtain them. This can be accomplished by hiring available competent personnel on a permanent basis from the labor market, or by employing consultant services. In any case, no matter how these skills may be acquired, it is still important to realize that another essential requirement for the small specialized team is a thorough knowledge of the company and its operations. The group must contain at least one person with a thorough understanding and knowledge of the company. Finally, this small initial group should be allowed to function at a sufficiently high level to be able to operate above any of the frictions and animosities that tend to develop in any investigation, and to be able to demand time and cooperation from any individual in the company.

The aim of this small specialized group is to establish quickly whether there is a possibility for the efficient use of electronic data processing equipment in accordance with the objectives that have been established by management. This method of study, the so-called exclusion method, attempts to ask strategic questions in such a way that a negative answer will exclude consideration of certain types of equipment, or of certain types of operations, or may even terminate the study. Only the facts that are needed to supply the answer to each question are examined, and the group does not get itself tied down in needless detail.

Assume that economy is the prime objective of management in a particular study. Then, an example of the type of question asked by the group could be, "Is the replaceable cost greater than the assumed equipment rental costs?" At the very first stage of investigation the words "replaceable cost" should be made to include all personnel and machines in the affected areas of operation. If this total personnel and machine cost is less than $200,000 annually, there is little point in looking at large-scale data processing equipment. The second stage of this particular investigation might then attempt to separate those employees and machines employed in well-governed and repetitive operations from those whose major function is to deal with irregularities and exceptions to the normal procedures to indicate a lower level of potential mechanization.

On the other hand, if the total cost of personnel and machines is in excess of $1,000,000 annually, and the cost of performing the routine type of operation is found to be above $500,000 annually, there is a good indication that the application warrants further investigation. At this point the study can be broadened by a statement of its objectives. These could be:

1. To determine all areas of the company's operations that can be processed by electronic equipment, to establish priorities for these operations, and to investigate possibilities of integrating operations by various systems approaches

2. To determine in these areas the relative advantages and disadvantages that may arise from the use of electronic data processing equipment and the possible savings in personnel, equipment, and purchased services

3. To decide upon the type of processor suited to the selected applications and the peripheral equipment that will be needed to completely process the applications

4. To calculate the time requirements for the selected operations

5. To determine the personnel requirments for the electronic and peripheral equipment, and the approximate programming and planning costs

The more detailed fact-finding stage will now start, and the small group can spread its work load by submitting questionnaires, of which the following is an example.

ELECTRONIC FEASIBILITY STUDY QUESTIONNAIRE

A. *General:*
1. Number and location of plants, offices, warehouses, etc.
2. Present or proposed system of communications between these units
3. Items produced at each plant with approximate volumes

B. *Personnel:*
1. Number of people employed at each plant or branch, etc.
   a. Management
   b. Clerical, including supervision
   c. Operational, including supervision
2. Number of people employed in head office
3. Number of people employed in sales office or other locations

C. *Equipment:*
1. List of all clerical equipment in use in all plants and offices
2. Approximate percentage of usage for this equipment. One or more shifts?
3. Cost price or monthly rentals of the equipment

D. *Clerical organization:*
1. Chart the clerical organization of each office, with job titles and number of persons in each job
2. Outline of the work of people shown in the chart, with an approximate percentage breakdown of their time
3. Salaries of all personnel

E. *Forms and reports:*
1. Copies of all forms and reports produced by the company
2. Frequency with which these forms and reports are prepared, and their disposition

F. *Systems department:*
1. Organization of department
2. Specialties of knowledge within the department

G. *Proposed electronics group:*
1. Names of proposed personnel
2. Specialized skills of personnel
3. Method of selection
4. Their systems background
5. Their programming background

An estimate of the machine capacity that will be taken up by the proposed applications is now needed. To estimate this requirement, both the processing cycle and the input-output requirements must be timed.

Because of fast internal operating speeds of electronics equipment, it might often be assumed that the total time of operation was that which was required to enter information into and receive information from the system, that is, that the system was input-output limited. This has sometimes proven to be an oversimplification, and the times so established for the applications might have been much lower than the times needed. Thus, it is often necessary to attempt to calculate processing time as well as the time for input and output of information, which is much simpler to estimate. A method that will allow a reasonable degree of accuracy in timing these operations is as follows (magnetic tape is assumed as both the input and the output medium, but similar calculations can be made for any other medium):

1. Estimate the time required for input of information and output of information to the system. This is a reasonably mechanical calculation to make, and depends on the length of items held within master files, the length of the transaction files, and the lengths of the required output tapes.

2. Write the program for the straightforward, or main line, processing. Allow program steps for exits to exception routines, but make no attempt to program these routines. Using the manufacturers' specifications, time the program that has been written, employing the volume statistics that are appropriate for the job to give the necessary weighting.

3. Estimate the number of major exceptions to these routines, and determine the ratio of work involved in the straightforward processing to that of handling exceptions. A detailed job analysis may be necessary at this point. If, for example, it is found that twice as many people are required to handle the exceptions, which constitute about a third of the work load, we have:

	% of employees	% of work	unit work load
Main line	33%	66%	2
Exceptions	66%	33%	½

This establishes that the effort to process exceptions is four times as great as the effort to process the main line work. This ratio is used to establish the program length required for each type of exception. This is further multiplied by the number of major exception paths to the main routine, since it is assumed that each path will require approximately the same number of instructions no matter what volume of work will be assigned to any given path. If the original program was of 1,000 steps, and if there are ten major exception paths, with the four to one work ratio we arrive at a final program length of 1,000 x 4 x 10 steps, or 40,000 program steps. This will indicate, from a knowledge of the machine's internal storage capacity, the probable number of passes through the computer necessary to complete the program. It will also give a good indication of programming costs, since current estimates show that a completed instruction, including planning, analysis, and conversion, costs about $4. The time estimate for processing can be made by applying the ratio determined before together with the appropriate volume figures to the main line and exception routine times, and adding the time required to unload and load the computer if multiple runs are necessary.

The replaceable costs can now be determined in greater detail, and a program should be drawn up to show when the equipment will be delivered, when gains will be forthcoming, and so on. If the analysis shows that a net savings will be made, and that the initial costs can be recouped in the period suitable to management, then detailed planning can be started. A sample analysis is shown in Table 13-4.

TABLE 13-4.

	machine I	machine II	machine III	machine IV	machine V
Site preparation	$100,000	$100,000	$100,000	$100,000	$100,000
Air conditioning	50,000	50,000	50,000	50,000	20,000
Document conversion	30,000	30,000	30,000	30,000	50,000
First-year programming	42,000	42,000	42,000	42,000	42,000
Position after one year	(222,000)	(222,000)	(222,000)	(222,000)	(212,000)
Second-year programming	42,000	42,000	42,000	42,000	42,000
Document conversion	30,000	30,000	30,000	30,000	20,000
(Equipment installed here)	— — —	— — —	— — —	— — —	— — —
Six months' rental	33,000	61,000	66,000	108,000	62,000
Six months' operation	18,000	18,000	18,000	18,000	18,000
Position after two years	(345,000)	(373,000)	(378,000)	(420,000)	(354,000)
Third-year programming	42,000	42,000	42,000	42,000	42,000
Rental	66,000	122,000	132,000	216,000	124,000
Operation	36,000	36,000	36,000	36,000	36,000
Gross savings	175,000	175,000	175,000	275,000	175,000
Position after three years	(314,000)	(398,000)	(413,000)	(439,000)	(381,000)
Fourth-year programming	42,000	42,000	42,000	21,000	42,000
Operation	36,000	36,000	36,000	36,000	36,000
Rental	66,000	122,000	132,000	216,000	124,000
Fourth-year second shift	7,200	9,000	1,800	—	1,800
Operation	13,200	30,500	6,600	—	6,200
Gross savings	300,000	300,000	300,000	300,000	300,000
Position after four years	(178,400)	(337,500)	(331,400)	(412,000)	(291,000)
Number of years to achieve break-even point	5 yrs.	7 yrs.	6½ yrs.	12 yrs.	6½ yrs.

After a decision has been made, through the feasibility study, to continue with the acquisition of electronic data processing equipment, many new major problems arise.

The first problem is that of reallocation of duties. Even with the comparatively simple transition approach, using the electronic processing system only as a service center for low-level departmental applications, some reorganization is necessary. Due to integration of both records and functions within the system, many jobs disappear, and also many departmental lines and responsibilities are crossed. The main impact is probably in the lower levels of work performed, that is, at clerical, supervisory, and junior management levels. Here, a major reallocation of work and responsibility may be necessary. For top management, the system acts as a superior managerial tool supplying better and faster information. Thus, in the transition phase, the impact on top management takes the form of a reallocation rather than a reorganization.

When the integrated coordinated systems approach is taken, however, a more serious disruption of management functions may take place. In addition to the reallocation problem, which would presumably still apply, there arises the reorganization problem. More and more functions would be stripped from management itself and incorporated into the system. The necessity for a new type of management may arise, one that is fully able to use the up-to-the-minute information received from the system.

The economic benefits from the answer to these problems may completely dwarf the returns available from the transition approach. These benefits are often intangible, and a dollar value cannot be assigned to them, but it is increasingly obvious that much can be done to decrease company overhead tied up in inventory and excess labor, and to increase company operating efficiency. The advent of the computer, even though first used by a company in its clerical areas, may well enable the right type of management to move into the MIS and operations research fields with its richer prizes.

The next problem is that concerned with the expansion of the original, small group of the feasibility study, into the larger group that will implement the installation. It is obvious from the importance of the operation, and from the amount of risk capital that the company must sink into it, that this group should be highly competent. At its head must be a man possessing managerial responsibility as well as good systems and technical knowledge. He must be able to cooperate well with other managerial personnel, and be able to sell the services that the electronic system can offer. Too often it is found that, although paying lip service to a system of mechanization, departments will maintain duplicate records in order to check on the work of the mechanized section, work that they often do not understand or trust. In order to achieve savings by electronic processing, this state of affairs cannot be tolerated. All affected departments must be convinced of the value of the service.

Lower in the group, at the analysis and coding levels, it is even more important to have competent personnel. The high man-hour figures that many companies require to program the operations may be due to this underestimation of the caliber of personnel required. One case is reported of an expert programmer doing in one week a job that had occupied others for a total time of three months. It is certain that a good group not only will cut expensive programming costs, but will also be able to achieve greater clerical savings when the operation is completed.

Application tests given to new people within the company, and the acquisition of those considered irreplaceable in other departments, will reduce the need to go outside of the organization. Even if the majority of the group can be obtained within the company, however, it is often desirable, in order that a high degree of computer knowledge be readily available to the group, that one or more experienced programmers be attracted into the company from outside. Every advantage should be taken of the assistance in training that the manufacturers of the equipment are willing to give.

The third major problem is the selection of equipment. It is assumed that the feasibility study has indicated the scale of equipment required, that is, whether the operation can support large-, medium-, or small-scale processors. Most business applications fall into one or more of the following four categories:

1. Problems involving much mathematical manipulation or internal processing. Among applications in which this type of problem is important are those involving operations research techniques, or those of a statistical nature, such as the preparation of actuarial tables.

2. Problems that involve processing a high ratio of transactions to a master file, but in which interrogations do not have to be answered immediately. Examples of this type of problem are public utility billing, insurance premium billing, and payroll and magazine subscription fulfillment.

3. Problems that involve processing a low ratio of transactions to a master file. These problems are typified by an accounts receivable procedure. The master file in this case may represent accounts receivable for a considerable period. Payments are received on any day for any, and probably all, days in the period. In order to perform the operation most efficiently, all items in the master file should be equally accessible for transaction processing, even though transactions will affect only a small part of the file at any given time. If this is not the case, a large part of the master file will have to be scanned sequentially, although it is otherwise unused, and transactions will have to be sorted to place them in the same order as the master file. Although both these operations can be done, of course, both can be avoided if all items in the master file are equally available on a random basis. Typical of these low activity problems are inventory control, parts requirements, such banking operations as Christmas clubs and special checking accounts, accounts receivable, and installment loans.

4. Problems in which no appreciable delay can be tolerated in answering interrogations to the system. In these problems, the entire master file must always be accessible for interrogation in order to provide an immediate answer. These problems can include both the high and low ratios of transactions to master file, but experience indicates that it is applications involving the low ratio of activity that are usually associated with random access requirements. Typical of the on-line problems are savings accounts, consumer credit accounting, installment loan accounting, and special checking accounts.

The equipment and the make of equipment to be chosen will depend on the type of operation predominating in any application. The wide range and variety of EDP equipment available today cannot be dealt with briefly here. A number of excellent reference sources, including those provided by the suppliers, are available. The most comprehensive are the publications of Auerbach Info, Inc., such as Standard EDP Reports, Data Communications Reports, and Data Handling Reports. Other excellent equipment information services are published by Office Automation and Charles Adams Associates.

INTEGRATING EDP

Besides the proper selection and operation of a computer, attention must also be given to the development of techniques for the integration of the computer within the over-all data processing system. Peripheral devices and automated processing techniques are available for integrating data processing which is an attempt to produce, at the first transcription, a machine-sensible or readable document, or record such as punched paper, mark sensing, magnetic tape keypunching, optical reading, etc. Such documents or records can be handled completely automatically as input to the computer from the initial source of preparation. Many of these records can be prepared as a by-product of a needed on-the-scene operation, such as preparing a purchase order to a forms manufacturer and simultaneously preparing punched paper tape for entry to a computer forms inventory control system as a record of the form and quantity on order.

In other words, the operation or record preparation prepares the necessary means for entry into an electronic system. The reverse is also possible when data or information requires transmission to a distant point or is to be produced in readable format away from the computer center itself.

The greatest strides being made in EDP (besides the installation of new and more modern computers) is in the reduction in costs and size of the computers, the integration of such units into an over-all computer teleprocessing system, and the automating of input and output. The "total systems" concept is becoming more and more a reality as peripheral equipment is integrated within the computer and MIS is utilized for both instantaneous information and decision-making.

Yet, in the final analysis, computer applications and electronic data processing systems are dependent upon human ingenuity to put the equipment to effective use. To a large extent, the computers with their peripheral equipment and devices have not been tested to their fullest capabilities. EDP seeks challenges to perform the most complex applications and sophisticated systems which the human mind can conceive.

14

Work Sampling in the Office

WILLIAM F. BUHL

B. F. Goodrich Company
Akron, Ohio

WILLIAM F. BUHL is a senior procedure analyst on the comptroller's staff of the B. F. Goodrich Company in Akron, Ohio; he joined the company in 1951. Prior to that time he was chief accountant and office manager for various companies, and also occupied positions as purchasing agent and mechanical engineer. For a number of years he was president of a metal products manufacturing company. He is a graduate engineer, and studied accounting and management at Rutgers University. He was one of the organizers and charter members of the Administrative Applications Division of the American Society for Quality Control, serving as secretary since its inception in 1955. He is also a member of the Akron-Canton Chapter of the Systems and Procedures Association of America, which he helped organize in 1957.

Mr. Buhl, the author of numerous articles on office and accounting procedures, also contributed a chapter on codes and numbering systems to the Tool Engineers Handbook. *He has spoken at several conventions and before many chapters of the American Society for Quality Control and of the Systems and Procedures Association on the subject of quality control in the office.*

CONTROL OF CLERICAL ERROR

The Need for Control

The basic clerical function is the creation of paper and the disposition of it to meet the needs of a business. It can be posting, typing, computing, or any other clerical function. After the first operation is completed, each paper moves on to the second stage, where another operation is performed, and so on until the paper is filed or otherwise disposed of. In these various operations, the problem has always been what to do about error. There is no doubt that error can occur each time an operation is performed, but what should be done about it? Research performed by many organizations has shown an error level in clerical work up to 5 per cent even after 100 per cent verification. Therefore, provision must be made in clerical operations to control this error.

This problem could be handled simply by counting errors, but the cost would be excessive in many cases. For example, if a group of people are making many mistakes, a manager will be concerned with the problem of improving their performance or determining the extent of their errors. If the manager is numbers-minded, he may start out by determining how many errors of each kind are being made. The results of such a survey will help the manager concentrate his approach on improving the quality of the work, or in determining the extent of error. Many a problem that seems difficult to handle can be made more manageable if one gets the "facts" by counting and comparing. But this can consume much time, especially when a manager must appraise the work and mistakes of many individuals or groups with a specific group to compare performance.

Thus, in the attempt to locate error, another operation is added: verification. This verification, or checking, isolates much of the error, but also adds to the cost of performing a clerical operation. Many times this doubles the cost of the operation because of the necessity of examining each piece of paper thoroughly. The question is always present of whether the cost justifies the additional effort. Another consideration is whether the recovery is sufficient to warrant the checking of each piece of paper. It has been found in many cases that the cost far exceeds the possible recovery. As a result, many companies do not check invoices of less than a specific dollar value. This method, however, has a certain element of risk, since one can never be certain that error has not entered the work at a later date. This error, if not detected, could add up to a considerable sum of money.

Costly Additional Operations

It has always been the opinion in industry that errors found by 100 per cent verification must be corrected. This opinion results more from psychology than from sound reasoning. However, it does add another operation: rework. The control of paper work now results in four operations—create, verify, rework, and dispose. It is obvious that the cost has been increased considerably. Some of this additional cost could be eliminated if certain types of errors were allowed to go by. The human mind, however, would have to be retrained to accept this philosophy. In normal verification work, it is not general practice to allow any error to go by uncorrected after it has been detected. There are errors that are often insignificant as far as loss is concerned that could be allowed to pass in order to minimize the cost of rework.

In general practice, therefore, the work is constantly checked and all located errors are corrected. The question of cost is not always considered, nor is it always known whether the operation results in a gain or a loss. More important is the fact that there is no control on the error, since checking is often performed long after the work was originally created. All that is gained is some control over errors getting by, but with more than twice the effort.

For an increase in office efficiency and the reduction of cost, it is important in the present-day office that some method be developed to eliminate the additional cost. This method should control the error at the source, as well as correct the work, with only a slight additional effort. Various methods have been developed in the past in an attempt to accomplish the desired results. Many of them fail to achieve the principal objective, which is to prevent error from happening.

Selective checking. Under this method certain items are not checked. The items not to be checked are determined by comparing the cost of checking against the recovery obtained in the past. If the cost of checking exceeds the recovery, no checking is performed in the future. This cost of checking is sometimes computed in groups of values, and compared against recoveries in those groups. Under this plan, only certain groups of values are not checked. In either case, considerable risk is present.

Spot checking. The system of spot checking was introduced to overcome the disadvantages of selective checking. The spot-checking method requires that only a portion of the work be observed for errors. Although this results in a better control with less effort by occasionally checking a portion of the work, there is always the question of whether a sufficient amount has been observed.

Since there is no uniform rule of spot checking, the selection could have been made from the top of the pile, from the middle, or from the bottom. The selection may also have been made haphazardly throughout the pile. This method is not true sampling as it is known today. True sampling is based on an orderly procedure in determining and selecting the required material. Spot checking ordinarily does not employ this procedure. The method of selection used is responsible for the considerable risk in spot checking. For a sample to be truly representative of the lot from which it is drawn, it is necessary that every piece of paper have an equal chance of being selected. It is this "randomness" of selection, together with the number of pieces observed, that results in the accuracy of true sampling.

Spot checking is not based on these two principles. In many cases, randomness is not insured and there is no method of determining the number of pieces that must be observed in order to obtain the desired accuracy. As the accuracy is based on the number of pieces observed, it is important to know the required sample size. With spot checking, it is possible to examine too many pieces and do unnecessary work, or examine too few and have the risk of overlooking error.

WORK SAMPLING

Advantages and Uses of Sampling

Work sampling is a shorter, less costly way to get satisfactory results. With it, instead of making total counts, a sample is taken according to a predetermined or systematic procedure, such as every tenth, hundredth, or thousandth item. Thus, with a minimum of counting, results as accurate as are required can be obtained, provided the sample is at random, that is, that every item has an equal chance of being included, and that the sample is of a sufficient size.

The advantages in sampling are numerous. From a periodic sampling of office work, any individual can analyze masses of information for purposes of decision-making and action-taking. With a minimum of regular checking, an over-all picture of the amount of work done can be obtained, as well as the error in the work performed. With this data, obtained right at the source, immediate action is possible. The work in error can be separated for close observation, or specific instructions can be given to prevent further error. Thus, error can be "stopped in its tracks," the cost of 100 per cent checking and later rework is reduced, and the work efficiency is increased with accuracy and quality under control.

Data obtained by work sampling can be used in any one of three ways:

1. *Quality control.* Samples are taken from the work examined and the amount of error posted to a graph (see lower left of Fig. 14-1), which is commonly referred to as a control chart. This control chart is continually observed, and when the error level goes beyond the limits set (out of control), corrective action is taken. Defective work lots may or may not be rejected (for 100 per cent verification to remove the error), depending upon the nature of the work. For example, if the work of reservation clerks for an airline were being sampled, it would not always be possible to correct the error.

2. *Work verification.* Samples are taken primarily to determine which lots are to be 100 per cent verified to maintain a specific quality level. This is similar to quality control, but a control chart is not always used.

3. *Data gathering.* Samples are taken solely for information purposes. It is used to obtain any analytical data desired, such as average number of items on an order, determination of the amount of error in work, or an indication of an employee's work load or job performance.

Sampling Defined

Sampling is defined as the random selection of a number of items from a larger group to determine the content of the larger group. Figure 14-1 illustrates this pictorially with a deck of cards. In a standard deck of fifty-two cards, each suit represents one fourth (25 per cent) of the deck. If the sampling plan specifies that the first card is to be drawn, and every seventh card thereafter, it will result in a sample of eight. For this sample to be truly representative of the deck from which it is drawn, it should contain two

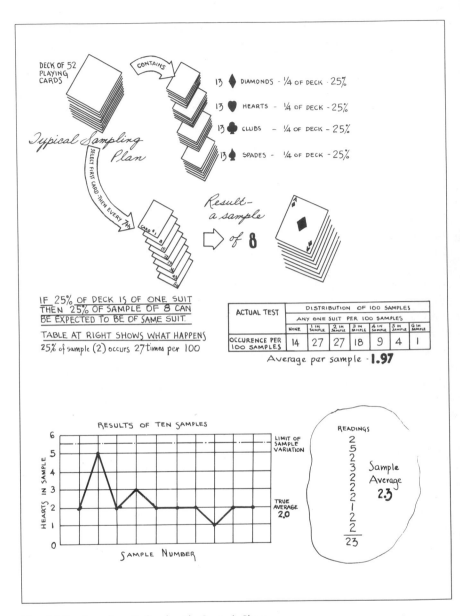

Fig. 14-1. Sampling Defined with Control Chart

hearts (one fourth of sample size, because hearts represent one fourth of the deck). In actual practice, this does not happen because of the probability of other combinations of cards appearing in the sample. It is possible to predict with 98 per cent accuracy the probabilities of each of the possible combinations appearing in a sample. Likewise, by the application of the principle of the stability of averages, it can be stated that the cumulative average in a number of samples will be one fourth (25 per cent) or two.

As will be seen later, it is possible to predict what will happen in a sample of eight, and find it correct in actual test. In Figure 14-1, the results of one hundred such tests are shown. It can be seen that twenty-seven times out of one hundred, the exact indication of the makeup of the deck was obtained, that is, two hearts. If a control were instituted to indicate when the heart content of the deck increased to more than one fourth, the table (mid-right of Fig. 14-1), shows that 68 per cent (27 + 27 + 14) of the time the sample would indicate that the deck contained one fourth or less (2, 1, and 0) of hearts. Thirty-two per cent of the time, the sample would indicate a higher heart content (three and over) than actually in the deck. In actual use, this generally does not present a serious problem, because of the stability of averages. In Figure 14-1 it can be seen that the cumulative average of the one hundred test samples is 1.97, compared to the actual sample average of two.

This stability of averages will apply whether ten persons each draw a sample of eight from ten different decks; one person draws a sample of eight, ten times from one deck; or one person draws a sample of eight each day for ten days from the same or ten different decks. The average will always come close to two if the number of hearts in the deck does not change. If the number of hearts in the deck is increased, then the cumulative average of the samples will also increase to conform to this change.

WORK SAMPLING FOR QUALITY CONTROL

History of Quality Control

Quality control applications have been more widely publicized than any other. This is because it came into the office by way of the plant, and was used in the plant to control the quality of the manufactured product. It was found that the quality of the product could be controlled by inspecting a small percentage of the total product with the resultant savings in inspection costs.

During the early part of World War II, the statistical methods used by statisticians for years were successfully applied to the control of quality in production. It was pioneered by Dr. Shewhart of the Bell Telephone Laboratories, and installed at the Western Electric plants. Dodge and Romig of Bell Laboratories continued his work and developed the first sampling tables. Since that time, quality control has been adopted by the leading industries in the country.

Office Applications

About fifteen years ago the technique developed and used in the plant was successfully applied to office operations. One of the early applications of this technique to the production of paper work was performed by Aldens, Inc., a Chicago mail-order house. Samples of the work were taken at intervals and posted to a control chart. If the points stayed within a predetermined limit, no action was taken. If the points went beyond, action was necessary.

To many individuals, the comparison between production operations and office operations is difficult. It is easy to understand the sampling of parts off the production line to determine the quality of units of production and the number of defective parts. However, when converting units of production and number of defective parts (errors) to office applications, the analogy becomes somewhat hazy. It has been argued that the two are not the same because in office work there is a variable dollar error not present in production operations. Four basic differences between plant and office installations are:

1. *Acceptance—rectification.* In office applications there cannot be a simple acceptance or rejection. Rejection usually implies scrapping, and office work cannot be scrapped. It is therefore necessary that all rejected work be rectified by verifying all rejected lots and removing the error.

2. *Dollar consideration.* In some office work, dollar error must be considered instead of quantitative error. It is not always a question of good or bad. Sometimes it is necessary to know how bad it really is. A 1 per cent error in a thousand dollar billing represents a different error than 1 per cent on a hundred thousand dollar billing, although both represent 1 per cent.

3. *Control by verification.* Prior to the development of quality control by work sampling, the control of the quality of clerical operations was obtained by a 100 per cent verification. Application of work sampling eliminates the need for such verification while still maintaining at least the same degree of control.

4. *Risk possibility.* Office plans must recognize the dollar error possibilities in certain cases. They must be designed to achieve control of this important factor, because in office work the range of error is greater (dollars) than it is in the plant (defectives). The comparable unit of measurement in office work therefore is dollars of error per hundred invoices rather than errors per hundred (per cent).

Other than the differences mentioned, the procedure in office applications is the same as in the plant. A sample is drawn from the work lot to determine the approximate error. From this determination one can decide whether to accept the work as is, or whether a complete verification is necessary or desirable. One may also use the data for informational purposes.

Quality control limits the level of error in work either by rejecting all bad work lots for 100 per cent verification or by providing a signal for action through the use of the control chart. Generally speaking, one is not concerned primarily with each individual error, only that the total error allowed to pass does not exceed a predetermined amount. By computation, it can be determined just how much error can appear in a sample before any corrective action is necessary. The limit of permissible error is determined by many factors, such as the cost of checking, the average recovery, and a management decision.

For illustrative purposes, Figure 14-1 shows a control chart on the ten samples of eight taken from the deck of cards. The tabulation shows the individual readings. Notice how many samples contained the exact amount of hearts (two), seven out of the ten samples. Also note that the average is 2.3, which is fairly close to the actual average, considering only ten readings have been used. The control chart shows these ten points in graphic form. The upper limit shown on this chart was determined mathematically (or from tables) and indicates the maximum number of hearts that should appear in a sample of eight when one fourth of the deck contains hearts. This is known as the sample variation, and in this case results in a reading of 3.7 hearts over or under the actual average of two (one fourth of the sample). This makes the high or upper limit 5.7, as shown on the chart. The lower limit or possible sample variation would be two minus 3.7. As this is less than zero, zero is set as the lower limit. If all of the sample readings remain within these limits, it indicates that in 98 per cent of all the cases the heart content (error) has not changed from one fourth of the deck. In this illustration, all readings remained within the limits.

To illustrate how a quality control program works, let it be assumed that a work lot of one hundred decks of cards (5,200) cards requires checking, and it is desired to limit the "heart" content to 12½ per cent, or not more than 650 hearts in the work lot. The sample size will be eight cards taken from each deck. If one heart appears in the sample, it will represent one out of eight or 12½. Using this as a basis, the sampling plan can state that if more than one heart appears in a sample, the entire deck will be rejected and all hearts removed. If, however, the sample shows one or less it will be safe to accept this deck without removing any hearts. Referring to the table in Figure 14-1, samples from forty-one decks (14 + 27) out of the hundred will show one or fewer hearts. These will be acceptable according to the plan. These forty-one decks will contain (41 × 13) 533 hearts. The remaining decks will be rejected and all hearts removed. Thus, only 533 hearts will remain in the original one hundred decks (5,200 cards) or 10¼ per cent. This is well below the limit of 12½ per cent set as a control. In actual practice the acceptance number is usually slightly higher than the control point. In this example, however, if the acceptance number was set at two, samples containing two or fewer hearts would result in sixty-eight of the decks $(14 + 27 + 27)$ being accepted containing 884 hearts or 17 per cent of the work lot.

This is the basis of a clerical quality control program. It is based on the random selection of a sample to obtain an indication of the error in the work and permit a decision to be made regarding further verification, and it provides the control chart, a visual means to create an incentive to improve work.

Reducing Error at Source

The reduction of error at the source is an important part of quality control. It eliminates the need for the rejection of all work, and the resultant verification. To reduce error at the source, the worker must be informed of the error, and must be given an incentive to produce better work; the supervisor must be kept informed of the error rate and the trend; and management must be informed of the cost of error to enable it to support the program, and to establish the policies necessary to implement it. The control chart is the medium used for this purpose.

Fig. 14-2. An Experience: Effect of Change in Error Rate on the Control Chart

WORK SAMPLING IN OTHER APPLICATIONS

Other Uses of Techniques

Many other uses can be made of these statistical techniques. Applications are not limited to office quality control or work verification. The techniques have been applied to sales analysis, sales forecasting, inventory control, computation of all types of averages, the costing of billing and production, actual billing by averages, and various types of auditing. These are but a few of the possible uses to which these techniques can be applied.

To illustrate the disadvantages of a 100 per cent check, let us assume one is standing on a street corner and decides to weigh the first ten adults passing by. Figure 14-3(a) shows such a tabulation of the weights of ten people. The total weight is 1,374 pounds or an average of 137.4 pounds. If every other person were weighed, the total would be 659 pounds for five people or an average of 131.8 pounds. This raises the question of whether it is worth twice the effort for 5.6 pounds.

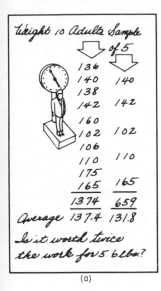
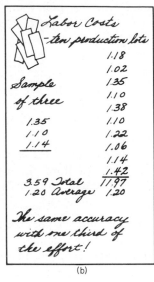
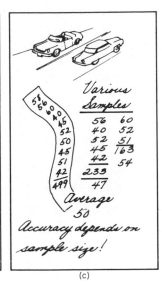

(a)   (b)   (c)

Fig. 14-3. Some Results of Sampling

Taking a similar case, Figure 14-3(b) tabulates the cost of ten production lots. It can be seen in the illustration that the total is $11.97 for an average cost of $1.20 per lot. To reduce effort, every third lot could be costed as it comes off the production line. This will result in a total of $3.59 for an average of $1.20. In this case, the same accuracy has been obtained with one third of the effort. Although it is true that the accuracy will vary from lot to lot, this can be controlled by the sample size. If sufficient accuracy cannot be obtained, it may be necessary to do a 100 per cent check. The principles outlined here can be easily checked in many ways. One method could be to take speedometer readings at regular intervals while driving along a superhighway. Figure 14-3(c) shows ten such readings for an average of fifty miles per hour. If five readings were taken in the same length of time, the average would forty-seven, a difference of three miles per hour. Three readings in the same length of time average fifty-four miles per hour in this example, a difference of four miles per hour. This results in an accuracy within 8 per cent with less than one third of the effort.

Research Reveals Applications

A review of the clerical operations in any office will reveal many possible applications of sampling techniques. A survey made at the B. F.

Goodrich Company located many possibilities that will require further exploration. A partial list is shown here to illustrate the extensive possibilities in the use of these techniques.

1. *Auditing.* One of the many methods used by auditors is the "test check." With this method, an auditor checks a number of transactions to determine if they are according to policy or procedure. The number of transactions to be reviewed is left to the discretion of the auditor. Unlike work sampling, this method does not provide the auditor with any guarantee that his examination was a sufficient coverage. Many times an auditor completes an assignment with a feeling that the audit was not sufficient, but he has no assurance to this effect. With work sampling, however, an auditor will be able to determine when he has examined a sufficient number of items to obtain the accuracy he requires. The audit could be completed with the assurance that the coverage is within a specific probability. It was found in one survey that the auditing time could be reduced by two thirds with the use of sampling. With one third of the previous effort, error to the extent of 0.283 per cent was located. Previously with a 100 per cent audit, the error rate located was 0.222 per cent.

2. *Costing production.* Another possible application was the costing of production. At this operation the standard cost of a manufactured part was multiplied by the total units produced. In an average lot, eighteen computations were required to complete the costing. With one sample, it was possible to compute an average, multiply it by the total production, and result in a total cost that was within $9 of the amount obtained with the previous method. An accuracy within 2/10 per cent was obtained with a 90 per cent reduction in computing time.

3. *Percentage comparison.* It is often necessary in accounting, and more particularly in cost accounting, to obtain percentages of one period to compare with the percentages of prior periods. In one case, it was necessary to estimate the gross income of five hundred units prior to the completion of all accounting work. By taking a sample of fifty of these units and computing an average percentage, it was possible to apply this percentage to all of the five hundred units and obtain a figure within 1.9 per cent of the final figure computed from all five hundred units. It is to be noted that this was done with a sample of only fifty. Larger sample sizes would result in a greater accuracy.

4. *Billing by averages.* In this test, the billings issued to one customer for a four-month period were gathered together and a sample of 450 invoices drawn. The next step was to total the dollar value of the invoices in the sample and divide by the number of units billed. This furnished an average billing price per unit. Multiplying the average by the total units billed resulted in the total billing price. Comparison between the sampling method and the 100 per cent method showed a discrepancy of only $69

over a four-month period. This method provided an accuracy within $5/100$ per cent with a fraction of the previous effort.

5. *Ratio delay*. Sampling can be an effective tool when it is necessary to determine how an employee spends his or her time. In the past, it was customary to conduct a detailed survey to determine the exact breakdown of how the time was being used. Using statistical methods, it can be determined that if thirty out of one hundred observations show a typist proofreading her work, it can safely be concluded that 30 per cent of her time is so spent. This technique is known as "ratio delay."

6. *Obtaining data quickly*. Management often requests data requiring extensive compilation, such as the average size of orders, average number of items per invoice, and number of dependents per employee. This information can be obtained with sufficient accuracy by sampling. In one case it was necessary to find out how many one-item purchases the corporation issues. A sample of 300 out of 3,000 purchase orders were taken, and the average was found to be 64 per cent. Not being satisfied with this result, all 3,000 orders were tabulated. This tabulation resulted in an average of 64.4 per cent. In this case, the 100 hundred per cent tabulation increased the effort ten times but only increased the accuracy $4/10$ per cent.

Users of Statistical Methods

Many companies, large and small, have adopted these techniques, and others are joining the ranks constantly. Aldens, Inc., as mentioned previously, was one of the pioneers in the adoption of statistical techniques in the office. Since that time, installations have been made in many organizations, some of which are: United Airlines at their various installations; A. B. Dick Company, Chicago; Prudential Insurance Company, Newark, N.J.; Metropolitan Life Insurance Company, New York City; and Standard Register Company, Dayton, Ohio.

UNITED AIRLINES. One of the installations at United Airlines that brought beneficial results was the sampling of the accuracy of the work of reservation clerks. Errors in three of their offices were reduced from 30 per cent to 5 per cent over a six-week period. Daily reduction of error in one office, over a two-month period, resulted in the error rate decreasing from 47 per cent to 15 per cent. This reduction in error rate is accomplished by watching the control chart. It enables action to be taken promptly to correct any difficulty. It also places a reminder of the error rate in front of the clerks, and gives them the incentive to "break the record." Figure 14-2 illustrates what happens when new agents are hired. The resultant error, owing to inexperience, is readily observed. In this case, when the new agents were hired, the chart went "out of control" until the agents were properly trained. A control chart will always indicate when a shift in error rate has occurred.

STANDARD REGISTER COMPANY. This firm has applied the techniques to the control of billing.[1] The control charts are based on accuracy instead of error (*see* Figure 14-4). Instead of showing 2 per cent error on their chart, they show 98 per cent accuracy. After several months of operation under this plan, they were maintaining a level of 98.7 per cent accuracy with one half of the previous effort.

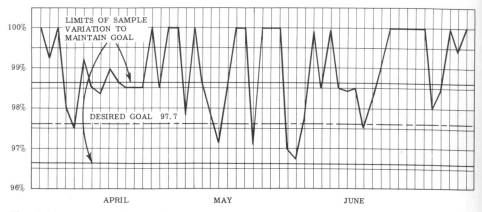

Fig. 14-4. Accounts Receivable Control Chart

THE B. F. GOODRICH COMPANY. A similar experience was realized by this company. Customer's invoices were grouped in lots of 1,000, and a sample of one hundred drawn. If the amount of error exceeded $2 in the sample, the entire lot was 100 per cent verified. Previously, with complete verification, error to the extent of 0.222 per cent was located. After the sampling plan was in effect three months, error to the extent of 0.218 per cent was being located with one third of the effort.

SAMPLING BASED ON STATISTICAL METHODS

Many terms have been applied to the techniques used in office applications. Statistical quality control, office quality control statistical methods, administrative applications of statistical quality control, and quality assurance are some of the terms used. How confusing these must be to the layman! What is actually meant by these terms is the application of statistical methods to office, management, clerical, and accounting operations. Quality control, or assurance, is the control of error at the source, and is but one of the many possible uses of statistical methods. There are many uses in the office, all based on the same techniques of random sampling and the stability of averages. All programs and uses require sampling as the starting point. It would, therefore, seem most appropriate to designate the technique

---

[1] Fred F. Shelton, "Quality Control for the Office," *NOMA Forum,* May, 1950.

and its use as "work sampling in the office." The phrase "quality control" is a carryover from the earliest applications of statistical methods in industry in the field of production control. At that time it was used to control the quality of the manufactured product without inspecting every piece. Since that time the techniques have been used for many purposes other than to control quality. "Work sampling" seems a more logical term to properly designate the wide range of applications possible.

Statistical Methods Applied

The statistical methods used are based on what is called the "normal curve of error." This is covered in detail in books on statistics and on quality control. The more familiar applications are the election polls, the mortality tables, and so on. Election polls are based on the sampling of the electorate and forecasting the results of such samples. What makes these polls go wrong at times is the result of either a shift of opinion after the sampling, or bias in the sampling. Bias enters a poll when the sample is not truly representative of the group to which the results are applied. In one such case, the sample was taken from the subscription list of a magazine and applied to the electorate. Here the electorate was not truly sampled. Actually, it was a select group not representative of the people who would determine the outcome.

It is possible to have a prediction upset by bias in other ways. For example, if a large group of men were asked to jot down the first color that came to their minds, the majority would say "red" (women would say "blue"). This can be safely predicted in advance. However, bias may result if the individuals are exposed to a green room for a period of time before they are asked this question. Bias is a factor that enters the normal random occurrence of an event, and which was not provided for in the sampling plan. Bias can be overcome if it is recognized in advance and the sampling procedure adjusted to meet it.

The Normal Curve of Error

In office work it has been found in many instances that any event occurring at random will be evenly distributed about its average. The number of values higher than average will equal the number below the average. This principle is illustrated in Figure 14-5, and is known as the "normal curve." In Figure 14-5(a) four unrelated occurrences are shown, all forming this normal curve:

1. *Soldiers by height.* A large number of soldiers were measured in height and the results tabulated. The curve shows just as many taller than average as shorter than average.

2. *One thousand shots from a gun.* Shots from a gun firing at a target were measured, and it was found that there were just as many shots too high as too low.

3. *Errors in measurement.* A manufactured part was measured with a micrometer and the various readings tabulated. It was found that just as many high readings were obtained as low readings.

4. *Tossing of coins.* Four coins were tossed many hundreds of times. Less than the average number of heads (two) appeared as many times or more than the average heads.

These all represent normal distributions. When sampling one piece from such a distribution [Figure 14-5(b)], it can come from anywhere within the confines of the curve. It may be a low value or a high value. The chances are, however, that it would come from a point near the center (the average), because there are more such points than any other. The odds are in favor of it. If we select more than one item, the odds of obtaining close to the average become greater. Thus, as the sample size is increased, the odds of getting a more accurate reading are more favorable. When one speaks of odds, he is dealing with the rules of chance, which are an important consideration in sampling. The law of averages and the rules of chance (probability) are the two factors that make sampling work.

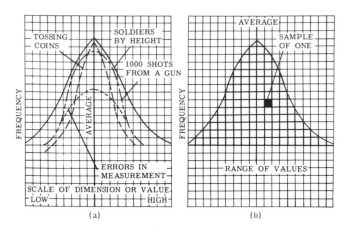

Fig. 14-5. Normal Curve of Error

Probability or Chance

Probability can be illustrated in many ways. One of the most effective ways is with coins. If a single coin is tossed, it can only land in either of two ways, heads or tails. This is known as a 50-50 chance, or the probability that heads will appear 50 per cent of the time. If four coins are tossed, they can land in five different ways, no heads, one head, two heads, three heads, and four heads. As each coin is independent of the other, it can land either heads or tails. Therefore, one head will result if any one of the four coins appears "heads up." Thus, one head can appear in four different combinations. Figure 14-6(a) shows the sixteen combinations possible when tossing four coins. The table shows that two heads can appear in six combinations, resulting in a probability of six of sixteen times. The probability of three heads appearing is four out of sixteen times, and no heads or four heads will appear rarely, once in sixteen times, or 6¼ per cent of the time for each.

Similar probabilities occur when dealing with office work. Figure 14-6(b) shows a pile of invoices, half of them in error. As in the case of one coin, if one invoice is drawn from the pile, there is a 50-50 chance that it will contain error, for it will either be right or wrong. When drawing a sample of four, each one of the four invoices will have the same chance of being in error (50-50) independently of the others. The table illustrates the number of different ways that error can appear in each of the four invoices drawn. There are sixteen combinations possible. Two errors will appear in six of sixteen combinations for a probability of 6-16, or 37½ per cent of the time. These probabilities are the same as for the coins, because the odds are the same, a 50-50 chance and the sample size of four.

Probabilities will change when the odds or the sample size change. Figure 14-6(c) illustrates what happens when there is only 10 per cent error in the work with a sample of four. With 10 per cent error, the odds will change. It will no longer be 50-50, because only one tenth of the invoices are in error. Instead of finding error or no error in a single invoice, there are nine chances of obtaining one invoice not in error to one chance of the invoice containing error. Thus, the probability of finding an error in each invoice drawn is one out of ten chances, or there is a nine times greater chance of finding invoices without error.

Based on these odds, the probabilities for a sample of four drawn from a work lot containing 10 per cent can be computed. Using Figure 14-6(b) as a guide, the probability can be computed. For example, in the figure, no error can appear only one way, that is, all four invoices without error. However, if the error rate is 10 per cent [Figure 14-6(c)], the probability of each one of the four invoices showing no error is nine times greater. This results in an occurrence of $9 \times 9 \times 9 \times 9$ or (9^4) or 6,561. In like manner, the four ways in which three errors can occur, when the work contains 50 per cent, are multiplied nine times when the error is only 10 per cent. The total number of combinations possible is $10 \times 10 \times 10 \times 10$ or (10^4) or 10,000. No error can appear in 6,561 of the 10,000 combinations, or 65.6 per cent of the time. This high probability of no error appearing in the sample can be more easily understood when it is realized that 10 per cent error in a work lot should result in approximately 10 per cent error in a sample. Ten per cent of a sample of four is four tenths. Obviously, it is not possible to obtain a fraction of one error. Therefore, no error will appear more times than any other combination.

It is not necessary to compute probability or to determine sample sizes in this fashion. It is demonstrated for illustrative purposes only. They can be computed mathematically, or published tables can be used.

Fig. 14-6(a). Four Coin Combinations. **(b)** What Determines Probability?

PROBABILITY TABLES. Mathematical computations for probability are involved and tiresome, whereas probability tables provide a ready reference. Examples of these tables can be found in Figure 14-7.

The tables shown in Fig. 14-7 are for a sample size of four, the same sample size as used in the illustration. Probabilities for this sample size with

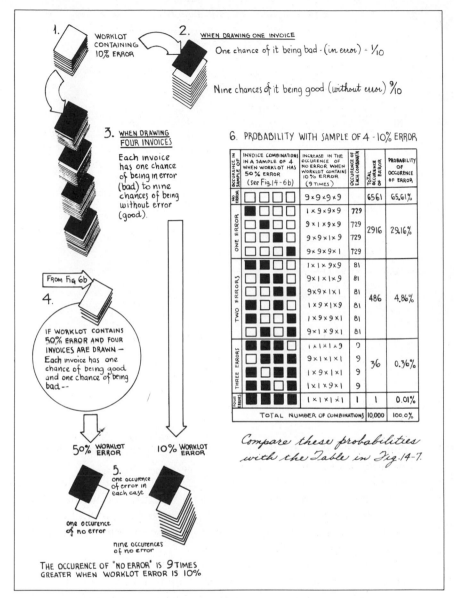

The table within the figure reads:

6. PROBABILITY WITH SAMPLE OF 4 - 10% ERROR

OCCURENCE IN SAMPLE OF	INVOICE COMBINATIONS IN A SAMPLE OF 4 WHEN WORKLOT HAS 50% ERROR (see Fig.14-6b)	INCREASE IN THE OCCURENCE OF NO ERROR WHEN WORKLOT CONTAINS 10% ERROR (9 TIMES)	OCCURENCE OF EACH COMBINATION	TOTAL OCCURENCE OF ERROR	PROBABILITY OF OCCURENCE OF ERROR
NO ERRORS	☐☐☐☐	9×9×9×9		6561	65.61%
ONE ERROR	■☐☐☐	1×9×9×9	729		
	☐■☐☐	9×1×9×9	729	2916	29.16%
	☐☐■☐	9×9×1×9	729		
	☐☐☐■	9×9×9×1	729		
TWO ERRORS	■■☐☐	1×1×9×9	81		
	☐■■☐	9×1×1×9	81		
	☐☐■■	9×9×1×1	81		
	■☐■☐	1×9×1×9	81	486	4.86%
	■☐☐■	1×9×9×1	81		
	☐■☐■	9×1×9×1	81		
THREE ERRORS	■■■☐	1×1×1×9	9		
	☐■■■	9×1×1×1	9		
	■☐■■	1×9×1×1	9	36	0.36%
	■■☐■	1×1×9×1	9		
FOUR ERRORS	■■■■	1×1×1×1	1	1	0.01%
	TOTAL NUMBER OF COMBINATIONS			10,000	100.0%

Figure text labels:

1. WORKLOT CONTAINING 10% ERROR

2. WHEN DRAWING ONE INVOICE
One chance of it being bad - (in error) - 1/10
Nine chances of it being good (without error) 9/10

3. WHEN DRAWING FOUR INVOICES
Each invoice has one chance of being in error (bad) to nine chances of being without error (good).

FROM FIG 6b

4. IF WORKLOT CONTAINS 50% ERROR AND FOUR INVOICES ARE DRAWN —
Each invoice has one chance of being good and one chance of being bad --

50% WORKLOT ERROR   10% WORKLOT ERROR

5. one occurence of error in each case
one occurence of no error
nine occurences of no error

THE OCCURENCE OF "NO ERROR" IS 9 TIMES GREATER WHEN WORKLOT ERROR IS 10%

Compare these probabilities with the Table in Fig. 14-7.

Fig. 14-6(c). Probability with Sample of Four and Ten Per Cent Work Lot Error

the error rate used in the examples can be found between the double lines. It should be noted that the probabilities developed pictorially in Figure 14-6 are identical to those shown in Figure 14-7, Table (a). Figure 14-7, Table (b), shows Poisson's approximation to the binomial, which is obtained by less involved computation. It can be seen that the approxima-

Table (a)—Binomial Probability Distribution

% error in work or permissible	errors appearing in sample				
	0	1	2	3	4
1	96.1%	3.9%	0.1%	—	—
2	92.2%	7.5%	0.2%	—	—
5	81.5%	17.1%	1.4%	—	—
10	65.6%	29.2%	4.9%	0.4%	—
15	52.2%	36.8%	9.8%	1.1%	0.1%
20	41.0%	41.0%	15.4%	2.6%	0.2%
25	31.6%	42.2%	21.1%	4.7%	0.4%
30	24.0%	41.2%	26.5%	7.6%	0.8%
40	13.0%	34.6%	34.6%	15.4%	2.6%
50	6.3%	25.0%	37.5%	25.0%	6.2%

Table (b)—Poisson's Approximation to the Binomial

1	96.1%	3.8%	0.1%	—	—
2	92.3%	7.4%	0.3%	—	—
5	81.9%	16.3%	1.7%	—	—
10	67.0%	26.8%	5.4%	0.8%	—
15	54.9%	32.9%	9.9%	2.0%	0.3%
20	44.9%	36.0%	14.4%	3.8%	0.8%
25	36.8%	36.8%	18.4%	6.1%	1.5%
30	30.1%	36.2%	21.6%	8.7%	2.6%
40	20.2%	32.3%	25.8%	13.8%	5.5%
50	13.5%	27.1%	27.1%	18.0%	9.0%

Fig. 14-7. Probability Tables—Sample Size of Four

tion is fairly close at 10 per cent, but at 50 per cent there is considerable variation from the actual binomial tables.

Probability tables are invaluable in the development of sampling plans. Reference to such tables will provide the various probabilities necessary to determine sample size and risk. In the majority of cases, however, the use of published sampling tables will be of considerable assistance in selecting proper sampling techniques.

SAMPLING TABLES. Many sources of sampling tables are available. They provide a handy guide to the development of a sampling plan.

Sampling tables are based on probability tables, and are developed for ready use. Through the use of the tables, the need for determining probability, which often requires extensive computation, is eliminated. Figure 14-8 shows a typical sampling table for a sample size of eight, for various acceptable error levels. For example, if it is desired to maintain an error level of 15 per cent with a sample of eight, all lots can be accepted (Acc.) when two or fewer errors appear in the sample. If three or more errors appear in the sample, it must be rejected and 100 per cent inspected to remove all error.

	ACCEPTABLE ERROR IN PER CENT														
LESS THAN 4.0		4.0		6.5		10.0		15.0		25.0		40.0		65.0	
ACC	REJ	ACC	REJ	ACC	REJ	ACC	REJ	ACC	REJ	ACC	REJ	ACC	REJ	ACC	REJ
0	1	0	1	1	2	1	2	2	3	3	4	5	6	7	8
ACC – DENOTES ACCEPT							REJ – DENOTES REJECT								

(a)

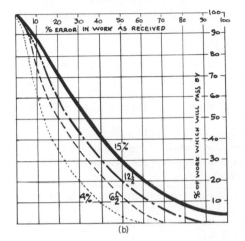

ERRORS IN SAMPLE	ERROR IN WORK – %
1	0.0-0.4
2	0.0-0.8
3	0.0-1.1
4	0.2-1.4
5	0.2-1.8
6	0.3-2.1
7	0.4-2.4
8	0.5-2.7
9	0.6-3.0
10	0.8-3.2
11	0.9-3.5
12	1.0-3.8
13	1.2-4.0
14	1.3-4.3
15	1.4-4.6
16	1.6-4.8
17	1.7-5.1
18	1.9-5.3

(b)

(c)

TYPE OF PLAN	TOTAL SAMPLE SIZE	ACCEPTABLE ERROR IN PER CENT											
		1.0		1.5		2.5		4.0		6.5		10.0	
		ACC	REJ	ACC	REJ	ACC	REJ	ACC	REJ	ACC	REJ	ACC	REJ
SINGLE	50	1	2	2	3	3	4	4	5	6	7	9	10
DOUBLE	35	0	3	1	3	1	5	2	7	3	12	6	15
	105	2	3	2	3	4	5	6	7	11	12	14	15
MULTIPLE OR SEQUENTIAL	14	–	2	–	2	–	2	–	3	0	4	1	5
	28	0	2	0	3	0	3	1	4	2	5	3	8
	42	0	2	1	3	1	4	2	4	4	8	5	10
	56	0	2	1	3	3	5	3	6	5	9	8	12
	70	1	3	2	4	3	5	4	6	7	10	11	14
	84	1	3	3	5	3	5	5	7	10	12	13	16
	98	2	3	4	5	4	5	6	7	11	12	15	16

(d)

Fig. 14-8(a), (b), (c), and (d). Typical Sampling Table

Referring to probabilities shown in Figure 14-1, samples containing two or fewer errors will occur sixty-eight times out of one hundred. Three or more errors will therefore occur 32 per cent of the time. If the work lot contains 25 per cent error (as in the case of the deck of cards, Figure 14-1), 32 per cent of the error will be removed. Thirty-two per cent of the error of 25 per cent is 8 per cent. Thus, the error remaining in the lots accepted will be 25 − 8 or 17 per cent. This approximates the acceptable error level selected in the sampling plan.

Sampling tables are available for a wide range of sample sizes and acceptable error levels. These tables are published for single, double, and sequential sampling. The aforementioned example is one of single sampling. In double sampling, two samples are taken, the first to determine if sufficient evidence is present to make a decision, and the second, if required, to make the final determination. Double sampling results in less work if the decision can be made on the first sample. If not, double sampling usually entails more work. Figure 14-8(d) shows the comparison between single and double plans. It shows clearly that if double sampling allows a decision on the first sample of thirty-five, it will be less effort than a single sampling plan of fifty. If, however, two samples are necessary, a total of 105 pieces will have been sampled.

The procedure used in double sampling is as follows (assuming the desired error level to be 1½ per cent):

> *First,* a sample of thirty-five pieces is taken and the number of errors counted.
> If one or less, work lot can be accepted.
> If three or more, work lot must be rejected.
> If exactly two errors appear in sample, no decision can be made, and therefore a
>
> *Second* sample of seventy pieces is drawn making a total of 105 pieces.
> If two errors or less appear in the sample of 105, work lot can be accepted. Three or more errors require the rejection of the lot.

Sequential, or multiple, sampling is similar to double sampling. In this case, however, a series of small samples are taken until sufficient evidence is accumulated to make a decision. If the error in the work lot is normally high or low (well beyond the desired error level), a decision can usually be made on the first sample. As the error in the work lot approaches the desired level, more samples are required under the multiple plan than in single sampling. In such cases, it may be necessary to take a sample twice the size in multiple sampling as in single sampling. The following steps illustrate the procedure used in multiple sampling as shown in Figure 14-8(d) (assuming the desired error level to be 1½ per cent):

> *First,* a sample of fourteen pieces is drawn and the number of errors counted.
> If two or more errors appear in sample, reject the lot.
> If less than two errors, a
>
> *Second* sample of fourteen pieces is drawn and added to the first.
> If no errors appear, accept the work lot.
> If three or more errors appear, reject the work lot.
> If one or two errors appear, proceed to take a
>
> *Third* sample of fourteen and add to previous samples.
> If one or fewer errors appear, accept work lot.
> If three or more errors appear, reject the work lot.
> If exactly two errors appear, proceed to take a
>
> *Fourth* sample of fourteen, and so on until the sixth sample is taken, if required.

All sampling plans have definite operating characteristics; that is, as the error rate in the work increases, more lots will be rejected. The rate of rejection varies from plan to plan depending upon the error level, the sample size, and the acceptance number (number of errors acceptable in a sample). This rate of rejection is usually shown in graph form, and is known as the operating characteristic curve. Figure 14-8(b) illustrates one of these curves, another tool of work sampling.

This curve indicates how many work lots can be expected to pass undetected with a given quality level. For example, in the deck of cards illustration, 25 per cent of the deck is comprised of hearts. If it is desired to limit the heart content of the deck to 12½ per cent using a sample of eight, the curve shows that 50 per cent of the work lots (decks) would be accepted, thus maintaining an error level of 12½ per cent. If, however, the error in the work lot was 80 per cent, then, according to the curve, 4 per cent of the work lots would be accepted, maintaining an error level of 3 per cent. Thus, if the error level in the work is consistently high, this sampling plan will result in maintaining a much lower error level than is required. In such a case, a larger sampling size or different acceptance number will provide a different operating curve more suited to the specific application.

Other sampling plans. Sampling plans are developed from probability tables that indicate the chances of one, two, or more errors appearing in a sample of a specific size when the error rate is known, or the desired level established. Occasionally, it is necessary to know the reverse information —that is, the range of error possible in the work when a specific sample size contains one, two, or more errors. The same basis of computation is used in either case, but with substitution of different unknown factors.

Figure 14-8(c) shows a table of this type. Based on a sample size of five hundred, it shows the range of error possible in a work lot when the sample contains the number of errors shown. For example, if ten errors appear in the sample, the error in the work lot from which this sample was taken will be from eight tenths of 1 per cent to 3.2 per cent. It is more likely to be midway (2 per cent), because of the tendency of readings to vary equally about the average.

Factors Affecting Sampling

There are several factors that affect the selection of a sample size.

1. *Range of values.* The range of values in the work being sampled has a definite effect on the size of the sample. Figure 14-9(a) shows the distribution curves of two different error ranges. If a sample of one were drawn from the narrow range, there would be a good chance of its approximating the actual average. If, however, the sample were drawn from the wider range, there would be less chance of this happening. To obtain the same odds or chance in the latter case, samples of two or more would be required.

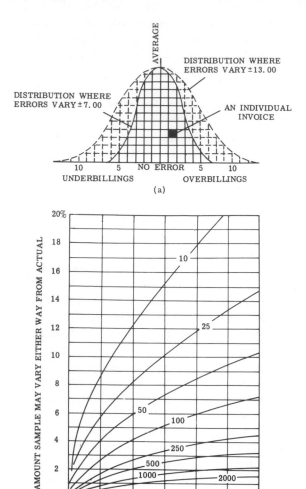

Fig. 14-9(a). Effect of Error Range (above); **(b)** Sample variations (below)

2. *Sample size.* The accuracy desired in sampling also determines the sample size. It is possible, therefore, to obtain a large degree of accuracy with a small sample size if the range is narrow. The graph in Figure 14-9(b) illustrates this point. When the error in the work is 1 per cent, and a sample of fifty is drawn, it will indicate the true error within 4 per cent; if the error in the work is 2 per cent, a sample slightly over one hundred pieces would be required for the same degree of accuracy. Obviously, the reason for this is that there is a greater range of error possible when it is 2 per cent than when it is 1 per cent.

3. *Lot size.* The question of lot size and the relationship of the lot size to the sample size has been much debated. The table, Figure 14-9(c),

LOT SIZE		RECOMMENDED SAMPLE SIZE
MORE THAN	LESS THAN	
	9	2
8	16	3
15	26	5
25	41	7
40	66	10
65	101	15
100	181	25
180	301	35
300	501	50
500	801	75
800	1301	110
1300	3201	150
3200	8001	225
8000	22001	300
22000	110000	450

Fig. 14-9(c). Selections of Sample or Lot Size

(c)

shows the recommended sample sizes as specified in MIL-Std 105. Whereas it is true that the sample size alone affects the accuracy of sampling, there are other considerations involved. Large sample sizes increase the accuracy of sampling, and thus maintain error levels closer to that desired. On the other hand, large sample sizes increase inspection costs. Large work lot sizes require the 100 per cent checking of more items if rejected.

The safest rule to follow is to select a work lot size that permits the smallest percentage of items to be checked and yet does not require a great amount of checking if the lot is rejected. This is the basis for the table in Figure 14-9(c). It is best applied by determining first the sample size necessary for the accuracy desired, and then selecting the approximate lot size from the table. This table also shows the inadvisability of setting sample sizes by percentage. It can be noted that as the lot size increases, the percentage sampled decreases.

There are, sometimes, other considerations used in determining the lot size. The clerical work may be done in batches, or represent a shift or a day's work. In such cases, it may be more convenient or practical to consider such factors as the basis for a work lot size.

As a general rule, the work lot size should not be such that the sample size to be taken from it amounts to almost a 100 per cent verification, such as eighty samples from a work lot of one hundred. Nor should the work lot size be so large that, if the sample indicates a rejection, there is an unusual amount of pieces to check, such as with a work lot of 10,000.

INSTALLING WORK SAMPLING

Selling the Program

The major obstacle in selling the program of quality control, or work sampling in the office, to management is the lack of literature comprehensible to the layman. Most of the available literature goes deeply into mathematics or statistics. To sell the program, the person being sold must understand it. Acceptance of the principles by all parties concerned insures cooperation and assistance if the program should develop flaws.

The reason for the limited number of applications of work sampling in the office field stems not from the lack of applications, but from the lack of knowledge of statistical methods by those individuals responsible for performing, planning, or supervising clerical and accounting functions. Some assistance on theory and application can be obtained from plant quality control men. Office problems, however, have more qualitative (personnel) factors involved than are in the usual plant quality control applications. The potentials in the use of work sampling in the office are enormous, not only in work verification and quality control, but in work analysis, administration, and forecasting. The task, then, is to provide an understanding of the principles of work sampling to those concerned with clerical and accounting operations, especially top management.

DEMONSTRATIONAL MATERIAL. Many types of demonstrational material are available.[2] For clerical operations, the most effective demonstrations have been made with ordinary playing cards. Another successful method has been the use of a bowl containing red and white beads. A paddle containing a number of depressions to catch the beads is inserted in the bowl to draw a sample, but it is usually difficult to associate the beads with paper work or invoices. Pictorial presentations similar to the illustrations shown in this chapter have also been used. One of these charts, shown in Figure 14-10(a), emphasizes the possible savings.

Another effective selling tool is the number selection test, shown in Figure 14-10(b). This test is used to illustrate the fact that error gets by even with 100 per cent verification. It proves that all errors will not be located in many instances by the complete checking of a work lot. Sampling, on the other hand, will furnish better accuracy in many cases. In sampling, the checking is confined to those lots in error as indicated in the sample. It is not necessary to check every lot, only those with concentrated error. Thus, with fewer papers to check, the certainty of locating errors without useless effort is increased. It also reduces boredom and fatigue, which are the psychological factors that contribute to the inability of obtaining 100 per cent accuracy with 100 per cent checking. Experience has shown that

---

[2] "Making Statistical Methods Easier to Understand," *Factory Management and Maintenance,* February, 1953.

STATISTICAL METHODS

Can eliminate 100% Verification

AND SAVE CONSIDERABLE TIME

IN LOTS OF 10,000
PIECES OF PAPER
ASSUMING 1% ERROR

10% SAMPLE (1000 PCS)
WILL INDICATE ERROR
WITHIN 1%

-5% SAMPLE (500 PCS)
WILL INDICATE ERROR
WITHIN 1 1/4 %

3% SAMPLE (300 PCS)
WILL INDICATE ERROR
WITHIN 1 3/4%

1% SAMPLE (100 PCS)
WILL INDICATE ERROR
WITHIN 3%

Saving 90 - 99% of effort

(a)

HOW EFFECTIVE IS 100% INSPECTION?

LISTED BELOW ARE 450 RANDOM THREE DIGIT NUMBERS. NUMBERS 851 THROUGH 900 ARE TO BE CONSIDERED ERRORS. GO THROUGH THIS LIST ONCE ONLY AND SEE HOW EFFECTIVELY YOU CAN SORT OUT THE ERRORS BY CHECKING EACH ONE YOU FIND. ALLOW A MAXIMUM OF THREE MINUTES TO COMPLETE THE INSPEC-TION.

```
921 250 401 976 121 931 084 435 980 428
335 142 212 842 282 741 402 418 924 039
867 499 018 496 589 317 233 381 802 534
612 066 927 222 975 211 952 217 027 398
348 893 048 826 241 306 031 430 511 286
763 952 862 501 877 996 868 497 892 057
726 240 548 655 566 285 818 168 339 336
163 824 321 659 840 869 749 481 071 519
830 005 048 960 745 405 000 941 357 655
836 903 857 701 436 065 589 010 329 548
669 694 623 459 203 856 420 896 285 588
808 944 999 972 868 685 424 087 676 190
631 000 298 526 684 774 797 753 643 469
230 928 563 137 649 101 322 494 828 103
483 588 637 632 572 459 293 074 803 481
108 685 213 691 120 502 835 122 362 556
704 807 865 878 848 775 658 499 298 055
770 445 079 672 226 741 216 653 051 411
734 019 267 479 654 794 897 965 998 997
960 890 786 648 477 272 035 766 464 131
765 369 941 482 992 472 922 342 732 093
424 726 000 245 462 650 811 944 049 127
178 202 199 170 115 033 926 792 634 449
240 006 747 463 154 822 465 084 680 251
800 325 827 305 761 195 605 994 260 704
026 326 604 861 097 311 504 677 828 959
069 158 228 277 306 315 304 277 224 154
065 957 830 684 519 335 133 912 672 414
138 844 532 202 854 489 160 705 287 852
400 930 444 940 420 883 330 759 173 570
951 315 664 997 313 614 899 169 423 661
884 092 285 462 624 771 904 021 124 212
285 344 389 419 434 436 423 396 356 301
232 150 053 943 820 683 532 368 191 796
579 349 160 850 581 299 004 697 377 044
699 341 971 588 194 787 367 936 492 037
569 090 599 096 581 054 516 966 405 832
248 652 045 427 797 156 505 842 167 482
786 079 362 633 894 144 383 611 829 037
234 420 597 762 918 063 198 323 437 542
636 721 795 860 914 959 994 019 034 040
036 022 999 966 924 872 811 741 661 572
473 365 248 122 987 842 689 526 355 174
985 787 579 363 139 905 663 412 152 884
607 321 027 725 414 094 766 430 086 733
```

(b)

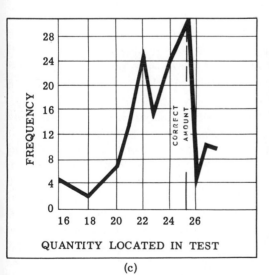

(c)

Fig. 14-10(a), (b), and (c). Selling Tools for Statistical Methods

checking large volumes of work and finding no error causes a relaxed vigilance that results in errors slipping by.

Surveys conducted by research organizations indicate that error up to 5 per cent remains in clerical work even after a 100 per cent check. To illustrate this fact dramatically, the test shown in Figure 14-10(b) was given to 133 people. Each participant was given a sheet of paper containing 450 three-digit random numbers, and told that all numbers from 851 through 900 represented errors. They were asked to see how many they could find in three minutes. The results of the test were quite interesting. Of the 133 people taking this test, only thirty obtained the correct answer, twenty-five. One hundred and three individuals gave answers ranging from a low of nine to a high of sixty-nine. A portion of the results of this test are shown in graph form in Figure 14-10(c). Some of the individuals missed 36 per cent of the error (6 per cent of the work lot). The majority of them missed three of the twenty-five errors in the work lot or 11 per cent. This test illustrates that variations exist between individuals checking clerical work. If this test of three minutes duration produces the variation shown, a checker working eight hours per day should have results of a much greater variation.

These are but a few of the many techniques that can be employed in selling the program.

Installing the Program

The steps involved in selecting and installing a sampling program are not difficult. The basic techniques outlined here and a set of probability tables should enable one to install a simple plan.

SURVEY AND ANALYSIS. A survey of the work is required to obtain the amount and extent of error and the frequency in which it occurs. It can be obtained from an analysis of prior work or current records kept until a representative amount of data has been accumulated. The amount of data required will vary with the complexity of the application.

After the survey has been completed, an analysis is made to determine the range of values represented and the amount and extent of error in such range. This will enable a decision to be made as to whether invoices should be grouped (stratification), whether the range of dollar error need be considered, and the amount of error that can remain in the work. Figure 14-11(a) shows the results of such a survey on vendors' invoices. It can be seen that only 11 per cent of the volume, but 84 per cent of the value, are represented by invoices of over $1,500. The invoices in this group contain 37 per cent of the errors, which represent 68 per cent of the total recovery. Thus, as the graph in Figure 14-11(b) shows, 100 per cent verification of all invoices over $1,500 would control 68 per cent of the dollar recovery, and yet represent only 11 per cent of the paper work.

The remainder of the invoices ($50 to $1,499) can be sampled. In addition, a further simplification can be made by eliminating the checking

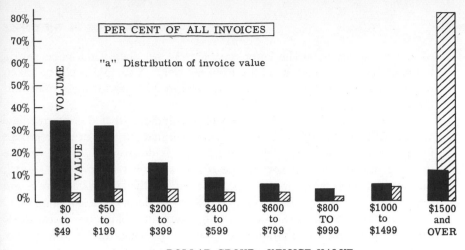

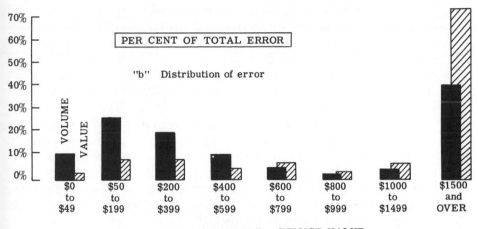

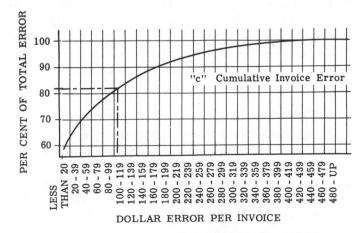

Fig. 14-11(a), (b), and (c). Typical Survey

of invoices under $50. The latter represent 34 per cent of the paper work, but contain only 1 per cent of the total recovery. A sample could be taken of this group every third month as a control to determine if the pattern has changed.

A review of Figure 14-11(a) will also indicate that the intermediate values ($50 to $1,499) could possibly be stratified into two or more groups for a sampling advantage. The final decision is determined by the volume involved and the cost of sorting the invoices against the benefits gained. Figure 14-11(c) shows that 84 per cent of all the individual errors are less than $100, an important consideration in the design of a sampling plan.

DESIGN CONSIDERATIONS. Although sampling plans are tailor-made for each particular installation, the example indicates that invoices over $1,500 should continue to be checked 100 per cent because of the recovery involved. Invoices under $50 would only require sampling every three months, whereas the balance ($50 to $1,499) would be sampled regularly. The error rate in dollars in this group averaged 67 cents per invoice or $67 per hundred invoices, and the total annual recovery was $28,000.

The primary consideration is the present cost of checking against the recovery obtained. This has the effect of reducing the recovery. This figure is then compared with the cost of checking under sampling and the amount of error allowed to pass. The net result will show whether sampling is advantageous in any specific case.

Sampling effects its greatest saving in verification when the error rate is low. If the error rate is high, most of the samples will be rejected, and 100 per cent verification will result. Under a 100 per cent verification plan, work is checked that does not contain error. If the error rate is low, this results in a large amount of unnecessary checking. Sampling, on the other hand, will isolate those work lots containing error for a 100 per cent check, allowing the others to pass by unchecked.

INSTALLATION. The installation of a sampling plan is no more complex than the installation of any other office procedure. It involves only four basic considerations: (1) how the work lot is to be accumulated, (2) how the sample is to be taken, (3) the size of the sample, and (4) the control point, or amount of error permitted to be in sample before the work is to be 100 per cent checked. In sampling for information, it is necessary only to consult the tables of probability to determine the size of sample necessary to provide the required accuracy.

Control of the Program

The control chart is the record kept to control a sampling program. Its purpose is to keep the people informed by recording the apparent error shown by each sample, and it is usually mounted on the department wall. Some companies use individual charts for each employee, but this is not recommended from an employee relations standpoint. Individual charts may be maintained by the supervisor and kept in his desk for merit rating purposes, but wall charts should be limited to departments or large segments of a department.

The control chart is nothing more than a graph of the sample readings for each of the sample intervals. A sample interval can be for each work lot, each day, each week, or on any other time or unit basis. A sample reading has been designated as the apparent error in this chapter to show the differences between actual error and the apparent error as shown by a sample. A sample drawn from a work lot will show error equal to, greater than, or less than the actual error in the work lot. The extent to which a sample reading will differ from the actual depends on the size of the sample and the range of the error in the work. The highest possible reading is known as the upper control limit, and the lowest is called the lower control limit. The error control point is in the center of this band, and is called the mean or average. It can be the actual error in the work, or the desired error level in the work.

The points on a control chart, if they remain within this band, indicate that the sample was taken from a work lot containing error equal to the mean. If points fall outside the band, it indicates that the sample came from a work lot having error higher or lower than the mean. The purpose of the control chart is to provide a visual means to show when error is under control. It provides a signal for action when the sample readings fall outside of the control band.

This action can take various forms. It will encourage a competitive spirit between groups of employees; it will result in additional instructions for the employee involved; it will serve as a signal for requiring verification; it will provide a control on error; and it will permit equitable merit rating of employees. Data from regular samples of office work can contribute to more objective merit ratings, fairer distribution of work loads, and a realistic appraisal of training needs. New job interest may be aroused when employees take a fresh look at their time and error goals. Assuring accuracy in office work offers promise, too, of improving customer relations.

15

Operations Research*

CLIFFORD J. CRAFT

Management Software Development Corporation
Los Angeles, California

GUY L. LANGSFORD

Management Technology Inc.
Washington, D.C.

CLIFFORD J. CRAFT is Vice President of Management Software Development Corporation, responsible for the firm's activities in the areas of electronic data processing, systems analysis, real time business systems, and management science. He holds a master's degree in electrical engineering from the University of Michigan and an MBA degree from the Wharton School, University of Pennsylvania.

Mr. Craft was formerly associated with Management Technology, Inc., as a Vice President and Director and his major assignments included the development of a simulation model of an automobile dealership; a survey of urban and regional planning activities by state and local governments; the design of a computer-based management system for the Navy for forecasting manpower requirements based upon workload indicators, and the design of multiple-regression procedures for the development of a Cost Estimating and PERT Scheduling System for the construction industry.

Prior to joining MTI, Mr. Craft served as Manager in Hughes Dynamics, where he conducted the feasibility study on the selection of a large-scale computer system for an on-line credit reporting system.

Mr. Craft served several years as Manager of the Management Controls Department of Peat, Marwick, Mitchell and Company in New York, where he led projects in areas of operations research, electronic data processing, and system and procedures. Earlier, Mr. Craft was Division Manager of the American Management Association, responsible for its activities in financial management, operations research, and data processing. At AMA, Mr. Craft was director of the project that led to the development of the first management game used in industry in executive development.

Mr. Craft is the author of two books, and has published many articles in the management sciences and electronic data processing field, where he is the holder of three patents. He also has been a speaker at

---

* This chapter is based in large part on Chapter 15: *Management Research* by Clifford J. Craft and David B. Hertz in the First Edition of this book.

many international, national, and regional meetings of leading professional organizations and universities, and was the originator of a widely circulated management publication. Books of which he is a co-author are: Management Games: A New Technique for Executive Development *by Joel M. Kibbee, Clifford J. Craft and Burt Nanus, Reinhold Publishing Company, New York, 1961, which has also been translated into Japanese; and* Top Management Decision Simulation: The AMA Approach, *Franc M. Ricciardi and Clifford J. Craft, American Management Association, Inc., New York, 1957.*

GUY L. LANGSFORD is a member of the professional staff of Management Technology, Inc. (MTI). He holds an M.S. degree from the School of Business Administration, San Diego State College, and a B.S. degree from the University of Missouri School of Business and Public Administration. At MTI, Mr. Langsford has served on numerous assignments, including forecasting future systems of management production control, automated shop loading, computerized staffing predictions, improved manufacturing methods and flow; and auditing existing management organization and methods, including the establishment of an internal audit function.

Prior to entering the consulting field, Mr. Langsford was with The Ryan Aeronautical Company of San Diego where he designed, developed, and implemented a management information system utilizing electronic data processing for engineering, manufacturing, and accounting data. The systems design and conversion of this management information system incorporated economic and statistical analysis (including real-time processing costs), design of computer reports, selection of processing methods, and programming specifications.

While with the Convair and Electronics Divisions of General Dynamics Corporation, Mr. Langsford designed and implemented systems for manpower forecasting, budgetary requirements and cost effectiveness, including evaluation of supporting systems of information such as personnel administration, human resources utilization, and statistical analysis of historical cost data. Additional responsibilities including the planning of research and development contracts using PERT/CPM, the electronic data processing of management information, and providing liaison between Electronics Division and service departments within Convair Division.

INTRODUCTION

Operations research is a management science which is being utilized profitably in an increasing number of companies.[1] Although this science is maturing as a field of endeavor, it was considered an emerging science until recently, and as such, was subject to most of the exaggerated claims which accompany any new and slightly-understood phenomenon. Many of the claims that were made for operations research sounded as promising as the early claims for automation and electronic data processing. Moreover,

---

[1] "Operations Research Is Growing Fast," by C. J. Craft, *Systems Magazine*, 1958.

some of this publicity has created the illusion that operations research is an entirely new kind of management process, and that the mathematical approach will eventually eliminate the need for judgment and executive experience.

Within this chapter, operations research is placed in proper perspective through an explanation of its history, its definition, and its relationship to the organization. Also the principal techniques used by operations research specialists are explained, and applications wherein some of these techniques can be used to advantage are discussed. In this way it is hoped that the management specialist can expand his capability through the use of operations research.

History of Operations Research

Operations research (more commonly referred to as "OR") is an extension of the scientific management movement which for more than sixty years has sought a wider application of advanced methods to the problems of management. In this respect, operations research is the present culmination of the quest that began with Frederick Taylor and his quantitative approach. Another early application of advanced mathematical techniques to business operations was made in the 1920's by Walter Shewhart of the Bell Telephone Laboratories. In analyzing telephone operations, Shewhart applied the theory of probability and statistics to the problems of sampling and quality control. These early applications were so successful that they sparked an increased use of mathematical techniques in such areas as industrial engineering, cost accounting, market research, and engineering development. Until the Second World War, however, there were relatively few successful applications of advanced mathematical techniques to the problems of management.

During the Second World War, the British and American military services recognized the value of an analytical approach to the complicated problems of war. This led to the organizing of scientists into so-called operations research or OR teams. These teams researched into operations for the purpose of providing military leaders with a factual or quantitative basis for making decisions. As a result of their prewar training and experience, these wartime researchers appreciated the value of a consistent and rigorous application of the scientific method, and they used whatever mathematical or analytical techniques were appropriate. Because the nature of many military situations required an explicit recognition of uncertainty, this research drew quite heavily upon the theory of probability and statistics.

In many of the wartime studies, an investigation required an integrated approach, using a team of specialists drawn from the various fields that might contribute to the solution of a particular problem. For example, a team composed of a mathematician, an aeronautical engineer, and a psychologist was required to determine the optimum height for a ship-bombing run in order to adequately consider all factors, such as the correlations of past experience with hits and plane losses, the capabilities of the various types of aircraft, and the relation of morale to over-all success. In some instances these scientists were even called upon to make specific recommendations regarding the best or "optimum" courses of action from among the various alternatives, and, as it turned out, the success of several important military campaigns resulted in large part from the adoption of the recommendations from the OR teams. Thus, it is generally recognized that scientific research into military operations during the Second World War was an unqualified success.

At the conclusion of the war it became apparent to these operations researchers that many business operations were very similar to the wartime situations that they had analyzed and solved. As a result, many of these scientists entered industry and commenced researching business operations, and within a few years a number of extremely complex business and industrial problems were brought under scientific analysis for the first time.

Definition of Operations Research

Operations research may be defined simply as the application of the scientific method to operational problems for the purpose of providing management with a quantitative basis for making decisions. Naturally, the development of quantitative material for decisions is also a function of accounting, market research, industrial research, and other similar areas of management analysis. The distinguishing characteristic of operations research, however, is the scientific method and the use of advanced mathematical techniques in the solution of operational problems.

Very briefly, the scientific method consists of seven basic steps: (1) observation and general survey of the problem area, (2) definition of the problem, (3) fact finding, (4) analysis of data and construction of a model, (5) comparison of the model with observed data, (6) repetition of the previous steps until a satisfactory model is constructed, and (7) use of the model to predict or forecast. In any area, the researcher using the scientific method begins his project by first defining the nature of the problem to be solved, the objective(s) to be reached, and the terms to be used. This is followed by observation and fact finding, which may even require the design of certain experiments involving actual operations for the purpose of gathering particular data. Next, the scientist analyzes the data, emphasizing: (1) the classification of data, (2) the isolation of patterns or trends, and (3) the determination of cause-and-effect relationships. After the data have been analyzed, the scientist usually constructs some kind of mathematical model designed to explain the observed facts.

As the final step of the scientific method, the model is tested to ascertain the degree to which it is capable of explaining past experience and forecasting future performance. If the model is not sufficiently accurate for this purpose, the various steps of the scientific method are repeated as often as is necessary to achieve a satisfactory model. At this point, creativeness plays an important role in the simplification of complex mathematics to permit practical computation; in the use of intelligent compromise in subsequent redefinitions of the problem; and in the insight into the likely areas of application, variables that can be ignored, limiting factors, and so forth.

The use of a model, once it has been developed, naturally depends on the purpose for which it has been developed. Generally, however, a model is used to predict future performance within the scope of the model—that is, performance which does not violate any of the assumptions or limitations incorporated into the model. More important, however, a model is useful as a basis for evaluating different possible courses of action in order to determine which alternative would best accomplish a particular objective, such as minimizing costs and maximizing profits. As a matter of fact, as will be seen later on, this is where the real power of some of the operations research techniques lies.

The operations research approach, with its emphasis on the scientific method, has the following characteristics:

1. OR can be applied to operations of all kinds of organizations.
2. OR studies operations in their entirety, thereby requiring for certain situations a team of specialists from all fields that might contribute to the solution of the problem.
3. OR emphasizes the development of a theory or model that symbolically represents all the important elements of the operation being studied.
4. OR is pragmatic in the sense that not only are constraints (such as the amount of resources available) incorporated into the theory or model, but also the goals and objectives of the operation are logically and consistently stated in order to provide a realistic basis for evaluating the effectiveness of the performance and the outcome of alternative courses of action.

Operations Research in the Organization

Ideally, the operations research approach to problems should be a part of the entire decision-making process of a company. That is, every manager, whatever his level, makes decisions. He likes to "optimize" the probable results of his decisions, he wants the "hard facts," he wants them "quantified," he attempts to use every relationship that seems relevant, and he wants to understand the over-all process that he is managing. The objectives at which operations research aims are of these same kinds, and, as a consequence, operations research is broadly compatible with all areas of company management. However, to achieve the state in which the operations research approach is used throughout a firm, one cannot "install" it simultaneously at all levels; one can only educate management in the operations research approach, and allow it to evolve. This is because the effective use of operations research requires a proper management philosophy and not a mere reliance upon techniques.

The location of the operations research function in the company is very important for several reasons. First, the initial cost of organizing the operations research group, installing the group, and educating the surrounding management is a significant cost. Second, operations research must be utilized, and this need is best served by a sponsor. Operations research does not have to report to this sponsor, but it is essential that OR be close to him in the administrative hierarchy. Thus, it is best to avoid having a company president order the installation of an operations research group in a manufacturing department several echelons below him without reference to the wishes of the departmental head. On the other hand, if the president wishes to sponsor an operations research department, and, working in cooperation with a factory manager who reports to him, he sets up such a group reporting to the factory manager, he is on the right track.

Another reason the location of the operations research group is important is that the group must have ready access to the data needed for viewing operational problems in their entirety. This requirement tends to raise the location of the OR group on the administrative ladder, but not necessarily to the top. The exact location will depend upon the sponsor and the types of problems to be undertaken. Whatever particular location in the administrative structure is selected, it also must be possible for the operations research group to be able to set up problem-solving teams that cut across both operating and staff lines.

TECHNIQUES OF OPERATIONS RESEARCH

It is not sufficient for the operations researcher simply to apply systematically and rigorously the scientific approach with its emphasis on objective and quantitative fact finding. The researcher must also be able to utilize a variety of complex mathematical and computational techniques. As a means of furnishing some insight into the tools of the operations research practitioner, the following techniques are presented.

Probability Theory

Many planning situations require an estimation of the likelihood of occurrence of particular variables in an operation. Consider, for example, the problem of staffing a maintenance or repair department to handle an unknown and variable level of machine breakdowns. A probabilistic model of such an operation would be a mathematical formulation containing all the important factors, with an explicit recognition of the element of uncertainty in machine breakdowns. Moreover, provided adequate data relating to the operation were available, the model would indicate the optimum level of repair facilities that would minimize the over-all cost of machine delays and repair facilities.

Probability theory has been applied to nearly every type of industrial operation. The most frequent areas of application are:

1. Inventory management
2. Accident or breakdown analysis

3. Short-range forecasting
4. Capital facilities planning
5. Allocation of marketing effort
6. Investment management
7. Behavioral studies
8. Long-range forecasting

The use of probability theory in inventory management is fairly well established. One company, for example, classifies its inventory into two categories:

1. Probability items which have a very low activity and which comprise about 25 per cent of the total dollar value that moves from stock into work-in-process
2. Planned items that represent about 75 per cent of the total dollar value

In this way, the company achieves effective control for the least cost. The planned items (about 25 per cent of the total) are carefully planned based upon known or forecasted requirements, whereas the probability items (those that move more slowly) are maintained on the basis of past activity. This is accomplished through a simple, more or less mechanical means of control based upon restocking and carrying costs and the probabilities of running out of stock.

In forecasting, the obvious problem is to predict future performance with a reasonable degree of accuracy. This is frequently accomplished by establishing mathematical relationships between the operation being studied and other known activities. For example, statistical correlations are used by public utilities in their planning for new facilities to meet the expected demand for services. These utilities forecast rather accurately their plant requirements, based upon such factors as the expected growth in family units, building plans, and value of the gross national product.

In analyzing its promotional methods, one company developed a probabilistic model based on existing data. This model was used to develop measures of the effectiveness of their promotion and the potential gain in sales through better promotion. The company also measured the effect of promotion on individual accounts, and, in so doing, obtained a broad view of the whole operation and an important part of a general theory of company operations.

Each of the foregoing applications is characterized by certain basic features. First, there is an element of uncertainty as to the occurrence of some future event(s). Second, it is possible to estimate the likelihood of the occurrence of the uncertain event(s). In most cases, such probabilities are determined from past experience; however, in some instances they are derived simply from estimates of future performance. Finally, in each of these situations it is possible to postulate different courses of future action. If one is not able to alter a future mode of operation, then the most he can do is to predict its consequences. However, where various alternatives exist, it is possible for one to improve his future position by choosing an optimum course of action.

Sampling Theory

Generally, wherever operations occur in a random fashion, statistical analysis becomes an essential part of the observational phase of management research. By analyzing a number of such events, using statistical methods, considerable insight can be gained into the relationships between the variables and over-all performance. Such analysis provides the basis for determining expected or average performance, and the likelihood that future operations will be similar to past experience. First of all, sampling is an economical and effective way of determining a representative picture of a universe. Moreover, this representation can be quite accurate as long as the sample size is adequate and the items are selected in a random fashion. Thus, sampling theory can be a very powerful tool in almost all data-gathering situations.

Many meaningful conclusions can be determined from random samples even when some or all of the characteristics of the universe (or total group from which the samples are taken) are not known. Very simply, sampling theory enables one to determine quantitative measures for an unknown universe of items or events based upon the results of one or more random samples. This is precisely what Walter Shewhart did in the early days at the Bell Telephone Laboratories. He was faced with the problem of determining the quality (or level of defectives) of lots of purchased items. In most cases, 100 per cent inspection was either too costly or not possible (as in the case of destructive testing), so it became necessary to use a sampling technique as a basis for estimating over-all quality.

Although the basic concepts of sampling theory are relatively simple, some of the practical business applications have been slow in developing. At persent, the most widespread use of this technique is in industrial quality control programs. Another type of application that is now coming into its own is quality control of clerical activities.

In the above situations, three important benefits are derived from the application of sampling theory. First of all, it enables management to establish an economical method of control (over clerical or industrial operations) that provides an accurate indication of an unsatisfactory operation. Second, it is possible to determine a statistical model of the operation (being sampled) that can be used to forecast future production or performance (provided, of course, that the operation remains in control). Finally, sampling provides a basis for incorporating feedback into a system by indicating promptly when an operation is going out of control. This indication can be derived from a continuing analysis of the reports of samples taken.

Up to now, sampling theory has been used mostly in the areas of production and inventory control. In addition to the application of this technique to quality control and inspection, it also has found use in the gathering of production data for control purposes and as a basis for constructing mathematical models. Many of these same types of applications are also finding their way into clerical operations. For example, sampling techniques have long been used to develop production or work standards for irregular operations like setup, stock, and toolroom control and maintenance. These same procedures are now being used to develop work standards for sales people and supervisors.

Some companies also use sampling as a basis for certain end-of-the-month or interim management reports. This is particularly true in the areas of production and cost reporting, where the accounting procedures are often costly, burdensome, and—more frequently the case—too time-consuming. As a means of cutting costs, speeding up cost accumulation and, at the same time, retaining reasonable accuracy, some companies are using periodic samples as a basis for allocating such items as maintenance costs and freight charges. In such applications, a sample is used to determine the pattern for distributing these charges, thereby simplifying the cost accumulation of cost data and speeding up its allocation.

The use of sampling in auditing and financial analysis is also increasing. Sampling is being used by auditors to confirm such operations as accounts receivable. It has also proven useful in verifying inter-line revenue settlements in the railroad and airline industries. Incidentally, this application is a good example of a practical use of stratified sampling. Different samples are used for different parts of the universe being studied, with the sample size for each section being determined by the importance, dollar value, and so on, of that section.

Finally, sampling has been used in forecasting and market research. Public opinion and market data may be obtained more economically and quickly, and frequently with greater accuracy, by using sampling techniques than by attempting to survey the complete universe. When the characteristics of a very large universe are changing rapidly, a sample is often the only feasible means of obtaining a timely picture of the facts.

Linear Programming

In those instances where the element of uncertainty is reasonably small and where the relationships between variables can be expressed with some degree of certainty, operations research utilizes exact models. This approach has received its greatest impetus from the development of linear programming—the technique for determining the best or optimum allocation of limited resources to accomplish specific goals. This benefit is achieved by maximizing a system of linear equations subject to limitations placed on the values of some or all of the variables.

The Simplex Method is a general method for solving any linear programming problem in a systematic manner. It is an iterative procedure, but is minimal in the sense that the solution of each stage or step is an improvement over the preceding step (or at least is equal to it). Also, this method assures one of an approach to the optimal solution.

For the purpose of demonstrating the Simplex Method of solution of linear programming problems, the following simple production planning problem will be used:

A paint manufacturer makes two brands of paint, A and B. These two paints are manufactured in three plants, each of which produces both brands. For a particular season, sales quotas are set on A and B. The total output of paint A should not exceed 100,000 gallons. There is a similar limitation on the production of B. The sales prices for A and B are $4 per gallon and $2 per gallon, respectively. The cost of raw material is $1 per drum, and labor cost is $2 per man-hour. Based upon the following input-output numbers, determine how much of each brand of paint should be produced and at which plants in order to maximize profits:

	Factory		
	#1	#2	#3
Inputs			
Material (drums)	7	6	5
Labor (man-hrs.)	1	1	1
Outputs			
Paint A (gals.)	3	2	1
Paint B (gals.)	1.5	2	3

The mathematical statement of this problem is as follows:

Restrictions: (1) $3X_1 + 2X_2 + X_3 \leqslant 100{,}000$ gallons of paint A

                (2) $1.5X_1 + 2X_2 + 3X_3 \leqslant 100{,}000$ gallons of paint B
Where X_1, X_2, and X_3 are the activity levels of factories 1, 2, and 3 respectively

Objective: (3) $P = 6X_1 + 4X_2 + 3X_3$ dollars of profit

Problem: To determine the (optimum) activity levels X_1, X_2, and X_3 which satisfy restrictions (1) and (2) and maximize the objective (3).

The introduction of (slack) variables X_4 and X_5 into the problem changes the restriction in equations (1) and (2) into the following equations:

         (4) $3X_1 + 2X_2 + X_3 + X_4 = 100{,}000$

         (5) $1.5X_1 + 2X_2 + 3X_3 + X_5 = 100{,}000$

SIMPLEX METHOD

Step 1.   Set up the problem in the following tabular or matrix form.

VALUES	6	4	3	0	0	
VARIABLES	X_1	X_2	X_3	X_4	X_5	Y
	3	2	1	1	0	100,000
	1.5	2	3	0	1	100,000

$\longleftarrow$ STRUCTURAL $\longrightarrow\longleftarrow$ SLACK $\longrightarrow$ $\uparrow$ REQUIREMENT

VARIABLES   VARIABLES   VARIABLE

Step 2.   Select the "basic" feasible solution with the slack variables equal to their corresponding requirement. In this case,

$$X_4 = 100,000$$
$$X_5 = 100,000$$

Since these slack variables enter into the "basis" at zero profit, there is no profit associated with this solution. In other words,

$$P = 0$$

Where slack variables do not exist, introduce them into the restriction equations and price them at a value which will insure their not being included in the optimum solution (e.g., at zero profit in the case of maximizing profits).

Step 3.   Form the first table as follows:

$\overline{\hspace{2cm}}$ j $\longrightarrow$

$j = 1 \quad j = 2 \quad j = 3 \quad j = 4 \quad j = 5$

	VALUES	$c_j \longrightarrow$	6	4	3	0	0		
	$c_i \downarrow$	VARIABLES	X_1	X_2	X_3	X_4	X_5	Y	R
$i = 4$	0	X_4	3	2	1	1	0	100,000	
$i = 5$	0	X_5	1.5	2	3	0	1	100,000	
		z_j	0	0	0	0	0	0	
		$z_j - c_j$	−6	−4	−3	0	0		

i with downward arrow spanning $i = 4$ and $i = 5$.

a.   Enter each slack variable into the table in the "VARI-ABLES" column in the same row in which it appears in the restriction equation.

b. Each element of the table is denoted by a_{ij} where the subscript i denotes the row and the subscript j denotes the column. In this case, for example $a_{43} = 1$.

c. Denote the column values by c_j and the row values by c_i. In this case, for example, $c_3 = 3$ and $c_4 = 0$.

d. Enter the slack values into the c_i column. (In the first table these are all zero.)

e. Compute $z_j = \sum_{\text{all } i} c_i d_{ij}$

In this case, for example $z_3 = \sum_{i = 4, 5} c_i a_{i3}$, or

$z_3 = c_4\ a_{43} + c_5\ a_{53} = 0\ (1) + 0\ (3) = 0.$

f. Compute $z_j - c_j$. In this case, for example,
$z_3 - c_3 = 0 - 3 = -3.$

Step 4. Determine the variable which should be brought into the "basis" for the next solution by choosing the variable with the most negative $z_j - c_j$. Denote this variable by X_K. In this case, $X_K = X_1$.

Step 5. Determine the variable which should be removed from the basis by calculating (for all positive a_{iK} values only) an index $R_i = Y_i/a_{iK}$, and removing the variable with the smallest R_i. Denote this variable by X_R. In this case for example, $R_4 = 100,000/3$ and $X_R = X_4$. The z_j value in the Y column indicates the profit associated with the solution table. In this case, profit is zero. Table 1 completed is shown below:

$$j = 1 \quad j = 2 \quad j = 3 \quad j = 4 \quad j = 5$$

VALUES	$c_j \longrightarrow$	6	4	3	0	0			
$c_i \downarrow$	VARIABLES	X_1	X_2	X_3	X_4	X_5	Y	R	
0	X_4	3	2	1	1	0	100,000	33,333	X_R ←
0	X_5	1.5	2	3	0	1	100,000	66,667	
	z_j	0	0	0	0	0	0		
	$z_j - c_j$	−6	−4	−3	0	0			

$i = 4$, $i = 5$ (row labels at left: $i \begin{cases} i = 4 \\ i = 5 \end{cases}$)

$X_K \uparrow$

Step 6. Form the next table with elements a_{ij} as follows:

a. Enter the variables from the preceding table into their corresponding rows with the exception that X_R is replaced by X_K.

b. Compute the elements in the row corresponding to X_K using:

$$a'_{Kj} = a_{Rj}/a_{RK}.$$

In this case, for example,

$$a'_{K4} = a_{R4}/a_{RK} = 1/3.$$

c. Compute the elements in the remaining rows using:

$$a'_{ij} = a_{ij} - (a_{Rj}/a_{RK}) a_{iK}.$$
$$a'_{ij} = a_{ij} - a'_{Kj} a_{iK}.$$

In this case, for example,

$$a'_{53} = a_{53} - a'_{K3} a_{5K}.$$
$$a'_{53} = 3 - (1/3)(3/2)$$
$$a'_{53} = 5/2$$

d. Compute $z'_j = \sum_{\text{all } i} c_i a_{ij}.$

In this case, for example,

$$z'_2 = 6(2/3) + 0(1) = 4$$

e. Compute $z'_j - c_j.$

In this case, for example,

$$z'_2 - c_2 = 4 - 4 = 0$$

f. Form the new table as follows:

$$j = 1 \quad j = 2 \quad j = 3 \quad j = 4 \quad j = 5$$

VALUES	$c_j \longrightarrow$	6	4	3	0	0		
$c_i \downarrow$	VARIABLES	X_1	X_2	X_3	X_4	X_5	Y	R
$i = K$ 6	X_1	1	2/3	1/3	1/3	0	33,333	
$i = 5$ 0	X_5	0	1	5/2	$-1/2$	1	50,000	
	z_j	6	4	2	2	0	200,000	
	$z_j - c_j$	0	0	-1	2	0		

(In this table the z_j value in the Y column is 200,000. This indicates the profit associated with this solution table.)

Step 7. Determine if this table is the optimum solution.

a. If for any $(z_j - c_j) < 0$, all a_{ij} in the corresponding column are $\leqslant 0$, then one or more of the activity levels and/or the objective function are infinite.

b. If all $(z_j - c_j) \geqslant 0$, the optimum activity levels and objective function have been reached.

c. If for a $(z_j - c_j) < 0$, some a_{ij} are $\geqslant 0$, then the optimum activity levels have not been reached. In this case return to Step 4, and repeat Steps 4 through 7.

COMPLETE SOLUTION TO ABOVE PROBLEM

VALUES	$c_j \longrightarrow$	6	4	3	0	0			
$c_i \downarrow$	VARIABLES	X_1	X_2	X_3	X_4	X_5	Y	R	X'_R
0	X_4	3	2	1	1	0	100,000	33,333	←
0	X_5	1.5	2	3	0	1	100,000	66,667	
	z_j	0	0	0	0	0	0		
	$z_j - c_j$	−6	−4	−3	0	0			
6	X_1	1	2/3	1/3	1/3	0	33,333	100,000	X_R
0	X_5	0	1	5/2	−1/2	1	50,000	20,000	←
	z_j	6	4	2	2	0	200,000		
	$z_j - c_j$	0	0	−1	2	0			
6	X_1	1	8/15	0	2/5	−2/15	26,667		
3	X_3	0	2/5	1	−1/5	2/5	20,000		
	z_j	6	22/5	3	9/5	2/5	220,000		
	$z_j - c_j$	0	2/5	0	9/5	2/5			

Table #1 (first block), Table #2 (second block), Table #3 / Optimum Solution (third block)

In Table #1, $X_K = X_1$
In Table #2, $X'_K = X_3$

Optimum solution from Table #3:

	Factory	#1	#2	#3
$X_1 =$ 26,667	Paint A	80,000 gal.	0	20,000 gal.
$X_2 =$ 0	Paint B	40,000 gal.	0	60,000 gal.
$X_3 =$ 20,000				

$P = \$220,000$ profit

NOTE:

A degeneracy occurs when more than one variable ties or qualifies for being removed from the basis, i.e., when there is more than one X_i for which $R_i = Y_i/a_{iK}$ is a minimum. In such a case the "tie" is broken as follows:

a. Divide all elements in the rows of the "tied" variables by a_{iK}.

b. Compare the two sets of ratios.

c. Determine the first position or element, starting from the left-hand side of the table, where the tie is broken and remove the basis variable associated with the smallest (algebraic) value of the ratio.

Another application of linear programming is in the area of planning and scheduling. In the past, the Gantt chart has been a well-known method for establishing schedules. Such a procedure, however, provides only one solution, or at most a few, that would meet the requirements. In addition, there is no guarantee that the Gantt chart will produce the optimum solution.

The linear programming model, on the other hand, enables one to determine an optimum solution. In one application of linear programming, the company reported savings of 10 per cent, equivalent to $1,000,000 per year. In this instance, the potential capacity of a group of machines was increased 10 per cent over what had been possible using a Gantt chart.

Queueing Theory

Queueing, or waiting-line, theory has found considerable use in personnel planning. This particular operations research technique, which draws heavily upon probability theory, was developed to solve certain waiting problems in an automatic telephone switching system. Since then, the theory has been applied to many other types of waiting-line or "bottleneck" problems, such as traffic congestion and machine feed and breakdown. Queueing theory is also applicable (1) to work flow, or to back-up of items to be worked on in a departmental situation, (2) to production control, and (3) to the proper staffing required to handle the flow of work within a department or organization.

A queueing situation has the following features: (1) customer or items (production or otherwise), (2) a gate or service point, (3) an input process, (4) a waiting-line discipline, and (5) a service mechanism. In other words, there are customers who desire service, and after each customer moves to the service point, there is a period of time required for the service operations, after which the customer leaves. Any customer who arrives while another customer is being served must wait his turn. In other words, there is a bottleneck, and a waiting line forms. (The "line" may consist of people, cars, products, calls, etc.) In such situations the major problem is a reduction in the waiting time of the customer, the number of customers in the waiting line, and the ratio of waiting time to service time.

The objective of using queueing theory is to minimize costs of investment and costs of operation while providing service in a timely manner to the customers. To accomplish this objective, the usual aim is to set the service rate equal to the average rate of arrivals. This, however, is not always a very satisfactory answer. As soon as customer arrivals start to fluctuate randomly, a waiting line usually forms. Consider, for example, the problem of check-out in a retail store. Figure 15-1 illustrates a situation in which customers are arriving randomly at two counters (which have a maximum servicing capacity of forty-eight customers per half-hour) at a rate of thirty-five per half-hour. Although the check-out operation has a capacity greater than the rate of arrival of customers, it should be apparent that a waiting line will form.

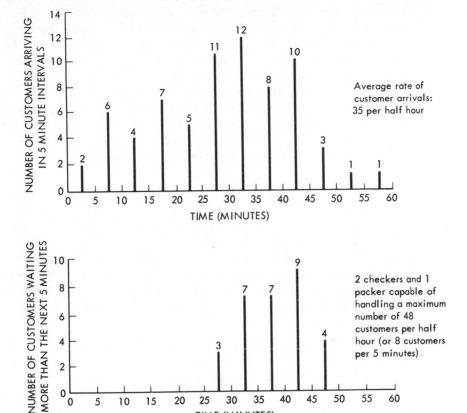

Fig. 15-1. Waiting Line at Two Check-out Counters in a Retail Store

One reason for the formation of waiting lines is that there are times when the number of customers arriving during a particular interval of time is less than the number of customers that can be serviced in that interval. As a result, there are times when more customers are waiting than can be served, and other times when no customers are waiting and no service is being provided. Such lost time reduces the effective capacity of a service-providing facility below the maximum capacity, and results in the formation of waiting lines. Thus, generally, whenever arrivals approach the maximum service rate, both the length of the lines and the waiting time increase drastically.

Simulation

Simulation has come to mean many different things to many different people, depending on the use to which they put simulation. It has been utilized for personnel selection and training, traffic control, war strategies, inventory distribution, logistics systems, job shop scheduling, and many other types of applications. It is much easier to characterize simulation in figurative terms than in literal terms. For example, an essential characteristic of a simulation is captured by the observation that a model *represents* a phenomenon, but that a simulation *imitates* it. This dynamic aspect of simulation is also caught in the figurative observation that models are photographs, and simulations are motion pictures. These figures of speech are not meant to imply that models and simulation are to be contrasted, because simulation is a way of using a model. It is, in effect, experimentation on a model rather than on the phenomenon itself; that is, it is vicarious experimentation. In principle, everything that can be accomplished by simulation can be accomplished by experimenting directly on the phenomena involved in the problem. In practice, however, it may be impossible or impractical to experiment on the phenomena directly. Moreover, one of the principal powers and advantages of simulation over other analytical tools is its ability to handle interacting elements in complex systems.

Simulation procedures can be classified into a number of main types, depending upon the type of model used. These types are iconic, analog, symbolic, and gaming. Since models may have a mixture of these characteristics, so may simulations.

1. An iconic model has the same essential properties as that which it represents, but with a transformation of scale. Such simulation is widely used in problems involving the construction or production of an object, in so-called hardware or design problems. For example, the testing of a small physical model of an aircraft in a wind tunnel is an iconic simulation. Testing ship models in tow tanks, and the operation of pilot plants in the chemical industries are other examples of iconic simulation.

2. Symbolic simulation is a process by which equations are evaluated numerically. An example would be:

$$\text{ROI} = \frac{\text{Profit}}{\text{Sales}} \times \frac{\text{Sales}}{\text{Investment}}$$

or *return on investment* is equal to *profitability of sales* times *investment turnover*.

3. A simulation in which decision-making is performed by one or more real decision-makers is called gaming. Gaming has come into increasing use in the last decade, particularly in the study of complex military and industrial operations. It is also being used in the study of governmental problems. Gaming, particularly in the military context, has a very long history, but its use as a research tool is quite recent.

The uses of gaming in problem-solving research fall into three general classes: (1) to help develop a decision model, (2) to help find the solution to such a model, and (3) to help evaluate proposed solutions.

With the advent of the computer, simulation has come to attract increasing attention in both research and management circles. One of the first applications of simulation to management endeavors was initiated in late 1957 by the American Management Association in its Top Management Decision Simulation Exercise. This exercise was designed to introduce top management to the concept of simulation and to provide a synthetic, or simulated, experience in the decision-making required to operate a large company. Decisions relating to marketing, research and development, plant expansion, production, pricing, and market intelligence were the main decisions involved. Performance was measured by the profit and loss and the return-on-investment achieved by the participant.

The success of this pioneering effort has been truly phenomenal.[2] By 1963, more than seventy of the nation's ninety leading schools of business administration were using business simulation exercises as a regular tool. Modern management needs to understand the sensitive control points in their businesses and to be able to evaluate quickly the effect of alternatives. Simulation exercises give the manager quick and specific experience in this way of thinking. Simulation is probably the most powerful tool available to management today for solving the complex problems confronting the firm.

The use of simulation in management training can be particularly helpful to the operations researcher in furthering his efforts in a company. Each organization may have somewhat different purposes for using simulation in training, but some of the main reasons for using it in this area are:

To provide for the practice of management principles

To clarify abstract managerial concepts

To get functional management to focus on profit and cost goals

To make "generalists" out of specialists

To remove attitude blocks and increase self-awareness

To deal with problems of conflicting goals and objectives

To teach individuals how to cope with advanced analytical tools

To familiarize managers with other operational areas and to foster teamwork

To demonstrate new management systems and controls

In general, the use of simulation provides the following advantages:

1. Simulation permits "cause" and "effect" to be felt. The user can appraise the effect of his actions immediately. It also excites participants so that they involve themselves, work more intently, and experience a more lasting effect.

---

[2] For a comprehensive discussion of the application of simulation to management development, refer to *Management Games: A New Technique for Executive Development,* by Joel M. Kibbee, Clifford J. Craft, and Burt Nanus. New York: Reinhold Publishing Corp., 1961.

2. Simulation poses a realistic situation rather than an academic one that may be full of exceptions. As such, it aids in judging what information is really important in making decisions and obtaining management control.

3. Simulation provides a good means of communication. It is something relatively easy to explain to superiors. In fact, it is also easier to talk about with managers (as well as with personnel at lower levels) as compared with, say, mathematical models. Simulation also provides some familiarization with electronic data processing.

4. Simulation provides a means for studying the transition of a particular phenomenon from one state to another. Such a transition can sometimes be studied analytically, but it is usually very difficult to do so.

Simulation, however, is not without its disadvantages. Some of the problems which the operations researcher should anticipate include the following:

1. The fact that simulations pique the interest of participants, and that they are easily talked about, may trap the user into thinking in terms of simulation instead of other, more useful, analytical tools. To a degree, simulation should be reserved only for those problems which are not amenable to the other methods of analysis. Also, there is some danger on the part of some people who are not completely familiar with simulation to expect too many answers from simulation.

2. Because gaming has a great deal of realism, it inspires its practitioners with remarkable confidence in its results. Sometimes an implausible result is accepted with special relish because of its implausibility. On the other hand, a fundamental weakness in current gaming lies in the inability of the player to draw strong inferences from the play of the game and to relate them to the making of decisions in the real-world situation that the game models.

3. Some simulations can get overly complex. It is said of a simulation used by one of the nation's leading graduate business schools that you have to go out into the real world in order to obtain sufficient experience to understand the model.

Operations Research and Electronic Data Processing

Operations research and electronic data processing are related to each other in three ways. First, operations research frequently utilizes selected data that has been accumulated, refined, and stored in the data processing system of information. Second, operations research depends more and more upon the high-speed capability of computers to process the large number of complex calculations required to convert raw data or unproven ideas into a refined and useful basis for decision-making. Third, electronic data processing frequently utilizes operations research methodology to design and develop new systems of information to be processed.

Computers are used in the formulation of problems and the creation of models that use such tools as linear programming, queueing theory, and simulation models. Once the preparation of a desired model is complete, the computer is called upon again—this time to manipulate the data in acordance with the model.

Until a few years ago, the use of certain operations research techniques was severely limited by the very substantial amount of time and skill required to apply them to some of the more complex management problems. With the advent of high-speed electronic computation, however, this serious limitation has been largely overcome. The speed of these machines now makes it possible to obtain solutions to very complex mathematical problems and to get the resulting information to management in time to be useful as a basis for administrative action.

An important feature of a computer is its low cost of computation. This permits the solution of problems that would ordinarily be too costly in terms of other forms of computation. Thus, electronic computers not only mean a release from mathematical drudgery, but they also make feasible the mathematical formulation of problems that up to now were dealt with in only a qualitative manner, or by only the most gross approximation to quantitative reasoning.

APPLICATIONS OF OPERATIONS RESEARCH

Requirements for Operations Research

At the present time, probably the two most important limiting factors in the application of operations research are: (1) the general lack of understanding by top management of the nature of its potential, and (2) the shortage of trained operations research personnel. Another limiting factor, which is related to the shortage of trained personnel, is the frequent need for an integrated team approach to large, complex, operational problems. It is certainly true that in many cases either the problem is not large enough, or the potential gain is too small to justify a team. Unfortunately, even for a really complex problem with a large potential payoff, it is often the case that there are just not enough trained specialists around to form a team. In such instances, however, this need not preclude an operations research approach to these problems. First of all, a committee of operating personnel is a practical alternative to a team of OR specialists—and it effectively extends the scope of an operations research specialist. More important, a single specialist, even without any assistance from such a committee, can often go a long way toward arriving at a practical solution to many problems.

Another fundamental requirement of operations research is adequate and reliable cost data. This is critical for two reasons. First of all, most problems are concerned with the realization of some objective, and this usually is a function of costs. Thus, one obviously needs to have the right kind of cost data to put into the mathematical model in order to obtain a solution to the problem.

A still more important reason why refined costs are important becomes apparent in any attempt to justify the use of operations research. Most of the areas of possible application of operations research techniques have been solved in the past, or are being solved at present, in what is sometimes surprisingly brute force fashion. The operations research specialist, on the other hand, is trying to persuade management to use better techniques, which presumably will result in lower costs or increased profits, and where the benefits and savings are quite often in the order of only a small percentage. If accurate cost figures are not available, or if the level of error approximates the expected improvement or saving, it will be very difficult to justify the operations research recommendations. In such a situation, a primary objective should be the collection of adequate and accurate cost data.

Even when accurate cost data are available, further refining is usually required. For example, it must be remembered that such cost data are usually allocated on the basis of a particular product mix, volume, and so forth. Therefore, if the operations research analysis involves a consideration of alternative product mixes or volumes, the original cost data must be modified accordingly. Very often this is difficult to do because of the many problems associated with obtaining the basic allocation data that are needed for such a redistribution of costs. This is one of the reasons why a cost accountant is frequently an essential member of an operations research team.

Administrative Planning and Control

The administration of any business is carried out by people who make a great number of day-to-day decisions. These range in scope from minor decisions to others that are very significant. The subject matter of these decisions is also quite varied, ranging from concerns such as assignment of effort, allocation of material and financial resources of the firm, personnel decisions, and choices of goods and services to be produced, to expansion or merger questions which affect the very structure of the firm itself. For the firm to survive and prosper there must be a method of relating these decisions to the welfare of the firm and to all other decisions. Although numerous techniques have been attempted from time to time, the most successful approach is to prepare a plan and then work according to that plan. Decisions, then, are made during the course of events in accordance with the predetermined plan. Since a plan is by nature a static entity in a dynamic environment of everyday activity, modifications will be required whenever the gap between the original plan and the most promising action

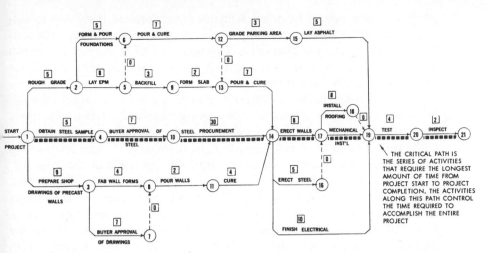

Fig. 15-2. Network for Erecting a Steel Structure

widens intolerably. Judgment is required in modifying the plan to distinguish between a reasonable revision that is required to accommodate a changed environment and a convenience revision that either compromises the objectives or allows the plan to drift due to insignificant fluctuations.

The development of a plan for use in the monitoring and control of a complex, dynamically changing program has been greatly facilitated by the development of time-scaled networking systems. (*See* Figure 15-2 for an actual example of a time-scaled network.) Names given to these systems include PERT (Program Evaluation and Review Technique), CPM (Critical Path Method), or simply Network Planning and Scheduling. Regardless of the name, however, each of these systems is based upon a visual presentation of activities, events, milestones, and their interrelationships plotted along a scale of time. Since time continues to pass, movement and progress along the chart should proceed from the past (left-hand side of the chart) to the future (right-hand side) at least as fast as predicted in the plan.

The network itself is an analytical device for planning a complex project by constructing an arrow diagram (network) made up of all the individual steps that must be taken to get to the end objective. The network also shows all of the interdependencies which exist between each individual task and all the other tasks that must be accomplished. In this manner, the network is a model and a master plan for the project that permits the manager to visualize the many facets as an integrated whole.

Once the network is defined, a calculating phase begins in which an electronic computer or manual methods may be used to sort the facts, to tell how long a project or other definable operation will take, and to calculate an earliest and latest calendar start date for each activity. The network is used to analyze alternative strategies and to evaluate their impact in terms of time and cost on the end objective—completion of the project on time and within cost targets.

Activities within the network relate to each other in a variety of ways, including dependency, restrictiveness, and concurrency. Obviously, there are trade-offs of time, skills, methods, and costs, which are possible because of the variety of these relationships. It is the optimizing of these relationship alternatives that can contribute to the profitable operation of the firm.

There are a number of significant benefits of networking. First, those activities that determine the length of time required to complete the project usually represent less than 10 per cent of all the tasks, but may require more than half the management effort that is expended during the life of the project. The positive identification of that series of strategic factors which comprise the critical path among all the activities can be of significant assistance to the manager in letting him know which, of all the problems to be solved, is the most deserving of his attention.

Second, network planning leads to a more critical analysis of the over-all project. This method of planning requires that each major task, regardless of its nature, be broken down into small enough increments so that a competent worker, as well as the manager, can visualize the task and make a realistic estimate of the time and cost to perform. Not only are more accurate estimates prepared, but pitfalls that otherwise would go unnoticed until too late can be identified and avoided.

Networks can be event oriented or activity oriented, or can be a combination of the two. Event orientation does not recognize the effort involved as a span of time, but instead locates an event which may be an act, such as "obtain approach," or merely the cessation of an act, such as "finish installing side panels." By contrast, the activity-oriented network focuses on the effort, such as "install side panels," and allows the activity to terminate when no more effort is needed to satisfy that activity.

Preparation of the network may begin with the first activity that is to be accomplished and proceed in a forward mode which permits a logical feel for the effort. Or the network may be prepared beginning with the last or ultimate activity, and regress step by step through the penultimate activity and so on backwards, until the network reflects the current state. The advantage of the last-first approach is that all activity tends to be more *objective* oriented or influenced and one incurs less risk of wandering astray into less efficient, unprofitable paths.

A network for erecting a steel structure is illustrated in Figure 15-2. It furnishes code numbers in the circles to assist in the identification of the named activities; time estimates are provided in the squares.

In summary, the networking approach, when properly used, provides management with advantages and benefits which include the following:

1. Provides an integrated "big picture" of the project
2. Forces a more logical approach to planning
3. Guards against omitting important jobs
4. Facilitates coordination between a prime contractor and his sub-contractors
5. Permits simulating the effect of changes and slippages
6. Simplifies replanning and rescheduling
7. Identifies who must be notified of schedule changes
8. Provides a means for project cost control
9. Provides a means for compressing schedules to meet deadlines and reduce total cost
10. Provides a means to estimate cash flow requirements

Linear Programming Application to Purchasing

A pharmaceutical manufacturer purchases an agricultural product from which two different products can be extracted for sale. This raw material comes in different varieties or species, depending on its source, and the amount of each product that can be extracted varies with the source. The following table shows the yield obtainable per pound of raw material for each of three major sources:

	source 1	source 2	source 3
Product A	0.10 lb.	0.08 lb.	0.07 lb.
Product B	0.06 lb.	0.07 lb.	0.05 lb.
Cost of raw material	$1.10/lb.	$1.00/lb.	$0.90/lb.
Maximum available (lbs/yr)	300,000	700,000	500,000

The processing of the material takes place in two steps. The first is essentially the preparation of a syrup. In the second step the two desired products are isolated. It is possible to isolate only product A, only product B, or both. The plant can handle up to 800,000 lbs. of raw material per year.

The processing costs for step 1 are: $0.100 per pound of raw material from Source 1 and Source 3, and $0.150 per pound of raw material from Source 2. The processing costs of step 2 are: $0.050 per pound of product A and $0.030 per pound of product B.

The products can be sold domestically as follows:

Product A—up to 10,000 lbs./year at $16.00/lb.
Product B—up to 30,000 lbs./year at $25.00/lb.

There is also a foreign market for product A at $4.50, up to 20,000 lbs./year. The company is contractually obliged to buy at least 100,000 lbs./year from Source 2.

Based upon these facts, the company wanted to know:

1. How much of each raw material should be contracted for?
2. How much of each product will be made, and in what market will it be sold?

This problem was formulated in terms of the linear programming model, and was solved using the Simplex Method. In summary, this problem involves eight restrictions, dealing with:

1. Availability of raw materials (one on each source)
2. Contractual purchase obligations (one)
3. Total plant capacity (one)
4. Market limitations (two for product A, one for B)

Also, there are a total of fifteen alternatives, dealing with:

1. Source of raw material (three alternatives)
2. Isolation of products (either A or B, or both)
3. Marketing of product A (domestic or export)

These may be tabulated as follows:

alternative	Source 1 raw material (RM1)	Source 2 raw material (RM2)	Source 3 raw material (RM3)
Make A only, sell domestically	1	6	11
Make A only, sell export	2	7	12
Make A + B, sell A domestically	3	8	13
Make A + B, sell A export	4	9	14
Make B only	5	10	15

The cost and profit calculations for each of these alternatives are:

RM1

Production system	1	2	3	4	5
Product A produced—lbs.	.10	.10	.10	.10	—
Product B produced—lbs.	—	—	.06	.06	.06
Sales return	1.60	.45	3.10	1.95	1.50
Raw materal cost—$	1.10	1.10	1.10	1.10	1.10
Processing cost—Step 1	.10	.10	.10	.10	.10
Processing cost—Step 2	.05	.05	.07	.07	.02
Total cost	1.25	1.25	1.27	1.27	1.22
Net profit	.35	−.80	1.83	.68	.28

RM2

Production system	6	7	8	9	10
Product A produced—lbs.	.08	.08	.08	.08	—
Product B produced—lbs.	—	—	.07	.07	.07
Sales return	1.28	.36	3.03	2.11	1.75
Raw material cost—$	1.00	1.00	1.00	1.00	1.00
Processing cost—Step 1	.15	.15	.15	.15	.15
Processing cost—Step 2	.04	.04	.06	.06	.02
Total cost	1.19	1.19	1.21	1.21	1.17
Net Profit	.09	−.83	1.82	.90	.58

	RM3				
Production system	11	12	13	14	15
Product A produced—lbs.	.07	.07	.07	.07	—
Product B produced—lbs.	—	—	.05	.05	.05
Sales return	1.12	.315	2.37	1.565	1.25
Raw material cost—$	.90	.90	.90	.90	.90
Processing cost—Step 1	.10	.10	.10	.10	.10
Processing cost—Step 2	.035	.035	.05	.05	.015
Total cost	1.035	1.035	1.05	1.05	1.015
Net Profit	.085	−.72	1.32	.515	.235

Note: All figures per pound of raw material charged.

The optimum solution is found to require the use of 428,600 lbs. of raw material from Source 2, and none from Source 1 or Source 3. This material is to be processed as follows:

pro-duction system	Level (lbs. of RM)	Production of A		Production of B	
		domestic sale	export sale	domestic sale	net profit
8	125,000 (RM2)	10,000 lbs.	—	8,750 llbs.	$227,500
9	250,000 (RM2)	—	20,000 lbs.	17,500 lbs.	225,000
10	53,600 (RM2)	—	—	3,750 lbs.	31,100
	428,600 lbs.	10,000 lbs.	20,000 lbs.	30,000 lbs.	$483,600

It should be noted that production system 3, which has the highest unit net profit ($1.83), does not appear in the solution. If it were used in place of production system 8, it would have to be used at a lower level, and the level of production system 10 would have to be increased, resulting in an over-all reduction of net profit, as follows:

pro-duction system	Level (lbs. of RM)	Production of A		Production of B	
		domestic sale	export sale	domestic sale	net profit
3	100,000 (RM1)	10,000 lbs.	—	6,000 lbs.	$183,000
9	250,000 (RM2)	—	20,000 lbs.	17,500 lbs.	225,000
10	92,900 (RM2)	—	—	6,500 lbs.	53,900
	442,900 lbs.	10,000 lbs.	20,000 lbs.	30,000 lbs.	$461,900

Similarly, the insertion of any of the other production systems will be found to reduce the total net profit.

Matrix Algebra Application to Information Processing

Suppose that there are two important types of information to be fitted into a sales catalogue program—the number of items to be contained on various catalogue pages and the estimated sales volume from each of these items. Call these types of information, I_1 and I_2 respectively. Also suppose that there are three reports circulated in the business, called R_1, R_2, and R_3.

Suppose that the firm has four administrators, M_1, M_2, M_3, and M_4. Information I_1 is contained in report R_2 only, information I_2 is in reports R_1 and R_3, but not in R_2. If administrator M_1 only receives R_2, administrator M_2 receives all three reports, and administrator M_3 receives reports R_1 and R_3, how can information that each of them receives be described, including duplications?

Define a table A that shows the information contained in each report by indicating with a "0" those reports not containing the given information, and by a "1" those reports containing the given information. Thus,

$$A = \begin{array}{c|ccc} & R_1 & R_2 & R_3 \\ \hline I_1 & 0 & 1 & 0 \\ I_2 & 1 & 0 & 1 \end{array}$$

Define a second table or matrix B that shows the reports received by each administration by indicating with a "0" those administrators not receiving a given report, and by a "1" those administrators receiving the given report, thus,

$$B = \begin{array}{c|cccc} & M_1 & M_2 & M_3 & M_4 \\ \hline R_1 & 0 & 1 & 1 & 0 \\ R_2 & 1 & 1 & 0 & 0 \\ R_3 & 0 & 1 & 1 & 1 \end{array}$$

To find the information received by each manager, we multiply the matrices A and B. This is done by multiplying each item of a row in A by each item in a column in B, adding the result and placing it in the resulting matrix at the intersection of the row and column multiplied.[3] Thus, letting C be the product matrix we have

$$C = AB = \begin{vmatrix} 0 & 1 & 0 \\ 1 & 0 & 1 \end{vmatrix} \begin{vmatrix} 0 & 1 & 1 & 0 \\ 1 & 1 & 0 & 0 \\ 0 & 1 & 1 & 1 \end{vmatrix} = \begin{vmatrix} 1 & 1 & 0 & 0 \\ 0 & 2 & 2 & 1 \end{vmatrix}$$

The interpretation of the result is seen when written with the appropriate row and column symbolism. Thus,

$$C = \begin{array}{c|cccc} & M_1 & M_2 & M_3 & M_4 \\ \hline I_1 & 1 & 1 & 0 & 0 \\ I_2 & 0 & 2 & 2 & 1 \end{array}$$

The matrix C says that administrators M_1 and M_2 receive information I_1, but M_3 and M_4 do not. Also M_1 does not receive information I_2, administrators M_2 and M_3 receive it from two sources, and M_4 receives information I_2 from one source.

---

[3] Matrix multiplication is performed as follows:

$$\begin{vmatrix} a & b & c \\ d & e & f \end{vmatrix} \times \begin{vmatrix} g & h & i & j \\ k & l & m & n \\ o & p & q & r \end{vmatrix} = \begin{vmatrix} (ag+bk+co) & (ah+bl+cp) & (ai+bm+cq) & (aj+bn+cr) \\ (dg+ek+fo) & (dh+el+fp) & (di+em+fq) & (dj+en+fr) \end{vmatrix}$$

The various reports and the needs of the administrators also can be classified according to time periods. In this way a logically consistent time sequence of information flow can be developed. The illustration indicates the formal procedure for determining:

1. Information received by administrators
2. Where duplication of information occurs
3. The sequence in which information is received
4. The way in which an information system may be designed to provide required information at the right place, at the right time, and with the greatest efficiency

Participative Forecasting

The forecasting function in business has evolved over the years into a specialized effort exhibiting a degree of sophistication which, while falling short of needs, is far superior to the absence of a forecasting function. As the techniques of forecasting have grown more complex—including operations research modeling and probability analysis—the forecasting function has grown more separate and specialized. Although this trend may produce forecasting information of greater reasonable accuracy, it has met increasing resistance or disregard.

This problem of resistance to "externally prepared" forecasting information is being resolved now by a fresh approach named "participative forecasting." Participation is an improvement over both the specialized function outside the mainstream of operations and its forerunner, where each administrator is responsible for his own forecasting. It is generally agreed that this latter approach to forecasting tends to produce a very parochial product, which in many cases is modified right out of recognition as it travels up the hierarchy to combine with the forecast of the total firm. Participative forecasting, on the other hand, involves those managers who are responsible for adhering to the forecasts that receive approval. This involvement results in both a better quality forecast and a willingness to press through obstacles to secure the realization of the forecast.

Participative forecasting can be used to forecast in any area of a firm's future—markets, products and processes, technological innovations, and future needs which are not yet apparent. By forecasting the future, which traditionally has seemed inevitable, a company discovers that there may be ways to alter or manipulate the future by intercepting anticipated conditions and influencing their occurrence.

The evolution of participative forecasting has been a logical extension from the single, incompletely informed forecaster, through the use of a committee which worked together to hammer out a common approach. The problem with a committee working face to face in forecasting is that information communicated among committee members is distorted by personality and status biases.

"...Therefore, you are asked to list below---all breakthroughs you believe are feasible within 50 years."

QUESTIONNAIRE II

a. ...List your judgement of the probability of implementation within each year.

Probability of Implementation During Period

	65-68	68-72	72-78	78-86	86-97	97-2013	Later	Not at anytime
Feasibility of chemical control over hereditary defects through molecular engineering								
Widespread socially accepted use of non-narcotic personality control drugs								

Note: Based upon the results from this second questionnaire, a statistical distribution can be formed by using as each forecaster's estimate of the year that the event, in his opinion, had a 50 percent chance of occurring.

QUESTIONNAIRE III

	Description of Potential Breakthrough	Consensus or dissensus to date	In your opinion, by what year does the probability of occurrence reach 50%	90%	If your 50% estimate falls within either the earlier or the later period indicated, briefly state your reason for this opinion
B1	Feasibility of chemical control over hereditary defects through molecular engineering	Consensus that it will occur; disagreement as to when			Why before 1987 or after 2013?
S8	Widespread socially accepted use of non-narcotic personality control drugs producing specific psychological reactions	Divergent opinions, possibly due to differing interpretations of the original question			Why before 1987 or after 2013, (or never)?

Note: Based upon this third round of questionnaires, a new distribution of estimates is prepared, and significant variations from this and the previous distribution are identified.

QUESTIONNAIRE IV

	Description of Potential Breakthrough	Majority Consensus to date	Minority Opinion	50%-year	90%-year
B1	Feasibility (not necessarily acceptance) of chemical control over some hereditary defects by modification of genes through molecular engineering	By 2000	Will take longer or occur never, because it would necessitate intervention during embryonic development, when the fetus is inaccessible, hence would require prior development of techniques of gestation in vitro		
S8	Widespread and socially widely accepted use of non-narcotic drugs (other than alcohol) for the purpose of producing specific changes in personality characteristics	By 2000	Will take 50 years or more, because research on psychopharmaceuticals has barely begun, and negative social reaction will cause delays		

Fig. 15-3. Example of an Application of Delphi Questionnaires in Long-range Technological Forecasting

FIRST-ROUND QUESTIONNAIRE

Series to be Forecasted	Your Forecast

SECOND-ROUND QUESTIONNAIRE

Series to be Forecasted	Your First-Round Forecast	Group Forecasts		Your New Forecast	Major Reasons Why You Feel Your Forecast Should Be Lower (or Higher) Than Those Forecasts Within the Interquartile Range If Your New Forecast Lies Outside the Interquartile Range
		Median	Interquartile Range		
Change in nonfarm business inventories		6.5	5.6 – 7.9		

THIRD-ROUND QUESTIONNAIRE

Forecasted	Forecast	Median	Interquartile Range	Major Reasons in the Opinion of D-Group Participants Whose Forecasts Are Lower (or Higher) Than Those Within the Interquartile Range, That Are Relevant and Useful in Making Forecasts of These Series	Your Opinion, for Each Reason You Find Unacceptable in Making Your Own Forecasts, as to Why It Is Unacceptable	Your New Forecast
Change in nonfarm business inventories		6.7	6.4 – 8.0	Reasons Given for Forecasts Lower Than Interquartile Range End of 1965 is going through period of liquidation due to stockpile buildup....		

FOURTH-ROUND QUESTIONNAIRE

Series to be Forecasted	Your Second Round Forecast	Group Forecasts		Summary of the Reasons Given by D-Group Members Whose Forecasts Were Lower (or Higher) Than Those Within the Interquartile Range, as Relevant and Useful in Making Forecasts of These Series	Summary of the Critiques of These Reasons Given by the D-Group Participants Who Found These Reasons to be Unacceptable in Making Their Own Forecasts	Your Final Forecast
		Median	Interquartile Range			
Change in nonfarm business inventories		7.0	6.8 – 7.5	Reasons Given for Forecasts Lower Than Interquartile Range End of 1965 is going through period of liquidation due to stockpile buildup....	Critiques of Reasons Given for Forecasts Lower Than Interquartile Range Liquidation should be over by First Quarter 1966 due to....	

Fig. 15-4. Example of the Use of Delphi Questionnaires in Short-range Forecasting for Corporate and Governmental Planning

Efforts made to eliminate this information distortion have resulted in, among others, a system called the Delphi process. This process retains the desirable features of receiving information input from various contributors and relying upon analytical tools to process the information while at the same time eliminating the detrimental effects of in-person group forecasting. The Delphi process requires complete anonymity of its contributor participants. This anonymity is accomplished by communicating through several rounds of very carefully worded questionnaires completed in private by each participant. (Examples of typical questionnaires used in the Delphi process are presented in Figures 15-3 and 15-4.)

The first round of Delphi questionnaires elicits ideas in a sort of brainstorming manner. The ideas contributed by individual participants are then related to other ideas being submitted and are subsequently recirculated to each of the participants. Judgment is brought into play by requiring participants who deviate radically from the central tendency of the group to explain and justify what may appear to be a deviant forecast but actually may be a well-chosen position. The explanations returned become the basis for successive refinements until the management of the firm believes that a detailed enough forecast has been achieved.

The Delphi process derives its strength from the multi-disciplinary input furnished by individuals representing diverse interests within the firm. Although experts from outside the organization can, and at times should, be engaged for forecasting in the Delphi group, in-house personnel have a more studied feel for future possibilities than is generally acknowledged. Tapping these resources certainly works to the best interests of the firm, and often the operations researcher can play a key role in introducing the Delphi process into an organization's forecasting.

PAYOFFS FROM OPERATIONS RESEARCH

There are three major areas in which operations research can provide payoffs. The first is advising management on which alternatives to a specific problem yield the best decisions or policies. For instance, specifying factory to warehouse shipping levels in a multi-plant warehouse operation would presumably yield an optimum freight bill. Second, operations research may develop methodologies for making various kinds of optimum decisions. An example of this would be a new method of sales forecasting. Finally, operations research may educate others in management to provide alternatives and to develop methods yielding the best decisions throughout a company.

Payoffs of the first kind—that is, specific decision-making in a given case—are usually measurable on a "before and after" basis. In the example given there would have been an actual or imputed freight to start with. The operations research solution would yield a new freight bill; the difference is the payoff. Such payoffs have been known to run from rather modest amounts to several hundreds of thousands of dollars a year. Also, the limitations of the payoff are generally well known in advance.

Payoffs of the second kind, the development of methodologies for making decisions, are very often measurable in similar terms. However, in many cases the methodologies themselves may be part of a larger system of studies, and may have only intangible results. Thus, the development of better forecasting methods extends its ramifications to all areas of a business, and the payoff, although clearly present, may not be easily determined. Similarly, development of methods for assisting in the making of broad strategic decisions will never be measurable on a "before and after" basis. One can only say that this probably would have happened if the study had not been undertaken. However, the payoffs are nonetheless real, and could make the difference between success and failure in the long run.

Similarly, the third kind of payoff, the education of others in management, is very much a matter of faith. Better equipped, we are in a better position to play; better trained, we are in a better position to win. In the long run, this payoff may exceed the other kinds by incalculable amounts, but we are in no position to put a capital value on it. Fortunately, it can be achieved concomitantly with problem solutions of both the above types, and, therefore, it is in an excellent position to pay its own way.

Conclusion

The foregoing sections have dealt with operations research by explaining the principal OR techniques that are available and by discussing several applications selected as examples. One point should be made clear: what has been presented here *does not cover all* of the useful techniques of the operations research field. Operations research methodology and its application are expanding rapidly, and it is reasonable to expect many significant new developments in the years ahead. For this reason it is wise for one to keep continually informed concerning progress in the state of the art for operations research. There is every reason to believe that, based upon progress since the Second World War, developments in the years ahead will be swift and substantial. It behooves the person in management or in staff support for management to keep his skills up to date and be prepared for whatever challenge may arise.

In trying to utilize operations research, one cannot overemphasize the creative imagination and ingenuity of the operations researcher himself, since he is the one who must exploit the possibilities that exist for profitable application of these important tools. Also, applications of operations research vary too widely to be defined once and for all. However, some of the key areas within the operation of a firm that provide opportunity for improvement through the application of operations research include:

1. Changes to the structure of the firm involving reorganization, merger, etc.
2. The production of new products or services
3. Changes to existing processes, such as building new production facilities, automating antiquated processes, or altering the state in which raw materials are received
4. Solution of problems posed by management or conflicts in management programs

In summary, then, the basic problem is the need to demonstrate to business executives and management researchers the possibilities of the new techniques of operations research. Long ago, alert industrial management became cognizant of the necessity for using the physical and mathematical sciences to solve practical problems. It is quite likely that the continued development of electronic data processing and automation will play a stimulating role in demonstrating to management the goals that can be reached by means of the more powerful tools and techniques of up-to-date scientific procedures, which might be referred to collectively as either operations research or modern management research.

16

Management Information Systems

PAUL R. SAUNDERS

American Airlines, Inc.
New York, N.Y.

PAUL R. SAUNDERS is director of management information systems for American Airlines. His primary responsibility is to develop and implement a corporate-wide total information system. This system will utilize the capability of the SABRE computers, American Airlines' commercial, large-scale, real-time data processing operation.

Mr. Saunders, a native of Nevada, graduated with a bachelor of science degree from the University of California, Los Angeles, and is currently writing his master's thesis at the City University of New York. He holds the DPMA Certificate in Data Processing. In addition to being a lecturer in systems analysis at the Management Institute of New York University, Mr. Saunders is a member of the editorial review board of the Systems and Procedures Journal, *and is active in the Systems and Procedures Association.*

Mr. Saunders, with more than twenty years' experience in systems and data processing, has done considerable public speaking and has published several articles relating to the field. Prior to joining American Airlines he was employed in various management positions for the Standard Oil Company of California, Colgate-Palmolive, and Continental Can Company, and also worked as a management consultant.

INTRODUCTION

Have you heard an executive complain that he is snowed under with paper work and reports, or read a recent article declaring that companies run on a sea of paper? These reports and paper work are part of "management information." Although the manager or executive may complain about the number of reports he sees, plus the meetings he attends or holds to obtain information, what would he say if he received no reports and no information? Can you imagine the initial reaction of relief when the IN basket is at last empty? Then the slow realization would come: "Without any information, how will I know what is going on? How can I plan, make operating decisions, and control my responsibilities and functions?"

Information is the major tool by which the management process is accomplished. The management process can be illustrated:

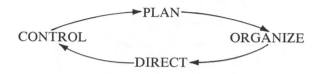

PLAN   Determine what to do and how it is to be done, establishing policy.

ORGANIZE   Obtain the necessary facilities, equipment, personnel, and material.

DIRECT   Set the time and cost framework for what is to be done; make operating decisions.

CONTROL   Measure performance against plan and take necessary action.

It is therefore apparent that management needs information to do its job. But a question may be raised at this point: "What is management?" The answer, in relation to informational needs, is: "Anyone who plans, decides, or exercises control in some area." This definition tends to include as part of management almost everyone in an organization, except perhaps the production-line worker and clerical employee. Is, then, all the data that flows through an organization management information? Yes, in one form or another.

The answers given to customers over the phone in regard to complaints about delivery dates is not management information, but the *number* of such calls *is* of definite concern to management. Similarly, an individual accounts payable voucher or check is not management information, but the sum of monies due on any one day *is*. The daily details that go into running a business, such as orders (sales), inventory changes, invoices, purchase orders, and accounts receivables, contain the data elements that build into information for management. This building of information starts at the lowest level, goes through producing levels, and eventually culminates in a top corporate report—often a single-page profit or loss statement. This can be illustrated as a pyramid, as shown in Figure 16-1.

Reports for the next higher level of management are not always the simple summaries of data contained in lower management level reports. New factors or information may be added or interpretation of data may be made, such as comparisons with other companies or industry. Top management will probably want to compare the company's relative sales growth with that of other companies in the same industry, while sales managers are more interested in comparative sales by salesman and sales territories.

We can define management information systems (MIS) as the total

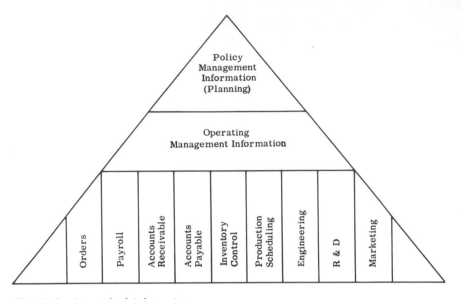

Fig. 16-1. Pyramid of Information

process by which raw rata is collected, summarized, or processed and reported—with the emphasis on the ultimate reporting to management. It should be noted that no mention of EDP or computers has been made in this definition of MIS.

Management information may be a simple manual process, or may involve the use of off-line or real-time computers or combinations of several systems and methods. In an MIS, we are primarily concerned with *information* rather than the method used to collect, accumulate, or interpret the data. The following explanations may help to clarify the point:

Data vs. information. The terms "data processing" and "information processing" are not interchangeable. Not all data is information, and information to one manager may be simply "data" to another. Data exist in a management information system, but the objective of such a system is to produce data which have meaning and usefulness, i.e., "information" for decision-making.

Information management vs. management information. Most commercial systems in use, and most of those still being designed, are concerned with the *managing* of information or the achievement of more economical methods of collecting, transporting, processing, and displaying information. Much of the information being generated by today's automated systems is valueless for decision-making.

Policy vs. operational decisions. The information requirements of executive management are different from those of middle managers, who are required to make the more immediate operational decisions. However, a management information system can be designed to serve either or both of these needs.

Decision-making vs. decision-supporting. Computers make management decisions only under restricted circumstances and, even then, only in relation to a highly routine process. Computers can and do perform decisions by observing prescribed threshold limits in instances such as the rating of applications of bank and department store customers for credit. But when introduced into a policy-level decision-making environment, the role of the computer is that of providing relevant information to support a higher, managerial level decision-making process.

In summary, a management information system is an organized method of providing each manager with all the data, *and only that data* which he needs to make decisions at the time he needs it, and in a form that aids his understanding and stimulates his action.

WHAT A MANAGEMENT INFORMATION SYSTEM DOES

Understanding the management process and the nature of management information, we now turn to what a management information system provides to the user. Such a system:

1. Considers the full effect of a decision in advance by supplying complete, accurate, and timely data for use in the planning and decision-making processes.
2. Eliminates from the planning and decision-making processes the problems associated with the use of inconsistent and incomplete data by providing a means for preparing and presenting information in a uniform manner.
3. Uses common data and methods in the preparation of long-range and short-term plans.
4. Identifies, organizes, and measures significant past relationships to forecast future relationships through the use of specialized or sophisticated mathematical techniques in analyzing data.
5. Merges financial, production, and marketing data to produce significant measures of performance in order to facilitate the controlling of present costs and the making of planning decisions with the minimum processing of data.
6. Meets the needs of each organizational unit with a minimum of duplication while at the same time serving the organization as a whole.
7. Reduces the time and volume of information required to make decisions by reporting to each level of management only the necessary degrees of detail, and usually only the exceptions from the standard or norm.
8. Uses personnel and data processing equipment effectively so that the optimum in speed and accuracy is achieved at the lowest cost.
9. Presents the data to those responsible for the decision-making and planning in a form that minimizes the time or effort needed for analysis and interpretation.

The concept of an MIS is one that is equally valid whether the company is small or large, or whether the data is obtained and processed through the most simple manual means or through the most sophisticated electronic devices. To design an MIS management must select at each level of control only required data. The data must be presented in a manner that facilitates understanding and action, and that provides a means for measuring the effectiveness of the action that has been and is being taken.

NEED FOR MANAGEMENT INFORMATION SYSTEM

Many companies have extensive (and expensive) data processing operations and are proud of their leadership in installing the latest EDP equipment. However, having the most current computer model does not guarantee that management is supplied with the information it needs. Despite the use of sophisticated equipment, there are frequently certain symptoms or indications of information deficiencies in a company. Some of these symptoms may arise from sheer poor management, even with an adequate MIS. Many managers simply do not realize that the information on which they are basing their most routine decisions may be dangerously inadequate or misleading, and that their information system is not geared to the current needs of the company. The major indications and symptoms of an inadequate MIS are:

A. *Operational indications*
   1. Large physical inventory adjustments
   2. Capital expenditure overruns
   3. Inability of executives to explain changes from year to year in operating results
   4. Unexplainable cost variances or inadequate cost information
   5. Unawareness of order backlogs
   6. Lack of communications among management personnel
   7. Insufficient knowledge about competition

B. *Psychological symptoms*
   1. Surprise at financial results
   2. Poor attitude of executives about usefulness of information
   3. Lack of understanding of financial information by executives
   4. Lack of concern for environmental changes

C. *Report content signs*
   1. Excessive use of tabulations of figures or details
   2. Multiple preparation and distribution of identical data
   3. Conflicting information generated from different sources
   4. Lack of periodic comparative information and trends or standards for comparison
   5. Lateness of information
   6. Inaccurate information
   7. Inadequate externally generated information

The symptoms of information deficiencies are the same both in growing and mature companies, whether large or small, and regardless of the state of EDP development within the company.

The logical question now is: "How does one develop an MIS to correct these information deficiencies?" Before ordering a new computer or hiring more clerks to prepare additional reports, a review should be made of the kinds of information needed at the respective managerial level.

Management reporting systems should provide four main types of reports:

1. Monitoring reports
2. Triggered reports
3. Demand reports
4. Planning reports

Monitoring Reports

Monitoring reports, or performance reports, are similar to the periodic reports currently being prepared for management. Such reports usually include end-of-month sales reports, expense reports, project progress reports, etc. These reports normally cover the complete performance for the activity being reported upon, and for the time period indicated.

Monitoring reports can be produced on a periodic scheduled basis, and/or on demand. They generally show both actual figures and plan figures, for both period-to-date and year-to-date. It is probable that significant differences between actual and plan would be highlighted.

In short, monitoring reports provide an overview of the whole performance of the activity being reported upon. If more detail is required to determine or explain differences between actual and plan, the feature of demand reports is brought into play.

Triggered Reports

Triggered reports are used for control purposes, and signal that a decision and/or action is needed. They require the existence of a well-defined plan or standard against which actual performance may be measured, and an allowed deviation from the standard. Only if the deviation exceeds this allowed variation should a report be prepared. If the operation stays within the prescribed limits during the time period, a triggered report is not necessary.

Triggered reports thus become a form of "exception" reports, produced only when an out-of-control condition is detected. The term "triggered reports" is used instead of "exception reports" because it implies that an alarm is sounded as a result of certain conditions. Such reports have been successful in making more effective use of EDP for management purposes by reducing the volume of data that the manager must peruse.

These exception reports cover such operations as production schedule control, efficiency control, quality control, inventory control, and machine down-time control.

Demand Reports

Demand reports make use of the on-line query and reponse feature of the future reporting systems, to allow manager(s) to systematically probe for more detail when analyzing a problem. Also, demand reports require the use of a content retrieval feature in the design of the data file.

These reports can be used for probing into the cause of deviations between actual and plan as highlighted in the monitoring reports. They are also used to probe into the causes of triggered reports. In short, they replace the detailed reports that currently back up the summary reports presented to management.

But demand reports should go far beyond these uses. They should be used (1) for probing into situations that may never be brought to light by the company's monitoring and triggered reports, but rather are brought to light less formally, and (2) in the planning function for uncovering challenges and opportunities facing the company. Examples of demand reports are capital equipment replacement analyses, costs per sales calls, machine utilization analysis, number of orders due for shipment but not shipped, and a variety of other reports.

Planning Reports

Variance reports and triggered reports require the existence of a standard or plan in order for the variance or exception to be reported. The function of planning is difficult to do since it is almost impossible to predict when certain time periods or events will occur, and unforeseen conditions may invalidate a set of plans. However, MIS can provide a real service because it can aid in formulating plans quickly and (hopefully) accurately.

One important element of planning is "exploding" proposed actions. For example, if management sets a goal for the forthcoming year of increasing sales by 10 per cent, more salesmen and more advertising may be required. Based on past experience (as indicated in historical records), "bills of resources" and lists of activities can be developed for supporting such action. When salesmen are needed, additional sales managers are often required (plus secretaries, office space, supplies, telephones, travel expenses, etc.). These resources must be developed in some logical sequence —the salesmen must be hired before they can be trained, for instance. Thus, bills of resources and lists of activities can gradually be developed from historical data and modified in the light of current knowledge.

Another important element of planning is simulating a schedule in order to develop realistic schedules and select the best among them. The planning function should provide the ability to test hypotheses—"what will happen if . . . ?" Computers have proved useful for simulation. (This should be a basic part of a future planning system.) Also desirable is the ability to develop PERT networks for projects. The planning function includes the ability to allocate resources within constraints. As plans are laid out, the utilization of the various resources are summed for each time period, to assure that none are over-committed.

The planning function should provide for maintaining a list of business opportunities, with weighted values assigned to each opportunity. The weights are usually set by management during opportunity review meetings. The system could provide for tracking the progress of investigating these opportunities.

With the types of reports listed above, produced on a more timely basis, management should be able to plan and control operations more effectively.

Report Timing

In present-day reporting systems, monthly reports are often not available to management until about fifteen days after the end of the month. Something could have happened during the first days of the month covered by the report, yet management may not know about it until almost forty-five days later. Even worse, if corrective action is taken, management will not know the effects of that action until thirty more days at the earliest, and more likely sixty more days. Therefore, it can be anywhere from seventy-five days to 105 days after something important has occurred before management has some feedback as to whether the corrective action was effective or not.

True, most organizations (including some of the largest corporations) have been operating (and many of them successfully) under these reporting conditions. But the situation is not by choice; it is often tolerated because of the limitations of the data processing tools in use. With the new tools available, more managements are taking steps to improve the timeliness of their reports.

Even if the data files of a fast response reporting system are updated daily, it is possible to improve the report timing system. For example, the files reflect the daily cumulative results of the business as of the prior business day, but management need not be flooded with reports. The information may stay in the system until the executives ask for it. Thus, if an executive has reason to ask: "How are sales so far this month?", he can obtain the information in a few moments' time. And if he sees a significant difference between actual and plan figures, he can interrogate the data file and trace the cause to a specific activity or condition. Nevertheless, a system can be set up to provide certain monitoring reports on a scheduled basis, such as the first of each month.

Where scheduled reports are desired, the user is faced with the decision of determining their frequency or period to be covered. An obvious ground rule is that a scheduled report should not be produced until there has been adequate time to act on the previous report. There is no purpose in acting on a suspended report. Daily reports tend to exhibit this characteristic: the executive is unable to completely analyze and act on each day's report before he receives the next one.

As an effective MIS is developed, executives are likely to make more use of the "on demand," in order to produce reports when desired and in the format desired rather than examine scheduled reports.

DEVELOPMENT OF A MANAGEMENT INFORMATION SYSTEM

Once the nature of an MIS has been defined and the company's needs in such a system have been outlined, the next step is to develop the system itself. However, there are often two factors present that complicate the development of a new management information system. The first factor is that a company is a going concern, and operations or business cannot be stopped while the new system is being developed and installed. The second factor is the general necessity for a computer to process the data.

In all probability, the company developing the MIS already has one or more computers. This necessitates long-range planning and coordination between the MIS group and the data processing personnel for proper computer selection and application. Frequently, an MIS program may point out that the present computer is not being fully utilized for profitable applications. This condition could create an organizational difficulty between those developing the management information system and the data processing group. These two factors, the going concern condition and current commitments for computers, relate mostly to the installation of an MIS.

The first step in developing an MIS is the same as the management process outlined earlier: Planning. For any systems project a plan must be developed and approved before work is undertaken. An MIS project plan might look like this:

Objective:

To develop an integrated management information system for the entire company.

Steps:

1. Organize a study team comprised of representatives from all major activities of the company. Most full-time members of the team should be experienced systems personnel from the corporate systems department (or management information systems division). Assign responsibilities and establish preliminary target dates for completion of each phase.

2. Review and document all present reporting systems and reports throughout the company. (It may not be necessary to detail each step of the data processing systems.)

3. Interview all levels of management concerning their information needs, in light both of the present reporting system and future requirements.

4. Develop recommendations for immediate improvements as they are recognized. After approval by management, schedule and oversee installation of these immediate improvements.

5. Design a new management information system as required and prepare a written proposal to management for approval. Include a schedule for installation, operating costs (and savings considerations), implementation costs, and personnel and data processing equipment requirements.

6. After appropriate approvals, install the new system.

This is a very general project plan and some elaboration on the element of time and responsibility involved is warranted in order to achieve success.

Time and Responsibility

The lengthy and far-reaching nature of a long-range information-handling system study requires that each step be carefully planned, responsibilities be assigned, and a schedule be developed for its accomplishment. These requirements become particularly critical when a multiplicity of functions is involved.

As in any major program, it is preferable that *responsibility* be vested with a single person. In this manner, the necessary coordination between functions and the resolution of different points of view can be achieved. Because all functions of a going organization are involved, this individual should be in a staff position, reporting no more than one step down from the operating head of the organization. In any case, it must be recognized that the responsibility requires the full time of one who knows the techniques of information systems design and analysis and who is capable of grasping new and advanced systems concepts.

Depending on the size of the operation, the program may require additional staff specialists. All functional departments will necessarily be part-time participants in the study, but in no case should additional functional personnel be required to carry out the program.

One of the first assignments of the director of the MIS program is to schedule time and responsibility. While he can do this in several ways, he must make perfectly clear who is going to do what and when. In scheduling responsibility, it is not unusual to find that an adequate amount of time has not been allowed for the transition planning (that is, for planning the moves from the present system to the new one).

If realistic budgets are not already available, the financial planning activity of the business during this first period must develop budgets that can be used to evaluate economically the cost of the new system, as well as possible transitional systems. Such a budget is necessary if the pay-as-you-go results are to be measured. These budgets must be structed to measure the resultant effect of the revised system design and the accompanying plans and schedules on the long-range financial objectives of the company.

Assuming that the manpower necessary to make the MIS study is available and the project team organized, the next step is the analysis of the present system. In a company of any size this review can be a staggering task, and care should be taken that the review or analysis is on a uniform basis and completed according to a schedule.

ANALYSIS OF PRESENT SYSTEM

The financial goals of nearly every business ordinarily call for year-by-year improvement in profitability. Therefore, any improvement program for a long-range information-handling system should be self-supporting. For this and other reasons, an important part of any long-range program is an analysis of the existing information-handling system to reveal improvements that can be made with little effort and expense. These are improvements from which savings can be realized quickly and in sufficient volume to make a start toward creating a self-supporting information system. Further, such analysis will provide the kind of information needed to plan the transition from the "old" to the "new" system, as well as provide an invaluable check list of system requirements.

Many techniques and methods for making systems analyses have been published or have gained wide acceptance. The persons analyzing the present information system in a company should be acquainted with the more practical and productive techniques in use.

Multi-dimensional Flow

One way of organizing facts is to trace the routing of information from origin to destination, and to arrange this routing in chronological sequence, showing how the information progresses through the organization. Delineation of information routing through an organization permits an objective study of all the steps.

To the flow-diagraming technique, the factors of *frequency, volume, time, cost,* and *physical distance* for each step are added. Since each of these factors is important in any plan considered for mechanization (or for other improvements), depicting them on the flow chart for each routing step aids in the objective analysis.

Input-output Data

An information input-output chart is a visual portrayal of the source information that is fed into a system and the output information that results. Each type of input or source data is listed along the left side, and each type of output document is listed across the top (*see* Figure 16-2).

A relationship of information input to information output can then be established by locating a dot at the point of intersection. For example, to produce shipping papers you need the information designated by the dot under customer order number, company order number, traffic routing, and

BEFORE ANALYSIS — OUTPUT DATA

INPUT & SUPPORTING DATA

	Invoices	Shipping papers	Shipping labels	Quantity shipped	Back orders	Replenishment orders	Net price	Shipping terms	Shipping register	Stock ledgers	Stock bulletin	Stock report	Billing & cost dist.	Price realization	Tax reports	Royalty reports	Face sheets	Unfilled orders ($)	Orders entered ($)	Statistical analysis
Customer orders																				
Order number		•	•			•														
Quantity ordered				•	•				•									•	•	•
Item ident.		•		•					•									•	•	•
List price						•												•	•	•
Company ord. no.	•	•	•		•		•	•												
Customer reg. record																				
Pricing policy (Dis.)	•						•	•										•	•	•
Traffic routing		•						•												
Tax data	•																			
Quantity shipped		•																		•
Net price	•																			•
Invent. cost at stand.										•	•	•								•
Stock replen. proc.					•	•			•											•
Receipts					•	•			•											
Invoices										•	•	•	•	•	•				•	•
Shipping papers	•		•				•	•												
Stock ledgers			•	•						•	•	•								
Price & cost refer.													•	•						
Peg board forms													•	•	•	•				
Royalty ident. codes																•				

AFTER ANALYSIS — OUTPUT DATA

INPUT & SUPPORTING DATA

	Invoices	Shipping papers	Shipping labels	Quantity shipped	Back orders	Replenishment orders	Net price	Shipping terms	Shipping register	Stock ledgers	Stock bulletin	Stock report	Billing & cost dist.	Price realization	Tax reports	Royalty reports	Face sheets	Unfilled orders ($)	Orders entered ($)	Statistical analysis
Customer order no.	•	•	•						•											
Cust. ident. no.	•	•	•		•		•	•	•					•				•	•	•
Item ident. no.	•	•		•	•	•	•	•		•	•	•	•	•	•	•	•	•	•	•
Quantity ordered	•	•		•	•	•				•	•	•	•	•	•	•	•	•	•	•
Receipts	•	•		•	•	•				•	•	•	•	•	•	•	•	•	•	•

Fig. 16-2. Input-output Chart (Customer Order Processing)

quantity shipped. Most of the information required for an information input-output chart can be taken directly from the multi-dimensional information flow chart, which shows the types of data used and generated in chronological sequence.

The information input-output chart brings this flow information together in terms of relationship without regard to time sequence. Analysis of such a chart often reveals some remarkable relationships. For example, by careful study of the information input and supporting data and the resulting output documents in the "before analysis," we can see that several items of output appear also as input.

For instance, take the shipping papers example: once the shipping papers have been produced, you will note that this becomes input data that can be subsequently used (as the dots point out) to produce invoices and shipping labels as well as to update the shipping register and the stock ledger. This indicates the rehandling and reprocessing of the same or similar data to produce the required output document. Obviously, some improvements could be achieved by redesigning the forms on an over-all systems basis. Permanent customer and product information could be listed on single source documents for easy transcription or reference.

A study of the same data, toward its possible application on electronic data processing equipment, may reveal additional possibilities for improvement. The customer and inventory information can be stored in a computer and may be recalled or processed as needed through the use of simple identification codes. Automatic typing of invoices, shipping papers, and shipping labels may be incorporated in the program. Inventories can be automatically updated; and, when necessary, back orders and replenishment orders are issued, providing a form of mechanized inventory control. Accounting and statistical reports can be mechanically produced from information output in the form of tabulating cards, paper tape, or magnetic tape. Such reports may be currently produced by handling great stacks of paper manually in order to obtain the needed information.

The second part of Figure 16-2 illustrates how this information input and output might appear after a complete input-output analysis. It is obvious that the input items have been reduced.

Short-range Improvements

The ability of a thorough systems analysis to contribute to immediate and short-range improvements is the heart of the pay-as-you-go concept of the program. During analysis of the existing system, factual information is being gathered and digested; good ideas are being sifted out and tentative improvements identified. Many of these are the kind that can be put into effect immediately without changing the long-range objectives. These improvements are made possible through the elimination or combination of steps, the alteration of the sequence of operations, the reduction of delay time, and other simplifications. Often these changes can be made without appreciably disturbing normal activities. Most systems analyses to date have demonstrated the ability to:

1. Produce immediate savings in excess of the cost of the program.
2. Contribute markedly to improve information-handling productivity *today*.

3. Provide step-by-step accomplishments toward the longer-range objectives.

4. Develop the knowledge and skill essential to an eventual integration of systems.

Care must be taken, however, to insure that these improvements are fully compatible with long-range objectives; otherwise they become false economies and impediments. Following are some very elementary examples of waste that a multi-dimensional information-flow analysis may point out:

1. A large proportion of elapsed time for the information-handling system is nonproductive delay time, due to losses in transporting the information between processing steps, and waiting for the processing to take place.

2. Physical relocation, job reassignment, elimination of nonproductive operations, and proper scheduling can frequently materially reduce this difference between productive and total elapsed time.

Some systems produce information that is not directly used to result in a product, insofar as total contribution to the process is concerned. Of course, this *may* generate necessary management information. However, showing these operations on the information flow chart together with their cost to produce will reveal that they represent a significant amount of the total cost. Duplication and overlap may also be noted.

The information flow chart is very effective in pointing out opportunities for doing work at the earliest stage of the system cycle, thereby reducing later work and preventing duplication. Once information has been supplied, it should be reduced to a form that will not require rework for use in later operations. For example, a field sales office should furnish all required customer, salesman, product, and billing information at the time of order entry. This would eliminate the need of turning to accounting or sales records for such data.

Consideration should be given to the end result of each step and how this might be achieved with less detail, time, and expense. For example, an information flow chart may show daily keypunching of sales orders to provide input data for a monthly orders-entered report. Since a high percentage of these orders will have a very short delivery time, many of them would also be reported as sales billings in the same month. In such a case, it is feasible to report an order as bookings at the same time it is reported as billings with no adverse effect on the resulting operations.

Subsystem Changes

Up to this point we have examined the individual steps of the existing system. Short-range improvements may be made by studying the existing system in somewhat broader scope. This involves a definition of the functional purpose of a discrete portion of the system, and an identification of the input available for it and the output required from it. A portion of the system identified and defined in this manner is termed a subsystem. For example, customer order processing and production control are major components or subsystems, of the total system.

Major subsystems may be referred to as building blocks used to make a total system. The building block concept—which requires that each subsystem be compatible with others in the totally integrated system—demands attention to the form and the content of information input and ouput data. Fitting each building block into the total system without overlap and duplication is a difficult task and requires care and skill.

To insure the proper compatibility between the system and the subsystem, the following two items should be considered:

1. The contribution of the subsystem to the total system must be examined. The information output data being generated in a subsystem can often be tailored to fit directly as information input to related subsystems. For example, the output of a production control system can be the input to a payroll system via the punched card used to record parts as they are completed and adding the worker's identification number.

2. Since one of the design objectives is to eliminate unnecessary records and reports, each element of information output should be scrutinized in terms of its specific contribution to subsequent steps.

The size and capabilities of the computer also exert an economic influence on the size of the system and its components. The computer's speed, its ability to get information in and out, and the cost of storage influence the size and complexity of the subsystem design and, therefore, of the overall system itself.

DETERMINING MANAGEMENT'S NEED

At this stage in the MIS project, the present system has been reviewed and documented. The recommendations to improve the present system in the short run will probably also have been made. The next step of the plan calls for interviewing managers to determine their information needs. It should be noted that the review of the present system can go on concurrently in several departments. However, the review and analysis of each department's reporting system should be completed prior to starting to interview the department's manager. In this manner the analyst knows what is currently available before asking the manager what he would like in the way of information.

It is difficult to describe the one best technique in determining a manager's information needs since the personality of the manager is also involved. Some executives are able to describe quite clearly what they want and why; others may not even want to talk with the interviewer. It is often necessary for the systems analyst to recommend reports and report formats in the preliminary design stage before a reaction can be obtained from the executive. Since this is part of the design phase, it cannot be accomplished at the interviewing stage. An attempt should be made, however, to discuss information concepts and needs with each department manager. Every report prepared for an executive should be discussed to determine: (1) does he use it; (2) what are its good and bad points; and (3) how receptive is the manager to a change in frequency, timeliness, content, or format. In the absence of a good interview it may be necessary for the systems analyst to define the function of the manager independently and then to synthesize the informational requirements for that position.

The basic purpose of interviewing the department management is to determine the type of output data required from the new system. In most cases, the information desired is a summary or comparison of detail operating data for the operation of the department or company, i.e. orders, invoices, inventory levels, etc. It is not possible at this stage to discuss with the executive detailed reports and detailed report formats of information he believes he desires. Proposed reports are developed during the design phase of the project and discussed with the executive for revision or acceptance. A second purpose of the interviews with management is to establish a good rapport with them. The review of what they currently receive in the way of information and what they think they should have presents a golden opportunity to discuss the entire MIS project and, accordingly, gain their support.

PRESENTING THE TOTAL PICTURE

As the analysis of each department's present reporting system and the management interviews proceeds, the over-all informational requirements should start to emerge. The problem at this point is to be able to understand the interrelationship of all the reporting system. One way to present the total picture is to list the major inputs, processing systems, and outputs as in Figure 16-3.

This is similar to the input-output chart illustrated earlier. The difference is that systems or subsystems are shown, rather than detail information on forms or reports. If required reports or information are shown on the output side, regardless of whether or not they are currently being produced, such a chart can point out the areas neglected in the present reporting systems. Once information output requirements are determined, attention should be concentrated on information input requirements. The objective here is twofold: to keep information inputs to a minimum, and to devise ways of generating these inputs in elemental forms most convenient for direct processing into as many of the required output documents as possible.

Another way to look at the over-all picture is to draw a general flow chart of all inputs, processing systems, and outputs. If this is done, only the major elements should be shown; otherwise the flow chart would become so huge as to be unmanageable. The objective of presenting the entire information flow in total is to be able to spot duplication and to aid in conceiving what the new system should include.

INPUT		PROCESSING SYSTEMS OUTPUT					OUTPUT
Form code	Basic forms used to originate system	Form codes affecting system			Various manual and EDP data processing systems		Major reports to management (present and desired)
A	Time card	C	B	A	Payroll		Personnel reports
B	Overtime slip			D	Order writing		Weekly sales report
C	Payroll change		D	E	Invoicing		Monthly sales report
D	Order			E	Sales analysis		Salesman report
E	Invoice		D	E	Inventory control		Overtime report
F	Inventory receipt			E	Accounts receivable		Past due A/R
G	Packing slip			D	Order analysis		
H	Cash receipt			C	Employee insurance		
	etc.					etc.	etc.

Fig. 16-3. Chart Showing Major Inputs, Processing Systems, and Outputs—Total Picture

DESIGN OF THE NEW SYSTEM

The present reporting systems, data collection procedures, processing systems, and reports of the entire company have all been analyzed. Information needs of all departments over and above the present reports have been determined. Short-range benefits have been obtained, or are in the process of being obtained. The next step is a proposal to management to design and install a new system. What should the new system look like? What will it cost? How long will it take to develop and install? Who will do it? What assurance will management have that the project will be successful? What organizational changes will the new system demand? The MIS project team must make its recommendations, in written form, as to what it believes should be done. The objective of the new information system must be clearly spelled out in accordance with the original project plan. The project team's proposal should answer management's questions concerning the work to be done, especially as to costs, benefits, and installation schedules.

What should the proposal say about the form the new system will take? It may not be possible at this stage to describe exactly what the new system will be like. Enough developmental design work must be completed, however, in order to satisfy management that the MIS proposal is valid. The proposal might include developing the following:

A corporate data file (or data bank)

Generalized computer routines for data retrieval

Output display and audio units

Time-shared computers

Better input methods

Improved reporting system structure

A CORPORATE DATA FILE

The success of any business is based on making sound and timely decisions based on accurate and current information. The corporate data file is one way to provide management with such information in that it represents a paper image of the business operation. If this image can be kept accurate, current, and easily accessible, it will be invaluable in making business decisions. The total information about a business could be pictured as a collection of containers or buckets, each containing information. A management information system would be represented by extracts of information from this collection of containers, properly organized and presented so as to show what is occurring at some point in the business.

The importance of collecting this detail, in volume, cannot be over-emphasized. Without it, problem areas cannot be pinpointed; therefore, it is essential to have a large amount of current and historical detail available to serve information needs properly. However, without the mass data storage capability of a computer-based system, this would be impractical. Therefore, the corporate data file (data bank) concept appears to be the most realistic way of accomplishing the task.

The data bank concept encompasses a central bank or file containing information about a business in a readily accessible form. Some specific points about a data bank serve to clarify the concept.

Informational Rather Than Functional Orientation

Most business organizations today use information that is functionally oriented. Functional concepts have been designed into systems, functional report requirements have been programmed into outputs, functional data have been incorporated into files, and any single file is unique to a functional organization and is not available (even for general information purposes) to other functions. The data bank system, in contrast, is concerned with total information rather than just data. It represents a total package of information, the pieces and parts of which are updated by various functional organizations. Any organization, at any time, is allowed to use any portion of the information base as desired. This use may be functionally oriented, but the pool of information serves over-all needs.

Single Record or Source of Information

All sorts of terms are in common use for the concept of a "record." In this discussion, the term "record" will be used to mean a selected group of fields of data, usually applying to some specific area—a customer, a shipment, a flight segment, an aircraft, or a part.

The idea of a data bank is founded on a single record concept. For example, in the case of personnel, there is a single record about an employee containing all necessary information about that employee (such as name, home address, employee number, date of birth, sex, marital status, payroll and department codes, skills, experience, and position). Contrast this with a typical situation of four different personnel files, maintained by four different functional units, all of which assumed they were keeping similar accurate data. It is not important how big or how long a record may be, or how many pieces of data are contained in this record—there is still basically only one record maintained within the entire system for any particular unit of information for reference purposes.

Information Storage Relative to Output

The storage level of information contained in a particular record is controlled by the output requirements from the system. In other words, if summary data is required on the output side, then this same summary information will be contained in the data bank record. This concept does not imply that summaries of individual records are not possible. It simply says that a summary or extension of information within any one record has already been made and is contained within the basic file, thus minimizing extracting and printing problems. If detail records are required, these will be maintained. The implication that storage requirements will be greatly increased is false, especially considering the typical ratio of four old files to one new file, as noted above.

Transaction—The Key to Input

Various input transactions represent the heart of a data bank system. All such transactions come into the system at a single point and have a path or flow that they follow. A single transaction may update any piece or part of the entire data bank, and which functional organization creates this input makes no difference to the system. Certain functional areas are responsible for certain input transactions, each of which is uniquely coded. This unique code determines the individual path or flow through the system and identifies the updating responsibility of that transaction. This approach says that any logic performed by the system takes place on the input side, whereas today's traditional systems normally contain a minimum amount of editing on files with logic being performed during output routines.

Extraction—The Key to Output

The ease of output reporting is an important factor in the data bank concept. Reporting from such a system should be done on an exception basis and, with adequate hardware and software capability, can be done by any user in a simple manner. The only basic requirement for reporting is that information must be contained in the system. Under these conditions, any report (regardless of format or sequence) can be obtained in a relatively short period of time. Extracts are made to take advantage of a generalized report generator program, and any information can be extracted, at any level, at any time a file is being processed, and provided to any functional organization.

Capabilities and Limitations of Data File

The data bank concept has many advantages and seems to be the most logical way of handling the paper work explosion. However, there are some important considerations and some short-term limitations involved in pursuing this approach. The pros and cons can be summarized as follows:

Pros

1. All relevant information in one file. All information about a company's operation is contained in the one readily accessible file, which is so arranged that duplication and redundancy are avoided. Information concerning on-going activity is captured only once, validated, and entered into the proper location in the data bank. Each department then utilizes the same central file in satisfying its total information needs, with an obvious improvement in accuracy and consistency. (The file constitutes the data bank and may consist of a number of subfiles.)

2. Elimination of filed and manual effort. Because of the single record concept, total file space is reduced and duplicate files previously maintained by various functional organizations can be completely eliminated. As a corollary to this fact, there should be a reduction in manual effort required in these same functional organizations, effort which was previously necessary to provide all the various inputs for the multiple files.

3. Inquiry and extraction potential. Having a central data bank file for all information about a business provides potential real-time inquiry capability to any functional organization that needs to determine the current status or history of any item contained in the total system. It also allows for extraction of summary information, on an exception basis, and provides consistent and timely status and historic information to all users.

Cons

1. Imposition of rigid input discipline. One of the basic requirements of a data bank system is that all incoming information be validated prior

to its having any updating effect on the system. This rule imposes a rigid discipline on the user or supplier of information. This user must be far more stringent in creating the input information or in providing some means of correcting errors and omissions that are detected. With this approach, the user may suddenly be placed in a position of needing to maintain a far greater degree of accuracy on information than ever before with the traditional functional systems. Any shirking of this responsibility on his part will mean the loss of timely and accurate output to many other users.

2. Installation timing. A data bank concept is most easily installed in a new organization or in an old one that can somehow be stopped for a period of time. However, such systems must usually be installed "on the fly," and, therefore, any potential conflict with the unique organizational dynamics of a particular company must be resolved before the system can produce any real benefits. Failure to recognize or resolve this potential conflict completely will either significantly delay the system installation or reduce its effectiveness below the acceptable minimum.

3. Hardware and software requirements. To achieve the total potential benefits of a data bank system, adequate hardware and software must be available. In the case of hardware, it is necessary to have modular equipment with a large mass storage capability. (Such equipment need not necessarily be in one location or facility, however.) This will allow for growth and for the true random access capability essential to an information system of this type. In the area of software, there must be a multi-programming or multi-processing capability and an operating system sufficient to allow adequate handling of the multiple files of a data bank system. Much of this hardware and software has only recently become available and some items are still under development.

GENERALIZED PROGRAMS

There are many common functions performed in the majority of file processing jobs. These functions include file creation, file maintenance, data retrieval, sorting, and report preparation. Every business-type file processing application has used these functions.

From the experience gained with batch-type applications performed on magnetic tape systems, companies are learning how to write generalized programs for performing these functions. The generalized programs allow the user to select options, so he may tailor the program to meet his own requirements. Application programming is thus either eliminated or largely reduced.

National Cash Register Company has developed the BEST technique, for programming business-type operations. NCR has been using BEST in its data processing centers for programming customer jobs. They report that programming time is cut to something like 10 per cent to 20 per cent of the time required using conventional programming techniques.

Other organizations have developed complete "file management" systems. For instance, Informatics, Inc., in Los Angeles, has developed and is marketing a series of file management software systems. The city of Alexandria (Virginia) has used one of these systems to set up and maintain two important data files for city management purposes—a street and intersection file and a land parcel file. Practically no special programming was required for getting these two files on the computer. Further, whenever a city official wants a special analysis made (such as street intersections that have had five or more traffic accidents in a period of six months), it takes only a few minutes to complete the forms that define the request. No special programming is required to create the report.

The systems developed to date have been based (generally) on batch-type processing, using magnetic tape systems. Rapid progress is being made in these systems, and in the next few years it is expected they will be extended to files in mass storage units, processing in an on-line fashion.

Thus, if the corporate data file is maintained on magnetic tape, generalized systems already exist that can greatly reduce the programming time required to convert an application to the computer. And it should not be too long before similar systems are available for at least some types of online processing.

DATA RETRIEVAL

An important element of the management information system will be the ability to pose inquiries to the computer and to have it retrieve the data and do the processing needed to answer the inquiry. Therefore, fast, flexible means are needed to retrieve data from the corporate data file.

Much progress has been made in this area. To date, most of the effort in developing data retrieval methods has been for batch-processed magnetic tape applications. The previously mentioned NCR's BEST technique and the Informatics' file management systems provide powerful data retrieval methods. Other systems have been developed that handle just the retrieval and reporting phase. One such, called SELECT, developed by the Standard Oil Company of California and available through IBM for 1401 and 360 users, usually takes only a few minutes to fill out the retrieval request forms; in the majority of cases, no special programming is needed.

OUTPUT DISPLAY AND AUDIO UNITS

Communication between man and the computer has been rather difficult in the past. Input data has had to go through a keypunch operation. Man has had to tell the computer what to do by means of tedious and meticulous programming. The computer has replied by printing volumes of data.

Because of the delays involved in getting information into a computer and receiving back the answers, specific answers to questions are generally not requested. Rather, a whole spectrum of answers is requested, so that the user can find the answers for variations of the questions. This approach has encouraged the development of high-speed printers. Of course, there have been other needs for high-speed printers, such as the printing of large volumes of invoices, paychecks, and so on.

New output devices speed the communication between machine and man by presenting information rapidly in "soft copy" (nonprinted) form. One such method is the Voice Answer-Back, using a recorded voice. Both the New York and American Stock Exchanges, for instances, are using this method for answering stock price inquiries. A subscriber dials the proper number, keys in the stock identification (via a Touch-Tone set attached to his telephone), and receives price and volume data via a recorded voice. The computer selects the proper set of pre-recorded words to create the desired message.

Perhaps the major development effort in output devices has been in the area of visual displays. Individual consoles, the furthest along, are already in use in some airline reservation systems, stock broker interrogation systems, and other inquiry systems. The cathode-ray tube is the heart of the console: while the CRT is not the ultimate for console use, it is good enough so that there is no great effort under way to replace it. The consoles often have keyboards attached by which data can be entered into the system, providing fast two-way communication between the man and the machine. This also provides a way of economically capturing input information. In fact, individual consoles are being considered for replacing key-punches; cards are not punched; rather, the data is entered directly into the computer, on a time-sharing basis.

Another area of development is the large screen display, suitable for group viewing. The military has supported a very large research and development effort on these devices for use in military command and control centers. While several promising new methods are well along in development, most current operating systems still depend upon photographic means. A message, graph, table, or map is created by the computer and displayed on a CRT. The output device photographs the CRT face, develops the picture, and displays it on a screen—all in ten seconds or so. In fact, by taking three pictures of the CRT and using three projectors, satisfactory color slides can be achieved. While a ten-second delay may be quite acceptable for business management displays, the military feels that it needs a screen that can be changed almost instantaneously.

TIME-SHARED COMPUTERS

The use of output displays implies that the display user can enter an inquiry or an instruction to the computer at random times. However, once the desired information has been displayed, the computer should be free to proceed with other jobs. This mode of operation involves the use of time-sharing principles.

The new computers now entering the market have, in general, at least limited time-sharing ability; some have been designed expressly for time-shared operation and perform it quite efficiently. Such computers can accept almost "continuous" interruption, as their attention is demanded by the various attached devices. They can handle many programs "simultaneously"—or so it seems.

Time-shared computers promise to play an important role in future management information systems. Current developments in time-sharing indicates that the computers will be available and capable of performing this function.

BETTER INPUT METHODS

The input of data to a mechanized data processing system has been an area of poor performance for years. The conventional method of input has been keypunching and key verifying. This method has been slow, has often created a bottleneck in the flow of data, and has been error-prone. One reason that environmental-type data have not been used more widely in data processing systems is that the input costs have been high while the likelihood of using specific data has been rather low. Instead, only data with a high probability of usage have been entered into the systems.

New developments are changing this picture and making the input operation more economical and faster. With these new methods, it will be more practical to enter into the system data that might have a low probability of usage. With both storage and processing costs coming down, it is more feasible to store and process such data.

One major development in this area is optical scanning. While optical scanning has been talked about during the past decade, it is only recently that its impact has begun to be felt. Most of the major computer manufacturers have devices that will read printed documents. In some cases, the readers are limited to reading only one or two lines of printing per document. These readers are used for applications such as reading utility bill-heads that are returned by customers with their payments. In other cases, the readers can read whole pages of printing or writings. Several manufacturers have readers that can read the imprinted journal tapes from cash registers and adding machines.

Another area of development is the on-line terminal. Examples of on-line terminals include the teller machines used in on-line savings bank systems, typewriter terminals such as used in IBM's Administrative Terminal System, the Telephone Company's Touch-Tone device for entering digital data, teletypewriter units used with on-line systems, and transaction recorders such as used in airline reservation systems.

The general characteristic of on-line systems is that they help the operating people in the performance of their jobs. Examples are found in the savings bank systems and airline reservation systems. The operating people are thus entering data into the system as part of their duties; further, the system can check the accuracy and completeness of the input. The manual costs of input are largely absorbed by what the operating people would have to do anyway; the cost of the terminals and communications are thus the major costs of this form of input. These latter costs are continuing to come down.

Still probably years away are such forms of input as the automatic reading of handwriting and hand printing, or the automatic recognition of spoken words. Development work is continuing in these areas, but the problems have proved to be quite difficult.

IMPROVED REPORTING SYSTEM STRUCTURE

All of the components discussed might be considered as "tools" for building and operating a management information system. But the heart of the MIS is the reporting system—and, at present, this is what each organization must work out for itself. The structure of a management reporting system should consist, however, of scheduled performance reports, triggered (exception) reports, demand reports, and the planning functions that have been discussed earlier.

The development of a new information-processing system that will meet desired specifications is the truly creative part of the project. If the objectives of the information system resulting from the study are to be achieved, systems design must provide a step-by-step plan. This may require discarding many traditions and taboos if the maximum benefit is to be achieved from an integrated systems concept. For example, some conventional organizational functions known today may cease to exist simply because there would be no clerical or low-level decision-making people involved in performing the functions in question. Thus, the remaining higher level personnel could evolve into a policy-making group.

Systems design requires (1) the analysis of information input data that are processed into information output documents, (2) the reduction of any manual handling, and (3) the logical analysis of decision-making tasks. At the same time, the resulting system must be flexible enough to furnish information that is not regularly required.

Because systems design is highly dependent on the equipment or techniques used to transmit and process data, there is a natural but dangerous tendency to select equipment—usually a computer—that is presumed to be capable of carrying out the information-processing needs and, after that, to design the system to utilize the capabilities of the machine.

Although this practice is generally criticized, and rightly so, it can actually be very effective if properly carried out, and if certain precautions are observed: the objectives of the system must be specified clearly and in as much detail as is practical before the matter of equipment selection is taken up, and as many different equipment configurations and system structures must be evaluated as can reasonably be expected to provide possible solutions to the system objectives. In such a process of evaluation, the objective must remain fixed; only the system design may be considered alterable.

Other considerations will influence the proposed design of the system and some will be influenced by it. But the most important of these considerations is the time and money needed to design a new system and to put it into operation. Therefore, changes in today's system should be made only when it is ascertained that the new system and the associated equipment are compatible with the requirements of future business conditions. This can be another short-range improvement; i.e., do not waste money working on present systems that are prone to change.

IMPLEMENTING THE SYSTEM

The proposal to management by the MIS project team recommending the development and installation of a new information system should answer the universal management questions: What is to be done, why should it be done, what will it cost, are there savings or benefits, who should or will do the work of installation, and how long will it take? It may not be easy to convince top management that the data bank concept should be embraced, especially where large-scale, time-sharing computers are tied into the proposal. Management may want better reports and a better reporting system but may balk at the cost of a new system. From the project team's standpoint, it will be difficult to estimate the cost of installing a total management information system. Every company will vary as to information requirements, sophistication of management and number of significant changes permitted, available systems personnel and their talent for designing a new system, and already available data processing equipment. With the best conditions possible within a company, the installation of a total MIS is still a long-range project and probably not achievable in less than three to five years, depending upon the size of the company, the industry, state of the art within the company, and other factors. Because the MIS project is a major change—and such a long-range program—the corporate data bank concept (as compared with individual EDP applications) and the pay-as-you-go concept should be stressed. The MIS proposal can recommend that the total system be installed in phases, with each phase to accomplish a certain objective. The installation plan should be a part of the proposal to management and outline either phase, stage, or step that can be used as control points to evaluate progress of the over-all project.

Implementing a total management information system differs from other systems or data processing projects only in its size and scope. The complexity requires that good planning be a reality and that the plan be followed.

A long-range information-handling system improvement plan can be achieved by applying new equipment and new technology to the solution of information-handling problems. But the planning and design of improved information-handling systems cannot be considered solely in terms of equipment, technology, and mathematical techniques. Systems improvement of the magnitude considered here will have inevitable impact on people and management because some jobs will be replaced or substantially altered. This impact must be recognized and planned for. Displacements will occur, naturally, but adverse effects can be minimized if the transition is effectively planned and managed. One thing is sure: *people* are going to be needed to operate the new information-handling system. And these people will be doing more demanding work at a higher intelligence level than before; therefore, they will be more highly skilled with commensurate salaries.

The personnel problem faced is of no less importance and is far more subtle than the problems encountered in the information systems study itself, because not all of the problems concerning people can be solved by logical analysis. There are psychological, sociological, and even philosophical implications to them. Not all human relations problems can be foreseen, and there are no simple answers to those that can be seen and identified. However, careful advance consideration must be given to the impact of a new system on that portion of the work force most likely to be affected by it.

CONCLUSION

Management is becoming more aware that computers can be utilized to produce meaningful information on which they can base their decisions, in addition to performing the detail paperwork functions of the company. This awareness has spurred the formation of Management Information Systems groups whose responsibility is to develop the reports. As a result, new concepts have emerged in the area of information processing. Foremost among these concepts is the corporate data file or data bank. The design and installation of a data bank is a long-term project often requiring years to complete. It is required however to serve as the base of a total Management Information System. Because of the scope of this work and amounts of money involved, a great deal of careful planning is required. There is no alternative to not improving a company's information system, as management must have good information on which to base its decisions.

17

Selecting and Training Systems Men

ELLES M. DERBY

Metropolitan Life Insurance Co.
New York, N.Y.

ELLES M. DERBY's career embraces experience in engineering, business administration, and education. He joined Metropolitan Life Insurance Company in 1942 as a procedures analyst, and later held posts as supervisor of home office systems work and supervisor of national advertising. He was promoted to his present position as administrative assistant, personnel, after twelve years as manager of management education in the Coordination (methods) Division of Metropolitan Life. In his new capacity he is charged with the development and administration of all management development programs at the upper middle management levels at the home office in New York.

Following his graduation from The Polytechnic Institute of Brooklyn with the degree of civil engineer, Mr. Derby was engaged for several years in bridge design for the Phoenix Bridge Company and the New York Central System. In 1932 he entered the life insurance field. He was executive manager of the New York City Life Underwriters' Association, general manager of the Fifth Avenue Association, special representative of the Mutual Benefit Life, and vice-president of the Life Extension Institute before joining Metropolitan Life.

He has been a member of the faculty, on a part-time basis, at Drexel Institute, Pratt Institute, New York University, and the N.Y. State School of Industrial and Labor Relations at Cornell University. He is a guest lecturer at New York University and the University of Pennsylvania, and holds the rank of adjunct professor of economics at his alma mater. In addition, Mr. Derby is a member of many business and engineering societies, and has served in official capacity in several of them.

INTRODUCTION

Systems work requires unusual people. The field of systems work is such that to compromise the basic requirements of systems men is equivalent to insuring that their work will be limited in concept, scope, or effectiveness. Although the tools and techniques of systems work are well defined and are not exceptionally complex, their application to the many classes of business problems requires a peculiar combination of skills. The individuals possessed of these skills are not a common commodity and are, therefore, difficult to find. Yet those not having these skills are seldom really successful.

Since this is the case, it seems desirable to give detailed consideration to the qualities that are found in the successful systems man and to the type of training that will enhance these qualities.

It should be understood that, in spite of the rather exacting qualities to be discussed, the selection and training of systems men can be prescribed. The selection requires a high degree of patience and a firm resolution not to compromise the standard needed. One large company engaged in the hiring of systems men has learned that ten applicants are interviewed to secure one qualified person. This ratio clearly indicates an unwillingness to compromise the specifications.

In the area of training, a similar patience must be exercised, because the easy method of training will not produce results. It is only by using original methods of training that systems men can be developed to the highest competency.

In this chapter will be discussed three major areas: (1) the qualities of a competent systems man, (2) the methods by which candidates can be selected, and (3) the type of training necessary. In discussing these three topics, one should keep in mind that the objective is to produce a man equipped to cope with management problems of broad scope, a man able to examine critically the smallest details.

Those interested only in the development of specialists in forms analysis, programming, cost analysis, machine procedures, and the like can take greater liberties with the principles presented. It must be realized, however, that this method will not produce a systems man; a team of specialists will be required to do the complete systems job.

THE REQUIREMENTS

The specific requirements for an effective systems man can be defined, in most cases, by a review of the steps found in most systems assignments. At one time or another the average assignment requires the systems man to:

1. Open the actual job
2. Secure information on the present situation
3. Analyze the data collected
4. Produce a statement of the problem
5. Investigate possible solutions
6. Synthesize a better way
7. Secure agreement from operating supervisors
8. Present the plan to management and gain approval
9. Install the system

Although these steps may be described in other words, and may be subject to elaboration or condensation by those who consider them, they constitute the basic steps of every systems job. They also describe the special qualifications of a systems man, for a review of these nine steps demonstrates that a systems man must be a salesman, an analyst, and a creator or innovator. Furthermore, the complete systems man encompasses the electronic systems man, the manual systems analyst, and the management information systems staff.

Salesmanship

Possibly the most important, and frequently unrecognized, talent demanded in systems work is salesmanship. From the time that he is assigned to a study until the completion of the installation, the systems man is constantly in a situation that requires salesmanship ability far in excess of that necessary to many sales situations.

Consider the first task of the job—getting the job under way. In only a few situations do we find the systems man brought into a line operating situation with a friendly welcome. In most situations the reception is passive at best. His first task is to secure acceptance of his physical presence. It is not within the scope of this chapter to discuss how this can best be done. It is a real and important challenge that occurs before anything else can be attempted.

Nor does it ever stop during the entire job. In securing information, a selling job is necessary. Otherwise, one merely secures specific answers to specific questions. It is the task of the systems man to establish himself in such a manner and to such a degree that he will discover not only the truth of a situation, but the whole truth.

During the course of an assignment, honest differences of opinion arise. To effectively reconcile these differences to the maximum extent possible, the qualities of a salesman—patience, tact, understanding, persuasiveness, expressiveness, and the like—are required.

Finally, there is direct selling, which is necessary to convince supervisors and management that the proposals developed are an improvement over systems in use. This tremendous sales problem becomes more apparent when one realizes that up to this point the new system has been merely an idea. Intangibles are always difficult to sell. In addition, the systems man frequently finds that those executives to whom the new system must be sold are those who designed and have administered the system to be replaced.

It seems clear that a systems man must be a salesman and, conversely, those not endowed with and trained in the skills of salesmanship will lack one of the most important characteristics for success. Even when authority stands back of the systems man on a study, the need for sales ability is plain and cannot be ignored in selection.

The Systems Man as an Analyst

Since a systems man is a technician to some degree, it follows that he must be an analyst. However, a review of the task may establish an unsuspected depth to this characteristic. In securing information one may not realize the necessity of an analytical talent for order and logic, perception, relation, and validity.

ORDER AND LOGIC. The interviewing of personnel in connection with a systems study can seldom be done in the easiest fashion, that is, by starting at the beginning of each procedure and tracing the work flow to the end. All too frequently, the data is received in unrelated sequence. An important aspect of the analytical problem is the ability of the systems man to give order to the material, mentally and in writing, and to develop the logic of the system.

PERCEPTION. The systems man must possess the ability to realize that something is missing, incompatible with other data, or partly so. Being a good listener is part of this talent, but a high degree of perception is required.

RELATION. As the data for the study is assimilated, it is necessary to relate it to data previously available. The quality needed to do this is not one utilizing routine comparison according to a preconceived notion, but rather the unusual, the innovated comparison that does not occur to everyone.

VALIDITY. One of the most difficult parts of the systems job is the establishment of a valid base from which to work. Testimony of others may be prejudiced, misleading, or misunderstood. The systems man must have the ability to collect data and test it to insure its worth.

In addition to the qualities that come into play during the collection of information, there is analysis. Analysis is the ability to break the whole into parts that can be related to each other and studied to produce the correct and complete statement of the current condition.

Creativity

In addition to the talents of a salesman necessary to conduct the systems job, and the talents of an analyst to develop a clear picture of a systems problem, the systems man must be a creator and an innovator. Certainly, little success will accrue to an individual who is unable to produce a "better way."

The development of new ideas and innovations in the solution of systems problems is something for which there are no rules. Time and again, productive ideas of great merit have come from those least qualified by schooling or experience. In fact, this has been the story of great inventions. Many believe that every man and woman possesses creative ability, though in many it lies dormant. Certainly it is a quality necessary to systems improvement.

The systems man must be able to take his knowledge of things outside the area of study and apply it to the problem at hand. For example, the electronic computer is the result of three major applications of non-business knowledge to a business problem. In 1642 Pascal used the characteristics of the wheel to invent a machine that would add. In 1942 Aiken used the characteristics of electrical paths (circuits) to quickly select those wheels (counters) that would be activated to perform arithmetic. In 1946 Eckert and Mauchly used the characteristics of electronic tubes to select circuits and perform arithmetic at fantastic speeds.

The systems man must have this same quality of productive imagination. He uses it following the analysis of the conditions for which he is expected to find a solution.

Other Qualities

It is evident that the systems man must have all the qualities that are common at the executive level. He must have the appearance, personality, confidence, and all of the other qualities that would make him acceptable to the upper strata of management. In addition, he needs to have inner qualities that are not usually identified with systems. A systems man must have ambition, because in systems work he may find many frustrations and disappointments. This ambition is more than patience, for it is no static thing, but a dynamic drive that takes a man forward in spite of setbacks and difficulties.

In addition, he must have the quality usually called integrity, because it is clearly detrimental if he lacks a reputation for honesty and directness. Of course, he can get into difficulty by being direct, but this sort of difficulty is more easily handled than that resulting from a lack of integrity in dealing with his fellow workers and with management. There must be complete confidence on the part of both that the individual with whom they are dealing is honest in his opinions, even though those opinions may differ widely from their own.

The systems man must be highly competent. It is not enough to know just enough to get by, he must be clearly outstanding in ability and, moreover, be willing to acknowledge when he does not know. Consequently, competence is one of the most important requisites; there is no substitute for it. Many so-called systems men have proven unsuccessful in their jobs because they are not willing to keep themselves informed, especially in keeping current with new electronic developments and managment information systems. They are unwilling to work to maintain the high degree of competence necessary, which requires extra study on a continuing basis.

In summation, the individuals who are most likely to succeed in systems work are people who are able to mix in higher managerial levels, men who have ambition, integrity, competence, an analytical mind, a high degree of creativity, and the personality and persuasiveness of a good salesman. This, indeed, is the complete systems man. Others may attempt to do systems work without one or more of these qualities, but it is unlikely that their work will ever reach the level of success found by the better-known people in the systems field.

THE PROBLEM OF SELECTION

Although the characteristics of a successful systems man have been defined, the problems they pose have not been discussed. The difficulty that is encountered in the process of selection is primarily a result of the psychological contradictions in the talents needed. Those responsible for the selection are well advised to be aware of these contradictions.

Consider the type of individual who is able to secure information, place it into correct relationship with other information, and then analyze it to tell the story of the present situation. He has what is generally referred to as an analytical type of mind. This is the individual who makes a good research man, mathematician, or engineer. He is a factual individual, a person who likes to deal with tangibles rather than intangibles. He is the man who likes to strip down automobile engines or take apart electrical appliances to see what makes them work, not to actually repair them. He has the searching, groping type of mind that always is aimed at a tangible object. There are many such individuals. However, it is when this quality is combined with others that one finds the individual not quite so common.

The second factor in this unusual combination is the need for a person who is a day dreamer, who likes to think in terms of possibilities. This person is frequently considered peculiar, or somewhat eccentric. Usually, he is not the least bit analytical. He does not like to analyze facts nor be bound by them. Therefore, the combination of the analytical quality already mentioned and this imaginative trait is somewhat of a rarity.

In addition to these two qualities, there is the need for salesmanship. The salesman is one who likes to deal with people and their emotions. He is the individual who takes keen delight in turning people to his own way of thinking. This kind of person is seldom bound by facts, very frequently is not imaginative, and is concerned primarily with the personal reactions of each individual to whom he speaks. Salesmanship, when combined with analytical and creative ability, reduces the area of probability in which the potentially successful systems man can be found.

Thus the problem of selection. Whatever method is used to implement selection must take these incompatibilities into consideration. Wherever embryonic systems men might be found, it is clear that there is no single source. Rather, it is mandatory that every qualified candidate be considered so that potentially successful men may not be passed over.

Sources of Systems Men

Inasmuch as there does not appear to be a single best source for the type of person described in the preceding paragraphs, it seems sensible to consider the three fields that are available: (1) present employees not engaged in systems work, (2) systems employees of other companies, and

(3) recent college graduates. Each source has both advantages and disadvantages.

As far as present employees are concerned, the most outstanding advantage is the familiarity of the employee with the company setup. He knows the kind of people who work there and what they think of the present systems of the company. They are already company oriented. The chances that they will not like the company's organization or atmosphere are minimized. They are quite likely to be permanent employees, and this in itself is an advantage. Conversely, the company employee, particularly if this is the only company for which he has ever worked, is probably highly indoctrinated with all of the taboos with which the company is infested. That is, he does not easily think in terms of possible change. He is continually balked in his own mind by a fear that he will step out of line, break some tradition, irritate some individual officer, or do some other unthinkable act. Obviously, a person with such mental taboos to overcome will rise less rapidly in systems work.

In the second source, that of experienced systems people who work for another company, there would seem to be the advantage of experience. They know what a system is, or at least it may be assumed that they do. They should be somewhat familiar with the difficulties faced by systems men in the documenting and analyzing of information. If they have been successful in their present positions, they have certainly demonstrated some creative ability. The ability to meet with various levels of management has been attested by success in the systems field. On the other hand, systems men are reasonably well paid, and, therefore, when one seeks a new connection, there is likely to be something wrong with the one he holds. It has been shown that many of those seeking to move from one systems job to another have found something in their present job that they do not like. It is usually not the salary situation, but some facet of the job itself that they find difficult to handle. In looking at potential systems men who are currently working for another company, one should be cautious of all records until they are investigated. Systems men are difficult to find and train. A company is not likely to treat those who are competent in other than a satisfactory manner.

A source not to be disregarded is the recent college or university graduate. These men are young, ambitious, and able to take an objective viewpoint. Since these factors are often lacking in candidates already within a company or from a similar company, the desirability of such qualities must be considered when making selections from such sources. Consequently, college or university graduates are a major source for candidates in this kind of work. The obvious disadvantage is the complete lack of experience in the company or in systems work. However, one should consider that the salary investment is considerably less than in using present employees or hiring experienced systems men. In no case can one be sure of the successful development of the systems man. In the case of the college man, less money is wasted in the failure of a man to develop. It is significant to note that some of the large systems consulting firms are now turning to this third source to meet their needs.

The Process of Selection

The selection of systems people is a three-part process. The first is gathering the facts, the second is personal contact with the individual, and the third is appraisal of the facts and the contact.

The basic fact-finding tool is an application form of some kind, and for this purpose the more detailed certain information is, the easier will be its use for selection. The application should have, in addition to identifying information, a complete record of the man's academic record. It should indicate the type of family from which he comes, the environment in which he has been raised, and the nature of the subjects in which he did well in his university or college. If the man has no academic degree, the application should indicate the type of work he is able to do best. Space should be provided for information as to honors secured, both in business and the academic world, the nature of the organizations to which he belongs, the degree of leadership he has exercised in those organizations, his military record, if any, and similar information.

A second tool in the fact-finding area is the psychological test. Opinion varies widely as to the importance of these tests, but it cannot be denied that they can be of some assistance in helping locate trouble spots. For example, properly designed tests can indicate that the applicant does not like detail of any kind. From what has already been said, this is an area that would have to be discussed in detail. Consequently, as a fact-finding device, the psychological test acts as a guide to the discussion, suggesting information to be secured from the candidate.

It is possible that, for some reason, a mercantile report may be desired on a particular candidate. Like the psychological tests, the purpose of such reports is to disclose background areas that might otherwise be overlooked.

The other fact-finding tool is really the second stage of the selection process. It is a personal interview with the candidate. This is a most important function, and very frequently follows the pattern of multiple interviews by persons who are intimately connected with the systems program. The personal interview is the opportunity to get the applicant to elaborate on basic facts. If it does not succeed in doing this, it is not accomplishing a worthwhile purpose in the selection process.

There are two types of interviews that can be conducted. The first of these, in which the interviewer follows a fixed pattern in his questioning, might be termed a planned interview. Many interviewers, particularly those who have had psychological training, prefer this type of interview because they are able to interpret psychological inferences in response to "patterned" questions.

On the other hand, many of those who are conducting interviews do not have this psychological background, and, therefore, are unable to take advantage of such knowledge. Consequently, their interviewing is usually much more informal in nature. There is, perhaps, a greater tendency to roam from subject to subject, depending on the normal flow of the conversation. However, in both types of interviews it is necessary that all of the factual information be explored to bring out the abilities of the candidate.

The most important ingredient in these interviews is the full participation of the applicant. Most interviewers develop a technique to get the interviewee to talk volubly. Means for accomplishing this lie in probing areas of common interest, such as athletic events, music, literature, and current events. When this technique is employed and the area of common interest is discovered, the interview proceeds somewhat along the lines of getting acquainted by means of the common interest.

On the other hand, certain interviewers have found it effective to take some of the least desirable characteristics disclosed by the factual information at hand and start probing into these areas first. The usual reaction to such probing is defensive. This reaction is considered important by many, because in systems work the individual is frequently under fire and in somewhat difficult circumstances. Consequently, if he does not have the ability to defend himself at the time of employment interview, it raises some question as to his potential to deliver under fire at a later date.

Identifying Analytical Ability

It should be clear that the individual who possesses the analytical type of mind is closely akin to the engineer, the scientist, the mathematician, and, to some degree, the accountant. All of these individuals have been trained to think in terms of forming a miscellany of information into an understandable, integrated story. The possession of an academic degree in any of these subjects is prima-facie evidence that the individual has analytical ability. Consequently, the facts that need to be developed in the resumé and personal interview are those that indicate that the candidate has this type of mind. Whether or not they actually possess an academic degree in any of these fields is not important; this point cannot be too heavily stressed. The four professional fields mentioned have one thing in common—they are all concerned with the analysis of tangibles rather than intangibles.

The engineer, the scientist, the mathematician, and the accountant deal largely with numbers. None of these professions can be carried on unless the person has a genuine ability to transform quantities into meaningful analyses. He must have a genuine liking for investigation of numerical relations. If he does not have this affinity, he will eventually get bored with such work and leave it. An interest in arithmetical, mathematical, and scientific subjects denotes such an interest. To a lesser degree, ability in accounting is desirable, but accounting is somewhat dominated by rules that must be followed to give uniformity to accounting interpretations.

The application blank should provide for answers to questions on the extent of knowledge of mathematics, the physical sciences, accounting, and so on. The applicant should have demonstrated a genuine ability, as well as a liking, in these areas. Failure to find these indications should be considered a danger signal against selection. Consequently, an effective application will ask for academic work and experience in these areas, as well as indication of the applicant's evaluation of these subjects.

In addition, there are a number of tests that disclose an individual's arithmetic ability and mechanical comprehension. In using such tests, the applicant should score quite well, because these are evaluations on which there is little room for misinterpretation of the aptitude characteristics. A suggested test in this area is the Engineering Aptitude of Moore, Lapham, and Capp, published by the Psychological Corporation in 1946, and recognized as one of the most effective tests. Parts 4, 5, and 6 of this test are sufficient to disclose such aptitude. It would be wise to consult with those qualified to evaluate available tests to supplement the application form and the interview.

In the course of the interview, and in a review of the factual information, there should develop certain very clear indications. If the interviewer is unable to find any place in which the applicant has ever dealt with tangibles, it is most likely that the candidate will not successfully handle this part of systems work. Many interviewees disclose that they find figures abhorrent to them, and that they want nothing to do with anything connected with numbers or machinery. Obviously, they disqualify themselves, but it is better to be so disqualified than to find themselves later engaged in a field in which they have no basic interest.

Identifying Creative Ability

The candidate for a systems job must be a person who continually sees that improvements are needed, and who has the ability to produce new ideas of high quality. This ability probably exists to some degree in most people, but not to the degree necessary to systems work. The candidate should be an individual who is not content with the things he experiences, but one who involuntarily dreams of the changes he would make if he were permitted. The candidates should be one with broad, and probably unrelated, interests, one who knows about many things, but not necessarily in depth.

Therefore, both the application form and the personal interview should point toward the identification of this quality. Creative ability is not as easily identified as analytical ability, particularly from the written record. Usually it is disclosed through the patient, persistent probing of the personal interview. The most productive topics to be probed are the leisure interests

—hobbies, do-it-yourself projects, community or campus activities, and such things.

Interviewers will have an advantage if they strike a response in some activity with which they are familiar. Familiarity enables the interviewer to better evaluate responses. For example, an interviewer familiar with auto mechanics is in an excellent position to weigh the creative degree of an applicant's attempts to improve the performance of his car.

Subjects that frequently produce the indications of creativity are: art, music, manual arts, automobile conversions, dramatics, committee work, social club activities, and home construction.

Psychological tests are also available in the area of creative potential. Notable among these are the Rorschach (inkblot) and Thematic Apperception tests. However, in this field it is necessary to use the services of a trained psychologist, both for the administration of the test and its interpretation.

In addition, there are certain basic philosophies of life that can be probed, such as whether the applicant is normally critical and quite likely to produce remedies for existing conditions without instructions. Many people do not have this faculty. They appear to be perfectly content with life exactly as it is at the present time. They never have the urge to change or improve or develop innovations, even as a mental exercise, and very definitely have never produced an idea of their very own.

Much has been said about the possession of creative ability by everyone, but there is no evidence that the degree of creative ability necessary to systems work is possessed by all individuals. There may be a latent creative urge in the minds of many people, and perhaps brainstorming and other techniques can bring creative urges to the surface. The systems man must have a creative urge far deeper than the sort of thing that results from a brainstorming session.

If in all of the probing, records, and tests there is little or no indication that the individual has ever in the past produced a genuinely original idea, or had the urge to do so, there is little reason to suppose that sometime in the future he is going to be able to produce high quality ideas.

Identifying Sales Ability

The sales job of the systems man is one of the most difficult in selling. The product that a systems man usually sells is an idea. That is, it is intangible in nature, and cannot be proven by its accomplishment. Salesmen of automobiles, soap, shoes, or other tangible products have a simple job compared to those who sell ideas.

In addition to the fact that the systems man is dealing in intangibles, he is also dealing in an area of multiple personalities—from those who willingly meet with and accept other people and their ideas to the individual who thinks that, when he had his own last idea, the well of new ideas dried up. The personality of the systems man must be an adaptable one, because he must succeed just as well with the one extreme as with the other, and with all the gradations between. He cannot be merely a back-slapper, because there are many people who do not like backslappers. He cannot, on the other hand, be a highly technical expert, because there are many people who not only dislike but actually fear highly technical experts. His character must be molded to meet the people with whom he comes into contact, and this requires a high degree of versatility.

The facts that must be uncovered to disclose sales ability are more likely to be brought out by personal contact than by the application form. The things that must be determined are whether the individual has a liking for people, whether this liking for people has been appraised well by his fellow workers, and whether he is able to direct his own personality to produce a favorable effect upon those with whom he comes in contact. Little of this is disclosed by the written record, and, therefore, the application form is of minor use for this particular quality. However, in the case of people who are or have been active in college or community life, the record should show whether the person generally likes to be with other people. If this indication is not present at all, the question is raised as to his true social awareness.

There are many psychological tests for salesmanship, and the results of many of these tests have had a high correlation with success in the sales field. However, one of the difficulties experienced in the use of tests is the difference already mentioned between selling a tangible and selling an intangible. However, for those who prefer to include tests in all areas, it is suggested that competent testing authorities be consulted on this matter.

The interview is of great importance in determining the sales ability of a candidate. It has already been suggested, in determining analytical ability, that undesirable items appearing in the record can be used to get the candidate to speak freely. These can also be used to stimulate the person's sales ability. If he finds that there are negative factors in his record that appear to have an adverse effect on the interviewer, he will disabuse the mind of the interviewer concerning the item being discussed. This is sales-manship, and the interview offers an excellent opportunity to test his salesmanship. In addition, during the interview, the interviewer has the chance to observe the candidate over a period of time sufficient to see whether he has unfortunate nervous habits that might detract from his usefulness in the systems field.

The ability to sell is one of the most important qualities of a systems man. There are many people who aspire to systems work who are extremely clever in both the analytical and creative phases of the work, but who are unable to present ideas to other people in a way that brings acceptance. Obviously, there is little point in spending time and money in developing ideas based on present difficulties if no one can understand the suggestions that are being made. In some few systems organizations, it is possible to specialize, and certain people are engaged for their selling ability. They are used primarily on this part of the systems job. Generally speaking, in the clerical field there is sufficient interest in the details of the present situation and the details of the new ideas to require the analyst who is doing the selling to have done the major part of the thinking all the way through the job. To have it otherwise is to flirt with danger, because at any time the job can be lost if the salesman is not able to produce the substantiating evidence in a way that is convincing.

Evaluating

In the preceding pages the characteristics of the complete systems man have been outlined, but no attempt has been made to weigh the relative importance of each characteristic. There is no single answer to the standards of selection that will be applicable to all companies or to all systems departments. However, in the following paragraphs an attempt has been made to define the conditions that have a bearing on the importance of certain qualities in comparison with others. These conditions involve the level at which the systems work takes place, the climate in which systems work is done, and the organizational complexities that will be encountered.

The level of work has a bearing on the selection process, for if the work is in a somewhat limited part of systems work, there is no necessity for the broad understanding that is necessary when the work covers all the facets of a business organization. For example, many organizations concentrate their systems work almost entirely on basic procedures, or, even more narrowly, on the actual processing of work. This requires a person who knows about basic methods of processing work, including computers, but it does not require deep knowledge in the areas of organization, finance, personnel, or many of the other factors in management work.

On the other hand, there are many organizations where the type of problem given to a systems man may be almost anything within the total scope of management. It may encompass personnel problems, organization problems, quality control problems, scheduling procedures, expenses, management information systems, and a hundred other areas. One of the conditions that should determine the selection of a systems man for a particular company is the level at which he will be expected to work. Possibly there may be more than one level of work, and two or three standards of selection are applicable.

The second condition that has a bearing on the standard of selection is the climate in which the individual is expected to work. There are companies in which systems work is welcomed or performed in a computer-oriented atmosphere, and there are companies in which almost all systems work is done under difficulties. Obviously, a person can be selected with less care when his transgressions are likely to be forgiven than in a company where many people are merely looking for an excuse to reject the systems analyst. This, of course, controls the type of individual who may be selected to do the work—one requiring a great deal more precision and accuracy in evaluation than the other.

What may be considered a third condition is the organizational structure in which the individual works. Many companies have a comparatively simple organizational structure. Others are extremely complicated, with a great deal of coordination necessary between departments. A person who finds difficulty in working through organizational patterns is quite likely to find himself in difficulty in the latter type of organization. Organization is a factor that should be taken into consideration in setting a standard of selection.

It is desirable that the selection of candidates be done through a rating of individuals. That is, there must be an appraisal sheet on which the various interviewers can express their appraisal of each candidate. After every interviewer has talked with a candidate, the various appraisals must be correlated. Prior agreement must be secured concerning the degrees of reservations permitted in the specifications. Some companies require unanimous approval of several interviewers before the candidate is accepted. Other companies permit minor reservations. In other situations, there may be conditions in which a considerably less rigid approval might be entirely satisfactory.

It is very important that a study be made from time to time of the selective data compared with the actual results of selection. In the case of psychological testing, this is the development of correlation, but the same idea should be applied to all selection qualities. Based on the appraisal forms, the systems men should be evaluated periodically as to how well they have made out in the areas of analysis, creativity, and salesmanship. If it appears that the interviewers are being misled in their appraisals, an adjustment needs to be made in the method of appraisal and selection for that quality.

THE BASIS OF SYSTEMS TRAINING

Systems work is one of the areas in management that requires a continuous training activity. Like many other aspects of management, it is not enough to train a man today and then assume he will remain highly competent. Over a period of time, new ideas, new machines, new applications of old techniques, and new needs develop. Constant training and retraining are necessary. The management of the systems department must plan a program not only for new men, but also one that insures all analysts will be kept up to date.

A complete program of training will cover two major areas, the analyst's personal qualities and his techniques. One must be aware of the many facets of the systems job that fall under these headings. For instance, the personal attributes of the analyst have already been discussed as to their impact on his success. He must display, and actually feel, an understanding of the problems discussed with him. He must be helpful in fact, not just as a front. While he is being both understanding and helpful, he must represent management. Consequently, during the development of a systems man, it is necessary to get him to understand this double relationship to the client and to management.

On the other hand, the techniques that need to be taught to a systems man depend more on the climate of application than upon the managerial objectives. For instance, the use of techniques such as stop watches or other precise measurement devices may very well be rejected because they make the individuals being time-studied very nervous. Consequently, the techniques that have to be used avoid these particular tools of measurement. The same thing is true in all of the areas of systems work, and we find a need for each systems man to fully appreciate that he needs in his repertoire not one but a number of techniques aimed at accomplishing the same end results.

The techniques in his portfolio are easier to teach than the attitudes he must acquire. The list is well known:

Work simplification	Mechanization—EDP—IDP
Statistical presentation	Budgeting and expense control
Work measurement techniques	Organization analysis
Procedure analysis	Forms, space, and equipment
Production control analysis	Communication analysis
Quality control analysis	Correspondence analysis
Performance analysis	Reports analysis

This is merely a list of the things the complete systems man must be able to do well. His technical competence depends on his theoretical knowledge of those subjects, and, of even greater importance, his ability to apply that knowledge.

Training is the method by which the systems man is taught both theory and the application. To be effective, this training needs to be done using a different approach than many systems supervisors try. The characteristics of a potential systems man and the means whereby one can select this potential from among aspirants have been covered.

Training Systems Men

The objective of training in systems is to produce a thinking management analyst, competent in both knowledge and in its application to the problems of management.

One is told that to teach others a task is a matter of instruction, demonstration, and supervision on the job. This method has been very successful when applied to the teaching of routine procedures. Its efficiency has been demonstrated again and again wherever it has been used correctly; it fails only when someone attempts to modify the basic psychological factors upon which such training is based.

Most training of systems men does not involve a formal breakdown of the job, but much of systems training is attempted that way. The manager takes the new systems man in tow and "teaches" him by revising everything that he has developed. After a while, if the new man is reasonably intelligent, he will realize what is happening and be able to produce answers identical to those that his superior would produce. This is the traditional method of developing systems men. It does not accomplish what should be accomplished.

If the training consists of reading of accepted texts, of following the words of senior men, of the solutions to problems of ten, twenty, or thirty years ago, all that will result will be a perpetuation of present attitudes, approaches, procedures, systems, personnel policies, and the like. Some people call this "getting experience," but such training has two disadvantages: (1) all management studies will be done according to a set of rules, and (2) the rule book eliminates any need for ability, since, if it is followed, every study will turn out the same way.

Fortunately, it doesn't seem to work that way. Troubles do arise, and they are not solved by a routine investigation. They require men who can think for themselves, and who have been trained to think outside of a pattern rather than within one. Systems men know this is true. Hours are spent in discussing the ways and means of approaching the multitude of problems that appear in every systems study. The competent systems man uses these hours of discussion not to imitate what others have done, but to dig out of the discussion the important principles by which he can be guided in making studies in his own company.

The objective of any training of systems men should be to encourage their thought processes rather than to teach them a set of techniques that are to be applied according to a set of rules. One should be interested in teaching these men to meet situations that require ingenuity and to have the capacity to develop these ingenious solutions and the ability to sell their solutions after they have been developed.

The means of training are many. They include such things as discussion groups, formal classes, programs designed for individuals, attendance at conferences and lectures, college courses, consideration of the techniques used in old studies, and instruction by the case method. These are all formal programs. By way of on-the-job training techniques, the trainee learns by doing. He is assigned to a senior analyst who guides him in what he does, and as he becomes more and more familiar with the company and its problems, he should become more and more effective.

Regardless of whether formal or on-the-job training is used, the aforementioned philosophy must be the guiding principle. It would be wise to establish a training rule to be used by all senior men or course instructors. This rule would provide that as each assignment is reviewed, the senior in charge or the instructor uses the indirect approach to correcting what has been put together by the trainee. The analyst who is doing the reviewing should question the trainee about his conclusions until one or the other of two terminal points is reached. Either the question of what has been done and what has been developed leads to the conclusion that there are no major omissions or flaws, or the second terminal point will be arrived at— the realization by the trainee that there are problems still unanswered in the solutions that he has advanced up to the time of review. At no point has the reviewer offered his own solution. He has used his experience solely to frame the kind of questions that he knows will cause the trainee to recognize that he does not have a good solution to the problem studied.

There are other benefits from this kind of training. The major one is that the competency of the systems men trained under such a philosophy will be far above that attained by merely parroting what someone else has thought to be a good solution to a problem. Secondly, the trainee himself has the feeling that he is not following theoretical patterns, but rather that systems work consists very largely of common sense and that the tools that he has been taught to use are merely a means to an end rather than an end in themselves.

A word of caution should be injected. The development of trainers who can teach this way is not easy. There is the general tendency among all teachers to tell rather than to guide, and this defect seems to have been adopted by everyone. It therefore becomes the duty of the head of a systems department to make sure that those senior men responsible for the guidance of new men are themselves exposed to the technique of guiding rather than telling. The questioning technique that has been described is time consuming. It is exhausting for the instructor, but it produces a thinking individual with confidence in his ideas and the ability to stand questioning of an extremely searching nature. The benefit is in the development of each individual's latent talents. Do not be content merely with making a new systems man no better than his trainer.

In the preceding illustrations, training by formal means has been inferred. Many systems departments are too small to use the formal class approach. However, the basic principle of teaching through guidance instead of by directives is just as applicable.

In the training area, there is the possibility of two general methods and the combinations thereof. There are those who feel that the systems man should first be put through a formal training period, during which time he is taught specific techniques. During the same period, he receives an intense orientation in the company and the systems department. Formal training means the use of classroom techniques modified to be palatable to adults, but essentially it is a schoolroom proposition.

There are some advantages to this technique. Among the advantages is the fact that equivalent training can be given in a shorter period of time. If a person is put through a planned course under experts, they can present to him, in a few hours, problems that he might not encounter for several months if he were to meet them in the normal course of events. Furthermore, the problems can be designed to give the new man more difficulty than he would find if he were to merely run into an on-the-job problem.

On the other hand, there are inherent disadvantages. The first is that the individual is not being productive during his period of training; therefore, the training course becomes an investment that may or may not pay off in the long run. If the time consumed in training is not substantial, this probably is a minor point, but in certain instances such training is given over a long period of time, and the investment amounts to several thousand dollars before any return to the company is experienced.

On-the-job training of systems people, conversely, has the advantage of being a pay-as-you-go plan. The trainee, or new man, is at least doing some productive work during the period in which he is learning how to do more complicated work. On the other hand, his development will normally consume a great deal more time. In the final analysis, it is somewhat problematical whether the company actually saves any money through a formal approach. Here again, no categorical answers can be given on whether formal training or on-the-job training is the better plan. It is suggested that in many instances a combination of the two methods is probably ideal.

Responsibility for Selection and Training

There appears to be no specific relationship between the effectiveness of selection and training and its organizational place in a company. However, certain key factors should be taken into consideration in deciding whether the program of selection and training should be done in a particular organizational unit.

On behalf of the systems department, it should be evident that they are probably more intimately aware of the precise needs than anyone else could be. They deal in the problems and shortcomings of their own men from day to day and have, through years of experience, a very clear idea of the exact qualities needed in their particular company situation. Consequently, they are very well equipped to ask the questions in connection with the selection process, and they should be able to evaluate the answers they receive better than those less familiar with the details of the work.

The systems department, on the other hand, is not normally geared to do a good training job, because of its own competence as much as anything. There appears to be a general tendency to shorten any instruction, since the trainee is supposed to be of superior intelligence and, therefore, should learn things upon the first presentation. For this reason, if the systems department is going to be charged with training its own men, it is important that the management of the department be very careful in the selection of those to do the training; otherwise, the training will consist largely of reading articles between intermittent spurts of direct personal training.

The personnel department of most companies is geared to the selective process. They are experienced in interviewing people and, on general employees, can interpret the responses quite accurately. In the selection of systems men, they are not quite so effective. It would seem desirable, if company policy indicates that the selection of all employees should be by a central personnel department, that the department add to its staff a well-qualified systems man to do the selecting of applicants.

The place of the personnel department in the training of systems men is generally one that can provide no more than classroom instruction. It is entirely possible, and it is frequently the fact, that the training activities of a company include work in the area of systems, but where this is the case, such training is necessarily limited to only the formal presentation of certain techniques previously mentioned.

18

The Network System –PERT/CPM*

MARVIN FLAKS

Booz, Allen & Hamilton, Inc.
New York, N.Y.

GLENN L. WHITE

Booz, Allen & Hamilton, Inc.
New York, N.Y.

MARVIN FLAKS has been a vice-president with Booz, Allen & Hamilton, management consultants, since 1964. He is the managing officer of the firm's Project Management and Control Division, which is responsible for all consulting activities related to the firm's project management work, and has had extensive experience in developing project management programs for business, industry, and government.

Before joining Booz, Allen & Hamilton in 1957, Mr. Flaks was associated with the Westinghouse Electric Corporation and with Rowe Manufacturing Company.

Mr. Flaks received his bachelor of science degree in mechanical engineering from the University of Connecticut and his master of science degree in industrial engineering from Ohio State University.

MR. WHITE is a vice-president in the Project Management and Control Division of Booz, Allen & Hamilton. He has directed the development of numerous project management control systems for government and manufacturing and construction companies throughout the United States.

Mr. White received his B.S. degree in mathematics from Millersville State College, Pennsylvania. He has taken graduate courses in mathematics and statistics at the University of Pennsylvania and Maryland University.

In 1963 Mr. White formed the Glenn L. White Co. to serve the management needs of the construction industry. He has written two books and numerous articles on PERT and CPM and has addressed national conventions of all major construction associations.

INTRODUCTION

Systems planners have found that most of their work, both in planning and implementation phases, is part of a project. Projects have become so important to business, industry, and government that much time and effort have been spent to develop adequate project management tools, since project management requires different tools and techniques than does day-to-day business or production management.

PERT (Program Evaluation and Review Technique) and CPM (Critical Path Method) are among the management tools which have evolved in recent years. These techniques have gradually merged into what is now commonly known as "network system." Properly applied, the network system insures thorough planning, scheduling, and control of complex projects. This approach provides:

1. A disciplined basis for planning the project
2. A clear, easily understood picture of the project's scope
3. A method for evaluating alternative plans and objectives
4. A realistic schedule for all operations
5. Effective communication among the various personnel involved in the project
6. An indication of activities or jobs that are critical from a schedule standpoint
7. Direction of management attention to critical areas
8. Precise evaluation of actual time and cost performance against schedule
9. A framework for improved scheduling of manpower, cash, equipment, supplies, and other resources

The network system can be applied to most management tasks to achieve lower costs and to reduce time and manpower needs. Its use is clearly indicated in the planning and management of complex projects that have many activities and interrelationships to be considered. It assists management by forcing complete and logical planning and by displaying all factors relating to a problem.

It is not a panacea but, when effectively used, it provides valuable and timely data for project management.

BACKGROUND AND HISTORY

The network approach is a major advance in the continuing development of improved management tools. For many years, bar charts have been used as a standard method of scheduling, displaying, and reviewing progress. However, it is difficult to measure progress during a project against a bar that represents a long period of time. Also, it is not possible to analyze or display by means of a bar chart the dependencies that govern project planning and schedule generation.

The bar chart technique was improved by inserting "milestones" to provide more detailed and specific control. These milestones were used to pinpoint significant events in the bar chart. While the addition of milestones was an improvement, the relationships *between* the milestones were still neglected. Thus, the next logical step was to diagram the sequence relationships among the milestones, or events, in a project. This "network" clearly described the interdependencies and interrelationships of the various tasks.

The basis for the network system was created in two parallel developments: a Du Pont Company chemical plant renovation project and the U.S. Navy's Fleet Ballistic Missile Project.

Du Pont, during the late 1950's, was interested in finding a way to schedule major renovation and maintenance projects so that a minimum amount of production was lost. With a team from the Univac Division of the Remington Rand Company, Du Pont developed a project planning and scheduling technique, based on network analysis, which came to be known as the Critical Path Method—abbreviated CPM. CPM was applied by Du Pont personnel with great success. By using this technique, they found that they saved a considerable amount of money as a result of reduced down-time.

At about the same time, the Navy Department was faced with the problem of overseeing the large, complex, and extremely important Fleet Ballistic Missile Project—the now-famous Polaris project. The problem was complicated because most of the work was new and there were several levels of subcontractors working within the many major divisions of the job. The Navy was seeking a way to calculate or predict the effect on one part of the project of developments in all other parts. The object was the isolation of trouble spots early enough to take appropriate action and to make most effective use of the available time and resources.

The U.S. Navy Special Projects Office, Lockheed Aircraft Company, and Booz, Allen & Hamilton developed, in January 1958, a technique they called Project Evaluation and Review Technique—PERT. This was a technique that produced a schedule for a project along with a statistical probability of meeting the schedule, and then evaluated and reviewed the progress of the project against this schedule. The Navy implemented the PERT system with much success on the Polaris project.

Both PERT and CPM utilize the same basic concepts, that is, the use of network analysis to plan and to schedule projects. The early differences between PERT and CPM have largely disappeared, and the term "network systems" is becoming widely used. The network system uses the features of PERT and of CPM as well as some new refinements in a continuing process of project time and cost control.

BASIC CONCEPTS

The network system is a management technique that enables a project manager to predict when the activities involved in his projects can be expected to occur. The technique uses actual job progress in a continuous process of schedule revision and improvement. It is a technique that, through this process of improvement and revision, enables the user to trust the schedule produced and make most effective use of whatever resources and limitations exist. Also, by refining and revising the schedule, the project manager is able to maintain control over rapidly changing conditions.

The system is capable of handling a high level of detail. Because of this, the user can break his project into as many activities as necessary to accurately and meaningfully describe it.

The network system consists basically of three phases:

1. Planning phase
2. Scheduling phase
3. Control-monitor phase

Note that the planning phase has been separated from the scheduling phase. One must finish the planning of the job before a schedule can be produced. Note also that the network system does not stop when the schedule has been produced, but rather continues into a control-monitor phase that remains throughout the life of the project. This phase gives the user the ability to manage his project under all circumstances, however unexpected.

The Planning Phase

During the planning phase, all necessary input data are developed. Because these inputs are crucial to the successful use of the network system, the planning phase must be performed by people completely familiar with the project.

One of the vital requirements of the network system is a complete and thorough job of project planning and analysis. *This is also one of its greatest benefits.* By performing the work required in this planning and analysis phase, one obtains intimate and early knowledge of the job and gains insights into details or anticipated problem areas that are not obtainable in any other fashion.

The planning phase consists of the following steps:

1. Determination of the scope and objectives of the project
2. Definition of activities necessary to accomplish these objectives
3. Construction of a network graphically portraying the interrelationships of the activities
4. Determination of duration estimates for each activity
5. Determination of cost and resource estimates for each activity
6. Determination of the items of material and equipment necessary for completion of the project.

Determining the scope of a project can best be accomplished by developing a work breakdown chart (*see* Figure 18-1).

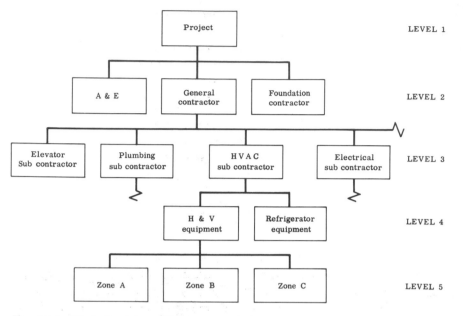

Fig. 18-1. Work Breakdown Chart

The planner prepares this chart by diagraming the various levels of work, starting with gross work groups at the top of the chart and breaking down these groups into smaller units as the chart is developed down the page. Notice in the Work Breakdown Chart that the second level consists of large, general, work categories and that lower levels break down these packages into more detailed tasks.

The project planner next constructs a network diagram for each task. This diagram graphically represents the sequence and interdependency of all the activities to one another. Additional activities are introduced to relate the various tasks. Duration estimates for each activity should not be considered at this stage of planning.

When the network diagram has been drawn and all dependencies have been indicated, resource requirements are determined and the activity durations are estimated and added to the diagram. If desired, the project planner may at this point make cost estimates for each activity and list the items of material and equipment necessary to be ordered and delivered.

The Scheduling Phase

In the scheduling phase, the input information included in the planning phase is used to produce schedules for the activities in the project.

Only simple arithmetic is necessary to prepare the schedule, and it can be done manually with pencil and paper. However, these computations are quite laborious and generally can be developed at less cost with the assistance of an electronic computer. Also, by allowing the computer to do the arithmetic, schedules can be produced faster and more accurately. The project manager can react quickly to unforeseen developments in the project, whereas manual revision of the schedule, when the unexpected occurs, is not so easily accomplished.

After schedules are produced, either by manual or computer methods, both the "Critical Path" and the "float" available to noncritical activities are known.

The Critical Path is defined as the longest path in time through the network from project start (or from "time now") to project completion. It is the sequence of activities which controls the over-all project duration. It is the path with least *float*.

Float is defined as the excess time, available within some time interval, to complete an activity. Float is further broken down into:

1. *Total float*—The difference between the amount of time available to accomplish an activity and the time estimated for that activity. It is the amount of extra time available to an activity assuming that all preceding activities have started as early as they can, and that all following activities will start as late as they can. It is the amount of time an activity could be delayed before it would delay the over-all project duration.

2. *Free float*—The amount of extra time available for an activity if every activity in the project starts as early as possible. Thus, it is the amount of float that can be allocated to an activity without interfering with subsequent work.

The Control-Monitor Phase

The control-monitor phase usually requires the use of an electronic computer. In this phase, the project manager is supplied with time status reports indicating the over-all status of the project and the status of individual activities. He is supplied with revised schedules that reflect actual job conditions. He can also obtain cost status reports that indicate how much money has been spent, and for what types of expenses. These reports can be supplied to the project manager as frequently as required to maintain control over the project.

All this information is based on the collection of actual job progress data. This data collection is a relatively simple task involving little effort.

PRODUCTS OF THE PLANNING PHASE. The planning phase has the following products:

A. A network diagram—defining the activities in the project
B. Duration estimates for each activity

C. Cost estimates for each activity (or group of activities)—for cost monitoring and cash requirement calculations

D. Manpower and other resource estimates—for resource requirement calculations

E. Responsibility indicators for each activity.

OUTPUT PRODUCED IN THE SCHEDULING PHASE. In the scheduling phase, many outputs can be produced, including:

A. A schedule for the activities described in the network diagram indicating:

    1. The critical activities

    2. The earliest start date for each activity

    3. The earliest finish date for each activity

    4. The latest start date for each activity

    5. The latest finish date for each activity

    6. The amount of extra time (float) available to an activity.

B. A bar chart for the project

C. A resource analysis—indicating the quantity of each resource to be required during each time period of the project

D. A cash requirement prediction—indicating how much money will be required to pay for the tasks in the project and the amount of money that will be coming in as a result of activity accomplishment

E. An order and delivery schedule—indicating the dates upon which each item of equipment is to be ordered and delivered

F. A daily log—showing the activities that should be in progress each day of the job. (This is available for other time units: hours, weeks, etc.)

INPUT/OUTPUT IN THE CONTROL-MONITOR PHASE. The following actual job progress data are *gathered* during the control-monitor phase:

A. Additions to the project—new activities

B. Additions to the project—new activities

C. Changes to duration, trade, description, or phase

D. Actual start dates

E. Actual finish dates or indications of partial completion

The following information can be *produced* during the control-monitor phase:

A. Time status reports

B. Revised schedules

C. Revised bar charts

D. Revised resource analyses

E. Revised cash flow predictions

F. Revised daily logs

G. Revised order and delivery schedules

H. Cost accumulation reports

I. Cost status reports

NETWORK DEVELOPMENT

A network must be drawn to identify, in graphic form, the individual items of work, services, or tasks—referred to as *activities*—that are involved in completing a project. Of equal importance, the network must show how each activity depends upon others during the sequence of the project.

In substance, the network graphically describes the sequence of activities as well as the interrelationships of activities within the project.

In a network, both arrows and circles are used to describe the sequence of work. An arrow represents an activity and a circle represents an *event*. An event is the starting point or ending point of an activity and occurs *only* when *all* the activities preceding it (which means all the arrows leading to the circle) have been completed.

In the sketch below, the starting point for the arrow marked "activity"

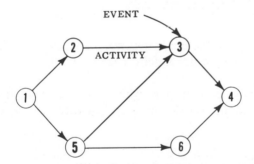

is the occurrence of event number②. Event number③ does not occur until the work represented by the arrow from② to③ *and* the work represented by the arrow from⑤ to③ has been completed—*and this means entirely completed.* This means then that the work represented by the activity from ③ to④ cannot start until② to③ and⑤ to③ have been finished. If this does not accurately describe the situation, the network must be redrawn.

Because the network system is based on dependency situations (i.e., one activity is dependent upon others), the network must be a meaningful description of the project. If it is not, less than satisfactory results will be obtained.

Network Rules and Practices

It is important that the following rules and practices be understood and applied completely:

1. Every arrow represents an item of work and is referred to as an activity. Activities are shown in the following manner:

2. An event is the starting point or ending point of an activity.

3. Each activity depends upon and cannot begin until the completion of all preceding activities.

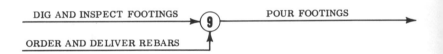

As illustrated, "pour footings" depends upon the completion of "dig & inspect footings" and "order & deliver rebars."

4. All activities that start with the same event depend upon and cannot begin until the completion of all activities that enter that event.

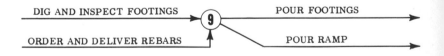

In the case illustrated above, "pour footings" and "pour ramp" depend upon the completion of the two activities that enter their common starting event. In other words, it is impossible to "pour footings" or to "pour ramp" until both "dig & inspect footings" and "order & deliver rebars" have been completed. The diagram indicates that all the footings (not just some) must be dug and inspected, and all necessary rebars must be on hand, before either of the two activities starting with event ⑨ can begin.

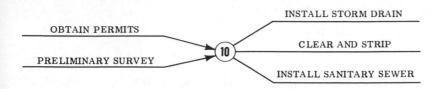

In the illustration above, all three activities that start with event ⑩ must wait until all activities that enter event ⑩ have been entirely completed. None of the three can possibly start until both "obtain permits" and "preliminary survey" have been finished. If one of three leaving ⑩ does not depend upon the completion of both these entering ⑩, the arrow diagram is misdrawn and the schedules produced from it will not be realistic.

5. An activity has a single definite starting point and a single definite ending point. In placing an arrow in a diagram, one must answer two basic questions. "What activities must be completed before this one can start?" (This indicates the event from which to start the activity.) "What activities cannot be started if this one is not completed?" (This indicates into which event the activity should enter.)

Suppose, for example, the following network had been drawn:

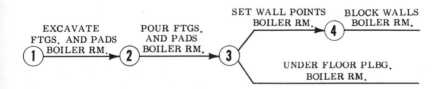

As shown above, excavating for the footings and pads for the boiler room is the first activity, followed by placing the concrete footings and pads. At event ③, and as a result of the completion of the previous activities, several independent work items can commence.

Suppose, however, that it is desired to add an activity to indicate delivery of concrete block for the walls of the boiler room. The first question asked about this new activity should be, "What must be finished before the block can be ordered and delivered?" Actually, there is nothing in the network that—if not accomplished—would hold up the ordering and delivery of block. Therefore, the starting point for this activity would be event ①.

The second question to be asked about the new activity is, "What cannot proceed until this activity is completed?" The answer is, of course, "block walls, boiler room." The termination point for this new activity then is event④, and the results of the analysis described above would look like this:

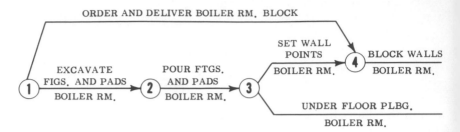

6. The network does not describe time relationships, but rather dependency relationships. Generally, the network is not drawn on a time scale. That is, the length and direction of an arrow has no relationship to the amount of time required to accomplish the work represented by it. Likewise, two activities starting with the same event do not necessarily commence simultaneously. In the diagram following, the only thing that is actually known about activities A and D is that they are independent. They may or may not take place at the same time.

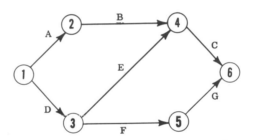

The time that an activity takes place is decided in the scheduling phase, not by the network. The network merely defines the dependency situations that exist. In the illustration involving the concrete block for the boiler room walls, for example, the activity "order and deliver boiler room block," starts with event 1 as does "excavate footings & pads," etc. This does not mean that both activities must be conducted at the same time. They might be, but probably will not be. The only thing indicated is that these two activities are independent.

7. Every activity must have a unique numeric identification. In the illustrations thus far, all the events are numbered. These numbers make it possible to identify each activity in a unique manner.

An activity is identified by using the event number at its head. In the boiler room illustration, "pour footings & pads, boiler room" could be identified as activity ② to ③. So that an activity can be uniquely identified, only one activity may have the same starting event and ending event numbers.

8. The assignment of event numbers must follow certain rules. When using a computer for scheduling, the numbers for the events can be chosen at random. The event number at the tail of an activity arrow does not have to be less than the event number at the head of the arrow.

For example, if the schedule for the network shown below is to be produced by a computer, the numbering of the events illustrated presents no problem. The only rule that must be followed in numbering the events for computer scheduling is that the same number may not be used more than once. This is so that the computer will not get dependencies confused.

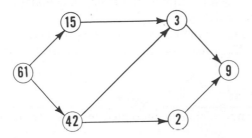

If the same number is used twice in the same network, the network would have a "loop." The numbering error would have to be located and corrected before the computer processing of the diagram could be continued.

To produce a schedule *by hand,* two rules must be followed: (1) event numbers should be sequential and (2) the number at the tail of any arrow should be less than the number at the head of that arrow.

The arithmetic necessary for the production of a schedule will be explained later. At that time the reasons for these two rules will be explained. The computer can work its way around these difficulties; therefore the rules need not be followed for computer processing. This difference between the computer and manual approaches to the scheduling phase becomes important when new activities must be added to an already numbered network. Since the rules must be followed, the whole project may need renumbering if the schedule is developed manually.

When numbering an arrow diagram, it is helpful to skip the groups of numbers containing, for example, 30's, 60's, and 90's. This will facilitate the subsequent addition of numbers anywhere in the network. If this practice is followed, the individual drawing the network will know that there are extra numbers available in the 30, -60, and 90-range.

Another helpful approach in numbering is to number events from the top to the bottom of the network vertically, moving from left to right, instead of using the traditional horizontal numbering system. This method of numbering aids in the location of an activity on the network.

It is advisable to number the network after it has been completed, reviewed, and approved.

9. A project should have only one starting event and only one ending event. When nothing is to be done prior to the start of an activity, the arrow representing that activity starts with the project's starting event. When nothing depends upon the accomplishment of an activity, its arrow ends with the project's ending event.

Actually, the computer can handle multiple starts and multiple finishes in a variety of ways, and therefore does not require a single starting event or finishing event on the network diagram. However, it has been found that when multiple start and finish events are used, an error in the network logic is often overlooked. Therefore, it is a good rule to tie all activities into the network, eliminating either intentional or erroneous multiple starts and endings.

It should be kept in mind that restricting the networks to one starting event and one ending event *does not limit the number of starting or ending activities.*

Illustration

The following example is presented to illustrate the preceding rules.

Create a network for a reinforced concrete equipment foundation to be built partially below ground level. Assume that all necessary tools, equipment, and materials (including concrete) are on the job site and that there is no limit to the number of workers. A rented backhoe is used for excavating. Use only the following activities:

1. Layout & excavate
2. Fine-grade
3. Prefabricate forms
4. Prefabricate rebar
5. Set forms
6. Set rebar & anchor bolts
7. Advise availability of backhoe
8. Pour concrete

For this problem, assume that "fine-grade" must be done before the forms are set.

One would start the network with three independent activities. Remember that the network does *not* indicate that these three items necessarily take place at the same time. It only shows that they are not dependent on the completion of any other activities.

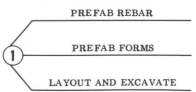

PREFAB REBAR

PREFAB FORMS

LAYOUT AND EXCAVATE

After "layout & excavate" has been completed, two activities could be started. "Fine-grade" would depend upon the completion of this activity, and the backhoe could be returned. The network would look like this:

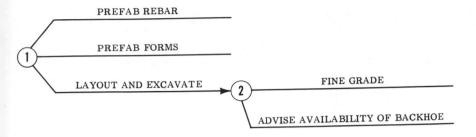

The network does not state that "fine-grade" and "advise availability of backhoe" occur simultaneously, but rather that they both depend upon and cannot start until the completion of "lay out & excavate."

After "fine-grade" had been completed and when "prefabricate forms" is finished, "set forms" could start. At its conclusion, and after "prefabricate rebar" had been completed, it would be possible to "set rebar & anchor bolts" and then finally "pour." The final network would look like this:

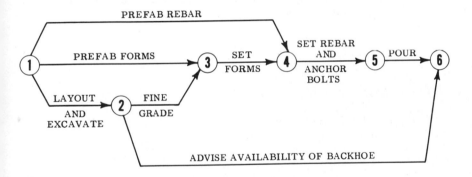

Dummy Activities

Occasionally, it is necessary to use a connector-type activity as mentioned earlier in this chapter to indicate a dependency relationship without causing confusion. This type of activity, which does not represent work and which has a duration of zero, is called a dummy and is shown on the network as a dotted line.

There are two reasons for using dummies. These two reasons can be illustrated by altering the previous example. Suppose that instead of having a single activity called "set rebar & anchor bolts," it was desired to make two activities, one called "set rebar" and the other called "set anchor bolts." Suppose that both depended upon "prefabricate rebar" and "set forms" and that both had to be completed before "pour." The affected part of the network would appear as follows:

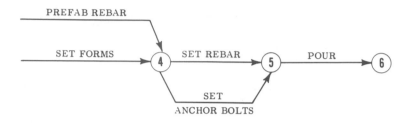

From a dependency point of view, there is nothing wrong with this kind of description. However, as mentioned earlier, it is not possible to have more than one activity with the same starting and ending event numbers. It is not clear which is activity ④-⑤. One of the two non-unique activities must be changed into two activities, one of which is a dummy.

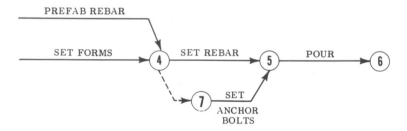

If this network is examined closely, the following points become clear.

1. Event ⑤ occurs when "set rebar" and "set anchor bolts" have been completed.
2. Since activity ④-⑦ is a dummy, it has zero duration and is completed at the same point in time as event ④ is completed.
3. For this reason, event ⑦ occurs when "set forms & prefabricate rebars" are finished; "set anchor bolts" can start at this time.
4. This is exactly the same dependency statement that was made in the incorrect solution above in which two activities from ④-⑤ appeared.

One reason for using a dummy then is to maintain the uniqueness of the activity identification system.

However, the major reason for using a dummy is somewhat more complex. A connector-type activity is sometimes needed to describe dependencies in such a way that nondependent activities are not shown as dependent. This can be also illustrated with the diagram from the previous example.

If the example were changed by eliminating the assumption that "fine-grade" had to precede the setting of the forms, one would be tempted to produce an arrow diagram that looked like the one shown below:

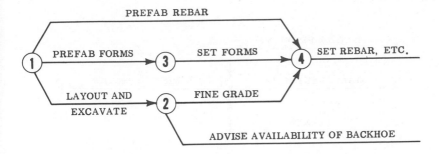

This approach, however, is incorrect because it is not possible to "set forms" until the excavating has been completed. Another solution—which is also incorrect—might be to combine event ② and event ③. Event ③ would then appear as below:

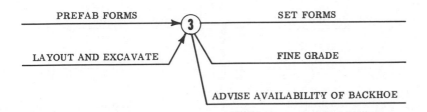

The error in this network exists because "fine-grade" and "advise availability of backhoe" do not depend upon the completion of "prefabricate forms" as indicated, but rather only on "lay out & excavate."

The correct solution is one in which "set forms" is indicated as depending upon both "prefabricate forms" and "lay out & excavate," and in which "fine-grade" and "advise availability of backhoe" depend only on "lay out & excavate." The proper way to show this situation is by using the first solution with a dummy from ② to ③, as illustrated below:

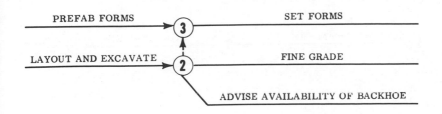

Because the dummy from ② to ③ has a zero duration, it is finished when event ② occurs. It merely transfers the desired dependency relationship—the sequence to event ③.

An example of partial dependency using a dummy is illustrated in the network below:

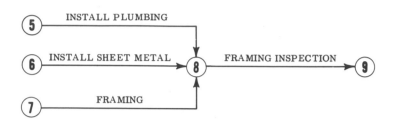

Suppose this network was found to contain the following error: The activity, "framing inspection," need not wait on the completion of all the plumbing represented by "install plumbing," but only on the completion of "plumbing top-out." This is a case of *partial dependency*. To show this concept, the network should be changed, as follows:

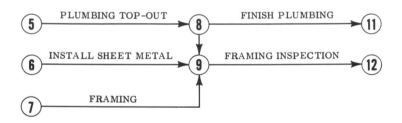

The dummy activity between events ⑧ and ⑨, and the redefinition of the activity, "install plumbing," have represented the situation accurately; that is, "framing inspection" cannot begin until "install sheet metal," "framing," and the first half of "install plumbing" are completed. The second half of "install plumbing" and "framing inspection" may proceed concurrently.

The careful use of dummies is essential. However, it is a poor practice to overuse dummies. Consider the following network:

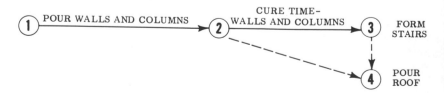

Evidently the activity, "pour roof," depends on "pour walls and columns" and "cure time—walls and columns." However, the dependency on "pour walls and columns" is shown by the links through ②—③—④. The dummy ② to ④ is unnecessary, or redundant, and should be omitted to avoid cluttering the network.

Consider also the following use of dummies:

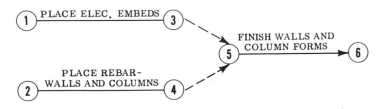

Dummies ③ to ⑤ and ④ to ⑤ are unnecessary and should be omitted for clarity. The network should be simplified as follows:

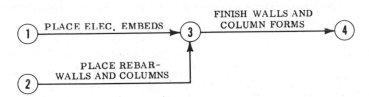

TIME ESTIMATES AND THE CRITICAL PATH

Time estimates for each activity are required to produce a schedule for the project.

The "normal" amount of time necessary to complete an activity under "normal" conditions with "normal" amounts of personnel and/or equipment is usually used as the duration estimate for an activity.

The Critical Path is the longest path, in time, through the network. It is that set of activities that controls the project's duration. It can be found by calculating and comparing the duration along all paths in the project. The one with the longest duration is the Critical Path. In the sketch below, the Critical Path includes events ①—④—③—⑥.

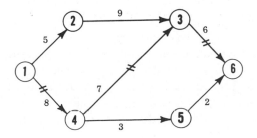

Generally, less than 30 per cent of the activities in a project become critical. It is possible to have more than one Critical Path. If a critical activity is accelerated, or if a noncritical activity is delayed, parallel Critical Paths can be produced.

NETWORK CALCULATIONS

The network calculations may be performed manually or with a computer. In a schedule, the following items of information about each activity are desired:

1. *Earliest start time (EST)*—The first day upon which work on the activity can be started if every preceding activity is finished as early as possible

2. *Earliest finish time (EFT)*—The first working day upon which no work is to be done for an activity, assuming it started on its earliest start date

3. *Latest allowable start time (LST)*—The latest possible point in time by which an activity must be started if the project is not to be delayed

4. *Latest allowable finish time (LFT)*—The latest point in time by which no further work must be done on an activity if the project is not to be delayed

5. *Float (FLT)*—The difference between the early start and the late start; the amount of extra time available to an activity; the difference between the time available and the time necessary to do a job

Manual Calculations

The first step in schedule production is the calculation of earliest start time for each event. This is calculated by determining the earliest finish time for each activity entering a given event and selecting the largest.

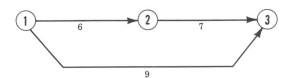

The earliest start time for event ① is zero. Event ② has only one activity entering—it can finish at time 6—so event ② can occur at time 6. Event ③ has two activities entering—②—③ can start at time 6 and finish at time 13, ①—③ can start at time zero and finish at time 9—since the maximum is 13; this is the earliest finish time for event ③.

The earliest occurrence time for each event is entered in a box beside each event, as shown at the top of the next page.

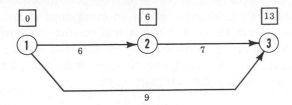

A further illustration is shown as follows:

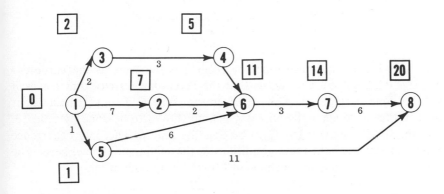

The earliest occurrence time for an event is the same as the earliest start time for all activities that start with that event.

The schedule is generated in tabular form (*see* Figure 18-2), for the network above.

starting event	ending event	time duration	EST	EFT
1	2	7	0	7
1	3	2	0	2
1	5	1	0	1
2	6	2	7	9
3	4	3	2	5
4	6	6	5	11
5	6	6	1	7
5	8	11	1	12
6	7	3	11	14
7	8	6	14	20

Fig. 18-2. Network Schedule in Tabular Form

The next step is the calculation for each event of the latest occurrence time. This is the point in time by which an event must occur so that all activities leaving it will be done in such time so that the project is not delayed. It is calculated by investigating all activities leaving an event, subtracting the duration of each from the latest finish time for the event that it enters, and choosing the minimum value.

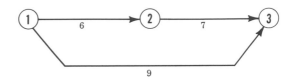

The latest occurrence time for event ③ is the same as the earliest—13. Event ② then must occur so that the seven-day activity that leaves it will be done by time 13. This is, of course, time 6. Event ① must occur at such time as to allow the nine-day activity ①—③ to be done by time 13, and the six-day activity ①—② to be done by time 6. The only occurrence time that satisfies both these conditions is the minimum choice, zero. The latest occurrence time for each event is entered by each event.

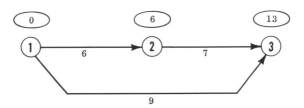

A further illustration is shown below.

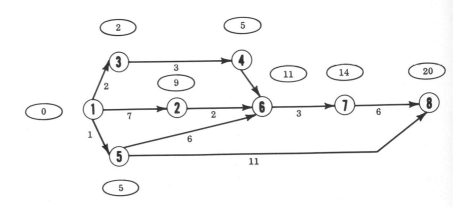

If the latest occurrence time for an event is known, the latest allowable finish time is also known. The latest start, LST, for each activity then is the duration subtracted from the LFT.

The amount of float is calculated by subtracting the early start, EST, from the latest start, LST. In some cases, this turns out to be zero. Those activities having zero float are critical.

These calculations are illustrated below for the network shown above:

starting event	ending event	time duration	EST	EFT	LST	LFT	FLT
1	2	7	0	7	2	9	2
1	3	2	0	2	0	2	0 *
1	5	1	0	1	4	5	4
2	6	2	7	9	9	11	2
3	4	3	2	5	2	5	0 *
4	6	6	5	11	5	11	0 *
5	6	6	1	7	5	11	4
5	8	11	1	12	9	20	8
6	7	3	11	14	11	14	0 *
7	8	6	14	20	14	20	0 *

* Critical Activities.

It must be noted that the schedule production described above is not quite complete. The times calculated are relative to time zero. An additional step would be required to translate the relative times into calendar dates. This step, while not difficult, is time-consuming.

Computer Calculations

When the computer is used, the same steps and arithmetic described above are performed. Input is submitted to the computer by means of punched cards containing data taken from the network. Additional input includes: the date the project is to start, the number of days in a work week, any holidays to be skipped, and any time to be allowed for weather considerations.

Computer output is the same as that worked out manually except that calendar dates are calculated instead of relative times, and float is broken down into free float as well as total float.

The computer can group activities in a variety of ways; e.g., by trade, responsibility, phase, float, etc. It is possible to delete any field of information not desired to be shown.

CONTROL-MONITOR PHASE

As the project proceeds, it tends to go out of date; thus, revision of the schedule is necessary. Data are collected about the progress of the work by marking up the schedule.

Five kinds of information can be collected.

1. *Additions*—new activities
2. *Deletions*—eliminated activities
3. *Changes*—to durations, descriptions, etc.
4. *Beginning dates*—actual information
5. *Ending dates*—actual information

The marked-up schedule can be used to produce a status report and a new schedule. The status report indicates the status of the project with respect to the original schedule. The new schedule produces the same information as the original schedule, but is updated to incorporate the data described above.

CONCLUSION

The preceding discussion contains a number of simple networks. However, in practice, networks may include hundreds or thousands of activities. A typical network is shown in Figure 18-3.

One of the new network applications is the planning and installation of new systems and procedures. Typically, systems work is project oriented; it involves many people performing tasks which are interrelated; it involves critical completion dates. The network system results in better planning, scheduling, and management of such projects. This, in turn, results in more rapid project completion and better utilization of resources. (*See* Figures 18-4 and 18-5.)

Figures 18-3, 18-4, and 18-5 appear on pages 493-497.

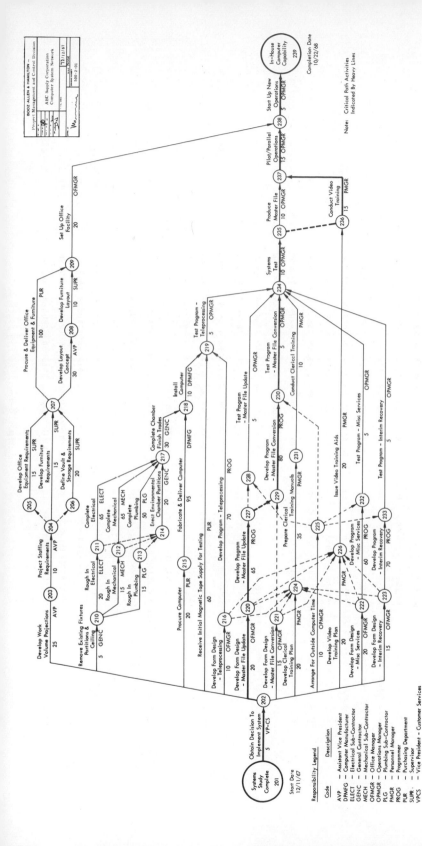

Fig. 18-3.

ABC SUPPLY CORPORATION
PHASE SCHEDULE

STARTING DATE 11DEC67
FINISH DATE 22OCT68

I	J	DESCRIPTION	DUR	TRADE	PHASE	EARLY START	EARLY FINISH	LATE START	LATE FINISH	TOTAL FLOAT	FREE FLOAT	STATUS	KEY
0202	0203	DEVELOP WORK VOLUME PROJECTION	25	AVP		18DEC67	24JAN68	07FEB68	14MAR68	35			
0203	0204	PROJECT STAFFING REQUIREMENTS	10	AVP		24JAN68	07FEB68	14MAR68	28MAR68	35			
0207	0208	DEV LAYOUT CONCEPT	30	AVP		07MAR68	18APR68	22JUL68	03SEP68	95			
0215	0218	FABRICATE + DELIVER COMPUTER	95	DPMFG		17JAN68	31MAY68	14MAR68	29JUL68	40	5		
0218	0219	INSTALL COMPUTER	10	DPMFG		07JUN68	21JUN68	29JUL68	12AUG68	35			
0210	0211	ROUGH IN ELECTRICAL	20	ELECT		26DEC67	24JAN68	14FEB68	14MAR68	35			
0211	0217	COMPLETE ELECTRICAL	65	ELECT		24JAN68	25APR68	14MAR68	14JUN68	35			
0202	0210	REM EXT FIX PARTNS + CEILING	5	GENC		18DEC67	26DEC67	07FEB68	14FEB68	35			
0214	0217	ERECT ENVIROMENT CHAMBER PARTN	20	GENC		24JAN68	21FEB68	16MAY68	14JUN68	80	45		
0217	0218	COMP CHAMBER FINISH TRADES	30	GENC		25APR68	07JUN68	14JUN68	29JUL68	35			
0210	0212	ROUGH IN MECHANICAL	15	MECH		26DEC67	17JAN68	21FEB68	14MAR68	40			
0212	0217	COMPLETE MECHANICAL	65	MECH		17JAN68	18APR68	14MAR68	14JUN68	40	5		
0202	0216	DEV FORM DESIGN TELEPROCESSING	10	OFMGR		18DEC67	03JAN68	18APR68	02MAY68	85			
0202	0220	DEV FM DESIGN MAST FILE UPDATE	20	OFMGR		18DEC67	17JAN68	18DEC67	17JAN68			CRIT	
0202	0221	DEV FM DESIGN MAST FILE CONVER	15	OFMGR		18DEC67	10JAN68	28MAR68	18APR68	70			
0202	0222	DEV FORM DESIGN MISC SERVICES	20	OFMGR		18DEC67	17JAN68	18APR68	16MAY68	85			
0202	0223	DEV FORM DESIGN INTERIM RECOV	15	OFMGR		18DEC67	10JAN68	11APR68	02MAY68	80			
0209	0238	SETUP OFFICE FACILITY	20	OFMGR		29JUL68	26AUG68	17SEP68	15OCT68	35	35		
0202	0225	ARRANGE OUTSIDE COMPUTER TIME	10	OPMGR		18DEC67	03JAN68	29JUL68	12AUG68	155			
0232	0234	TEST PROGRAM MISC SERVICES	5	OPMGR		11APR68	18APR68	12AUG68	19AUG68	85	85		
0228	0234	TEST PROG MASTER FILE UPDATE	5	OPMGR		18APR68	25APR68	12AUG68	19AUG68	80	80		
0233	0234	TEST PROGRAM INTERIM RECOVERY	5	OPMGR		18APR68	25APR68	12AUG68	19AUG68	80	80		
0219	0234	TEST PROGRAM TELEPROCESSING	5	OPMGR		21JUN68	28JUN68	12AUG68	19AUG68	35	35		
0230	0234	TEST PROG MAST FILE CONVERSION	5	OPMGR		12AUG68	19AUG68	12AUG68	19AUG68	35	35	CRIT	

Fig. 18-4A.

I	J	DESCRIPTION	DUR	TRADE PHASE	EARLY START	EARLY FINISH	LATE START	LATE FINISH	TOTAL FLOAT	FREE FLOAT	STATUS KEY
0234	0235	SYSTEMS TEST	10	OPMGR	19AUG68	03SEP68	19AUG68	03SEP68			CRIT
0235	0237	PRODUCE MASTER FILE	10	OPMGR	03SEP68	17SEP68	10SEP68	24SEP68	5	5	
0237	0238	PILOT/PARALLEL OPERATIONS	15	OPMGR	24SEP68	15OCT68	24SEP68	15OCT68			CRIT
0238	0239	START UP NEW OPERATIONS	5	OPMGR	15OCT68	22OCT68	15OCT68	22OCT68			CRIT
0210	0213	ROUGH IN PLUMBING	15	PLG	26DEC67	17JAN68	14MAR68	04APR68	55		
0213	0217	COMPLETE PLUMBING	50	PLG	17JAN68	28MAR68	04APR68	14JUN68	55	20	
0202	0224	DEV CLERICAL TRAINING PLAN	20	PMGR	18DEC67	17JAN68	16MAY68	14JUN68	105		
0202	0226	DEV VIDEO TRAINING PLAN	20	PMGR	18DEC67	17JAN68	08JUL68	05AUG68	140		
0224	0231	PREP CLERICAL TRAINING MANUALS	35	PMGR	17JAN68	07MAR68	14JUN68	05AUG68	105		
0226	0236	ISSUE VIDEO TRAINING AIDS	20	PMGR	17JAN68	14FEB68	05AUG68	03SEP68	140	140	
0231	0234	CONDUCT CLERICAL TRAINING	10	PMGR	07MAR68	21MAR68	05AUG68	19AUG68	105	105	
0236	0237	CONDUCT VIDEO TRAINING	15	PMGR	03SEP68	24SEP68	03SEP68	24SEP68			CRIT
0216	0219	DEV PROGRAM TELEPROCESSING	70	PROG	03JAN68	11APR68	02MAY68	12AUG68	85	50	
0223	0233	DEV PROGRAM INTERIM RECOVERY	70	PROG	10JAN68	18APR68	02MAY68	12AUG68	80		
0220	0227	DEV PROG MASTER FILE UPDATE	65	PROG	17JAN68	18APR68	17JAN68	18APR68			CRIT
0222	0232	DEV PROGRAM MISC SERVICES	60	PROG	17JAN68	11APR68	16MAY68	12AUG68	85		
0229	0230	DEV PROG MAST FILE CONVERSION	80	PROG	18APR68	12AUG68	18APR68	12AUG68			CRIT
0202	0215	PROCURE COMPUTER	20	PUR	18DEC67	17JAN68	14FEB68	14MAR68	40		
0202	0219	REC INL MAG TAPE SUPL FOR TEST	60	PUR	18DEC67	14MAR68	16MAY68	12AUG68	105	70	
0207	0209	PROC + DELIV OFF EQUIP + FURN	100	PUR	07MAR68	29JUL68	25APR68	17SEP68	35		
0204	0207	DEV FURNITURE REQUIREMENTS	15	SUPR	07FEB68	29FEB68	04APR68	25APR68	40	5	
0205	0207	DEV OFFICE EQUIPMENT REQUIRE	15	SUPR	07FEB68	29FEB68	04APR68	25APR68	40	5	
0206	0207	DEFINE VAULT + STORAGE REQUIRE	20	SUPR	07FEB68	07MAR68	28MAR68	25APR68	35		
0208	0209	DEV FURNITURE LAYOUT	10	SUPR	18APR68	02MAY68	03SEP68	17SEP68	95	60	
0201	0202	OBT DECISION TO IMPLEMENT SYSM	5	VP-CS	11DEC67	18DEC67	11DEC67	18DEC67			CRIT

Fig. 18-4B.

ABC SUPPLY CORPORATION
FLOAT SCHEDULE

STARTING DATE 11DEC67
FINISH DATE 22OCT68

I	J	DESCRIPTION	DUR	TRADE PHASE	EARLY START	EARLY FINISH	LATE START	LATE FINISH	TOTAL FLOAT	FREE FLOAT	STATUS	KEY
0201	0202	OBT DECISION TO IMPLEMENT SYSM	5	VP-CS	11DEC67	18DEC67	11DEC67	18DEC67			CRIT	
0202	0220	DEV F4 DESIGN MAST FILE UPDATE	20	OFMGR	18DEC67	17JAN68	18DEC67	17JAN68			CRIT	
0220	0227	DEV PROG MASTER FILE UPDATE	65	PROG	17JAN68	18APR68	17JAN68	18APR68			CRIT	
0229	0230	DEV PROG MAST FILE CONVERSION	80	PROG	18APR68	12AUG68	18APR68	12AUG68			CRIT	
0230	0234	TEST PROG MAST FILE CONVERSION	5	OPMGR	12AUG68	19AUG68	12AUG68	19AUG68			CRIT	
0234	0235	SYSTEMS TEST	10	OPMGR	19AUG68	03SEP68	19AUG68	03SEP68			CRIT	
0236	0237	CONDUCT VIDEO TRAINING	15	PMGR	03SEP68	24SEP68	03SEP68	24SEP68			CRIT	
0237	0238	PILOT/PARALLEL OPERATIONS	15	OPMGR	24SEP68	15OCT68	24SEP68	15OCT68			CRIT	
0238	0239	START UP NEW OPERATIONS	5	OPMGR	15OCT68	22OCT68	15OCT68	22OCT68			CRIT	
0235	0237	PRODUCE MASTER FILE	10	OPMGR	03SEP68	17SEP68	10SEP68	24SEP68	5	5		
0202	0203	DEVELOP WORK VOLUME PROJECTION	25	AVP	18DEC67	24JAN68	07FEB68	14MAR68	35			
0202	0210	REM EXT FIX PARTNS + CEILING	5	GENC	18DEC67	26DEC67	07FEB68	14FEB68	35			
0210	0211	ROUGH IN ELECTRICAL	20	ELECT	26DEC67	24JAN68	14FEB68	14MAR68	35			
0203	0204	PROJECT STAFFING REQUIREMENTS	10	AVP	24JAN68	07FEB68	14MAR68	28MAR68	35			
0211	0217	COMPLETE ELECTRICAL	65	ELECT	24JAN68	25APR68	14MAR68	14JUN68	35			
0206	0207	DEFINE VAULT + STORAGE REQUIRE	20	SUPR	07FEB68	07MAR68	28MAR68	25APR68	35			
0207	0209	PROC + DELIV OFF EQUIP + FURN	100	PUR	07MAR68	29JUL68	25APR68	17SEP68	35			
0217	0218	COMP CHAMBER FINISH TRADES	30	GENC	25APR68	07JUN68	14JUN68	29JUL68	35			
0218	0219	INSTALL COMPUTER	10	DPMFG	07JUN68	21JUN68	29JUL68	12AUG68	35			
0219	0234	TEST PROGRAM TELEPROCESSING	5	OPMGR	21JUN68	28JUN68	12AUG68	19AUG68	35	35		
0209	0238	SETUP OFFICE FACILITY	20	OFMGR	29JUL68	26AUG68	17SEP68	15OCT68	35	35		
0202	0215	PROCURE COMPUTER	20	PUR	18DEC67	17JAN68	14FEB68	14MAR68	40			
0210	0212	ROUGH IN MECHANICAL	15	MECH	26DEC67	17JAN68	21FEB68	14MAR68	40			
0212	0217	COMPLETE MECHANICAL	65	MECH	17JAN68	18APR68	14MAR68	14JUN68	40	5		

Fig. 18-5A.

I	J	DESCRIPTION	DUR	TRADE PHASE	EARLY START	EARLY FINISH	LATE START	LATE FINISH	TOTAL FLOAT	FREE FLOAT	STATUS	KEY
0215	0218	FABRICATE + DELIVER COMPUTER	95	DPMFG	17JAN68	31MAY68	14MAR68	29JUL68	40	5		
0204	0207	DEV FURNITURE REQUIREMENTS	15	SUPR	07FEB68	29FEB68	04APR68	25APR68	40	5		
0205	0207	DEV OFFICE EQUIPMENT REQUIRE	15	SUPR	07FEB68	29FEB68	04APR68	25APR68	40	5		
0210	0213	ROUGH IN PLUMBING	15	PLG	26DEC67	17JAN68	14MAR68	04APR68	55			
0213	0217	COMPLETE PLUMBING	50	PLG	17JAN68	28MAR68	04APR68	14JUN68	55	20		
0202	0221	DEV FM DESIGN MAST FILE CONVER	15	OFMGR	18DEC67	10JAN68	28MAR68	18APR68	70			
0202	0223	DEV FORM DESIGN INTERIM RECOV	15	OFMGR	18DEC67	10JAN68	11APR68	02MAY68	80			
0223	0233	DEV PROGRAM INTERIM RECOVERY	70	PROG	10JAN68	18APR68	02MAY68	12AUG68	80			
0214	0217	ERECT ENVIROMENT CHAMBER PARTN	20	GENC	24JAN68	21FEB68	16MAY68	14JUN68	80	45		
0228	0234	TEST PROG MASTER FILE UPDATE	5	OPMGR	18APR68	25APR68	12AUG68	19AUG68	80	80		
0233	0234	TEST PROGRAM INTERIM RECOVERY	5	OPMGR	18APR68	25APR68	12AUG68	19AUG68	80	80		
0202	0216	DEV FORM DESIGN TELEPROCESSING	10	OFMGR	18DEC67	03JAN68	18APR68	02MAY68	85			
0202	0222	DEV FORM DESIGN MISC SERVICES	20	OFMGR	18DEC67	17JAN68	18APR68	16MAY68	85			
0216	0219	DEV PROGRAM TELEPROCESSING	70	PROG	03JAN68	11APR68	02MAY68	12AUG68	85	50		
0222	0232	DEV PROGRAM MISC SERVICES	60	PROG	17JAN68	11APR68	16MAY68	12AUG68	85			
0232	0234	TEST PROGRAM MISC SERVICES	5	OPMGR	11APR68	18APR68	12AUG68	19AUG68	85	85		
0207	0208	DEV LAYOUT CONCEPT	30	AVP	07MAR68	18APR68	22JUL68	03SEP68	95			
0208	0209	DEV FURNITURE LAYOUT	10	SUPR	18APR68	02MAY68	03SEP68	17SEP68	95	60		
0202	0219	REC INL MAG TAPE SUPL FOR TEST	60	PUR	18DEC67	14MAR68	16MAY68	12AUG68	105	70		
0202	0224	DEV CLERICAL TRAINING PLAN	20	PMGR	18DEC67	17JAN68	16MAY68	14JUN68	105			
0224	0231	PREP CLERICAL TRAINING MANUALS	35	PMGR	17JAN68	07MAR68	14JUN68	05AUG68	105			
0231	0234	CONDUCT CLERICAL TRAINING	10	PMGR	07MAR68	21MAR68	05AUG68	19AUG68	105	105		
0202	0226	DEV VIDEO TRAINING PLAN	20	PMGR	18DEC67	17JAN68	08JUL68	05AUG68	140			
0226	0236	ISSUE VIDEO TRAINING AIDS	20	PMGR	17JAN68	14FEB68	05AUG68	03SEP68	140	140		
0202	0225	ARRANGE OUTSIDE COMPUTER TIME	10	OPMGR	18DEC67	03JAN68	29JUL68	12AUG68	155			

Fig. 18-5B.

497

Outline for Conducting and Implementing a Systems Study

V. LAZZARO

*Merrill Lynch, Pierce, Fenner
and Smith Inc.
New York, N.Y.*

The following outline serves to guide the systems analyst in the proper undertaking and implementation of a systems project. Though this outline covers conditions and areas that an analyst may not necessarily apply in the usual situation, it does highlight the factors which must be or should be taken into consideration either subconsciously or knowingly when undertaking a major study.

Experience indicates that there is no short cut to a complete and comprehensive systems study, whether it is a general systems project, an EDP project, or an integrated data processing assignment. The bypassing of a specific item should be done with the understanding that it does not apply to the areas being analyzed. Suffice it to say that the analyst should review each phase of the outline in relation to the study and then take action accordingly.

I. MAJOR AREAS OF STUDY

1. Define the Assignment—Determine Objectives
2. Prepare Outline of Study
3. Schedule Phases of the Project
4. Get Facts—Fact Finding
5. Analyze Data
6. Develop Proposed Method or New System
7. Prepare Cost Analysis—Present versus Proposed
8. Sell the Idea
9. Testing and Implementing Proposed Method
10. Follow up and Re-evaluate

II. DEFINE THE ASSIGNMENT—DETERMINE OBJECTIVES

1. Source of Assignment:
   A. PRODUCT CHANGE
   B. MANAGEMENT DECISION
   C. NEW EQUIPMENT—COMPUTER
   D. CUSTOMER COMPLAINTS, ERRORS
   E. RELOCATION OF DEPARTMENT
   F. TIME SCHEDULE
   G. IMPROVED PROCEDURE TO REDUCE COSTS

2. Define the Project
   A. HOLD PRELIMINARY DISCUSSION OF PROJECT WITH ORIGIN OF STUDY
       AND KEY MANAGEMENT INDIVIDUALS AFFECTED BY STUDY.
   B. GET THEIR INTERPRETATION OF PROBLEM.
   C. ARRIVE AT MEETING OF MINDS AS TO OBJECTIVES, SCOPE, ETC.

3. Undertake Preliminary Study—Reconnaissance Survey. Make Brief
   Review of Facts and Problem Situation.

4. Re-define Problem from Systems Department Viewpoint:
   A. TYPE OF STUDY:

   (a) Is this a systems study?
   (b) Is this a procedure study?
   (c) Is this an equipment replacement study?
   (d) Is this an integrated data processing study?

   B. DEFINE OR RE-DEFINE PROBLEM
   C. ESTIMATE MANPOWER REQUIREMENTS AND TIMETABLE
   D. ESTABLISH ATTENTION AREAS
   E. DETERMINE LIKELY COST
   F. DETERMINE SPECIAL SKILLS REQUIRED BEYOND ABILITY OF SYSTEMS
       STAFF
   G. ESTABLISH OBJECTIVES:

   (a) To lower costs
   (b) To improve flow of data
   (c) To strengthen operating controls
   (d) To automate
   (e) To meet external requirements
   (f) To meet customer requirements, new regulations, etc.

5. Compare Objective to cost of Study. (*Should One Spend $20,000 to
   Save $10,000?*)

6. Obtain Agreement and Approval on:
   A. NEW DEFINITION OF PROBLEM
   B. LATITUDE OF STUDY
   C. DESIRED RESULTS
   D. COST OF STUDY
   E. USE OF CONSULTANTS

III. PREPARE OUTLINE OF STUDY. PLAN THE ATTACK TO SUCCEED! (*DON'T BE TOO AMBITIOUS.*) AIM AT ACHIEVABLE RESULTS AND SALABLE APPROACHES FOR IMPLEMENTATION! USE TOTAL SYSTEMS CONCEPT

1. Breakdown Study into Major Phases:

   A. PERSONNEL
   B. EQUIPMENT, PHYSICAL FACILITIES, TOOLS
   C. SPACE, LAYOUT
   D. PRODUCTS
   E. PRODUCTIVITY
   F. COMMUNICATIONS
   G. PROCEDURES
   H. AUTOMATED DATA PROCESSING
   I. ORGANIZATIONAL SETUP
   J. POLICIES, RULES, REGULATIONS
   K. MARKETING (*Sales*) ASPECT
   L. RECORDS (*Type, storage, retention*)

2. Establish Outline in Sequence of Information Needed. Confine Limits of Study to Area Under Survey.
3. Define Each Phase and Determine Necessity for:

   A. WRITE-UP OF PRESENT PROCEDURES (*If not available*)
   B. WORK DISTRIBUTION CHART
   C. WORK FLOW DATA
   D. WORK MEASUREMENT DATA
   E. PRODUCTIVITY RECORDS
   F. COST RECORDS

4. Ascertain Timetable of Each Phase.
5. Ascertain Funds and Manpower Available.
6. Develop Final Outline.
7. Submit Progress Reports. (*Keep management informed!*)

IV. SCHEDULE PHASES OF THE PROJECT

1. Use Schedule Graphs:

   A. GANTT CHARTS
   B. PERT (*Program evaluation and review technique*)
   C. CPM (*Critical path method*)

2. Determine Areas That Can Be Worked on Simultaneously.
3. Assign Phases to Analyst, Team, or People Working on Project.
4. Use Project Control and Progress Charts.

V. GET FACTS—FACT FINDING

1. Notify All Concerned Based on New Definition. Hold Meetings with Department Managers, Supervisors and Employees as Warranted.

   A. EXPLAIN REASONS FOR STUDY.
   B. OBTAIN COOPERATION OF EMPLOYEES.
   C. NOTIFY EMPLOYEES ON DATA TO BE COLLECTED BY THEM. GIVE EMPLOYEES A ROLE.

2. Record Facts:

    A. IN SIMPLEST MANNER POSSIBLE.
    B. TO BE UNDERSTOOD BY ALL.
    C. TO BE ABLE TO PUT DATA TOGETHER.
    D. TO LOCATE EASILY AND FOR REFERENCE PURPOSES.

3. Use Questionnaires, and Interview Affected Personnel.
4. Develop Work Distribution Chart(s).
5. Ascertain Productivity, Unit Time, Cycle Time, etc. (*Utilize work measurement, time studies*).
6. Ascertain Equipment Utilization, Ratio Delay Studies.
7. Study Existing Records.
8. Develop:

    A. MAN MACHINE CHARTS
    B. FLOW PROCESS CHARTS
    C. LOGICAL DIAGRAMS
    D. TOOLS
    E. GRAPHS

9. Examine Equipment on the Market.
10. Visit Other Companies and Installations.
11. Study Company Policies, Rules, Regulations, Regulatory Rules. Follow Cycle from Beginning to End. Separate Fact from Fiction.

VI. ANALYZE DATA

1. Arrange Data in Logical Sequence of Analysis and Relationship.
2. Verify Facts as Necessary. Is Data Complete?
3. Answer All Questions—What, Where, When, Who, and Why—for Each Step or Fact, Not only for Process Charts but for Other Areas Such as Policies, Layout, Organizational Structure, Equipment.
4. Discuss Facts with Line People to Ascertain Accuracy and Agree on Possible Solutions.

VII. DEVELOP THE PROPOSED METHOD OR NEW SYSTEM

1. Initially, Let Imagination Run Wild! Consider Several Solutions. What is One Best Way?
2. Refine One Best Way to Practical Application.
3. Consider Various Proposals to Objectives.
4. Relate Possible Solutions for Effect on

    A. EMPLOYEES
    B. PROFITS
    C. SCHEDULES
    D. CUSTOMERS

5. Are Solutions Attainable and Feasible?
6. Evaluate Proposed Methods as to:

    A. FEASIBILITY (*Degree of success 50-100 per cent?*)
    B. LIKELY INSTALLATION COSTS, EQUIPMENT, ETC.
    C. POSSIBILITY OF ACHIEVING OBJECTIVES OF STUDY

7. Decide on Best Workable Method and Refine it for Implementation.

8. Develop Models for Test.
9. Prepare New Procedures and Forms to Conform to Proposed Method. Decide on New Equipment, Layout, etc.

VIII. PREPARE COST ANALYSIS—PRESENT VS. PROPOSED

1. For Present and Each Likely Proposed Plan Ascertain:
   A. SALARIES
   B. SPACE
   C. MATERIAL AND SUPPLIES (*Postage, telephone*)
   D. LOSS IN BUSINESS
   E. OVERHEAD—TAXES, LIGHT, INSURANCE
   F. COST OF CAPITAL
   G. PROFITS EARNED ON CAPITAL
2. Compare Costs (*Investment recovery in three to five years*).
3. Compare Costs of Each Plan Suggested.
4. Consider Equipment:
   A. PURCHASE
   B. RENTAL
5. Develop Savings Anticipated.

IX. SELL THE IDEA

1. Report Approach:
   A. VERBAL
   B. WRITTEN
2. Conferences and Discussions with Affected People
3. Dropping Suggestions
4. Using Trial Approach
5. Emphasizing Savings and Advantages
6. Relating Expected Results in Profits, Income, Number of Sales Orders

X. TESTING AND IMPLEMENTING PROPOSED METHOD

1. Should Test be Made? If "Yes," Determine Limits.
2. Dual Operation
3. Complete Conversion
4. New Machines
5. New Forms
6. New Policies
7. New Skills, Training
8. Organizational Change
9. Layout
10. Necessity to Coordinate Printing of Forms, Arrival of New Equipment, Training, New Space Layout, etc.
11. Ten Guides to Installation:
    A. BE READY BEFORE STARTING.
    B. MAINTAIN INSTALLATION SCHEDULE.

    C. AVOID RASH, EMERGENCY DECISIONS.

    D. ANTICIPATE AND ELIMINATE CRISES.

    E. DON'T LOSE CONFIDENCE AND ENTHUSIASM.

    F. KEEP EVERYONE CONCERNED COMPLETELY INFORMED OF CHANGE-OVER PROGRESS.

    G. BE CAREFUL TO PREVENT DISSENSION AMONG PERSONNEL DURING INSTALLATION.

    H. AVOID OVERTIME TO ACCOMPLISH CHANGEOVER. USE TEMPORARY HELP IF NECESSARY.

    I. AVOID DISRUPTION OF DATA FLOW AND SERVICE DURING INSTALLATION.

    J. DO NOT SACRIFICE THOROUGHNESS FOR SPEED.

XI. FOLLOW UP AND RE-EVALUATION

1. Examine Installation.
2. What Further Improvements Are Possible?
3. Refine Problem Areas. Obtain Reaction of Employees and Management.
4. Re-evaluate Achievements to Objectives and Costs. Did Savings, etc., Materialize? If Not, Why Not?
5. Prepare Final Report.

Case Study—
The Walnut Furniture
Company

EUGENE V. REDMOND

Sterling Drug Inc.
New York, N.Y.

EUGENE V. REDMOND has had experience in both factory and office systems applications including such companies as Emerson Radio Corp. and Lily Tulip Cup Corp. Since 1960, as director of systems and planning for Sterling Drug Inc., he has been responsible for developing a wide range of automated and manual systems applications.

Mr. Redmond has a B.S. degree in industrial engineering, and is an adjunct assistant professor of management at the Management Institute of New York University. He is a member of the editorial review board of the Systems and Procedures Journal, *and former chairman of the Metropolitan Systems Council of the Systems and Procedures Association of America. He has lectured at the American Management Association, and is a charter member and former officer of the Knickerbocker Chapter of the Systems and Procedures Association.*

The Walnut Furniture Company has been manufacturing furniture at its original location in South Carolina for almost 100 years. During that period it has grown steadily from a family-owned maker of children's school desks to a major factor in the retail furniture industry. Recently, there has been a change in management as a result of the retirement of the last of the original family owners.

The new management decided to make a fundamental analysis of the retail furniture industry and its growth possibilities. In a study by a reputable consultant, the following points were emphasized:

1. Retail furniture sales of WFC are made either direct (60 per cent) or through jobbers (40 per cent). Industrial sales are made 100 per cent through jobbers.
2. Many jobbers handle competitive lines.
3. Jobbers do not warehouse stock, but retailers do.
4. Delivery time is *not* the major factor in closing a retail sale, while it *is* the major factor in closing an industrial sale.

5. Competitors' merchandise may possibly be more advantageously displayed in retail showrooms.
6. Retail buyers of major furniture pieces are often in the market for other major home furnishing items.

It was decided that the timely acquisition, manipulation, and control of all management information would be essential to the successful penetration of competitive markets. A management information specialist was hired to develop, where needed, economically sound systems consistent with the stated objectives. He met and conferred with the sales, manufacturing, and financial vice-presidents.

In order to accomplish his assignment, the information specialist decided to survey the major systems now utilized within the company. Following is a summary of his findings.

ORDER PROCESSING PROCEDURE

Orders are received by mail and phone at the South Carolina plant (100,000 per year). Mail orders are separated from correspondence, edited for acceptability and clarification of item groups ordered (two clerks). Unclarified orders are referred to the sales division for a decision.

A billing clerk sorts edited orders alphabetically at the FlexoWriter work station. Edge-punched header cards are selected from a tub file and placed on top of the order document. NOTE: The credit department removes header cards daily for accounts that have been placed on the referral list. If no header card, the billing clerk sends this order to credit. Orders are held there, for accounts on the referral list, until collection is completed. If a new account, the new account procedure is instituted (unless there is an unfavorable decision on opening the account, in which case, the order is returned with a letter).

Orders are passed to the inventory clerk, who reduces the perpetual inventory record balance. If an item is out of stock, the ordered item is marked "BO". If special routing instructions (not on header card) are requested, the order is sent to the traffic department; otherwise it is returned to the billing clerks.

A billing clerk places the header card in the feed and selects the first product card while the FlexoWriter types the heading data. The machine is programmed to stop for operator's entry of customer order number and special instructions. The header card is then replaced by the first product card and refiled. The billing clerk enters the ordered quantity of the first product on the keyboard. While the FlexoWriter extends and types the line-item data, the billing clerk selects the next product card and enters the appropriate quantity on the keyboard for the next line-item. This cycle is repeated until the last line-item has been entered. The operator then depresses the required sales tax, discount and/or total keys to complete the invoice. Nonrepetitive special instructions are manually typed at this point.

Periodically, groups of billed orders are detached by the billing clerk and brought with the original orders to the proofreaders. At the end of each day, all punched paper tapes are placed in an envelope and delivered to data processing. The proofreader checks heading and product data, account identification, special instructions, application of proper discount and sales tax percentages, and adherence to minimum sale policy requirements ($100). If an error is detected, the order is returned to the billing clerk; otherwise, the order is released to the warehouse. Invoices that do not meet minimum order requirements are sent to the manager for customer notification. The order processing (including billing) and sales control functions are responsible to the Comptroller.

WAREHOUSE PROCEDURE

The warehouse scheduling clerk detaches the top two (invoice) copies and places them in an envelope marked "Invoice Inside" and staples the envelope behind the invoice set. The date and time are stamped on the top shipping copy; the routing is typed on this copy using a standard routing guide as reference (unless special routing instructions are noted by traffic clerk). A bill of lading is typed indicating the shipper, shipper's number, destination, routing, and number of packages by class. A shipping stencil is handprinted, specifying shipper's number, name, and destination. The shipping set and stencil are given to a warehouseman and the bill of lading is pended by carrier (freight is prepaid).

The warehouseman selects the item(s) ordered and, using a fork lift truck, delivers the order to the shipping dock (all large packages are palletized). Each item delivered is stenciled and checked off; the completed shipping order is initialed and dated. The "Invoice Inside" envelope is detached and stapled to the largest package of the order. If the company is unable to ship the entire order, the item is lined-out on the shipping set, and the "Invoice Inside" envelope does not accompany the merchandise but remains attached to the shipping set. All shipping sets are picked up periodically by the control clerk.

After loading the carrier, the driver signs and dates the bill of lading pended in the warehouse office. One copy is filed in the warehouse by date; two copies are sent to sales control and the fourth copy remains with the driver.

The warehouse manager supervises all receiving, shipping, and order picking activities, and is responsible to the manufacturing vice-president.

SALES CONTROL

Each morning, the previous day's shipping sets are accumulated; if any have the "Invoice Inside" envelope attached, they are separated and given to a billing operator for re-billing. All other invoice-shipping sets are pended awaiting return of the re-bills.

Shipping sets requiring re-billing are processed as outlined previously, except that all copies, save the top shipping set copy, are destroyed. The new invoice-shipping set, together with the saved shipping set copy, is given to the proofreaders, and, if found to be correct, is sent to the availability desk for adding back into inventory. The documents are returned to sales control for inclusion in the day's sales.

An adding machine tape is made of all the shipping set copies reflecting the entire day's billing (invoice number and dollars). The adding machine tape is sent to data processing. One signed bill of lading copy is matched and stapled to the shipping copy before sending it to the file clerk; the other bill of lading copy is forwarded to the traffic department.

Data processing converts the punched paper tapes to punched cards (interpreted) daily, adding in the sales (shipping) date after the matching card is selected. Card totals (for the batch) are summarized and compared to the adding machine tape for validation of discrepancies and/or missing invoices. Cards are sorted alphabetically to prepare the daily order register.

The original copy is sent to the order processing department and the duplicate is filed in data processing.

After preparation of the daily order register, sales summary cards are converted to magnetic tape (medium-size computer) and balanced to the control total. The daily sales tapes are sorted alphabetically to update the customer master tape. A product sort is made to update the product master tape. Data is sorted by salesman and/or jobber to update the salesman's tape. Sales summary cards are sent to accounts receivable with the adding machine tape prepared by order processing.

ACCOUNTS RECEIVABLE

Accounts receivable summary cards (400/day) are manually inserted into the tub files (alphabetical sequence). The number of open items average about 20,000.

Payments are received daily (200/day), separated, sorted and matched to the appropriate open item (three clerks). Unmatched payment items that are within $1 of the correct amount are credited as payment in full. Remaining unmatched items (unearned discounts, partial payments, overpayments, etc.) are mark-sensed for the payment amount received.

A tape of the card payments (gross and discount) is balanced to a tape of the daily cash receipts. A deposit slip is prepared on a bank designated by the treasurer.

A typed listing is made of the unmatched receipt items in excess of $1, with a copy to the credit section as notification to contact the customer. Matched payment cards are sent to data processing with the adding machine tape, mark-sensed cards and a copy of the unmatched receipts listing.

Data processing converts mark-sensed unmatched payment cards to reflect the amount received. Cards are balanced to the adding machine tape. A daily listing of remittances is prepared by the day following the completion of the matching operation. New transaction cards for the balance due are punched at this time and sent to accounts receivable. Old transaction cards with the payment date gang-punched are returned to accounts receivable as a record of the completed transaction.

Monthly statements and an aged trial balance are prepared from the unmatched open item cards in the accounts receivable tub files at the cut-off date. Statements are sent to the mailroom where they are mailed in window envelopes to the customer.

A payment activity card is prepared monthly for all accounts, summarizing the monthly amount outstanding, and the amounts paid promptly, thirty, sixty, or ninety days past due (one printed line on the card per month). The card contains a two-year payment history of the account when completely posted.

COLLECTIONS, REFERRALS AND NEW ACCOUNTS

Customer payments that do not match the accounts receivable open item amount are listed on a report from the accounts receivable department. Such unmatched items are reviewed against the aged trial balance report (monthly) and the current correspondence file. If the variance is not readily explainable (i.e., deduction for a return, etc.) the credit man writes the customer, requesting the balance due. If the amount in question is large in relation to the account's line of credit, the customer is placed on the referral list by removing the header card from the tub file.

Payments received by the credit man are forwarded to the accounts receivable department with a copy of the customer's letter and an adding machine tape of the payment batch. Correspondence is continued on uncollected remittance until the transaction is satisfactorily concluded.

The credit department receives customer orders which are lacking header cards in the billing tub file. If the account is delinquent (determined by a review of the aged trial balance and correspondence file), the order is pended and the credit man notifies the customer, usually in conjunction with the next collection letter.

If the order is from a new account, it is checked against trade credit sources to determine acceptability. If the account is acceptable, approval is indicated on the order and returned to the billing clerk (one) after sales approval. A new account form is sent to data processing to update the master files. If the account is unacceptable, the order is returned to the order processing supervisor for notification of the customer.

Additions or deletions are made to the referred list daily, based on the most current information. All referred header cards are kept in one file tray in the credit department regardless of who is responsible for the account.

SALES AND INVENTORY REPORTS

Product and Customer sales data are accumulated daily, using the computer tape equipment configuration. At the end of every ten-day, twenty-day, and monthly period, a listing is made of product sales (product code, description, quantity and dollars).

Monthly, customer sales reports are prepared listing product quantity and dollars by customer within each sales territory. Summaries are prepared for regional and U.S. sales activity.

Similarly, item inventory balances are computed at the same periods. Inventory reports include allocations covering orders received but not shipped due to out-of-stock condition. Such balances are recorded as minus quantities.

INVENTORY CONTROL

Inventory reports are received from data processing at ten-, twenty-, and thirty-day intervals. Notification is received whenever a shortage condition develops for more than twenty-four hours during the filling of customer orders. In such instances, it is the responsibility of the inventory section to ascertain a definite production date (in coordination with the scheduling function) or to seek transfer of the merchandise from a customer's warehouse having excess stock to the customer that is temporarily short. To meet these responsibilities, the inventory function needs information on inventory levels both in the company warehouse and in major customer storage points. It requires up-to-date knowledge of items short, orders unshipped, and production scheduled.

Upon receipt of a shortage notification, the inventory supervisor requests a confirming stock search from the warehouse manager. A check is made with the scheduling supervisor to determine if finished stock is expected within twenty-four hours. If either source indicates a positive answer, notification is made to release the order; if both sources are negative, a search is made of customer inventory reports (received quarterly). If a customer's inventory indicates possible availability, the customer is contacted for transfer authority at WFC expense. Failure of these procedures results in querying the scheduling supervisor for the best available date which is passed on to the order processing supervisor for customer notification. Unresolvable situations are brought to the attention of the manufacturing vice-president who is responsible for inventory control, traffic, and scheduling activities.

Every ten days, the inventory and scheduling supervisors meet to review production priorities using the ten-day sales and inventory reports as guides. A back order report is issued listing the scheduled quantity and date for all items on allocation.

Purchasing consists of two basic categories: raw and semifinished materials, and office supplies.

Raw and semifinished material are purchased on a bid system. All purchase orders over $200 require three bids. The typical raw material purchase order is about $300. Approximately 450 quotation requests are mailed out per week and these result in about 150 purchase orders per week (exclusive of office supplies). There are two buyers, two assistant buyers, one control clerk, and two typists for raw materials (although the same typists also prepare office supply purchase orders). The manager of purchasing has a secretary and believes that he now requires an additional buyer and control clerk. Purchasing policies are set by the president who is directly responsible for the purchasing function.

Buyers receive a weekly inventory position of all raw and semifinished materials from data processing. This report is reviewed by the control clerk (3,000 items) for minimum balance conditions, which are flagged to the appropriate buyer for purchasing action. In addition, there are requisitions for special items or telephone notifications of out-of-stock conditions for inventoried stock. If a buyer has reason to believe replenishment is not needed now, he may hold up an order pending a storage check or a necessity evaluation.

If the order is less than $200, he will approve the requisition (if there is one) or note the quantity, description, vendor, and price on a slip of paper which goes to the purchase order typists.

If more than one vendor is indicated, the purchase order typist prepares a five-part quotation form. Parts one, two, and three are mailed to the vendors (a separate vendor name—one only—appears on each of these copies), and two copies are pended. Returned bids are attached to the fifth (file) copy and the approved bid (or requisition, or notation from the buyer) is used to type a six-part purchase order (two copies to vendor, one each to receiving, accounting, originator and file). Quotation copies are attached to the file copy of purchase order and pended by vendor name awaiting the acknowledgment and invoice.

When received, vendor invoices are matched to the pended purchase order copy, initialed for price verification and the original invoice is released to accounts payable with the number four quotation copy (the duplicate invoice is retained by purchasing). Price discrepancies are resolved before releasing to accounts payable.

Office supplies are purchased on authority of a signed purchase requisition (two copies to purchasing, one copy for file). The office supplies buyer approves the requisition, indicates price (after phone check, if needed) and vendor. Purchase order typing (100/week) is the same as outlined previously, except that only one copy is sent to the vendor (no acknowledgment copy is used).

TRAFFIC PAYMENTS

Bills of lading received from sales control are pended by carrier name (3,000 a month). Upon receipt of the freight (way) bill, it is matched to the pended bill of lading (two rate clerks). The rate is validated, using ICC published rate schedules, and the initialed invoice is sent to the extension clerk. If there is no matching bill of lading, the shipment is verified through the warehouse bill of lading file. If there is no record of the bill of lading, the freight bill is returned to the carrier by the supervisor.

Freight bill extensions and totals are checked for accuracy (using a comptometer), and, if correct, are initialed and dated by the extension clerk. If inaccurate, corrections are indicated on the freight bill before approving. Waybills are accumulated in batches, and totaled on an adding machine.

Validated freight bills are paid, using a bookkeeping machine coupled to a keypunch to capture statistical data. A vendor code is first applied from a Wheeldex type file (1,500 vendors). The bookkeeping machine operator then records the division, point of origin, and amount of each bill being paid. The total of the voucher is computed by the machine and the check amount and date is automatically printed. The operator enters vendor number, name, and address. Total disbursements are checked against the batch tapes prepared by the comptometer operator. Vouchers are sent to the disbursement section.

Supporting documents (waybill, B/L) are filed by carrier upon return from disbursements. A copy of the check is filed by date.

ACCOUNTS PAYABLE

Purchase order copies are received from the purchasing department and filed alphabetically in the open order file (one clerk). Upon receipt of an approved invoice from the purchasing department, it is matched to the open purchase order. A date stamp and block stamp are applied to the vendor invoice, which is attached to the purchase order. If an invoice is received directly from a vendor and is supported by a purchase order, it is routed to purchasing for price validation before any further processing. If the invoice does not require a purchase order (telephone bill, etc.), it must be signed for receipt and approved for payment before further processing.

The original copy of a three-part receiving report is matched to the open file (copy number two is sent to originator). When all supporting data is present, a voucher number is assigned from the voucher register, the block stamp is initialed and the payment file is sent to the extension clerk.

If the receipt and invoice is for a partial amount of the order, duplicate copies of the purchase order (and requisition, if any) serve as the payment support, with the originals remaining in the file. If the invoice is made out for the full amount, and the receipt is for a partial quantity, the actual amount received is noted on the invoice. If the invoice cannot be validated to the receipt, it must be approved by the originating department before initiating payment. If more than one payment item for a vendor is ready for payment, they are processed together.

The extension clerk multiplies the quantity received by the unit price, using a desk calculator. Invoices are totaled and discounts computed. If the invoice is in error, the correction is made on the document. The payable amount is circled and the invoice is initialed. Approved payment files are forwarded to the code clerk.

The code clerk enters the proper account distribution in the space provided on the block stamp. The chart of accounts serves as the guide for assigning the proper code (one clerk). Coded invoices are forwarded to the bookkeeping machine operator. If more than one distribution, the amount applicable to each code is entered. If unable to apply the appropriate distribution, the payment file is sent to the supervisor.

The bookkeeping machine operator processes an average of 300 four-part checks per week. Each payment includes the date, vendor name and address, amount charged to each account, amount of check, and voucher number (checks are prenumbered). Upon completion of a payment batch, the check set, together with supporting documents and the check register prepared on the bookkeeping machine, are sent to the payables supervisor.

The payables supervisor validates each payment item in the batch for:

1. Complete and correct coding
2. Proper discounts
3. Agreement between the check amount and the circled payment amount on the invoice

He is responsible for random testing of extensions and payment support documents. In the event of an error, the check is marked "void" and documents are returned to the bookkeeping machine operator for reprocessing. The original check set is returned with the reprocessed documents to the payables supervisor.

The payables supervisor initials the duplicate voucher copy of approved documents and forwards them to the chief accountant. After approval by the chief accountant, payment documents are sent to the disbursement section (the check register is filed by date).

Upon return of canceled documents, the distribution ledger is posted on the bookkeeping machine (date, account name, debit or credit amount). After posting, the distribution control sheet is filed by date, and the number two copy of the check is stapled on top of supporting invoice, purchase order and receiving copies for filing by voucher number. The number three copy is filed alphabetically by vendor name, and the number four copy by check number.

DISBURSEMENTS

The disbursement section detaches the original check from the approved voucher set and applies an authorized signature to the check, using a check-signing device (one clerk). Checks are folded and inserted in a window envelope for mailing (one clerk). All supporting documents are canceled and returned to the payment section for filing. A daily record is kept of the number of checks signed. The originals of voided checks are filed in the disbursement section after cancellation.

The disbursement section is responsible for microfilming financial records. Every quarter, the payment section releases canceled voucher documents more than two years old. These are filmed along with supporting ledgers and registers (one clerk). Records are returned for filing and eventual destruction after the seven-year retention period. The treasurer is responsible for disbursements in addition to credit activities.

FINANCIAL REPORTS

At the close of each month, the distribution ledgers (1,750) are summarized to the general ledger, using the bookkeeping machine. The total debit or credit amount outstanding for each account is copied to a preprinted financial statement form with a monthly comparison and computation of variances (two clerks). The financial statement is typed and distributed to management (one clerk). In a similar manner, statements of monthly profit and loss and cash position are prepared. Finally, all reports are summarized for quarterly and annual comparisons. The comptroller is responsible for financial reports preparation as well as accounts payable, accounts receivable, data processing, and mail room activities.

Analyses of a nonrepetitive nature are prepared as needed. Such reports usually analyze return on existing investments in the form of plant and equipment, as well as operating profit of various product lines. Industry-wide profitability comparisons and projected return on new major expenditures are made (two clerks).

CUSTOMER SALES CALLS (RETAIL TRADE)

Retail salesmen's orders are written at the time of his periodic sales call.

NOTE: With 10,000 accounts and 100 salesmen, it is the sales policy to call on an account at least once every third month, an average of two calls/day.

The order is a four-part form (original to plant, duplicate to the customer, triplicate to the sales office, and quadruplicate for the salesman) that requires the customer's signature. Orders are not priced or extended unless a special arrangement is indicated. Usually, the salesman takes the customer inventory which accompanies the order to the plant. A duplicate copy remains with the customer.

If the customer has any damage complaints that, upon inspection, the salesman deems justified, he prepares a damage repair form (in duplicate). The original is forwarded to the traffic department.

If the salesman has received any correspondence relating to unpaid bills, he reviews the transaction with the customer and reports any factual data that would shed light on the problem. In the event that orders are being held, the salesman is instructed to so inform the customer.

If an order is received from a new account, or if he is otherwise directed to a new account, the salesman prepares the new account form in quadruplicate (original to credit, duplicate to order processing, and triplicate to sales office).

SELLING INDUSTRIAL ACCOUNTS

Industrial accounts are sold through jobbers or directly through the national accounts sales group. It is the policy of the industrial group to call on accounts at least every month. In addition, the industrial salesmen make retail calls at the direction of regional managers, depending upon the urgency of the situation.

Industrial salesmen make customer calls with the jobber as the occasion demands. Whenever a jobber is invited to bid on an order, he contacts his salesman, who may help prepare a bid which the jobber uses as the basis for his submission. Special bid information is transmitted to the jobber by mail or phone, with prices determined by the size of the order. The buyer's credit is checked before releasing bid information.

If successful, the jobber mails his order to the main office, including any special shipping instructions or design modifications. The order is confirmed by the industrial sales supervisor's secretary. Large industrial orders are cleared with the scheduling supervisor to assure meeting delivery dates.

All damage or quality complaints received by the jobber are referred to the industrial salesman who makes a personal inspection at the customer's premises. If the complaint is warranted, but less than an estimated $10, a local serviceman is engaged (through the jobber, if possible). If the cost appears more than $10, consultation is made with the factory before taking corrective action (e.g., return and replace, fix locally, or allow credit).

MAIL ROOM

The mail room supervisor is responsible for mail, duplicating, and office supply services. It is the policy to charge mail room expense to the user department.

Mail services consist of receiving and distribution of the U.S. mails, collection and distribution of inter-office mail, and the application of postage to outgoing mail (four mail clerks). In connection with the latter, a separate daily record is kept of postage dispensed by each department incurring the expense.

This record is accumulated to the monthly postage expense report. The total accumulated for each department is posted to the monthly mail room expense.

The duplicating department consists of two offset duplicators (two operators), a metal platemaker, a paper cutter, a padding table (one assistant operator) and an office copier (one operator). Duplicating or copying services are requisitioned by the appropriate two-part form approved by the department head.

Upon receipt of a copying order (500/month), it is delivered to the photocopy operator along with the original document. After copying, all documents are returned to the originator with the copy order.

Upon receipt of a duplicating order (250/month), a two-part job order is prepared by the control clerk, specifying each job to be done (i.e., duplicating, collating, cutting, inserting, mailing, etc.). One copy of the job order acts as the signed delivery receipt of the completed order, while the second copy is pended by the mailroom.

At the end of each month, the control clerk prices and totals the pended job orders, using standard job rates (job time has been recorded by the operators to the nearest quarter-hour). The job orders are sorted by department, and the totals taped. The amount charged to each department is posted to the monthly mail room expense. Job orders are pended for three months and destroyed.

Stationery and supplies are ordered as required from the supply room, using a three-part requisition—two copies to supply clerk, one copy retained as a follow-up—(40/week). The original and duplicate requisitions accompany the completed order to the originator who receipts the duplicate copy, which is returned to the supply room. If unable to complete the order, the quantity delivered is noted in place of the quantity ordered. If out of stock, the item is lined out (there are no back orders). If the item is not carried in stock, the requisition is marked "Special Order," indicating it must be ordered from purchasing.

Completed duplicate copies of the stationery requisition are pended by the control clerk until the end of the month, when they are priced (based on costs supplied by purchasing), extended, totaled, and accumulated by department. A tape of the department total is made and the amount is posted to the monthly mail room expense. The latter document is totaled for the department and is sent to accounting for posting.

Supply room replenishment is made through the purchasing department, whenever noticed, by preparation of the three-part requisition. A copy of the requisition and its matching purchase order serve as a follow-up.

SAMPLE PROJECT ASSIGNMENTS

1. If you were the information specialist, prepare an outline of how ou would proceed to undertake the study in order to achieve the desired objectives.

2. Prepare an organization chart that conceivably reflects the performance of responsibilities at the Walnut Furniture Company. How would you reorganize the company for more effective operation?

3. Where would you recommend placing the systems function on the organization chart? Give advantages and disadvantages for this recommendation.

4. Prepare a flow chart of each major function as now performed, using a conventional technique for the graphic representation of the work done.

5. State the problem at the Walnut Furniture Company in one paragraph.

6. Prepare a process chart of the customer billing operation.

7. Prepare a work distribution chart of the accounts payable function. Explain how a work distribution chart is useful in analyzing this function.

8. Outline a work measurement program for the customer billing function. State objectives, procedures for setting up and operating the program, the type of forms needed, and the type of data you would gather. If you were responsible for the customer billing function, would you adopt the program, and why or why not?

9. Why would the billing function be a logical place to conduct a work sampling program? What would you expect to learn? Explain the type of work sampling you would use. What is the critical factor in work sampling?

10. Prepare an evaluation of the Walnut Furniture Company systems and recommend the changes you consider warranted. Support your proposal with flow charts, forms, cost, or other statistical comparisons deemed useful.

11. Analyze each of the forms used and design improved forms where warranted. If you consider the forms in use satisfactory, prepare a design of the forms and explain why they do not need to be revised.

12. Outline a plan for the implementation of your previously recommended systems proposals. Include such factors as sequence of installation, data control, and conversion techniques.

13. What type of management information system would you recommend for this company? Outline the management information data you would consider essential to such a system and to whom it should be directed. What hardware capabilities would be required to meet your information system recommendations?

Index

Access:
random, 336
time, 336
Accounting:
labor distribution, 315
relationship with management audit, 90
Accounting machine:
control panel, 301
tabulating, 299
Account posting program, computer, 341
Accounts payable, 277
Accounts receivable, 374
Activity:
analysis chart, 79
list, 129
network systems, 479
Administering Systems and Procedures department, 27
Administration, work measurement, 175
Administrative Issuances:
classification, 223
filing, 224
program, 225
standard format, 223
Administrative programming, operations research, 412
Advertising Budget, 265
Allowances:
determining, 167
work standard, 166
American Bankers Association MICR, 202
American Management Association:
management games, 409
simulation exercise, 409
Analog computers, 330
Analysis:
management audit, 109
motion, 159
procedure work sheet, 41
process work sheet, 69
project data analysis, 47
systems facts, 41
work sheet, 41
Analysis chart:
activity, 79
forms, 44

Analyst, systems, 37 (*see also* Systems man)
Appraisal, manuals, 260
Architectural chart, 67
Assembly line in office, 139
Assignment:
case study, 517
defining systems, 500
project, 32, 33
Audio Units in MIS, 445
Audit: (*see also* Management Audit)
accounting, 90
policies of management, 99
purpose of, 91
relationship with accounting, 91
write-ups of management, 111
Auditing by work sampling, 372
Auditor:
management, 100
sampling by, 400
AUTOCODER, 345
Auxiliary Memory Systems, 336

Balance sheet, 271
Barish, Norman N., 52
Batch Type in MIS applications, 444
BEST technique (NCR), 414
Billing by averages, 372
Binomial probability distribution, 380
Birn, Serge A., 85
Block diagram, 76
Brush, William H., 143
Budget, budgets: 262-283
advertising, 265
balance sheet, 277
cash, 265
control vs. prediction, 263
cost control, 265
supervisory participation in, 281
data needed for, 274
definition, 264
developing format, 269
estimating, 276

Budget, budgets (*Cont.*)
expense allocation, 280
flexible, 265, 280
human factors involved with, 263
inventory, 265
necessity for, 262
net earnings trend, 273
objectives of, 263
production, 265
profit planning, 265
reports, 283
by responsibility, 281
sales, 265
schedule captions, 275
why prepared, 263
Budget forecast, 263
accuracy, 268
definition, 264
details, 268
length of period, 268
necessity for, 266
preparation of, 266
procedure for preparing, 268
report schedules, 269
what it discloses, 267
Buffer units, electronic, 335
Buhl, William F., 362
Bulletins (*see* Administrative Issuances)
Business computers, 331

Calculating machine, tabulating, 298
Cameras, microfilm, 232
Capital expenditure data, 274
Cards:
design of tabulating, 199
IBM tabulating, 287, 288
layout of tabulating, 304
punched, 334
Remington Rand tabulating, 287, 288
Systems and procedures project status, 16
tabulating, 287, 288 (*see also* Tabulating Cards)
classification of, 289
Carriage attachments, tabulating machines, 300

Case study:
project assignments, 517
Walnut Furniture Co., 505
Cash budget, 265
Cash receipts and disbursements statement, 272
Cathode-Ray tube, 446
Centralized Stenographic department, 227
Centralized Systems and Procedures department, 17
Central processor, electronics, 335
Chance (probability), 376
Channels in punched paper tape, 317
Character recognition:
forms, 202
magnetic ink, 323
Characteristics of electronic equipment, 370
Characteristics of systems man, 463
Characters, optically recognizable, 319
Chart, charts:
activity analysis, 79
architectural, 67
batch billing, 303
block diagram, 76
computer procedure, 76
critical path method (CPM), 87, 474, 476
electronics flow, 339
flow, 68, 69, 70, 259
batch billing, 303
layout of, 43, 45
process, 132
types of, 68
forms analysis, 44
forms distribution, 43, 77, 80
forms flow, 72-75
functional, 79
Gantt, 86-89, 406
horizontal vs. vertical, 71
layout flow, 43, 45, 73, 75
linear responsibility, 84
line-drawing flow, 76
logical diagram, 76
MIS input-output, 435
multi-column flow process, 131, 134, 136
network systems (CPM/PERT), 87, 474, 476
operational, 67
flow, 68
organization, 43, 68, 77, 82, 217
paperwork simplification, 230
personnel, 67
PERT, 87, 474, 476
planning, 62
procedural flow, 70
process, 43, 68
right and left hand, 45, 79, 81, 134
sampling control, 390
scheduling, 86
simo, 81
special purpose, 79
staffing requirements, 82
statistical, 45, 67
symbols of flow process, 71, 130
in systems studies, 39
tabulating card procedure, 76

Chart, charts (Cont.)
types of, 67
work distribution, 39, 43, 47, 79, 83, 126
work sampling control, 366
workplace, 131
Charting:
aids, 66
applications, 60
codes, 71
conventions, 78
cost, 63
in design phase, 60, 61
information, 64
in installation phase, 62
layout conventions, 71
materials, 65
methods, 62
need for, 59
preparation for, 63
in presentation phase, 61
procedures, 43
standards for procedures, 42
symbols, 46, 65, 71, 76
systems, 43
tabulating cards volume, 307
techniques, 64
template, IBM, 76
tools, 65
when to use, 62
Check, work sampling test, 372
Checking:
forms proofs, 205
sequence, programming, 352
work sampling, 364
Check list, management audit, 112, 118
Checks:
programming, 350
use of MICR on, 319
Classification:
of administrative issuances, 223
forms, 187
punched cards, 294
tabulating cards, 291
Clerical:
cost reduction, 133
employee in relation to records preparation, 216
error control, 262
function definition, 362
work control units, 145
work standards (see Work standards)
COBOL, 345
Codes, coding: (see also Programming)
charting, 71
Dewey decimal system, 224
forms, 187, 188, 189, 219
MICR optical, 320
optically recognizable, 320
releases, 223
tabulating, 304
Coding data for tabulating cards, 291
Collating machine, tabulating, 297
Company:
manuals, 240-261
policies, 53
Communications within organization, 97
Comptometer, select time standard for, 173
Computation of performance effectiveness, 177

Computers: (see also Electronic data processing machines)
accounting flow chart, 341
analog, 330
business, 331
checking, programmed, 349
controls, 349
data bank in, 441
digital, 330
feasibility study, 352
general purpose, 331
input cards, 296
large scale, 332
management information systems, 445
medium scale, 332
network systems, 481, 491
operations research, 410
procedure charts, 76
programming, 338
random access, 336
scientific, 331
size, 332
small scale, 332
special purpose, 331
staffing, 333
systems (see Electronic data processing machines)
time shared, 446
types of, 330
Concepts:
management information systems, 438
network systems, 473
Conducting systems study, 499
Console, electronics, 334
Consultants, systems, 21
Continuous:
forms, 201
operation sheet, 158
recording in time study, 157
timing, 156
Control:
in computer programming, 349
cost, 278 (see also Cost control)
of electronic machines, 328, 334
elements of, 93
evaluation of, 93
forms, 182, 183
program, 212
management, 92
audit, 96
methods assignments, 22
paperwork, 363
quality (see Quality control)
stockroom, stationery, 205
Systems and Procedures department, 27
systems projects, 20
tabulating:
operations, 300
procedures, 311
work sampling, 362, 390
Control-monitor phase in network systems, 475, 492
Control panel and wiring diagram, 300, 302
Conversion to electronic systems, 330
Conway, Benjamin, 327
Corporate:
data file, 441
organization, 249
Correspondence:
form letters, 227

Correspondence (*Cont.*)
letter contents in, 225
management, 225
production, 226
semantics of, 226
Correspondex, definition and advantages, 228
Cost:
analysis in systems study, 503
charging forms, 220
charting, 63
clerical error, 363
Cost control, 262-283
budget, 265, 281
computers, 332
of electronic machines, 329
of errors in office, 368
factors, 278
feasibility study, 354
forms, 133
in management audit, 103
microfilm, 232
necessity for, 262, 264
paperwork, 217
of proposed method, 39, 52
records, 215
reduction in:
work measurement, 180
work sampling, 364
of sales, estimating, 276
standards, 171
Costing production in work sampling, 372
CPM (Critical Path Method), 87
history of, 472
Craft, Clifford J., 392
Critical Path Method (CPM), 87, 446
network systems, 475
operations research, 412
time estimate, 487
Cross footing balance checks, programming, 352

Data:
bank, 441, 443
budget requirements, 274
for charts, 63
display equipment, 326
file, 441, 443
obtaining via work sampling, 373
processing:
integrated, 183
machines, 322 (*see also* Electronic data processing machines)
peripheral equipment, 321
vs. information processing, 426
recording chart, 44
retrieval, 445
sheet, time study, 157
storage, electronic machines, 329
transmission equipment, 325
vs. information, 426
work sampling, gathering, 365
Decentralized Organization Manual, 243
Decimal system, Dewey, 224
Decimal watch, 155

Decisions, electronic machine, 329
Decision making:
MIS, 427
operations research, 412
Defining systems study, 35
Demand reports, 429
Delay, ratio, 373
Delphi Questionnaire, 420
Depository, records, 235
Derby, Elles M., 451
Design:
Management information system, 432
manual, 245
punched card, 290, 305
tabulating card, 305
of work measurement plan, 170
Design techniques, forms, 189
Determining management needs in MIS, 438
Developing:
Management information system, 432, 440
operations research model, 396
proposed method, 502
Dewey decimal system, 224
Diagram, networks, 375
Diazo process, 200
Digital:
computer, 330
position in tabulating card, 291
Direct charges report, 317
Direction, definition of, 91
Directives (*see* Administrative Issuances)
Direct labor, 282
cost, 282
report, 282
Disc files, 346
Display:
data equipment, 326
output, 445
Disposition of forms and record files, 234, 235
Distribution:
mail, 228
management audit report, 117
reports, 224
sampling, 384
work, 127
Distribution chart:
activity list, 129
forms, 43, 77, 80
work, 39, 40, 43, 47, 79, 83
work simplification, 126
Draftsman, charting, 64
Drums, magnetic, 337
Dummy activities in network systems, 483
Duplicating, time standard for, 176

Earnings, budgeted trend net, 273, 275
Earnings statement, 270
Economy, principles of motion, 137
Effectiveness, per cent, 169
Electrical impulse counters, 146
Electronic computer in operations research, 410

Electronic data processing:
consultants for, 21
forms, 183
integrating systems, 360
Electronic data processing machines and systems (EDPM), 327-361
accuracy, 328, 349
advantages, 328
background, 327
buffer units, 335
central processor, 335, 339
challenge, 361
checking:
built-in, 356
programmed, 358
components, 333
controls, 328, 349
console, 334
conversion to, 330
cost, 329, 332, 357
decision making ability, 329
disadvantages, 329
feasibility study, 352 (*see also* Feasibility study)
flow chart, 339
hypothetical illustration of, 339
input and input devices, 317, 321, 334
integrating systems, 360
keyboard devices for, 334
keypunching for, 330
label, 351
magnetic tape, 335
Management information systems applications, 328, 426
manufacturers, 370
operating staff, 333
operations research applications, 410
operating concepts, 346
output and output devices, 321, 334
paper tape, 334
printers, 335
problem solution, 342
processor, 339
program:
account posting, 341
hypothetical, 339
programming (*see* Programming)
publications and references, 360
punched cards, 334
random access, 336
record count, 350
references and publications, 360
software, 342
speed, 328
staff, 333
storage, 328, 329, 336
system components, 333
time sharing, 347
transition to, 365
types, 342
Electronics, 327-361 (*see also* Electronic data processing machines)
Elemental:
motions, 159, 161
time analysis, 163
times, 152, 155, 159
Employee:
payroll tabulating procedure, 315

Employee (*Cont.*)
service activities, 104
systems, procedures effect on, 7
tabulating payroll procedure, 323
task list, 38
Engineer, information, 217
Engineered standards, 152, 279
Engineering:
manual, 242
work standards, 152
Equipment:
computers (*see* EDPM)
data processing (*see* EDPM)
data display, 326
data transmission, 325
economic justification of, 52
electronic (*see* EDPM)
feasibility study for (*see* Feasibility study)
forms control, 206
internal forms printing, 220
justifying purchase of, 52
office, 140, 231
operating standards for office, 231
optical scanning, 323
peripheral, data processing, 321
proper, 51
rate of return, 52
recognizable reading, 322
reproduction, 220
selecting proper, 51
standards program, 24
tabulating, 285, 295 (*see also* Tabulating equipment)
Error notches in IBM cards, 296
Error rate control chart, 370
Errors:
controlling clerical, 362, 363
quality control for reducing, 370
Evaluating forms, 219
Examination: (*see also* Management Audit)
of forms, 219
of notes, etc., in fact gathering, 37
Executive training, source of, 22
Expense allocation budget, 280
Expenses:
determining, 282
fixed, 280
variable, 280
Extraction, data, 443

Fact gathering:
examining papers and notes in, 37
objectives of, 37
recording data in, 39
for systems study, 37, 501
task list, 38
Fair day's work concept, 147
Feasibility study:
cost analysis, 357
electronics, 352
objectives, 353
programming for, 356
questionnaire, 355
time operations in, 356
File systems for records, 228

Filing releases, 224
Finance Manual, 243
Financial program data, 274
Fixed expenses, 280
Flaks, Marvin, 470
Flexible budgets, 265, 280
"Float" in network systems, 475
Flow charts, 70, 73, 259
electronics, 339
forms, 73, 74
layout, 43, 45, 68, 73, 75
line drawing, 76
operational, 68
procedural, 70
tabulating operation, 303
types of, 68
Flow diagram, schematic, 72
Flow of information in MIS, 434
Flow process charts, 46, 130, 132 (*see also* Process chart)
multicolumn, 131, 136
paper work simplification, 230
symbols of, 130
Follow-up:
management audit, 108, 117
need for, 57
systems installation, 504
work measurement, 179
Forecast, budget, 263, 267 (*see also* Budget forecast)
Forecasting:
operations research, 398, 421
participative, 419
short range, 421
Form letters, 227
Format:
administrative issuances, 223
organization manual, 249
Forms:
analysis chart, 44
appearance of, 194
charging cost of, 220
checking proofs, 205
classification of, 187, 189
clerical cost of, 133
coding, 189
control, 190-221
equipment, 206
installing, 185
number assignment, 219
procedure, 185
program results, 212
responsibilities, 184
revision, 184
by systems staff, 184
construction, 197
continuous printing, 201
co-ordinating, 25
cost, 133
cylinder press, 201
definition, 183
design, 182, 213
colored inks and paper, 190
distribution chart, 43, 77, 80
electronic data processing, 183
emergencies, 212
evaluating and improving, 219
flow chart, 73, 75
functional file for, 219
gang runs printing, 201

Forms (*Cont.*)
hectographic, 199
improvement program, 220
inspecting, 210
inventorying, 210
layout, 192
layout sheets, 194
lead times for re-ordering, 208
management, 218
minimum quantity, 207
necessity of, 39
NCR (no carbon required) paper, 197
numbering systems, 187
ordering, 199, 207
procedure for, 208
output and input in EDP, 183
paper grades, 195, 197
printing techniques and processes, 200
problems and crises, 211
processing equipment, 300
project assignment, 33
purchasing department, 204
purposes of, 188
quantity order, 199
report on program, 212
revision, 210
scrapping, 210
sizes, 192
specifications, 192
specification sheet, 196
stock record, 205, 209
stockroom control, 210
storage, 187, 212, 220
systems project assignment, 33
tabulating cards, 199, 292
for tabulating source information, 304, 305
tags, 200
work measurement, 145
work simplification, 133
Formula for computing investment interest charge, 52
Formula development, operations research, 418
FORTRAN, 345
Functional chart, 79
Functional files for forms, 219
Functions:
in management manuals, 250
Systems and Procedures department manager, 29
Tabulating department, 295

Gang runs, printing, 201
Gantt charts, 85, 86, 87, 406
Gathering facts for surveys, 37, 110
Gilbreth, Dr. Frank, 71
Gilbreth, Dr. Lillian M., 123
Gill, William A., 39

Hamman, Paul E., 262
Hash totals checks, programming, 350
Haslett, John W., 11
Hectographic:
forms, 199
process, 200
Hendrick, James G., 240
Hijmans, Ernst, 85
Horizontal chart, 72

IBM:
  407 wiring diagram, 301
  origin of, 286
  tabulating card, 287, 288
Implementing:
  management information
    system, 449
  systems study, 499, 503
Imprinters, 324
Impulse counters, mechanical,
  146
Incentives, wage, 171, 280
Index, report, 222
Industrial engineering, 4
Information:
  chart in MIS, 435
  engineer, 217
  functionally oriented, 441
  management, 426
  Management information
    systems, 425, 440
  obtaining for MIS, 439
  output, 441
  storage, 441
  source, 442
  system, 229
  vs data, 426
Input:
  equipment, electronics, 321,
    334
  key to, 442
  management information
    system, 434
  methods, 447
  in network systems, 476
Inspecting forms, 210
Inspecting quality of paperwork, 231
Inspection sampling, 399
Installation:
  charting in, 62
  work measurement, 174
  work sampling, 386, 388
Instructions, programming,
  336
Integrated data processing, 299,
  360 (see also Electron-
  ics)
Interest charge, formula for
  computing investment,
  52
Internally stored program, 329
Internal printing, 220
Interrogation, 337
Interviews:
  management audit, 109
  for selecting systems men,
    459
Inventory:
  balances estimating, 277
  budget, 265
  data, 274
Investigation (see Management audit)
Issuances, administrative, 222

Jacquard, Joseph Marie, 286
Job breakdown:
  steps, 149
  work measurement, 149

Kearny, Paul W., 215
Keyboard devices, electronics,
  334
Keypunch machines, tabulat-
  ing, 293, 295 (see also
  Tabulating machines)

Keypunching for electronic
  system, 330
Key verifiers, tabulating, 295

Labor, direct, 282
Labor distribution, tabulating
  procedure for, 315
Langsford, Guy L., 392
Layout:
  flow charts, 43, 45, 73, 75
  form, 192
  sheets for forms, 194
  of tabulating:
    card, 292, 305
    form, 305
Lead time for ordering forms,
  207
Left and right hand chart, 45
Leonard, William P., 90
Lettering devices, 65
Letters, contents of, 225
Letters, guide, 227
Leveling time data, 165
Limit checks, programming,
  351
Linear programming, 400
  application, 415
  simplex method, 401
Linear responsibility chart, 79,
  84
Line-drawing flow chart, 76
Literal block diagram, 78
Logical diagram, 76, 77
Long range:
  information system, 450
  planning, operations re-
    search, 420
  procedure manual program,
    256
Lot size, sampling, 383, 385

Machine language, 343
Machine recognizable media,
  317
Machines:
  electronic (see EDPM)
  punched card, 285
  tabulating (see Tabulating
    equipment)
Magnetic:
  drums, 337
  ink character recognition,
    202, 319
  tape, 321, 335
    auxiliary memory system,
      336
    input-output devices, 323
Mail distribution, 228
Management:
  benefits derived from con-
    sultants, 23
  control, 92
  co-ordinated, 92
  correspondence, 225
  definition of, 425
  elements of, 91
  engineering, 4
  factors, 92
  forms, 218
  function, prime, 260
  management information
    system relations to,
      425, 428
  methods appraisal, 91, 93
  paperwork, 239
  performance appraisal, 93
  personnel, 19

Management (Cont.)
  philosophy in operations re-
    search, 396
  of records program, 25 (see
    also Records manage-
    ment)
  reports, 221
  responsibility of S & P, 13
  systems and procedures re-
    sponsibilities, 8
  systems role in, 2
  tools, 144
    PERT/CPM, 471
Management audit, 90-121
  analysis for, 105
  area of study, 95, 98
  auditor, 100
  benefits, 94
  check lists, 112, 118
  conducting, 11, 107, 108
  control, 96
  cost control, 103
  definition, 93
  difficulties encountered, 112
  discussion with management
    and supervisors, 115,
      117
  evaluating policies and prac-
    tices, 99
  examination, 100
  facts, gathering, 110, 115
  findings, 108, 114
  follow-up, 117
  interviews, 109
  investigation, 109
  operations appraisal, 102
  organization principles, 96
  organizing program, 105
  outline, 107
  personnel for, 105
  policies, 104
  program, 94, 106
  purpose, 94
  recommendations, 116
  report, 113, 114, 117
  review and appraisal, 108
  scope, 95
  specialized service, 93
  systems and procedures, 101
  techniques, 110
  time involved, 107
Management information systems (MIS), 424-450
  analysis of present system,
    434
  applications, 445
  audio units, 445
  definition of, 425
  designing, 440
  developing, 432
  hardware requirements, 444
  implementing, 449
  need for, 428
  operational indications in,
    428
  personnel phases, 450
  proposal for, 441
  psychological symptoms, 428
  relationship to management,
    438
  report content signs, 428
  reports in, 429
  software requirements, 444
  sub-system changes, 437
  uses of, 427
  what it does, 427
Management needs, determining, 438
Manager, functions of, 244

Manager, Systems and Procedures department:
qualifications, 19
project approval by, 34
write-up of, 29
Managers, systems and procedures effect on, 6
Manning tables, 282
Manpower requirements, 282
Manpower utilization, 171
Manual procedure, 252, 325
Manuals, 240-261
appraisal program, 260
benefits, 241
design, 244, 245
distribution, 248, 260
engineering, 242
finance, 243
industrial relations, 243
limitations, 241
job responsibilities in, 247
maintenance, 247, 258, 260
for management functions, 242
organization, 243, 244
policy, 252
potentials, 241
procedure for preparing, 5, 253
production, 242, 249
program outline, 253
research, 261
sales, 242
staff and line definition in, 246
systems and procedures, 28
tabulating, 313, 314
training, 55
uses of, 24
Mark-sensed cards, 246
Material accounting on tabulating machines, 315
Materials, charting, 65
Materials control procedure, 312
Mathematical formula, developing operations research, 418
Matrix formula, operations research, 417
Matrix multiplication, 418
Measurement: (see also Work measurement)
of tabulating work volume, 307
Measuring operating time on tabulating machines, 309
Mechanical impulse counters, 146
Mechanics, charting, 64
Mechanization, office, 139
Memory systems, auxiliary, 336
Method:
scientific, steps of, 395
work count, 146
Methods:
assignment procedure, 22
charting, 62
function, 12
man (see Systems analyst)
management, 92
statistical, 373
Methods analysis:
one best way, 148
work measurement, 148
Methods department on organizational chart, 15

Methods man (see Systems man)
Methods and Procedures manager responsibilities, 29
Methods time measurement, 159
Mettler, Armond L., 30
MICR:
forms, 202
magnetic ink character recognition, 319
recording and processing equipment, 322
specifications, 203
Microfilming, 232
records prohibited from, 232
Mimeograph process, 201
MIS (see Management information systems)
Mnemonic code, 344
Mode, programming, 336
Model construction, operations research, 396, 415, 418
Mogensen, Allan H., 123
Monitoring reports in MIS, 429
Motion:
analysis, 159
economy, principles of, 137
elemental, 159
times, predetermined, 155, 159, 166
MTM (Methods Time Measurement), 159
Mullee, William R., 122
Multi-column process chart, 131, 136
Myers, Dr. Gibbs, 182

National Archives, 238
NCR paper, 197
Network systems (PERT/CPM), 87, 470-492 (see also PERT)
activity, 479
advantages, 415
approach to developing, 471
arrow diagrams, 481
background, 471
calculations, 488
computer, 491
concepts, 473
critical activities, 491
development, 477
dummy activities, 483
illustration of rules for, 482
management information reports, 430
number assignments, 481
planning, 478
practices, 478
project diagram, 492
project planning, 471
rules, 478
schedule development, 476, 489
time estimates, 487
uses, 471
work breakdown chart, 474
Neumaier, Richard, 122
Neuschel, Richard F., 57
Non-productive materials report, 284
Normal curve of error, 375
Numbering systems for forms, 187 (see also Codes)

Objectives of systems study, 500
Observation sheet, time study, 158
OCR (Optical Character Reading), 202
Office:
appraisal program, 25
assembly line in, 139
equipment, 140, 231
control program, 231
incentive report, 178
mechanization, 139
orderliness in, 138
quality control, 368
standards, 154
systems program, 20, 24
tools, 140
One best way, 148
On-job training, systems man, 466
Operating:
staff for computer systems, 333
standards, office equipment, 231
Operation:
codes, 344
sheet, 164
time development, 308
Operational decisions vs policy, 426
Operations:
appraisal of, 102
chart, 67
feasibility study, 356
flow chart, 68, 69
Operations research, 392-323
administrative programming, 412
applications, 415, 423
basic steps, 395
case studies, 415
characteristics of, 396
definition, 395
developing model, 396
forecasting, 398
formula development, 418
history, 394
linear programming, 400
long-range application, 420
mathematical formula, 418
matrix multiplication, 418
organization, 396
payoff, 422
philosophy, 395
probability theory, 397
queuing theory, 406
random sampling, 399
requirements for, 411
sampling accounts receivables, 400
sampling theory, 399
teams, 394
techniques, 397
Optical:
character reading, 202
scanning, 447
Optically recognizable characters, 320
OR (see Operations research)
Ordering procedure for forms, 207
Organization:
analysis, 97
charts, 43, 68, 79, 82, 128, 246, 256, 262
definition, 91

Organization (*Cont.*)
  growth, systems and procedures effect on, 12
  manual, 244
  operations research, 396
  principles, 96
  records management program, 216
  systems and procedures, 15, 17
Origin of punched cards, 286
Outlines:
  for systems study, 34, 499
  management audit, 98, 106, 107
    report, 114
  manuals program, 253
  of report, 55
  of systems study, 34
Output equipment, electronics, 334
Output:
  information storage, 442
  in network systems, 476

Paper, grades of, 195, 197
Paper punched tape, 317, 334
  (*see also* Punched tape)
Paperwork:
  automation, 239
  cost, 217
  flow process chart, 238
  simplification, 229
    symbols, 230
Parallel plan work flow, 48
Participative forecasting, 419
Payroll:
  check, 316
  systems and procedures, 253
  tabulating procedure for, 315
Percentage comparison, work sampling, 372
Perforated:
  tags, 321
  tape (*see* Punched tape)
Performance effectiveness, computation of, 177
Performance rating, 165
Peripheral devices in data processing, 285, 321
Personnel:
  appraisal of, 104
  chart, 67
  for management audit, 105
  policies, 104
  for simulation, 407
  for systems work, 18
  training for:
    management audit, 106
    systems work, 19
Pilot run of proposed method, 54
Planning:
  budget for profit, 265
  charts, 62
  definition, 91
  Delphi questionnaire in, 421
  linear programming, 401
  long range, 458
  management audit, 105
  management information system, 432
  manual content, 253
  net work systems, 473, 475
  office systems program, 24

Planning (*Cont.*)
  organization, 248
  production, 401
  reports, 429, 430
  systems program, 14, 23
  systems study or project, 23, 27, 34
  tabulating procedure, 302
Point of sale recorders, 324
Poisson's approximation, 380
Policies:
  company, 53
  compliance with, 100
  management and organizational, 99
  organizational, 246
  personnel, 104
    vs procedures, 261
  vs operational decisions, 426
Policy manual, 251
  contents of, 252
  interpreting policy in, 252
Pomeroy, Richard W., 59
Porter, David B., 123
Pre-determined motion times, 155, 159, 166
Preliminary:
  planning of audit, 105
  survey, systems, 34
Prepunched cards, 294
Principles of motion economy, 137
Principles of tabulating process, 286
Printers, electronic, 335
Printing:
  continuous forms, 201
  facilities, internal, 220
  gang runs, 201
  presses, 200
  processes, 200
  techniques, 200
    diazo, 200
    hectographic, 200
    mimeograph, 200
    offset, 200
    Xerox, 200
Probabilistic model, 397
Probability, 376
  binomial, 380
  determining, 377
  tables, 380
  theory, 397, 398
Problem solution, 342
Procedure:
  analysis of, 39, 41
  analyst selection, 458
  budget forecast, 268
  charts, 42, 55, 76
  computer, 76
  employee tabulating, 315
  flow chart, 70
  forms control, 185
  forms ordering, 208
  manuals, 252
    preparation and maintenance of, 5
  for methods assignments, 22
  payroll, 252
  preparing the, 5
  proposed, 54
  records depository, 235
  reports control, 221
  for selecting systems analyst, 58
  standard, 261
  standard practice, 149
  for tabulating:
    applications, 302

Procedure (*Cont.*)
  for tabulating (*Cont.*)
    batch billing, 303
    controls, 311
    time study, 155
    writing tabulating, 313
Procedures (*see also* Systems and Procedures)
  analyst (*see* Systems man)
  interdepartmental, 257
  departmental, 257, 258
  standard practice, 149
  writing, 54
Process chart, 43, 68 (*see also* Flow process charts)
  flow, 46, 130, 132
  paperwork simplification, 230
  right- and left-hand, 134
  symbols (ASME standard), 71
Processes, reproduction, 66
Processing:
  basic operations in work, 51
  data via punched cards, 317
  electronic, 328, 331
  tabulating machine, 311
Processor, electronics data, 339
Production:
  budget, 265
  correspondence, 226
  costing by work sampling, 372
  manual, 242, 249, 256
  planning and control, 48
  report:
    daily, 177
    work measurement, 175
PERT/CPM (Program Evaluation Review Technique), 87, 470 (*see also* Network systems)
  advantages, 415
  in MIS reports, 430
  operations research, 413
Profit planning budget, 265
Program (*see also* Programming)
  account posting, 341
  developing survey, 34
  evaluation (PERT), 87, 470-492 (*see also* Network systems)
    advantages, 415
    in MIS reports, 430
    operations research, 413
  forms control, 185, 212, 218
  forms disposal, 235
  languages, 343
  long range systems, 31
  management audit, 94, 105, 106
  management information system, 432
  office:
    appraisal, 25
    equipment, 231
  planning systems and procedures, 14, 23
  procedure manual, 256
  records management, 25, 216
  systems man training, 464
  systems research, 26
  work measurement, 174
    installation of, 386
    selling, 386
  work simplification, 141

Programming:
  addressing, 336
  computer, 338, 344
  checks and controls:
    cost, 356
    cross footing balance, 352
    hash totals, 350
    limit checks, 352
    proof figures, 351
    record count, 349
    sequence check, 350
  cost, 329
  facilities, software, 343
  in feasibility study, 356
  flow of account posting program, 341
  for hypothetical process, 338
  instructions, 336, 343
  internally stored program, 329
  linear, operations research, 400, 415
  mode, 336
  staff, 333
  stored addresses, 342
  word length, 336
Project assignments, 32
Projects:
  approach to systems, 31
  clearance of systems, 32
  conducting systems, 27
  control of systems, 20
  defining, 32, 35
  developing solutions to, 54, 58
  planning, 23, 27
  requests for S & P, 31, 32
  solutions to, 47, 54
  status card, 16
Proof figures, computer, 351
Proofs, forms, 205
Protection records, 233, 237
Publications, co-ordinating, 25
Punched cards, 285, 334
  classifying, 294
  coding, 291
  concepts, 287
  design of, 290
  format of, 287
  input-output, 286
  layout, 292
  machines (see Tabulating machines)
  origin, 286
  procedure charts, 76
  types of, 287, 288
  in U.S. Census Bureau, 286
Punched tape, 317, 334
  five and eight channel, 318
  paper, 334
  processing equipment for, 322
Punches, summary, 299
Purchasing department, 204

Qualifications of systems personnel, 18
Quality control, 365, 367, 399
  applications in office, 367
  for error reduction, 370
  history, 367
  used by, 373
Questionnaire:
  Delphi, 420, 421
  for feasibility study, 355
  for management audit, 118

Queuing theory:
  case application, 406
  objectives, 406

Random access systems, 336
Random sampling, 399
Rapid access, 337
Rate of return on equipment investment, 52
Rating, performance, 165
Ratio delay, 373
Reading:
  printed code, 320
  punched cards, 289
  punched tape, 318
Readers, MICR, 318
Recognition, MICR, 319
Recognizable media for data processing, 317
Recommendations, putting into effect, 56
Record:
  source of information, 442
  stock form, 209
Recording:
  continuous, 156
  repetitive, 156
Recording data chart, 44
Recording facts in systems study, 39
Records:
  analysis formula, 216
  barrier, 216
  costly problem, 215
  depository procedure, 235
  disposal, 233
  file, 228
  microfilming, 232
  prohibited from microfilming, 232
  protection, 233, 237
  reducing size of, 232
  research, 215
  retention regulations, 235
  storage, 233
  study, 133
Records management, 214-239
  areas, 218
  files disposition, 234
  organizing program, 216
  program, 25
  science of, 216
Re-defining systems problem, 35
Redmond, Eugene V., 505
Reducing errors by quality control, 370
Re-evaluation system study, 504
References, electronic computers, 360
Regulations for records retention, 235
Reitzfeld, Milton, 214
Releases:
  administrative
    coding, 223
    filing, 224
Remington Rand tabulating card, 287
Remote processing, 348
Repetitive data sheet, 157
Reporting:
  by exception, 222
  system, 221, 448
Reports:
  basic elements of, 113

Reports (Cont.)
  budget, 283
    forecast, 269
  daily production, 177
  for direct charges, 317
  direct labor, 282
  distribution of, 224
  essential parts of, 55
  index for, 222
  management, 221, 222
  management audit, 114-116
  MIS:
    demand, 429
    monitoring, 429
    planning, 430
    timing, 431
    triggered, 429
    use of, 429
  network systems, 476
  non-productive materials report, 283
  office incentive, 178
  outline of, 55
  preparing, 55
  progress, MIS, 431
  systems study of, 28, 133
  work measurement, 175
Reproducing machine, tabulating, 296
Reproduction equipment, 220
Reproduction processes, 60
Research:
  manuals, 260
  operations (see Operations research)
  records, 215
  systems, 26
Resistance to change, 124
Responsibilities:
  definition of, 246
  forms control, 184
Responsibility:
  budgeting by, 281
  chart, linear, 85
  for MIS, 433
Retention schedules of records, 234
Retrieval, data, 445
Revising forms, 210
Right- and left-hand chart, 45, 79, 81, 134

Safe guarding records, 233
Sales budget, 265
Sales forecast data, 274
Salesman, systems man as, 453
Sales manual, 242
Sampling, 362-391 (see also Work sampling)
  applications, 399
  benefits, 399
  factors, 383
  lot size, 385
  plans, 382
  range of values, 383
  sequential, 382
  size of, 383
  tables, 380
  theory, operations research, 399
Saunders, Paul R., 424
Savings, estimating, 53
Scanning, 337
  optical, 319
Schedule captions, budget, 275
Schedules:
  budget forecast, 269

Schedules (*Cont.*)
network systems, 476
records retention, 234
of tabulating:
machines, 308
operations, 310
Scheduling:
charts, 79, 85
systems studies, 501
Schematic flow diagram, 72
Science of records, 216
Scientific:
computers, 331
method, 395
Scope of management audit, 95
Selecting:
consultants, 23
equipment, 51
feasibility study for, 357, 359
management audit personnel, 105
sampling lot size, 385
systems man, 445, 451-469
work count, 145
work simplification job, 125
Selection interview, systems man, 459
Selective checking, 364
Select times for key punching operations, 172
Selling:
statistical methods, 387
systems, 37, 503
work sampling program, 386
Senensieb, W. Louis, 285
Sequence check, programming, 352
Serial plan work flow, 48
Shewhart, Walter, 394
Shortage of forms, 212
Short range:
forecasting, 421
MIS improvements, 436
Simo-chart, 81
Simplex method calculations, 401
Simplification:
paperwork, 229
work (*see* Work simplification)
Simulation, 407, 410
symbolic, 408
Single record, MIS, 442
Snap-back method of time study, 155
Snap out forms, 198
Software, 342
Solutions, project, 47
Sorting machine, tabulating, 297
Source:
data, recording equipment, 323
documents, 319
information, 442
Sources for systems men, 456
Space requirements for electronic system, 330
Specialist:
operations research, 411
systems and procedures, 9
Specification forms, 196, 306
Specifications, MICR forms, 203
Spot checking, work sampling, 364

Staff:
function of Systems and Procedures department, 9, 14
needed for electronics installation, 333
programming, 333
requirements chart, 82
Standard:
ASME flow chart symbols, 71
cost, 171
data, 154, 159
predetermined, 166
equipment program, 24
format for administrative issuances, 223
practice instructions and procedures, 149
Standards:
definition of work, 147
developing work, 149, 165, 167
engineered, 152, 279
equipment, 231
establishing work, 168
for keypunch operation, 172
maintenance of work, 177
objective of, 152
office, 154
for procedure chart, 42, 261
unit data, 281
work, 147
work measurement (*see* Work standards)
Statement:
cash receipt and disbursements, 272
earnings, 270
preparation of, 275
Stationery stockroom control, 205
Statistical analysis work standards, 151
Statistical charts, 45, 67
Statistical methods:
applications, 375
chance, 376
normal curve of error, 375
probability, 376
tables, 378
sampling, 380, 383
selling tools, 387
work sampling, 373
Statistical sampling techniques, 152
Stenographic department, centralized, 227
Stocking forms, 187
Stockroom records and control, 205, 209, 220
Storage:
of data in electronic machines, 329, 336, 342
of forms, 187, 220, 300
records, 233
tabulating cards, 300
Study:
conducting systems, 27
feasibility (*see* Feasibility study)
gathering facts for, 37, 110
outline of systems, 34
preliminary systems, 34
recognizing problem in, 35
systems (*see* Systems study)
systems report, 28
Subjective work standard, 150

Sub-system changes in MIS, 437
Summary punch machine, 299
Supervisors:
management audit discussion with, 115
systems and procedures effect on, 6
systems and procedures responsibilities of, 7
work measurement follow-up by, 179
Supply room forms, 187
Survey:
charting, 60
preliminary systems, 34
work sampling, 388
Symbolic block diagram, 78
Symbolic simulation:
illustration, 408
problem solving, 408
Symbols:
charting, 65, 71
flow process chart, 130, 230
paperwork simplification, 230
process chart, 71
therbligs, 71
Systems: (*see also* Procedures; Systems and Procedures; and Systems study)
analysis of facts, 39, 41
analysis work sheet, 39
assignment, staff, 14
"blue collar," 3
charting, 43
co-ordinating overall, 26
cost of electronic, 332
design requirements, 448
fact gathering for, 37
field of, 1
implementing MIS, 449
network, 470, 473, 477, 478
office, 3
PERT/CPM, 470
personnel training, 19
project planning, 27
reporting, 221
savings, 28
task list, 38
"white collar," 3
"who, what, how long," 27
Systems Analyst, 37 (*see also* Systems man)
Systems charting, 59-89
Systems man:
as analyst, 453
characteristics, 463
as innovator, 454
qualifications of, 18, 452, 455
as salesman, 453
selecting, 456, 458-461, 468
source of supply, 456
as technician, 453
training, 19, 26, 468
work simplification, 123
Systems personnel (*see* Systems man)
Systems and Procedures, 1-10
activities involved, 4
analyzing, 5
appraising, 101
approach to, 10
centralized versus decentralized, 17
classifications, 3
complete study concept, 15

Systems and Procedures
(Cont).
concept of, 10
considerations, 2, 10
consultants, 21
controls, 5
definition, 11
designing, 5
effectiveness of, 101
effect on, 12
employees, 7
  managers, 6
  supervisors, 6
implementing, 6
improving, 5
industrial engineering, 4
management:
  responsibilities in, 8
  responsibilities to, 13
  role in, 2
  support, 13
manual of techniques, 28
meeting requirements, 101
organization for, 12, 17
principles of, 8, 12
program, 7 (see also Systems
  program)
projects, 32
  requests for, 31
  status card, 16
recommendations, 15
reporting officer, 15
resistance to change, 17
responsibilities, 6
reviewing, 5
specialist, 9
staff, 19
studies, 30 (see also Systems
  study)
supervisor's responsibilities
  for, 8
Systems and Procedures department, 11-29
activities, 17
administering, 28
controls, 27
design of, 13
forms control by, 184
foundation for, 10
location in company, 15
manager:
  qualifications of, 19
  write-up for, 29
manual, 28
organizational status, 15
planning, 14
relationship to other departments, 13
set-up, 13
size of, 17
staff function, 14
staffing, 19
Systems program:
co-ordinating, 25
equipment standards, 24
long range planning, 131
management approval of, 31
office, 25
planning, 23
project control, 20
records management, 25
research, 26
Systems project:
analyzing data, 502
assignment, 22, 32, 34
control card, 28
defining, 32
developing solutions to, 47,
  54

Systems project (Cont.)
planning, 27
practical approach to, 31
reviewing, 101
Systems study, 30-58
assignment, 500
background, 27
case problem, 35, 505
changeover to new method,
  57
consultants, 21
cost analysis, 503
fact finding, 37, 501
firm policies, 53
follow-up, 504
fulfilling objectives, 50
implementing, 503
major areas of, 499
objectives, 500
outline for, 499-504
planning, 34
preliminary, 34
recognizing problem, 35
recording facts, 39
re-evaluation, 504
scheduling, 501
selling, 503
solutions to problem, 51, 53
total systems concept, 501
types of, 500
Systems training (see Training)

Tabulating:
applications, 313
coding, 304
flow chart, 303
manual, 313
Tabulating cards:
codes for, 291, 304
design and layout, 199, 290,
  304
development, 286
fields, 289
IBM, 287
origin, 286
procedure chart, 76
punching, 293
Remington Rand, 287
storage, 300
types, 287
work sheet, 305
Tabulating equipment:
form processing, 300
objectives of, 285
types of, 295
Tabulating forms:
handling, 306
layout, 305
source information, 304
specifications, 306
Tabulating machines: (see also
  Tabulating equipment)
accessories, 300
accounting machine, 299
attachments, 300
advantages, 329
applications, 313
calculators, 298
collators, 297
employee payroll on, 315
interpolators, 299
keypunch, 295
key verifiers, 295
labor distribution on, 315
processing, 311
reproducers, 296
sorters, 297, 307

Tabulating machines (Cont.)
summary punches, 299
tabulators, 299
timing and scheduling of,
  308
verifiers, 295
work flow, 317
Tabulating manual, 313
Tabulating procedures:
analysis, 302
control of, 311
development, 302
employee payroll, 315
machine processing and specifications, 311
material control, 315
objectives, 302
for payroll, 315
Tabulating wiring diagram,
  301
Tabulating work measure-
  ments, 307
Tags, design of, 200
Tape:
magnetic, 321, 335
punched paper, 317, 334
recording for manuals, 261
Task lists, 38, 129
Taylor, Frederick W., 123, 394
Technician, systems man as,
  453
Techniques:
charting, 64
management audit, 110
network systems, 471
operations research, 397
printing, 200
systems man, 465
work sampling, 370
work simplification, 125
Telpak, 325
Telprocessing, 348
Template, charting, 76
Terminals, 348
Test check, work sampling,
  372
Testing, systems study, 503
Therbligs, 71
Time:
data leveling, 165
elemental, 159
estimates for network system, 487
measurement methods, 159
for operation, 308
predetermined motion, 159
sharing, computer, 446
Time standard:
for comptometer, 173
for duplicating, 176
Time study:
continuous, 155
cycle of, 156
decimal watch, 155
for developing standards,
  152
explanation of, 155
observation sheet, 158
procedure, 155
repetitive cycle data sheet,
  157
snap back, 155
Time table for plan of action,
  56
Time values, developing, 161
Timing of changeover to new
  method, 57
Timing operations in feasibility study, 356

Timing tabulating machines, 308
Tools:
  forms design, 194
  charting, 64
  CPM, 471
  management, 425
  MIS, 425
  network systems, 471
  office, 140
  PERT, 471
  work simplification, 125
Total systems concept, 501
Training:
  executive personnel, 19
  management audit personnel, 106
  manuals, 55
  systems, 26, 464
  systems man, 19, 451-469
Transaction:
  key to input, 442
  recorders, 323
Transmission, data, 325
Transmitting devices, 325
Triggered reports, 429
Types, punched cards, 294

Unit assembly plan work flow, 49
Unit data, 281
Unit times, 151
Urwick, L. F., 216

Value of work count, 147
Variable expenses, 280
Variance reports, 430
Verification, work sampling, 365
Verifying machine, tabulating, 296
Vertical chart, 71, 72
Volume measurements, tabulating, 307

Wage incentives, 171, 280
Waiting line theory, 406
White, Glenn L., 470
Wiring diagram, tabulating, 301
Word length, 336
Work count:
  assigning value, 147
  methods for making, 146
  selecting unit for, 145
  uses, 147
  using existing records for, 145
  value of, 147
  in work measurement, 145
Work cycle, 164
Work distribution chart, 39, 43, 47, 79, 83, 126
  activity list, 129

Work distribution chart (Cont.)
  organization unit, 128
  task list, 129
  work simplification, 126
Work effectiveness report, 177
Work flow:
  importance of proper, 48
  parallel plan for, 48
    serial plan for, 48
    unit assembly plan, 48
  tabulating machines, 317
Work measurement, 141-181
  administration of, 175
  benefits, 179, 181
  comparison with:
    methods analysis, 148
    other management tools, 144
  compilation of data, 177
  concepts, 143
  cost reduction, 180
  definition, 143
  design plan for, 170
  developing work standards, 150
  follow-up on program, 179
  forms, 145
  installing program, 174
  job breakdown steps, 149
  objectives, 144
  philosophy, 144
  policing, 150
  production report, 175
  supervisory follow-up, 179
  time report, 175
  uses for, 181
  work count (see Work count)
  work place chart, 131
  work standards (see Work standards)
Work processing, basic operations for, 51
Work sampling, 362-391
  advantages, 164, 365
  applications, 365, 373
  in auditing, 372
  in billing by averages, 372
  checking, 364
  control, 362
    chart, 366
    program, 390
  for cost reduction, 364
  in costing production, 372
  definition, 365
  installing, 386
  limitations, 164
  in obtaining data quickly, 373
  in percentage comparison, 372
  program:
    considerations, 390
    control, 390
    installation, 386
  for quality control (see Quality control)

Work sampling (Cont.)
  in ratio delay, 373
  selective checking, 364
  selling program, 386
  spot checking, 364
  statistical methods, 373 (see also Statistical methods)
  survey, 388
  terminology, 374
  verification, 365
  work standards, 161
Work sheet:
  procedure analysis, 39
  process analysis, 69
Work simplification, 122-142
  application of, 51
  factors, 125
  five-step program, 125
  forms design, 133
  open-mindedness, 124
  paperwork, 229
  philosophy, 123
  program, 141
  resistance to change, 124
  round table, 123
  selecting job for improvement, 125
  systems man relationship, 123
  tools and techniques, 125
  work distribution chart, 129
Work standards, 147, 167
  allowances, 166
  applications, 169, 186
  comparison with actual time, 169
  for cost standards, 171
  criteria, 168
  definition, 147
  developing, 154, 167
  elements of motion, 161
  engineering approach to, 152
  fair day's work concept, 147
  maintenance, 177
  for manpower utilization, 171
  in sampling (see Work sampling)
  setting, 154
  standard data, 159
  statistical approach, 151
  subjective approach, 150
  time study for establishing, 155
  for wage incentives, 171
Working papers, examination, 113
Workplace chart, 131
Work volume, tabulating, 307

Xerox process, 200

"Zero times," 87